US Navy
& Marine Corps
AIR POWER DIRECTORY

Editors: David Donald & Jon Lake

Aerospace Publishing London
Airtime Publishing USA

Published by
Aerospace Publishing Ltd
179 Dalling Road
London W6 0ES
England

Published under licence in USA
and Canada by
Airtime Publishing Inc.
10 Bay Street,
Westport, CT 06880
USA

Distributed in the UK,
Commonwealth and Europe by
Airlife Publishing Ltd
101 Longden Road
Shrewsbury SY3 9EB
England
Telephone: 0743 235651
Fax: 0743 232944

Distributed to retail bookstores in
the USA and Canada by
Abbeville Press Inc.
488 Madison Avenue
New York, NY
10022
USA

US and Canadian readers wishing
to order by mail, please contact
Airtime Publishing Inc. at (203)
226-3580. The publishers also
welcome inquiries from model and
hobby stores.

Copyright © 1992 Aerospace
Publishing Ltd

First published 1992

Aerospace ISBN: 1 874023 26 3
Airtime ISBN: 1 880588 02 1

Publisher: Stan Morse
Editors: David Donald and
          Jon Lake
Production Editor:
          Karen Leverington
Picture Researcher and
Editorial Assistant: Tim Senior
Design: David Donald
          Robert Hewson
Authors: Bob Archer
          Chris Bishop
          Chris Chant
          David Donald
          Robert F. Dorr
          Jon Lake
          Peter B. Mersky
          Lindsay Peacock
          Tim Ripley
Artists: Chris Davey
          Rob Garrard
          Grant Race
          John Weal
Typesetting: SX Composing Ltd
Origination and printing by
   Imago Publishing Ltd
Printed in Singapore

The publishers gratefully
acknowledge the assistance given
by the units of the US Navy, US
Marine Corps and US Coast
Guard, and aviation corporations,
who have generously helped with
this publication.
   We would like particularly to
thank Lieutenant Commander Rick
Burgess (the Editor of *Naval
Aviation News*) and Lieutenant Fred
Henney, US Navy, and Major
Rick DeChaineau and Master
Sergeant Paul Earle of the US
Marine Corps for their invaluable
work in ensuring the accuracy of
our text. Any remaining errors are
ours!
   We would also like to thank the
many squadron commanders and
public affairs officers, and the base
and command PAOs whose help
with information and photographs
has been greatly appreciated. It is
impossible to name them all, but
they include Ensign Dan Abrams,
AW-2 Roger Anderson, Lieutenant
Jeff Bartowski, Mr Fred Bradshaw,
Commander R. E. Davis, JO2
James Knott, Lieutenant Jesus
Lavandera, ACC Tom O'Leary,
ACC Guy McMillan, Lieutenant
Mark Muzii, Lieutenant Dave
Nelson, Lieutenant junior grade
Cathy Ring, Commander
Santapola, Lieutenant Larry Slade,
Lieutenant junior grade Eric
Venema, Rear Admiral Joseph
Walker, PH3 Markus White,
Lieutenant Commander Lyn
Whitmer, and Mr Nick Young.

**World Air Power Journal is
published quarterly and provides
an in-depth analysis of
contemporary military aircraft
and their worldwide operators.
Superbly produced and filled
with extensive color
photography, World Air Power
Journal is available by
subscription from:**

**UK, Europe and Commonwealth:
Aerospace Publishing Ltd
179 Dalling Road
London W6 0ES
England**

**USA and Canada:
Airtime Publishing Inc.
Subscription Dept
10 Bay Street
Westport, CT 06880
USA**

US Navy
& Marine Corps
AIR POWER DIRECTORY

CONTENTS

US NAVAL AVIATION

US Naval Aviation has a long and proud history as the United States' most visible form of global power projection. From full-scale wars to minor 'brushfire' incidents, the carriers and their air wings have never been far away, ready to bring their enormous power to bear at short notice.

Below right: If one aircraft was chosen to represent US naval air power, it would have to be the Grumman F-14 Tomcat. In terms of weapons it is the world's top fighter, these ranging from an internal cannon to ultra-long-range Phoenix missiles. Here the America's air wing puts up a quartet from VF-33 and VF-102.

Below: Launching a large strike package from an aircraft carrier involves a carefully-choreographed operation that requires each individual to perform his allotted task correctly, safely and on time. The result appears to be a chaotic flurry of activity, but in reality is a highly effective means of launching the maximum number of aircraft in the shortest possible time.

Many US Navy admirals are proud to point out that the usual Presidential reaction to crisis has always been to ask "Where are the carriers?". Such a question is a natural one to ask, since the carrier force represents one of the most powerful military weapons ever seen. With some 250 squadrons and more than 1,500 front-line aircraft and helicopters, the US Navy has the world's third-largest air arm, whose capability even includes the capacity for launching independent strategic nuclear strikes. And unlike a conventional air force, the bulk of US Naval Aviation takes its own airfields with it, wherever it goes, in the shape of the fleet of carriers. This allows it to operate almost anywhere in the world, without having to find bases in friendly countries.

However, the US Navy is now entering a difficult period, which may turn out to be its toughest battle. With an ever-tightening budget, and a perceived reduction in the military threat facing the United States, defense expenditure has been dramatically trimmed and funding for any program has to be fought for with tenacity, and justified convincingly. In such an atmosphere the US Navy's ineptitude in publicizing itself may well prove damaging. During Desert Storm, for example, the USAF tasked, controlled and coordinated coalition air power assets while simultaneously releasing spectacular film of its successes; the US Navy fulfilled its tasking in an exemplary fashion, but made few efforts to ensure that it received any media exposure at all. The question "Where are the carriers?" took on a new meaning, almost gaining the suffix "and what are they doing in the Gulf?"

This was particularly unfortunate, since in fact the US Navy and Marine Corps aircraft deployed to the Gulf played a major role in the war against Iraq, with many types proving themselves in action for the first time. Poor public relations meant that these facts remained largely unknown, however, and this mistake may well bring severe repercussions when the funding battle gets fiercest. Already the US Navy has lost its A-12 Avenger (designed as an A-6 replacement) and the P-7 patrol aircraft (destined to replace the Orion), and cancellation of both the V-22 and the F-14D have been recommended. Since FY 1985, the percentage of Pentagon funding allocated to naval aviation has shrunk more than twice as quickly as the overall defense budget, giving the US Navy's aviators an ever-shrinking slice of a diminishing pie.

Naval aviation, the projection of naval warfare in the air, has had a revolutionary impact on the conduct of the war at sea. On 7 December 1941, the Imperial Japanese Navy mounted an impressive demonstration of what the aircraft could achieve against vulnerable surface ships, and that les-

son was taught again and again, by all the combatants, during the long war that followed. Perhaps most impressively, the Japanese bombers which struck against the ships at Pearl Harbor had themselves been ship-launched. It was the US Navy which was to develop carrier warfare to its logical conclusion, using these versatile ships to bludgeon their way across the Pacific to the Japanese homeland itself. Having followed European developments during the 1920s and 1930s with great interest, the US embarked on a massive aircraft carrier construction program of its own. By the end of World War II, the US Navy had 41,000 aircraft on strength, and nearly 140 aircraft carriers. In fighting a 'carrier war' in the Pacific, the US Navy developed naval aviation from an arm designed to support the war at sea into a weapon capable of independent use and of carrying the war to the enemy country, and not just the enemy fleet.

Humble beginnings

Since then the US Navy has continued to develop the concept of carrier warfare, becoming in the process the most powerful naval air arm in history. From its humble beginnings in 1910, when civilian Eugene Ely made the first take-off in a fixed-wing aircraft (a Curtiss) from a ship (from the battleship USS *Birmingham*), US Naval Aviation has come a long way. (It is interesting to note that some date the birth of US Naval Aviation to 8 May 1911, when a USN captain signed the requisition to purchase two Curtiss pushers.)

US Navy interest in aviation really dated back to 1908, when two Navy officers were members of the board which convened at Fort Myers, VA, to assess the suitability of the Wright flyer for military use. The demonstrations killed a US Army officer, but this was not sufficient to prevent Lieutenant George C. Sweet from recommend-

ing the purchase of four aircraft. The Secretary of the Navy was affected by the fatal crash, however, and took no further action.

After the famous demonstration by Ely aboard the USS *Birmingham* (intended as a sales demonstration to the Navy for the Curtiss aircraft), Glenn Curtiss offered to train a USN officer to be a pilot free of charge, in another attempt to interest the US Navy in his aircraft. Thus a submariner,

Below: Despite the introduction of mirror landing systems, the Landing Signals Officers (LSOs) remain vital to the safe recovery of the aircraft. The LSO has a back-up, each able to immediately order a wave-off.

Above: US Naval Aviation is more than just the steam and excitement of the carrier deck. Long hours are put in by the patrol community, keeping watch on submarine and maritime forces around the globe. The patrol units universally fly the P-3 Orion.

Right: Support forces are vital to keep any major fighting machine at the peak of effectiveness. The Navy has many support helicopter units, flying a variety of types including the Sikorsky CH-53E (illustrated), which mainly fly logistic supply missions, including the vertical replenishment of ships at sea.

Lieutenant 'Spuds' Ellyson, was ordered to report to the Curtiss camp at North Island, CA. Further demonstrations by Curtiss and Ely (assisted by Ellyson) included the landing of an aircraft on a platform built on the USS *Pennsylvania*.

These demonstrations finally bore fruit in 1911, when the Navy ordered two Curtiss aircraft and one Wright, the manufacturers agreeing to train a mechanic and a pilot for each type. In January 1914 the infant air arm moved to Guantanamo Bay, Cuba, for practical tests with the Fleet, exploring the practicalities of scouting, submarine hunting and artillery spotting. By 1914, the Navy was experimenting with the use of catapults for take-off from ships and in 1916 the formation of a naval flying corps was authorized. When America entered the war on 6 April 1917, the Navy had 54 aircraft, three balloons and a single blimp, organized into aerial coast patrol units at Yale, Harvard, Princeton and Columbia Universities. Initially, priority was given to combating the German U-boat menace, using flying boats. Navy pilots did deploy to France, where some flew bombing sorties against the Germans. Plans for a fleet of aircraft carriers for use against the Austrian navy came to nothing.

Postwar, the US Navy continued to support development of new tactics, techniques and equipment. In January 1919 a squadron of flying boats conducted Fleet exercises off Cuba, supported by a seaplane tender so that they could travel with the Fleet. They were joined by a detachment of Sopwith Camels, which were flown from a platform built on the No. 2 turret of the battleship *Texas*.

Perhaps the most important inter-war development was the birth of the aircraft carrier fleet. Influenced by British experiments, and suddenly left with two partially-completed battlecruisers which were in excess of treaty limitations, the US Navy converted the two ships to become the carriers *Lexington* and *Saratoga*, commissioned in 1927. They were followed by purpose-designed aircraft carriers.

Carrier war in the Pacific

By 1941, the US Navy had eight aircraft carriers and 5,260 aircraft. The Japanese attack on Pearl Harbor fortunately found the carriers at sea. The US Navy, and in particular its aircraft carriers, played a major part in the long war against Germany and Japan, keeping the Atlantic supply routes open and eventually driving back the Japanese from their conquests in the Pacific. One early highlight of the carrier war included Doolittle's epic raid, mounted with USAAC B-25s from the carrier *Hornet*. The Battle of the Coral Sea was the first naval engagement decided entirely by air power, the opposing fleets never closing to within gunnery range of each other. Coral Sea was followed by Midway, which smashed the Japanese carrier fleet; actions at Guadalcanal and the Marianas further reinforced US maritime air superiority.

Throughout the postwar period, the US Navy's aircraft carriers and land-based aircraft have provided the 'tip of the spear' for US foreign policy makers, making an incalculable contribution during the Cold War and a more concrete one in Korea, Vietnam and, most recently, the Persian Gulf. In the 1950s, the US Navy was enthusiastic in embracing British developments like the angled deck, the steam catapult and the mirror landing sight.

Perhaps above all else, the US Navy has kept its faith in the very concept of the aircraft carrier as a major capital ship, and in the versatility and usefulness of Naval Aviation. Technological and tactical developments have kept the huge carriers from becoming mere obsolete behemoths, and even in the post-Cold War 1990s the question is not whether the USA needs a carrier force (and its associated aviation) but how large that force needs to be. Whatever the eventual answer, US Naval Aviation will continue to play a crucial role in both the defense of the USA and its interests, and in maintaining world peace.

The 'Peace Dividend'

The end of the Cold War immediately brought forth demands for defense cuts and a reduction in force levels. Dramatic proof of increased instability (and a telling demonstration of the increasing importance of out-of-area operations) came in 1991 with the Gulf War against Iraq, but this was not enough to prevent reductions in the level of US Naval Aviation forces. By FY 1996, defense spending will be down to 3.6 per cent of GNP, the lowest level since before World War II and marking a reduction of more than one-third since the late 1980s. Even

with the proportion of US GNP allocated to defense spending falling, US Naval Aviation should have been safe, since it represents the most cost-effective and versatile way of meeting the worldwide threat. US Navy aircraft carriers were involved in some 200 crises during the Cold War, most of them low-intensity, Third World brushfire situations which perfectly replicate the most likely future threat.

As a trading nation, the United States of America depends absolutely on keeping the sea lanes open, since 95 per cent of imports and exports still travel by sea. The aircraft carrier is an excellent way of keeping the seas safe for such traffic. While it is undoubtedly true that the aircraft carrier is large, and to a certain extent vulnerable, it is much less vulnerable than the closest equivalent, a land airfield on overseas territory. Conventional airfields cannot move to respond to a changing threat, and are more exposed to terrorist action or even natural disaster. (The eruption of Mt Pinatubo closed Clark AFB, for example.)

Carrying its own air force, the aircraft carrier is a most persuasive implement of foreign policy. This is USS Dwight D. Eisenhower, complete with Air Wing Seven, assigned to the Atlantic Fleet.

Below: While the US Air Force has virtually ended its aggressor program, the Navy has expanded its own adversary fleet. Recently added are F-14 Tomcats, this being one of two NFWS ('Top Gun') aircraft painted to resemble Su-27 'Flankers'.

Powerplant
The A-6E is powered by a pair of Pratt & Whitney J52-P-8E turbojets, each developing 9,300 lb (41.38 kN) thrust.

TRAM turret
The Target Recognition and Attack Multisensor turret incorporates a FLIR and laser designator, permitting the A-6 to acquire targets at night and to autonomously aim laser-guided weapons such as Paveway bombs and Skipper missiles.

Another advantage of the aircraft carrier is that the USA has no need to take into account local sensibilities when it is used, whereas opposition can render an air base unusable (Britain was the only country prepared to allow US warplanes to use bases during the strikes against Libya) or can even force the withdrawal from such a base, as happened in Libya (Wheelus AFB) and as is happening in the Philippines and Spain. As the use of overseas fixed bases becomes more and more uncertain, the carriers become increasingly important as a force capable of showing the flag, deterring aggression or undertaking a rapid military response to any threat to US interests.

Deterrent effect

Critics of the aircraft carrier point to the small number of aircraft deployed, many of which serve a defensive role. This fundamentally misses the point. Even one squadron of nuclear-capable A-6 bombers (to say nothing of the two F/A-18 strike/fighter squadrons) can make a dramatic difference to the balance of power in a region, exercising a huge deterrent effect. Nevertheless, two aircraft carriers, the *Enterprise* and the *John F. Kennedy*, now look as if they may retire early, and one air wing, CVW-6, has already been disestablished. Critics ask whether the USA can afford its fleet of aircraft carriers. A wiser question might be whether it can do without them. Vice Admiral Richard Dunleavy, Assistant Chief of Naval Operations for Air Warfare said: "Although the phrases 'downsizing' ... and 'reductions in force' seem firmly ingrained in the military lexicon, I am, more than ever, absolutely confident (that) Naval Aviation is the sharp and convincing point of the Navy spear."

Secretary of Defense Dick Cheney had similar words: "The emphasis on regional conflicts, the kind of thing we did in the Persian Gulf, for example, means that carrier battle groups will continue to be an absolutely vital part of the force. They're always available to us on short notice, you can project power regardless of what the situation might be on shore, so I cannot foresee a set of circumstances (certainly not in my lifetime) when we're not going to want a robust carrier force."

The argument in favor of the carriers (and Naval

Aviation) is not uncontested, and powerful interests have proposed many alternative ways of spending the 'Defense Dollar'. The US Air Force has argued strongly for funding for the Northrop B-2 'Stealth Bomber' instead of for the AX and F/A-18E/F, stating that a force of 120 B-2s would represent a $44-billion saving. Alternatively, the USAF avers, a saving of $102 billion would result from procurement of 75 B-2s instead of the AX, the F/A-18E/F and three carrier battle groups.

In today's economic climate, it was inevitable that Naval Aviation would suffer some losses. Perhaps most importantly, these have included several ambitious future aircraft projects, around which the US Navy was planning its 21st century carrier air wings. The first and most obvious casualty was the troubled A-12, whose cost overruns and poor progress made it an obvious target. Cancellation allowed increased funding for smart weapons, more F/A-18Cs and procurement of the advanced F/A-18E and F/A-18F. The A-12 itself is to be replaced by the AX, which retains the same 700-nm radius of action and night/all-weather capability, but the specification has been significantly relaxed in other areas.

Advanced Hornet

While the advanced Hornet derivative has survived, the F-14D Tomcat has not. The nominal air wing of the future was once intended to have comprised an equal mix of 20 F-14Ds and 20 F/A-18E/Fs, but elimination of the F-14D in favor of an air wing containing 40 F/A-18E/Fs will save $13.2 billion over 20 years. The F/A-18E/F has the same 700-nm radius of action as the F-14D, and can meet the relaxed long-range intercept requirement even without the cancelled Advanced AAM. The advanced Hornet derivative is a much more effective attack aircraft, with greater accuracy, better night-attack capability and more advanced weapons systems. It is also cheaper, costing only $6,150 per hour (compared with $7,650 for the F-14D) to run, with a maintenance man hours per flight hour figure of 24.4 compared with 37.3 for the F-14D. Manning levels will also be lower, with an F/A-18E/F squadron requiring 22 officers and 174 enlisted men rather than the 31 officers and 214 enlisted men required by an F-14D unit. The new Hornet promises to be safer and more reliable, with a time between aircraft losses of 22,000 flying hours (compared with 13,300 for the F-14D) and an MTBF of 2.16 hours (compared with 0.87 hours). The cost of 13 F/A-18E/F wings will be $44.3 billion, compared with $53.8 billion for a similar number of mixed F-14D and F/A-18E/F wings.

The killing-off of the A-12, the F-14D and the Advanced AAM have not saved today's front line from deep cuts. With the diminution of the Soviet ballistic missile submarine threat the patrol/ASW community will bear a substantial proportion of the cuts presently envisaged, while corresponding reductions in frigate/destroyer numbers will lead to the loss of some LAMPS assets, perhaps casting doubt on the future of Kaman's Seasprite. In the Orion world, 24 regular and 13 Reserve units will be trimmed to 18 regular and nine Reserve by FY 1993. The disbandment of Air Wing Six has also resulted in the disestablishment of some units. The exact situation *vis à vis* unit disbandments changes frequently, and several squadrons have been mooted for disbandment only to gain a sudden reprieve.

Below: The Navy's carrier training program is in the process of a considerable upgrade. The veteran training carrier Lexington has finally given way to the Forrestal, while the T-45 Goshawk is being procured for advanced training, replacing the T-2 Buckeye and TA-4J Skyhawk.

Gruman A-6E Intruder

Elderly it may be, but the tough Intruder remains the spearhead of US Naval Aviation. Just one squadron is included in the standard air wing, tasked with providing the main strike/attack element with weapons ranging from anti-personnel cluster weapons to nuclear bombs. Plans to replace the aircraft with a stealthy attacker were dealt a blow by the cancellation of the A-12.

Weapon load
One centerline and four wing pylons are available for weapons carriage, although the outer wing pylons are usually occupied by fuel tanks. This aircraft is shown carrying 18 Mk 82 500-lb ow-drag general-purpose bombs.

Fuel
Fuel is held in integral tanks in the wings, including the outer folding portions and in the central fuselage. A prominent refueling probe is mounted directly in front of the windscreen.

Crew
The Intruder is operated by a pilot and bombardier/navigator. The B/N's seat is lower and set back from the pilot's. Both have Martin-Baker GRU-7 ejection seats.

Markings
A-6Es are marked in the standard tactical gray scheme, although some of the KA-6D tankers retain some vestiges of the previous gray/white paint. This aircraft is marked for VA-42 'Green Pawns', the Atlantic FRS unit.

Radar
The principal attack sensor is the Norden APQ-156 radar. In addition to providing attack and search functions, it incorporates terrain avoidance.

Airbrakes
The trailing edges of the wingtips split open to form airbrakes, slowing the Intruder to acceptable speeds for carrier approaches or weapon runs.

Below: The Navy's best-known aircraft are the F/A-18As of the 'Blue Angels' flight demonstration team, based at Pensacola. The 'Blues' previously flew the A-4 Skyhawk.

By May 1992, it seemed likely that force reductions would include the following casualties:

FY 1992:

31 May 1991	VP-44
28 June 1991	VP-56
31 August 1991	VP-19; VP-48; VA-185
31 March 1992	VMFA-333; VMFA-531
33 May 1992	VT-26
1 June 1992	VFA-132; VAQ-133; VF-24?
30 June 1992	VMA-322; VP-50
31 August 1992	VC-5
30 September 1992	VMA-133
1 October 1992	VA-176; VMA-331; VS-28; VAW-122
Others in FY 1992:	VT-24 (by October); VT-25 (by October); HSL-31

FY 1993:
HS-?? (TBA); HM-18 (Reprieved?); HM-19 (Reprieved?); HSL-74; HSL-35; HSL-36; VA-155; VP-6; VP-64; VP-67; VP-90; VP-93; VC-1; VR-22; VR-24; VXN-8; VMO-1

FY 1994:
VMO-2; VMO-4; VP-31; VF-43; VF-126; VC-10

ORGANIZATION, WARFIGHTING ROLES AND ORDER OF BATTLE

Carriers

The US Navy has two separate chains of command: operational and administrative. An individual squadron will be thus assigned to a 'type commander' for administrative control during training and other periods spent ashore. The same squadron may also be assigned to a carrier air wing (CVW) for advanced training and operations prior to deployment. Thirdly, the CVW itself may be assigned to an individual aircraft carrier (CV or CVN) for operations.

Operationally, like Air Force, Army and Marine assets in a given area, all US Navy assets come under one of three unified commands: CINCLANT in the Atlantic, CINCPAC in the Pacific, and CINCENT in the Middle East. All carrier- and most land-based US Navy aircraft are operationally controlled through the numbered operational fleets: the Second (headquartered at Norfolk, VA, and known to NATO as Striking Fleet Atlantic) a roving fleet in the Atlantic; the Third (now

headquartered at San Diego, CA) in the eastern Pacific; the Sixth (headquartered at Gaeta, Italy and known to NATO as Naval Striking and Support Forces South) permanently deployed in the Mediterranean; and the Seventh (headquartered at Yokosuka) in the western Pacific and Indian Ocean. Each is commanded by a four-star admiral.

Each numbered Fleet parents a number of forces. The Sixth Fleet is typical in having a battle force (CTF-60), an amphibious force (CTF-61), a landing force (CTF-62), a service force (CTF-63), a submarine force (CTF-64), an ASW force (CTF-66), a maritime surveillance and reconnaissance force (CTF-67), and special operations (CTF-68) and attack submarines (CTF-69) forces. The core of each Fleet is provided by aircraft carriers, which are usually deployed with a number of other vessels as a carrier battle group, forming the backbone of the Fleet's battle force. A battle force is a fluid and changing organization, which can fluctuate in size and composition, with one or more carrier battle groups within it.

There are four carrier groups in the Pacific, and another four in the Atlantic. A carrier will be assigned to one of these groups or to the commander of a cruiser/destroyer group on reporting to the Fleet. The eight carrier groups are 2, 4, 6 and 8 in the Atlantic and 1, 3, 5 and 7 in the Pacific. The group commander is responsible for operational planning and for coordination of air, surface and sub-surface operations, as well as for readiness, training and administration.

The aircraft carrier had effectively displaced the battleship as the capital ship by the end of World War II. The key to that success was versatility. A carrier's air group could strike at almost any kind of target at 10 times the range of even the biggest battleship guns. Combining the air groups of several carriers greatly enhanced their striking power. This was demonstrated from day one of the war in the Pacific, when Japan used a six-carrier force to launch the devastating strike on Pearl Harbor. How-

America *(top)*, Saratoga *(middle)* and John F. Kennedy *sail in the Red Sea during Desert Shield operations, making an impressive force with over 240 aircraft. 'JFK' was carrying the A-7E Corsair on its last cruise.*

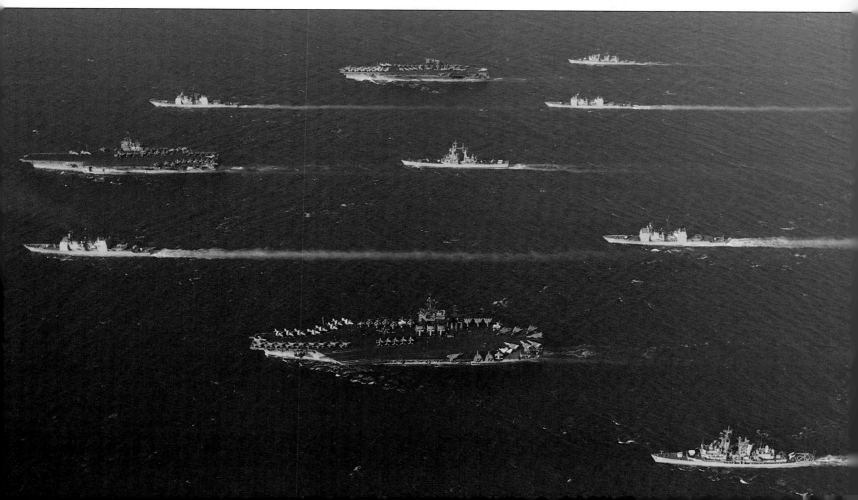

ever, it was the US Navy's fast carrier task forces which were to be the ultimate expression of the concept.

By the end of the war, carriers and surface escorts alike worked beneath an umbrella of CAPs, or Combat Air Patrols, while the strike squadrons ranged far and wide. Surface targets were overwhelmed, the enemy air forces shot out of the skies, beach defenses were softened up before amphibious assaults, and Japanese industry was starved of materials before being bombed and strafed to rubble. Seapower had never been so flexible and devastating. The carrier was so successful that the US Navy has continued to develop and refine the concept for the next half century.

Postwar aircraft, capable of deploying nuclear weapons and of rapidly increasing size and performance, combined higher landing speeds with much greater catapult weights. The wartime straight-deck carriers could handle the new aircraft with difficulty, but the British developments of the steam catapult, the angled deck and the mirror landing system made life simpler, and the entry into service in 1955 of the USS *Forrestal* pointed the way ahead. The *Forrestal* was the first of the super-carriers, dramatically larger than wartime vessels, and the design has been the basis for all subsequent US Navy carriers.

Follow-on supercarriers

The 'Forrestal' class was completed with construction of three sister ships, the USS *Ranger*, the USS *Saratoga*, and the USS *Independence*. All featured the armored flight deck, sealed hurricane bow, angled deck and self-folding mast as the *Forrestal* herself. The 'Forrestal' class was followed by the externally similar 'Kitty Hawk'-class ships (USS *Kitty Hawk* and USS *Constellation*) and the USS *America*, which differed from the earlier 'Kitty Hawk' class in detail only. The 'Kitty Hawk' class and the *America* provided more aircraft parking area, and had relocated aircraft lifts. Completed at the same time as the *Kitty Hawk* and *Constellation*, the USS *Enterprise* shared the same flight deck layout as these ships but introduced a nuclear powerplant, albeit one with eight separate reactors. The elimination of the smoke-stack gave the island of the *Enterprise* a unique shape, with a distinctive narrow base and a square top. The elimination of boilers and fuel bunkers allowed a huge increase in aviation fuel and ammunition capacity. Ordinary fuel is often carried as ballast, allowing *Enterprise* to refuel her own escorts on occasion! High construction costs led to the abandonment of five proposed sister-ships.

The next supercarrier was the *John F. Kennedy*, which had originally been intended to be powered by nuclear reactors. In the event it was completed as virtually a fourth member of the 'Kitty Hawk'/'America' class, with detail changes and revised defensive systems. The almost total absence of development costs was not enough to persuade the US Navy to build more of these cheap but effective carriers, since

their sights were already set on an ambitious new class of nuclear-powered carriers, which began with the USS *Nimitz*.

The advantages of the nuclear-powered aircraft carrier quickly became apparent through operational experience with *Enterprise*, and after a major Congressional battle for funds (eventually won by Admiral Rickover) three new ships (*Nimitz, Dwight D. Eisenhower* and *Carl Vinson*) were authorized (another, *Theodore Roosevelt*, followed soon after.) These ships were built on the proven supercarrier configuration, but with many internal improvements giving much extra space. By comparison with *Enterprise*, *Nimitz* and her sisters have only two nuclear reactors, with uranium cores which need replacing every 13 years. Two further 'Nimitz'-class carriers (*Abraham Lincoln* and *George Washington*) were authorized in the FY 1983 budget. Current plans call for a seventh and an eighth ship in the class (the USS *John Stennis* and the USS *United States*).

Multi-role ships

The first of the big-deck carriers were originally classified as attack carriers or CVAs, while the older, smaller vessels handled ASW or training roles. The phasing out of the World War II-vintage 'Essex' class in the 1960s and 1970s meant that the supercarriers had to assume both attack and ASW functions, and they became multi-role ships (in doing so the simple designation CV or, for nuclear-powered ships CVN, was adopted). In some respects, this led to a diminution of their fighting power, since each carrier's attack potential was diluted with the addition of ASW aircraft, and the logistics problems of operating a wide range of aircraft were increased. Attack numbers have been diluted still further by the need to carry aircraft to perform auxiliary but nevertheless vital functions, such as airborne early warning, inflight refueling, electronic warfare

support, and on-board delivery. Even so, while a modern air wing is numerically inferior to that of yesteryear, it is vastly superior in quality. And it remains the main strike asset of the carrier battle group.

Carrier battle groups, or CVBGs, are essential to the naval strategies of force projection and sea control. There are no precise definitions of either concept, but sea control involves using the oceans for one's own purposes while denying the enemy the same. A carrier battle group is well capable of establishing local superiority over 800 to 2,000 square miles of ocean, thereby allowing the passage of an important convoy, covering an amphibious landing or mounting a major evacuation.

Force projection involves using the CVBG offensively, taking the war to the enemy and defeating him. The essence of the CVBG is balance, with the carrier being at once the group's heart and its sword. The air wing is the

CVBG's offensive arm, while at the same time it is used to defend the carrier and its escorts. Some of the lessons learned during World War II still apply, especially the idea that the larger the air component the better its chance of success. To deliver a strike in any real strength calls for at least a second carrier, and for major operations even more are required. However, there is no single formula for the ideal carrier battle group, which, like any other task group, may be tailored to suit a particular mission. The Gulf War of 1991 saw no less than six US Navy carriers launching attacks against the Iraqi invaders of Kuwait.

Ideally, the composition of a carrier battle group provides a multi-layer defense, a steel onion where to penetrate one layer is to run up against another. Grumman E-2C Hawkeye Airborne Early Warning (AEW) aircraft fly in the outer ring, 180 miles from the carrier. With their radar capable of peering out a further 250 miles, the AEW aircraft stretch the carrier's horizon out to 450 miles, which is well beyond the range of most anti-ship missiles. The AEW aircraft are accompanied in the outer zone by pairs of Grumman F-14 Tomcat fighters, which use their unique long-range radar/missile mix to fight the 'outer air battle'. The Tomcats were designed to destroy enemy bombers or long-range missiles before they can become a threat.

Attackers which penetrate the outer defensive ring will be engaged by the carrier's F/A-18 Hornets, patrolling 90 miles from the carrier. They might be supported by Grumman EA-6B Prowlers, using powerful jammers to confuse enemy radar and missile control signals. Within this layer, any penetrators will have to deal with the long-range surface-to-air missiles fired by the carrier's escorts. Each carrier battle group will have at least one AEGIS cruiser, whose powerful computerized radar and battle management systems can track and engage hundreds of targets simultaneously. Anything which gets through that layer has to run the gauntlet of small, short-range missiles, more fighters mounting CAPs over the CVBG, and a last-ditch defense provided by fast-firing radar-guided multi-barrelled cannon.

Attack ability

The carrier air wing is far from just a defensive weapon, however. Grumman A-6E Intruders form the offensive backbone of the wing, providing genuine all-weather, long-range precision attack capability. They are usually backed by two squadrons of McDonnell Douglas F/A-18 Hornet light attack fighters, which can be used in the air-to-air and air-to-ground roles. In the mud-moving role, the Hornet can carry a heavy load of ordnance, although the type's range has always been criticized. In fact, the Hornet's precision in weapons delivery allows single-pass attacks using less ordnance than some previous light attack types, and its self-escort capability can save fuel for a given strike package, making a KA-6D's fuel load go that much further. The ASW-optimized S-3 Viking can also be used for ground attack and anti-shipping strike missions.

Having chosen excellence in developing the huge supercarriers, with their multi-role cap-

abilities, the US Navy has to live with a number of shortcomings. Big carriers are expensive, both to build and equip and to operate. Even at the height of the Reagan expansion of the American armed forces, the US Navy could not afford more than 15 carriers. Financially-straitened circumstances were already putting pressure on that force level when the end of the Cold War and the collapse of the Soviet Union took away a major opponent, and the USA is likely to end the 1990s with less than a dozen carriers. The concentration on quality rather than quantity has also meant that CVBGs have occasionally been risked in brushfire situations, which could have been influenced quite as effectively by smaller shows of force.

This leads to the vexed question of vulnerability, the 'all eggs in one basket' syndrome. While the supercarriers are huge, heavily-armored vessels, with extensive compartmentalization and sophisticated damage control systems, and which should therefore prove very difficult to sink, they also represent an enormous high-value target. In any case all an enemy has to do is damage a carrier enough to interrupt flying, and it becomes little more than a large floating lump of metal. There is also the problem of supply. A crew of 6,000 goes through an enormous quantity of supplies, and the aircraft eat fuel and ordnance at a great rate during combat operations. Even if the carrier is nuclear powered, it is still dependent upon oil-fueled escorts. The whole group needs topping up once or twice a week, so if an enemy can interfere with the supply train, he will sharply reduce the whole battle group's effectiveness.

Even with these handicaps, the fact remains that large-deck carriers are the only vessels able to deploy aircraft of sufficiently high performance to pose a credible threat in any scenario, and the carrier battle group's unique ability to provide area superiority should ensure its survival in the US Navy for many years to come.

While aircraft carriers tend to remain allocated either to the Atlantic or Pacific, they do often move between the numbered fleets on an as-required basis. The maintenance of a huge fleet of expensive, nuclear-powered supercarriers is becoming increasingly hard to justify. The dramatic reduction in tension with the former USSR has largely removed any challenge to US maritime superiority, lending weight to the arguments of those who believe that smaller ships should be built which are cheaper to maintain and to run. Others believe that large aircraft carriers are simply too vulnerable to contemporary anti-ship missiles. US

Right: A typical battle group surrounds USS Abraham Lincoln. Two frigates, a destroyer, two cruisers and a supply vessel accompany the carrier for a WestPac cruise.

Below: A Tomcat lands on the crowded flight deck of USS Theodore Roosevelt during North Atlantic operations.

Navy plans to have a 15-carrier navy in the 1990s have thus been dramatically downgraded, and even a 12-carrier force is beginning to look optimistic.

Unfortunately for the supporters of the aircraft carrier, these arguments have coincided at a time that more than half the present fleet have reached the midway point in their nominal 45-year lifespan, the very point at which replacements should be in the planning stage. Although there are now three CVNs under construction, further vessels will find it very hard to attract funding.

Carrier changes

The last of the wartime carriers (*Lexington* fought in the Pacific, including the ferocious Marianas Turkey Shoot, while *Midway* was launched in March 1945) have now finally been retired. *Lexington*, the training carrier since 1962, has been replaced by USS *Forrestal* which was redesignated from CV-59 to AVT-59, retaining a measure of operational capability for contingencies. USS *Midway* became the first carrier home-ported outside the USA by being based at Yokosuka, Japan. This allowed the ship to be readily available for rapid deployments in the Pacific. USS *Independence* has now taken over *Midway*'s role and its Air Wing Five, leaving its own CVW-14 (which played a major part in Operation Desert Storm) ashore for subsequent re-assignment to *Vinson*.

The remaining three 'Forrestal'-class carriers, USS *Saratoga*, USS *Ranger* and USS *Independence*, along with the USS *America* (essentially an improved *Forrestal*), are now scheduled to decommission during the remainder of the decade: *Ranger* in FY 1993, *Saratoga* in FY 1995, *America* in FY 1996 and *Independence* in FY 1998. The USS *America* is being retired ahead of the other three 'Kitty Hawk'/'John F. Kennedy'-class ships because it

has not undergone the SLEP (Service Life Extension Program) which can extend a carrier's normal 30-year life by some 15 years.

Plans for USS *John F. Kennedy* to undergo a SLEP were vigorously discussed before it was decided to send the ship through a $491-billion overhaul in 1993, which will give an eight- or nine-year life extension. Sister-ship USS *Kitty Hawk* received her SLEP at Philadelphia between January 1988 and August 1991, while *Constellation* is currently in SLEP and due to rejoin the fleet in 1993.

Most of the newer nuclear-powered carriers seem to have a long life stretching ahead of them, although a cloud hangs over *Enterprise*, presently laid up for the nuclear refueling which would provide power for another 13 years in operation. This simple-sounding operation is in fact very costly and complex. When she was last refueled, in 1971, the eight new nuclear cores cost $80 million and installation came to $17 million. *Enterprise* is unique, built to a modified *Forrestal* design, and has two reactors for each of the ship's four shafts. The newer 'Nimitz'-class ships have only two reactors in total.

Three nuclear-powered carriers have yet to commission. These are CVN-73 *George Washington* (due to commission on 4 July 1992), CVN-74 *John Stennis* (due to commission in 1994) and CVN-75 USS *United States*, scheduled to commission in 1998. This leaves five front-line carriers (*America, Kennedy, Saratoga, Roosevelt* and *Eisenhower*, to be joined by *Washington* in 1992) presently in service in the Atlantic Fleet, with six (*Ranger, Independence, Kitty Hawk, Nimitz, Vinson* and *Lincoln*) in the Pacific.

ATLANTIC FLEET

USS *Saratoga* (CV-60)

Service notes: The USS *Saratoga* entered service with the Atlantic Fleet in 1958. In 1962 she was involved in the blockade of Cuba during the Cuban missile crisis. *Saratoga* saw the first operational deployment of the Grumman A-6 Intruder, in 1963. The carrier was used to conduct trials into the multi-purpose carrier concept in 1970. She made one combat deployment to Southeast Asia, from May 1972 to January 1973. *Saratoga* underwent the first SLEP refit between 1981 and 1983, extending her potential service career by 10-15 years. Three Mediterranean deployments followed, and she was involved in the confrontations with Libya in 1985 and 1986. In August 1990, *Saratoga* made the fastest Atlantic crossing by a carrier since World War II, to reach the Persian Gulf in seven days. In a cruise lasting from August 1990 to March 1991, the carrier participated fully in Operations Desert Shield and Desert Storm. During the cruise, her air group flew 12,664 sorties. In the sea-control role, the *Saratoga* battle group challenged 1,500 cargo ships, intercepting and boarding 242, while enforcing the blockade of Iraq.

Air wing:
USS *Saratoga*'s Air Wing Seventeen included, in 1992, the following squadrons:

VF-74 'Bedevilers'	F-14B
VF-103 'Sluggers'	F-14B TARPS
VFA-83 'Rampagers'	F/A-18C
VFA-81 'Sunliners'	F/A-18C
VA-35 'Black Panthers'	A-6E, KA-6D
VAW-125 'Tigertails'	E-2C
VAQ-132 'Scorpions'	EA-6B
HS-9 'Sea Griffins'	SH-3H
VS-30 'Diamondcutters'	S-3B

Specification
USS *Saratoga* CV-60

Dimensions: length 1,063 ft (324 m); beam 129 ft 6 in (39.5 m); flight deck width 252 ft (76.8 m); draft 37 ft (11.3 m)
Displacement: 59,060 tons standard and 75,900 tons full load

Part of the ship's complement rings the deck of 'Sara' following Desert Storm duty.

Performance: maximum speed 34 kt (39 mph; 63 km/h); range 13,800 miles (22200 km) at 20 kt (23 mph; 37 km/h)
Notional air wing: 84 aircraft, as USS *Forrestal*, including 20 Grumman F-14 Tomcats, 20 McDonnell Douglas F/A-18 Hornets, 20 Grumman A-6E Intruders (including some KA-6D tankers), 10 Lockheed S-3A/B Vikings, four Grumman EA-6B Prowlers, four Grumman E-2C Hawkeyes and six Sikorsky SH-3H Sea King or SH-60F Ocean Hawk helicopters
Aviation load: 5,500 tons of fuel and 1,650 tons of ordnance
Combat persistence: 8-10 days of normal operations without replenishment
Complement: 5,249 including 2,279 air wing and 70 flag staff

USS *America* (CV-66)

Service notes: USS *America* was commissioned into the Atlantic Fleet in January 1965, and operated on the East Coast and in the Mediterranean. Although similar in general to the two preceding 'Kitty Hawk'-class ships, she has a revised island and also features a bow anchor indicating the presence of a sonar dome. *America* made three combat deployments to Southeast Asia, relieving Pacific Fleet carriers, between May 1968 and March 1973. In 1975 she was modified to allow the operation of the F-14 Tomcat fighters and S-3A Viking ASW aircraft then entering fleet service. In 1980 the *America* was the first vessel to receive the Mk 15 Phalanx CIWS (Close-In Weapon System). She made three more Mediterranean cruises in the 1980s, operating off Lebanon and in the confrontation with Libya. *America* has not yet received a SLEP refit, and may not do so as the US Navy's carrier force is reduced in the 1990s. The carrier was involved in the Gulf War, arriving in-theater in January 1991 and launching aircraft from Air Wing 1 as part of Operation Desert Storm.

Air wing:
USS *America*'s Air Wing One included, in 1992, the following squadrons:

VF-102 'Diamondbacks'	F-14A TARPS
VF-33 'Starfighters'	F-14A
VFA-82 'Marauders'	F/A-18C
VFA-86 'Sidewinders'	F/A-18C
VA-85 'Buckeyes'	A-6E, KA-6D
VAW-123 'Screwtops'	E-2C
VAQ-137 'Rooks'	EA-6B
HS-11 'Dragonslayers'	SH-3H
VS-32 'Maulers'	S-3B

Specification
USS *America* (CV-66)

Dimensions: length 1,047 ft 6 in (319.3 m); beam 130 ft (39.6 m); flight deck width 252 ft (76.8 m); draught 37 ft (11.3 m)
Displacement: 60,300 tons standard and 81,500 tons full load
Performance: maximum speed 33 kt (38 mph;

A TARPS pod image from a Tomcat shows America's plan view. Note the Tomcat on alert on the forward cat.

61 km/h); range 13,800 miles (22200 km) at 20 kt (23 mph; 37 km/h)
Notional air wing: 84 aircraft, as USS *Forrestal*, including 20 Grumman F-14 Tomcats, 20 McDonnell Douglas F/A-18 Hornets, 20 Grumman A-6E Intruders (including some KA-6D tankers), 10 Lockheed S-3A/B Vikings, four Grumman EA-6B Prowlers, four Grumman E-2C Hawkeyes and six Sikorsky SH-3H Sea King or SH-60F Ocean Hawk helicopters
Aviation load: 5,900 tons of fuel and 2,150 tons of ordnance
Combat persistence: 8-10 days of normal operations without replenishment
Complement: 5,480 including 2,480 air wing and 70 flag staff

USS *John F. Kennedy* (CV-67)

Service notes: Completed in 1968, the USS *John F. Kennedy* was commissioned into the Atlantic Fleet. Originally intended to be nuclear powered, the *Kennedy* was eventually, after considerable delay, built with a conventional powerplant. Generally similar to the 'Kitty Hawk'-class vessels, the carrier has better underwater protection and a revised deck layout. *Kennedy* has spent much of her career in the Mediterranean. In 1970 she was dispatched to the Middle East at short notice in response to a crisis. Her third Mediterranean cruise was extended to almost one year's duration to cover for carriers sent to Southeast Asia

after the 1972 Communist invasion of Vietnam. *Kennedy* was the first carrier to take the Lockheed S-3 Viking to sea, in 1975. Three more cruises in the 1970s were followed by a further four in the 1980s, during which *Kennedy* and her air wing saw action over Lebanon and against Libyan fighters. For much of that time, she was operating the so-called 'all Grumman' air wing. *Kennedy*, along with Air Wing Three, were once again in Mediterranean waters in September 1990, as part of the US Navy's response to the Iraqi invasion of Kuwait. The air wing was unusual in containing no Hornets, with the Vought A-7 Corsair II attending its last war in their place. During the Gulf War, the

Kennedy battle group flew 11,000 combat sorties, mainly from the Red Sea, during which CVW-3 made the first operational use of the SLAM missile.

Air Wing Three was in the process of changing its A-7s for F/A-18s when the Gulf War began. The ship is to undergo what has been referred to as a 'complex overhaul' at Philadelphia from September 1993. This will cost $491 billion and last some 24 months. It will result in an eight- or nine-year life extension.

Air wing:
USS *John F. Kennedy*'s Air Wing Three included, in 1992, the following squadrons:

'Big John' heads home after Desert Storm, carrying the A-7E (from VA-46 and VA-72) on its last active duty with the Navy.

VF-14 'Top Hatters'	F-14A
VF-32 'Swordsmen'	F-14A TARPS
VFA-37 'Bulls'	F/A-18C
VFA-105 'Gunslingers'	F/A-18C
VA-75 'Sunday Punchers'	A-6E, KA-6D
VAW-126 'Seahawks'	E-2C
VAQ-130 'Zappers'	EA-6B
HS-7 'Big Dippers'	SH-3H
VS-22 'Vidars'	S-3B

Specification
USS *John F. Kennedy* (CV-67)
Dimensions: length 1,052 ft (320.7 m); beam 130 ft (39.6 m); flight deck width 260 ft (79.25 m); draft 35 ft 11 in (10.9 m)
Displacement: 61,000 tons standard and 82,561 tons full load

Performance: maximum speed 34 kt (39 mph; 63 km/h); range 13,800 miles (22200 km) at 20 kt (23 mph; 37 km/h)
Notional air wing: 84 aircraft, as USS *Forrestal*, including 20 Grumman F-14 Tomcats, 20 McDonnell Douglas F/A-18 Hornets, 20 Grumman A-6E Intruders (including some KA-6D tankers), 10 Lockheed S-3A/B Vikings, four Grumman EA-6B Prowlers, four Grumman

E-2C Hawkeyes and six Sikorsky SH-3H Sea King or SH-60F Ocean Hawk helicopters
Aviation load: 5,900 tons of fuel and 2,150 tons of ordnance
Combat persistence: 9-10 days of normal operations without replenishment
Complement: 5,279 including 2,279 air wing and 70 flag staff

USS *Dwight D. Eisenhower* (CVN-69)

Service notes: Commissioned into the Atlantic Fleet in 1977, USS *Dwight D. Eisenhower* became fully operational in 1978, and began her first Mediterranean cruise in January 1979. In 1980, *Eisenhower* made the first all-nuclear carrier change-over when she relieved *Nimitz* in the Indian Ocean battle group. *Eisenhower* made three deployments to the Mediterranean in the early 1980s, before entering Newport News for a refit. In 1988, the carrier was deployed to the Caribbean. *Eisenhower*'s 1990 Mediterranean deployment was extended unexpectedly when Iraq invaded Kuwait at the beginning of August. *Eisenhower*'s air wing, CVW-9, formed part of the force defending Saudi Arabia for the first month. However, having already been overseas for six months the carrier played no part in the actual war. She

returned to the USA in September, after being relieved by *Saratoga* and *John F. Kennedy*.

Air wing:
USS *Dwight D. Eisenhower*'s Air Wing Seven included, in 1992, the following squadrons:

VF-143 'Pukin' Dogs'	F-14B TARPS
VF-142 'Ghostriders'	F-14B
VFA-136 'Knighthawks'	F/A-18C
VFA-131 'Wildcats'	F/A-18C
VA-34 'Blue Blasters'	A-6E, KA-6D
VAW-121 'Blue Tails'	E-2C
VAQ-140 'Patriots'	EA-6B
HS-5 'Night Dippers'	SH-3H
VS-31 'Top Cats'	S-3B

'Ike' was committed to the first phase of Desert Storm, with CVW-7 aboard. Here it transits north through the Suez Canal.

Specification
USS *Dwight D. Eisenhower* (CVN-69)
Dimensions: length 1,092 ft (332.9 m); beam 134 ft (40.8 m); flight deck width 252 ft (76.8 m); draft 37 ft (11.3 m)
Displacement: 72,916 tons standard and 91,487 tons full load
Performance: maximum speed +35 kt (+40 mph; +65 km/h); range 1.15 million miles (1.85 million km) at 20 kt (23 mph; 37 km/h)
National air wing: 86 aircraft, as USS *Enterprise*, including 20 Grumman F-14 Tomcats, 20 McDonnell Douglas F/A-18 Hornets, 20 Grumman A-6E Intruders (including some KA-6D tankers), 10 Lockheed S-3A/B Vikings, five Grumman EA-6B Prowlers, five Grumman E-2C Hawkeyes and six Sikorsky SH-3H Sea King or SH-60F Ocean Hawk helicopters
Aviation load: 9,000 tons of fuel and 2,570 tons of ordnance
Combat persistence: 16 days of normal operations without replenishment
Complement: 6,054 including 2,800 air wing and 70 flag staff

USS *Theodore Roosevelt* (CVN-71)

Service notes: Operation Desert Storm, January to April 1991.

Air wing:

USS *Theodore Roosevelt*'s Air Wing Eight included, in 1992, the following squadrons:

VF-41 'Black Aces'	F-14A	VA-65 'Tigers'	A-6E
VF-84 'Jolly Rogers'	F-14A TARPS	VA-36 'Roadrunners'	A-6E
VFA-15 'Valions'	F/A-18C	VAW-124 'Bear Aces'	E-2C
VFA-87 'Golden Warriors'	F/A-18C	HS-3 'Tridents'	SH-60F/HH-60H
		VAQ-141 'Shadowhawks'	EA-6B
		VS-24 'Scouts'	S-3B

Performance: maximum speed +35 kt (+40 mph; +65 km/h); range 1.15 million miles (1.85 million km) at 20 kt (23 mph; 37 km/h)
Notional air wing: 86 aircraft, as USS *Enterprise*, including 20 Grumman F-14 Tomcats, 20 McDonnell Douglas F/A-18 Hornets, 20 Grumman A-6E Intruders (including some KA-6D tankers), 10 Lockheed S-3A/B Vikings, five Grumman EA-6B Prowlers, five Grumman E-2C Hawkeyes and six Sikorsky SH-3H Sea King or SH-60F Sea Hawk helicopters
Aviation load: 9,000 tons of fuel and 2,570 tons of ordnance
Combat persistence: 16 days of normal operations without replenishment
Complement: 6,054 including 2,800 air wing and 70 flag staff

Specification
USS *Theodore Roosevelt* (CVN-71)
Dimensions: length 1,092 ft (332.9 m); beam 134 ft (40.8 m); flight deck width 252 ft (76.8 m); draft 38 ft 6 in (11.8 m)
Displacement: 73,973 tons standard and 96,396 tons full load

PACIFIC FLEET

USS *Ranger* (CV-61)

Service notes: *Ranger* was commissioned into the Atlantic Fleet in 1956, but was transferred to the Pacific in 1957. She made eight combat deployments to Southeast Asia between August 1964 and September 1974. She was the first carrier to operate the Vought A-7 Corsair II, taking the new attack bomber into action in 1967 during the third deployment to Vietnam. *Ranger* made several deployments to the western Pacific and the Indian Ocean in the 1980s. The carrier was heavily involved in Operation Desert Storm between January and April 1991, cruising with the veteran USS *Midway* as part of the Persian Gulf task force. They were the only two carriers to be forward deployed in the Gulf itself. *Ranger* has not undergone a SLEP refit. She was scheduled to receive a 'complex overhaul' early in 1993, but is now scheduled to be decommissioned in 1993.

Air wing:

In 1991, *Ranger* shipped Air Wing Two. Differing from the notional air wing, which includes F/A-18 Hornets, Air Wing Two comprises the following squadrons:

VF-1 'Wolfpack'	F-14A
VF-2 'Bounty Hunters'	F-14A TARPS
VA-155 'Silver Foxes'	A-6E, KA-6D
VA-145 'Swordsmen'	A-6E, KA-6D
VAW-116 'Sun Kings'	E-2C
VAQ-131 'Lancers'	EA-6B

Ranger *at rest near Hong Kong. The carrier's Air Wing Two was unique in being an 'all Grumman' wing, with two squadrons of Tomcats and two of Intruders – no light attack assets being assigned. However, two Hornet squadrons are now in the process of joining the wing at the expense of one A-6 unit.*

HS-14 'Chargers'	SH-3H
VS-38 'Red Griffins'	S-3A

Specification
USS *Ranger* (CV-61)

Dimensions: length 1,071 ft (326.4 m); beam 129 ft 6 in (39.5 m); flight deck width 252 ft (76.8 m); draft 37 ft (11.3 m)
Displacement: 60,000 tons standard and 79,300 tons full load
Performance: maximum speed 34 kt (39 mph; 63 km/h); range 13,800 miles (22200 km) at 20 kt (23 mph; 37 km/h)
Notional air wing: 84 aircraft, as USS *Forrestal*, including 20 Grumman F-14 Tomcats, 20 McDonnell Douglas F/A-18 Hornets, 20 Grumman A-6E Intruders (including some KA-6D tankers), 10 Lockheed S-3A/B Vikings, four Grumman EA-6B Prowlers, four Grumman E-2C Hawkeyes and six Sikorsky SH-3H Sea King or SH-60F Ocean Hawk helicopters
Aviation load: 5,500 tons of fuel and 1,650 tons of ordnance
Combat persistence: 8-10 days of normal operations without replenishment
Complement: 5,249 including 2,279 air wing and 70 flag staff

USS *Independence* (CV-62)

Service notes: The USS *Independence* was commissioned into the Atlantic Fleet in 1959. She took part in the missile crisis blockade of Cuba in 1962. *Independence* was the first Atlantic Fleet carrier to make a combat deployment to Southeast Asia, being used to relieve the overstretched Pacific Fleet carriers. The Grumman A-6 Intruder flew its first combat missions during the carrier's sole Vietnam cruise, between June 1965 and November 1965. *Independence* supported the US invasion of Grenada in 1983, and in the same year was in operation in support of the Multinational Peacekeeping Force in the Lebanon. She underwent a SLEP refit between 1985 and 1988. The carrier transferred to the Pacific Fleet in 1988, and in 1990 she deployed to the Mediterranean and the Red Sea as part of Operation Desert Shield. *Independence* left the Middle East in November 1990, without taking part in the active phase of the

war. In 1991, *Independence* replaced the aging USS *Midway* as the only non-US-based carrier, home-ported at Yokosuka in Japan.

Independence carried the standard Air Wing Fourteen in the Middle East, but on transferring to Japan she took Midway's old wing, Air Wing Five, which did not fly Tomcats or Vikings. However, two of Midway's three Hornet squadrons were exchanged for F-14s from the spare CVW-14.

Air wing:

USS *Independence*'s Air Wing Five included, in late 1991, the following squadrons:

VF-154 'Black Knights'	F-14A TARPS
VF-21 'Freelancers'	F-14A
VFA-192 'World Famous Golden Dragons'	F/A-18C
VFA-195 'Dam Busters'	F/A-18C
VA-115 'Eagles'	A-6E
VS-21 'Fighting Redtails'	S-3B
VAW-115 'Sentinels'	E-2C
VAQ-136 'Gauntlets'	EA-6B
HS-12 'Wyverns'	SH-3H

Specification
USS *Independence* (CV-62)

Dimensions: length 1,070 ft (326.1 m); beam 129 ft 6 in (39.5 m); flight deck width 252 ft (76.8 m); draft 37 ft (11.3 m)
Displacement: 60,000 tons standard and 79,300 tons full load
Performance: maximum speed 34 kt (39 mph; 63 km/h); range 13,800 miles (22200 km) at 20 kt (23 mph; 37 km/h)
Notional air wing: 84 aircraft, as USS *Forrestal*, including 20 Grumman F-14 Tomcats, 20 McDonnell Douglas F/A-18 Hornets, 20 Grumman A-6E Intruders (including some KA-6D tankers), 10 Lockheed S-3A/B Vikings, four Grumman EA-6B Prowlers, four Grumman E-2C Hawkeyes and six Sikorsky SH-3H Sea King or SH-60F Ocean Hawk helicopters
Aviation load: 5,500 tons of fuel and 1,650 tons of ordnance
Combat persistence: 8-10 days of normal operations without replenishment
Complement: 5,249 including 2,279 air wing and 70 flag staff

USS *Kitty Hawk* (CV-63)

Service notes: *Kitty Hawk* commissioned into the Pacific Fleet in 1961. Built to a modified 'Forrestal' design, she has a more efficient layout of flight deck, island, catapults and elevators. She was the first carrier to be equipped with surface-to-air missiles, although the original medium-range Terrier SAM system was replaced by Sea Sparrow point-defense missiles in the late 1970s. Between 1962 and 1978 *Kitty Hawk* operated on the West Coast and in the Pacific, cruises often going on into the Indian Ocean and the Gulf of Oman. She made seven combat deployments to Southeast Asia between November 1965 and June 1974. The first Vietnam cruise also saw the first operational use of the Grumman E-2 Hawkeye airborne early warning aircraft. Deployments in the Pacific and Indian Oceans continued through the 1970s and 1980s, culminating in a round-the-world cruise in 1987 as the carrier was transferred from the Pacific Fleet to the Atlantic Fleet. In January 1988, *Kitty Hawk* began a SLEP refit. She was temporarily assigned to AIRLANT for this, and returned to AIRPAC in December 1991. Air Wing Fifteen was assigned to *Kitty Hawk* in 1992.

Air wing:

USS *Kitty Hawk*'s Air Wing Fifteen included, in 1992, the following squadrons:

VF-51 'Screaming Eagles'	F-14A
VF-111 'Sundowners'	F-14A TARPS
VFA-27 'Chargers'	F/A-18C
VFA-97 'Warhawk'	F/A-18C
VA-52 'Knight Riders'	A-6E, KA-6D
VAW-114 'Hormel Hawgs'	E-2C
VAQ-134 'Garudas'	EA-6B
HS-4 'Black Knights'	SH-6-F, HH-60H
VS-37 'Sawbucks'	S-3B

Specification
USS *Kitty Hawk* (CV-63)

Dimensions: length 1,046 ft (318.8 m); beam 130 ft (39.6 m); flight deck width 252 ft (76.8 m); draft 37 ft (11.3 m)

Displacement: 60,100 tons standard and 80,800 tons full load

Performance: maximum speed 34 kt (38 mph; 63 km/h); range 13,800 miles (22200 km) at 20 kt (23 mph; 37 km/h)

Notional air wing: 84 aircraft, as USS *Forrestal*, including 20 Grumman F-14 Tomcats, 20 McDonnell Douglas F/A-18 Hornets, 20 Grumman A-6E Intruders (including some KA-6D tankers), 10 Lockheed S-3A/B Vikings, four Grumman EA-6B Prowlers, four Grumman E-2C Hawkeyes and six Sikorsky SH-3H Sea King or SH-60F Ocean Hawk helicopters

Aviation load: 5,900 tons of fuel and 2,150 tons of ordnance

Combat persistence: 9-11 days of normal operations without replenishment

Complement: 5,480 including 2,480 air wing and 70 flag staff

Kitty Hawk *deck crew spell out 'Bye SD' as the carrier leaves San Diego in 1987 to join the Atlantic Fleet. It returned to Pacific service in late 1991.*

USS *Nimitz* (CVN-68)

Service notes: Largely completed by 1973, USS *Nimitz* was not commissioned until 1975 due to the late delivery of essential components for her nuclear powerplant. In 1975, *Nimitz* joined the Atlantic Fleet, ending *Enterprise*'s reign as the largest warship in the world. The carrier's flight deck is generally the same as that of the *Kitty Hawk*, but with the cut-off forward flight deck first seen on the *John F. Kennedy*. Between 1975 and 1985, *Nimitz* made numerous cruises in the Atlantic and the Mediterranean. In 1980, the carrier made a round-the-world deployment. While in the Indian Ocean, she served as the seaborne base for the abortive Teheran hostage rescue mission, Operation Eagle Claw. At the start of the 1981 Mediterranean cruise, the F-14 made its air-to-air combat debut when two VF-41 Tomcats from *Nimitz* shot down two attacking Libyan Sukhoi Su-22 fighters. In 1987, *Nimitz*

transferred from the Atlantic Fleet to the Pacific Fleet, embarking Air Wing Nine which had previously been attached to the USS *Kitty Hawk*. Due to a shortage of F-14Bs, *Nimitz*'s two Tomcat units transitioned back to the F-14A in early 1992.

Air wing:

USS *Nimitz*'s Air Wing Nine included, in 1992, the following squadrons:

VF-24 'Fighting Renegades'	F-14A
VF-211 'Fighting Checkmates'	F-14A TARPS
VFA-146 'Blue Diamonds'	F/A-18C
VFA-147 'Argonauts'	F/A-18C
VA-165 'Boomers'	A-6E, KA-6D
VAW-112 'Golden Hawks'	E-2C
VAQ-138 'Yellow Jackets'	EA-6B
HS-2 'Golden Falcons'	SH-60F, HH-60H
VS-33 'Screwbirds'	S-3A

With F-8 Crusaders aboard, Nimitz maneuvers hard during sea trials in 1975. It and its sisters remain the world's largest warships.

Specification
USS *Nimitz* (CVN-68)

Dimensions: length 1,092 ft (332.9 m); beam 134 ft (40.8 m); flight deck width 252 ft (76.8 m); draft 37 ft (11.3 m)

Displacement: 72,916 tons standard and 91,487 tons full load

Performance: maximum speed +35 kt (+40 mph; +65 km/h); range 1.15 million miles (1.85 million km) at 20 kt (23 mph; 37 km/h)

Notional air wing: 86 aircraft, as USS *Enterprise*, including 20 Grumman F-14 Tomcats, 20 McDonnell Douglas F/A-18 Hornets, 20 Grumman A-6E Intruders (including some KA-6D tankers), 10 Lockheed S-3A/B Vikings, five Grumman EA-6B Prowlers, five Grumman E-2C Hawkeyes, and six Sikorsky SH-60F Ocean Hawk helicopters

Aviation load: 9,000 tons of fuel and 2,570 tons of ordnance

Combat persistence: 16 days of normal operations without replenishment

Complement: 6,054 including 2,800 air wing and 70 flag staff

VFA-25 'Fist of the Fleet'	F/A-18C
VA-196 'Main Battery'	F/A-18C
VAW-113 'Black Hawks'	A-6E
VAQ-139 'Cougars'	E-2C
HS-8 'Eight Ballers'	SH-60F, HH-60H
VS-35 'Blue Wolves'	S-3A

Specification
USS *Carl Vinson* (CVN-70)

Dimensions: length 1,092 ft (332.9 m); beam 134 ft (40.8 m); flight deck width 252 ft (76.8 m); draft 37 ft (11.3 m)
Displacement: 72,916 tons standard and 91,487 tons full load
Performance: maximum speed +35 kt (+40 mph; +65 km/h); range 1.15 million miles (1.85 million km) at 20 kt (23 mph; 37 km/h)
Notional air wing: 86 aircraft, as USS *Enterprise*, including 20 Grumman F-14 Tomcats, 20 McDonnell Douglas F/A-18 Hornets, 20 Grumman A-6E Intruders (including some KA-6D tankers), 10 Lockheed S-3A/B Vikings, five Grumman EA-6B Prowlers, five Grumman E-2C Hawkeyes and six Sikorsky SH-60F Ocean Hawk helicopters
Aviation load: 9,000 tons of fuel and 2,570 tons of ordnance
Combat persistence: 16 days of normal operations without replenishment
Complement: 6,054 including 2,800 air wing and 70 flag staff

USS *Carl Vinson* (CVN-70)

Service notes: The USS *Carl Vinson* was commissioned in 1982. Shakedown and training cruises in the Atlantic were followed in 1983 by a deployment to the Mediterranean, before continuing around the world to join the Pacific Fleet. Since then, the *Carl Vinson* has made regular deployments to the west Pacific and the Indian Ocean, with Air Wing Fifteen embarked. Air Wing Fourteen was assigned in 1992.

Air wing:
USS *Carl Vinson*'s Air Wing Fourteen included, in 1992, the following squadrons:

VF-11 'Red Rippers'	F-14D
VF-31 'Tomcatters'	F-14D TARPS
VFA-113 'Stingers'	F/A-18C

USS *Abraham Lincoln* (CVN-72)
Service notes: The USS *Lincoln* commissioned into the Pacific Fleet in November 1989.

*Abraham Lincoln **has been in Pacific Fleet service since 1989. At 102,000 tons fully loaded, it is heavier than its predecessors.***

Air wing:
USS *Abraham Lincoln*'s Air Wing Eleven included, in 1992, the following squadrons:

VF-114 'Aardvarks'	F-14A
VF-213 'Black Lions'	F-14A TARPS
VFA-22 'Fighting Redcocks'	F/A-18C
VFA-94 'Shrikes'	F/A-18C
VA-95 'Green Lizards'	A-6E, KA-6D
VAW-117 'Wallbangers'	E-2C
VAQ-135 'Black Ravens'	EA-6B
HS-6 'Indians'	SH-60F, HH-60H
VS-29 'Screaming Dragon Fires'	S-3A

Specification
USS *Abraham Lincoln* (CVN-72)

Dimensions: length 1,092 ft (332.9 m); beam 134 ft (40.8 m); flight deck width 252 ft (76.8 m); draft 39 ft (11.9 m)
Displacement: 74,000 tons standard and 102,000 tons full load
Performance: maximum speed +35 kt (+40 mph; +65 km/h); range 1.15 million miles (1.85 million km) at 20 kt (23 mph; 37 km/h)
Notional air wing: 86 aircraft, as USS *Enterprise*, including 20 Grumman F-14 Tomcats, 20 McDonnell Douglas F/A-18 Hornets, 20 Grumman A-6E Intruders (including some KA-6D tankers), 10 Lockheed S-3A/B Vikings, five Grumman EA-6B Prowlers, five Grumman E-2C Hawkeyes and six Sikorsky SH-3H Sea King or SH-60F Sea Hawk helicopters
Aviation load: 9,000 tons of fuel and 2,570 tons of ordnance
Combat persistence: 16 days of normal operations without replenishment
Complement: 6,054 including 2,800 air wing and 70 flag staff

CARRIERS UNDER CONSTRUCTION, IN SLEP OR REFUELING

USS *Constellation* (CV-64)

Service notes: *Constellation* suffered a major dockyard fire while fitting out, which put her completion back by several months. She commissioned into the Pacific Fleet in October 1961. Aircraft from the carrier were involved in the 1964 Tonkin Gulf incident which spurred American participation in the Vietnam War. *Constellation* made eight combat deployments to Southeast Asia between June 1964 and October 1974, possibly the most successful cruise being in May 1972 when her aircraft scored numerous kills of North Vietnamese aircraft. After the war, *Constellation* continued to deploy in the Pacific and Indian Oceans. The carrier underwent a major refit at Bremerton between 1982 and 1984. In February 1985 *Constellation* was host to the first operational deployment of the McDonnell Douglas F/A-18 Hornet. In 1990 the carrier began a SLEP refit, and is temporarily assigned to AIRLANT while undergoing this. It will return to AIRPAC by December 1993.

Constellation's last regular air wing was CVW-14, which briefly served aboard *Independence* before its transfer to Japan. Air Wing Fourteen is now assigned to *Carl Vinson*. No air wing is currently assigned to USS *Constellation*.

Specification
USS *Constellation* (CV-64)

Dimensions: length 1,072 ft (326.7 m); beam 130 ft (39.6 m); flight deck width 260 ft (79.25 m); draft 37 ft (11.3 m)
Displacement: 60,100 tons standard and 80,800 tons full load
Performance: maximum speed 33 kt (38 mph; 61 km/h); range 13,800 miles (22200 km) at 20 kt (23 mph; 37 km/h)
Notional air wing: 84 aircraft, as USS *Forrestal*, including 20 Grumman F-14 Tomcats, 20 McDonnell Douglas F/A-18 Hornets, 20 Grumman A-6E Intruders (including some KA-6D tankers), 10 Lockheed S-3A/B Vikings, four Grumman EA-6B Prowlers, four Grumman E-2C Hawkeyes and six Sikorsky SH-3H Sea King or

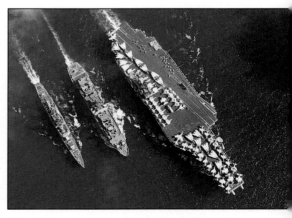

'Connie' replenishes under way during a 1979 cruise, which was followed by a refit.

SH-60F Ocean Hawk helicopters
Aviation load: 5,900 tons of fuel and 2,150 tons of ordnance
Combat persistence: 9-11 days of normal operations without replenishment
Complement: 5,480 including 2,480 air wing and 70 flag staff

USS *Enterprise* (CVN-65)

Service notes: Commissioned into the Atlantic Fleet in 1961, the nuclear-powered USS *Enterprise* was the largest warship in the world. In 1962, the huge carrier was involved in the blockade of Cuba. In May 1963 she demonstrated the capabilities of nuclear power when she formed a task group with the nuclear-powered cruiser *Long Beach* and the nuclear-powered frigate *Bainbridge*, in a non-stop cruise around the world. After her first refueling in 1964, *Enterprise* joined the Pacific Fleet. She was the first nuclear-powered vessel to see action, making eight combat deployments to Southeast Asia between November 1965 and May 1975. *Enterprise* was severely damaged off Hawaii in February 1969, in a fire caused by the accidental detonation of an aircraft rocket. Twenty-seven sailors died, 344 were injured and 15 aircraft were destroyed. After repairs she underwent her second refueling. In 1973, aircraft from *Enterprise* mounted the US Navy's final air attacks on Vietnamese targets. In 1974 the carrier hosted the first operational deployment of the Grumman F-14 Tomcat, and in 1975 those Tomcats provided top cover to the evacuation of Saigon. Between 1979 and 1982 *Enterprise* underwent a major overhaul, during which she was again refueled and from which she emerged with a radically different island superstructure. Through the 1980s the carrier continued to undertake deployments to the northern and western Pacific and to the Indian

Ocean. In 1991 she was laid up for a 'complex overhaul', during which a fifth set of reactor cores were to be fitted, to provide power for another 13 years in operation. This simple-sounding operation is in fact very costly and complex, and casts a shadow on the carrier's future. The one-of-a-kind *Enterprise* is built to a modified *Forrestal* design and is powered by eight reactors (unlike the two reactors of the newer 'Nimitz' class). She is temporarily assigned to AIRLANT while undergoing nuclear refueling and modernization, and her area of service is to be decided in 1994. No air wing is currently assigned to *Enterprise*.

Specification
USS *Enterprise* (CVN-65)

Dimensions: length 1,102 ft (335.9 m); beam 133 ft (40.5 m); flight deck width 252 ft (76.8 m); draft 35 ft

Enterprise undergoes sea trials in 1983 following a major reworking which altered the original superstructure. Again the ship is in dock, for refueling and modification.

9 in (10.9 m)
Displacement: 75,700 tons standard and 93,970 tons full load
Performance: maximum speed 35 kt (40 mph; 65 km/h); range 466,000 miles (750000 km) at 20 kt (23 mph; 37 km/h)
Notional air wing: 86 aircraft, including 20 Grumman F-14 Tomcats, 20 McDonnell Douglas F/A-18 Hornets, 20 Grumman A-6E Intruders (including some KA-6D tankers), 10 Lockheed S-3A/B Vikings, five Grumman EA-6B Prowlers, five Grumman E-2C Hawkeyes and six Sikorsky SH-3H Sea King or SH-60F Ocean Hawk helicopters
Aviation load: 8,500 tons of fuel and 2,520 tons of ordnance
Combat persistence: 12-14 days of normal operations without replenishment
Complement: 5,765 including 2,480 air wing and 70 flag staff

USS *George Washington* (CVN-73)

Service notes: Commissioning date 4 July 1992.

Specification
USS *George Washington* (CVN-73)

Dimensions: length 1,092 ft (332.9 m); beam 134 ft (40.8 m); flight deck width 252 ft (76.8 m); draft 39 ft (11.9 m)
Displacement: 74,000 tons standard and 102,000 tons full load
Performance: maximum speed +35 kt (+40 mph; +65 km/h); range 1.15 million miles (1.85 million km) at 20 kt (23 mph; 37 km/h)
Notional air wing: 86 aircraft, as USS *Enterprise*, including 20 Grumman F-14 Tomcats, 20 McDonnell

The Navy's latest carrier is George Washington, seen here in late 1991 undergoing final construction at Newport News shipyard at Norfolk prior to commissioning. Two more supercarriers are planned, the John C. Stennis and United States.

Douglas F/A-18 Hornets, 20 Grumman A-6E Intruders (including some KA-6D tankers), 10 Lockheed S-3A/B Vikings, five Grumman EA-6B Prowlers, five Grumman E-2C Hawkeyes and six Sikorsky SH-3H Sea King or SH-60F Sea Hawk helicopters
Aviation load: 9,000 tons of fuel and 2,570 tons of ordnance
Combat persistence: 16 days of normal operations without replenishment
Complement: 6,054 including 2,800 air wing and 70 flag staff

TRAINING CARRIER

USS *Forrestal* (CV-59)

Service notes: The USS *Forrestal* entered service with the Atlantic Fleet in 1956. The carrier deployed to the Mediterranean that year in response to the Suez crisis. *Forrestal* covered the evacuation of foreign nationals from the Lebanon during the 1958 Lebanese civil war, and later made one combat deployment to Southeast Asia. That deployment was cut short in August 1967 after a catastrophic explosion and fire during operations off the coast of North Vietnam. One hundred and thirty-four seamen were killed and 64 were wounded. The badly damaged vessel returned to Norfolk for repair. *Forrestal* then returned to the Atlantic Fleet. Four Mediterranean cruises in the early 1980s were followed by an 18-month SLEP refit between 1983 and 1985. *Forrestal* is no longer an operational carrier, having been designated the

US Navy's training carrier from 1992. This follows the withdrawal from service of the 'Essex'-class carrier USS *Lexington*. The last operational air wing carried by *Forrestal* was Air Wing Six.

Air wing:

USS *Forrestal*'s Air Wing Six included, at the time of its disestablishment on 1 April 1992, the following squadrons:

VF-11 'Red Rippers'	F-14A
VF-31 'Tomcatters'	F-14A TARPS
VFA-132 'Privateers'	F/A-18A
VFA-137 'Kestrels'	F/A-18A
VA-176 'Thunderbolts'	A-6E, KA-6D
VAW-122 'Steeljaws'	E-2C
VAQ-133 'Wizards'	EA-6B
HS-15 'Red Lions'	SH-3H
VS-28 'Gamblers'	S-3B

Specification
USS *Forrestal* (CV-59)

Dimensions: length 1,086 ft (331 m); beam 129 ft 6 in (39.5 m); flight deck width 252 ft (76.8 m); draft 37 ft

(11.3 m)
Displacement: 59,060 tons standard and 75,900 tons full load
Performance: maximum speed 33 kt (38 mph; 61 km/h); range 13,800 miles (22200 km) at 20 kt (23 mph; 37 km/h)
Notional air wing: 84 aircraft, including 20 Grumman F-14 Tomcats, 20 McDonnell Douglas F/A-18 Hornets, 20 Grumman A-6E Intruders (including some KA-6D tankers), 10 Lockheed S-3A/B Vikings, four Grumman EA-6B Prowlers, four Grumman E-2C Hawkeyes and six Sikorsky SH-3H Sea Kings or SH-60F Ocean Hawks
Aviation load: 5,500 tons of fuel and 1,650 tons of ordnance
Combat persistence: 8-10 days of normal operations without replenishment
Complement: 5,249 including 2,279 air wing and 70 flag staff

RECENTLY RETIRED CARRIERS

USS *Midway* (CV-41) was decommissioned in April 1992 and its air wing transferred to *Independence* (CV-62). USS *Lexington* (AVT-16) was retired in November 1991.

Organization

Carrier air wings and aircraft

The *raison d'être* of the aircraft carrier lies in the aircraft which it carries. The squadron is the usual deployed unit, although some aircraft types can deploy in flights. (The ES-3A will operate in flights aboard carriers, for example, as did Elint-configured A-3 Skywarriors.) The squadron is the smallest independent naval aviation unit, and typically consists of between nine and 12 aircraft (though S-3A Viking, E-2C Hawkeye, EA-6B Prowler and SH-3 Sea King or SH-60F Ocean Hawk units are appreciably smaller) with perhaps 200 personnel, officers and enlisted men. Except for a handful of (normally shore-based) larger squadrons, a regular squadron will typically be led by a commander, usually between 38 and 42 years old and with between 15 and 17 years in the Navy. Known as the Commanding Officer, or CO, he will usually be assigned the aircraft whose 'Modex' ends in the digits '01'. His deputy, the Executive Officer, or XO, is usually also a commander, slightly younger, and waiting to 'fleet up' to fill the CO's slot.

Depending on the size and mission of the unit, there may be another commander on board as Operations Officer, but this position will usually be held by a lieutenant commander, as are the other department heads (maintenance and administration). These officers each have lieutenants and lieutenants (junior grade) as assistants. All aircrew on board a carrier, with the exception of some Viking, Hawkeye and helicopter crew members, are officers. The number of such officers in a squadron depends on the aircraft type in use, with a typical F-14 unit having twice as many aircrew as an F/A-18 unit.

The largest portion of any squadron is the enlisted cadre, which consists of various rates (job specializations) and grades (ranks). They range in age from young 18-year-olds fresh from training to grizzled 'chiefs' (chief petty officers) who may have more than 30 years' experience. After the first three *ab initio* grades (E-1 to E-3) there are three petty officer grades: third class (E-4), second class (E-5) and first

class (E-6). There are also three grades of chief petty officer: chief petty officer (E-7), senior chief petty officer (E-8) and master chief petty officer (E-9). Senior enlisted men may also gain commissions as warrant officers, within certain specialities, including weapons, photography and administration. Some enlisted men can also be commissioned as limited duty officers.

The squadron is thus a varied yet homogenous group, whose morale and achievements depend on the leadership at the top. However, while the CO is firmly in command, and very much king of his domain, he has senior officers to whom he must report. His immediate superior is his wing commander. Since the US Navy is administered through two separate (but often connected) administrative systems, there are actually two types of wing, and the average squadron commander will have two wing commanders. While shore-based he will report to the commander of the relevant administrative or functional wing (known as Func-Wings), or when deployed to the commander of the carrier air wing (CVW). The CVW commander is inevitably known as the CAG (Commander Air Group), a historical anomaly dating from when such organizations were known as air groups and not air wings.

The CAG will typically be a junior captain, with at least one tour as a squadron CO under his belt. The tour as CAG is usually an officer's last flying assignment, although there are a handful of flying billets for captains and admirals, and those officers lucky enough to gain such a post take full advantage to maintain their flying proficiency. Even as a CAG, responsibilities usually prohibit an individual from spending much time in the cockpit although, to compensate, most CAGs will be checked out on several of the types under their command. Each squadron will have an aircraft nominally allocated to the CAG, usually with the 'double nuts' ('00') modex and often painted in some kind of special color scheme. The 'CAG bird' in a squadron will often be the only aircraft with 'high-vis' markings.

While on deployment, the CAG and his wing (normally between six and eight squadrons) report to the battle group commander, the CO of the aircraft carrier, who is always a designated Naval Aviator (either pilot or NFO) and a captain in rank. The carrier's XO is usually a captain, too, although he might begin his XO tour as a senior commander or captain (selectee). Command of a carrier is the most

A greenshirt checks the pressure on the catapult before launching a Lockheed Viking. The catapult has to be reset for different types of aircraft and for different launch weights.

prized goal in an ambitious Naval Aviator's career, and marks an individual as a front-runner whose further rise to flag rank is likely, if not inevitable.

The carrier captain will typically have amassed some 4,000-6,000 flying hours, with between 800 and 1,200 traps (carrier landings) in three or four squadron tours. Many will have previously been CAGs, and most will have completed a tour of duty as a department head aboard a carrier. The captains of nuclear-powered carriers will have also completed 16 months of specialized training after their tours as squadron XO and CO.

The aircraft carrier is administered through departments, one of which is the air department. Headed by the air officer (better known as the air boss) the air department is further subdivided into five divisions which look after aircraft handling on the flight deck, catapults and arrester gear, hangar deck aircraft handling, aviation fuels and primary air traffic control. A separate aircraft intermediate maintenance department looks after the intensive engineering effort.

The US Navy's remaining carriers share 11 air wings (nominally six per fleet), with two Reserve air wings. These air wings are not all of the same composition, since different types of ships can accommodate different numbers of aircraft, and since not all carriers can accommodate all aircraft types in use. In addition, there have been experiments in air wing composition in order to try to find the most efficient type, and some non-standard air wings are still deployed. The eventual aim, however, is to end up with a standard air wing, with the same number of aircraft of the various different types. This will bring great benefits in training and operationality.

Nine of the existing air wings are similar in composition (known as conventional CVWs), with a total of 86 aircraft. This total includes two long-range all-weather fighter/intercept squadrons equipped with 24 F-14 Tomcats, two fighter/light attack squadrons equipped with 24 F/A-18 Hornets, a single medium attack squadron equipped with 10 A-6E and four KA-6D Intruders, and single ECM/EW,

Full afterburner combines with the throw of the catapult to hurl a Tomcat off the deck. Plane-guard helicopters stand by in case the aircraft suffers a 'cold cat' shot, which deposits the aircraft into the water.

Above: Intruders, Vikings, Tomcats and a Greyhound maneuver on the cramped deck of USS America. The deck movements are carefully controlled using a scale model of the carrier to ensure safety and efficiency.

Above right: Steam from the previous cat shot hangs over the deck as a 'Pukin' Dogs' Tomcat is prepared for launch. A series of signals between air and deck crew ends with the traditional salute to the cat officer.

Right: Dedicated refueling for the carrier air wing is provided by the Grumman KA-6D Intruder, which has a hose-drum unit in the rear fuselage. Other types, such as regular Intruders and Vikings, can augment the tanking effort.

ASW, AEW and SAR/ASW squadrons equipped respectively with four or five EA-6B Prowlers, six (previously 10) S-3 Vikings, four or five E-2C Hawkeyes and six SH-3H Sea King or six SH-60F Ocean Hawk helicopters, and two HH-60H 'Rescue Hawk' helicopters.

The 'attack heavy' CVW-8 on board the USS *Roosevelt* represents the future composition of the air wing, which again has a total of 86 aircraft. It differs in having a second A-6E Intruder squadron, with a total of 20 of these powerful aircraft on charge, some equipped with buddy refueling pods. Hornet and Tomcat numbers are reduced by four aircraft of each type, and no dedicated KA-6Ds are carried. An extra EA-6B and an extra E-2C make up the total. Very recently, however, plans have been set in motion for a 'Power Projection' air wing, with 24 F/A-18s and 16 'exceptionally offensive aircraft': A-6s or AXs.

The 66-aircraft CVW-5 previously on USS *Midway* also had a second Intruder unit (with a total of 16 of these aircraft) and an extra Hornet unit (bringing the total to 36 F/A-18s), but lacked any F-14s or S-3s. The air wing was otherwise identical to the Conventional type.

CVW-2 on *Ranger* has two Intruder units (24 A-6Es, four KA-6Ds) and no Hornets, but is otherwise similar to the conventional wing, albeit with a total of only 76 aircraft. The impending early retirement of *Ranger* makes its conversion to a more standard CVW (incorporating Hornets) unlikely.

Perhaps the biggest change on US Navy carrier decks in recent years has been the substitution of the ageing A-7 Corsair II by the multi-role F/A-18 Hornet. The last A-7 units remained in service just long enough to participate in Desert Storm, but all have now been replaced. Although it lacks range (a fault admitted by even its most devoted admirers) the F/A-18 has revolutionized the light strike community, bringing an undreamed-of measure of versatility and survivability. Every Hornet on a

carrier deck represents both a modern ground attack aircraft, capable of precisely delivering the most modern types of ordnance, and also a highly effective air combat aircraft.

The original F/A-18A and its two-seat equivalent, the F/A-18B, have now been replaced on the production line by the F/A-18C and F/A-18D. The first 137 F/A-18Cs and 31 F/A-18Ds incorporated improved avionics and featured AMRAAM and IR-Maverick compatability, while the latest aircraft have been equipped to full night attack standard, with a Kaiser AV/AVQ-28 raster HUD, thermal imaging and color MFDs.

Future projects

The proposed F/A-18E and F/A-18F offer increased range, two extra stores stations and enhanced performance with uprated engines and a bigger wing. The US Navy currently plans to procure some 800, with deliveries from 1998. Research and development of the new-extended range Hornet will cost $4.88 billion. The two-seat F/A-18D has already started to replace the A-6E Intruder in US Marine Corps all-weather attack units, trading a slight reduction in range and endurance for survivability and accuracy. The F/A-18 (and Marine AV-8Bs) will eventually be replaced by an Advanced STOVL strike fighter. Two technology demonstrators for such an aircraft have already been funded in a joint NASA/DARPA project. The aircraft is likely to be a short take-off (90 m/300 ft) and vertical landing type, in broadly the same class as the F/A-18.

The importance of the F/A-18 Hornet to the

US Navy of the 1990s cannot be understated. Although the engine problems which crippled the F-14 Tomcat were finally solved in the F-14A (Plus), since redesignated F-14B, the aircraft is increasingly being seen as an expensive luxury which is no longer needed with the demise of the Soviet Union and Warsaw Pact, and whose fleet defense role can be as effectively fulfilled by AMRAAM-equipped Hornets operating in conjunction with ship- and land-based AEW platforms. Plans to build 127 advanced F-14Ds and produce 400 more by conversion were dramatically cut back, and now only 37 of these aircraft will be built, with 18 more produced by conversion of F-14As. The F-14D introduces new avionics, including APG-71 radar and a new IRST set. Even the interim re-engined F-14B (which retains F-14A avionics) will now only equip four front-line squadrons, with 38 being built new and 32 more being produced through conversion of F-14A airframes. The F-14 will remain in service for many years to come, but procurement was halted in May 1992, and the size of some F-14 squadrons has been reduced, making room for more multi-role Hornets and A-6E Intruders. Money is still being spent on the F-14, however, with $50 million for the Quick-strike program and $946 million for the conversion of F-14As to F-14D configuration. Four Atlantic Fleet F-14 squadrons have now undergone air-to-ground training and the Mk 80 series of bombs has already been cleared for carriage by the F-14 when operating from a land base. The 'Bombcat' will be in the Fleet by FY-93 and the first F-14 strike/fighter air wing will deploy in October 1992.

With less emphasis on the 500-nm outer air battle, the Advanced Air-to-Air Missile has now been cancelled and Admiral Dunleavy has publicly stated his preference for F/A-18 procurement. The reduced Soviet long-range aircraft/missile threat, he affirmed, "was one of the reasons that drove us to the F/A-18. We are more concerned in having a strike fighter than simply an aircraft that is built to shoot down other aircraft." The USN and the USAF still hope to develop improved propulsion and seeker for the AMRAAM, which is applicable to both the F/A-18 and F-14.

The A-6E Intruder, despite its age, remains crucially important. All operational aircraft are now to A-6E TRAM standard, although most A-6 units also include a handful of dedicated KA-6D tankers. Some 80 of the remaining 300 A-6E airframes are now severely *g*-limited because of fatigue problems and, during Desert Storm, many had to be relegated to performing tanker duties only. Cancellation of the A-12 leaves re-winging these aircraft as the only realistic option apart from replacing them by the two-seat all-weather F/A-18D (or a more advanced Hornet derivative) or one of the proposed strike versions of the Tomcat, for which Grumman is lobbying hard, but which would offer little more than an F/A-18 apart from (irrelevant) supersonic performance. One hundred and seventy-eight sets of new composite wings have been contracted for, and options on 72 or 144 more may be exercised. Ninety-four wing sets had been delivered by the beginning of 1990, and 22 sets had been fitted by Grumman and the two Naval Air Depots at Norfolk and Alameda. Current plans call for Grumman to install three sets per month, and for each of the NADEPs to install one set.

Intruder enhancement

Various improvements have already been, or are being, incorporated into the A-6. The Block 1A upgrade gives a new mission computer, a new HUD, new MFD, GPS, Integrated Defense Avionics Package and CAINS II ring laser gyro. The E-250 operational flight pro-

Weapons
The Hornet can carry a wide range of weapons, including AGM-84 Harpoon/SLAM and AGM-88 HARM air-to-surface missiles. Shown here is a typical short-range bombing load consisting of four Mk 82 500-lb bombs on the four wing pylons, and two AIM-9M and a single AIM-7M for self-defense or opportunist fighter engagements.

Powerplant
Two of General Electric's F404-GE-400 turbofans are fitted to the Hornet, each producing a thrust of 17,600 lb (78.32 kN). The F404-GE-402 EPE is now being delivered.

gram gives expanded weapons capability, improving FLIR tracking and simplifying the use of smart weapons. NVG compatibility is already well underway, with five Atlantic Fleet units declared NVG capable by the beginning of 1992.

In the longer term, the A-6 will be replaced by the AX (for which a navalized version of the USAF's F-22 could form the basis) during the early years of the next century (2007-2008). The Navy has a preliminary 700-nm range requirement, which may be relaxed as a trade-off for 'supercruise' capability. The US Navy

Approaching the carrier with everything dangling and flapping, it's easy to see how the F-14 picked up the 'Turkey' nickname. This 'Diamondback' F-14A carries a TARPS pod between the engine nacelles.

hopes to deploy some 16 A-6 or AX aircraft (both of which are classed as 'exceptionally offensive aircraft' by Assistant Chief of Naval Operations Admiral Richard Dunleavy) alongside 24 F/A-18s in the new 82-aircraft 'power projection air wing' mix.

The US Navy is moving further and further away from 'dumb' ordnance which requires an aircraft to overfly its target. Accordingly, the US Navy hopes to procure different stand-off weapons to fulfill several slightly different requirements. For short-range use, there is the Joint Direct Attack Munition, while the Joint Stand-Off Weapon (hitherto known as the Advanced Interdiction Weapon System) will be used to fill the medium-range requirement. For long-range use the USN will procure the Tri-Service Stand-off Attack Missile and Stand-off Land Attack Missile.

Mainstream US Navy carrier air wings adopted the ASW role (previously assigned mainly to shore-based aircraft, ship-based helicopters and a handful of specialist carriers) during the mid-1970s, and what had been attack carriers (CVAs) became general-purpose carriers (CVs). ASW aircraft are used alongside a core of fighter and strike aircraft, with the various support types. Thus all cur-

In the event of hook or undercarriage failure, the naval aviator always has the barrier as a last resort. These prove remarkably effective at recovering a stricken aircraft with little damage.

Sensor pods
Three pods are available to the Hornet to enhance night attack capability. These are mounted on the intake pylons and are the Ford Aerospace AAS-38 FLIR, Hughes AAR-50 TINS (Thermal Imaging Navigation Set) and Martin Marietta ASQ-173 LDT/SCAM (Laser Designator Tracker/Strike Camera).

Radar
The principal sensor is the Hughes APG-65 multi-mode radar, providing a full range of functions for both air-to-air and air-to-surface (including sea search and terrain avoidance) roles.

McDonnell Douglas F/A-18C Hornet

Procured to replace the Vought A-7 on light attack squadrons, and the last remaining F-4 Phantoms aboard the Japan-based *Midway*, the F/A-18 Hornet has introduced considerable upgrades in capability in both the attack and secondary air defense roles. The Hornet airframe is seen as the basis for the Navy's future plans in the form of the F/A-18E/F, an enlarged and enhanced Hornet which will assume the roles of the current Hornet and Tomcat squadrons. This F/A-18C is marked as the CAG-bird of VFA-87 'Golden Warriors'.

Intakes
No Mach 2 performance was required of the Hornet, so the intakes did not need variable ramps. A simple 'D'-shaped intake is mounted under the leading edge root extension, with a splitter plate to separate boundary layer air.

Cannon
Mounted in the nose ahead of the cockpit is the M61A1 Vulcan cannon. A rotary weapon with six barrels, the Hornet's gun is armed with a maximum of 578 rounds.

Flight control
A digital fly-by-wire system controls all Hornet flight operations, including a return to straight and level function if the pilot lets go of the controls. Roll control is performed by ailerons and tailerons, aided by flaperons at low speeds.

rent types of CVW include six helicopters (with a dual SAR and ASW role) or eight where the SH-60F is in use. All wings also include between six and 10 S-3 Vikings.

The remarkable Viking (affectionately dubbed the 'Hoover' because of the peculiar hoot of its turbofan engines) has proved extraordinarily successful in service, and has even been pressed into service as a bomber (this latter role being demonstrated during the Gulf War). The Viking is unique among US Navy carrierborne aircraft in that its crew includes an enlisted man, the only 'White Hat' to fly in an

Moving aircraft, tow trucks, live ordnance, hungry air intakes, tie-down cleats and parking chains can make the carrier deck a highly unsafe place for the unwary deck crew. Safety training is therefore of the highest order.

ejection seat. In 1981, Lockheed received a contract to upgrade 160 of the 187 S-3As built to S-3B standard, with increased acoustic processing capacity, expanded ESM, better radar processing, provision for the Harpoon missile and a new sonobuoy telemetry receiver. These modifications are being incorporated at NAS Cecil Field, FL, and at the time of writing all Atlantic Fleet units have S-3Bs, with some Pacific Fleet units having also transitioned.

The basic S-3 airframe has been used to provide a COD platform (the US-3A) and was used when the USN needed a replacement for the ageing Skywarrior in the carrierborne Elint role, producing the ES-3A, which has recently flown in prototype form. This will allow new squadrons VQ-5 and VQ-6 to form at Agana and Cecil. These will operate Elint aircraft from carriers for the first time since 1987, when a Skywarrior crash (on 21 November) on the USS *Nimitz* led to the type being restricted to shore bases. VQ-1 discarded its Skywarriors in December 1988, followed by VQ-2 in October 1991, leaving these units operating only the EP-3 Orion. VQ-2 used the EA-3B operationally in the Gulf, but all have now been retired. A handful of Skywarriors are used by civilian contractors for a variety of trials duties.

The carrierborne inner zone ASW role is handled by helicopters. The trusty Sikorsky SH-3H Sea King is only now being replaced by the SH-60F version of the Sea Hawk, known as the Ocean Hawk. This newer helicopter has made one deployment with HS-2 aboard the USS *Nimitz* and is entering service with HS-3, HS-4, HS-6, HS-8 and HS-15. By comparison with the SH-60B used for outer-zone ASW work and deployed on smaller ships, the SH-60F lacks MAD gear, ESM and datalink, and carries only eight sonobuoys. The aircraft lacks the SH-60B's underfuselage radar scanner, and instead has a dunking sonar. The SH-60F can carry the Mk 46 or Mk 50 homing torpedo. When they deploy, SH-60F units will eventually have six Ocean Hawks and two HH-60Hs for combat SAR.

Another vitally important support type is the Grumman E-2C Hawkeye. Deployed aboard every carrier in fours (or fives), the turboprop-

powered 'hummer' serves as an airborne early warning and radar command post, and is chiefly used for the control of F-14 interceptors. The aircraft is reputed to be one of the most difficult types to bring aboard a carrier. Early E-2Cs were equipped with the AN/APS-139 radar, but all will be retrofitted with the newer AN/APS-145. Preliminary plans for a Hawkeye replacement were reviewed during early 1992 and a mission statement for a follow-on (dubbed EX) was issued. A SLEP (Service Life Extension Program) is likely to be instituted to prolong service life until at least 2010, and the EX requirement could be fulfilled by an E-2C derivative or even by conversion of existing Hawkeyes with new computers and sat-comms.

Hawkeye replacement

Senior officers seem to have dismissed the use of satellites, airships or UAVs in the AEW role, and the use of a common airframe to replace all carrierborne EW and AEW types seems to have been killed off on grounds of practicality and expense. A possible Hawkeye replacement is a Lockheed/LTV Viking derivative, with an electronically-scanned, fixed, phased-array radar in a triangular fairing above the fuselage. Whatever the outcome of current EX plans, Grumman is engaged in a program which will bring all surviving E-2Cs to Group II standards, with extended-range radar, IFF, improved engines, JTIDS and GPS by 2000. A total of 54 aircraft will be retrofitted to this standard, while the last 21 E-2Cs built for the USN are built with Group II equipment. The last E-2C will be delivered during 1993.

To support and protect packages of strike aircraft, every carrier has a detachment of EA-6B Prowler ECM/EW aircraft. Developed from the A-6 Intruder, the Prowler is a dedicated electronic warfare platform, with four crew sitting in tandem pairs of side-by-side ejection seats. First deployed in Vietnam, the aircraft has been continuously updated and upgraded, so that several standards of Prowler are now in use. Representing today's baseline is the EA-6B ICAP-1, which introduced increased jamming capability with an eight-band

The hardest part of the naval pilot's job is trapping back aboard the carrier, especially when it is pitching in a heavy sea at night. This VF-33 CAG-bird makes it look easy.

expanded jamming system, reduced response time, and a multi-format display, along with an automatic all-weather carrier landing system, and new navigation and communications systems. Twenty-three basic aircraft were followed by 25 EXCAP EA-6Bs, all of which have now been retired or upgraded. Twenty-one surviving basic production aircraft were modified to ICAP-1 standard, followed by 45 new-build aircraft. The ICAP-2 modification further enhanced jamming capability with a new AYK-14 computer with four times the memory and three times the processing speed. This enables the system to operate effectively across nine frequency bands. Each of the five external jammer pods can generate signals in one of seven frequency bands (instead of one) and can jam in two frequency bands simultaneously. New-build ICAP-2 aircraft began rolling off the line during 1984. EA-6Bs have also carried the HARM missile since 1986, using them successfully in the Gulf War.

The latest EA-6B equipment standard is known as ADVCAP. ADVCAP aircraft are compatible with the HARM missile (two extra underwing hardpoints are provided to make up for the use of the two inboard pylons for the missile), and incorporates the new Lockheed-Sanders AN/ALQ-149 communications jammer, with its distinctive underfuselage antenna. Various other new jammers are incorporated, along with extra chaff/flare dispensers, Navstar GPS and JTIDS. The increased weight is compensated by uprated engines and a host of aerodynamic improvements, including an increased-height tailfin, recontoured slats and flaps, drooped wing leading edges and new strakes on the forward fuselage. Some 100 ADVCAPs are to be converted from ICAP-2 standard aircraft.

One EA-6B has been modified to serve as the Vehicle Improvement Program (VIP) testbed, aimed at improving low speed and maneuvering limitations by using modified slats and flaps, and airbrakes which also act as ailerons.

AIRLANT

Air Wing One (USS *America*)

VF-102	'Diamondbacks'	F-14A TARPS	Codes commence AB/100
VF-33	'Starfighters'	F-14A	Codes commence AB/200
VFA-82	'Marauders'	F/A-18C	Codes commence AB/300
VFA-86	'Sidewinders'	F/A-18C	Codes commence AB/400
VA-85	'Buckeyes'	A-6E/KA-6D	Codes commence AB/500
VAW-123	'Screwtops'	E-2C	Codes commence AB/600
VAQ-137	'Rooks'	EA-6B	Codes commence AB/620
HS-11	'Dragon Slayers'	SH-3H	Codes commence AB/610
VS-32	'Maulers'	S-3B	Codes commence AB/700

(VF-33 were previously known as the 'Fighting Tarsiers')
(VA-85 have been known as the 'Black Falcons')

Air Wing Three (USS *John F. Kennedy*)

VF-14	'Tophatters'	F-14A	Codes commence AC/100
VF-32	'Swordsmen'	F-14A TARPS	Codes commence AC/200
VFA-37	'Bulls'	F/A-18C	Codes commence AC/300
VFA-105	'Gunslingers'	F/A-18C	Codes commence AC/400
VA-75	'Sunday Punchers'	A-6E/KA-6D	Codes commence AC/500
VAW-126	'Seahawks'	E-2C	Codes commence AC/600
VAQ-130	'Zappers'	EA-6B	Codes commence AC/620
HS-7	'Big Dippers'	SH-3H	Codes commence AC/610
VS-22	'Vidars'	S-3B	Codes commence AC/700

Air Wing Six (Disestablished 1 April 1992)

VF-11	'Red Rippers'	F-14A	Transferred to CVW-14
VF-31	'Tomcatters'	F-14A TARPS	Transferred to CVW-14
VFA-132	'Privateers'	F/A-18C	Disestablished
VFA-137	'Kestrels'	F/A-18C	Transferred to CVW-2
VA-176	'Thunderbolts'	A-6E/KA-6D	Disestablished
VAW-122	'Steeljaws'	E-2C	Disestablished
VAQ-133	'Wizards'	EA-6B	Disestablished
HS-15	'Red Lions'	SH-3H	Transitioning to SH-60F/HH-60H
VS-28	'Gamblers'	S-3B	Disestablished

Air Wing Seven (USS *Dwight D. Eisenhower*)

VF-143	'Pukin' Dogs'	F-14B TARPS	Codes commence AG/100
VF-142	'Ghostriders'	F-14B	Codes commence AG/200
VFA-136	'Knighthawks'	F/A-18C	Codes commence AG/300
VFA-131	'Wildcats'	F/A-18C	Codes commence AG/400
VA-34	'Blue Blasters'	A-6E/KA-6D	Codes commence AG/500
VAW-121	'Bluetails'	E-2C	Codes commence AG/600
VAQ-140	'Patriots'	EA-6B	Codes commence AG/620
HS-5	'Night Dippers'	SH-3H	Codes commence AG/610
VS-31	'Top Cats'	S-3B	Codes commence AG/700

Air Wing Eight (USS *Theodore Roosevelt*)

VF-41	'Black Aces'	F-14A	Codes commence AJ/100
VF-84	'Jolly Rogers'	F-14A TARPS	Codes commence AJ/200
VFA-15	'Valions'	F/A-18A	Codes commence AJ/300

All US Navy carrier air wings include a detachment of Grumman EA-6B Prowlers for ECM and EW duties. A squadron is the usual deployed unit, although a Prowler squadron has only a handful of aircraft (usually four). Here a Prowler of CVW-1's VAQ-137 'Rooks' is captured seconds before it takes that elusive OK 3 Wire. Although Prowlers operate on every carrier, with both Atlantic and Pacific Fleets, the EA-6B is shore-based at a single location, NAS Whidbey Island in Washington state.

Below: In addition to its internal drogue system, this KA-6D tanker carries a buddy refueling pod under the centerline. It is from VA-85, part of Air Wing One.

Air Wing Seventeen (USS *Saratoga*)

VF-74	'Bedevilers'	F-14B	Codes commence AA/100
VF-103	'Sluggers'	F-14B TARPS	Codes commence AA/200
VFA-83	'Rampagers'	F/A-18C	Codes commence AA/300
VFA-81	'Sunliners'	F/A-18C	Codes commence AA/400
VA-35	'Black Panthers'	A-6E/KA-6D	Codes commence AA/500
VAW-125	'Tigertails'	E-2C	Codes commence AA/600
VAQ-132	'Scorpions'	EA-6B	Codes commence AA/620
HS-9	'Sea Griffins'	SH-3H	Codes commence AA/610
VS-30	'Diamondcutters'	S-3B	Codes commence AA/700

Air Wing Eight (continued)

VFA-87	'Golden Warriors'	F/A-18A	Codes commence AJ/400
VA-65	'Tigers'	A-6E	Codes commence AJ/500
VA-36	'Roadrunners'	A-6E	Codes commence AJ/530
VAW-124	'Bear Aces'	E-2C	Codes commence AJ/600
HS-3	'Tridents'	SH-60F/HH-60H	Codes commence AJ/610
VAQ-141	'Shadowhawks'	EA-6B	Codes commence AJ/620
VS-24	'Scouts'	S-3B	Codes commence AJ/700

AIRPAC

Air Wing Two (USS *Ranger*)

VF-1	'Wolfpack'	F-14A	Codes commence NE/100
VF-2	'Bounty Hunters'	F-14A TARPS	Codes commence NE/200
VA-155	'Silver Foxes'	A-6E/KA-6D	Codes commence NE/400
VA-145	'Swordsmen'	A-6E/KA-6D	Codes commence NE/500
VAW-116	'Sun Kings'	E-2C	Codes commence NE/600
VAQ-131	'Lancers'	EA-6B	Codes commence NE/620
HS-14	'Chargers'	SH-3H	Codes commence NE/610
VS-38	'Red Griffins'	S-3A	Codes commence NE/700
VFA-137	'Kestrels'	F/A-18C	To join CVW-2 from CVW-6
VFA-151	'Vigilantes'	F/A-18C	To join CVW-2 from CVW-5

Air Wing Five (USS *Independence*)

VF-154	'Black Knights'	F-14A TARPS	Codes commence NF/100
VF-21	'Freelancers'	F-14A	Codes commence NF/200
VFA-192	'World Famous Golden Dragons'	F/A-18A	Codes commence NF/300
VFA-195	'Dambusters'	F/A-18A	Codes commence NF/400
VA-115	'Eagles'	A-6E	Codes commence NF/500
VAW-115	'Sentinels'	E-2C	Codes commence NF/600
VAQ-136	'Gauntlets'	EA-6B	Codes commence NF/604
HS-12	'Wyverns'	SH-3H	Codes commence NF/610
VS-21	'Fighting Redtails'	S-3B	Codes commence NF/700
VFA-151	'Vigilantes'	F/A-18A	Transferred to CVW-2
VA-185	'Knighthawks'	A-6E/KA-6D	Decommissioned 1991 NF/400

Air Wing Nine (USS *Nimitz*)

VF-24	'Fighting Renegades'	F-14A*	Codes commence NG/100
VF-211	'Fighting Checkmates'	F-14A* TARPS	Codes commence NG/200
VFA-146	'Blue Diamonds'	F/A-18C	Codes commence NG/300
VFA-147	'Argonauts'	F/A-18C	Codes commence NG/400
VA-165	'Boomers'	A-6E/KA-6D	Codes commence NG/500
VAW-112	'Golden Hawks'	E-2C	Codes commence NG/600
VAQ-138	'Yellow Jackets'	EA-6B	Codes commence NG/620
HS-2	'Golden Falcons'	SH-60F/HH-60F	Codes commence NG/610
VS-33	'Screwbirds'	S-3A	Codes commence NG/700

(*VF-24 and VF-211 transitioned back to the F-14A from the F-14B in 1992 due to a shortage of F-14Bs)

Air Wing Eleven (USS *Abraham Lincoln*)

VF-114	'Aardvarks'	F-14A	Codes commence NH/100
VF-213	'Black Lions'	F-14A TARPS	Codes commence NH/200
VFA-22	'Fighting Redcocks'	F/A-18C	Codes commence NH/300
VFA-94	'Shrikes'	F/A-18C	Codes commence NH/400
VA-95	'Green Lizards'	A-6E/KA-6D	Codes commence NH/500
VAW-117	'Wallbangers'	E-2C	Codes commence NH/600
VAQ-135	'Black Ravens'	EA-6B	Codes commence NH/604
HS-6	'Indians'	SH-60F/HH-60H	Codes commence NH/610
VS-29	'Screaming Dragon Fires'	S-3A	Codes commence NH/700

Above: The standard air wing has one squadron of A-6E Intruders for the heavy attack mission, although Ranger's CVW-2 has an extra A-6 unit in place of the Hornet squadrons. This Desert Storm veteran is from VA-145.

Below: Hornets from VFA-92 enter the landing pattern for Midway, which had four F/A-18 squadrons. This carrier has been replaced at Yokosuka by Independence, while resident CVW-5 has returned to a standard complement.

Right: Lockheed's versatile S-3 Viking has the primary role of providing outer zone ASW protection for the carrier battle group, but can also tote bombs, anti-shipping missiles or air-to-air refueling pods. The 'Hoover' has also spawned a dedicated Elint sub-variant, the ES-3A, which is entering service with two squadrons.

Air Wing Fourteen (USS *Carl Vinson*)

VF-11	'Red Rippers'	F-14D	Codes commence NK/100
VF-31	'Tomcatters'	F-14D TARPS	Codes commence NK/200
VFA-113	'Stingers'	F/A-18C	Codes commence NK/300
VFA-25	'Fist of the Fleet'	F/A-18C	Codes commence NK/400
VA-196	'Main Battery'	A-6E	Codes commence NK/500
VAW-113	'Black Hawks'	E-2C	Codes commence NK/600
VAQ-139	'Cougars'	EA-6B	Codes commence NK/620
HS-8	'Eight Ballers'	SH-3H	Codes commence NK/610
VS-35	'Blue Wolves'	S-3A	Codes commence NK/700

Air Wing Fifteen (USS *Kitty Hawk*)

VF-51	'Screaming Eagles'	F-14A	Codes commence NL/100
VF-111	'Sundowners'	F-14A TARPS	Codes commence NL/200
VFA-27	'Chargers'	F/A-18C	Codes commence NL/300
VFA-97	'Warhawks'	F/A-18C	Codes commence NL/400
VA-52	'Knight Riders'	A-6E/KA-6D	Codes commence NL/500
VAW-114	'Hormel Hawgs'	E-2C	Codes commence NL/600
VAQ-134	'Garudas'	EA-6B	Codes commence NL/605
HS-4	'Black Knights'	SH-60F	Codes commence NL/610
VS-37	'Sawbucks'	S-3A	Codes commence NL/700

Above: Sikorsky's ancient SH-3 Sea King is now nearing the end of its carrierborne career, with replacement by the newer SH-60 Ocean Hawk well underway. The aircraft performs inner zone ASW, Vertrep, plane-guard and combat rescue duties. The gray and white color scheme seen here has largely given way to an overall gray tactical scheme.

Below: Nosewheel compressed, tailerons up, a VF-2 'Bounty Hunters' Tomcat strains against its brakes as a crewman sprints clear. In seconds the cat officer will drop his arm, the catapult will fire, the flimsy holdback will snap, and several tons of fighter will hurtle into the air. One of every carrier's two F-14 units has a secondary recce role using the TARPS pod. VF-2 is CVW-2's recce unit.

Gaps in the sequence of air wings have been caused by a number of decommissionings. Most recent was CVW-6, which decommissioned in 1992 after *Forrestal* was reassigned as an AVT. CVW-13 was disestablished after *Coral Sea* was retired in 1989. CVW-10 had a brief existence in the late 1980s, but never deployed, while CVW-16, CVW-21 and CVW-19 decommissioned in 1971, 1975 and 1977 respectively. The designation CVW-18 has never been used. This gives the 11 CVWs required for the likely 10-carrier Navy of the late 1990s.

Organization

ADMINISTRATIVE COMMAND

Although the prototype first flew as long ago as July 1959, the Kaman Seasprite still plays a large part in US Naval Aviation, sharing the task of deploying to ships with the SH-60B Seahawk. These undertake a wealth of duties from their parent vessel, the primary task being antisubmarine patrols. Secondary roles include rescue and general light transport.

Administratively, command originates with the Chief of Naval Operations, and then runs through two area fleet commanders (Atlantic and Pacific), who control surface vessels, submarines, the Marines and Aviation. These are responsible for training and readiness. Aviation comes under the Commander Naval Air Force Atlantic (COMNAVAIRLANT) and the Commander Naval Air Force Pacific (COMNAVAIRPAC), headquartered respectively in Norfolk, Virginia, and San Diego, California.

Each has administrative control over some 2,300 aircraft and is headed by a three-star admiral. (In time of war, however, the organizations 'fade' somewhat, and operational control is exercised directly by CINCLANT and CINCPAC.) They control the various aircraft carriers, and naval air stations and naval air facilities worldwide. In the administrative 'wiring diagrams' of COMNAVAIRLANT and COMNAVAIRPAC, different aircraft types are divided by community and report to a confusing array of wings, whose designations owe little to any desire for commonality or logic. In the main, however, most of these wings exercise control over shipborne squadrons only while these are shore-based between cruises.

Apart from the carrier-based units, this includes the various ship-based helicopter units operating aircraft as diverse as the SH-2F and SH-60B LAMPS platforms and transport aircraft like the CH-46 and CH-53. The various HSLs deploy helicopters to various types of ships on an as-required basis. SH-2Fs only go to the 'Knox'- and 'Kidd'-class frigates, and to the Truxton nuclear-powered cruiser.

'Spruance'-class ASW destroyers accept the SH-60B. The first two 'Ticonderoga'-class Aegis cruisers take SH-2Fs but others in the class take SH-60Bs. Of the 'Oliver Hazard Perry'-class ASW frigates, the first and third through 25th ships carry SH-2Fs, but the second and the 25th through 51st take SH-60Bs. The *Belknap* cruiser itself carries an SH-3G as a transport, but the other eight vessels in the class embark an SH-2F.

Despite the widespread introduction of the SH-60B, the Seasprite still has a long life ahead of it. A life extension program incorporating new GE T700 engines and revised avionics has resulted in the SH-2G. Six have been newly-built, but most of the 97 required are to be produced by conversion of existing SH-2Fs.

The exceptions to this rule are provided by the patrol wings, which often conduct operations and train from the same shore bases. On deployment the wings and their squadrons report to the area operational commanders. Atlantic Fleet Patrol squadrons currently maintain permanent deployments at NAS Bermuda (manned only by Reserve units), NAS Roosevelt Roads, Puerto Rico, NAS Rota, Spain, NAF Lajes in the Azores and NAS Sigonella, Sicily. Pacific units staff deployments at NAS Adak, Alaska, NAF Misawa, Japan, NAF Kadena, Okinawa, and NAF Diego Garcia. The regular detachment to NAS Cubi Point, Philippines, ended in early 1992. The patrol community has undergone a number of recent changes in the drive towards modernization. In order to free late Orions for the re-equipment of some Reserve units, the patrol wings have been reduced from six to five squadrons, and squadron establishments have dropped from nine to eight aircraft.

The other community which uses the Orion is more secretive. Elint is the role of the EP-3E-II Aries II aircraft used by VQ-1 and VQ-2 at Agana and Rota, while highly modified P-3Bs are used by VPU-1 and VPU-2 at Brunswick and Barbers Point. The latter aircraft are painted to resemble standard P-3Cs and often carry spurious serials and squadron insignia.

Naval Aviation is administered overall by a three-star Assistant Chief of Naval Operations (ACNO Air Warfare or Op 05) in Washington, DC. His task is to implement the programs of the CNO with respect to naval aviation, determining support requirements for aircraft and ships, and acting as CNO's principal advisor on aviation matters. The present incumbent is Vice Admiral Richard M. Dunleavy, a former A-3 and A-6 NFO, who is scheduled to retire and to be replaced by Vice Admiral Jerry D. Tuttle. The ACNO does not exercise operational control, however, which lies in the hands of CINCLANT and CINCPAC, who are four-star Admirals.

Naval Air Systems Command

Inevitably referred to as Navair, the Naval Air Systems Command, headed by a three-star (aviator) Admiral, oversees the development, production and procurement of all air-related equipment, including aircraft, aircrew and support equipment and armaments. Navair also oversees all modification programs relating to existing aircraft and systems. Navair was created in 1966 from the Bureau of Naval Weapons which, in turn, was formed in 1959 from the Bureau of Aeronautics and the Bureau of Ordnance.

After gaining Congressional approval, all US Naval Aviation research and development has now been concentrated under a new

organization headquartered at Crystal City near Washington, DC: the Naval Air Warfare Center, which stood up on 1 January 1992. This was part of a wider program, under which 32 organizations were streamlined into four 'full spectrum' Warfare Centers. The Naval Air Warfare Center will oversee the work of an Aircraft Division (at Lakehurst, Warminster and Patuxent River) and a Weapons Division (split between China Lake and Point Mugu). The existing separate technical commands will lose their present status and will report to the new organization.

These commands were, for the record, the Naval Weapons Evaluation Facility at Kirtland AFB, NM (which will close); the Naval Air Development Center at Warminster, PA (also due to close); the Naval Air Propulsion Center at Trenton, NJ; the Naval Avionics Center at

Indianapolis, IN; the Naval Weapons Center at China Lake, CA; the Naval Air Engineering Center at Lakehurst, NJ; the Naval Ordnance Missile Test Station at White Sands, NM; and the Pacific Missile Test Center at Point Mugu, CA. The Naval Air Test Center, Naval Air Development Center, Naval Air Engineering Center, Naval Air Propulsion Center, Naval Avionics Center, Naval Research Laboratory and Navy Test Pilot's School form the Aircraft Division, while the other organizations form the Weapons Division.

Naval Air Warfare Center Aircraft Division, Warminster, PA

The broad task of the Naval Air Warfare Center (previously the Naval Air Development Center) at Warminster is to enhance technology, improving existing aircraft and systems by refining equipment already in use. This involves a great deal of software and avionics integration work. Heavily involved with ASW development, their work led to the P-3C updates and to the LAMPS project. The NAWC is also involved with the Aries Elint/EW modifications to the Orion, and with instrument and avionics development.

| NAWC | UP-3A (with S-3 avionics), P-3C, F-14A, T-2C | Warminster, PA |

Naval Air Warfare Center Aircraft Division, Lakehurst, NJ
The Naval Air Warfare Center (previously the Naval Engineering Center) at Lakehurst conducts programs of research, engineering development, testing, evaluation and systems integration, as well as procurement and fleet engineering support for aircraft launching and recovery systems, landing aids and support equipment for aircraft and weapons systems.

Naval Air Warfare Center Aircraft Division, NAS Patuxent River, MD
The NAWC at Patuxent River, previously the Naval Air Test Center, is home to the Flight Test and Engineering Group, which tests and evaluates aircraft, systems and weapons systems to determine their suitability for service use. The center's prime responsibility is for strike and ASW aircraft and helicopters, but it also tests and develops systems, servicing procedures and even computers. The NAWC has a wide variety of aircraft types on charge for trials, and to support such trials. In the latter category is the service's sole Convair 880, used as an inflight-refueling tanker and for ASW trials. VX-4 'Evaluators', based at Point Mugu, operates as part of the NAWC.

| FTEG | F-14A, NF-14D, F/A-18A/C, AV-8B, A-6E, E-2C, S-3B, AH-1W, SH-2F, SH-3H, NVH-3A, CH-53E, SH-60B, HH-60H, HH-60J, T-45A, Cv.880, P-3B, P-3C, E-6A | Patuxent River, MD |

Naval Air Warfare Center Weapons Division, China Lake, CA
The Naval Air Warfare Center (previously the Naval Weapons Center) at China Lake is a major research development and test center for naval weapons, primarily concerned with naval air warfare. It includes full range facilities (including nuclear range facilities) and deals with all types of ordnance, guided and unguided, powered and free-fall. To support these tasks, the NAWC operates a large fleet of aircraft including substantial numbers of unmanned target drones. The NAWC parents a number of smaller units, including VX-5 'Vampires'.

| NAWC | F/A-18A/C/D, AV-8B, A-6E, TA-7C, NTA-4J, QF-4N/S, QF-86F, T-39D, AH-1W, UH-1N | China Lake, CA |

Naval Air Warfare Center Weapons Division, Point Mugu, CA
Previously known as the Pacific Missile Test Center, the NAWC's Weapons Division at Point Mugu tests and evaluates naval missiles, including air-to-air and air-to-ground

weapons, providing development, engineering, logistic, training and range support. It parents the Pacific Missile Range Facility at Barkings Sands, HI, which operates RC-12Ms and UH-3As. F/A-18s and F-14s are used as launch aircraft and for chase duties. The various Orions and the RC-12M are used for range control duties.

| NAWC | F-14A, NF-14D, F/A-18A/B, F/QF-4N/S, A-6E, EP-3A, RP-3A, RC-12M, A-7E/TA-7C, EA-7L | Point Mugu, CA |

Naval Weapons Evaluation Facility, Kirtland, NM
The Naval Weapons Evaluation Facility is based at Kirtland AFB, near Albuquerque. Its task is to test, evaluate and support nuclear and conventional weapons. The facility assists in the trials of some naval aircraft, its duties being mainly to support the development of delivery methods. Recently, the NWEF has carried out work on both SLAM and Harpoon.

| NWEF | A-6E, F/A-18A/B | Kirtland, NM |

Naval Research Laboratory, Washington, DC
NRL is a scientific research facility, consisting of several laboratories, whose assigned aircraft are operated by the NRL Flight Support Detachment from Patuxent River, MD

| NRL | EP-3A, RP-3A, EP-3B, P-3B | Patuxent River, MD |

Naval Coastal Systems Center, Panama City, FL
The Naval Coastal Systems Center incorporates the Naval Diving and Salvage training center, and the Navy Experimental Dive Unit. Aircraft operate in a purely support role.

| NCSC | MH-53E | Panama City, FL |

NAWC has many constituent parts, including the former NATC at Patuxent River (P-3s, top) and the former PMTC at Point Mugu (F/A-18, above).

Naval Test Pilot's School, Patuxent River, MD
With so many test establishments, the US Navy has a requirement for large numbers of test pilots and flight test engineers. It therefore trains its own at the Naval Test Pilot's School at Patuxent River. The school enjoys an excellent reputation, and receives students (on an exchange basis) from the US Air Force, Britain, France and a number of other countries. The unit operates a large and varied fleet of aircraft and helicopters to give students the broadest possible experience. TA-4s and TA-7s have recently been retired, leaving four T-38As and two F/A-18Bs as the prime fast-jet type. Many types stay with the NTPS for only a short time. The types listed are the 'regulars'.

| NTPS | F/A-18B, T-2C, T-38A, T-39D, OH-6A/B, UH-60A, HH-65A, NU-1B, U-6A, U-21A, X-26A | Patuxent River, MD |

Miscellaneous units

AUTEC detachment Andros Island, Bahamas	UH-3A	
BF NAF Atlanta, GA	UC-12B	'7B'
BF NAS Norfolk, VA	UC-12B/M	'7C'
BF NAF Dallas, TX	A-4M, UC-12B	'7D'
BF NAS Jacksonville, FL	UC-12B, SH-3D	'7E'
BF NAF Brunswick, ME	UC-12B, HH-1N	'7F'
BF NAS Whidbey Island, WA	UC-12B, SH-3D	'7G'
BF NAF Fallon, NV	UC-12B, HH-1N	'7H'
BF NAF Alameda, CA	UC-12B	'7J'
BF NAF Memphis, TN	UC-12B	'7K'
BF NAF Point Mugu, CA	UC-12B, HH-46D	'7L'
BF NAS North Island, CA	UC-12B	'7M'
BF NAF Washington, DC	UC-12B	'7N'

BF NAS Key West, FL	UC-12B, SH-3D	'7Q'
BF NAS Oceana, VA	UC-12B, SH-3D	'7R'
BF NAS Lemoore, CA	UC-12B, HH-1N	'7S'
BF NAS Moffett, CA	UC-12B	'7T'
BF NAS Cecil Field, FL	UC-12B	'7U'
BF NAS Glenview, IL	UC-12B	'7V'
BF NAF Willow Grove, PA	UC-12B	'7W'
BF NAF New Orleans, LA	UC-12B	'7X'
BF NAF Detroit, MI	UC-12B	'7Y'
BF NAF South Weymouth, ME	UC-12B	'7Z'
BF NAF Sigonella, Sicily	UC-12M	'8C'
BF NAF Rota, Spain	UC-12M	'8D'
BF NAF Roosevelt Roads PR	UC-12B, RC-12M	'8E'
BF NAF Guantanamo Bay, Cuba	UC-12B	'8F'
BF NAF Mildenhall, UK	UC-12M	'8G'
BF NAF Kadena, Okinawa	UC-12B	'8H'
BF NAS Agana, Guam	UC-12B	'8J'
BF NAF Misawa, Japan	UC-12B	'8M'
BF NAS Patuxent River, MD	SH-3D/G	'7T'
NAS Bermuda	UP-3A, HH-1N	
NAS Keflavik, Iceland	UP-3A	
CINCAFSE, Sigonella, Sicily (operated by NAS Sigonella)	VP-3A	
CINCLANT FLT, Norfolk, VA (operated by VP-30)	VP-3A	
CINCPAC FLT, Barbers Point, HI (operated by NAS Barbers Point)	VP-3A, UP-3A	
CNO, NAF WAshington, DC (operated by VP-30)	VP-3A	

BF = Base Flight

The vast majority of NAS Base Flights are equipped with the Beech UC-12B or UC-12M, this aircraft being from New Orleans. Rescue or transport helicopters also serve.

Commander Naval Forces Atlantic (COMNAVAIRLANT)

The mission of COMNAVAIRLANT is to provide combat-ready forces to Fleet commanders operating from the North Pole to the Antarctic, between the East Coast of the USA and the Indian Ocean. These forces fall under the operational control of the Second Fleet in the Atlantic, and the Sixth in the Mediterranean.

Reporting directly to COMNAVAIR-LANT are Commander Tactical Wings Atlantic at Oceana, Commander Strike Fighter Wings Atlantic at Cecil, Commander Helicopter Wings Atlantic at Jacksonville, Commander Patrol Wings Atlantic at Brunswick and Commander Fleet Air Mediterranean at

Naples, Italy. The constituent wings of these organizations are: **Commander Tactical Wings Atlantic, NAS Oceana, VA:** Fighter Wing One; Medium Attack Wing One; Carrier Airborne Early Warning Wing 12; Fleet Area Control and Surveillance Facility, Virginia Capes. **Commander Strike Fighter Wings Atlantic, NAS Cecil Field, FL:** Light Attack Wing One; Sea Strike Wing One; Fleet Area Control and Surveillance Facility, Jacksonville; FEWSG; NAS Key West. **Commander Helicopter Wings Atlantic, NAS Jacksonville, FL:** NAS Jacksonville; NAS Mayport; Helicopter Tactical Wing One; Helicopter Antisubmarine Warfare Wing One; Helicopter Antisubmarine Light Wing One. **Commander Patrol Wings Atlantic, NAS Brunswick, ME:** NAS Brunswick; NAS Bermuda; NAS Lajes; VXN-8; VQ-4; Patrol Wing Five; Patrol Wing Eleven; VP-30. **Commander Fleet Air Mediterranean:** NS Rota; NAS Sigonella; VQ-2; VR-22; VR-24.

Commander, Tactical Wings Atlantic

Fleet Area Control and Surveillance Facility, Virginia Capes, VA

Commander, Fighter Wing One, NAS Oceana, VA

VF-43	'Challengers'	A-4E/F, TA-4J, F-5E/F, F-16N, TF-16N, T-2C	NAS Oceana	'AD'
VC-8	'Redtails'	TA-4J, SH-3G	NAS Roosevelt Roads, PR	'GF'
VC-10	'Challengers'	TA-4J	NAS Guantanamo Bay, Cuba	'JH'
VF-101	'Grim Reapers' (FRS)	F-14A/B	NAS Oceana	'AD'

Plus deployed Atlantic Fleet Tomcat units, nominally shore-based at Oceana:

VF-14	'Top Hatters'	F-14A	CVW-3	'AC'
VF-32	'Swordsmen'	F-14A TARPS	CVW-3	'AC'
VF-33	'Starfighters'	F-14A	CVW-1	'AB'
VF-41	'Black Aces'	F-14A	CVW-8	'AJ'
VF-74	'Bedevilers'	F-14B	CVW-17	'AA'
VF-84	'Jolly Rogers'	F-14A TARPS	CVW-8	'AJ'
VF-102	'Diamondbacks'	F-14A TARPS	CVW-1	'AB'
VF-103	'Sluggers'	F-14B TARPS	CVW-17	'AA'
VF-142	'Ghostriders'	F-14B	CVW-7	'AG'
VF-143	'Pukin' Dogs'	F-14B TARPS	CVW-7	'AG'

Two units have moved to Miramar to join the Pacific Fleet and re-equip with the F-14D:

VF-11	'Red Rippers'	F-14A	ex CVW-6	'AE'
VF-31	'Tomcatters'	F-14A TARPS	ex CVW-6	'AE'

Commander Medium Attack Wing One, NAS Oceana, VA

VA-42	'Green Pawns' (FRS)	A-6E/KA-6D, TC-4C,T-34C	NAS Oceana	'AD'

Plus deployed Atlantic Fleet Intruder units, nominally shore-based at Oceana:

VA-34	'Blue Blasters'	A-6E/KA-6D	CVW-7	'AG'
VA-35	'Black Panthers'	A-6E/KA-6D	CVW-17	'AA'
VA-36	'Roadrunners'	A-6E	CVW-8	'AJ'
VA-65	'Fighting Tigers'	A-6E	CVW-8	'AJ'
VA-75	'Sunday Punchers'	A-6E/KA-6D	CVW-3	'AC'
VA-85	'Buckeyes'	A-6E/KA-6D	CVW-1	'AB'
VA-176	'Thunderbolts'	A-6E/KA-6D	CVW-6	'AE'

VA-176 disestablished 1 October 1991

Commander Carrier Airborne Early Warning Wing 12, NAS Norfolk, VA

VAW-120	'Cyclones' (FRS)	E-2C/C-2A	NAS Oceana	'AD'

Plus deployed Atlantic Fleet Hawkeye units, nominally shore-based at Norfolk:

VAW-121	'Bluetails'	E-2C	CVW-7	"AD'
VAW-122	'Steeljaws'	E-2C	CVW-6	'AE'
VAW-122 is scheduled to disestablish during October 1992				
VAW-123	'Screwtops'	E-2C	CVW-1	'AB'
VAW-124	'Bear Aces'	E-2C	CVW-8	'AJ'
VAW-125	'Tigertails'	E-2C	CVW-17	'AA'
VAW-126	'Seahawks'	E-2C	CVW-3	'AC'
VRC-40	'Rawhides'	C-2A	NAS Oceana	'JK'

Commander Strike Fighter Wings Atlantic

Directly assigned:

VF-45	'Blackbirds'	F-16N, TF-16N, A-4F, TA-4J, F-5F	NAS Key West, plus det at Cecil Field	'AD'
VAQ-33	'Firebirds'	EA-6A, EP-3J, P-3B	NAS Key West	'GD'

VF-43 at Oceana supplies dissimilar air combat training to Atlantic fighter squadrons. The principal equipment is the A-4F Skyhawk, F-5E Tiger II and F-16N Fighting Falcon.

Top: Atlantic Fleet units were heavily involved in Desert Storm, John F. Kennedy being one of the carriers deployed to the Gulf region. Here a KA-6D of VA-75 takes on fuel from a USAF KC-135R, watched by a 'Swordsmen' Tomcat from VF-32.

Above: ComLatWing One has control of the 10 F/A-18C units that deploy to Atlantic Fleet carriers, plus the FRS. This VFA-82 CAG-bird displays the maximum air combat persistence load of six AIM-9Ms and two AIM-7Ms.

Fleet Tactical Readiness Group

	EC-24A,	Waco, TX
	NKC-135A	

Fleet Area Control and Surveillance Facility, NAS Jacksonville, FL

Commander Light Attack Wing One, NAS Cecil Field, FL

VFA-106	'Gladiators' (FRS)	F/A-18A/B/ C/D, T-34C	NAS Cecil Field	'AD'
VQ-6	'Sea Shadows'	S-3A, ES-3A	NAS Cecil Field	'ET'

Plus deployed Atlantic Fleet Hornet units, nominally shore-based at Cecil Field:

VFA-15	'Valions'	F/A-18C	CVW-8	'AJ'
VFA-37	'Bulls'	F/A-18C	CVW-3	'AC'
VFA-81	'Sunliners'	F/A-18C	CVW-17	'AA'
VFA-82	'Marauders'	F/A-18C	CVW-1	'AB'
VFA-83	'Rampagers'	F/A-18C	CVW-17	'AA'
VFA-86	'Sidewinders'	F/A-18C	CVW-1	'AB'
VFA-87	'Golden Warriors'	F/A-18C	CVW-8	'AJ'
VFA-105	'Gunslingers'	F/A-18C	CVW-3	'AC'
VFA-131	'Wildcats'	F/A-18C	CVW-7	'AG'
VFA-136	'Knighthawks'	F/A-18C	CVW-7	'AG'
VFA-137	'Kestrels'		moved to Lemoore 1992 (ex CVW-6 'AE')	
VFA-132	'Privateers'		disestablished 1992 (ex CVW-6 'AE')	

Commander Sea-Strike Wing One, NAS Cecil Field, FL

VS-27	'Seawolves' (FRS)	S-3B	NAS Cecil Field	'AD'

Plus deployed Atlantic Fleet Viking units, nominally shore-based at Cecil:

VS-22	'Vidars'	S-3B	CVW-3	'AC'
VS-24	'Scouts'	S-3B	CVW-8	'AJ'
VS-28	'Gamblers'	S-3B	CVW-6	'AE'

VS-28 is scheduled to disestablish during 1992

VS-30	'Diamondcutters'	S-3B	CVW-17	'AA'
VS-31	'Top Cats'	S-3B	CVW-7	'AG'
VS-32	'Maulers'	S-3B	CVW-1	'AB'

Commander Patrol Wings Atlantic

Directly assigned:

VXN-8	'World Travellers'	RP-3D, P-3B	NAS Patuxent River	'JB'
VQ-4	'Shadows'	E-6A	NAS Patuxent River	'HL'

VQ-4 will move to Tinker AFB, OK, during FY 1993 under the command of Strategic Communications Wing One

VP-30	'Pros' (FRS)	P-3C, TP/UP-3A	NAS Jacksonville	'LL'

Commander Patrol Wing Five, NAS Brunswick, ME

VP-8	'Tigers'	P-3C	NAS Brunswick	'LC'
VP-10	'Red Lancers'	P-3C	NAS Brunswick	'LD'
VP-11	'Pegasus'	P-3C	NAS Brunswick	'LE'
VP-23	'Sea Hawks'	P-3C	NAS Brunswick	'LJ'
VP-26	'Tridents'	P-3C	NAS Brunswick	'LK'
VPU-1	'Association of Old Buzzards'	P-3B, UP-3A	NAS Brunswick	'SP'

Commander Patrol Wing Eleven, NAS Jacksonville, FL

VP-5	'Mad Foxes'	P-3C	NAS Jacksonville	'LA'
VP-16	'Eagles'	P-3C	NAS Jacksonville	'LF'
VP-24	'Batmen'	P-3C	NAS Jacksonville	'LR'
VP-45	'Pelicans'	P-3C	NAS Jacksonville	'LN'
VP-49	'Woodpeckers'	P-3C	NAS Jacksonville	'LP'

Commander Fleet Air Mediterranean

Directly assigned:

VQ-2	'Batmen'	EP-3E, P-3B	NAS Rota, Spain	'JQ'
VR-22	'Med Riders'	C-130F, KC-130F	NAS Rota, Spain	'JL'
VR-24	'Lifting Eagles'	C-2A, CT-39G	NAS Sigonella, Sicily	'JM'

Commander Helicopter Wings Atlantic

Directly assigned:

VX-1	'Pioneers'	P-3, S-3, SH-2, SH-3, SH-60B	NAS Patuxent River	'JA'

Commander Helicopter Tactical Wing One, NAS Norfolk, VA

HM-12	'Sea Dragons' (FRS)	CH/MH-53E	NAS Norfolk	'DH'
HM-14	'Sea Stallions'	MH-53E	NAS Norfolk	'BJ'
HC-2	'Circuit Riders'	CH-53E, SH-3G, VH-3A	NAS Norfolk, det Bahrain det Naples	'HU'
HC-6	'Chargers'	CH-46D, HH-46D, UH-46D	NAS Norfolk	'HW'
HC-8	'Dragon Whales'	CH-46D, HH-46D, UH-46D	NAS Norfolk	'BR'
HC-4	'Black Stallions'	CH-53E	NAS Sigonella, Sicily	'HC'
HC-16	'Bullfrogs'	SH-3D, UH-1N	NAS Pensacola	'BF'
VC-6	'Skeet of the Fleet'	Pioneer RPVs	NAS Norfolk	

Commander Helicopter Antisubmarine Warfare Wing One, NAS Jacksonville, FL

HS-1	'Sea Horses' (FRS)	SH-3G/H	NAS Jacksonville	'AR'

Plus deployed Atlantic Fleet Sea Kings and SH-60Fs, nominally shore-based at Jacksonville:

HS-3	'Tridents'	SH-60F, HH-60H	CVW-8	'AJ'
HS-5	'Night Dippers'	SH-3H	CVW-7	'AG'
HS-7	'Big Dippers'	SH-3H	CVW-3	'AC'
HS-9	'Sea Griffins'	SH-3H	CVW-8	'AJ'
HS-11	'Dragonslayers'	SH-3H	CVW-1	'AB'
HS-15	'Red Lions'	SH-60F, HH-60H	unassigned	'AE'

One HS squadron to disestablish during 1993

Commander Helicopter Antisubmarine Light Wing One*, NAS Norfolk, VA

HSL-30	'Scooters' (FRS)	SH-2F	NAS Norfolk	'HT'

Plus deployed Atlantic Fleet SH-2F squadrons, nominally shore-based at Norfolk:

HSL-32	'Tridents'	SH-2F	NAS Norfolk	'HV'
HSL-34	'Gray Checkers'	SH-2F	NAS Norfolk	'HX'
HSL-36	'Lamplighters'	SH-2F	NAS Mayport	'HY'
HSL-40	'Air Wolves' (FRS)	SH-60B	NAS Mayport	'HK'

Plus deployed Atlantic Fleet SH-60 squadrons, nominally shore-based at Mayport:

HSL-42	'Proud Warriors'	SH-60B	NAS Mayport	'HH'
HSL-44	'Swamp Foxes'	SH-60B	NAS Mayport	'HP'
HSL-46	'Grandmasters'	SH-60B	NAS Mayport	'HQ'
HSL-48	'Vipers'	SH-60B	NAS Mayport	'HR'

*The wing was formed on 1 July 1992 by the absorption of Commander Helicopter Sea Control Wing Three, NAS Mayport, FL, by Commander Helicopter Sea Control Wing One at NAS Norfolk, VA.

Organization

Commander Naval Forces Pacific (COMNAVAIRPAC)

COMNAVAIRPAC trains and administers all Naval Aviation units in the Pacific, administering all aircraft, carriers and aviation units assigned to the Pacific Fleet. It also provides combat-ready forces for the Third and Seventh Fleets, operating between the Indian Ocean and the West Coast of the USA. The Third Fleet exercises control over forces on the West Coast and in the Hawaiian area, while the Seventh looks after forces in the Far East and Indian Ocean.

Reporting directly to COMNAVAIRPAC are Commander Fighter/Airborne Early Warning Wing Pacific at Lemoore, Commander Medium Attack/Tactical Electronic Warfare Wing Pacific at Whidbey Island, Commander Light Attack Wing Pacific at Lemoore, Commander Antisubmarine Warfare Wing Pacific at North Island, Commander Patrol Wings Pacific at Moffett Field (incorporating Patrol Wings One, Two and Ten) and Commander Fleet Air Western Pacific at NAF Atsugi (incorporating Patrol Wing One).

Interestingly, COMNAVAIRPAC looks after all Fleet EA-6Bs (based at Whidbey Island when not deployed) including those assigned to Atlantic Fleet air wings.

The 'Gunbearers' of HC-11 fly various Sea Knight versions from North Island in support of the Pacific Fleet. The 'VR' tailcode is apt for the primary mission: vertical replenishment of vessels at sea.

Commander Fighter/Airborne Early Warning Wing Pacific

Directly assigned:

Navy Fighter Weapons School	A-4E/F, TA-4F, F-14A, F-16N, TF-16N	NAS Miramar	
VF-126	'Bandits'	A-4E/F, T-2C, F-16N, TF-16N	NAS Miramar	'NJ'
VC-1	'Blue Alii'	A-4E, TA-4J	NAS Barbers Point	'UA'
VX-4	'Evaluators'	F-14A/B/D, F/A-18A/C	NAS Point Mugu	'XE'
VF-124	'Gunfighters' (FRS)	F-14A/B/D, T-34C	NAS Miramar	'NJ'

Plus deployed Pacific Fleet Tomcat squadrons, nominally shore-based at NAS Miramar:

VF-1	'Wolfpack'	F-14A	CVW-2	'NE'
VF-2	'Bounty Hunters'	F-14A TARPS	CVW-2	'NE'
VF-11	'Red Rippers'	F-14D	CVW-14	'NG'
VF-21	'Freelancers'	F-14A	CVW-5	'NF'
VF-24	'Renegades'	F-14A*	CVW-9	'NG'
VF-31	'Tomcatters'	F-14D TARPS	CVW-14	'NG'
VF-51	'Screaming Eagles'	F-14A*	CVW-15	'NL'
VF-111	'Sundowners'	F-14A* TARPS	CVW-15	'NL'
VF-114	'Aardvarks'	F-14A	CVW-11	'NH'
VF-154	'Black Knights'	F-14A TARPS	CVW-5	'NF'
VF-211	'Flying Checkmates'	F-14A* TARPS	CVW-9	'NG'
VF-213	'Black Lions'	F-14A TARPS	CVW-11	'NH'

*Transition of VF-51 and VF-111 to F-14D cancelled; VF-24 and VF-211 have reverted to F-14A (from F-14B) because of a shortage of F-14Bs.

Three of CVW-14's constituent squadrons are VAQ-139 with Prowlers and VFA-25 and -113 with Hornets. All of the Navy's active-duty Prowlers are shore-based at Whidbey Island but deploy to both fleets.

VAW-110	'Firebirds' (FRS)	E-2C, E-2C+, C-2A	NAS Miramar	'NJ'

Plus deployed Pacific Fleet Hawkeye squadrons, nominally shore-based at NAS Miramar:

VAW-112	'Golden Hawks'	E-2C+	CVW-9	'NG'
VAW-113	'Black Hawks'	E-2C+	CVW-14	'NK'
VAW-114	'Hormel Hawgs'	E-2C+	CVW-15	'NL'
VAW-115	'Eagles'	E-2C	CVW-5	'NF'
VAW-116	'Sun Kings'	E-2C	CVW-2	'NE'
VAW-117	'Wallbangers'	E-2C	CVW-11	'NH'

Commander Medium Attack/Tactical Electronic Warfare Wing Pacific

Directly assigned:

VA-128	'Golden Intruders' (FRS)	A-6E, TC-4C	NAS Whidbey Island	'NJ'

Plus deployed Pacific Fleet Intruder squadrons, nominally shore-based at NAS Whidbey Island:

VA-52	'Knight Riders'	A-6E, KA-6D	CVW-15	'NL'
VA-95	'Green Lizards'	A-6E, KA-6D	CVW-11	'NH'
VA-115	'Eagles'	A-6E	CVW-5	'F'
VA-145	'Swordsmen'	A-6E, KA-6D	CVW-2	'NE'
VA-155	'Silver Foxes'	A-6E, KA-6D	CVW-2	'NE'
VA-165	'Boomers'	A-6E, KA-6D	CVW-9	'NG'
VA-196	'Main Battery'	A-6E	CVW-14	'K'
VAQ-129	'New Vikings' (FRS)	EA-6B	NAS Whidbey Island	'NJ'

Plus all deployed Fleet Prowler squadrons, nominally shore-based at NAS Whidbey Island:

VAQ-130	'Zappers'	EA-6B	CVW-3	'AC'
VAQ-131	'Lancers'	EA-6B	CVW-2	'NE'
VAQ-132	'Scorpions'	EA-6B	CVW-17	'AA'
VAQ-134	'Garudas'	EA-6B	CVW-15	'NL'
VAQ-135	'Black Ravens'	EA-6B	CVW-11	'NH'
VAQ-136	'Gauntlets'	EA-6B	CVW-5	'NF'
VAQ-137	'Rooks'	EA-6B	CVW-1	'AB'
VAQ-138	'Yellowjackets'	EA-6B	CVW-9	'NG'
VAQ-139	'Cougars'	EA-6B	CVW-14	'NK'
VAQ-140	'Patriots'	EA-6B	CVW-7	'AG'
VAQ-141	'Shadowhawks'	EA-6B	CVW-8	'AJ'

VAQ-133 'Wizards' disestablished June 1992

Commander Light Attack Wing Pacific

Directly assigned:

VX-5	'Vampires'	TA-4J, A-6E, AV-8B, F/A-18, OV-10D, AH-1W	NAWC China Lake	'XE'
VAQ-34	'Flashbacks'	F/A-18A/B	NAS Lemoore	'GD'
VAQ-35	'Gray Wolves'	EA-6B	NAS Whidbey Island	'GD'
VFA-127	'Cylons'	F/A-18A/B	NAS Fallon	'NJ'
NSWC		F/A-18A/ B/C, A-6E, SH-3H	NAS Fallon	'STRIKE'
VFA-125	'Rough Riders' (FRS)	F/A-18A/B/ C/D, T-34C	NAS Lemoore	'NJ'

Plus deployed Pacific Fleet F/A-18 squadrons, nominally shore-based at NAS Lemoore:

VFA-22	'Fighting Redcocks'	F/A-18C	CVW-11	'NH'
VFA-25	'Fist of the Fleet'	F/A-18C	CVW-14	'NK'
VFA-27	'Chargers'	F/A-18C	CVW-15	'NL'
VFA-94	'Shrikes'	F/A-18C	CVW-11	'NH'
VFA-97	'Warhawks'	F/A-18C	CVW-15	'NL'
VFA-113	'Stingers'	F/A-18C	CVW-14	'NK'
VFA-137	'Kestrels'	F/A-18A	for CVW-2	'NE'
VFA-146	'Blue Diamonds'	F/A-18C	CVW-9	'NG'
VFA-147	'Argonauts'	F/A-18C	CVW-9	'NG'
VFA-151	'Vigilantes'	F/A-18A	for CVW-2	'NE'
VFA-192	'Golden Dragons'	F/A-18C	CVW-5	'NF'
VFA-195	'Dambusters'	F/A-18C	CVW-5	'NF'

Commander Antisubmarine Warfare Wing Pacific

Directly assigned:

VS-41	'Shamrocks' (FRS)	S-3A/B	NAS North Island	'NJ'

Plus deployed Pacific Fleet Viking squadrons, nominally shore-based at NAS North Island:

VS-21	'Fighting Redtails'	S-3B	CVW-5	'NF'
VS-29	'Screaming Dragon Fires'	S-3A	CVW-11	'NH'
VS-33	'Screwbirds'	S-3A	CVW-9	'NG'
VS-35	'Blue Wolves'	S-3B	CVW-14	'NC'
VS-37	'Sawbucks'	S-3B	CVW-15	'NL'
VS-38	'Red Griffins'	S-3A	CVW-2	'NE'
VRC-30	'Providers'	C-2A, UC-12B, CT-39E	NAS North Island	'RW'
HS-10	'Taskmasters' (FRS)	SH-60F	NAS North Island	'RA'

Plus deployed Pacific Fleet Sea King and SH-60F squadrons, nominally shore-based at NAS North Island:

HS-2	'Golden Falcons'	SH-60F, HH-60H	CVW-9	'NG'
HS-4	'Black Knights'	SH-60F, HH-60H	CVW-15	'NL'

The Hornet has completed the replacement of the Vought A-7 on light attack squadrons, dramatically increasing the precision attack capability while adding a full air-to-air function. This is VFA-147's CAG-bird firing a 5-in Zuni rocket during training over the desert ranges.

HS-6	'Indians'	SH-60F, HH-60H	CVW-11	'NH'
HS-8	'Eight Ballers'	SH-60F, HH-60H	CVW-14	'NK'
HS-12	'Wyverns'	SH-3H	CVW-5	'NF'
HS-14	'Chargers'	SH-3H	CVW-2	'NE'
HSL-31	'Archangels' (FRS)	SH-2F	NAS North Island	'TD'

HSL-31 scheduled to disestablish during FY 1992
Plus deployed Pacific Fleet Seasprite squadrons, nominally shore-based at NAS North Island and Barbers Point:

HSL-33	'Sea Snakes'	SH-2F	NAS North Island	'TF'
HSL-35	'Magicians'	SH-2F	NAS North Island	'TG'
HSL-37	'Easy Riders'	SH-2F, SH-60B	NAS Barbers Point	'TH'
HSL-41	'Sea Hawks' (FRS)	SH-60B	NAS North Island	'TS'

Plus deployed Pacific Fleet SH-60B squadrons, nominally shore-based at NAS North Island:

HSL-43	'Battle Cats'	SH-60B	NAS North Island	'TT'
HSL-45	'Wolfpack'	SH-60B	NAS North Island	'TZ'
HSL-47	'Saberhawks'	SH-60B	NAS North Island	'TY'
HSL-49	'Scorpions'	SH-60B	NAS North Island	'TX'
HC-1	'Angels'	CH-53E, SH-3G, SH-3H	NAS North Island	'UP'
HC-3	'Pack Rats'	CH-46D, HH-46A/D	NAS North Island	'SA'
HC-11	'Gunbearers'	CH/UH-46D, HH-46D	NAS North Island	'VR'
HM-15	'Blackhawks'	MH-53E	NAS Alameda	'TB'
VXE-6	'Puckered Penguins'	LC-130F/R, HH-1N	NAS Point Mugu	'XD'

Commander Fleet Air Western Pacific

NAS Agana, Guam
NAS Cubi Point, Philippines (to close December 1992)
NAF Atsugi, Japan
NAF Kadena, Japan
NAF Misawa, Japan
NAF Diego Garcia

Directly assigned:

VC-5	'Checkertails'	A-4E, TA-4J, SH-3G	NAS Cubi Point	

VC-5 disestablished in August 1992

HC-5	'Providers'	HH-46A	NAS Agana	'RB'
VQ-1	'World Watchers'	EP-3E	NAS Agana	'PR'
VQ-5	'Black Ravens'	ES-3A, S-3A	NAS Agana	'SS'
VRC-50	'Foo Dogs'	C-2A, US-3A, C-130F	NAS Cubi Point	'RG'

VRC-50 moved to Andersen AFB, Guam, in August 1992

HSL-51	'Warlords'	SH-60B	NAF Atsugi	'TA'

Commander Patrol Wings Pacific

NAS Adak, Alaska
NAS Barbers Point, Hawaii
NAS Moffett Field, CA
NAF Midway Island

Directly assigned:

VP-31	'Black Lightnings' (FRS)	P-3C,UP/ TP-3A	NAS Moffett Field	'RP'

Commander Patrol Wing One, Kamiseya, Japan

COMPATWING det Diego Garcia
COMPATWING det Misawa
COMPATWING det Cubi Point
COMPATWING det Agana

Commander Patrol Wing Two, NAS Barbers Point, HI

VP-1	'Screaming Eagles'	P-3C	NAS Barbers Point	'YB'
VP-4	'Skinny Dragons'	P-3C	NAS Barbers Point	'YD'
VP-6	'Blue Sharks'	P-3C	NAS Barbers Point	'PC'

VP-6 is due to deactivate in May 1993

VP-17	'White Lightnings'	P-3C	NAS Barbers Point	'ZE'
VP-22	'Blue Geese'	P-3C	NAS Barbers Point	'QA'
VPU-2	'Wizards'	P-3B, UP-3A	NAS Barbers Point	'SP'
VQ-3	'Tacamopac'	E-6A	NAS Barbers Point	'TC'

VQ-3 to move to Tinker AFB, OK, in summer 1992 to join Stategic Communication Wing One, due to be established in June 1992.

Commander Patrol Wing Ten, NAS Moffett Field, CA

VP-9	'Golden Eagles'	P-3C	NAS Moffett Field	'PD'
VP-40	'Fighting Marlins'	P-3C	NAS Moffett Field	'QE'
VP-46	'Gray Knights'	P-3C, TP-3A?	NAS Moffett Field	'RC'
VP-47	'Golden Swordsmen'	P-3C	NAS Moffett Field	'RD'
VP-50	'Blue Dragons'	P-3C	disestablished June 1992	

The Pacific Fleet Tomcat community resides at NAS Miramar when not afloat, based alongside the Hawkeyes. Basing the fighters and AEW aircraft together heightens the coordination between the two.

Organization

US Naval Air Reserve

The US Navy has a substantial reserve, the air elements of which report directly to Commander Naval Air Reserve, who in turn reports to ACNO Air Warfare in Washington, or to their respective operational commanders. The task of the Naval Air Reserve is to maintain a civilian force of qualified aviation officers and enlisted personnel who are able to be mobilized to support and augment the active Navy at short notice. The establishment of such a force was initiated in 1914, and the first unit was established in 1916. Aircraft for the naval militia were first funded in 1917, the same year in which a naval flying corps was established. The Naval Air Reserve expanded throughout the 1920s and 1930s, and was recalled to active duty during World War II. Forty Reserve squadrons were recalled during the Korean War, and one entire aircraft carrier was made up wholly of recalled Reserve units. Reserve squadrons were later called up during the Berlin crisis, the *Pueblo* crisis and for service in Vietnam.

Since 1970, the Naval Air Reserve (which includes vital medical and intelligence units, as well as aircraft/helicopter operators) has been reorganized to reflect a mirror image of the front-line Fleet it is tasked with supporting and augmenting. It has two full carrier air wings, backed by patrol and support wings. The carrier air wings CVWR-20 and CVWR-30 are not assigned to an individual ship, but would be recalled to serve with AIRLANT and AIRPAC respectively. They undergo their necessary periodic CQs (Carrier Qualifications or Carquals) with carriers as they become available. At one time, it was proposed that one of the older carriers, eg. *Coral Sea* or *Midway*, should be kept in service as a dedicated Reserve carrier, but these plans proved too ambitious.

The Naval Air Reserve has six dedicated naval air stations at Dallas, TX, New Orleans, LA, Glenview, IL, Atlanta, GA, Willow Grove, PA, and South Weymouth, MA, and has units stationed at various regular Navy NAFs and NASs. The 22,000 Naval Air Reservists constitute some 17 per cent of total Navy aviation personnel, providing about one-third of maritime patrol wings, more than one-tenth of tactical carrier air wings, and all combat SAR and heavy logistic airlift assets.

Naval Air Reservists are normally expected to attend a minimum of 48 drills per year (a drill weekend consisting of four four-hour drills) and undergo a 12- to 14-day period of active duty training. TARs (Training and Administration of the Reserve) are full time Reservists who allow units to be properly organized, administered and trained, activities which cannot be completed on a part-time basis.

For a brief period beginning in the mid-1980s, in order to keep Reserve aircrew current on aircraft types which could not be made available full-time, squadron augmentation units (SAUs) were formed as shadow identities for the relevant (F-14, A-6 and S-3) FRS training units. The MAU was the patrol community's equivalent. Financial constraints led to the disbandment of these units in September 1991.

The Naval Air Reserve contributed seven squadrons to Operation Desert Storm, and 2,942 Reservists were mobilized, many of them medical and intelligence personnel. The seven squadrons included four transport units, an ASW unit and two new combat support helicopter units.

VR-48 is presently training C-130T aircrew for VR-53, a new Reserve squadron slated to stand up as a Reserve unit at Martinsburg, WV. The 'Sky Pigs' will continue to operate two C-20G Gulfstream IV aircraft.

In addition to its two carrier air wings and patrol wing, the Navy Reserve operates some support units. VFC-13 at Miramar has Skyhawks to augment the adversary training effort.

Commander Carrier Air Reserve Wing Thirty, NAS Miramar, CA

VF-301 'Devils Disciples'	F-14A	Codes from ND/100	NAS Miramar
VF-302 'Stallions'	F-14A TARPS	Codes from ND/200	NAS Miramar
VFA-303 'Goldenhawks'	F/A-18A	Codes from ND/300	NAS Lemoore
VFA-305 'Lobos'	F/A-18A	Codes from ND/400	NAS Point Mugu
VA-304 'Firebirds'	A-6E, KA-6D	Codes from ND/420	NAS Alameda
VAW-88 'Cottonpickers'	E-2C	Codes from ND/600	NAS Miramar
VAQ-309 'Axemen'	EA-6B	Codes from ND/604	NAS Whidbey Island

Commander Reserve Patrol Wing Atlantic, NAS Norfolk, VA

VP-62 'Broadarrows'	P-3C	NAS Jacksonville	'LT'
VP-64 'Condors'*	P-3B	NAS Willow Grove	'LU'
VP-66 'Liberty Bell'	P-3B	NAS Willow Grove	'LV'
VP-68 'Blackhawks'	P-3C	NAF Washington	'LW'
VP-92 'Minutemen'	P-3C	NAS South Weymouth	'LY'
VP-93 'Executioners'*	P-3B	NAF Detroit	'LH'
VP-94 'Crawfishers'	P-3B	NAS New Orleans	'LZ'

* scheduled to disestablish during FY 1993

Commander Reserve Patrol Wing Pacific, NAS Moffet Field, CA

VP-60 'Cobras'	P-3B	NAS Glenview	'LS'
VP-65 'Tridents'	P-3C	NAS Point Mugu	'PG'
VP-67 'Golden Hawks'*	P-3B	NAS Memphis	'PL'
VP-69 'Totems'	P-3B	NAS Whidbey Island	'PJ'
VP-90 'Lions'*	P-3B	NAS Glenview	'LX'
VP-91 'Stingers'	P-3C	NAS Moffett Field	'PM'

* scheduled to disestablish during FY 1993

Commander Fleet Logistic Support Wing, NAS Dallas, TX

VFC-12 'Fighting Omars'	A-4F/M	NAS Oceana	'JY'
VFC-13 'Saints'	A-4F/M	NAS Miramar	'UX'
VR-46 'Peach Airlines'	DC-9	NAS Atlanta	'JS'
VR-48 'The Sky Pigs'	C-20G, C-130T	NAF Washington	'JR'
VR-51 'Flamin' Hookers'	C-9B	NAS Glenview	'RV'
VR-52 'Taskmasters'	DC-9	NAS Willow Grove	'JT'
VR-54 'Revellers'	C-130T	NAS New Orleans	
VR-55 'Bicentennial Minutemen'	C-9B	NAS Alameda	'RU'
VR-56 'Globemasters'	C-9B	NAS Norfolk	'JU'
VR-57 'Conquistadors'	C-9B	NAS North Island	'RX'
VR-58 'Sun Seekers'	C-9B	NAS Jacksonville	'JV'
VR-59 'Lone Star Express'	C-9B	NAS Dallas	'RY'
VR-60 'Volunteer Express'	DC-9	NAS Memphis	'RT'
VR-61 'Islanders'	DC-9	NAS Whidbey Island	'RS'
VR-62 'Motowners'	DC-9	NAS Detroit	'JW'
CFLSW det NOLA	CT-39G	NAS New Orleans	
CFLSW det WASH	C-20F, CT-39G	NAF Washington	

Commander Helicopter Wing Reserve, NAS North Island, CA

HCS-4 'Red Wolves'	HH-60H	NAS Norfolk	'NW'
HCS-5 'Fire Hawks'	HH-60H	NAS Point Mugu	'NW'
HM-18 'Norsemen'	RH-53D	NAS Norfolk	'NW'
HM-19 'Golden Bears'	RH-53D	NAS Alameda	'NW'
HS-75 'Emerald Knights'	SH-3H	NAS Jacksonville	'NW'
HS-85 'Golden Gaters'	SH-3H	NAS Alameda	'NW'
HSL-74 'Demon Elves'	SH-2F	NAS South Weymouth	'NW'
HSL-74 to disestablish during FY 1993			
HSL-84 'Thunderbolts'	SH-2G	NAS North Island	'NW'
HSL-94 'Titans'	SH-2F	NAS Willow Grove	'NW'

Commander Naval Air Reserve Force, New Orleans, LA

Commander Carrier Air Reserve Wing Twenty, NAS Cecil Field, FL

VF-201 'Hunters'	F-14A	Codes from AF/100	NAS Dallas
VF-202 'Superheats'	F-14A TARPS	Codes from AF/200	NAS Dallas
VFA-203 'Blue Dolphins'	F/A-18A	Codes from AF/300	NAS Cecil Field
VFA-204 'River Rattlers'	F/A-18A	Codes from AF/400	NAS New Orleans
VA-205 'Green Falcons'	A-6E, KA-6D	Codes from AF/500	NAS Atlanta
VAQ-209 'Star Warriors'	EA-6B	Codes from AF/610	NAS Washington
VAW-78 'Fighting Escargots'	E-2C	Codes from AF/600	NAS Norfolk

The Atlantic Fleet Reserve Tomcats are based at Dallas, and both squadrons show allegiance to the 'Lone Star' state in their unit markings. This is VF-202's CAG-bird.

Chief of Naval Air Training

Training Command's most famous aircraft are the Hornets of the 'Blue Angels' display team, which give worldwide displays of formation aerobatics.

Naval Aviation's many achievements, together with magazine articles, coffee table books and Hollywood movies like *Top Gun* and *An Officer and a Gentleman*, have ensured that the US Navy is never short of applicants to become naval aviators. Recruiting, selecting and training the right candidates is, however, a challenging and difficult task, requiring a large, dedicated training organization.

The Chief of Naval Education and Training reports directly to the Chief of Naval Operations, and controls the various Training departments of the Atlantic and Pacific Fleets (COMTRALANT and COMTRAPAC), the Chief of Naval Technical Training (whose responsibilities include the training of air traffic controllers, aviation engineer and technical officers, and enlisted personnel), and the Chief of Naval Air Training (CNATRA).

CNATRA is responsible for the training of all pilots and NFOs, and for the indoctrination of flight surgeons and aerospace experimental psychologists. Engineer officers are trained at the Naval Post Graduate School at Monterey, CA, while maintenance officers undergo training at Pensacola, FL. Supply officers are trained at Athens, GA. Enlisted personnel attend Naval Air Technical Training Centers at Memphis, TN, Lakehurst, NJ, and Meridian, MS, while further specialist training is conducted at an ever-varying number of Naval Air Maintenance Training Group Detachments.

The US Navy trains some 2,000 pilots and NFOs (Naval Flight Officers) per year. Recruiters operate a fleet of blue-painted piston-engined T-34B Mentors. Students join the program either from the US Naval Academy at Annapolis (after a four-year, university equivalent course), or from the Naval Reserve Officer Training Candidate Scholarship program (conducted in 60 mainstream universities and colleges). On graduation from either of these programs, the student is commissioned as an ensign in the regular Navy. The third source of students is the Aviation Officer Candidate Program, which takes enlisted personnel or civilians through the Officer Candidate School at Pensacola, these emerging as Reserve Ensigns.

A six-week Aviation Preflight Indoctrination course follows before students are streamed to pilot or NFO training. Pilot training begins with a 20-week Primary Flight Training course on the T-34C Turbo-Mentor at NAS Whiting Field, FL, or at NAS Corpus Christi, TX. Those destined for jet aircraft then go to Meridian, Chase Field or Kingsville for a 24-week Intermediate Jet (Intermediate Strike) training course on the T-2 Buckeye. All T-2s remaining in the inventory are T-2Cs, although a handful of less-powerful T-2Bs served until recently with the undergraduate NFO training squadron, VT-10. The T-2C is used for the great milestone of the naval aviator's student career: carrier qualifications (Carquals or CQs). Carquals follow 10 field-practise periods, and the shipboard qualification flight requires them to complete two touch-and-go landings, four arrested landings and

four catapult launches. A 21-week Advanced Jet (Advanced Strike) training course follows at the same bases, with students transitioning to the TA-4J Skyhawk. The T-45 Goshawk is being introduced to replace both Buckeye and Skyhawk. On successful completion of the course, pilots are posted to fleet replenishment squadrons for the F-14, F/A-18, A-6, EA-6B, S-3 or C-9.

Pilot trainees destined for larger, heavier aircraft stay at Whiting Field or Corpus Christi for a five-week Intermediate Prop course before transitioning to the T-44 King Air at Corpus Christi for a 19-week Multi-engine course. Successful students go on to the E-2C or C-2, or to the P-3 or C-130. E-2 and C-2 pilots go to VT-4 at Pensacola for carrier qualifications in the T-2C. Future helicopter pilots undergo the same Intermediate Prop course at Whiting Field, before transitioning to the TH-57 with HT-8 for a six-week/39-flying hour Helicopter Transition course and a 12-week/66-flying hour Advanced Helicopter course at Whiting Field on the TH-57 with HT-18.

An increasing number of pilot trainees are female, who can be assigned to various shore-based aircraft types (theoretically including Adversary units) and to the C-2 VRC units with which they can at least fly onto aircraft carriers in the COD role.

All NFOs undergo the same 15-week Basic course in the T-34 and T-2C at Pensacola, before some are sent for the 22-week/85-flying hour Interservice Undergraduate Navigator Training on USAF T-43s at Mather AFB, CA. This will move to Randolph AFB, TX, in 1993. These NFOs return to the Navy C-130 and P-3 fleets. All other NFOs undergo a seven-week Intermediate course on the T-34C (10 hours), the T-2 (12 hours) and T-39N (12 hours) at Pensacola, before being streamed. The T-47s of Training Wing Six have been replaced by T-39Ns modified by Sabreliner Corporation. Contract irregularities mean that the T-39s will be used for only 18 months, after which Flight International will take over the contract using modified Learjets. Future F-14 Radar Intercept Officers stay at Pensacola on the T-2 (six flights) and T-39N (46 hours) for a further 17 weeks. A-6 tactical navigators also stay at Pensacola, but their course lasts only 11 weeks (49 hours on the T-39N, 11 hours on the T-2). EA-6B crews undergo the same tactical navigator course, before a 12-week Electronic Warfare course. Overwater jet navigators for the S-3 also undergo an 11-week course at Pensacola. Future airborne tactical data systems officers for the E-2C go directly to one of the two FRSs at Miramar or Norfolk.

Other naval aviators receive their 'Wings of Gold' at the end of the appropriate training course, and before proceeding to an FRS for type conversion. The training world has not been immune to the effect of defense cuts, and TRAWING 3 was scheduled to disestablish in August 1992, with VT-26 having disbanded on 22 May 1992 and the other two units following by October.

Commander Naval Air Training, NAS Corpus Christi, TX

Commander Training Wing One, NAS Meridian, MS

VT-7 'Eagles'	TA-4J	Intermediate Jet	'A'
VT-19 'Fighting Frogs'	T-2C	Advanced Jet	'A'

Commander Training Wing Two, NAS Kingsville, TX

VT-21 'Red Hawks'	TA-4J, T-45A	Advanced Jet	'B'
VT-21 became the first T-45 unit during January 1992			
VT-22 'King Eagles'	TA-4J	Advanced Jet	'B'
VT-23 'Professionals'	T-2C	Intermediate Jet	'B'

Commander Training Wing Three, NAS Chase Field, Beeville, TX

VT-24 'Bobcats'	TA-4J	Advanced Jet	'C'
VT-25 'Cougars'	TA-4J	Advanced Jet	'C'
VT-26 'Tigers'	T-2C	Intermediate Jet	'C'
VT-26 disestablished 22 May 1992			

Commander Training Wing Four, NAS Corpus Christi, TX

VT-27 'Boomers'	T-34C	Primary Turbine	'D'
VT-28 'Rangers'	T-44A	Multi-Engine Turbine	'D'
VT-31 'Wise Owls'	T-44A	Multi-Engine Turbine	'D'

Commander Training Wing Five, NAS Whiting Field, FL

VT-2 'Doer Birds'	T-34C	Primary Turbine	'E'
VT-3 'Red Knights'	T-34C	Primary Turbine	'E'
VT-6	T-34C	Primary Turbine	'E'
HT-8	TH-57B	Basic Rotary	'E'
HT-18	TH-57B/C	Advanced Rotary	'E'

Commander Training Air Wing Six, NAS Pensacola, FL

VT-4 'Rubber Ducks'	T-2C	E-2/C-2 Carquals	'F'
VT-10 'Cosmic Cats'	T-2C, T-34C	NFO syllabus	'F'
VT-86 'Sabre Hawks'	T-2C, T-39N	RIO, tactical and overwater navigation	'F'
NFDS 'Blue Angels'	F/A-18A/B	Naval Flight	'BA'
	TC-130G	Demonstration Squadron	

Recruiting Command aircraft

In order to screen candidates for naval aviator training, Recruiting Command operates some 51 piston-engined Beechcraft T-34B Mentors. Based singly (90 per cent of them at civilian airfields) close to major population centers, these aircraft are used to weed out applicants who may be prone to air sickness or who have any other aversion to flying. Four aircraft are based at Pensacola for training and as a reserve for when others are being serviced. The others are at the following locations: **Area 1:** Albany, NY; Boston, MA; Buffalo, NY; Harrisburg, PA; Newark, NJ; New York, NY; Philadelphia, PA; Pittsburgh, PA. **Area 3:** Macon, GA; Atlanta, GA; Columbia, SC; Jacksonville, FL; Louisville, KY; Miami, FL; Montgomery, AL; Nashville, TN; Raleigh, NC; Richmond, VA; Washington, DC. **Area 5:** Great Lakes, Chicago, IL; Cleveland, OH; Columbus, OH; Detroit, MI; Indianapolis, IN; Milwaukee, WI; Minneapolis, MN; Omaha, NE. **Area 7:** Albuquerque, NM; Dallas, TX; Denver, CO; Houston, TX; Kansas City, MO; Little Rock, AR; Lubbock, TX; Memphis, TN; New Orleans, LA; Oklahoma City, OK; San Antonio, TX; St Louis, MO. **Area 8:** Los Angeles, CA; Phoenix, AZ; Portland, OR; Salt Lake City, UT; San Diego, CA; San Francisco, CA; Seattle, WA.

US MARINE CORPS AVIATION

Priding themselves on their rapid reaction, ability to fight in any terrain or climate, and a reputation for being the President's global 'fire brigade', the US Marines are first and foremost a ground-fighting organization, and to that end the aviation assets are dedicated to troop support.

The United States' Naval Forces are subordinate to the Department of the Navy, and are composed of two forces: the US Navy and the US Marine Corps. Although the Marine Corps is smaller than the US Navy, it is no less important, and is in no way subordinate to the larger organization, fulfilling a different, though often complementary, function. Although the Marine Corps operates within the Fleet, and often under the operational control of the Atlantic and Pacific Fleet Commanders, its purpose is to act as an expeditionary force, deploying logistically-sustainable forces into areas with no existing US logistical network.

As a maritime nation, with two ocean coastlines and dependent on sea trade, the United States has a vested interest in keeping the sea lanes open to US commercial ships and in keeping large areas of ocean 'sanitized' of hostile naval forces with an offensive capability. As a net importer of many vital raw materials, the USA also has legitimate interests in maintaining stability and trade in many parts of the world. The US Navy is a prime instrument in achieving these aims and protecting these interests. There are, however, choke points on the various sea lines of communication and areas where land-based forces can threaten the security of the sea lanes, and these necessitate the employment of an armed force which can mount expeditionary-type operations from sea bases provided by the Navy.

Because of its ability to act independently of fixed US bases, the Marine Corps has always had a particular importance in between-wars conflicts and brushfire situations. The break-up of the Warsaw Pact and virtual disappearance of the Soviet threat has been accompanied by a general increase in tension and instability leading to, if anything, an increase in the importance of this role.

The US Marine Corps has always been characterized by tremendous *esprit*, devotion to duty and self sufficiency. The *raison d'être* of the Corps has always been to function as a self-contained military force, capable of going into battle with all its support arms under a single command. This tradition of self sufficiency makes the Corps ideal for expeditionary operations and for operations away from traditional rear echelon support, and led to the Marines embracing aviation from a very early date.

The Marine Corps' first aviator (and actually only the fifth naval aviator) was First Lieutenant Alfred A. Cunningham, who constantly requested aviation duty because of his own interest in aviation. He was eventually told to report for training with the US Navy on 22 May 1912, subsequently regarded as the birthdate of Marine aviation. He ensured that the third US naval aircraft, the B-1, was allocated to the Marines. Marine aviators supported landing forces at Tampico and Vera Cruz, among other early operations.

The landplane-equipped First Aviation Squadron was

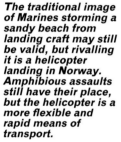

The traditional image of Marines storming a sandy beach from landing craft may still be valid, but rivalling it is a helicopter landing in Norway. Amphibious assaults still have their place, but the helicopter is a more flexible and rapid means of transport.

expanded to force strength, with four squadrons, and was deployed to France during World War I, while the First Marine Aeronautic Company, with seaplanes, deployed to the Azores for ASW patrols. The Marine aviators in France were hampered by a shortage of aircraft but solved this problem by trading Liberty engines (which they had in abundance) for Royal Flying Corps D.H.4s and D.H.9s. Thirty-six aircraft were eventually acquired by these means. Initially flying with RAF D.H.9 squadrons, the Marines began independent operations during October 1918.

Between 9 August and the Armistice, the Marines flew 43 missions with the RAF and 14 on their own, dropping 34,000 lb (15400 kg) of bombs and gaining four confirmed victories over enemy fighters. Four pilots were killed and another (and two gunners) wounded. One pilot was killed in an accident, while four officers and 21 enlisted men died in the influenza epidemic which swept through the western front.

After the war, Marine aircraft demonstrated their usefulness several times. In 1927 Marine D.H.4s kept insurgents from overwhelming a USMC garrison in Nicaragua. During World War II close air support techniques were honed and refined, and Marine aviators played a major role in supporting the 'grunts' as they swept through the Pacific.

Marines to the fore

Since the end of World War II, the Marines (with their own aviation units) have fought in Korea, Vietnam, Grenada and the Gulf, with the aviators repeatedly proving their value to the Corps. In Vietnam, the case for a Marine 'air force' was conclusively proved. In the early days, Marine aircraft operated in support of Marine ground forces in the traditional way, even establishing at Chu Lai a forward base, known as a Short Airfield for Tactical Support (SATS), with catapults and arrester gear. Later in the war, the USAF 7th Air Force assumed responsibility for planning and coordinating all air operations, and direct Marine air support of Marine ground forces virtually ceased. Marine commanders learned a valuable lesson, and vowed never to lose control of their air assets again.

The 1991 war in the Persian Gulf necessitated the deployment of the largest contingent of Marine Corps aircraft since Vietnam, and validated the Corps' Total Force Employment policy, demonstrating its rapid-response capability convincingly. The Gulf War also provided a useful opportunity to combat test a number of new US

Marine Corps aircraft, including the F/A-18D and the AV-8B.

The size and structure of the Marine Corps today conforms to the dictates of the National Security Act amended in 1952 by Title 10 of the US Code. In one of the Marine Corps' own publications this is quoted as stating that the Marine Corps should include: "not less than three combat divisions, three air wings, and such other land combat, aviation and other services as may be organic therein. . . and to provide fleet marine forces of combined arms, together with supporting air components, for service with the fleet in the seizure and defense of advanced naval bases and for the conduct of such land operations as may be essential to the prosecution of a naval campaign. . . and to develop, in coordination with the Army, Navy and Air Force, the doctrines, tactics, techniques and equipment employed by landing forces in amphibious operations."

The Headquarters US Marine Corps in Washington, DC, administers its assets through two Fleet Marine Forces, which equate broadly to the US Navy's Atlantic and Pacific Fleets. Under the FMFs are Marine Air-Ground Task Forces (MAGTFs) which include infantry, artillery, armor, engineer, reconnaissance, aviation and logistics components. More specialized surveillance, reconnaissance and intelligence elements are drawn from MEF command elements. MAGTFs can vary enormously in size and composition. The subordinate Ground Combat Element can comprise an infantry platoon or one or more divisions, while the Air Combat Element can be anything

Top: In most air arms the fighters and strike aircraft are the raison d'être of that force, but with the Marines they are there in a support function. F/A-18 Hornets can provide close support and ward off enemy attack aircraft.

Above: The Marine Corps has for many years operated a small but highly effective electronic warfare force, and like the Navy has settled on the EA-6B Prowler to perform the task. A single active-duty squadron (VMAQ-2, illustrated) is augmented by a Reserve unit (VMAQ-4).

Above: The Marines' standard heavylift helicopter is the Sikorsky CH-53E, used principally for the distribution of heavy loads. A great advantage of the Super Stallion is its ability to refuel in flight from the Lockheed Hercules, as demonstrated here by a VMGR-252 KC-130R over the Florida Keys.

Above right: The two-seat Hornet has a wide-ranging combat role within the Marine Corps structure. Equipped with 5-in rockets, the aircraft is used in the fast FAC role to control other attack aircraft. This machine is from the training unit, VMFAT-101.

Markings
This aircraft is shown in the markings of VMA-211 'Wake Island Avengers', based at Yuma as part of MAG-13. The two-tone gray scheme is now standard.

from a reinforced helicopter squadron to a number of MAWs. A Combat Service Support Element provides the full range of necessary support functions, from supply and engineering to health and graves registration.

Although the MAGTF can be of any size, there are four standard types. These are the Marine Expeditionary Force (MEF), the Marine Expeditionary Brigade (MEB), the Marine Expeditionary Unit (MEU) and the special purpose force. The MAGTF will often be a composite of several of these types of organization, perhaps with a pair of MEBs and MEUs coming together as an MEF, or with elements of several MEFs combining, as happened during Desert Storm.

The MEF is the largest type of MAGTF. Commanded by a lieutenant general it usually includes one or more Marine Divisions and a Marine Air Wing. The MEF is usually deployed with sufficient supplies for 60 days, allowing both sustained operations ashore and amphibious operations. The Marines have three MEFs, based at Camp Pendleton, Camp Lejeune and Okinawa. An MEF will typically contain 60 AV-8B Harrier IIs, 48 single-seat F/A-18 Hornets and 34 A-6Es and/or F/A-18Ds, six EA-6Bs and 12 KC-130 Hercules tankers, as well as 12 OV-10 Broncos. Helicopter strength will typically include 24 AH-1Ws, 60 CH-46Es, 44 CH-53s and 24 UH-1Ns. Other assets would include 44 tanks, 66 155-mm howitzers, 16 Hawk missile launchers and 90 Stinger teams.

An MEB usually represents the forward echelon of an MEF, and usually consists of a reinforced infantry regiment supported by a Marine Aircraft Group and support elements. There are various slightly different types of MEB. The amphibious MEB in many ways represents the standard, consisting of an assault echelon (deployed as a balanced force on board Navy amphibious ships) and an assault follow-on echelon. The amphibious MEB is commanded by a brigadier general and typically consists of

nearly 17,000 Marines and 900 Navy personnel. Air power assets typically include 40 AV-8Bs, 24 F/A-18Cs, 22 A-6Es (and/or F/A-18Ds), six KC-130s, six OV-10s, 12 AH-1Ws, 48 CH-46Es, 28 CH-53s and 12 UH-1s. The amphibious MEB would typically have 14 tanks and 47 AAVs.

The Maritime Prepositioning Force MEB is larger than a standard amphibious MEB and has a greater allocation of armor (44 tanks and 109 AAVs). It is designed to project combat power into an area extremely rapidly, and to be capable of combat against a sophisticated mechanized enemy. Designed to be prepositioned afloat, the MPFMEB does not require strategic airlift to get it where it is needed. Once ashore, the MPFMEB can be ready for combat within seven days, and can sustain operations for up to 30 days. The MPFMEB will operate in conjunction with a US Navy maritime prepositioning ship's squadron. There are three of these organizations: MPSRON-1 in the Atlantic, with four Military Sealift Command chartered ships; MPSRON-2 at Diego Garcia, with five ships; and MPSRON-3 at Guam with four ships. An MPFMEB will usually be commanded by a brigadier general. The air-power assets of an MPFMEB are similar in composition to those of an amphibious MEB, although with only 20 AV-8Bs and 16 CH-53s, and with only 12 CH-46s.

The smallest type of MEB is the Norway Airlanded MEB (NALM). Developed following a memorandum of understanding between the US and Norwegian govern-

Cannon
The port underfuselage pod is fitted with the 25-mm GAU-12/A Equalizer cannon, a five-barrelled rotary weapon.

ments in January 1981, the NALM consists of some 150 aircraft and 30 days of supplies, and deploys to Norway in USAF Air Mobility Command transport aircraft. It is designed for rapid reinforcement of NATO's northern flank. Much equipment is supplied by Norway or stored in-country, considerably easing the burden on strategic airlift assets. Air power assets allocated to the NALM are similar to those for a typical amphibious MEB, but with no A-6Es, 12 fewer CH-53s and only half as many (24) CH-46s.

Every MEF includes an Air Contingency Force (ACF) MEB, which functions as a short-notice, airlifted light MEB ready for deployment by strategic airlift. Capable of being employed as a distinct force, the ACFMEB can also be used as part of a composite force.

Next down the scale from the Marine Expeditionary Brigade is the Marine Expeditionary Unit (MEU), which is usually a 1,000 to 4,000-strong MAGTF consisting of a reinforced infantry battalion and a reinforced helicopter squadron. The latter would normally parent six AV-8Bs, some four CH-53s, four AH-1Ws, 12 CH-46Es and four UH-1Ns. Pairs of OV-10s and KC-130s are sometimes also included. The MEU is usually commanded by a colonel, and is normally forward deployed as an on-station

sea-based component of a fleet commander's amphibious and power projection force. MEUs are continuously deployed in the Mediterranean and Pacific, and periodically deployed elsewhere. The MEU is most useful for raid-type operations rather than for assaults. For missions where an MEF, MEB or MEU is inappropriate, small specialized MAGTFs, known as Special Purpose Forces, can be formed.

All US Marine Corps aviation units report to the FMFs (or to MAGTFs when deployed), and are administratively divided into four marine aircraft wings and one brigade, which are subdivided into various marine aircraft groups (broadly equivalent to a US Navy carrier air wing), then further subdivided into squadrons.

The USMC is rapidly moving towards a two-type offensive force, based on the Hornet and the AV-8B Harrier II. This example of the latter serves with VMA-311, part of MAG-13 at Yuma.

Weapons
This AV-8B carries a typical CAS/BAI load of two AGM-65 Maverick anti-armor missiles and two cluster bombs. The AIM-9 Sidewinders provide a useful self-defense capability.

Chaff/flare
Unusual features of the AV-8B are the upward-firing chaff/flare dispensers on the rear fuselage, providing protection against look-down/shoot-down attacks. Further dispensers are located underneath the rear fuselage.

Powerplant
Current delivery AV-8Bs are fitted with the latest Rolls-Royce F402-RR-408 engine (Pegasus 11-61), rated at 23,800 lb (106 kN) thrust. Twenty-five per cent of the engine parts for US aircraft are made by Pratt & Whitney.

McDonnell Douglas/BAe AV-8B Harrier II Night Attack

For direct support of Marines on the ground, the Corps chose the AV-8B. This Harrier II is of inestimable value, for it can happily operate from assault carriers or from makeshift airstrips in the field. By basing the aircraft close to the troops in contact, the aircraft's sortie rate can be vastly increased. Offering a major enhancement to the USMC's close support force is the Night Attack version of the AV-8B. This adds a GEC FLIR in a small protuberance forward of the cockpit, and NVG-compatible cockpit lighting. Further development of the AV-8B has resulted in the Harrier II Plus, which integrates a Hughes APG-65 radar, as used by the Hornet. The first was due for delivery in October 1992.

In many ways the cornerstone of Marine Corps aviation, the Boeing Vertol CH-46 Sea Knight serves in large numbers as the main assault helicopter. Marine commanders would like to replace these veterans with the revolutionary V-22 Osprey tilt-rotor for the assault mission, but this program faces a long haul through the budgetary mire.

The MAW is usually commanded by a two-star major general, or very occasionally by a one-star senior brigadier general. The MAW uses its assets to provide whatever services the ground forces require, from transport to close air support and air defense. The MAG exercises operational and administrative control over its constituent squadrons whether afloat or ashore. MAGs usually have a specific mission and operate similar aircraft types; thus, helicopters will tend to be clustered in one MAG while fixed-wing aircraft will be in another. Mixed MAGs (like MAG-70 in the Gulf War) may be formed to meet a particular need.

Regular deployment

Marine squadrons are usually commanded by a lieutenant colonel, with a junior lieutenant colonel (or sometimes a senior major) as executive officer (XO). The squadron commander reports directly to the MAG commander, usually a colonel.

Marine Corps squadrons are nominally shore-based at a particular airfield, but they exist to deploy, and most units will undergo regular six-month deployed tours. The 2d and 3d MAWs in particular regularly deploy units to bulk out the skeletal 1st MAW. (Marine organizations are always referred to as 2d and 3d and not 2nd or 3rd.) Many fixed-wing units have undertaken deployments aboard US Navy carriers, and carrier qualifications are regularly renewed.

Two Special Operations Capable Marine Expeditionary Units are permanently deployed, 365 days per year, each with an aviation composite element typically consisting of a composite squadron of 12 CH-46s, four CH-53s, six AH-1s, three UH-1s and six AV-8Bs. One of these serves in the Mediterranean and another in the Pacific, typically carried aboard an example of the 'Wasp'-, 'Tarawa'- or 'Iwo Jima'-class amphibious assault ships. The original 'Iwo Jima'-class ships are known as LPHs and embark up to 27 Sea Knight-sized helicopters, and are scheduled for retirement during the mid-1990s. They are augmented by five 'Tarawa'-class LHAs, which have full-length flight

decks and half-length hangar decks. This reflects the growing importance of VTOL/STOVL Harrier operations during the 1970s, when the ships were delivered. The LHAs can carry up to 38 CH-46s, but usually deploy a slightly smaller composite squadron including Harriers, AH-1s and CH-53s. The newer 'Wasp'-class vessels are similar, but offer improved facilities for STOVL and helicopter operations. The 'Whidbey Island' class of LSDs (Dock Landing Ships) can also embark and operate Harriers and helicopters. (Four of a planned five 'Wasp'-class have now been laid down but only one 'Wasp'-class ship has been commissioned, while five of the smaller 'Tarawa'-class and seven 'Iwo Jima'-class vessels are operational.)

US Marine Corps aviation tackles all roles except flying training (which is undertaken by the US Navy) and strategic airlift (which is undertaken by the USAF when necessary). Marine aviation displays great flexibility and has tremendous capability. There is, however, no ethos of independent air action, and the primary mission of Marine aviation is to support the 'grunt' on the ground. The marine air wings and air groups are thus seen as an integral part of the Corps, and aviation is not seen as a separate 'service within a service'. The secondary role of augmentation of US Navy aviation is seldom practised, although squadrons do occasionally deploy for cruises aboard US Navy aircraft carriers. Recently, however, (on 13 January 1992) the Secretary of the Navy directed that VMFA and VMAQ squadrons should be more closely integrated into the US Navy carrier air wings. Every pilot, navigator and maintenance man is a Marine first and foremost, and all undergo the same basic training as those who serve in infantry units. For pilots this means the Officers Land Course or Platoon Leaders Course followed by Basic School at Quantico before undergoing the appropriate flying training with the Navy.

Ongoing modernization

Although the end of the Cold War has led to some cutbacks in Marine Corps strength, Marine aviation has emerged remarkably unscathed, with an ongoing modernization program transforming the capability of the various MAGs and MAWs. The F-4 Phantom was the first of the 'old faithfuls' to bow out, being replaced by the versatile F/A-18 Hornet. These now equip 12 front-line squadrons. The Marines actually started forming their first Hornet units before the Navy, and VMFA-314 and VMFA-323 deployed aboard the USS *Coral Sea* for its 1983 Mediterranean cruise, during which the aircraft received its baptism of fire in operations against Libya. The Marines were pleased with the Hornet's performance in the Gulf, although Lieutenant General Duanne Wills, Deputy Chief of Staff for Aviation, admitted that Desert Storm "confirmed some deficiencies we knew we had, and have been working to fix." In the case of the Hornet this includes the provision of radar upgrades, the service entry of the much-delayed ATARS, and the provision of FLIRS and GPS for all aircraft. Two F/A-18 squadrons (VMFA-333 'Shamrocks' and VMFA-531 'Gray Ghosts') were stood down in FY 1992 (on 31 March 1992) as part of the general round of defense cuts, leaving 10 active-force single-seat Hornet squadrons.

The Corps' first-generation AV-8A and AV-8C Harriers and A-4M Skyhawks have now given way in the front line to second-generation AV-8B Harrier IIs, including aircraft equipped with comprehensive night attack avionics (all AV-8Bs from the 167th airframe). Future Harrier II deliveries may include at least 24 (and perhaps 72) new-build APG-65 radar-equipped Harrier II Plus airframes, plus those produced by conversion of 114 existing 'day attack' AV-8Bs. Total procurement of the AV-8B/TAV-8B is planned to reach 328 aircraft. This will extend the life of the AV-8B until the new STOVL strike fighter

AH-1s, UH-1s, CH-46s and CH-53s on board the USS Iwo Jima, one of the Marine Corps' main assault carriers. AV-8Bs are also carried so that the LHAs can operate as a small but complete battle force, with full air support.

can enter service in about 2010. Two of the existing AV-8B squadrons are to be disestablished during 1993.

All-weather attack squadrons have begun to convert from the ageing Grumman A-6E Intruder to the F/A-18D Hornet, sacrificing some range for survivability, accuracy and an unrestricted new airframe. In fact, five 10-aircraft A-6 Intruder units, a single 21-aircraft RF-4B Phantom squadron, and 27 OA-4Ms (these latter being spread between a number of MALS units) are being replaced by six 12-aircraft F/A-18D squadrons. The new variant (a two-seat, night-attack equipped derivative of the F/A-18C) was blooded during the Gulf War, operating largely in the fast FAC role. A similar variant, the F/A-18D(CR), will replace the RF-4B (now retired from VMFP-3) in the photo recce role. The remaining A-6Es are being transferred back to the US Navy to alleviate shortages caused by fatigue problems and the cancellation of the A-12. Marine Intruder units do not include KA-6D tankers, which are borrowed from the US Navy to support carrier deployments as required. The F/A-18D will also take over some of the roles of the OV-10A and OV-10D Bronco, with other roles being taken over by AH-1W and UH-1N helicopters. This will allow the Bronco to be retired by FY 1994. Six former USAF Broncos transferred to the Corps during 1991 are now unlikely to be converted to OV-10D standard.

Helicopter assault

Marine Corps aviation is not only about close air support. Enormous numbers of helicopters serve in the transport, attack and various other roles. Numerically most important are the 17 squadrons (including two Reserve units) of CH-46 Sea Knights, known to the Marines as 'Frogs'. Augmenting these are five units equipped with the CH-53D and five units equipped with the second-generation CH-53E. Six composite light attack squadrons fly the AH-1W and various UH-1 sub-variants. All surviving AH-1Ts have now been converted to AH-1W standards. Two Reserve units operate the AH-1J, but are converting to the AH-1W. The Marine Corps still wants to replace its ageing CH-46 and CH-53 helicopters with 552 V-22 Osprey tilt-rotor aircraft, but funding difficulties continue to dog this vital program and the production future of the

aircraft remains in doubt. Lieutenant General Wills described the CH-46E replacement as "our most critical aviation requirement" and as "our number one aviation priority," explaining that "we are experiencing a shortfall now in the numbers and capability of our medium lift assault support force, and the situation will worsen in the next few years unless we can produce an adequate medium lift replacement." Continued development funding has kept alive Marine hopes that this vital and versatile tool will eventually be funded for production.

As with the US Navy, the toughest battle facing the Marines is that for funding, although Marine aircraft procurement has been cut less deeply than that of the other services. The Marines are adapting to the shrinking budget by emphasizing the maintenance of all combat capabilities in a leaner, more efficient force. The Marines aim to maintain their contributions to joint and combined operations, and to remain fully capable of mounting expeditionary operations.

Lieutenant General Wills, Deputy Chief of Staff for Aviation, should have the final word. "Re-entering a period of peace does not mean that our job stops. We will continue to maintain Marine Forces on alert, worldwide, ready to respond on a moment's notice to protect our nation's interests."

Armed with 5-in rockets and Mk 83 1,000-lb low-drag bombs, a Marine Corps F/A-18D rolls on to a target. The D-model Hornet has taken over from the Intruder in precision attack duties, equipped with laser tracking and FLIR pods to enhance its night attack capabilities.

Most useful to the Marine Corps are the KC-130 Hercules which serve with three active-duty and two Reserve units. Tanking is provided for tactical aircraft and CH-53 helicopters, while the ability to carry cargo worldwide is retained.

US Marine Corps Aviation

Fleet Marine Force Atlantic (FMFLant)
HQ: Norfolk, VA

As well as the 2d Marine Division at Camp Lejeune, FMFLant controls the 2d Marine Expeditionary Force (II MEF) and Force Troops FMFLant at the same base. II MEF is responsible for the European theater, and for operations on the west coast of Africa and the coastline of South America.

2nd Marine Air Wing
HQ: Cherry Point, NC

The 2d Marine Air Wing exists to support the 2d Marine Division at Camp Lejeune, NC, which provides Marine forces to support the US Navy's 2d Fleet in the Atlantic and Sixth Fleet in the Mediterranean. Operations in Norway and Turkey are usually supported by 2d MAW. During the Gulf War several 2d Marine Air Wing squadrons deployed to Saudi Arabia with 3d Marine Air Wing MAGs. Marine Air Group 40 was newly formed to parent various squadrons deployed with the 4th Marine Expeditionary Brigade on board the vessels of Marine Amphibious Group 2.

Directly assigned:

SOES	C-9B,CT-39G	Cherry Point	'5C'
Cherry Point Base Flight	UC-12B	Cherry Point	'5C'
Cherry Point SAR Flight	HH-46D	Cherry Point	
Beaufort Base Flight	UC-12B	Beaufort	'5B'
Beaufort SAR Flight	HH-46D	Beaufort	
New River Base Flight	UC-12B	New River	'5D'
VMGRT-253	KC-130F	Cherry Point	'GR'

Marine Air Group 14, Cherry Point, NC

VMGR-252 'Heavy Haulers'	KC-130F/R	Cherry Point	'BH'
VMAQ-2 'Playboys'	EA-6B	Cherry Point	'CY'
VMA(AW)-224 'Bengals'	A-6E	Cherry Point	'WK'
VMA(AW)-332 'Polka Dots'	A-6E	Cherry Point	'EA'
VMA(AW)-533 'Hawks'	A-6E	Cherry Point	'ED'

(VMAQ-2 to split on 1 July 1992 to form VMAQ-1, -2, -3 and, on 1 October, -4, which will re-activate as an active unit)

Marine Air Group 26, New River, NC

HMLA-167	UH-1N/AH-1W	New River	'TV'
HMM-261 'Bulls'	CH-46E	New River	'EM'
HMM-264 'Black Knights'	CH-46F	New River	'EH'
HMM-266 'Griffins'	CH-46E	New River	'ES'
HMM-362 'Ugly Angels'	CH-53D	New River	'YL'
HMM-461 'Sea Stallions'	CH-53E	New River	'CJ'
HMT-204	CH-46E/CH-53D	New River	'GX'

Marine Air Group 29, New River, NC

VMO-1 'Yazoo'	OV-10A/D/D+	New River	'ER'
HMM-162 'Doughboys'	CH-46E	New River	'YS'
HMM-263 'Thunder Chickens/Red Lions'	CH-46E	New River	'EG'

FMFLant has the 2d Marine Air Wing assigned, with helicopters concentrated at New River. HMM-365 is primarily a CH-46E assault helicopter unit, but also has some UH-1Ns assigned when afloat.

HMLA-269 'Sea Cobras'	UH-1N/AH-1W	New River	'HF'
HMM-365	CH-46E	New River	'YM'
HMH-464 'Condors'	CH-53E	New River	'EN'

Marine Air Group 31, Beaufort, SC

VMFA-115 'Silver Eagles'	F/A-18A	Beaufort	'VE'
VMFA-122 'Crusaders'	F/A-18A	Beaufort	'DC'
VMFA-251 'Thunderbolts'	F/A-18A	Beaufort	'DW'
VMFA-312 'Checkerboards'	F/A-18A	Beaufort	'DR'
VMFA-451 'Warlords'	F/A-18A	Beaufort	'VM'

(VMFA-333 'Shamrocks' deactivated 31 March 1992)

Marine Air Group 32, Cherry Point, NC

VMAT-203 'Hawks'	AV-8B/TAV-8B	Cherry Point	'KD'
VMA-223 'Bulldogs'	AV-8B	Cherry Point	'WP'
VMA-231 'Ace of Spades'	AV-8B	Cherry Point	'CG'
VMA-331 'Bumblebees'	AV-8B	Cherry Point	'VL'

VMA-331 to deactivate 1 October 1992

VMA-542 'Flying Tigers'	AV-8B	Cherry Point	'WH'

Fleet Marine Force Pacific (FMFPac)
HQ: Camp Smith, CA

FMFPac controls Force Troops FMFPac at Twentynine Palms, the 1st Marine Division (Reinforced) and the 1st Marine Expeditionary Force (I MEF) at Camp Pendleton, CA; the 3d Marine Division (Reinforced) and 3d Marine Expeditionary Force (III MEF) at Camp S. D. Butler on Okinawa; and the 1st Marine Brigade at Kaneohe Bay, HI. These units are supported by the 3d Marine Air Wing (in the case of the CONUS-based forces) and by rotational deployments by the 3d and 2d Marine Air Wings (in the case of the Far East units). Hawaii's 1st Marine Brigade has its own organic aviation force. I MEF provides forces for commitment into the Pacific and for reinforcement of NATO's southern flank.

1st Marine Air Wing
HQ: Iwakuni, Japan

The 1st Marine Air Wing has only two permanently assigned squadrons, the CT-39-equipped liaison squadron at Futemma and the co-located KC-130R tanker unit. The two constituent MAGs receive aircraft on rotation from 2d and 3d Marine Air Wings, such that MAG-12 always includes a VMAQ detachment and MAG-36 always includes aircraft from VMO-1 and VMO-2. The wing's role is to support the Okinawa-based 3d Marine Division, which provides Marine forces for the US Navy's 7th and 3rd Fleets. Due to Desert Storm commitments the VMAQ-2 detachment was replaced by a detachment from the Reserve VMAQ-4 for six months from March 1991, while three Reserve helicopter units were also deployed.

VMGR-352 is the KC-130 unit assigned to FMFPac's 3d MAW. Here an aircraft practises rough field landings, a tactic used when the Hercules is employed in the direct support of ground troops.

Directly assigned:

Iwakuni Base Flight	UC-12B	Iwakuni	'5G'
Iwakuni SAR Flight	HH-46D	Iwakuni	

Marine Air Group 12, Iwakuni, Japan

VMAQ- (det)*	EA-6B	Iwakuni
VMFA- *	F/A-18C	Iwakuni
VMFA- *	F/A-18C	Iwakuni
VMFA(AW)- *	F/A-18D	Iwakuni
VMA- *	AV-8B	Iwakuni

* = Rotational

Marine Air Group 36, Futemma, Japan

VMO-2 (det) 'Hostage'	OV-10A/D/D+	Futemma	'UU'
VMGR-152	KC-130R	Futemma	'QD'
MWHS-1	CT-39G	Futemma	'SZ'
HMM- *	CH-46E	Futemma	
HMH- (det)*	CH-53D, UH-1N	Futemma	
Futemma Base Flight	UC-12B	Futemma	'5F'

* = Rotational

3d Marine Air Wing
HQ: El Toro, CA

The 3d Marine Air Wing exists to support the 1st Marine Division, whose primary role is as an intervention force assigned to the joint-service Central Command, ready to send a combat force anywhere at very short notice. In August 1990 a new Marine air group, MAG-70, was formed as the aviation vanguard of the 7th Marine Expeditionary Brigade (1st Marine Expeditionary Force) then disbanded in September, when MAG-11 took over responsibility for Marine F/A-18s in the Gulf. MAG-13 looked after four AV-8B and two OV-10 units and MAG-16 parented eight helicopter units (some of them Reserve). Marine Air Group 50 was newly formed to parent various squadrons deployed with the 5th Marine Expeditionary Brigade on board the vessels of MAG-3.

Directly assigned:

El Toro Base Flight	UC-12B	El Toro	'5T'
El Toro SAR Flight	HH-1N	El Toro	
Yuma Base Flight	UC-12B	Yuma	'5Y'
Yuma SAR Flight	HH-1N	Yuma	

Marine Air Group 11, El Toro, CA

VMFAT-101 'Sharpshooters'	F/A-18A/B/C/D, T-34C	El Toro	'SH'
VMFA-314 'Black Knights'	F/A-18A	El Toro	'VW'
VMFA-323 'Death Rattlers'	F/A-18A	El Toro	'WS'
VMFA-531 'Gray Ghosts'	F/A-18A	El Toro	'EC'

VMFA-531 deactivated 31 March 1992

VMFA(AW)-121 'Green Knights'	F/A-18D	El Toro	'VK'
VMFA(AW)-225 'Vagabonds'	F/A-18D(CR)	El Toro	'CR'

VMA-223 (top) and VMA-542 (bottom) are two East Coast AV-8B squadrons from MAG-32 at Cherry Point, seen during training at Yuma.

Norway is a major operational area for the USMC, as emphasized by regular exercises. Marines reinforce NATO's weak northern flank.

US Marine Corps Aviation

Regiment, largest infantry unit in the Corps. Hawaii is an excellent training area for the Corps, with plentiful remote and isolated countryside which includes some stretches of coastline. It is also ideally located as a base for rapid response forces, and in this connection the 1st MEB supports the Marine Prepositioning Ships Program, under which pre-loaded container ships (carrying ordnance and supplies) patrol strategically vital areas. If trouble flares the 1st MEB simply rendezvous with the nearest ship and go into action. Several 1st MEB aviation units were deployed to the Gulf, temporarily attached to 3d MAW MAGS.

VMFA(AW)-242 'Batmen'	F/A-18D	El Toro	'DT'
VMGR-352	KC-130F/R	El Toro	'QB'

Marine Air Group 13, Yuma, AZ

VMA-211 '(Wake Island) Avengers'	AV-8B*	Yuma	'CF'
VMA-214 'Black Sheep'	AV-8B*	Yuma	'WE'
VMA-311 'Tomcats'	AV-8B	Yuma	'WL'
VMA-513 'Flying Nightmares'	AV-8B	Yuma	'WF'
* = AV-8B Night Attack version			

Marine Air Group 16, Tustin, CA

HMT-301 'Windwalkers'	CH-46E	Tustin	'SU'
HMT-302 'Phoenix'	CH-53A	Tustin	'UT'
HMM-161	CH-46E	Tustin	'YR'
HMM-163 'Ridgerunners'	CH-46E	Tustin	'YP'
HMM-164 'Flying Clamors'	CH-46E	Tustin	'YT'
HMM-166 'Sea Elk'	CH-46E	Tustin	'YX'
HMM-268 'Red Dragons'	CH-46E	Tustin	'YQ'

HMH-361 'Pineapples'	CH-53E	Tustin	'YN'
HMH-363 'Lucky Red Lions'	CH-53D	Tustin	'YZ'
HMH-462 'Heavy Haulers'	CH-53D	Tustin	'YF'
HMH-465 'Warhorses'	CH-53E	Tustin	'YJ'
HMH-466	CH-53E	Tustin	'YK'

Marine Air Group 39, Camp Pendleton, CA

VMO-2 'Hostage'	OV-10A/D	Camp Pendleton	'UU'
HMLA-169	UH-1N/AH-1W	Camp Pendleton	'SN'
HMLA-267 'Black Aces'	UH-1N/AH-1J	Camp Pendleton	'UV'
HMLA-367 'Scarface'	UH-1N/AH-1W	Camp Pendleton	'VT'
HMLA-369	UH-1N/AH-1J	Camp Pendleton	'SM'
HMT-303	UH-1N/AH-1J	Camp Pendleton	'QT'

1st Marine Expeditionary Brigade
HQ: Kaneohe Bay, HI

The 1st Marine Expeditionary Brigade incorporates fighter-bomber and helicopter units and is tasked with supporting the 3d Marine

Directly assigned:

Kaneohe Bay SAR Flight 'Kaneohe Bayhawks'	HH-46D	Kaneohe Bay	'KB'

Marine Air Group 24, Kaneohe Bay, HI

VMFA-212 'Lancers'	F/A-18C	Kaneohe Bay	'WD'
VMFA-232 'Red Devils'	F/A-18C	Kaneohe Bay	'WT'
VMFA-235 'Death Angels'	F/A-18C	Kaneohe Bay	'DB'
HMM-165	CH-46E	Kaneohe Bay	'YW'
HMM-262 'Flying Tigers'	CH-46E	Kaneohe Bay	'ET'
HMM-265	CH-46E	Kaneohe Bay	'EP'
HMM-364 'Purple Foxes'	CH-46E	Kaneohe Bay	'PF'
HMH-463 'Heavy Haulers'	CH-53D	Kaneohe Bay	'YH'
HMLA-367 det B	AH-1W/UH-1N	Kaneohe Bay	'VT'

US Marine Corps Reserve

4th Marine Air Wing
HQ: New Orleans

Marine Reserve forces are supported by the 4th Marine Air Wing. This organization is now following the rest of Marine Corps aviation in a program of intensive modernization and re-equipment. Inadequacies in the Reserve were underlined by Operation Desert Storm, during which, with over 80 per cent of regular units deployed worldwide, mobilized Reserve squadrons became a crucial part of US Marine Corps aviation strength. Some units, however, could not be mobilized because their equipment was not compatible with newer active force equipment, and would have been difficult to support. Well-trained, highly-motivated and much-needed units were unable to deploy. The phasing out of the AH-1J, CH-53A, A-4M and F-4S was accelerated as a result of this sobering experience, so that only the A-4M remained in use by the early summer of 1992.

The 4th MAW will lose one of its fast jet units, but will eventually be left with five F/A-18- and two AV-8B-equipped units, allowing the final retirement of the long-serving A-4 Skyhawk.

The F-4 Phantom, long a backbone of the USMC Reserve, has now finally retired, with VMFA-112 at Dallas withdrawing its final two aircraft on 29 January 1992, after an official 'Phantom Pharewell' on 18 January, when four were still active. With the withdrawal of the F-4S from the Naval Air Warfare Center Weapons Division at Kirtland, NM (formerly the Pacific Missile Test Center), and the NAWC Weapons Division at China Lake, CA (formerly the Naval Weapons Center) holding only one F-4J in storage as a potential ejection seat test aircraft, all Navy and Marine F-4s are now drones.

Similarly, units operating the EA-6A and KC-130F are re-equipping with newer versions of the Prowler and Hercules, and even helicopter units are transitioning onto newer variants of the CH-53 and AH-1. As well as supporting Reserve forces, units are sometimes deployed in place of regular aviation units. During the summer of 1991, for example, a VMAQ-4 detachment replaced one from VMAQ-2 at Iwakuni, and helicopter squadrons HML-771, HML-776 and HMH-772 sent aircraft and crews to reinforce the 1st MAW.

The reduction from five to four Reserve MAGs has led to the loss of MAG-48 and a wholesale shuffle of units between the surviving MAGs.

Directly assigned:

MWHS-4	UC-12B, CT-39G	NAS New Orleans	'EZ'

Marine Air Group 41, NAS Dallas, TX

VMFA-112 'Cowboys'	F/A-18A	NAS Dallas	'MA'
HMH-777	CH-53A/D	NAS Dallas	'QM'
(HMM-777 was previously HMH-772 det B)			
MAG-41 det A, NAS Memphis, TN			

VMA-124 'Whistling Death'	A-4M/TA-4J	NAS Memphis	'QP'
MAG-41 det B, NAS Glenview, IL			
HML-776	UH-1N	NAS Glenview	'QL'
VMGR-234 'Bears'/ 'Thundering Herd'	KC-130F/T	NAS Glenview	'GH'

Marine Air Group 42, NAS Atlanta, GA

HMA-773	AH-1W	NAS Atlanta	'MP'
VMO-4	OV-10A/D+	NAS Atlanta	'MU'

MAG-42 det A, NAS Cecil Field, FL			
VMFA-142 'Flying Gators'	F/A-18A	NAS Cecil Field	'MB'
MAG-42 det B, NAS Norfolk, VA			
HMM-774 'Honkers'	CH-46E	NAS Norfolk	'MQ'
MAG-42 det C, NAS New Orleans, LA			
HML-767	UH-1N	NAS New Orleans	'MM'

Marine Air Group 46, MCAS El Toro, CA

VMFA-134 'Smokes'	F/A-18A	MCAS El Toro	'MF'
HMM-764 'Moonlight'	CH-46E	MCAS El Toro	'ML'
VMFT-401 'Snipers'	F-5E/F-5F	MCAS Yuma	'WB'
MAG-46 det A, MCAS Camp Pendleton, CA			
HMA-775	AH-1J	MCAS Camp Pendleton	
MAG-46 det B, NAS Alameda, CA			
HMH-769	RH-53D	NAS Alameda	'MS'
(HMH-769 was previously HMH-772 det A)			
VMA-133 'Golden Gaters'	A-4M	NAS Alameda	'ME'
(VMA-133 to deactivate 30/9/92)			
MAG-46 det C, NAS Whidbey Island, WA			
VMAQ-4 'Seahawks'	EA-6B	NAS Whidbey Island	'RM'
(VMAQ-4 to deactivate 30/4/92, and become an active-duty unit on 1/10/92 at MCAS Cherry Point)			

Marine Air Group 49, NAS Willow Grove, PA

VMA-131 'Diamondbacks'	A-4M/TA-4F	NAS Willow Grove	'QG'
HMH-772 'Flying Armadillos'	CH-53A	NAS Willow Grove	'MT'
MAG-49 det A, NAF Washington, MD			
VMFA-321 'Hell's Angels'	F/A-18A	NAF Washington	'MG'
MAG-49 det B, Stewart Field, NY			
VMGR-452 'Yankees'	KC-130T	Stewart Field	'NY'
MAG-49 det C, to form at Johnstown, PA, with HMLA-77X			
MAG-49 det D, NAS South Weymouth, VA			
HML-771 'Hummers'	UH-1N	NAS South Weymouth	'QK'
VMA-322 'Gamecocks'	A-4M/TA-4F	NAS South Weymouth	'QR'

Miscellaneous units

HMX-1	VH-3D, CH-46E, CH-53D, VH-60D	Quantico	'MX'
FMFPAC VIP Flight	UC-12B	Camp Smith	'BZ'
HQMC VIP Flight	UC-12B	Washington	'5A'

US COAST GUARD

Often neglected in reviews of US armed services, the Coast Guard is a military force despite being administered by a civilian department, as opposed to the Department of Defense. It has fought in every major US war, and has among its wartime tasks direct support of the Navy and Air Force. Even in peacetime, the USCG is 'at war' – against drug importers.

Although the US Coast Guard falls under, and is tasked by, the Department of Transportation during peacetime, according to Title 14 of the US Code it is "at all times an armed force of the United States," enjoying equal status with the US Air Force, Navy, Army and Marine Corps. In wartime, or by Presidential Decree, the Coast Guard can be placed under the command of the Department of the Navy. It has in fact fought in every conflict involving the USA since 1790, including the recent war in the Gulf. The entire service came under US Navy control during World War II, and some units were placed under Navy control during the Vietnam War.

Despite its name, the Coast Guard's responsibilities are not limited to the coastlines of the USA, but include the whole country and some overseas territories. Responsible for, among other things, protection of the MDZ (Maritime Defense Zone) stretching 200 miles out from the US coast, the Coast Guard also conducts drug interdiction, anti-smuggling and a variety of other missions. In wartime, some US Coast Guard aircraft would be seconded to the USAF for SAR work. To fulfill its responsibilities, the Coast Guard operates 250 ships and 2,000 other vessels, and its aviation element (operating some 190 aircraft) ranks as the world's seventh largest naval air arm.

The alarming increase in drug smuggling into the USA has resulted in a tremendous growth in Coast Guard activity, and the aviation elements have gained in importance. Always eager to take on new challenges, the

Coast Guard is also taking on the 'Hurricane Hunter' role from the USAF.

Coast Guard aircrew come from many sources, although all wear the traditional 'Wings of Gold' worn by US Naval and Marine aviators. The Coast Guard itself sends 60 pilots per year through the US Navy's flying training program, and more pilots transfer from the other armed forces. Many of the latter are former Army Warrant Officer pilots. The Coast Guard also operates reciprocal exchange programs with other US service branches, the RAF, the Royal Navy, and the Canadian Forces. Advanced training is conducted by the Coast Guard itself, and presently includes an ambitious NVG training program.

The largest aircraft in Coast Guard Service is the Lockheed C-130 Hercules. Twelve HC-130Bs were delivered between 1959 and 1963, serving until 1986. These allowed the Coast Guard to conduct eight-hour (on station) searches up to 1,000 miles from base. The aircraft frequently patrolled with two engines shut down. At least one of the early HC-130Bs was fitted with SLAR on the undercarriage fairings, and with underwing sensor pods. Other Coast Guard Hercules have since operated with SLAR mounted on the undercarriage fairings, and two are in use at Elizabeth City, NC. A single EC-130E was delivered in 1966 for calibration work and was retired in 1986. The present Coast Guard variant is the HC-130H, based on the USAF combat rescue HC-130H but without provision for the Fulton STAR ground-air recovery system, without

refueling pods and without the AN/ARD-17 Cook Aerial Tracker. Thirty-five were delivered, some of them HC-130H-7s with standard 'Pinocchio' nose and T56-A-7 engines. One was lost during 1989. Today the Hercules serves at Elizabeth City (six aircraft), Clearwater (six aircraft), Sacramento (four aircraft), Kodiak (six aircraft), Barbers Point (three aircraft) and Borinquen (three aircraft). Three more form a reserve to fill gaps caused by servicing, and the last delivered has been converted to EC-130V standard, with a rotodome above the fuselage housing an E-2C type radar.

The Sacramento-based aircraft carry a FLIR turret, while those from Clearwater, Barbers Point and Borinquen are fitted with the same AN/APS-137 radar as the P-3 Orion and ES-3A Viking. They retain the standard AN/APN-215 weather radar.

Coast Guard procurement of the Dassault Falcon 20G, known as the HU-25A and B Guardian (and HU-25C Interceptor) in Coast Guard use, resulted from a 1967 requirement for a medium-range surveillance type to replace the ageing Grumman HU-16 Albatross amphibian. Various aircraft types were evaluated, before the choice was narrowed to a turbofan-powered 'bizjet' type. The basic HU-25A differed from civil Falcon 20s in having a full mission avionics suite, cabin

Procured to replace the Sikorsky HH-52, the Aérospatiale HH-65A Dolphin undertakes the short-range SAR role. In this task it regularly operates with cutters and patrol boats.

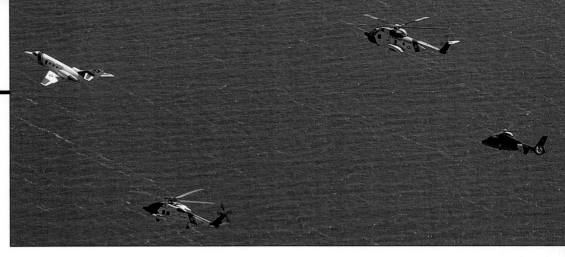

Four of the USCG's five main mission aircraft are represented in this formation, only the HC-130H Hercules being absent. An HU-25A leads an HH-3F, HH-60J and HH-65A.

search windows, an air delivery drop hatch, hardpoints and various sensor systems. Forty were delivered. Seven Guardians were modified to HU-25B configuration, with a SLAR under the starboard forward fuselage, and an APS-131 IRLS pod under the starboard wing. This equipment was primarily intended for the identification of ships causing oil spills. Two of these aircraft were deployed to Bahrain during Operation Desert Storm to monitor the oil slick pumped into the Gulf by the Iraqis.

Nine Guardians were later more extensively modified for the drug interdiction role, with a Westinghouse AN/APG-66 radar (as used by the F-16) and a WF-360 FLIR, as well as comprehensive communications equipment including military UHF and secure VHF. These aircraft are often reassigned between districts in response to specific requests.

Until recently, the US Navy's standard shipborne Airborne Early Warning platform, Grumman's E-2C Hawkeye, was in service with the Coast Guard as the backbone of the air interdiction effort against drug runners. Four E-2Cs were in use, allowing the Coast Guard to monitor up to 150,000 miles of ocean and 3,000,000 cubic miles of airspace. Operating as Coast Guard Air Wing One, the E-2C unit frequently deployed aircraft from its base at CGAS St Augustine, FL (and previously NAS Norfolk, VA) to bases fringing the Caribbean and Gulf of Mexico. The Hawkeyes were augmented by Aerostat units. Five of these are ship-based, while two, Cariball One and Cariball Two, are located at High Rock, Bahamas, and on the old Georgetown Airport, Great Exuma, Bahamas. The E-2C operation ended in October 1991, when the aircraft were returned to the Navy. CGAS St Augustine was disestablished in November 1991.

Drug interdiction

The Coast Guard currently operates a pair of Schweizer RG-8As on covert surveillance patrols connected with the drug interdiction program. Acquired from the US Army, these motor gliders have an exceptionally quiet engine and propeller, and are inaudible from the ground when flying at altitudes of around 2,000 ft. They also have a very long endurance and a 65 cubic feet equipment bay which can accept a wide variety of palletized sensors. The exact equipment fit and mission of these, the Coast Guard's most mysterious aircraft, remains unknown. The aircraft are painted in low-visibility gray, and can be fitted with cockpit armor. The two pilots wear NVGs during night operations.

The single-turbine HH-52 Seaguard is now retired, leaving the Sikorsky HH-3F Pelican (and a handful of similar ex-USAF CH-3Es procured in 1989) as the Coast Guard's only fully amphibious 'flying life boat'. Forty HH-3Fs were delivered between 1969 and 1973, their twin engines giving greater reliability and safety and conferring a 700-mile range. They carried radar and various navaids, dramatically improving capability. The HH-3F can refuel from a surface vessel while in the hover. The

three similar CH-3Es were fitted with a nose-mounted APN-215 radar, Loran C navigation system and an auxiliary fuel tank. So modified, they were sent to serve at CGAS Traverse City, MI.

The Coast Guard announced a requirement for a new short-range recovery helicopter to replace the HH-52 in 1978. The resulting competition was won by Aérospatiale, who put forward a variant of their SA 365 Dauphin. Ninety-five SA 365G/HH-65A Dolphins were ordered, powered by US Lycoming engines, with a high level of US equipment and assembled in Texas. Since it entered service in 1984, the HH-65A has been plagued by problems, especially with its engines. A single HH-65A has been converted to the T800 engine in a joint Coast Guard/US Army test program, but re-engining of the whole fleet is not to be undertaken.

To replace the larger HH-3F the Coast Guard has selected a dedicated rescue version of the Sikorsky Black Hawk. Similar to the HH-60H acquired by the US Navy for combat SAR duties, the HH-60J Jayhawk can operate up to 300 miles from the shore, and has an on-scene endurance of 45 minutes. Advanced navaids and avionics allow the aircraft to operate effectively in what would previously have been very marginal conditions. The only lack by comparison with the older HH-3F is the inability to actually land on the water during routine operations. The Coast Guard has ordered 32 of these advanced $12-million helicopters, and requested funding for a further 12.

Two unique aircraft conversions in use with the Coast Guard in the VIP transport role are the Gulfstream I (VC-4A) and Gulfstream II (VC-11A). These were delivered in 1963 and 1969 respectively. The single CASA C.212 in Coast Guard service is used for low-cost logistics support operations in the Caribbean, mainly in support of helicopter operations.

Above: The USCG celebrated its 200th anniversary in 1990, and adorned an HU-25A with this smart logo.

Two special Guardian variants are the HU-25B (above) with SLAR and the HU-25C (below) with APG-66 radar and FLIR turret.

Below: Long a cornerstone of the USCG, the HH-3F Pelican is being slowly replaced by the HH-60J Jayhawk.

US Coast Guard Headquarters, Washington, DC

The USCG HQ in Washington controls 10 Coast Guard Districts, listed below. These are subdivided between two area commands, serving the Atlantic and Pacific.

Commander Atlantic Area, Governors Island, NY: 1st Coast Guard District HQ Boston, ME; 2nd Coast Guard District HQ St Louis, MI; 5th Coast Guard District HQ Portsmouth, VA; 7th Coast Guard District HQ Miami, FL; 8th Coast Guard District HQ New Orleans, LA; 9th Coast Guard District HQ Cleveland, OH.

Commander Pacific Area, Alameda, CA: 11th Coast Guard District HQ Long Beach, CA; 13th Coast Guard District HQ Seattle, WA; 14th Coast Guard District HQ Honolulu, HI; 17th Coast Guard District HQ Juneau, AK; Marianas Section, Guam; Far East Section, Tokyo.

Below: The sole VC-4A Gulfstream I is based at Elizabeth City for staff transport duties. A VC-11A Gulfstream II is at Washington.

Commander Atlantic Area

1st Coast Guard District HQ Boston, ME

The 1st District administers the air stations in the area covering the states of Maine, New Hampshire, Vermont, Massachusetts, Rhode Island, Connecticut and New York. The Cape Cod HH-3Fs are due for replacement by HH-60Js by May 1994.

CGAS Brooklyn, NY	HH-65A
CGAS Cape Cod, MA (Otis ANGB)	HH-60J,
'Guardians of New England'	HU-25
CGAS Salem, MA	

2nd Coast Guard District HQ St Louis, MS

Since the 2nd Coast Guard District takes responsibility for those central states that have no coastline, it has no air stations.

5th Coast Guard District HQ Portsmouth, VA

The 5th District covers the central part of the Eastern seaboard, taking responsibility for Coast Guard activities in Pennsylvania, New Jersey, the District of Columbia, Delaware, Virginia, Maryland and North Carolina. Elizabeth City, NC, is the district's largest air station and is a very active SAR and patrol center. It also acts as the primary maintenance and aircrew standardization center for the Hercules in Coast Guard service. The air station is home to the Aviation Technical Training Center (ATTC) and the Aircraft Repair and Supply Center. Opened in 1978, the ATTC in-cludes five separate schools for the training of aviation survivalmen, electronics technicians, electrician's mates, structural mechanics and machinist's mates. Active since the late 1940s, the Coast Guard Aircraft Repair and Supply Center overhauls, repairs and modifies Coast Guard aircraft and helicopters. Today, the ARSC mainly maintains HH-65s and HU-25s, but also overhauls and reworks C-130 and HH-3F powerplants. The unit coordinates requisition and purchase orders from individual air stations.

CGAS Elizabeth City, NC	VC-4A, HC-130H, HH-3F, HH-65A, HH-60J
CGAS Cape May, NJ	HH-65A
CGAS Washington, DC (Washington National Airport)	VC-11
Aviation Technical Training Center (Elizabeth City)	
Aircraft Repair and Supply Center (Elizabeth City)	

7th Coast Guard District HQ Miami, FL

The 7th District comprises Florida, South Carolina and Georgia, and also takes responsibility for Puerto Rico and the Greater Antilles. Drug interdiction is a vital secondary role for the district's air stations, which include dedicated surveillance aircraft. SAR capabilities will be dramatically improved in May 1992, when Clearwater trades its HH-3Fs for new HH-60Js. Clearwater is expected to be the home of the sole EC-130V. The huge fleet of HH-3Fs presently based at Clearwater is comprehensively equipped, with Nitesun searchlights and other sensors. They are heavily committed to OPBAT operations against drug traffic.

CGAS Borinquen, PR 'Les SAR Frogs'	HC-130H, HH-65A
CGAS Clearwater, FL (St Petersburg IAP) 'Anywhere, Anytime'	HC-130H, HH-3F
CGAS Miami, FL (Opa Locka IAP)	HH-65A, HU-25A/B/C, CASA C.212-300, RG-8A
NAS Key West, FL	Aerostat
CGAS Savannah, GA	
CGAS Charleston, SC	

Left: For long-endurance sea searches, the USCG uses the HC-130H, this being an HC-130H-7 with standard nose. Two of the Hercules are fitted with SLAR.

Left: The USCG's latest type is the HH-60J Jayhawk, procured to replace the HH-3F Pelican. Complete with search radar, the Jayhawk carries external fuel tanks.

Right: For medium-range sea search the USCG chose the Dassault HU-25A Guardian, which differs primarily from the civil Falcon 20 by having large observation windows.

8th Coast Guard District HQ New Orleans, LA

Because of its position on the coast of the Gulf of Mexico (transit route for many of the illegal narcotics smuggled into the USA) the 8th District, covering New Mexico, Texas, Louisiana, Mississipi and Alabama, is of particular importance. Its five active air stations each cover a substantial area, and all are generously equipped. CGAS New Orleans (the first air station to re-equip with the HH-65A) provides 24-hour SAR cover for the Gulf of Mexico area from the Texas/Louisiana borders to Apalahicola, FL. Drug interdiction and environmental patrols are important secondary roles. The unit makes four deployments on US Navy and Coast Guard ships every year in the battle against drug runners. The station holds one HH-65 at 30-minute readiness, with a second at two-hour standby.

CGAS Biloxi, MS (Keesler AFB)	HC-130H
CGAS Corpus Christi, TX	HH-65A, HU-25
CGAS Houston, TX (Ellington AFB)	HH-65A
CGAS Mobile, AL	HH-65A, HH-60J, HU-25A/B/C
CGAS New Orleans, LA (NAS New Orleans)	HH-65A
Aviation Training Center (Mobile)	

9th Coast Guard District HQ Cleveland, OH

The 9th District looks after the Great Lakes and covers the states of Minnesota, Wisconsin, Illinois, Indiana, Michigan and Ohio, and parts of Pennsylvania and New York.

CGAS Chicago, IL (NAS Glenview)	HH-65A
CGAS Detroit, MI (Selfridge ANGB) 'Motor City SAR'	HH-65A
CGAS Traverse City, MI 'Great Lakes Guardian'	HH-60J

Commander Pacific Area

11th Coast Guard District HQ Long Beach, CA

The 11th Coast Guard District covers California, Nevada, Utah and Arizona. Sacramento-based HC-130Hs are fitted with a FLIR turret for night operations, and can carry the strap-on SAMSON pod underwing.

CGAS Humboldt Bay, CA	HH-65A
CGAS Los Angeles, CA (International Air Port)	HH-65A
CGAS Sacramento, CA (McClellan AFB)	HH-65A, HU-25B, HC-130H (SAMSON)
CGAS San Diego, CA (Lindbergh Field)	HH-65A, HU-25
CGAS San Francisco, CA (International Air Port)	HH-60J

13th Coast Guard District HQ Seattle, WA

The western seaboard is divided in two areas for Coast Guard purposes, with the 13th District covering the northern portion. The states which comprise this district are Washington, Idaho, Montana and Oregon.

CGAS Astoria, OR 'Guardian of the Sunset Empire'	HH-65A, HU-25
CGAS North Bend, OR	HH-65A
CGAS Port Angeles, WA 'Still the Best'	HH-65A

14th Coast Guard District HQ Honolulu, HI

Hawaii's single Coast Guard air station is administered by the 14th District.

CGAS Barbers Point, HI (NAS Barbers Point) 'Semper Paratus'	HC-130H, HH-65A

17th Coast Guard District HQ Juneau, AK

Coast Guard aviation in Alaska is administered by the 17th District. The ageing HH-3F Pelicans are scheduled for replacement by new HH-60Js during 1995.

CGSC Kodiak, AK	HC-130H, HH-3F
CGAS Sitka, AK	HH-3F
CGAS Casco Cove, AK	

Flying from CGAS Miami at Opa Locka are the Coast Guard's two Schweizer RG-8A motor-gliders. These super-quiet sensor platforms are dedicated to surveillance of drug-smuggling.

AIRCRAFT OF THE
US NAVY, MARINE CORPS AND COAST GUARD

McDonnell Douglas
A-4 Skyhawk

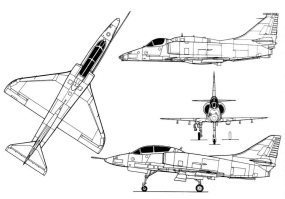

Now no longer a part of the first-line inventory, the **McDonnell Douglas A-4** – still affectionately known as 'Heinemann's Hot Rod' in recognition of its creator – continues to make a most valuable contribution to fleet readiness in a number of ways and is unlikely to disappear from the scene in the immediate future.

Arising out of Ed Heinemann's determination to reverse the trend towards ever more complex and heavier combat aircraft, the machine that eventually became the Skyhawk was conceived to satisfy a Navy requirement of the early 1950s. This called for a carrier-based attack aircraft weighing somewhere in the region of 30,000 lb (13600 kg) and the service also anticipated that it would be powered by a turboprop engine. Payload criteria laid down by the Navy required the ability to operate with an ordnance payload of 2,000 lb (900 kg).

In pursuing a very different line of thought, the Douglas chief engineer responded with a turbojet-powered machine which handsomely exceeded payload and performance stipulations, while weighing only half of the specified amount. Needless to say, the Navy was extremely interested and promptly ordered two **XA4D-1** prototypes and 18 **YA4D-1** (later **YA-4A**) test specimens. In prototype form, the Skyhawk made its maiden flight on 22 June 1954, with production-configured **A4D-1**s (**A-4A**s) beginning to join Fleet units just a couple of years later.

Subsequent development resulted in the appearance of ever more sophisticated variants, with some of the changes incorporated during a 26-year production run including a different powerplant and increasingly capable avionics kit. By the time manufacture terminated with the delivery of the final **A-4M** to the Marine Corps in 1979, no fewer than 2,960 Skyhawks had been built for home and export customers.

Today, four basic versions of the Skyhawk are still operated by Navy and Marine Corps units, specifically the **A-4E**, **A-4F** and A-4M single-seaters and the **TA-4J** two-seater. All are powered by variants of the Pratt & Whitney J52 turbojet, which replaced the original Wright J65 from, with effect, the **A-4E** version.

In Navy service, the Skyhawk fulfils two very important training functions which are, perhaps paradoxically, at opposite ends of the skill spectrum. The first version that will be encountered in a Navy pilot's career is the TA-4J, which presently serves with four training wings, these being located at Meridian, Mississippi (TW-1), Kingsville, Texas (TW-2), Chase Field, Texas (TW-3), and Pensacola, Florida (TW-6).

The first three of these wings are solely concerned with transforming the still relatively raw students into qualified naval aviators, these 'tyros' coming to the Skyhawk directly from the rather more sedate T-2 Buckeye. The final wing is involved with training Naval Flight Officers who eventually emerge from the pipeline as Radar Intercept Officers, Bombardier/Navigators and the like. In due course, both types are to be replaced by the T-45A Goshawk but, for the moment, the Skyhawk is the first 'hot ship' to be encountered during a Navy or Marine Corps flying career and students will become well acquainted with its vices and virtues as they move towards a Fleet billet.

Once they have reached a squadron, there is a strong possibility that they will encounter the Skyhawk at later stages in their career. It continues to be one of the handful of types that are used as dissimilar aircraft in air combat training and several squadrons presently use A-4Es, A-4Fs and TA-4Js for this valuable work.

Countless Navy and Marine Corps pilots have encountered the TA-4J Skyhawk while under training, but this long-serving machine is now in the process of giving way to the McDonnell Douglas T-45A Goshawk.

McDonnell Douglas A-4M Skyhawk

For many years the mainstay of the US Navy and Marine Corps light attack squadrons, the 'Scooter' is now all but out of service in its offensive role, serving with a handful of Marine Reserve units.

Markings
This A-4M wears the standard USN/USMC two-tone gray tactical camouflage, and carries the 'QP' tailcode of Marine Attack Squadron 124, which operates under the nickname 'Whistling Death'. The squadron reports to MAG-42 at Alameda, as part of the USMC's Reserve organization.

Weapons
In its day the A-4 could carry a large load for the size of aircraft, but today the loads are much less. This aircraft carries single Mk 7 cluster bombs on the external wing pylons, sacrificing the internal pylons for fuel tanks.

Fuel
Internal fuel is carried in self-sealing integral wing tanks and a tank aft of the cockpit. Wing and centerline tanks of varying sizes can be carried, and the Skyhawk can inflight-refuel using the nose-mounted boom.

Avionics
Introduced on the A-4F model, the characteristic fuselage hump houses much of the electronics package. Chief among these items is the Angle Rate Bombing System, which gives the A-4M excellent accuracy in the bombing role, a highly necessary factor given its close support role. Fin-tip and nose fairings house antennas for an electronic warfare suite.

Cockpit
The pilot sits on a Douglas Escapac 1-G3 zero-zero lightweight ejection seat. The cockpit of the A-4M is more bulged than on previous variants, giving better visibility.

Wings
The diminutive wings are almost of delta planform, featuring a sweepback of 33° at the quarter-chord and built around a three-spar structure. Ailerons, split trailing-edge flaps, leading-edge slats and overwing spoilers are all incorporated into the design to give excellent maneuverability and high lift.

Guns
For strafing attacks in the close support role, the A-4M is fitted with a pair of 20-mm Mk 12 cannon which project forward from the wing roots. Each weapon is armed with 200 rounds.

Powerplant
Marking the A-4M apart from other Skyhawk variants is the Pratt & Whitney J52-P-408 engine, with thrust increased to 11,200 lb (50 kN). A brake chute is housed below.

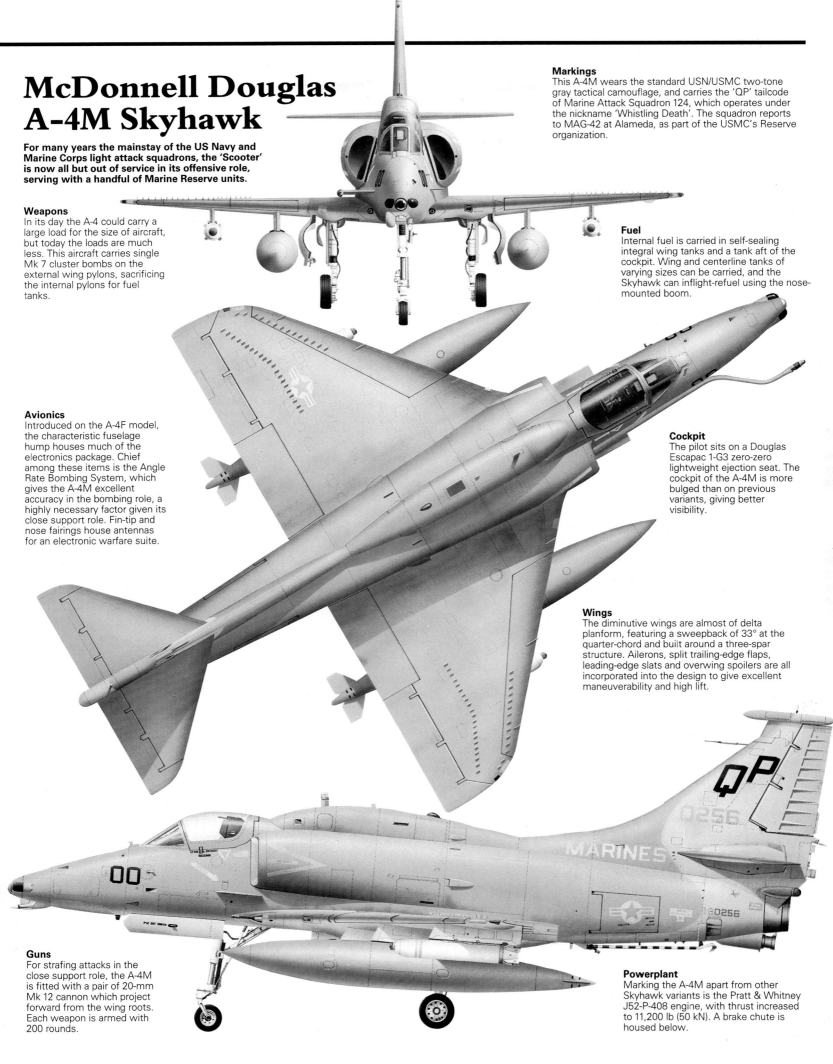

Left: Better known as 'Top Gun', the Navy's Fighter Weapons School at Miramar also operates in support of Marine Corps units, and a Skyhawk usually wears Marines titles. This camouflaged machine is an A-4F.

VARIANTS AND SERIALS

A-4E: This was the improved version of the Skyhawk, introducing a Pratt & Whitney J52-P-6A turbojet engine and five external stores stations. Two A-4Cs (148613 and 148614) were converted as prototypes, leading to the production of 498 A-4Es for service with the Navy and Marine Corps.
149647 to 149666; 149959 to 150138; 151022 to 151201; 151984 to 152101

A-4F: The updated version of A-4E had a J52-P-8A engine and additional avionics among other improvements. The final A-4E (152101) served as a prototype, and subsequent production totaled 146 aircraft.
154172 to 154217; 154970 to 155069

A-4M: This was the final development of the Skyhawk family for US service. It used the more powerful J52-P-408A engine and also introduced numerous other refinements, including a braking parachute and enhanced avionics suite. Production was undertaken solely for the Marine Corps, which received 162 examples. The production A-4F (155049) was modified to serve as the NA-4M prototype.
158148 to 158196; 158412 to 158435; 159470 to 159493; 159778 to 159794; 160022 to 160045; 160241 to 160264

TA-4E: Two examples were completed to serve as prototypes for the two-seat trainer version, and both were subsequently redesignated TA-4F.
152102 to 152103

TA-4F: This was the initial trainer derivative, and 239 examples were built for service with the Navy and Marine Corps. Many were later converted to the TA-4J by the deletion of guns and weapons delivery equipment.
152846 to 152878; 153459 to 153531; 153660 to 153690; 154287 to 154343; 154614 to 154657; 155071

NTA-4F: This two-seater was modified for special permanent test duties with the former NWC, China Lake. It is probably no longer in use.
152102.

TA-4J: A simplified version of the TA-4F which was intended initially for service with the Naval Air Training Command. It lacks cannon armament and weapons delivery capability. Production totaled 281.
New build: 155070; 155072 to 155119; 156891 to 156950; 158073 to 158147; 158453 to 158527; 158712 to 158723; 159099 to 159104; 159795 to 159798
Conversions: 152847; 152848; 152850; 152853; 152855; 152858; 152861; 152863; 152864; 152868; 152872; 152877; 152878; 153459; 153462; 153469; 153471; 153477 to 153479; 153481; 153482; 153484; 153492; 153495; 153497; 153498; 153500; 153502; 153504 to 153506; 153509; 153512; 153513; 153515 to 153518; 153521; 153522; 153524; 153528; 153530; 153661; 153663; 153667; 153669 to 153672; 153674 to 153676; 153678 to 153681; 153683; 153685; 153689; 153690; 154287; 154289 to 154293; 154296 to 154298; 154300; 154303; 154305; 154310 to 154313; 154315; 154318; 154319; 154322; 154323; 154327; 154330; 154332; 154334; 154342; 154343; 154614; 154618; 154619; 154626; 154631; 154632; 154634; 154650; 154656; 154657

NTA-4J: This two-seater was modified for special permanent test duties.
154332

SPECIFICATION

McDonnell Douglas A-4M
Wing: span 27 ft 6 in (8.38 m); area 260.0 sq ft (24.155 m²)
Fuselage and tail: length excluding probe 40 ft 3.5 in

Above: Examples of both the single- and two-seat Skyhawk are flown for 'aggressor' tasks and usually feature very distinctive camouflage, as portrayed here on a TA-4J.

A-4 Skyhawk (continued)

Some of these squadrons are to be found at the major Fleet fighter bases at Miramar, California, and Oceana, Virginia, where they are instantly available to the 'customer' looking for a fight. Others are at or close to fighter/attack bases such as Cecil Field, Florida, while still others are located overseas, in key areas of interest like Guantanamo Bay, Cuba.

Marine Corps use of the Skyhawk centers on the A-4M version. This is no longer a part of the front-line force, having been replaced entirely by the AV-8B Harrier II during the 1980s, but it is still employed by four Reserve light attack (VMA) squadrons. Primary task is close

Below: A 'Double Nuts' modex on the nose and a Russian republic flag on the tail are unusually carried by this A-4F of the Miramar-based Navy Fighter Weapons School.

air support of ground forces but it seems that the end is in sight for the A-4M in Reserve service, since current plans anticipate that two squadrons will transition to the AV-8B. A third looks set for redesignation as a fighter-attack unit with F/A-18 Hornets, while the remaining unit is almost certain to be disestablished. These changes are expected to take place during the next three or four years.

A few assorted Skyhawks continue to operate with research, development, test and evaluation organizations like the Naval Air Warfare Center Weapons Division and VX-5 at China Lake, California, plus the NAWC Aircraft Division at Patuxent River, Maryland. These probably fulfil support functions, perhaps acting as high-speed chase aircraft or as camera ships for photography. Single- and two-seat versions have been observed but numbers are extremely limited and probably do not exceed a dozen.

The Marines also make limited use of the Skyhawk as an adversary aircraft for dissimilar air combat training, in much the same way as the Navy. However, the numbers involved are far fewer and are confined to a handful of TA-4s which serve with regular Marine Aviation Logistics Squadrons (MALS) at Kaneohe Bay, Hawaii, and Beaufort, South Carolina. Reserve Force MALS exist at Alameda, California, and Willow Grove, Pennsylvania, but it is doubtful if these devote much effort to aggressor duties – instead, any operational-type flying they do is probably more oriented towards forward air control since both bases also host A-4M squadrons of the Reserve.

MISSION PROFILE

Threat simulator: As a threat simulator for air-to-air training, the A-4 carries a single AIS pod suspended from one or the other underwing pylon by a Sidewinder launcher rail. These missions seldom last more than an hour. For ferry purposes it carries up to three 450-US gal (1700-liter) fuel tanks.

Primary trainer: The TA-4J is the primary jet trainer for new Navy and Marine fighter pilots. They are most often seen with two underwing fuel tanks and fly missions lasting about 1.0 to 1.5 hours.

Above: The slender pod carried by this A-4F of VA-127 is used to relay data to ground stations during air combat training. Later redesignated VFA-127, this squadron has now relinquished its Skyhawks and operates both the F-5 and F/A-18.

(12.27 m); height 15 ft 0 in (4.57 m); tailplane span 11 ft 3.5 in (3.44 m)
Powerplant: one Pratt & Whitney J52-P-408 rated at 11,200 lb (50.0 kN) dry thrust
Weights: empty 10,465 lb (4747 kg); maximum take-off 24,500 lb (11113 kg)
Fuel and load: internal fuel 4,434 lb (2011 kg); external fuel up to three 300-US gal (1136-liter) drop tanks; maximum ordnance 9,155 lb (4153 kg)
Speed: maximum level speed 'clean' at 25,000 ft (7620 m) 625 mph (1006 km/h); maximum speed 'clean' at sea level 685 mph (1102 km/h)
Range: ferry range 2,000 miles (3225 km); combat radius with a 4,000-lb (1814-kg) warload 340 miles (547 km)
Performance: maximum rate of climb at sea level 10,300 ft (3140 m) per minute; service ceiling 38,700 ft (11795 m); take-off run 2,730 ft (832 m) at 23,000-lb (10433-kg) weight

McDonnell Douglas A-4F
generally similar to the A-4M except in the following particulars:
Fuselage and tail: length excluding probe 40 ft 1.1 in (12.22 m)
Powerplant: one Pratt & Whitney J52-P-8A rated at 9,300 lb (41.3 kN) dry thrust
Weights: empty equipped 10,448 lb (4739 kg); maximum take-off 27,420 lb (12437 kg)
Fuel and load: internal fuel 770 US gal (2915 liters); maximum ordnance 8,200 lb (3720 kg)
Speed: maximum level speed with 4,000-lb (1814-kg) warload at 34,000 ft (10365 m) 593 mph (954 km/h)
Range: ferry range 2,055 miles (3307 km)
Performance: maximum rate of climb at sea level 5,620 ft (1713 m) per minute

McDonnell Douglas TA-4F
generally similar to the A-4M Skyhawk II except in the following particulars:
Fuselage and tail: length 42 ft 7.25 in (12.98 m); height 15 ft 3 in (4.65 m)
Powerplant: one Pratt & Whitney J52-P-8A rated at 9,300 lb (41.3 kN) dry thrust
Weights: empty 10,602 lb (4809 kg); normal take-off 15,783 lb (7159 kg)
Fuel and load: internal fuel 660 US gal (2498 liters)
Speed: maximum level speed 'clean' at sea level 675 mph (1086 km/h)
Range: ferry range 2,200 miles (3540 km); normal range 1,350 miles (2175 km)
Performance: maximum rate of climb at sea level 5,750 ft (1753 m) per minute; take-off run 3,380 ft (1030 m) at 23,000-lb (10433-kg) weight

McDonnell Douglas TA-4J
generally similar to the TA-4F Skyhawk except in the following particulars:
Powerplant: one Pratt & Whitney J52-P-6 rated at 8,500 lb (37.7 kN) dry thrust

McDonnell Douglas OA-4M
generally similar to the A-4M except in the following particulars:
Fuselage and tail: length 42 ft 7.25 in (12.99 m); height 15 ft 5.5 in (4.71 m)
Weights: empty equipped 10,740 lb (4872 kg)
Fuel and load: internal fuel 770 US gal (2915 liters); maximum ordnance 6,500 lb (2948 kg)
Speed: maximum level speed 'clean' at low altitude 670 mph (1078 km/h)
Range: combat radius with a 150-US gal (568-liter) ventral drop tank 230 miles (370 km)

OPERATORS

US Navy (USN)

VFC-12	Oceana, VA	A-4F, TA-4J
VFC-13	Miramar, CA	A-4F, TA-4J
VF-43	Oceana, VA	A-4E, A-4F
VF-45	Key West, FL	A-4E, TA-4J
VF-126	Miramar, CA	A-4E, A-4F, TA-4J
VT-7	Meridian, MS	TA-4J
VT-21	Kingsville, TX	TA-4J
VT-22	Kingsville, TX	TA-4J
VT-24	Chase Field, TX	TA-4J
VT-25	Chase Field, TX	TA-4J
VC-1	Barbers Point, HI	A-4E, TA-4J
VC-5	Cubi Point, RP	A-4E
VC-8	Roosevelt Roads, PF	TA-4J
VC-10	Guantanamo Bay, Cuba	TA-4J
VX-5	China Lake, CA	TA-4J
NARU	Dallas, TX	A-4M
NFWS	Miramar, CA	A-4F
NTPS	Patuxent River, MD	TA-4J
NAWC/WD	China Lake, CA	NTA-4J

US Marine Corps (USMC)

VMA-124	Memphis, TN	A-4M, TA-4F
VMA-131	Willow Grove, PA	A-4M
VMA-133	Alameda, CA	A-4M
VMA-322	South Weymouth, MA	A-4M
MALS-42	Alameda, CA	TA-4F, TA-4J
MALS-49	Willow Grove, PA	TA-4J

Below: Even though its is painted in a 'low-viz' tactical color scheme, the VT-7 TA-4J depicted here is normally employed on pilot training.

Grumman

A-6 Intruder

Development of the **Intruder** was launched in the mid-1950s in response to a Navy and Marine Corps requirement for a new attack aircraft with the ability to operate equally effectively by both day or night and in all sorts of weather conditions. One of a number of companies that submitted proposals during the course of 1957, Grumman's G-128 was judged to be the most suitable candidate. An initial batch of eight **A2F-1** development aircraft was ordered in March 1959, with the first of these getting airborne on 19 April 1960.

Intended to replace the veteran piston-powered Douglas Skyraider with medium attack echelons of both services, the first examples of the Intruder were assigned to training squadron VA-42 at Oceana, Virginia, in February 1963. Just over two years later, in March 1965, VA-75 claimed the distinction of introducing the **A-6A** (as it had been re-signated in 1962) to combat duty when it deployed to the South China Sea aboard the USS *Independence*.

Early experience with the A-6A revealed it to be a superb aircraft when everything was working well, but in-commission rates of parts of the Digital Integrated Attack Navigation Equipment (DIANE) were not always satisfactory. There were also some problems with weapons racks, a few aircraft being lost to premature detonations when bombs collided moments after they were released. Nevertheless, there were few aircraft that could match the Intruder's ability to find and attack targets in the often-murky weather that prevails in Southeast Asia, nor did many possess its potential as a bomb-carrier, since the A-6 could operate with ordnance loads that exceeded 17,000 lb (7700 kg).

The A-6A has, however, long since disappeared from the operational inventory, as also have the specialist **A-6B** and **A-6C** versions. The first of these was primarily a missile-armed model which employed weapons like the AGM-78 Standard ARM (anti-radiation missile) to destroy hostile SAM sites, while the second incorporated a bulky ventral turret housing TRIM (Trails, Roads, Interdiction Multi-sensor) equipment - basically a FLIR and LLLTV – which bestowed superior night attack capability, especially in interdiction of the celebrated Ho Chi Minh Trail. Quantities procured were small, at 19 and 12 respectively.

Efforts to develop improved **A-6F** and **A-6G** models during the latter half of the 1980s failed to come to fruition, although the A-6F did make it as far as flying in prototype form before it was cancelled in favor of the 'stealthy' A-12 Avenger II, which was itself destined for cancellation. As a consequence, apart from a few **EA-6A** ECM aircraft with a Marine Corps Reserve unit and, possibly, a Navy ECM aggressor outfit, the only Intruder models to be found in today's inventory are the **KA-6D** and the **A-6E**.

Of the two, the principal version in US Navy service is the A-6E. This also remains active with the Marines, but numbers are declining fast following the decision to replace them with two-seat F/A-18D Hornets configured specially for the all-weather/night attack mission. As a result, Marine Corps A-6Es are progressively being turned over to the Navy as they become redundant, a transfer that will allow the Navy to retain a worthwhile force until it is able to invest in a replacement.

Close to 450 examples of the A-6E have been obtained but procurement has now terminated after a 20-year run. Many of them were built as such by Grumman but some 240 existing A-6As, A-6Bs and A-6Cs were also retrospectively modified to this standard. Flown in prototype form in 1970, the A-6E introduced a new and much more reliable package of avionics which made extensive use of the latest solid-state technology. Key components included a Norden AN/APQ-148 multi-mode nav/attack radar, an IBM/Fairchild AN/ASQ-133 computerized nav/attack system and a Conrac Corporation armament control unit.

Otherwise, it was largely unchanged, with the two crew members – a pilot and a bombardier/navigator – continuing to sit more or less side by side in the bulbous forward fuselage. Power continued to be furnished by a pair of Pratt & Whitney J52 turbojet engines which provided respectable, but far from startling, performance. Since then, further refinements have been added, with one of the most valuable and most obvious being the Target Recognition and Attack Multi-sensor (TRAM), an undernose turret containing FLIR and laser detection equipment which is fully integrated with the Norden radar.

Use of this kit and other elements of the complex avionics suite allows the Intruder to navigate to a distant target at low level, execute a blind first-pass attack and then withdraw to safety, again at low level. Once back in the vicinity of the parent carrier, it can then perform a wholly-automatic 'hands-off' landing.

Improvements aimed at enhancing the A-6's effectiveness at finding and attacking its targets have been accompanied by steady growth in the diversity of the weaponry that it can

Below: Intruder four-ship. Three A-6Es with a KA-6D in the slot position overfly their parent carrier, the USS Dwight D. Eisenhower, during a routine peacetime deployment.

employ from its total of five external stores stations, each of which has a capacity of 3,600 lb (1633 kg) and each of which is 'plumbed' for the carriage of external fuel tanks. In the early days, ordnance options were mostly conventional 'iron' bombs plus, of course, tactical nuclear devices.

Now, however, the list is much longer. Bombs still figure prominently but the Intruder is compatible with a variety of types of bomb, ranging from old-fashioned 'dumb' ordnance in either slick or retarded form through to the newest 'smart' weapons which embody laser guidance for extreme accuracy. As a bomb-carrier, the A-6E can operate with up to 18,000 lb (8160 kg), typical loads comprising 28 500-lb (227-kg) Mk 82s or anything up to five 2,000-lb (907-kg) Mk 84s. Other, more sophisticated weapons include the AGM-84 Harpoon anti-ship attack missile. The A-6E is also the subject of an ongoing Systems Weapon Integration Program (SWIP) which will provide compatibility with both the AGM-65 Maverick and AGM-88 HARM. AIM-9 Sidewinders are also on the 'menu' for self-defense. During the recent Gulf War some aircraft were pressed into service in a deception role, using the TALD (Tactical Air-Launched Decoy) glider to saturate the Iraqi defense networks by providing multiple 'targets'.

As with other front-line types, Intruder units of the two major Fleets are grouped into 'communities', with Atlantic assets based at Oceana, Virginia, and their Pacific counterparts at Whidbey Island, Washington. Each has eight squadrons, including a training unit, and normal deployment practise involves one squadron being assigned to each active CVW, although a couple of wings do have two. When embarked, squadron strength usually numbers 10 A-6Es plus a quartet of KA-6D tankers, but some squadrons have recently deployed with only attack-dedicated machines, 'buddy'-refueling pods being employed to fill the tanker requirement.

The KA-6D model is actually a conversion, just over 80 examples of the A-6A having been fitted with a single point hose-and-reel assembly in the lower aft fuselage. Removal of some of the avionics kit was necessary to accommodate the refueling equipment, with the result that the KA-6D features only a limited attack potential. In the normal course of events it is confined to the tanker task, supporting all elements of a CVW. In service, the KA-6D was primarily a Navy machine, only ever being operated by Marine Corps squadrons on the few occasions that these deployed for sea duty as part of a fully-fledged CVW.

Other units that fly the Intruder comprise two Reserve Navy squadrons, with A-6Es and KA-6Ds at Atlanta, Georgia, and Alameda, California, and three Marine Corps outfits, all of which are resident at Cherry Point, North Carolina. As already noted, the Intruder is disappearing from the Marine inventory and two of the three remaining squadrons are slated for transition to the Hornet during 1993-95.

Intruders also operate with several test organizations, including VX-5 and the NAWC/WD at China Lake, and the NAWC/AD at Patuxent River.

The aging process has inevitably resulted in

fatigue-related problems manifesting themselves in recent times, but that is hardly surprising, since some Fleet aircraft are now almost 30 years old. In consequence, *g*-force limitations have been imposed, these restrictions greatly impairing capability. Efforts to address these problems have involved fitting some Intruders with new wings made of graphite/epoxy composite materials. Manufactured by Boeing, testing of the new wing was accomplished during 1989-90 and contracts have so far been awarded for at least 80 sets. Of these, 21 were installed on new-build A-6Es with the balance destined for retrofitting to existing metal-winged examples. Further orders seem certain to follow if the Navy is to retain a viable medium attack force.

Below: Pre-deployment training often involves a visit to Fallon, NV, for live weapons work. This A-6E of VA-85 is carrying a GBU-12 Paveway II laser-guided bomb.

Grumman A-6E Intruder

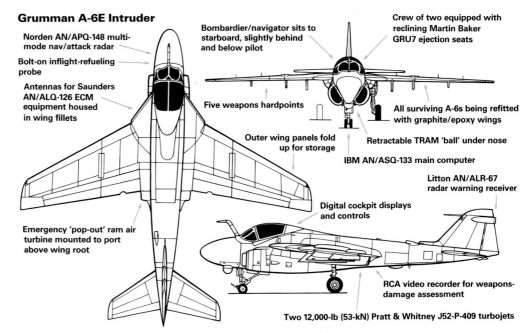

Norden AN/APQ-148 multi-mode nav/attack radar

Bolt-on inflight-refueling probe

Antennas for Saunders AN/ALQ-126 ECM equipment housed in wing fillets

Emergency 'pop-out' ram air turbine mounted to port above wing root

Bombardier/navigator sits to starboard, slightly behind and below pilot

Crew of two equipped with reclining Martin Baker GRU7 ejection seats

Five weapons hardpoints

All surviving A-6s being refitted with graphite/epoxy wings

Outer wing panels fold up for storage

Retractable TRAM 'ball' under nose

IBM AN/ASQ-133 main computer

Litton AN/ALR-67 radar warning receiver

Digital cockpit displays and controls

RCA video recorder for weapons-damage assessment

Two 12,000-lb (53-kN) Pratt & Whitney J52-P-409 turbojets

MISSION PROFILE

Armament options: The A-6E has five weapons pylons each capable of carrying 3,600 lb (1630 kg) of stores, including 300-US gal (1135-liter) fuel tanks which are most commonly seen on the centerline pylon. All are equipped with the AAS-33 TRAM housed in a turret mounted just behind and below the aircraft radome. As they are equipped with the SWIP, they become capable of employing the AGM-65, AGM-84E, AGM-88 and AIM-120.

Ground attack: In its primary role as a bomber, the Intruder delivers heavier loads of bombs further than any other carrier-based aircraft. Typical of these would be up to 22 Mk 82 general-purpose bombs and/or Mk 7 dispensers, 10 Mk 83 GP bombs or four Mk 84 GP bombs. For high-threat scenarios, the bombs on the right inboard pylon are replaced with an ALQ-167 ECM pod.

Precision attack: The A-6E is also capable of delivering the GBU-10, -12, and -16 laser-guided bombs in certain scenarios. Its normal load of these would be one bomb per pylon. It can also serve as a delivery platform for the AGM-62 Walleye and AGM-94E SLAM. However, it apparently cannot guide them once launched unless this capability is part of SWIP.

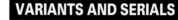

Above: A KA-6D of VA-34 tops up the tanks of an A-6E from the same outfit, while a second A-6E awaits its turn to replenish its fuel. Close to 90 Intruders have been modified to serve in the inflight-refueling role as KA-6Ds.

A-6 Intruder (continued)

SEAD: All A-6Es can deliver as many as 26 ADM-141 TALDs to confuse enemy radars. SWIP aircraft are capable of employing up to four AGM-88 HARMs.

Anti-ship: A typical high-threat anti-ship mission would employ two AGM-84 Harpoons on the inboard and two AIM-9L Sidewinders on the outboard pylons. In a lower threat arena the Harpoons could be moved to the outboard pylons to make room for 10 Mk 82 GP bombs or Mk 20 Rockeye II dispensers.

Below: In addition to the specialist KA-6D, the A-6E may also function as a tanker, using D-704 buddy refueling pods. These invariably occupy the centerline stores station, as depicted here on an A-6E from VA-176.

Armed surface reconnaissance: This anti-ship mission is employed in a low threat scenario where friendly ships outnumber enemy targets, making Harpoon attacks impractical. Extensively used in the 1991 Gulf War, a wide variety of bomb loads were carried to attack Iraqi patrol boats attempting to flee to Iran. A typical load was two Mk 82 GP bombs on one outboard pylon, two Mk 20 Rockeye II dispensers on the other, an AGM-123 Skipper II rocket-powered GBU-16, and one or two fuel tanks.

Mine laying: Used in both Vietnam and the 1991 Gulf War for this little noticed, but strategically significant, task, the Intruder can deliver as many as five purpose-built mines, or as many Quickstrike/Destructor mines as they can carry, or their Mk 80 series bomb equivalents.

Air refueling: Commonly accomplished by KA-6Ds with their built-in refueling equipment and five external fuel tanks. If needed, these can be supplemented by A-6Es using a D-704 air-refueling store on the centerline and four external fuel tanks.

VARIANTS AND SERIALS

YA-6A: Eight pre-production examples of the Intruder initially used the YA-6A designation, although they were later reclassified as A-6As.
147864 to 147867; 148615 to 148618

A-6A: This was the initial production model of the Intruder all-weather attack aircraft for service with the Navy and Marine Corps units. A total of 488 was ordered but not all were completed as such, some being produced in EA-6A, A-6B and A-6C configurations. No A-6As remain active, with almost all having been subsequently modified to either KA-6D or A-6E standard.
149475 to 149486; 149935 to 149958; 151558 to 151600; 151780 to 151827; 152583 to 152646; 152891 to 152954; 154124 to 154171; 155581 to 155721; 156994 to 157029

EA-6A: The initial electronic warfare version of the Intruder, which was based on the original A-6A derivative and developed for service with the Marine Corps. Manufacture of new-build aircraft totaled 15, while a further 12 resulted from the conversion of A-6A airframes.
New build: 156979 to 156993
Conversions: 147865; 148616; 148618; 149475; 149477; 149478; 151595 to 151600

A-6B: A total of 19 A-6As was converted to three different A-6B configurations for defense suppression tasks, using AGM-45 Shrike and AGM-78 Standard anti-radiation missiles. The 14 survivors were all subsequently updated to A-6E standard.
149944; 149949; 149955; 149957; 151558 to 151565; 151591; 151820; 152616; 152617; 155628 to 155630

A-6C: Following a prototype conversion (151568) a dozen A-6As were completed to A-6C standard, incorporating a belly-mounted TRIM turret. They were used for night interdiction of the Ho Chi Minh Trail. Eventually, the 11 survivors were subjected to modernization as A-6Es.
151568; 155647; 155648; 155653; 155660; 155662; 155667; 155670; 155674; 155676; 155681; 155684; 155688

KA-6D: This was a specialized inflight refueling model, featuring a hose-and-drogue assembly in the aft avionics bay and with only limited attack capability. Despite plans to purchase some new airframes, the 87 tanker Intruders that have been identified all originated from the conversion of A-6A and A-6E aircraft.
From A-6A: 149482; 149484 to 149486; 149936; 149937; 149940; 149942; 149945; 149951; 149952; 149954; 151566; 151568; 151570; 151572; 151575; 151576; 151579 to 151583; 151589; 151783; 151787; 151789; 151791 to 151793; 151795; 151796; 151801; 151806; 151808 to 151810; 151813; 151818; 151819; 151821; 151823 to 151827; 152590; 152592; 152597; 152598; 152606; 152611; 152618; 152619; 152624; 152626; 152628; 152632; 152637; 152892 to 152894; 152896; 152906; 152910; 152911; 152913; 152914; 152919 to 152921; 152927; 152934; 152939; 154133; 154147; 155686; 155691
From A-6E: 151814; 154154; 155583; 155584; 155597; 155598; 155604; 155619; 155638

A-6E: The definitive version of the Intruder, featuring revised avionics equipment. Procurement of approximately 450 examples of this model was accomplished in new-build form and through the conversion of existing A-6A/B/C aircraft.
New build: 158041 to 158042; 158528 to 158539; 158787 to 158798; 159174 to 159185; 159309 to 159317; 159567 to 159579; 159895 to 159906; 160421 to 160431; 160993 to 160998; 161082 to 161093; 161100 to 161111; 161230 to 161235*; 161659 to 161690*; 162179 to 162182; 162188 to 162212*; 164376 to 164385
(* = batch possibly incomplete)
Conversions: 149941; 149943; 149944; 149946; 149948 to 149950; 149953; 149955 to 149957; 151558; 151562; 151564; 151565; 151573; 151591 to 151593; 151782; 151784; 151790; 151802; 151804; 151807; 151811; 151812; 151814; 151820; 152583 to 152585; 152587; 152591; 152593; 152596; 152599; 152600; 152603; 152607; 152610; 152614; 152617; 152620; 152621; 152623; 152630; 152634; 152635; 152640 to 152642; 152645; 152895; 152902; 152904; 152905; 152907; 152908; 152912; 152915; 152916; 152918; 152923 to 152925; 152928 to 152931; 152933; 152935; 152936; 152941; 152942; 152945; 152947; 152948; 152950; 152953; 152954; 154124; 154126; 154128; 154129; 154131; 154132; 154134 to 154137; 154140; 154142; 154144; 154146; 154148; 154151; 154154; 154156; 154158; 154159; 154161 to 154163; 154167 to 154171; 155581 to 155586; 155588 to 155592; 155595 to 155600; 155602; 155604; 155606; 155608; 155610; 155612; 155615 to 155617; 155619 to 155621; 155623 to 155625; 155627 to 155633; 155635 to 155638; 155642 to 155646; 155648; 155649; 155651; 155653 to 155662; 155664; 155665; 155667 to 155670; 155672 to 155676;

Reserve force units also operate the A-6E. These are represented here by an Intruder of VA-304, which is getting down to some serious low-level training over the inhospitable desert terrain near El Centro, CA.

155678 to 155685; 155687 to 155689; 155692; 155694; 155695; 155697 to 155699; 155702 to 155704; 155706 to 155708; 155710 to 155719; 156995 to 156997; 157000 to 157006; 157009 to 157014; 157016; 157019; 157091; 157021; 157023 to 157027; 157029

SPECIFICATION

Grumman A-6E
Wing: span 53 ft 0 in (16.15 m); width folded 25 ft 4 in (7.72 m); area 528.9 sq ft (49.13 m²)
Fuselage and tail: length 54 ft 9 in (16.69 m); height 16 ft 2 in (4.93 m); tailplane span 20 ft 4.5 in (6.21 m); wheel base 17 ft 2.25 in (5.24 m)
Powerplant: two Pratt & Whitney J52-P-8B rated at 9,300 lb (41.4 kN) dry thrust
Weights: empty 26,746 lb (12132 kg); maximum take-off 58,600 lb (26580 kg) for catapult launch or 60,400 lb (27397 kg) for field take-off
Fuel and load: internal fuel 15,939 lb (7230 kg); external fuel up to 10,050 lb (4558 kg) in five 400-US gal (1514-liter) drop tanks; maximum ordnance 18,000 lb (8165 kg)
Speed: never exceed 806 mph (1297 km/h); maximum level speed 'clean' at sea level 644 mph (1037 km/h); cruising speed at optimum altitude 474 mph (763 km/h)
Range: ferry range 3,245 miles (5222 km) with empty tanks dropped or 2,740 miles (4410 km) with empty tanks retained; range with maximum military load 1,011 miles (1627 km)
Performance: maximum rate of climb at sea level 7,620 ft (2323 m) per minute; service ceiling 42,400 ft (12925 m); minimum take-off run 3,890 ft (1185 m); take-off distance to 50 ft (15 m) 4,560 ft (1390 m); minimum landing run 1,710 ft (521 m); landing distance from 50 ft (15 m) 2,540 ft (774 m)

Grumman KA-6D
Wing: span 53 ft 0 in (16.15 m); width folded 25 ft 4 in (7.72 m); area 528.9 sq ft (49.13 m²)
Fuselage and tail: length 54 ft 9 in (16.69 m); height 15 ft 7 in (4.75 m); tailplane span 20 ft 4.5 in (6.21 m); wheel base 17 ft 2.25 in (5.24 m)
Powerplant: two Pratt & Whitney J52-P-8B rated at 9,300 lb (41.4 kN) dry thrust

The underfuselage fairing for the hose and drogue is clearly visible on this KA-6D from VA-176.

Weights: empty about 25,684 lb (11650 kg); maximum take-off 58,600 lb (26580 kg) for catapult launch or 60,400 lb (27397 kg) for field take-off
Fuel and load: internal fuel 15,939 lb (7230 kg); external fuel up to 10,050 lb (4558 kg) in five 300-US gal (1136-liter) or 400-US gal (1514-liter) drop tanks
Speed: never exceed 806 mph (1297 km/h); maximum level speed 'clean' at sea level 644 mph (1037 km/h); cruising speed at optimum altitude 474 mph (763 km/h)
Range: ferry range 3,245 miles (5222 km) with empty tanks dropped or 2,740 miles (4410 km) with empty tanks retained; radius to transfer 16,000 lb (7258 kg) of fuel 300 miles (483 km)
Performance: maximum rate of climb at sea level 6,950 ft (2118 m) per minute; service ceiling 41,660 ft (12700 m); minimum take-off run 1,630 ft (497 m); take-off distance to 50 ft (15 m) 2,200 ft (670 m)

OPERATORS

US Navy (USN)

VA-34	Oceana, VA	A-6E, KA-6D
VA-35	Oceana, VA	A-6E, KA-6D
VA-36	Oceana, VA	A-6E
VA-42	Oceana, VA	A-6E
VA-52	Whidbey Island, WA	A-6E, KA-6D
VA-65	Oceana, VA	A-6E
VA-75	Oceana, VA	A-6E, KA-6D
VA-85	Oceana, VA	A-6E, KA-6D
VA-95	Whidbey Island, WA	A-6E, KA-6D
VA-115	Atsugi, Japan	A-6E
VA-128	Whidbey Island, WA	A-6E
VA-145	Whidbey Island, WA	A-6E
VA-155	Whidbey Island, WA	A-6E
VA-165	Whidbey Island, WA	A-6E, KA-6D
VA-196	Whidbey Island, WA	A-6E, KA-6D
VA-205	Atlanta, GA	A-6E, KA-6D
VA-304	Alameda, CA	A-6E, KA-6D
VAQ-33	Key West, FL	EA-6A
VX-5	China Lake, CA	A-6E
NAWC/AD	Patuxent River, MD	A-6E
NAWC/WD	China Lake, CA	A-6E
NAWC/WD	Point Mugu, CA	A-6E
NSWC	Fallon, NV	A-6E

US Marine Corps (USMC)

VMA(AW)-224	Cherry Point, NC	A-6E
VMA(AW)-332	Cherry Point, NC	A-6E
VMA(AW)-533	Cherry Point, NC	A-6E

Grumman
EA-6B Prowler

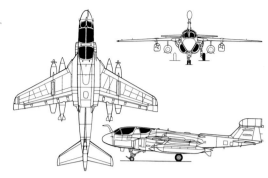

Stemming from the Grumman A-6 Intruder, to which it bears a strong family resemblance, the **EA-6B** differed sufficiently from its medium attack forebear to merit the allocation of a different name. Intended from the outset to undertake electronic countermeasures tasks, the Prowler was initially unarmed, although it has recently acquired some 'punch' and is now compatible with the AGM-88A HARM, an anti-radar missile that is just one of a number of weapons used in the suppression of enemy air defenses (SEAD). SEAD is basically the *raison d'être* behind the Prowler, which is arguably the most capable aircraft of its type in the world.

Development of electronic warfare versions of the Intruder actually predated the advent of the Prowler by several years, with the two-seat **EA-6A** being conceived and produced in modest quantities specifically to replace old and obsolescent EF-10B Skyknights with the Marine Corps. Less capable than the Prowler, these aircraft did nevertheless see extensive combat action in Vietnam, as did the EA-6B, even though it arrived much later in the day.

When the time came for the Navy to obtain a new EW/ECM platform to take over from the EKA-3B Skywarrior, it opted for a radically revamped version of the trusty Intruder. The result was a four-place aircraft which was somewhat longer so as to provide crew accommodation for a pilot and three ECMOs (electronic countermeasures operators). Apart from the additional cockpit, the most visible evidence that this was a very different machine was to be seen at the top of the fin, which was capped by a bulbous fairing containing receivers for the AN/ALQ-99 Tactical Jamming System (TJS) that lies at the heart of Prowler capability.

Flown in prototype form during May 1968, the EA-6B underwent a fairly lengthy trials period and it was not until 1972 that it finally attained operational status, in time to participate in the closing stages of the Vietnam War, where it soon proved its worth. Subsequent production, which was due to terminate in 1991, raised total procurement to around the 180 mark, this quantity including about 15 examples for service with the Marine Corps.

Throughout the period of production, numerous initiatives aimed at enhancing the Prowler's impressive capability have been implemented, and the contemporary EA-6B is infinitely superior to the original 'basic' model that was introduced in the early 1970s. Along the way, the EA-6B has progressed via an EX-CAP (Expanded Capability) version through ICAP-1 (Improved Capability-1) to today's ICAP-2. The latter sub-type appeared at the beginning of the 1980s and is now the major Prowler version in service, having been procured in both new-build form and by means of a retrofit program affecting older aircraft.

Changes incorporated in the successive variations on the Prowler theme were mostly concerned with refining its abilities as an EW/ECM platform, ICAP-2 introducing power management and improved emitter identification as well as greater reliability and maintainability. A more recent addition allowed the EA-6B to play a fuller SEAD role, for it may now operate as a 'shooter', using the AGM-88A HARM to target hostile radars.

Even though production has now ceased, still more improvements are in the pipeline. The next step in the evolutionary process will be the introduction of the ADVCAP (Advanced Capability) version. Litton Industries is at the heart of this project, which was launched in 1983 and will lead to new receiver/processing equipment being installed. Flight trials began in 1988 and ADVCAP should begin to join Fleet units during 1993. In obtaining ADVCAP Prowlers, the Navy has elected to return to the CILOP (Conversion In Lieu Of Procurement) concept. Most EA-6Bs should eventually be remanufactured to this standard.

With the Navy, the Prowler community has always been concentrated at Whidbey Island, Washington, even though it provides assets to carriers of both major Fleet organizations. Today, this base is home to a dozen fully-operational Tactical Electronic Warfare Squadrons (VAQ-130 to VAQ-141 inclusive), plus a training unit (VAQ-129) and a recently established outfit (VAQ-35) which operates as part of the Fleet Electronic Warfare Support Group in the important ECM aggressor training role. Efforts to update Reserve forces have also extended to the EA-6B. This type now equips single squadrons within each Reserve CVW, specifically VAQ-209 at NAF Andrews and VAQ-309 at Whidbey Island.

So far, normal deployment practise has required Navy Tactical Electronic Warfare Squadrons to embark with a complement of four Prowlers. That places a heavy burden on the units concerned but things should improve before too much longer, since this number is expected to rise to five as the service moves towards a standardized CVW structure.

The Marines have just one active-duty Prowler squadron, namely VMAQ-2 at Cherry Point, North Carolina. In Marine Corps service, normal operating policy entails the use of detachments (usually of five aircraft). One detachment is invariably forward deployed to Iwakuni, Japan, where it supports rotational fighter and attack elements of the 1st Marine Air Wing. Reserve squadron VMAQ-4, which currently flies from Whidbey Island, has acquired Prowlers to replace EA-6As.

EW/ECM missions can vary to a quite significant degree, depending on circumstances. The Prowler may, for instance, be used purely as an intelligence gatherer, by flying in the proximity of areas of interest and using its TJS equipment in purely passive mode to build up a picture of the electronic order of battle by detecting, locating and analyzing signals. Alternatively, it can furnish support to friendly strike forces, which may be accomplished in several ways.

ECM escort is most probably the preferred option when operating against high-value targets which are extremely well defended. In

Left: Electronic countermeasures units of the Navy Reserve have recently been given a major boost with the assignment of the EA-6B Prowler as a replacement for the EA-6A. VAQ-309 is one of two second-line units to benefit and one of its Prowlers is depicted here carrying a brace of AGM-88A HARMs for defense suppression.

Intakes
With subsonic performance, the Prowler has no requirement for variable-geometry intakes. Simple D-shaped inlets have a small splitter plate to separate boundary layer airflow.

Undercarriage
The stalky mainwheels retract forwards to lie in wells in the intake/wing fairing.

Pods
The main active jammers of the Prowler are carried on the four underwing or centerline pylons, three being a usual number. Designated ALQ-99F, they are better known as TJS, and are equipped with external ram air turbines to provide power.

Wings
The wings are equipped with comprehensive lift devices, including nearly full-span leading-edge slats, flaps and drooping ailerons. The speed brakes are at the wingtips, splitting into the airflow above and below the wing.

Grumman
EA-6B Prowler

Serving with carrier air wings and with Marine Corps formations, the EA-6B is a highly advanced electronic warfare platform used for the SEAD (Suppression of Enemy Air Defenses) role. In addition to electronic jamming, the EA-6B can also fire the AGM-88 anti-radiation missile, giving it a hard-kill option against enemy radars.

Cockpit
The EA-6B has a crew of four, comprising a pilot and three Electronic Countermeasures Officers. ECMO 1 in the forward starboard station provides navigation duties and works the ALQ-92 comms jamming system, while ECMOs 3 and 4 in the rear compartment work the TJS.

Fuselage plug
In order to house the two extra cockpit stations, the fuselage of the basic A-6 airframe had to be extended. This adds 4 ft 4 in (1.32 m) to the overall length.

Fin-tip fairing
The large 'football' fairing at the fintip houses the main SIR (System Integration Receivers) antennas, which detect hostile radars. Information is passed to the central onboard computer for analysis before the jammers are instructed to operate.

DECM
The small prong at the base of the refueling probe and the fairing at the base of the fintip fairing house the ALQ-126 deception ECM system, which interrupts and confuses hostile radars.

Equipment platform
Mounted in the lower rear fuselage is a rack which hinges downwards for access. Known as the 'birdcage', this mounts much of the special equipment, including the APN-153 Doppler navigation system.

Markings
For several years VMAQ-2 has been the sole Marine Corps Prowler squadron, identified by the well-known Playboy insignia. It detached aircraft to other units and to Navy carriers as and when required. In 1992 the Marines are introducing three more active-duty squadrons to spread the tasking of VMAQ-2.

Powerplant
Compared to the standard A-6 Intruder, the Prowler has uprated engines to cope with the considerable extra weight. The engines in question are the Pratt & Whitney J52-P-408, rated at 11,200 lb (50 kN) thrust.

Jamming pods and fuel tanks are visible beneath the wings of a pair of VAQ-130 EA-6Bs during Desert Storm, when they played a key role in rendering Iraq electronically 'blind'.

EA-6B Prowler (continued)

this, the Prowler will accompany a strike package to the target area, initially monitoring for hostile signals and in the later stages actively countering them with jamming signals radiating from the pod-mounted emitters that are associated with the ALQ-99 TJS package. It is in this role that HARM is particularly useful, and Prowler squadrons are known to have expended their fair share of missiles during the recent Gulf War when most of the handful of units that were involved configured their aircraft as 'shooters'.

In instances where multiple strikes are being staged against several targets in the same general area, the EA-6B will most likely be utilized in a stand-off capacity, whereby a couple of jammers orbit at some distance from the target area as they set about the job of disrupting enemy radar networks. The result is a sort of electronic 'smoke-screen' which effectively masks the intentions of strike elements as they approach, execute their respective attacks and then withdraw to safety.

MISSION PROFILE

Armament options: Up to four AGM-88A HARM missiles can be carried on the EA-6B's four wing pylons, along with external AN/ALQ-99 emitter pods or Aero-1D 300-US gal (1136-liter) drop tanks. A further AN/ALQ-99 pod is carried on the centerline pylon. An AN/ALQ-126 DECM system is carried internally. AN/ALE-39 expendable countermeasures dispensers are also installed in the rear fuselage, with a mix of chaff, flares and expendable jammers, to decoy IR-guided SAMs or AAMs. ADVCAP EA-6Bs will be configured with the AN/ALQ-149 jamming system.

Armed SEAD: As an integral part of USN/USMC strike packages, HARM-armed EA-6Bs fly ahead of the main attack force to destroy SAM guidance radars protecting the target area. EA-6Bs then remain on station in racetrack patterns to neutralize any radars directing SAMs at the main attack force, either firing their own HARMs or downloading 'threat' information to HARM-armed F/A-18s. The HARM's 49-mile (80-km) range allows EA-6Bs to stay out of the firing envelopes of most Soviet-made SAMs.

Jamming/Elint: With a combination of three or five AN/ALQ-99 pods, EA-6Bs are employed to provide blanket jamming ahead of strike packages or over designated areas. This mission can be accomplished without having to penetrate enemy air space. By using the TJS equipment in passive mode, Elint can be gathered on enemy radars.

Battlefield support: USMC Prowlers are heavily tasked to provide battlefield electronic warfare support for Marine ground units. Enemy tactical communication nets are jammed and artillery locating radars attacked with HARM missiles. Direct radio links are set up between Prowlers and Marine artillery units so fire can be called down instantaneously when enemy artillery-locating radars start emitting.

VARIANTS AND SERIALS

EA-6B: This was a dedicated four-seat electronic warfare platform based on the Intruder and manufactured for service with Navy and Marine Corps units. Updating of the EW suite was undertaken throughout production history, the types recently acquiring HARM capability. Three early A-6As were converted to serve as prototypes before the manufacture of 170 production aircraft.
Prototypes: 148615; 149479; 149481 (latter two later NEA-6B)
New build: 156478 to 156482; 158029 to 158040; 158540 to 158547; 158649 to 158651; 158799 to 158817; 159582 to 159587; 159907 to 159912; 160432 to 160437; 160609; 160704 to 160709; 160786 to 160791; 161115 to 161120; 161242 to 161247; 161347 to 161352; 161774 to 161779; 161880 to 161885; 162223 to 162230; 162934 to 162939; 163030 to 163035; 163044 to 163049; 163395 to 163406; 163520 to 163531; 163884 to 163892; 164401 to 164403

SPECIFICATION

Grumman EA-6A
generally similar to the A-6E except in the following particulars:
Fuselage and tail: length 55 ft 3 in (16.84 m); height 16 ft 3 in (4.95 m); tailplane span 20 ft 8.5 in (6.31 m)
Powerplant: two Pratt & Whitney J52-P-8A rated at 9,300 lb (41.4 kN) dry thrust
Weights: empty 27,769 lb (12596 kg); maximum take-off 56,500 lb (25628 kg)
Fuel and load: internal fuel 15,857 lb (7193 kg)
Speed: maximum level speed 'clean' at sea level more than 620 mph (998 km/h); normal cruising speed at optimum altitude 481 mph (775 km/h)

Range: ferry range 2,995 miles (4820 km)
Performance: service ceiling 38,960 ft (11875 m); minimum take-off run 2,100 ft (640 m); take-off distance to 50 ft (15 m) 2,700 ft (823 m)

Grumman EA-6B
Wing: span 53 ft 0 in (16.15 m); width folded 25 ft 10 in (7.87 m); area 528.9 sq ft (49.13 m²)
Fuselage and tail: length 59 ft 10 in (18.24 m); height 16 ft 3 in (4.95 m); tailplane span 20 ft 4.5 in (6.21 m); wheel base 17 ft 2 in (5.23 m)
Powerplant: two Pratt & Whitney J52-P-408 rated at 11,200 lb (49.8 kN) dry thrust
Weights: empty 32,162 lb (14588 kg); carrier take-off in stand-off jamming configuration with five jammer pods 54,461 lb (24703 kg); maximum take-off 60,610 lb (29483 kg)
Fuel and load: internal fuel 15,422 lb (6995 kg); external fuel up to 10,025 lb (4547 kg) in five 400-US gal (1514-liter) drop tanks
Speed: never exceed 817 mph (1315 km/h); maximum level speed 'clean' at sea level 651 mph (1048 km/h) or with five jammer pods 610 mph (982 km/h); cruising speed at optimum altitude 481 mph (774 km/h)
Range: ferry range 2,399 miles (3861 km) with empty tanks dropped or 2,022 miles (3254 km) with empty tanks retained; range with maximum external load 1,099 miles (1769 km)
Performance: maximum rate of climb 'clean' at sea level 12,900 ft (3932 m) per minute or with five jammer pods 10,030 ft (3057 m) per minute; service ceiling 'clean' 41,200 ft (12550 m) or with five jammer pods 38,000 ft (11580 m); take-off run with five jammer pods 2,670 ft (814 m); take-off distance to 50 ft (15 m) 'clean' 2,850 ft (869 m) or with five jammer pods 3,495 ft (1065 m); landing run 'clean' 1,900 ft (579 m) or with five jammer pods 2,150 ft (655 m); landing distance from 50 ft (15 m) 2,700 ft (823 m)

OPERATORS

US Navy (USN)

VAQ-35	Whidbey Island, WA	EA-6B
VAQ-129	Whidbey Island, WA	EA-6B
VAQ-130	Whidbey Island, WA	EA-6B
VAQ-131	Whidbey Island, WA	EA-6B
VAQ-132	Whidbey Island, WA	EA-6B
VAQ-134	Whidbey Island, WA	EA-6B
VAQ-135	Whidbey Island, WA	EA-6B
VAQ-136	Whidbey Island, WA	EA-6B
VAQ-137	Whidbey Island, WA	EA-6B
VAQ-138	Whidbey Island, WA	EA-6B
VAQ-139	Whidbey Island, WA	EA-6B
VAQ-140	Whidbey Island, WA	EA-6B
VAQ-141	Whidbey Island, WA	EA-6B
VAQ-209	Washington/Andrews, MD	EA-6B
VAQ-309	Whidbey Island, WA	EA-6B
VX-5	China Lake, CA	EA-6B
NAWC/AD	Patuxent River, MD	EA-6B

US Marine Corps (USMC)

VMAQ-2	Cherry Point, NC	EA-6B
VMAQ-4	Whidbey Island, WA	EA-6B

Below: Prowlers also serve with one front-line Marine Corps unit, specifically VMAQ-2 headquartered at Cherry Point, although it does usually keep a detachment at Iwakuni in Japan.

Vought
A-7 Corsair

Bearing a strong family resemblance to the classic F-8 Crusader, the **A-7 Corsair II** is one of that rare breed of warplanes that found acceptance with both the US Navy and the US Air Force and its stubby shape was a familiar sight aboard carrier flight decks for more than two decades. Familiarly known as the 'SLUF' – 'Short Little Ugly Fella' or 'Short Little Ugly Fucker', depending on the company one keeps – its rather undistinguished appearance tends to mask the fact that it is a most potent attack aircraft, able to carry a substantial ordnance payload over long distances, penetrate hostile airspace and deliver that payload on target with remarkable accuracy.

In US Navy service, the Corsair was viewed from the outset as a replacement for the diminutive A-4 Skyhawk. It represented a quantum leap over that much-loved type in terms of payload and capability. Its Navy career began during one conflict, with the initial **A-7A** variant joining the fleet at the height of the Vietnam War. It still figured in the operational force during the Desert Storm air campaign which paved the way for the liberation of Kuwait.

Then, the two dozen **A-7E**s shared by light attack squadrons VA-46 'Clansmen' and VA-72 'Bluehawks' aboard the USS *John F. Kennedy* flew hundreds of combat missions, setting the seal on this type's impressive record. Sadly, these two squadrons did not have long to bask in recent glory for within weeks of returning home to Cecil Field, Florida, both were disestablished. This action signalled the end of an era, since they were the last two squadrons to deploy operationally with the Corsair.

Even though it was no longer a part of the front-line inventory, the A-7 continued to serve with the Navy in fairly modest quantities, primarily in support functions. As far as squadron use is concerned, this was extremely limited and was confined to VAQ-33 at Key West, Florida, which flew a few **TA-7C** two-seaters on tasks that are concerned with the ECM 'aggressor' role, such as chaff laying and anti-ship missile attack simulation. A few specially modified two-seaters known as

EA-7Ls were also used until recently by VAQ-34 at Lemoore, but these have now been replaced by the F/A-18 Hornet.

In addition, a number of test agencies also retained examples of the EA-7 and TA-7C for various projects. These organizations included the Naval Air Warfare Center Weapons Divisions at China Lake and Point Mugu, California, and the NAWC Aircraft Division at Patuxent River, Maryland. Finally, a number of redundant A-7Es are employed by the Naval Air Technical Training Center at Memphis, Tennessee, for ground instructional duties.

MISSION PROFILE

The handful of Corsairs which remain in use are shared between a number of second-line and trials units. A handful may still be in use as as hacks or general trials platforms.

VARIANTS AND SERIALS

YA-7A: Three prototypes were ordered for development tasks.
152580 to 152582

A-7A: This was the initial production model, powered by a Pratt & Whitney TF30 turbofan and incorporating dual gun armament. A total of 196 examples was produced, but none remain active with the Navy.
152647 to 152685; 153134 to 153273; 154344 to 154360

A-7B: This was the second major production version, with a more powerful variant of TF30 turbofan. Production terminated after the 196th example was delivered.
154361 to 154556

A-7C: This designation was allotted to 67 aircraft from the initial A-7E contract which retained the TF30 engine but embodied other changes planned for the A-7E.
156374 to 156800

NA-7C: At least two A-7Cs were modified for permanent test duty as NA-7Cs with the former Naval Weapons Center at China Lake.
156734; 156739

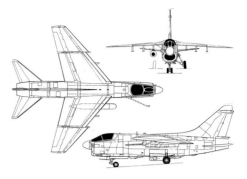

TA-7C: This was a two-seat conversion of 61 A-7B and A-7C aircraft. One or two may still be in use with Navy test agencies.
154361; 154377; 154379; 154402; 154404; 154407; 154410; 154412; 154424; 154425; 154437; 154450; 154455; 154458; 154464; 154467; 154471; 154477; 154489; 154500; 154507; 154536; 154537; 154544; 156737; 156738; 156740; 156741; 156743 to 156748; 156750; 156751; 156753; 156757; 156761; 156764 to 156768; 156770; 156773; 156774; 156777; 156779; 156782; 156784; 156786 to 156791; 156793 to 156795; 156800

A-7E: This was the definitive USN version of the Corsair II, introducing an Allison TF41 turbofan as well as the Vulcan cannon, improved avionics and anti-skid brakes first fitted to A-7C. Production totaled 541 aircraft but very few remain active today.
156801 to 156890; 157435 to 157594; 158002 to 158028; 158652 to 158681; 158819 to 158842; 159261 to 159308; 159638 to 159661; 159668 to 159679; 159967 to 160002; 160537 to 160566; 160613 to 160618; 160710 to 160739; 160857 to 160880

YA-7H: This was the prototype two-seat trainer conversion of the A-7E.
156801

EA-7L: A few TA-7C aircraft were modified for use as electronic countermeasures platforms by Navy ECM aggressor squadron VAQ-34 at Point Mugu. These aircraft have now been withdrawn from service following replacement by the F/A-18 Hornet.
156741; 156743; 156745; 156757; 156786; 156791; 156794

SPECIFICATION

Vought A-7E
Wing: span 38 ft 9 in (11.81 m); width folded 23 ft 9 in (7.24 m); aspect ratio 4.0; area 375.0 sq ft (34.83 m²)
Fuselage and tail: length 46 ft 1.5 in (14.06 m); height 16 ft 0 in (4.88 m); tailplane span 18 ft 1.5 in (5.52 m); wheel base 15 ft 10 in (4.83 m)
Powerplant: one Allison TF41-A-2 rated at 15,000 lb (66.6 kN) dry thrust
Weights: empty equipped 19,915 lb (8988 kg); normal take-off 29,000 lb (13154 kg); maximum take-off 42,000 lb (19050 kg)
Fuel and load: internal fuel 9,263 lb (4202 kg); external fuel up to four 300-US gal (1136-liter) drop tanks; maximum ordnance 20,000 lb (9072 kg) nominal, about 15,000 lb (6804 kg) practical with reduced internal fuel and 9,500 lb (4309 kg) practical with maximum internal fuel
Speed: maximum level speed 'clean' at sea level 698 mph (1123 km/h)
Range: ferry range 2,871 miles (4621 km) with external fuel or 2,281 miles (3671 km) on internal fuel; combat radius 715 miles (1151 km) on a hi-lo-hi mission
Performance: maximum rate of climb at sea level 15,000 ft (4572 m) per minute; service ceiling 42,000 ft (12800 m); take-off run 5,000 ft (1524 m) at maximum take-off weight; take-off distance to 50 ft (15 m) 5,865 ft (1790 m); landing distance from 50 ft (15 m) 4,695 ft (1430 m)

Left: The final active examples of the Corsair were assigned to test units such as the NAWC/AD at Patuxent River.

McDonnell Douglas/British Aerospace
AV-8 Harrier II

The unique V/STOL capability of the Harrier made it an attractive proposition to the Marine Corps from the very earliest days, since it appeared in many respects to be almost tailor-made for the traditional 'Flying Leatherneck' mission of furnishing support to ground forces in and around a beachhead. Flying from the decks of amphibious assault ships or from semi-prepared strips, the Harrier had the potential to provide tactical 'air' where it was most wanted, while at the same time eliminating the need for lengthy transit flights to and from the battlefield. Thus, it would be able to employ greater firepower and be more responsive to the requirements of the forces on the ground.

At least, that was the theory, but the initial Marine Corps purchase of 102 **AV-8A**s (plus eight **TAV-8A** two-seaters for training purposes) fell short of satisfying the service's needs. Further development, undertaken jointly by British Aerospace and its American partner, McDonnell Douglas, led to the **AV-8B**, which began to enter service in 1984. Introduction of this far superior version of the Harrier allowed the original machines to be progressively retired, and these have now all disappeared from the inventory.

Procurement is continuing towards the present target of purchasing 300 AV-8Bs and 28 examples of the two-seat **TAV-8B**. This quantity should be sufficient to support eight front-line squadrons as well as a training unit and two second-line squadrons of the Marine Corps Reserve.

At present, the front-line units are close to

being fully equipped, with each of the two US-based marine air wings possessing four squadrons. Normal complement is around 20 aircraft per squadron, FMFLant units (VMA-223, -231, -331 and -542) being concentrated at Cherry Point, North Carolina, while FMFPac units (VMA-211, -214, -311 and -513) can be found at Yuma, Arizona. One of these eight squadrons is, however, usually forward deployed to Iwakuni, Japan, as part of the 1st Marine Air Wing on a rotational basis, while elements of others are often embarked upon amphibious assault vessels, operating alongside assorted helicopter types.

Cherry Point is also home for VMAT-203, unique in being the only Harrier training squadron and the only one to use the TAV-8B version. These two-seaters are operated alongside a number of single-seaters in the task of supplying fully-trained air and ground crews to operational units of both FMFLant and FMFPac.

As far as the **Harrier II** is concerned, three distinct versions are expected to eventually see service with the Marine Corps. Initially, the Anglo-American manufacturing team produced a version which might best be referred to as the baseline aircraft. This employs the Hughes AN/ASB-19 ARBS (Angle Rate Bombing Set) as the main weapon delivery sensor system. However, with effect from the 167th Harrier II, enhanced night attack capability was incorporated through fitment of a GEC Sensors FLIR in the nose section, a Smiths Industries wide-angle HUD, a digital color moving-map display, and cockpit light-

A much improved variant of the Harrier, the AV-8B entered service with the Marine Corps in 1984 and was a key type in Desert Storm.

ing compatible with pilot's night-vision goggles. Both of these versions are now well established in service under the common AV-8B designation.

The third variant – currently referred to as the **AV-8B Harrier II Plus**, although it may acquire a new designation – will enjoy even better night attack potential by virtue of possessing a Hughes AN/APG-65 radar. Originally conceived as a private venture, the consortium's design work was rewarded in September 1990 by a contract for one prototype and two dozen production examples for service with the Marines. Italy and Spain may also obtain aircraft to this standard in due course. Expected to make its maiden flight in October 1992, the Harrier II Plus should begin to enter service in the late spring or early sum-

AV-8Bs from two of the four front-line units based at MCAS Cherry Point are seen here, these being VMA-223 and VMA-542. A further four deployable squadrons are stationed at Yuma, the Marine Corps Harrier force being completed by a training outfit at Cherry Point.

mer of 1993 and it is conceivable that others will follow as a result of a CILOP program.

Perhaps the most startling improvement in the AV-8B concerns its payload ability, which is significantly superior to that of the AV-8A. Maximum external stores load is in excess of 13,000 lb (5900 kg), carried on six wing stations (three on each side) plus one located under the fuselage between the two belly packs which house a 25-mm rotary cannon and 300 rounds of ammunition. The two inner wing stations on each side are 'plumbed' for the carriage of auxiliary fuel tanks, although in combat they would usually be used for ordnance.

That was certainly the case during Operation Desert Storm when five AV-8B squadrons contributed to the coalition cause, four flying from King Abdul Aziz air base in Saudi Arabia and one from the USS *Nassau* operating in the waters of the Persian Gulf. Weapons employed during six weeks of war were mostly of the 'dumb' type and included Rockeye CBUs, Mk 82 500-lb (227-kg) and Mk 83 1,000-lb (454-kg) bombs. All of these were put to good effect in battlefield air interdiction and close air support missions, with dive-bombing from medium altitude being the preferred method of delivery. Other ordnance options available to the Harrier II consist of unguided rockets and fire bombs, which may have been expended in the Gulf in fewer numbers.

During the early phase of the war, when the threat from Iraqi fighter aircraft was perceived to be at its height, at least one AIM-9M Sidewinder heat-seeking air-to-air missile was also carried for defensive purposes. Once air supremacy had been achieved, these were removed, allowing extra bombs to be carried, a typical load consisting of one bomb or CBU per pylon, for a maximum of six. Although a handful of Marine Corps Harriers was lost in combat, all apparently fell foul of ground defenses and there is no evidence that any Sidewinders were ever fired.

AV-8Bs are also fully able to deliver a variety of types of 'smart' weapons, such as the Paveway laser-guided bomb and the Hughes AGM-65 Maverick air-to-surface missile. During Desert Storm, however, responsibility for using those was entrusted to other aircraft types, freeing the Harrier to concentrate on what it does best: daylight battlefield air interdiction.

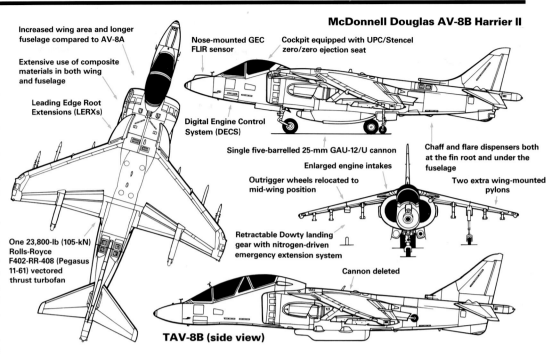

McDonnell Douglas AV-8B Harrier II

Increased wing area and longer fuselage compared to AV-8A

Extensive use of composite materials in both wing and fuselage

Leading Edge Root Extensions (LERXs)

Nose-mounted GEC FLIR sensor

Cockpit equipped with UPC/Stencil zero/zero ejection seat

Digital Engine Control System (DECS)

Single five-barrelled 25-mm GAU-12/U cannon

Enlarged engine intakes

Outrigger wheels relocated to mid-wing position

Retractable Dowty landing gear with nitrogen-driven emergency extension system

One 23,800-lb (105-kN) Rolls-Royce F402-RR-408 (Pegasus 11-61) vectored thrust turbofan

Chaff and flare dispensers both at the fin root and under the fuselage

Two extra wing-mounted pylons

Cannon deleted

TAV-8B (side view)

300-US gal (135-liter) fuel tanks can be carried, but the latter are normally used only for ferry flights.

Night attack: The night attack Harrier II Plus will feature additional pylons in front of the outrigger wheel fairing and have the capability to employ the AIM-7L/M, AGM-84, and AIM-120 missiles. A typical mission configuration might be two fuel tanks inboard, plus two Harpoons and AIM-9Ls outboard.

VARIANTS AND SERIALS

YAV-8B: Two of the original early production AV-8A Harriers were modified by McDonnell Douglas to serve as YAV-8B prototypes for the Harrier II derivative. One was destroyed during the flight test program and the other was later transferred to NASA, with which it is still active.
158394; 158395

AV-8B: Production of the AV-8B is continuing to satisfy a Marine Corps requirement for 300 aircraft. Roughly 250 examples have now been ordered, with the most recent deliveries being completed to night attack standard, incorporating FLIR, NVG compatibility and a modified HUD, among other improvements. Early production machines are to be retrospectively brought

to this standard and plans are also in hand to fit APG-65 radar.
161396 to 161399; 161573 to 161584; 162068 to 162088; 162721 to 162746; 162942 to 162962; 162964 to 162970; 162972; 162973; 163176 to 163179; 163181 to 163185; 163187 to 163190; 163192 to 163195; 163197 to 163201; 163203 to 163206; 163419 to 163426; 163514 to 163519; 163659 to 163690; 163852 to 163855; 163862 to 163883; 164115 to 164121; 164123 to 164154*; 164540 to 164571*
(* = probably includes some TAV-8B two-seaters)

TAV-8B: Intended for pilot training in support of operational forces, the Marine Corps expects to obtain a total of 28 examples of the two-seat TAV-8B.
162747; 162963; 162971; 163180; 163186; 163191; 163196; 163202; 163207; 163856 to 163861; 164113; 164114; 164122 (plus others from later batches)

AIM-9 Sidewinders, unguided rocket pods and Mk 82 500-lb bombs are visible beneath this AV-8B as it gets airborne from a short strip. A key feature of Marine Corps Harrier operating doctrine is this type's unparalleled ability to make use of remote locations, but it also flies regularly from the flight decks of amphibious assault ships. The latter activity is commonly demonstrated in the course of major exercises, such as those tasked by NATO.

MISSION PROFILE

Armament options: Despite being capable of mounting weapons from TERs, in practice the weight and drag involved do not make this a viable option. The weapon loads seen during Desert Storm are probably the extent of the AV-8B's abilities. The GAU-12 gun system, while not mandatory, appeared to be virtually standard in combat. ALQ-167s were seen on the centerline of some aircraft. AIM-9Ls could be carried on any pylon, but in practice only on the left one, with a launcher rail mounted on the right.

Day attack: The four inboard pylons carried four of the same kind of weapon on any given sortie. During Desert Storm these were primarily cluster and general-purpose bombs, with fire bombs and FAE also being seen. Although capable of delivering laser-guided bombs, as well as AGM-65Es, fewer than 10 Mavericks were reported as having been delivered by AV-8Bs during Desert Storm. Rocket pods and up to four

Above: Four VMA-231 AV-8Bs model the original color scheme applied to Marine Corps aircraft.

Below: Updating work has resulted in the night attack version, which features extra equipment.

SPECIFICATION

McDonnell Douglas AV-8B

Wing: span 30 ft 4 in (9.25 m); aspect ratio 4.0; area 338.7 sq ft (22.18 m^2) including two 4.35-sq ft (0.40 m^2) LERXes

Fuselage and tail: length 46 ft 4 in (14.12 m); height 11 ft 7.75 in (3.55 m); tailplane span 13 ft 11 in (4.24 m); wheel base 11 ft 4 in (3.45 m)

Powerplant: one Rolls-Royce F402-RR-406A rated at 21,450 lb (95.42 kN) dry thrust

Weights: operating empty 13,086 lb (5936 kg); normal take-off 22,950 lb (10410 kg) for 9-*g* operation; maximum take-off 31,000 lb (14061 kg) for 1,330 ft (405 m) STO or 18,950 lb (8595 kg) for VTO

Fuel and load: internal fuel 7,759 lb (3519 kg); external fuel up to 8,070 lb (3661 kg) in four 300-US gal (1136-liter) drop tanks; maximum ordnance 9,200 lb (4173 kg)

Speed: maximum level speed 'clean' at sea level 661 mph (1065 km/h)

Range: ferry range 2,418 miles (3891 km) with empty tanks dropped or 2,015 miles (3243 km) with empty tanks retained; combat radius 103 miles (167 km) with a 1-hour loiter after a 1,200-ft (366-m) STO with 12 Mk 82 Snakeye bombs, or 553 miles (889 km) on a hi-lo-hi mission after a 1,200-ft (366-m) STO with a 4,000-lb (1814-kg) load including seven Mk 82 Snakeye bombs, or 722 miles (1162 km) on a deck-launched interception mission with two AIM-9 Sidewinders and two drop tanks; combat air patrol radius with a 3-hour patrol 115 miles (185 km)

Performance: maximum rate of climb at sea level

Above: Transition training for pilots who are new to the V/STOL world is accomplished on the two-seat TAV-8B, which serves only with VMAT-203 at Cherry Point.

14,715 ft (4485 m) per minute; service ceiling more than 50,000 ft (15240 m); STO distance 1,330 ft (405 m) at maximum take-off weight

McDonnell Douglas/British Aerospace TAV-8B

generally similar to the AV-8B except in the following particulars:

Fuselage and tail: length 50 ft 3 in (15.32 m)

Weights: operating empty 14,223 lb (6451 kg)

OPERATORS

US Navy (USN)

NAWC/AD	Patuxent River, MD	AV-8B
NAWC/WD	China Lake, CA	AV-8B

US Marine Corps (USMC)

VMAT-203	Cherry Point, NC	AV-8B, TAV-8B
VMA-211	Yuma, AZ	AV-8B
VMA-214	Yuma, AZ	AV-8B
VMA-223	Cherry Point, NC	AV-8B
VMA-231	Cherry Point, NC	AV-8B
VMA-311	Yuma, AZ	AV-8B
VMA-331	Cherry Point, NC	AV-8B
VMA-513	Yuma, AZ	AV-8B
VMA-542	Cherry Point, NC	AV-8B

Grumman
C-2A Greyhound

Evolved from the Grumman E-2 Hawkeye airborne early warning platform, the **C-2A Greyhound** is now the US Navy's principal COD (Carrier Onboard Delivery) aircraft and recently achieved the rare distinction of being reinstated in production to satisfy US Navy needs to update its capability in this role.

Development of the Greyhound dates back to the early 1960s, when the first two C-2As to appear were nothing more than conversions of early production E-2A Hawkeyes. Testing of these proved the validity of the Greyhound and production contracts were subsequently placed for a total of 29 new-build examples. As it transpired, only 17 of these were completed, which began to enter service during the course of 1966. Firmly based on the Hawkeye, the C-2A differed mainly in having a new, deeper fuselage able to accommodate about 30 passengers or up to 10,000 lb (4500 kg) of cargo when operating from carriers at sea. Loading is effected by means of a ramp situated in the sharply upswept aft fuselage, and the type is fully carrier-compatible.

Attrition and old age means that few, if any, of the original 19 Greyhounds now remain in active service, current requirements in the COD role being satisfied by 39 much newer aircraft that were obtained during the second half of the 1980s, primarily to replace the veteran C-1A Trader. Embodying uprated Allison T56 turboprop engines and revised avionics as well as an auxiliary power unit to allow operations from austere sites, the first of the new-build machines was handed over to the Navy in January 1985. C-2As now serve with four specialist transport squadrons which are located close to the main carrier operating areas.

Two of the squadrons reside in the USA, comprising VRC-30 at North Island, California, and VRC-40 at Norfolk, Virginia, from where they respectively support carriers with the Pacific 3rd Fleet and the Atlantic 2nd Fleet. Elsewhere, in Europe, VR-24 flies in support of 6th Fleet operations from a main operating base at Sigonella, Sicily, while WestPac's 7th Fleet is serviced by VRC-50 at Cubi Point in the Philippines. Normal C-2A complement appears to be about eight aircraft per unit, with the few remaining examples being assigned to VAW-110 at Miramar and VAW-120 at Norfolk for training of replacement air and ground crew destined to join the COD community.

As far as the overseas-based units are concerned, in the normal course of events the Greyhound tends to lead a somewhat nomadic existence, by virtue of the need to 'follow the fleet'. This entails operating mostly from shore facilities and flying out to a carrier or carriers to deliver and collect personnel, equipment and mail before heading back to a land base. However, in special circumstances – such as a short cruise to participate in a major exercise – it is not unknown for a Greyhound to be attached to a carrier air wing for the duration of the cruise.

MISSION PROFILE

Configuration options: The C-2A has a rear ramp to allow for bulky cargo items, such as aircraft engines or ordnance, weighing up to 10,000 lb (4500 kg) to be loaded easily. The passenger-configured version can carry 39 persons. Some 20 casualty litters can also be installed. Provision of arrester hook gear allows for aircraft carrier operations.

Carrier onboard delivery COD: The delivery of high-priority cargo or passengers to and from aircraft carriers at sea. The C-2A's 1,200-mile (1900-km) range, while fully loaded, allows it to support carriers operating far outside the range of land-based helicopters.

VARIANTS AND SERIALS

C-2A: This was a carrier onboard delivery version of the E-2 Hawkeye developed in the 1960s. Two prototype YC-2As were converted from E-2A test aircraft as a prelude to the procurement of the initial batch of 17. A second batch of 39 aircraft was obtained later to replace the C-1A Trader.
148147; 148148; 152786 to 152797; 155120 to 155124; 162140 to 162178

SPECIFICATION

Grumman C-2A
Wing: span 80 ft 7 in (24.56 m); width folded 29 ft 4 in (8.94 m); aspect ratio; area 700 sq ft (65.03 m²)
Fuselage and tail: length 56 ft 7.5 in (17.26 m); height 16 ft 11 in (5.16 m); tailplane span 26 ft 2.5 in (7.99 m); wheel base 23 ft 2 in (7.06 m)
Powerplant: two Allison T56-A-425 rated at 4,912 ehp (3663 kW)
Weights: empty 36,346 lb (16486 kg); maximum take-off 57,500 lb (26081 kg)

Fuel and load: internal fuel 12,400 lb (5625 kg); maximum payload 10,000 lb (4536 kg) for carrier operation and 15,000 lb (6804 kg) for land operation
Speed: maximum level speed at optimum altitude 395 mph (636 km/h); maximum cruising speed at optimum altitude 299 mph (482 km/h)
Range: ferry range 1,796 miles (2891 km); range with a 10,000-lb (4536-kg) payload more than 1,200 miles (1930 km)
Performance: maximum rate of climb at sea level 2,610 ft (796 m) per minute; service ceiling with maximum payload 28,800 ft (8780 m); minimum take-off run 2,180 ft (665 m); take-off distance to 50 ft (15 m) 3,060 ft (932 m) at maximum take-off weight; minimum landing run 1,428 ft (435 m); landing distance from 50 ft (15 m) 2,666 ft (691 m) at maximum landing weight or 1,735 ft (529 m) at maximum arrested landing weight

OPERATORS

US Navy (USN)

VAW-110	Miramar, CA	C-2A
VAW-120	Norfolk, VA	C-2A
VR-24	Sigonella, Sicily	C-2A
VRC-30	North Island, CA	C-2A
VRC-40	Norfolk, VA	C-2A
VRC-50	Cubi Point, RP	C-2A

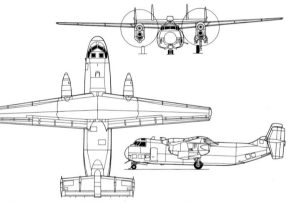

Based on the E-2 Hawkeye, the C-2A has been employed on carrier onboard delivery tasks for more than 25 years.

Grumman
C-4

Taking to the air for the first time in August 1958, the Grumman G-159 Gulfstream met with considerable success as an executive transport, this Rolls-Royce Dart-powered twin-turboprop remaining in production until well into the 1960s when it was supplanted by the Gulfstream II. Most of the examples built were delivered to civilian customers, but the US Navy obtained nine for use in the training of A-6 Intruder bombardier-navigators.

Using the designation **TC-4C** and known by the popular name 'Academe', these machines are extensively modified and feature a bulbous nose fairing housing an Intruder radar as well as other avionics equipment associated with the Intruder's sophisticated nav/attack package. The interior also bears little resemblance to the plush cabins of the executive transports, its spartan layout instead containing a number of consoles that are used to provide tuition to as many as six students at a time.

Until the late 1970s, three TC-4Cs were allocated to each of the three Intruder-equipped training units, specifically VA-42 and VA-128 of the US Navy plus VMAT(AW)-202 of the US Marine Corps. Then, following a decision to transfer to the Navy responsibility for training Marine personnel, VMAT(AW)-202 ceased operations and the surviving eight aircraft are now distributed equally between the two Navy squadrons.

Improvements in the Intruder's avionics suite have been matched by modernization of the TC-4C so as to enable it to remain an effective training tool. As a consequence, most if not all of the survivors now incorporate such items as the undernose TRAM (Target Recognition and Attack Multi-sensor) turret.

Two other models of the C-4 have also existed. One is the **VC-4A** of the US Coast Guard, which ordered two examples in the early 1960s although, as it turned out, only one was actually delivered. Fitted out as a VIP

Instruction of bombardier/navigators for the Intruder force begins on the TC-4C Academe. Based on the Gulfstream turboprop, this carries radar equipment in a modified nose and is able to accommodate up to six students at a time.

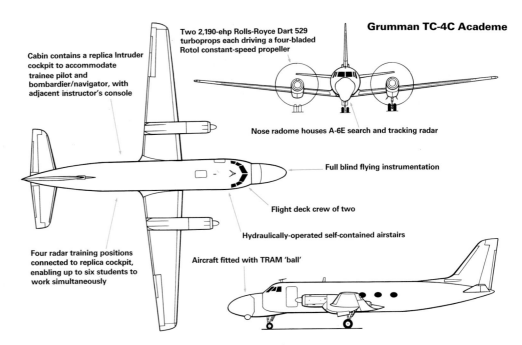

Grumman TC-4C Academe

Two 2,190-ehp Rolls-Royce Dart 529 turboprops each driving a four-bladed Rotol constant-speed propeller

Cabin contains a replica Intruder cockpit to accommodate trainee pilot and bombardier/navigator, with adjacent instructor's console

Nose radome houses A-6E search and tracking radar

Full blind flying instrumentation

Flight deck crew of two

Hydraulically-operated self-contained airstairs

Four radar training positions connected to replica cockpit, enabling up to six students to work simultaneously

Aircraft fitted with TRAM 'ball'

transport, this was handed over to the USCG in 1963 and stationed at Washington's National Airport, conveniently close to this agency's headquarters. It remained in use from Washington until it was replaced by a VC-11A Gulfstream II and was last noted in service at the Coast Guard overhaul and repair facility at Elizabeth City, North Carolina, during 1990.

The other version stemmed from Navy plans to buy Gulfstream Is for use as navigational trainers, an order for 10 aircraft being placed in the early 1960s. Initially known as the T-41A, the designation of this proposed model was changed to **TC-4B**; it would also have featured radar in an extended nose had it not been cancelled before the first example was completed.

MISSION PROFILE

Configuration options: One VC-4A is used by the USCG as a VIP transport/general liaison aircraft. Its internal configuration corresponds to the commercial Gulfstream 1 civilian executive jet.

Intruder training: Up to six student A-6E bombardier/navigators operating the TC-4C's training systems are able to simulate using the A-6E's complex night-attack systems such as the TRAM and Norden

APQ-148 multi-mode nav/attack radar. Instructors monitor a student's progress throughout training missions.

VARIANTS AND SERIALS

VC-4A: A single example of the Grumman Gulfstream I was obtained by the US Coast Guard and used as a VIP staff transport by the Washington headquarters between 1963 and 1969, when it gave way to a Gulfstream II. It is now stationed at Elizabeth City, NC. 02 (originally 1380)

TC-4C: A total of nine Grumman Gulfstreams was obtained for use as radar systems trainers in support of Intruder communities of both the Navy and Marine Corps. Eight remain active with the Navy's two Intruder-equipped fleet replenishment squadrons. 155722 to 155730

SPECIFICATION

Gulfstream Aerospace TC-4C
Wing: span 78 ft 4 in (23.88 m); area 610.3 sq ft (56.70 m²)
Fuselage and tail: length 67 ft 10.75 in (20.69 m); height 23 ft 4 in (7.11 m)
Powerplant: two Rolls-Royce Dart Mk 529-8X rated at 2,210 ehp (1648 kW)
Weights: empty 24,575 lb (11114 kg); maximum take-off 36,000 lb (16330 kg)
Fuel and load: internal fuel 1,550 US gal (5867 liters); maximum payload 4,270 lb (1937 kg)
Speed: maximum speed at 15,000 ft (4570 m) 365 mph (587 km/h); maximum cruising speed at 25,000 ft (7620 m) 348 mph (560 km/h); economical cruising speed at 25,000 ft (7620 m) 298 mph (480 km/h)
Range: typical range at 30,000 ft (9145 m) 1,980 miles (3186 km); typical range at 5,000 ft (1525 m) 1,145 miles (1843 km)
Performance: maximum rate of climb at sea level 1,900 ft (579 m) per minute; service ceiling 33,600 ft (10240 m); take-off distance to 35 ft (10.7 m) 3,000 ft (914 m) at maximum take-off weight; landing distance from 50 ft (15 m) 2,180 ft (664 m) at maximum landing weight

OPERATORS

US Navy (USN)

VA-42	Oceana, VA	TC-4C
VA-128	Whidbey Island, WA	TC-4C

US Coast Guard (USCG)

CGAS	Elizabeth City, NC	VC-4A

de Havilland Canada
UC-8A Buffalo

Originating in response to a 1962 US Army requirement for a turboprop-powered STOL tactical transport aircraft, the de Havilland Canada DHC-5 Buffalo bore a strong family resemblance to the DHC-4 Caribou and, indeed, was known for a time as the 'Caribou II'. Powered by two General Electric CT64 engines, it flew for the first time in April 1964 and went on to achieve a reasonable degree of success. US Army interest was sufficient to merit a contract for four aircraft; these were exhaustively evaluated but the subsequent decision to transfer larger Army fixed-wing aircraft to the US Air Force in the mid-1960s effectively killed off any hope for major orders.

US Navy operation of the **UC-8A Buffalo** is limited to a single example which was obtained in the mid-1980s. This presently forms part of the fleet of utility and communications aircraft operated by the NAWC Weapons Division at China Lake. Its reasonably large hold capacity, rear loading ramp and STOL capability may well have influenced its selection for use in range support operations in and around the China Lake complex, and it is probably also used for longer-haul transport tasks.

MISSION PROFILE

The sole UC-8A serves in the general trials support role with the NAWC at China Lake.

VARIANTS AND SERIALS

UC-8A: A single example of the Buffalo was obtained

Acquired during the mid-1980s, the sole example of the UC-8A Buffalo operates on miscellaneous support duties with the NAWC/WD at China Lake.

for service with the Naval Air Warfare Center on general transport tasks.
161546

SPECIFICATION

de Havilland Canada UC-8A
Wing: span 96 ft 0 in (29.26 m); aspect ratio 9.75; area 945.00 sq ft (87.79 m²)
Fuselage and tail: length 77 ft 4 in (23.57 m); height 28 ft 8 in (8.73 m); tailplane span 32 ft 0 in (9.75 m); wheel track 30 ft 6 in (9.29 m); wheel base 27 ft 11 in (8.50 m)
Powerplant: two General Electric T64-GE-10 each rated at 2,850 ehp (2125 kW)
Weights: empty 16,795 lb (7618 kg); normal take-off 26,000 lb (11794 kg); maximum take-off 38,000 lb (17237 kg)

Fuel and load: internal fuel 2,087 US gal (7900 liters); external fuel none; maximum payload 11,200 lb (5080 kg)
Speed: maximum level and maximum cruising speed 'clean' at 10,000 ft (3050 m) 271 mph (435 km/h); economical cruising speed at 10,000 ft (3050 m) 208 mph (335 km/h)
Range: range 2,170 miles (3492 km) with maximum fuel and a 4,000-lb (1814-kg) payload, or 5,176 miles (815 km) with maximum payload
Performance: maximum rate of climb at sea level 1,890 ft (576 m) per minute; service ceiling 30,000 ft (9145 m); take-off run 1,040 ft (317 m) at maximum take-off weight on grass; take-off distance to 50 ft (15 m) 1,540 ft (470 m) at maximum take-off weight from grass; landing distance from 50 ft (15 m) 1,020 ft (342 m) at normal landing weight on grass; landing run 610 ft (186 m) at normal landing weight on grass

OPERATORS

US Navy (USN)

NAWC/WD	China Lake, CA	UC-8A

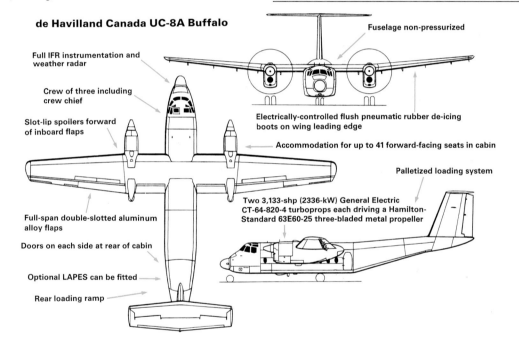

de Havilland Canada UC-8A Buffalo

Fuselage non-pressurized

Full IFR instrumentation and weather radar

Crew of three including crew chief

Slot-lip spoilers forward of inboard flaps

Electrically-controlled flush pneumatic rubber de-icing boots on wing leading edge

Accommodation for up to 41 forward-facing seats in cabin

Palletized loading system

Full-span double-slotted aluminum alloy flaps

Doors on each side at rear of cabin

Optional LAPES can be fitted

Rear loading ramp

Two 3,133-shp (2336-kW) General Electric CT-64-820-4 turboprops each driving a Hamilton-Standard 63E60-25 three-bladed metal propeller

McDonnell Douglas
C-9B Skytrain II

Efforts to modernize the Navy's small but important fleet of transport and logistics support aircraft resulted in the April 1972 order for the first examples of the **C-9B Skytrain II**. At that time, procurement plans anticipated a total of 12 aircraft to be obtained for service with the Navy plus two for the Marine Corps. That program was adhered to, with delivery of these brand new machines being accomplished by McDonnell Douglas between May 1973 and March 1976.

Based on the commercial DC-9 Srs 30, the C-9B features identical dimensions and is powered by a pair of Pratt & Whitney JT8D-9 turbofan engines. Additional fuel capacity was provided so as to extend range. It also possessed a forward cargo door as standard, allowing it to operate in all-cargo, all-passenger or mixed cargo/passenger configurations, according to requirements.

For the first few years of service, the Navy C-9Bs were distributed equally between regular squadrons VR-1 and VR-30, but a reappraisal of service transport needs in the latter half of the 1970s resulted in these two squadrons progressively turning their aircraft over to the Navy Reserve, which established four new units specifically to operate them.

Then, in March 1981, the first of a number of additional C-9Bs were obtained to replace the long-serving C-118B Liftmaster. The Navy fleet has since grown to around 30 aircraft, with most of the recent acquisitions being purchased second-hand and still know as **DC-9**s.

Today, the Navy C-9B fleet is still operated entirely by Reserve outfits, but the number of squadrons involved has grown and some 11 are currently active. These are mostly to be found at major centers of Reserve activity and the normal complement is just two or three aircraft per squadron. In addition to supporting the regular Navy, the C-9Bs are also used to airlift Reservists to their stations so that they can satisfy AcDuTra (Active Duty Training) commitments.

The pair of aircraft delivered to the Marine Corps is still very much part of the line-up. These airplanes have spent their entire service careers with the SOES (Station Operations and Engineering Squadron) at MCAS Cherry Point, North Carolina. Duties are principally oriented towards general-purpose transport tasks, but these aircraft are also often required to act as 'navigation leaders' for Marine Corps fighter and attack aircraft which are deploying to overseas bases.

MISSION PROFILE

Configuration options: Removable seating allows the C-9B to be configured for both passenger and cargo operations, in which a maximum of 32,500 lb (14700 kg) of cargo can be carried. By use of the forward cargo door eight standard-type 463L cargo pallets can be loaded. A maximum of 90 seats can be fitted. Often the aircraft is configured for a mix of seating and cargo.

Fleet logistic support: In peacetime, Navy Reserve C-9Bs provide heavy logistic airlift on a 365-day basis. Single aircraft are regularly rotated through the Mediterranean and Western Pacific theaters in support of Fleet deployments. In wartime, units deploy en masse to support forward-based naval forces.

VARIANTS AND SERIALS

C-9B: Some 33 examples of the DC-9 commercial airliner have seen service with the Navy and Marine Corps and 29 of these are still active, mostly with second-line units of the Navy Reserve. Tasks include transport duties which involve movement of men and material, while the USMC machines are often used as pathfinders to escort attack and fighter aircraft engaged on transoceanic ferry flights.
159113 to 159120; 160046 to 160051; 161266; 161529; 161530; 162753; 162754; 163036; 163037; 163208; 163511 to 163513; 164605 to 164608 (latter four aircraft marked as DC-9)

SPECIFICATION

McDonnell Douglas C-9B
Wing: span 93 ft 5 in (28.47 m); aspect ratio 8.71; area 1,000.7 sq ft (92.97 m²)
Fuselage and tail: length 104 ft 4.75 in (31.82 m); height 27 ft 6 in (8.38 m); tailplane span 36 ft 10.25 in (11.23 m); wheel base 43 ft 8.5 in (13.32 m)
Powerplant: two Pratt & Whitney JT8D-9 rated at 14,500 lb (64.5 kN) dry thrust
Weights: operating empty 65,283 lb (29612 kg) in passenger configuration or 59,706 lb (27082 kg) in freight configuration; maximum take-off 110,000 lb (49900 kg)
Fuel and load: internal fuel 3,679 US gal (13925 liters); maximum payload 32,444 lb (14717 kg)
Speed: maximum cruising speed at 25,000 ft (7620 m) 576 mph (927 km/h); long-range cruising speed at between 30,000 and 35,000 ft (9145 and 10670 m) 504 mph (811 km/h)
Range: range at long-range cruising speed with a 10,000-lb (4536-km) payload 2,023 miles (4704 km)
Performance: maximum rate of climb at sea level 3,400 ft (1035 m) per minute; service ceiling 37,000 ft (11280 m); military critical field length 7,410 ft (2259 m); landing distance 2,580 ft (786 m) at maximum landing weight

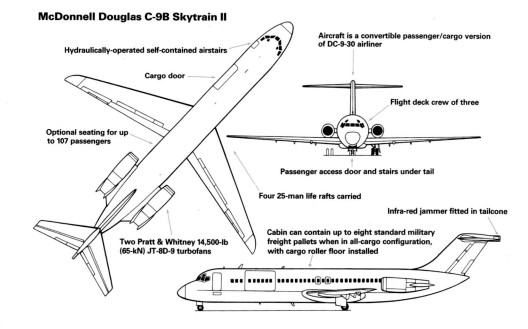

McDonnell Douglas C-9B Skytrain II

Hydraulically-operated self-contained airstairs

Cargo door

Optional seating for up to 107 passengers

Two Pratt & Whitney 14,500-lb (65-kN) JT-8D-9 turbofans

Aircraft is a convertible passenger/cargo version of DC-9-30 airliner

Flight deck crew of three

Passenger access door and stairs under tail

Four 25-man life rafts carried

Infra-red jammer fitted in tailcone

Cabin can contain up to eight standard military freight pallets when in all-cargo configuration, with cargo roller floor installed

OPERATORS

US Navy (USN)

VR-46	Atlanta, GA	DC-9
VR-51	Glenview, IL	C-9B
VR-52	Willow Grove, PA	DC-9
VR-55	Alameda, CA	C-9B
VR-56	Norfolk, VA	C-9B
VR-57	North Island, CA	C-9B
VR-58	Jacksonville, FL	C-9B
VR-59	Dallas, TX	C-9B
VR-60	Memphis, TN	DC-9
VR-61	Whidbey Island, WA	DC-9
VR-62	Detroit, MI	C-9B

US Marine Corps (USMC)

SOES	Cherry Point, NC	C-9B

Left: Carrying the name 'Spirit of Kuwait', the C-9B Skytrain II illustrated here was one of a number that were deployed to Europe for airlift duties the Gulf War.

Grumman
VC-11A Gulfstream II

The **Gulfstream** ranks as one of the most elegant and successful executive jets. Later versions of the family have found favor with all branches of the US armed forces, but the original production model operates only with the Coast Guard, which acquired a solitary example in the late 1960s for VIP transport tasks.

Development began in the early 1960s and the resulting design retained many features of the **Gulfstream I** turboprop, combining these with a new wing and tail structure. A production go-ahead was announced in May 1965 and the Coast Guard was among the early customers. Adopting the military designation **VC-11A**, the Coast Guard aircraft has spent its entire service life operating from Washington's National Airport, close to the office of the Commandant and the Secretary of Transportation, who are among its most regular users.

Powered by two Rolls-Royce Spey Mk 511-8 turbofan engines, the type possesses transatlantic capability and has been a frequent visitor to Europe in more than two decades of service, a notable milestone being passed early in 1988 when it completed 10,000 flying hours. In normal operation, it usually has a crew of four and is able to carry a maximum of 12 passengers. At the time of writing, there appear to be no plans to acquire a replacement aircraft and Coast Guard 'Zero-One' should remain a familiar sight for many years to come.

MISSION PROFILE

Configuration options: Up to 12 passengers can be carried in executive luxury on the VC-11A up to a 2,930-mile (4700-km) range.

Executive transport: The USCG's single VC-11A is kept on alert at Washington National Airport to transport the US Secretary of Transport and US Coast Guard Commandant anywhere in the world.

Below: VIP airlift and movement of senior Coast Guard personnel are the primary duties assigned to the solitary VC-11A Gulfstream II.

VARIANTS AND SERIALS

VC-11A: One example of the Gulfstream II executive jet transport was delivered to the Coast Guard in the late 1960s for use as a VIP transport by Washington-based officers. It is still operated from Washington's National Airport at the present time.
01

SPECIFICATION

Gulfstream Aerospace (Grumman) VC-11A
Wing: span 68 ft 10 in (20.98 m); aspect ratio 5.97; area 793.50 sq ft (73.72 m²)
Fuselage and tail: length 79 ft 11 in (24.36 m); height 24 ft 6 in (7.47 m); tailplane span 27 ft 0 in (8.23 m); wheel track 13 ft 8 in (4.16 m); wheel base 33 ft 4 in (10.16 m)
Powerplant: two Rolls-Royce Spey RB.168 MK 511-8 each rated at 11.400 lb (50.71 kN) dry thrust
Weights: maximum take-off 57,500 lb (26081 kg)

Fuel and load: internal fuel 22,500 lb (10206 kg); external fuel none
Speed: maximum level speed 'clean' at 25,000 ft (7620 m) 585 mph (941 km/h); maximum cruising speed at optimum altitude 565 mph (909 km/h)
Range: range 3,460 miles (5568 km)
Performance: maximum rate of climb at sea level 5,050 ft (1539 m) per minute; service ceiling 43,000 ft (13105 m); take-off field length 4,070 ft (1240 m) at maximum take-off weight; landing field length 3080 ft (939 m) at normal landing weight

OPERATORS

US Coast Guard (USCG)

CGAS	Washington, DC	VC-11A

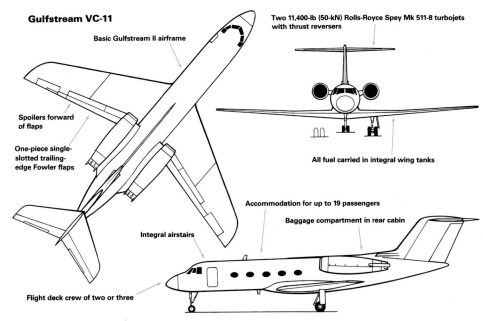

Gulfstream VC-11

Basic Gulfstream II airframe

Spoilers forward of flaps

One-piece single-slotted trailing-edge Fowler flaps

Two 11,400-lb (50-kN) Rolls-Royce Spey Mk 511-8 turbojets with thrust reversers

All fuel carried in integral wing tanks

Accommodation for up to 19 passengers

Baggage compartment in rear cabin

Integral airstairs

Flight deck crew of two or three

Beech
C-12 Super King Air

Below: Examples of the C-12 Super King Air are flown by both the Navy and Marine Corps from a number of locations around the world.

Beech's family of light twins has long been popular with the various elements of the US armed forces. Versions of the **Super King Air** are certainly no exception, being used for a variety of tasks which range from humble general-purpose light transport duties through battlefield surveillance to the acquisition of intelligence and electronic warfare.

The US Navy and Marine Corps lagged behind the other services when it came to acquiring the Super King Air, and it was only as recently as 1979 that the first examples were taken on charge. The initial order covered exactly 66 aircraft – 49 for the Navy and 17 for the Marines – and delivery of these machines was completed in May 1982. In military service, they adopted the designation **UC-12B**, indicating their primary utility transport mission. A maximum of 13 passengers can be accommodated in a high-density layout but it is doubtful if that configuration is used very often, especially as the UC-12B was the first version of the Super King Air to benefit from provision of a port fuselage cargo door.

Once introduced to service, the UC-12Bs replaced such older types as the Grumman US-2B Tracker, and further orders have seen the number on hand rise towards the 100 mark. The first such contract was placed in 1985 and covered a dozen **UC-12F**s which were also distributed between the Navy and Marine Corps. More recently, a batch of 11 **UC-12M**s has been received, all of which are operated by the Navy, as are two **RC-12M**s. One is very

much a 'one-off' machine, being specially instrumented for work connected with missile trials, and it presently serves with the NAWC Weapons Division at NAS Point Mugu, California. The other flies from NAF Roosevelt Roads.

UC-12s of the Navy and Marine Corps are to be found at a large number of home and overseas air bases, where they function principally as 'station hacks', being engaged on

routine communications and liaison tasks. Normal complement of a 'station flight' varies from one to three aircraft. A few also serve with VRC-30 from NAS North Island, California, with other operators including USMC headquarters organizations at NAF Andrews, Washington, and MCAS El Toro, California. In addition, two UC-12Fs are attached to the Pacific Missile Range Facility support element located at Barking Sands, Hawaii.

Seen under test from Patuxent River, the initial example of the UC-12B is still assigned to the NAWC/AD which uses it for routine transport tasks. Navy procurement of this model totalled no fewer than 66, and three other versions have also been purchased.

MISSION PROFILE

Configuration options: A number of internal seating and cargo configurations are available. UC-12Bs, Fs and Ms all have two aircrew, with passenger seats or cargo capacity and a cargo door. The UC-12B can carry 2,000 lb (900 kg) of cargo or up to 13 passengers. UC-12F/Ms have provision for eight passengers and two casualty litters.

Fleet logistic support: The UC-12B is used for a wide range of transport missions at ranges of up to 2,022 miles (3250 km). The more powerful UC-12F has greater reach.

VARIANTS AND SERIALS

UC-12B: A total of 66 Beech Super King Airs was acquired for use in the liaison and communications role, primarily by station flights at Navy and Marine Corps bases in the United States and at overseas locations. 161185 to 161206; 161306 to 161327; 161497 to 161518

UC-12F: Follow-on contracts for derivatives of the Super King Air included a dozen UC-12Fs used on duties identical to those of the UC-12B. 163553 to 163564

UC-12M: The most recent order for the Super King Air involved 11 UC-12Ms for liaison and communications. 163836 to 163846

RC-12M: Two RC-12Ms were obtained for telemetry relay tasks in support of missile testing programs. 163847; 163848

SPECIFICATION

Beech UC-12B
Wing: span 54 ft 6 in (16.61 m); aspect ratio 9.8; area 303.0 sq ft (28.15 m²)
Fuselage and tail: length 43 ft 9 in (13.34 m); height 15 ft 0 in (4.57 m); tailplane span 18 ft 5 in (5.61 m); wheel base 14 ft 11.5 in (4.56 m)
Powerplant: two Pratt & Whitney Canada PT6A-41 rated at 850 shp (634 kW)
Weights: empty 7,315 lb (3318 kg); maximum take-off 12,500 lb (5670 kg)
Fuel and load: internal fuel 544 US gal (2059 liters); maximum payload 2,000 lb (907 kg)
Speed: never exceed 310 mph (499 km/h); maximum level speed at 15,000 ft (4570 m) 333 mph (536 km/h); economical cruising speed at 25,000 ft (7620 m) 313 mph (503 km/h
Range: range at economical cruising speed at 31,000 ft (9450 m) 2,172 miles (3495 km); range at maximum cruising power at 31,000 ft (9450 m) 2,022 miles (3254 km)
Performance: maximum rate of climb at sea level 2,450 ft (747 m) per minute; service ceiling more than 31,000 ft (9450 m); take-off run 1,942 ft (592 m); take-off distance to 50 ft (15 m) 2,579 ft (786 m) at maximum take-off weight; landing run 1,120 ft (341 m) with propeller reversal; landing distance from 50 ft (15 m) 2,074 ft (632 m) with propeller reversal

Beech UC-12F
generally similar to the UC-12B except in the following particulars:
Powerplant: two Pratt & Whitney Canada PT6A-42 rated at 850 shp (634 kW)
Weights: operating empty 8,060 lb (3656 kg)
Fuel and load: internal fuel 3,645 lb (1653 kg); maximum payload more than 2,300 lb (1043 kg)
Speed: maximum level speed at 25,000 ft (7620 m) 339 mph (545 km/h); maximum cruising speed at 25,000 ft (7620 m) 336 mph (536 km/h); economical cruising speed at 25,000 ft (7620 m) 325 mph (523 km/h)
Range: range with maximum fuel at 35,000 ft (10670 m) 2,263 miles (3641 km)
Performance: service ceiling more than 35,000 ft (10670 m); take-off distance to 50 ft (15 m) 2,579 ft (786 m)

Beech UC-12M
generally similar to the UC-12F

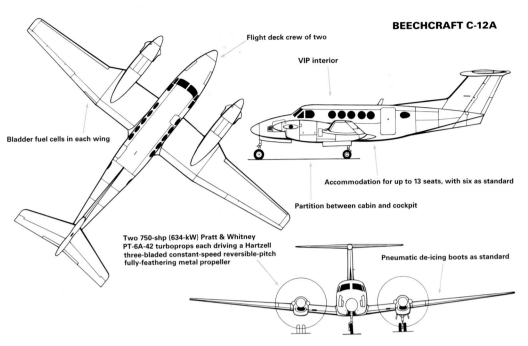

BEECHCRAFT C-12A

Flight deck crew of two
VIP interior
Bladder fuel cells in each wing
Accommodation for up to 13 seats, with six as standard
Partition between cabin and cockpit
Two 750-shp (634-kW) Pratt & Whitney PT-6A-42 turboprops each driving a Hartzell three-bladed constant-speed reversible-pitch fully-feathering metal propeller
Pneumatic de-icing boots as standard

OPERATORS

US Navy (USN)

VRC-30	North Island, CA	UC-12B, UC-12F
TW-1	Meridian, MS	UC-12B
TW-4	Corpus Christi, TX	UC-12B
TW-6	Pensacola, FL	UC-12B
PMRF	Barking Sands, HI	UC-12F
NAWC/WD	Point Mugu, CA	RC-12M
CMEF	Manama, Bahrain	UC-12B
NAS	Agana, Guam	UC-12B
NAS	Alameda, CA	UC-12B
NAS	Atlanta, GA	UC-12B
NAF	Atsugi, Japan	UC-12F
NAS	Brunswick, ME	UC-12B
NAS	Cecil Field, FL	UC-12B
NAS	Cubi Point, RP	UC-12B, UC-12F
NAS	Dallas, TX	UC-12B
NAF	Detroit, MI	UC-12B
NAF	El Centro, CA	UC-12B
NAS	Fallon, NV	UC-12B
NAS	Glenview, IL	UC-12B
NAS	Guantanamo Bay, Cuba	UC-12B
NAS	Jacksonville, FL	UC-12B
NAF	Kadena, Okinawa	UC-12B
NAS	Key West, FL	UC-12B
NAS	Lemoore, CA	UC-12B
NAS	Mayport, FL	UC-12B
NAS	Memphis, TN	UC-12B
NAF	Mildenhall, England	UC-12M
NAF	Misawa, Japan	UC-12B
NAS	Moffett Field, CA	UC-12B
NAS	New Orleans, LA	UC-12B
NAS	Norfolk, VA	UC-12B, UC-12M
NAS	North Island, CA	UC-12B
NAS	Oceana, VA	UC-12B
NAS	Point Mugu, CA	UC-12B
NS	Roosevelt Roads, PR	UC-12B, RC-12M
NS	Rota, Spain	UC-12M
NAS	Sigonella, Sicily	UC-12M
NAS	South Weymouth, MA	UC-12B
NAF	Washington/Andrews, MD	UC-12B
NAS	Whidbey Island, WA	UC-12B
NAS	Willow Grove, PA	UC-12B

US Marine Corps (USMC)

MWHS-4	New Orleans, LA	UC-12B
HQ USMC	Washington/Andrews, MD	UC-12B
MCAS	Beaufort, SC	UC-12B
MCAS	Cherry Point, NC	UC-12B
MCAS	El Toro, CA	UC-12B
MCAS(H)	Futemma, Okinawa	UC-12B
MCAS	Iwakuni, Japan	UC-12F
MCAS(H)	New River, NC	UC-12F
MCAS	Yuma, AZ	UC-12B

Below: In addition to pure transport models, two RC-12Ms have been acquired by the Navy for service with the missile test facility at Point Mugu. It is equipped with an underbelly radar and is normally employed on range control tasks during missile trials.

Gulfstream Aerospace

C-20D Gulfstream III

Continued development of this highly successful family of corporate jet aircraft has resulted in the appearance of the **Gulfstream IV**, which differs from its predecessor by virtue of relying upon a pair of Rolls-Royce Tay turbofans rather than the Spey as a means of propulsion. Procurement for the US armed forces has been undertaken in a fairly limited fashion, primarily for the USAF VIP transport role.

US Navy operation of the **Gulfstream III** was confined to just a pair of aircraft that was obtained in the late 1980s and allocated to the Fleet Logistic Support Wing, a Reserve organization headquartered at Dallas, Texas. Designated the **C-20D**, they are normally resident at the Naval Air Facility at Andrews AFB on the outskirts of Washington and conveniently close to Navy headquarters elements in the Pentagon, as well as to the seat of government. More recently, two C-20Gs have been taken on charge by VR-48 'Sky Pigs' at Andrews AFB, MD.

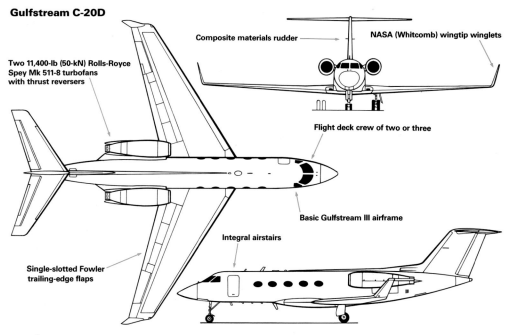

Gulfstream C-20D

Composite materials rudder

NASA (Whitcomb) wingtip winglets

Two 11,400-lb (50-kN) Rolls-Royce Spey Mk 511-8 turbofans with thrust reversers

Flight deck crew of two or three

Basic Gulfstream III airframe

Integral airstairs

Single-slotted Fowler trailing-edge flaps

MISSION PROFILE

Configuration options: up to 14 passengers and five aircrew can be carried by the C-20D.

Fleet logistic support (VIP transport): VIP-style internal fitting is standard on US Navy C-20Ds to provide comfortable travel at ranges up to 4,100 miles (6600 km).

VARIANTS AND SERIALS

C-20D: Two examples were acquired for high-speed executive transport tasks in support of command echelons located in Washington. 163691; 163692

C-20G: Two examples were acquired for VIP duties and are based at Andrews.

SPECIFICATION

Gulfstream Aerospace C-20B
Wing: span 77 ft 10 in (23.72 m); area 934.6 sq ft

(86.82 m²)
Fuselage and tail: length 83 ft 1 in (25.32 m); height 24 ft 4.5 in (7.43 m)
Powerplant: two Rolls-Royce Spey Mk 511-8 rated at 11,400 lb (50.7 kN) dry thrust
Weights: manufacturer's empty 32,300 lb (14651 kg); operating empty 38,000 lb (17236 kg); maximum take-off 68,200 lb (30936 kg)
Fuel and load: internal fuel 28,300 lb (12836 kg); typical payload 1,600 lb (726 kg)
Speed: maximum cruising speed at 30,000 ft (9145 m) 576 mph (928 km/h); long-range cruising speed at 30,000 ft (9145 m) 508 mph (818 km/h)
Range: maximum range 4,721 miles (7598 km); typical range 4,200 miles (6760 km)
Performance: maximum rate of climb at sea level 3,800 ft (1158 m) per minute; maximum operating altitude 45,000 ft (13715 m); balanced take-off field length 5,700 ft (1738 m); landing distance 3,400 ft (1040 m)

Gulfstream Aerospace C-20G
generally similar to the C-20B except for the following particulars:
Wing: span over winglets 77 ft 10 in (23.72 m); aspect ratio 6.0; area 950.39 sq ft (88.29 m²)

Fuselage and tail: length 88 ft 4 in (26.29 m); height 24 ft 10 in (7.57 m); tailplane span 32 ft 0 in (9.75 m); wheel base 38 ft 1.25 in (11.61 m)
Powerplant: two Rolls-Royce Tay Mk 611-8 rated at 13,850 lb (61.6 kN) dry thrust
Weights: manufacturer's empty 35,500 lb (16102 kg); operating empty 42,500 lb (19278 kg); maximum take-off 73,200 lb (33203 kg)
Fuel and load: internal fuel 29,500 lb (13381 kg); maximum payload 4,000 lb (1814 kg)
Speed: maximum cruising speed at 30,000 ft (9145 m) 586 mph (943 km/h); normal cruising speed at 45,000 ft (13715 m) 528 mph (850 km/h)
Range: range with maximum fuel and eight passengers 4,859 miles (7820 km); range with maximum payload 4,254 miles (6845 km)
Performance: maximum rate of climb at sea level 4,002 ft (1220 m) per minute; balanced take-off field length 5,250 ft (1600 m); landing distance from 50 ft (15 m) 3,366 ft (1026 m)

OPERATORS

US Navy (USN)

CFLSW det	Washington/Andrews, MD	C-20D
VR-48	Washington/Andrews, MD	C-20G

Left: The primary duty of the C-20D Gulfstream III is high-speed transportation. Two examples are in use and both are assigned to the Fleet Logistic Support Wing Detachment at Andrews AFB on the outskirts of Washington, DC.

Below: Although it is also on the charge of the Fleet Logistic Support Wing Detachment, one of the two C-20Ds actually displays Marine Corps titles and insignia.

Douglas
EC-24A

Even though the USA was responsible for the design and construction of the Douglas DC-8 commercial jet transport, it is only relatively recently that this type has found its way into service with the armed forces of its country of origin. This situation came about when the US Navy obtained a solitary example in the latter part of the 1980s to supplement the pair of NKC-135As that operated with the Fleet Electronic Warfare Support Group (FEWSG). In Navy service, the DC-8 has been given the designation **EC-24A** in recognition of its electronic mission and beginnings as a pure transport aircraft.

Somewhat ironically, in view of the fact that they were built by the 'opposition', the two Boeings (and two B-47E Stratojets which undertook similar duties at an earlier date) were actually maintained by a McDonnell Douglas facility at Tulsa, Oklahoma, under the terms of a Navy contract for many years, but this company's involvement may well go some way towards explaining why the EC-24A was eventually added to the fleet. Responsibility for this unusual trio of aircraft has, however, now passed to the Chrysler Corporation, and the operation is presently centered upon Waco, Texas.

Like the NKC-135As, the Douglas-built machine has been extensively modified in order to undertake electronic countermeasures and electronic counter-countermeasures duties. These are fundamentally concerned with providing training opportunities for elements of the fleet, a task that has grown in importance in recent times and one which requires periodic overseas deployments in order to exercise with far-flung elements of the Navy. Europe is one area where it has been seen actively supporting major Naval exercises, and it is likely that it has also visited the

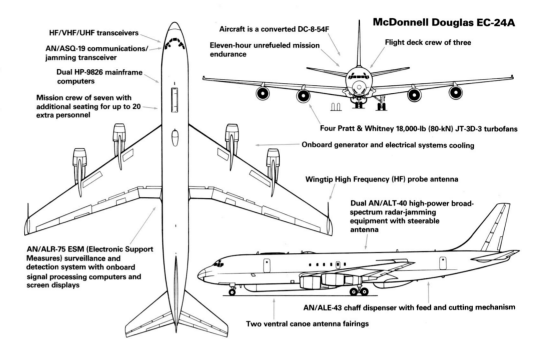

HF/VHF/UHF transceivers

AN/ASQ-19 communications/ jamming transceiver

Dual HP-9826 mainframe computers

Mission crew of seven with additional seating for up to 20 extra personnel

AN/ALR-75 ESM (Electronic Support Measures) surveillance and detection system with onboard signal processing computers and screen displays

McDonnell Douglas EC-24A

Aircraft is a converted DC-8-54F

Eleven-hour unrefueled mission endurance

Flight deck crew of three

Four Pratt & Whitney 18,000-lb (80-kN) JT-3D-3 turbofans

Onboard generator and electrical systems cooling

Wingtip High Frequency (HF) probe antenna

Dual AN/ALT-40 high-power broad-spectrum radar-jamming equipment with steerable antenna

AN/ALE-43 chaff dispenser with feed and cutting mechanism

Two ventral canoe antenna fairings

Far East on a number of occasions.

Little is known of the electronic suite carried by the EC-24 but there is every reason to believe that it incorporates a highly comprehensive array of kit. This certainly features numerous emitters so as to offer realistic training across all areas of the electronic spectrum.

MISSION PROFILE

The sole EC-24A on USN charge operates in the electronic warfare training role, providing 'hostile' jamming for Fleet units at sea. Details of the internal layout and details of typical sortie lengths remain unknown. The aircraft carries powerful twin AN/ALT-40

jammers, and has the AN/USQ-113 communications intrusion, deception and jamming set.

VARIANTS AND SERIALS

EC-24A: One DC-8 commercial transport was obtained for service with the Fleet Electronic Warfare Support Group and fitted out with numerous items of EW equipment.
163050

SPECIFICATION

Electrospace Systems (McDonnell Douglas) EC-24A
Wing: span 142 ft 5 in (43.41 m); area 2,868.0 sq ft (266.44 m²)
Fuselage and tail: length 150 ft 6 in (45.87 m); height 42 ft 4 in (12.91 m); tailplane span 47 ft 6 in (14.48 m); wheel base 57 ft 6 in (17.52 m)
Powerplant: four Pratt & Whitney JT3D-3 rated at 18,000 lb (79.9 kN) dry thrust
Weight: maximum take-off 325,000 lb (147415 kg)
Fuel and load: internal fuel 23,390 US gal (88531 liters); maximum payload 3,000 lb (1361 kg)
Speed: maximum cruising speed at 30,000 ft (9145 m) 545 mph (877 km/h)
Range: ferry range about 5,527 miles (8895 km); endurance 11 hours 0 minutes
Performance: take-off field length 10,560 ft (3220 m) at maximum take-off weight; landing field length 5,620 ft (1713 m) at maximum landing weight

OPERATORS

US Navy (USN)

FEWSG	Waco, TX	EC-24A

Augmenting a brace of NKC-135 Stratotanker aircraft with the Navy Fleet Electronic Warfare Support Group, the solitary EC-24A is also much modified and features numerous bumps and bulges. These are associated with its specialized task of providing electronic warfare training for elements of both major Fleet organizations.

Lockheed
C-130 Hercules

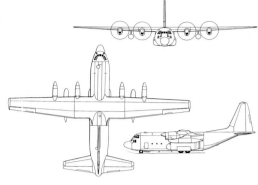

Without doubt one of the most successful transport aircraft of all time, the **Lockheed Hercules** has seen service with the Navy, Marine Corps and Coast Guard in a variety of configurations for a variety of roles. Today, all three services continue to operate the type in modest quantities on missions that range from support of Antarctic exploration through air refueling to search and rescue, and the 'Herky-bird' is expected to remain in use for the foreseeable future.

US Navy operation of the Hercules dates back to the late 1950s when two very different models were obtained for pure transport duties, most of which are still active today. The initial Navy contract covered four **UV-1L**s (later **LC-130F**) which featured a combined wheel/ski undercarriage so as to allow them to operate safely from the Antarctic ice in support of Operation Deep Freeze. Roughly comparable to the US Air Force's **C-130B**, the sometimes hazardous nature of the task has resulted in numerous accidents over the years. Perhaps the most remarkable story relates to the recovery of one machine after no less than 16 years stuck in the snow following a take-off accident in September 1971. Retrieved in 1987, this aircraft was subsequently repaired and returned to service with VXE-6.

Expansion of Antarctic operations resulted in half a dozen **LC-130R**s being purchased during the 1970s, these being fundamentally similar to the **C-130H** but also incorporating skis. Like the LC-130Fs, these have had their share of mishaps. Four are still in use alongside three LC-130Fs and the months of the Antarctic summer are routinely spent in the region, with a VXE-6 detachment operating from the main base at McMurdo Sound in support of remote scientific outposts on the ice.

Transport duties of a more conventional nature are performed by the Navy's seven **C-130F**s. Also acquired in the late 1950s, these began their careers as **GV-1U**s and they now serve with VR-22 at Rota, Spain, and VRC-50 at Cubi Point in the Philippines, respectively supporting Sixth and Seventh Fleet activities. Again, they are basically similar to the C-130B version.

Other models which have been operated by the Navy in reasonable quantities comprise the **EC-130G** and **EC-130Q**, which were used for the vital role of communications between National Command Authorities and nuclear-armed submarines. Four EC-130Gs were the first examples to assume this duty and were originally purchased as **C-130G**s for conventional transport tasks. Based on the **C-130E**, they were soon modified to EC-130G TACAMO (TAke Charge And Move Out) standard, using an extensive array of communications equipment, with the most visible evidence of change centering around fitment of a trailing antenna for the VLF radio. One was destroyed and plans to convert the survivors to **TC-130G** trainer/utility transports have evidently lapsed.

Following on from the original quartet of TACAMO aircraft, the Navy eventually obtained a total of 18 EC-130Qs. Based on the C-130H airframe, these were otherwise little different from the EC-130G and provided good service to VQ-3 and VQ-4 squadrons for many years until replaced by the Boeing E-6A Hermes (recently renamed Mercury). A few may still be active in the TACAMO role with VQ-4 from Patuxent River, but their days are numbered and most of the redundant aircraft have been consigned to storage after surrendering their specialized communications gear for fitment in the E-6A. At least one is, however, still flying and this, now known as a **TC-130Q**, is assigned to VXE-6, which uses it as a 'bounce bird' for crew training at Point Mugu when not deployed to the Antarctic.

Procurement of pure transport versions of the Hercules for the Navy resumed fairly recently, with the placing of a contract for two examples of a new variant known as the **C-130T**. These are destined to join VR-54, a Reserve unit stationed at New Orleans, Louisiana, and are similar to the **KC-130T** of the Marine Corps although they lack air-refueling equipment.

Of the three services, the Marine Corps is easily the major operator of the Hercules, obtaining its first examples during the late 1950s. It continues to buy newer models today. Three basic versions have been purchased, beginning with the **GV-1** (later **KC-130F**) in the late 1950s and progressing via the **KC-130R** to the contemporary KC-130T. Respective quantities are 46, 14 and (to date) 22 and all three models are still very much in service with three front-line squadrons, a training unit and two Reserve outfits.

Although perhaps best known as tankers by virtue of featuring dual pod-mounted underwing hose-and-drogue assemblies which are used to transfer fuel from one or two tanks housed in the hold, the KC-130 may be reconfigured for pure transport tasks without too much difficulty. Indeed, a good proportion of the workload is concerned with conventional airlift duties, especially in support of routine deployments of fighter and attack aircraft. Another task, and one that was undertaken by one aircraft from VMGR-452 during the Gulf War, relates to use as an intelligence-gathering platform using 'Senior Warrior' equipment.

As far as the regular forces are concerned, these are solely equipped with the KC-130F and KC-130R. VMGR-152 at Futemma, Okinawa, utilizes only the F model, while the other two squadrons - VMGR-252 at Cherry Point, North Carolina; and VMGR-352 at El Toro, California – have fleets that include both sub-types. KC-130Fs also serve with training unit VMGRT-253 at Cherry Point, while the 16 or so KC-130Ts that have been delivered so far have been allocated in their entirety to the Reserve Force, operating with VMGR-234 at Glenview, Illinois, and and VMGR-452 at Stewart, New York. The most recent examples –

Left: First ordered for use as tanker aircraft in the late 1950s, the KC-130 Hercules is still the primary Marine Corps tanker today. Here, a KC-130R of VMGR-252 tops up the fuel tanks of a two-seater Hornet from VMFAT-101.

Above: This DC-130A, once flown by the Navy, it is now bailed to Tracor, which operates it on behalf of the NAWC/WD at Point Mugu.

handed over in late 1991 – are 'stretched' aircraft and should more properly be known as **KC-130T-30**s.

In Coast Guard service, the Hercules has been almost as durable, a batch of 12 aircraft initially being obtained as the **R8V-1G** during the late 1950s for long-range search-and-rescue missions. A derivative of the C-130B, these machines were subsequently redesigned as **HC-130B**s during 1962 and remained in service until the early 1980s, principally from the stations at Barbers Point, Hawaii, and Elizabeth City, North Carolina.

They were joined in the summer of 1966 by a single **EC-130E** which was obtained mainly for LORAN calibration tasks on a global basis but this, too, has now been retired, leaving just the **HC-130H** and **HC-130H-7** variants in Coast Guard service. Procurement has so far totalled 35 examples, of which 31 are known to remain in use, flying from locations in North Carolina, Hawaii, California, Alaska, Florida and Puerto Rico. Long-range SAR is still the prime task for these aircraft but some effort is also directed towards drug interdiction, the type's long duration on station being particularly useful in surveillance tasks. Special sensors associated with anti-smuggling operations include optional 'bolt-on' SLAR pods that are fitted adjacent to the wheel wells and a pod-mounted FLIR housed in what looks like a modified auxiliary fuel tank. Equipment associated with the FLIR package includes a datalink and an operator's console incorporating display and recording apparatus.

Above: Low visibility tactical colors have now spread as far as the support aircraft for the 'Blue Angels' aerobatic display team, although evidence of ownership is rather more prominent.

MISSION PROFILE

Configuration options: In USN, USMC, and USCG service the C-130 is configured for cargo, troop transport, search and rescue, Antarctic development, air refueling and strategic communications. USN, USMC and USCG C-130s are highly specialized aircraft and are rarely switched between roles.

Fleet logistic support: US Navy C-130Fs provide heavy logistic support for Fleet operations on an intercontinental basis. Their large rear ramps allow for the loading of bulky items such as ordnance, ship engine components and helicopters. Up to 92 passengers or 74 casualty litters can be carried.

Refueler-transport: USMC KC-130F/Ts are tasked to support transoceanic deployments of Marine Corps tactical aircraft. Up to 31,000 lb (14060 kg) of fuel is carried. KC-130s also fly combat refueling missions in support of fighter, strike and electronic warfare aircraft. Up to two aircraft can be refueled at a time from the KC-130's two underwing drogue refueling pods. Cargo hold fuel tanks can be removed to allow 26,913 lb of (12200 kg) cargo to be carried. Some 64 paratroopers can be dropped.

Antarctic development: LC-130F/Rs support American Antarctic research effort, flying from ice runways with the aid of skis and JATO rocket systems. Special scientific equipment is installed to monitor pollution and carry out other research.

Above: Primarily employed in support of the 6th Fleet, VR-22 is equipped with examples of the pure cargo C-130F and the tanker KC-130F.

Strategic communications: The EC-130Q's main mission is post-nuclear strike communications, using trailing wire Airborne Very Low Frequency (AVLF) radio antenna and relaying messages to ballistic missile-firing submarines when shore-based communications systems are put out of action. Backup communications with submarines and ships out of range of shore-based VLF transmitters during peacetime is a secondary task for the EC-130Q force.

Long-range search/drug interdiction: USCG HC-130H/H-7 aircraft provide search coverage up to 4,894 miles (7870 km) from shore. Survival equipment and marking devices can be dropped to survivors of maritime or air disasters. USCG HC-130H/H-7s fly drug interdiction missions over the Gulf of Mexico and the Caribbean. The new EC-130V airborne early warning version is soon to enter USCG service to provide long-range surveillance of large areas of ocean as part of the US drug interdiction effort.

VARIANTS AND SERIALS

HC-130B: A total of 12 examples of this version of the Hercules was acquired by the US Coast Guard for long-range search and rescue tasks. They were referred to as SC-130Bs upon delivery and were subsequently known as HC-130Gs, until adopting the designation HC-130B. None now remain in use.
1339 to 1342; 1344 to 1351

EC-130E: One aircraft was obtained by the US Coast Guard for the calibration of LORAN navigation aids during the latter half of the 1960s. This machine is no longer in service.
1414

Left: Antarctic exploration and support are the primary tasks undertaken by the 'ski-birds' of VXE-6. High-visibility orange areas are prominent aspects of the LC-130R color scheme.

C-130 Hercules (continued)

KC-130F: A total of 46 KC-130F tanker/transports was purchased for service with the Marines, these featuring pod-mounted hose-reel assemblies under each wing and a fuel tank in the hold. When used as tankers, they can refuel two receivers simultaneously.
147572; 147573; 148246 to 148249; 148890 to 148899; 149788; 149789; 149791; 149792; 149795; 149796; 149798 to 149800; 149802 to 149804; 149806 to 149816; 150684 to 150690

C-130F: Seven aircraft were diverted from an early contract and assigned as pure cargo transports.
149787; 149790; 149793; 149794; 149797; 149801; 149805

LC-130F: Featuring a ski/wheel undercarriage assembly, four aircraft were obtained for Antarctic airlift tasks in support of Project Deep Freeze.
148318 to 148321

EC-130G: Four suitably modified airframes were acquired for use in the VLF communications role, operating in support of nuclear-armed and -powered strategic submarines.
151888 to 151891

TC-130G: At least one EC-130G was converted to this configuration for use as a crew trainer and in support of the Navy aerobatic team. Modification entailed removal of specialist communications equipment.
151891

HC-130H: A total of 35 HC-130Hs has been delivered to the US Coast Guard, although the original batch of three aircraft has now been disposed of. The primary mission is that of long-range search and rescue, but other duties include drug interdiction and surveillance, for which SLAR and FLIR pods may be carried.
1452 to 1454; 1500 to 1504; 1600 to 1603; 1700 to 1721; 1790

EC-130Q: A follow-on version to the EC-130G, 17 examples of the EC-130Q were purchased for SSBN communications duties.
156170 to 156177; 159469; 160608; 161223; 161494 to 161496; 161531; 162312; 162313

TC-130Q: At least three EC-130Qs were converted to this standard for use in crew training. Modification entailed removal of the specialist VLF communications equipment, much of which has been installed in Boeing's E-6A.
156170; 156174; 159348

KC-130R: The second tanker/transport version to enter service, some 14 examples of this model were acquired for the Marines.
160013 to 160021; 160240; 160625 to 160628

LC-130R: LC-130F attrition and expanded Antarctic exploration activity resulted in a further six ski/wheel examples of the Hercules being obtained.
155917; 159129 to 159131; 160740; 160741

KC-130T: Procurement of the newest tanker/transport model is continuing and some 22 examples have so far been purchased, with the most recent deliveries being stretched KC-130T-30s. All are assigned to second-line units of the Marine Corps Reserve force.
162308 to 162311; 162785; 162786; 163022; 163023; 163310; 163311; 163591; 163592; 164105; 164106; 164180; 164181; 164441; 164442; 164597; 164598; 164759; 164760

C-130T: Two pure transport equivalents of the KC-130T have been acquired for a Navy Reserve squadron but current planning anticipates that at least 20 more examples will be obtained as replacements for C-9Bs of the Reserve force.
164762; 164763

EC-130V: One Coast Guard HC-130H has been modified to EC-130V configuration for use in the battle to interdict drug-smuggling activities in the Gulf of Mexico. The principal identifying feature of this machine is the AN/APS-125 radar antenna mounted AWACS-fashion above the fuselage. Further conversions are likely to follow in due course.
1721

SPECIFICATION

Lockheed C-130F
Wing: span 132 ft 7 in (40.41 m); aspect ratio 10.1; area 1,745.0 sq ft (161.12 m²)
Fuselage and tail: length 97 ft 9 in (29.79 m); height 38 ft 3 in (11.66 m); tailplane span 52 ft 8 in (16.05 m); wheel base 32 ft 0.75 in (9.77 m)
Powerplant: four Allison T56-A-7 rated at 4,050 ehp (3020 kW)
Weights: empty equipped 69,300 lb (31434 kg); maximum take-off 135,000 lb (61236 kg)
Fuel and load: internal fuel 5,050 US gal (19116 liters); external fuel two 450-US gal (1703-liter) underwing tanks; maximum payload 35,700 lb (16194 kg)
Speed: maximum cruising speed at 30,000 ft (9145 m) 370 mph (595 km/h)
Range: range with maximum fuel 4,850 miles (7805 km); range with maximum payload 2,200 miles (3540 km)

Left: Tasks undertaken by the Coast Guard fleet of Hercules include surveillance, interdiction of drug smugglers and search and rescue.

Left: Configuration as a tanker aircraft has not impaired the KC-130R when it comes to operating from unimproved surfaces, as this view of a Hercules from VMGR-352 shows.

Performance: maximum rate of climb at sea level 2,000 ft (610 m) per minute; service ceiling 34,000 ft (10365 m); take-off distance to 50 ft (15 m) 4,300 ft (1311 m) at maximum take-off weight

Lockheed KC-130F
generally similar to the C-130F except in the following particulars:
Powerplant: four Allison T56-A-16 rated at 4,910 ehp (3661 kW)
Fuel and load: maximum payload 3,600 US gal (13627 liters) of additional fuel in a removable cargo-hold tank
Speed: maximum cruising speed at 30,000 ft (9145 m) 380 mph (612 km/h); refuelling speed 355 mph (571 km/h)
Range: typical range to transfer 31,000 lb (14061 kg) of fuel 1,000 miles (1609 km)

Lockheed EC-130G
generally similar to the C-130F except in the following particulars:
Powerplant: four Allison T56-A-7A rated at 4,050 ehp (3020 kW)
Weights: normal take-off 155,000 lb (70310 kg); maximum take-off 175,000 lb (79380 kg)
Fuel and load: internal fuel 6,960 US gal (26346 liters); external fuel two 1360-US gal (5145-liter) underwing tanks

Lockheed EC-130Q
generally similar to the EC-130G

Lockheed LC-130R
generally similar to the C-130F except in the following particulars:
Powerplant: four Allison T56-A-15 rated at 4,508 ehp (3362 kW)
Weights: empty equipped 78,492 lb (35604 kg); maximum take-off 175,000 lb (79380 kg)
Fuel and load: internal fuel 45,240 lb (20520 kg); external fuel up to 17,680 lb (8020 kg) in two 1,360-US gal (5148-liter) underwing tanks

Lockheed KC-130R
generally similar to the KC-130F except in the following particulars:
Powerplant: four Allison T56-A-15 rated at 4,508 ehp (3362 kW)
Weights: operating empty 79,981 lb (36279 kg); normal take-off 109,744 lb (49780 kg); maximum take-off 166,301 lb (75433 kg)
Fuel and load: internal fuel 45,240 lb (20520 kg); external fuel up to 17,680 lb (8020 kg) in two 1,360-US gal (5148-liter) underwing tanks; maximum payload 3,600 US gal (13627 liters) of additional fuel in a removable cargo-hold tank
Speed: maximum cruising speed at 30,000 ft (9145 m) 374 mph (602 km/h)
Range: radius with maximum payload 2,952 miles (4751 km); typical range to transfer 52,000 lb (23587 kg) of fuel or 1,150 miles (1850 km)

Lockheed KC-130T
generally similar to the KC-130R

Below: One of the Coast Guard HC-130Hs has been modified to EC-130V standard, incorporating the APS-125 radar in a rotodome above the fuselage.

Lockheed LC-130R Hercules

The US Navy maintains a small fleet of Hercules for the pure cargo role, including those intended for Antarctic support. Three LC-130Fs serve alongside four LC-130Rs on this mission, permanently based at Point Mugu but deploying operationally to McMurdo Sound to support scientific research outposts.

Engines
The LC-130R is based on the C-130H airframe, and has the same Allison T56-A-16 turboprops. These develop 4,910 eshp (3662 ekW) at maximum rating but are usually derated to 4,508 eshp (3362 ekW). The LC-130Fs are based on the C-130B, and are powered by the T56-A-7 rated at 4,050 eshp (3021 ekW).

Markings
The most distinctive of US Navy Hercules, the LC-130s wear a bright scheme of orange, gray and white for maximum conspicuity should they be forced down in the icy wastes of Antarctica. All wear the 'XD' tailcode of VXE-6.

Fuel
The C-130H airframe offers a good internal capacity, but this is usually augmented by the carriage of two 1,360-US gal (5150-liter) underwing tanks to cope with the extra demands of long-range polar flying.

Antarctic equipment
The most visible modification for the polar exploration role is the undercarriage skis, similar to those fitted to the C-130Ds and LC-130Hs of the US Air Force. These entail a certain amount of redesign of the fuselage, notably the additional fairing to house the nose ski when retracted. Other equipment includes the fitment of JATO rockets for take-offs from icefields.

Cockpit
The standard Hercules cockpit has four crew stations. The two pilots face forward, behind and between whom sits the flight engineer on a raised seat. Facing outward on the starboard side is the navigator.

OPERATORS

US Navy (USN)

VR-22	Rota, Spain	C-130F, KC-130F
VRC-50	Cubi Point, RP	C-130F
VR-54	New Orleans, LA	C-130T
VXE-6	Point Mugu, CA	LC-130F, LC-130R
'Blue Angels'	Pensacola, FL	TC-130G

US Marine Corps (USMC)

VMGR-152	Futemma, Okinawa	KC-130F
VMGR-234	Glenview, IL	KC-130T
VMGR-252	Cherry Point, NC	KC-130F, KC-130R
VMGRT-253	Cherry Point, NC	KC-130F
VMGR-352	El Toro, CA	KC-130F, KC-130R
VMGR-452	Stewart, NY	KC-130T

US Coast Guard (USCG)

CGAS	Barbers Point, HI	HC-130H
CGAS	Borinquen, PR	HC-130H
CGAS	Clearwater, FL	HC-130H, EC-130V
CGAS	Elizabeth City, NC	HC-130H
CGAS	Kodiak, AK	HC-130H
CGAS	Sacramento, CA	HC-130H

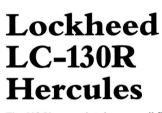

Boeing
C-135 Stratotanker

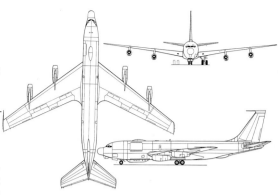

Obtained during 1977-78 to replace a pair of Boeing EB-47E Stratojets, the two **NKC-135A**s that continue to form part of the US Navy inventory are both former tankers. They have been extensively modified to undertake electronic warfare simulation duties and are reported to carry as much as 12,500 lb (5670 kg) of specialized EW equipment. Most of this is housed internally but both aircraft also feature underwing pods containing mission-related apparatus, and the standard nose-mounted weather radar is thought to have given way to sea-search radar.

Assigned to the Fleet Electronic Warfare Support Group (FEWSG), responsibility for maintenance and operation has always been undertaken on a contract basis by civilian agencies. Initially, a McDonnell Douglas facility at Tulsa, Oklahoma, looked after this program but management is now entrusted to the Chrysler Corporation, this change being accompanied by a move to new quarters at Waco, Texas.

Beyond the fact that they are mainly concerned with providing opportunities for elements of the Fleet to train in a realistic EW environment, little is known about the precise nature of the duties that the two aircraft perform, but it seems that these may also extend to include research, development, test and evaluation projects. As for the equipment carried, even less is known, but it appears that their jamming capability exceeds that of any other aircraft now flying. There have also been reports that some fuel cells have been removed to allow extra equipment to be installed.

MISSION PROFILE

Both of the US Navy's NKC-135As are used by FEWSG for electronic warfare training duties. Details of the internal layout and details of typical sortie lengths remain unknown. The aircraft carries powerful twin AN/ALT-40 jammers, and can carry 'Tree' series jamming pods underwing.

VARIANTS AND SERIALS

NKC-135A: Two former USAF KC-135 Stratotankers were transferred to the Navy for service with the FEWSG as replacements for the B-47 Stratojet. Both machines are extensively modified and incorporate much specialized electronic equipment.
553134; 563596

SPECIFICATION

Boeing NKC-135A
Wing: span 130 ft 10 in (39.88 m); area 2,433.0 sq ft (226.03 m²)
Fuselage and tail: length 136 ft 3 in (41.53 m); height 41 ft 8 in (12.70 m); tailplane span 40 ft 3 in (12.27 m); wheel base 46 ft 7 in (14.20 m)
Powerplant: four Pratt & Whitney J57-P-59W rated at 13,750 lb (61.1 kN) dry thrust
Weights: operating empty 123,000 lb (55793 kg); maximum take-off 270,000 lb (122472 kg)
Fuel and load: internal fuel 189,702 lb (86047 kg)
Speed: maximum level speed at high altitude 610 mph (982 km/h); cruising speed at 35,000 ft (10675 m) 532 mph (856 km/h)
Range: ferry range 9,200 miles (14806 km); typical operational range 5,067 miles (8154 km)
Performance: maximum rate of climb at sea level 1,290 ft (393 m) per minute; service ceiling 41,000 ft (12495 m); typical take-off distance 10,700 ft (3260 m)

OPERATORS

US Navy (USN)

FEWSG	Waco, TX	NKC-135A

Below: Acquired as replacements for a pair of EB-47E Stratojets, two examples of the NKC-135A Stratotanker are flown by the Fleet Electronic Warfare Support Group from Waco, TX. Duties are mostly concerned with providing realistic training in the EW environment for elements of the Fleet at home and overseas.

Convair
UC-880

One of a number of commercial jet transports that were developed and manufactured in the USA during the late 1950s and 1960s, the **Convair 880** was specifically designed to meet the demand for a medium-range airliner. It met with only limited success, being overshadowed by the Boeing 707 and Douglas DC-8. The 880 bore a strong resemblance to both types in that its quartet of General Electric CJ-805 turbojet engines was housed in pods that were suspended beneath a low-slung wing structure. The maiden flight took place on 27 January 1959 and deliveries to airline customers – which included Trans-World Airlines, Delta and Northeast – began little more than a year later, in February 1960.

Today, few if any remain in regular commercial service but the US Navy did obtain a single example in the 1980s. This machine is currently operated by the NAWC Aircraft

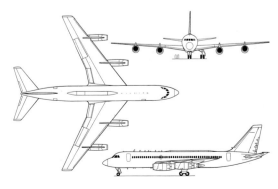

Right: Designated as a UC-880, the Navy's sole Convair 880 has spent its entire service career operating from Patuxent River, MD, and has recently acquired a handsome new paint job.

Division's Anti-Submarine Aircraft Test Directorate at Patuxent River, Maryland, on trials and development projects that are related to this mission.

MISSION PROFILE

The sole Navy Convair 880 is used for trials work by the Naval Air Warfare Center. It can be configured as an inflight-refueling tanker aircraft, but details of its other tasks remain unclear.

VARIANTS AND SERIALS

UC-880: One Convair 880 commercial jet transport was obtained for operation with the NAWC/AD on various test taskings.
161572

SPECIFICATION

Convair UC-880
Wing: span 120 ft 0 in (36.58 m); area 2,000 sq ft (185.80 m²)
Fuselage and tail: length 129 ft 4 in (39.42 m); height

Right: Although little is known of the tasks of the UC-880, it has been modified to serve as an aerial tanker and does feature a single-point hose-reel assembly, seen in use here to transfer fuel to a TA-4J Skyhawk.

36 ft 4 in (11.07 m)
Powerplant: four General Electric CJ805-3 rated at 11,200 lb (49.7 kN) dry thrust
Weights: empty 81,800 lb (37104 kg); basic empty 89,000 lb (40370 kg); maximum take-off 189,500 lb (85957 kg)
Speed: maximum level speed at optimum altitude 615 mph (990 km/h); cruising speed at optimum altitude 605 mph (974 km/h)
Range: range at 35,000 ft (10670 m) with a 23,150-lb

(10501-kg) payload 3,200 miles (5150 km)
Performance: maximum rate of climb at sea level 3,500 ft (1067 m) per minute

OPERATORS

US Navy (USN)

NAWC/AD	Patuxent River, MD	UC-880

CASA
C.212

Despite the fact that it has met with considerable success on world markets, the **CASA C.212** remains a rare sight in US military markings, with barely a handful of machines currently active. Most of those are operated by the Air Force but a single example of the Series 300 utility transport version is presently being flown by the Coast Guard facility at Opa Locka on the outskirts of Miami, Florida. Obtained under the terms of a leasing arrangement concluded with CASA during the summer of 1990, this aircraft is essentially undergoing trials to determine its suitability for the logistics support role.

Powered by a pair of Garrett TPE331 turboprop engines and featuring a greater maximum take-off weight, the Series 300 is rather more attractive to potential customers, especially as recent improvements have resulted in increased range and payload capacity. The latter is now a maximum of 6,217 lb (2820 kg) but a more practical idea of its worth is provided by the fact that it can carry 6,108 lb (2770 kg) a distance of 254 miles (408 km). Alternatively, it may accommodate up to 26 passengers.

As yet, there is no indication that it will be widely adopted by the US Coast Guard, even though CASA reached an agreement with Fairchild in June 1989 covering manufacture and marketing rights in the USA for both commercial and military customers.

MISSION PROFILE

The single Coast Guard CASA C.212 is being evaluated to ascertain the type's suitability for the logistics support role.

VARIANTS AND SERIALS

CASA C.212: A single example of the Series 300 has recently been operating with the US Coast Guard on a trial basis in the light transport and logistics support role, but it is not yet known if this evaluation will lead to further procurement.
0393

SPECIFICATION

CASA C.212 Series 300
Wing: span 66 ft 6.5 in (20.28 m); aspect ratio 10.0; area 441.33 sq ft (41.00 m²)
Fuselage and tail: length 53 ft 1.75 in (16.20 m); height 20 ft 8 in (6.30 m); tailplane span 27 ft 6.75 in (8.40 m); wheel track 10 ft 2 in (3.10 m); wheel base 18 ft 2.5 in (5.55 m)
Powerplant: two Garrett TPE331-10R-513C each flat-rated at 900 shp (671 kW) without automatic power reserve and 925 shp (690 kW) with automatic power reserve
Weights: empty equipped 9,700 lb (4400 kg) in freight configuration; operating empty lb (kg); normal take-off lb (kg); maximum take-off 17,637 lb (8000 kg)
Fuel and load: internal fuel 3,527 lb (1600 kg) plus provision for one 264-US gal (1000-liter) or two 198-US gal (750-liter) ferry tanks in the cabin; external fuel up to 1,764 lb (800 kg) in two 132-US gal (500-liter) underwing tanks; maximum payload 5,952 lb (2700 kg)
Speed: maximum operating speed 'clean' at optimum altitude 230 mph (370 km/h); maximum cruising speed at 10,000 ft (3050 m) 186 mph (300 km/h)
Range: range about 1,125 miles (1811 km) with maximum fuel or 403 miles (648 km) with maximum payload
Performance: maximum rate of climb at sea level 1,630 ft (497 m) per minute; service ceiling 26,000 ft

(7925 m); take-off run 1,115 ft (340 m) at maximum take-off weight; take-off distance to 50 ft (15 m) 1,837 ft (560 m) at maximum take-off weight

OPERATORS

US Coast Guard (USCG)

CGAS	Miami, FL	CASA C.212 Srs 300

Above: US Coast Guard operation of the CASA C.212 Aviocar is limited to a single example.

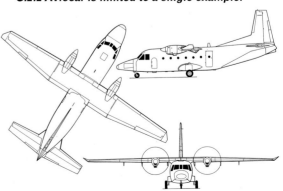

Grumman
E-2 Hawkeye

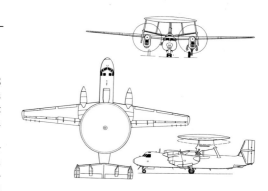

Known colloquially as the 'Hummer' (an allusion to the noise made by its pair of Allison T56 turboprop engines), the **Hawkeye** was conceived as a replacement for the piston-powered Grumman Tracer in the airborne early warning (AEW) role and made its maiden flight as long ago as October 1960. Beginning life as the **W2F**, it was redesignated as the **E-2** in 1962 and entered service with elements of the Pacific Fleet some two years later, during 1964. Subsequent efforts at improving its capability have met with considerable success and the Hawkeye is still being manufactured today for service with both the US Navy and overseas customers.

Initial production was of the **E-2A** model but most of the 50 or so examples that were built were eventually updated to **E-2B** standard with effect from the late 1960s, the principal changes being internal in nature and intended to bolster computer processing capability. None remains in service with the Navy.

Further efforts at enhancing Hawkeye resulted in the advent of the **E-2C** model which flew for the first time in prototype form on 20 January 1971, with the initial production-configured example making its debut in the autumn of 1972, paving the way for operational deployment in late 1974. A significant improvement over its predecessors, the E-2C married a new APS-125 radar with far superior computing capability. That original package has been the subject of continuing development, and current production aircraft are very different from early E-2Cs.

One particular noteworthy area of change relates to the radar, with the original APS-125 system initially being replaced by APS-138 and, more recently, by APS-139, which was included on new-build Hawkeyes with effect from 1989. Existing airframes have also been updated by means of a retrofit program.

Looking ahead, an even more capable radar is expected to be adopted by all Hawkeyes during the next few years. This is the Grumman/General Electric APS-145, which was evaluated during 1986. Able to track more targets at greater distances, APS-145 is more resistant to jamming and offers better overland resolution. It was due to be installed on new-build aircraft produced during 1991 and is also earmarked for 'back fitting' to older Hawkeyes. Other improvements in the pipeline are aimed at boosting detection and processing capabilities, trials having been conducted with JTIDS (Joint Tactical Information Distribution System) as well as new IFF (Identification Friend or Foe) equipment.

Production of the E-2C for the Navy seems certain to surpass the 150 mark. It currently serves with some 16 squadrons in airborne early warning 'communities' that are concentrated at Norfolk, Virginia, and Miramar, California. The former station is home to Atlantic Fleet elements, which comprise a training outfit (VAW-120, which also has some C-2As), half a dozen deployable squadrons (VAW-121 to VAW-126 inclusive) and a Reserve unit (VAW-78). With the Pacific Fleet, Miramar hosts a similar line-up, this consisting of VAW-110 (training unit), VAW-112 to VAW-117 inclusive (deployable units) and VAW-88 (Reserve unit).

Training unit complements are somewhat larger than their sea-going counterparts, with the latter normally embarking with a total of four aircraft. One of these will be airborne at all times during flight operations and it is usual to use a 'doublecycle' method, whereby the E-2C launches at the start of one wave and stays aloft until it recovers at the end of the next wave. Thus, typical mission duration slightly exceeds three hours.

Carrying a crew of five – consisting of a pilot, co-pilot, combat information center (CIC) officer, air control officer and radar operator – the Hawkeye is capable of performing a variety of tasks. AEW is perhaps the best known and this mission normally requires the Hawkeye to extend the range of the parent carrier's own radar by moving to a position ahead of the battle group. Once there, it usually sets up an orbit at an altitude of around 30,000 ft (9150 m) and employs its own radar to detect potentially hostile sea and air traffic. At that altitude the E-2C is able to observe aircraft at ranges of up to 300 miles (480 km) and the latest APS-148 radar has demonstrated that it

Below: An E-2C Hawkeye in landing configuration hangs apparently motionless above a carrier as it makes its final approach for another 'trap', or arrested landing.

Left: Progressive refinement of the Hawkeye has mainly been concerned with improving the radar sensor. Initial E-2C aircraft relied on APS-125 but this was replaced by APS-138. The current equipment is APS-139, which is to be retrofitted across the entire fleet in order to achieve standardization.

can detect incoming cruise missiles at distances which exceed 160 miles (258 km). Constant communication with the carrier's own CIC staff by means of a secure datalink facility ensures that they are kept fully 'in the picture' with regard to information gathered by the Hawkeye's primary radar sensor.

The E-2C may also be used as a fighter control platform, with the datalink facility allowing it to furnish information on heading, altitude and speed of targets to F-14 Tomcats undertaking combat air patrol duty. Since the datalink is a two-way facility, the E-2C may also receive information from the fighters, allowing the detection range to be extended by F-14s operating at the outer limits of the E-2C's surveillance capability.

Command post activity also comes within the remit of the Hawkeye and is of particular value in assisting attack forces. In much the same way as it relays information to F-14s, the datalink facility can be used to direct a strike package to a rendezvous area and then issue course instructions towards the target. Post-strike activity includes identifying returning aircraft and vectoring them to either a tanker for fuel or directly to the aircraft carrier for recovery. In addition, the CIC personnel will maintain a watch for hostile fighters, alerting TarCAP-assigned Tomcats to their presence so that they may take action to counter any threat that might appear.

Last, but by no means least, the E-2C can also function in the air traffic control task. This may be undertaken to assist controllers on board the carrier by stacking returning aircraft. Alternatively, should the carrier be unable to recover its aircraft for any reason, the Hawkeye can assist by diverting them to a suitable land base – again, this would entail the provision of headings to steer and, almost certainly, altitudes to maintain during the transit.

Although the US Navy is the principal operator of the Hawkeye, a handful of E-2Cs were until recently also active with the US Coast Guard. Obtained from the Navy, these were assigned to Coast Guard Air Wing One and operated from a facility at St Augustine, Florida, in the continuing battle to disrupt drug-smuggling operations in the southeastern corner of the USA. They were mainly tasked with area surveillance, using the radar as a tool to observe air and sea traffic routes and using communications equipment to direct drug interdiction forces to intercept contacts suspected of being engaged in illegal activities. These aircraft have been replaced by the EC-130V.

MISSION PROFILE

Configuration options: The E-2C is configured as an airborne early warning (AEW) aircraft. Two flight crew and three battle management staff are carried. The provision of arrester hook gear allows for aircraft carrier operations.

AEW: Air defense of carrier battle groups is the primary mission of the E-2C, with detection of aircraft and missile threats over land and sea at ranges of up to 300 miles (480 km) possible when operating at 30,000 ft (9100 m). Automatic datalinks pass target information to F-14 Tomcat fighter CAPs.

Battle group management: Surface radar surveillance and automated datalinks enable the E-2C to coordinate the surface warfare operations of USN battle groups.

Strike control: E-2Cs operate as AEW and command platforms in support for USN strike packages penetrating deep into enemy territory, detecting air and other threats. If any friendly aircraft are shot down E-2Cs provide strike rescue coordination, calling in rescue helicopters and strike aircraft to protect downed fliers from capture.

VARIANTS AND SERIALS

E-2C: Developed from earlier versions of the Hawkeye which are no longer in service, the E-2C has been vastly improved since it joined the Fleet in the mid-1970s. Recent deliveries embody a far more sophisticated and capable radar package. Two early E-2A aircraft (148712 and 148713) were modified to serve as prototypes and at least 142 production examples have since been delivered.
158638 to 158648; 159105 to 159112; 159494 to 159502; 160007 to 160012; 160415 to 160420; 160697 to 160703; 160987 to 160992; 161094 to 161099; 161224 to 161229; 161341 to 161346; 161547 to 161552; 161780 to 161785; 162614 to 162619; 162797 to 162802; 163024 to 163029; 163535 to 163540; 163565; 163693 to 163698; 163848 to 163851; 164107 to 164112; 164352 to 164357; 164483 to 164518*; 164621 to 164626 (* = batch 164483 to 164518 not built in entirety)

TE-2C: Both E-2C prototypes and two early production airframes were modified for use as crew trainers. These no longer appear to be in Fleet service, although one has apparently been bailed to Grumman for test duties. 148712; 148713; 158639; 158648

Left: Watched by a deck-edge crewman, a VAW-113 E-2C winds up to full power in preparation for launch, while another Hawkeye with wings still folded trundles towards the catapult. The Hawkeye's size makes it a difficult aircraft to operate from carrier decks, and it is reputed to be the most tricky to land as wingtip clearance is minimal.

Above: AEW assets assigned to the Navy Reserve comprise two squadrons, both of which presently operate the E-2C Hawkeye.

SPECIFICATION

Grumman E-2C

Wing: span 80 ft 7 in (24.56 m); folded width 29 ft 4 in (8.94 m); aspect ratio 9.3; area 700.0 sq ft (65.03 m²)
Fuselage and tail: length 57 ft 6.75 in (17.54 m); height 18 ft 3.75 in (5.58 m); tailplane span 26 ft 2.5 in (7.99 m); wheel base 23 ft 2 in (7.06 m)
Powerplant: two Allison T56-A-425 rated at 4,910 ehp (3661 kW)
Weights: empty 38,063 lb (17265 kg); maximum take-off 51,933 lb (23556 kg)
Fuel and load: internal fuel 12,400 lb (5624 kg)
Speed: maximum level speed 372 mph (598 km/h); maximum cruising speed 358 mph (576 km/h); ferry cruising speed 308 mph (496 km/h)

Above: Responsibility for the training of crews for Pacific Fleet airborne early warning units is entrusted to VAW-110 at Miramar, CA, one of whose E-2Cs is the subject of this fine study. Similar duties are undertaken by VAW-120 at Norfolk, VA, although this squadron is active in support of the Atlantic Fleet which also has half a dozen deployable units.

Range: ferry range 1,605 miles (2583 km); endurance with maximum 6 hours 6 minutes; time of station at 200 mile (322 km) radius between 3 and 4 hours
Performance: service ceiling 30,800 ft (9390 m); minimum take-off run 2,000 ft (610 m); take-off distance to 50 ft (15 m) 2,600 ft (793 m) at maximum take-off weight; minimum landing run 1,440 ft (439 m) at maximum landing weight

OPERATORS

US Navy (USN)

VAW-78	Norfolk, VA	E-2C
VAW-88	Miramar, CA	E-2C
VAW-110	Miramar, CA	E-2C
VAW-112	Miramar, CA	E-2C
VAW-113	Miramar, CA	E-2C
VAW-114	Miramar, CA	E-2C
VAW-115	Atsugi, Japan	E-2C
VAW-116	Miramar, CA	E-2C
VAW-117	Miramar, CA	E-2C
VAW-120	Norfolk, VA	E-2C
VAW-121	Norfolk, VA	E-2C
VAW-122	Norfolk, VA	E-2C
VAW-123	Norfolk, VA	E-2C
VAW-124	Norfolk, VA	E-2C
VAW-125	Norfolk, VA	E-2C
VAW-126	Norfolk, VA	E-2C
NAWC/AD	Patuxent River, MD	E-2C

Left: Until recently, the Coast Guard was also ranked among the E-2C users, operating a small number of Hawkeyes on loan from the Navy. These have now been returned, with surveillance duties likely to pass to the EC-130V Hercules.

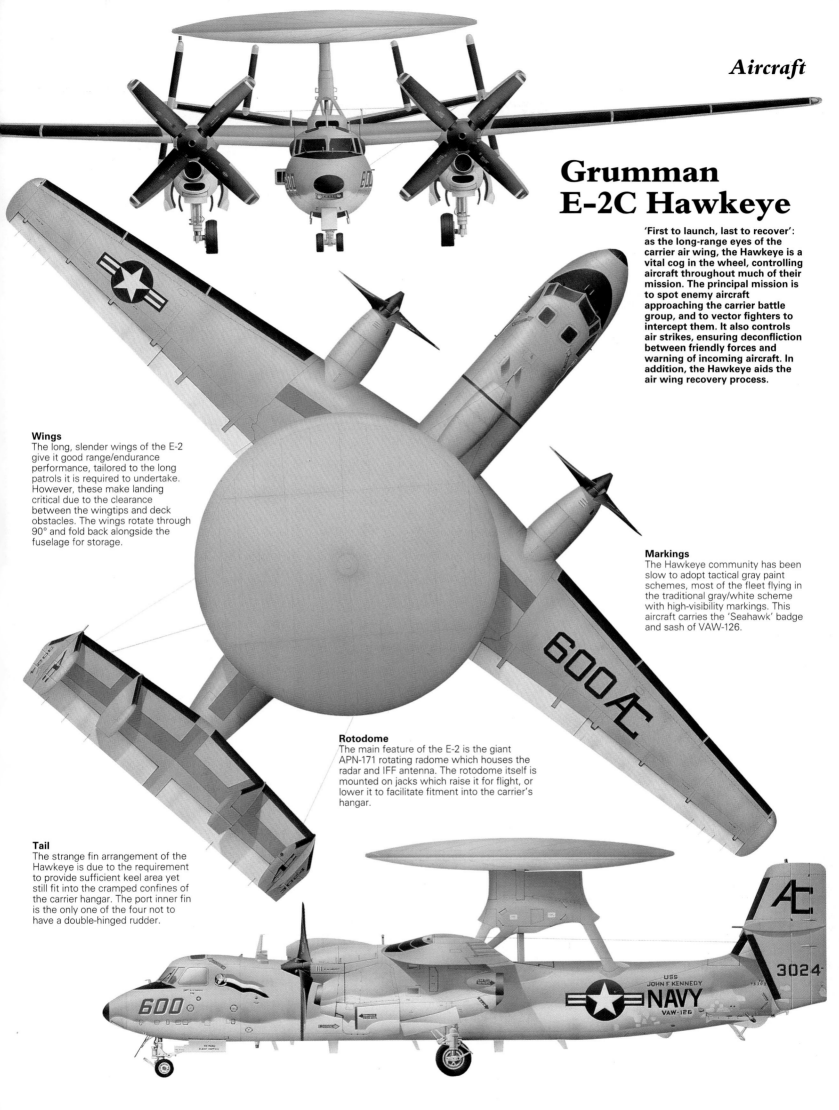

Grumman E-2C Hawkeye

'First to launch, last to recover': as the long-range eyes of the carrier air wing, the Hawkeye is a vital cog in the wheel, controlling aircraft throughout much of their mission. The principal mission is to spot enemy aircraft approaching the carrier battle group, and to vector fighters to intercept them. It also controls air strikes, ensuring deconfliction between friendly forces and warning of incoming aircraft. In addition, the Hawkeye aids the air wing recovery process.

Wings
The long, slender wings of the E-2 give it good range/endurance performance, tailored to the long patrols it is required to undertake. However, these make landing critical due to the clearance between the wingtips and deck obstacles. The wings rotate through 90° and fold back alongside the fuselage for storage.

Markings
The Hawkeye community has been slow to adopt tactical gray paint schemes, most of the fleet flying in the traditional gray/white scheme with high-visibility markings. This aircraft carries the 'Seahawk' badge and sash of VAW-126.

Rotodome
The main feature of the E-2 is the giant APN-171 rotating radome which houses the radar and IFF antenna. The rotodome itself is mounted on jacks which raise it for flight, or lower it to facilitate fitment into the carrier's hangar.

Tail
The strange fin arrangement of the Hawkeye is due to the requirement to provide sufficient keel area yet still fit into the cramped confines of the carrier hangar. The port inner fin is the only one of the four not to have a double-hinged rudder.

Boeing
E-6A Mercury

Specially configured to provide the Navy with a survivable means of communicating with its fleet ballistic missile submarine (SSBN) force, the **Boeing E-6A** TACAMO is essentially a derivative of the hugely successful 707-320 commercial jetliner. The type has benefited from hardening initiatives incorporated on the E-3 Sentry to provide added protection against the EMP (electromagnetic pulse) effects that are encountered in nuclear blasts. Flying for the first time in February 1987, it began to enter service in August 1989. All 16 of the aircraft on order are due to be fully fitted out and in use by 1993.

Development in fact originated with studies at the Naval Air Development Center (NADC) which launched the search for a suitable platform to take over responsibility for the TACAMO mission from the EC-130Q Hercules. NADC attentions soon focused on a version of the 707-320 which seemed to offer sufficient space and payload capacity for the sophisticated communications equipment, while at the same time providing a far more comfortable working environment for crew members. By 1984, the project had progressed sufficiently far to warrant the issue of a contract covering the first two aircraft, both of which were intimately involved in service trials with the Naval Air Test Center and development squadron VX-1 from Patuxent River, Maryland, during 1987-89.

Powered by four General Electric-SNECMA F108-CF-100 high bypass ratio turbofans, the E-6A inherited most of the major components of its communications suite from the EC-130Qs that it was to replace. Part of the deployment planning was based upon the need to remove this equipment from the

Hercules and then instal it in the E-6A.

Elements of the package include AN/USC-13 very low frequency transmit/receive equipment and an AN/USC-14 communications center, plus two trailing wire antennas which on the E-6A are located in the extreme tail cone and beneath the center fuselage section. Special flight profiles are required when these antennas are deployed, possibly comparable to those of the Hercules, which is understood to have flown a fairly tight circular pattern so as to allow the trailing antenna (which is reportedly more than 6 miles/10 km long) to hang vertically.

If, as seems likely, a similar profile is used by the E-6A, this could well have been responsible for two instances of vertical tail surface failure which resulted in operations being curtailed during the spring of 1990. Subsequent in-

vestigation and testing by Boeing seems to have resulted in a satisfactory 'fix' for this problem.

Specialized electronic equipment of an as-yet unspecified nature is housed in a pair of wingtip pods. The E-6A is also compatible with the 'flying boom' method of aerial refueling, allowing it to remain on station for extended periods of time. The latter is particularly valuable since the TACAMO mission is thought to require at least one aircraft of each squadron to be airborne at any given time. In normal operation the E-6A carries a crew of 18

Below: Trailing a pair of antennas associated with the very low frequency communications gear used for contacting SSBNs, an early production example of the E-6A cruises serenely along. Two Navy squadrons are equipped with the E-6A, so as to cover the Atlantic and Pacific Oceans.

Boeing E-6A Hermes
TACAMO II

- Wingtip-mounted General Instruments AN/ALR-66(V)4 ESM and SatCom pods with HF communications antennas
- All electronic systems EMP hardened
- Three Collins AN/ARC-182 VHF/UHF transceivers and five Collins AN/ARC-190 HF coms
- VLF STWA (Short Trailing Wire Antenna) 4000 ft (1220 m) in length
- VLF (Very Low Frequency) LTWA (Long Trailing Wire Antenna) 26,000 ft (7925 m) in length
- TWAs transmit signals to fleet SSBNs (ballistic missile submarines) with 200 kW of power
- Bendix/King AN/APS-133 color weather radar with limited terrain-mapping capability
- Four-man flight deck with rest area
- Four 24,000-lb (106-kN) CFM International F108-CF-100 turbofans
- Forward freight door retained
- Inflight-refueling receptacle
- Specially developed Bendix/King AFCS (Automated Flight Control System)
- Crew access ladder under nose
- Triplex Litton LTN-90 laser gyro navigation system with VLF/Omega
- 600-kVa electrical power generator
- Increased corrosion protection; fuselage strengthened to alleviate stress caused by banked orbit when trailing wire antenna is deployed
- Main mission compartment with five operations consoles

personnel, eight of whom are relief members; this, too, will ease the workload of long missions.

Training of personnel was accomplished on standard 707-320s and was undertaken in such a way as to eliminate the need for a stand-down while transition took place. Thus, operational sorties continued to be flown on the EC-130Q until such time as the E-6A could take over responsibility. As noted elsewhere, deliveries to the fleet began in August 1989. The E-6A is eventually to be flown by two units, these, perhaps confusingly, referred to as Fleet Air Reconnaissance Squadrons even though they do not actually engage in reconnaissance duties.

VQ-3 at Barbers Point, Hawaii, was the first squadron to enter the process of conversion from the EC-130Q, and it is now understood to be fully operational with a fleet of eight E-6As. Elsewhere, its East Coast counterpart – VQ-4 at Patuxent River, Maryland – began receiving its new equipment in 1990 but is not expected to complete the transition process until some time in 1993. Again, when fully up to strength, it should eventually have a complement of eight aircraft.

MISSION PROFILE

Configuration options: Hardened trailing wire AVLF radio equipment is carried by the E-6A to enable its 18-man crew to communicate with ballistic missile-firing submarines in a post-nuclear strike environment. Aerial refueling and the carrying of relief aircrew allows the aircraft to stay on-station for up to 72 hours.

Strategic command/communications: While the wartime mission is the main rationale for the E-6A's procurement, they have a secondary mission of providing backup VLF communications to submarine and surface units in parts of the world out of range of shore-based VLF transmitters. When the USAF retires its EC-135 Silk Purse aircraft, E-6As will take over their alternate command post mission for the new US Strategic Command.

VARIANTS AND SERIALS

E-6A: Based on the Boeing 707 commercial jetliner, the E-6A has replaced the EC-130Q in the SSBN

Above: The wingtip pods fitted to the E-6A are clearly visible in this view but no details are available as to what these contain, nor of what their precise purpose is.

communications role and embodies much of the specialized equipment that was fitted to the Hercules for this role. A total of 16 examples has been obtained. 162782 to 162784; 163918 to 163920; 164386 to 164388; 164404 to 164410

SPECIFICATION

Boeing E-6A
Wing: span 148 ft 2 in (45.16 m); area 2,050.0 sq ft (283.35 m^2)
Fuselage and tail: length 152 ft 11 in (46.61 m); height 42 ft 5 in (12.93 m); tailplane span 45 ft 9 in (13.95 m); wheel base 57 ft 0 in (17.98 m)
Powerplant: four CFM International F108-CF-100 (CFM56-2A-2) rated at 22,000 lb (97.9 kN) dry thrust
Weights: operating empty 172,795 lb (78378 kg); maximum take-off 342,000 lb (155128 kg)
Fuel and load: internal fuel 155,000 lb (70305 kg)
Speed: dash speed 610 mph (981 km/h); maximum cruising speed at 40,000 ft (12190 m) 523 mph (842 km/h)
Range: mission range without aerial refueling 7,307 miles (11760 km); unrefueled endurance 15 hours 24 minutes; on-station endurance at 1,150-mile (1850-km) radius 10 hours 30 minutes without aerial refueling, or 28 hours 54 minutes with one aerial refueling, or 72 hours 0 minutes with multiple aerial refuelings
Performance: service ceiling 42,000 ft (12800 m); patrol altitude between 25,000 and 30,000 ft (7620 and 9145 m); maximum effort take-off distance 5,400 ft (1646 m); maximum effort take-off run with fuel for 2,875 miles (4630 km) 2,400 ft (732 m); landing distance 2,600 ft (793 m) at maximum landing weight

OPERATORS

US Navy (USN)

VQ-3	Barbers Point, HI	E-6A
VQ-4	Patuxent River, MD	E-6A

Left: Seen at its Seattle birthplace, the first of 16 E-6As is towed to the flight line during the course of trials with Boeing. Deliveries of these aircraft began in August 1989 to VQ-3 at Barbers Point, while VQ-4 at Patuxent River got its first example in 1990.

McDonnell Douglas

F-4 Phantom II

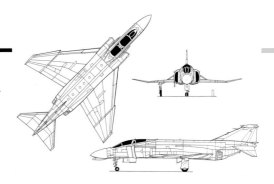

Approximately 1,250 examples of the **Phantom** were produced for service with both the Navy and Marine Corps, and it was for many years the principal fighter with both of these organizations. Today, however, it has long since disappeared from front-line service. A few aircraft are still active with one Marine Corps Reserve fighter-attack squadron and others are to be seen on the charge of test agencies in fairly limited quantities.

Development was initiated by McDonnell during the course of 1953, but the gestation period was fairly protracted by the standards of the day and it was not until May 1958 that the first of two prototype **XF4H-1**s (later **XF-4A**s) got airborne. Three years of development testing followed, paving the way for production copies of the **F4H-1F** (**F-4A**) to join the Navy in June 1961. This model was never deployed operationally and the first true combat-ready Phantom was the **F4H-1** (**F-4B**), which had more powerful J79-GE-8A engines, a modified cockpit canopy and AN/APQ-72 radar. This was the first version to join the Marine Corps, which began receiving Phantoms about a year after the Navy, at roughly the same time that US Air Force interest culminated in major orders.

Subsequent developments for the Navy and Marine Corps resulted in the appearance of the **F-4J**, which had a new radar and additional thrust as well as slatted tailplanes, larger mainwheels and extra fuel cells, among other refinements. The only other new-build model to be procured was the **RF-4B**. Beginning life as the **F4H-1P**, this was a dedicated photo-reconnaissance derivative which was unique to the Marines, and which remained in use until quite recently.

Although no more new aircraft were obtained, the two services did make extensive use of the **F-4N** and the **F-4S**, versions which arose from a CILOP program intended to enhance capability and extend service life throughout the latter half of the 1970s and into the 1980s. The F-4N was the first to appear and was basically an updated F-4B, some 228 examples being so modified. They were followed by just over 260 examples of the F-4S, fundamentally a revamped F-4J with maneuvering slats and other improvements. Update initiatives also extended to the RF-4B but were mostly concerned with the sensor fit and did not warrant redesignation.

Today, even the F-4S has been retired from squadron service with VMFA-112, a Dallas-based Marine Reserve fighter-attack outfit, presently acquiring F/A-18 Hornets. Normal peacetime flying training is predicated upon Marine Corps doctrine of supporting ground forces. Another squadron – VMFA-321 at Andrews, Washington – also utilized the F-4S until the summer of 1991, when they were disposed of in anticipation of obtaining the Hornet at the beginning of 1992.

As far as research and development organizations are concerned, the Pacific Missile Test Center at Point Mugu, California, still featured two examples of the F-4S in its assorted fleet as recently as summer 1991.

Other than that, the only Phantoms that still fly regularly with the Navy are the **QF-4N** drones which are instantly recognizable by virtue of featuring a vivid red colour scheme. Conversion to this configuration for live missile trials is continuing and a substantial number of redundant F-4Ns are held in storage at China Lake, California, in order to support drone operations for the foreseeable future. QF-4Ns are currently used by the NAWC Weapons Divisions at Point Mugu and at China Lake.

MISSION PROFILE

The US Navy's surviving Phantoms are now used only as drones or chase aircraft.

VARIANTS AND SERIALS

QF-4N: Capable of being flown remotely, the QF-4N is a drone target conversion of the F-4N Phantom II that is used for trials of air-to-air missile systems. At least 31 aircraft have been modified for this task but other F-4Ns are presently held in storage at China Lake until such time as they are required.
Already converted: 150419; 150432; 150456; 150464; 150475; 150630; 150993; 151406; 151415; 151463; 151465; 151469; 151476; 151484; 151503; 152214; 152226; 152235; 152246; 152253; 152269; 152272; 152277; 152282; 152303; 152968; 153034; 153056; 153059; 153065; 153914
In store awaiting conversion: 150412; 150415; 150423; 150489; 151002; 151004; 151007; 151430; 151435; 151440; 151449; 151455; 151461; 151471; 151475; 152217; 152221; 152222; 152223; 152229; 152230; 152243; 152258; 152279; 152281; 152323; 152326; 153011; 153030; 153053; 153064

F-4S: A total of 265 F-4Js was converted to F-4S configuration, modification work including fitment of updated avionics systems and maneuvering slats. All have now been consigned to storage but the following examples were recently reported in service.
153792; 153809; 153814; 153823; 153833; 153851; 153860; 153882; 153884; 153887; 153904; 153911; 155524; 155527; 155561; 155573; 155580; 155740; 155741; 155759; 155829; 155834; 155847; 155864; 155878; 155900; 157261; 157293; 158360

SPECIFICATION

McDonnell Douglas F-4S
Wing: span 38 ft 7.5 in (11.77 m); width folded 27 ft 7 in (8.41 m); aspect ratio 2.82; area 530.0 sq ft (49.24 m²)
Fuselage and tail: length 58 ft 4 in (17.78 m); height 16 ft 5.5 in (5.02 m); tailplane span 17 ft 11.5 in (5.47 m); wheel base 23 ft 4.5 in (7.12 m)
Powerplant: two General Electric J79-GE-10B rated at 11,870 lb (52.7 kN) military and 17,900 lb (79.48 kN) afterburning thrusts
Weights: empty about 28,000 lb (12701 kg); maximum take-off 62,390 lb (28300 kg)
Fuel and load: internal fuel 2,000 US gal (7569 liters); external fuel up to one 600-US gal (2271-liter) and two 370-US gal (1401-liter) drop tanks; maximum ordnance about 16,000 lb (7258 kg)
Speed: maximum level speed 'clean' at 40,000 ft (12190 m) 1,470 mph (2360 km/h); cruising speed at maximum take-off weight 571 mph (919 km/h)
Range: ferry range with drop tanks 2,300 miles (3701 km); radius with four AIM-7 Sparrows, four AIM-9 Sidewinders, six 500-lb (227-kg) bombs and one 600-US gal (2271-liter) drop tank 263 miles (423 km), or with four AIM-7 Sparrows and eight 1,000-lb (454-kg) bombs 157 miles (253 km), or with five 1,000-lb (454-kg) bombs and two 370-US gal (1401-liter) drop tanks 385 miles (620 km)
Performance: maximum rate of climb at sea level about 28,000 ft (8534 m) per minute; service ceiling 61,000 ft (18590 m)

McDonnell Douglas QF-4N
generally similar to the F-4S except in the following particulars:
Fuselage and tail: height 16 ft 3 in (4.95 m)
Powerplant: two General Electric J79-GE-8 rated at 10,900 lb (48.5 kN) military and 17,000 lb (75.6 kN) afterburning thrusts
Weights: (F-4B) 28,000 lb (12701 kg); normal take-off 44,600 lb (20230 kg)
Speed: maximum level speed 'clean' at 48,000 ft (14630 m) 1,485 mph (2390 km/h)
Range: typical radius 400 miles (644 km)

OPERATORS

US Navy (USN)

NAWC/WD	China Lake, CA	QF-4N
NAWC/WD	Point Mugu, CA	QF-4N

Below: Once the backbone of the Fleet fighter force, the Phantom has now all but disappeared from the scene and remains active only in QF-4N guise as a pilotless target drone.

Northrop
F-5 Tiger II

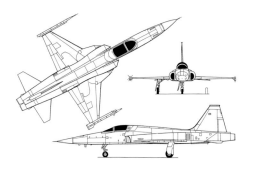

Evolved from the F-5A Freedom Fighter as a private venture, the **Northrop F-5E Tiger II** represented a significant improvement in terms of performance and capability when it was eventually ordered into quantity production for supply to friendly nations in December 1970, after emerging victorious in the International Fighter Aircraft competition. Among the new features were more powerful General Electric J85-GE-21 afterburning turbojet engines, full-span leading-edge maneuvering flaps, leading edge extensions, an integrated fire control system and greater internal fuel capacity.

The initial production example made its maiden flight on 11 August 1972. Deliveries to friendly air arms got under way the following year, early customers in what eventually grew to be a long list of recipients including Thailand, South Vietnam and South Korea. Later, the type was also selected to equip a small number of US Air Force aggressor training units, functioning in that role until replaced by the F-16 Fighting Falcon in the late 1980s.

US Navy operation of the Tiger II has also been confined to aggressor outfits and began in the mid-1970s when an initial batch of five former Vietnamese examples was obtained for service with the Naval Fighter Weapons School (NFWS, alias 'Top Gun') at Miramar. This unit received five more F-5Es fairly soon afterwards, as well as a trio of **F-5F** two-seaters for pilot conversion and proficiency duties in about 1977. More recently, the availability of surplus USAF F-5Es resulted in approximately two dozen examples being transferred to the Navy and Marine Corps. The combined current Tiger II fleet is just under three dozen strong, including the three F-5Fs.

The Miramar-based NFWS no longer operates the Tiger II, but the type does still make an important contribution to the task of teaching air combat doctrine with four units. Two are located on the East Coast in support of Atlantic Fleet elements, these comprising VF-43 'Challengers' at Oceana, Virginia, and VF-45 'Blackbirds' at Key West, Florida. In both cases, the Northrop machine is operated alongside other types like the General Dynamics F-16N Fighting Falcon and the McDonnell Douglas A-4 Skyhawk, with each of these two squadrons usually having about four F-5E single-seaters and one F-5F two-seater on charge.

The other F-5 unit is stationed in the western USA and has more Tiger IIs assigned, using about a dozen examples.

The specialist Marines unit VMFT-401 'Snipers' was formed as the service's sole DACT outfit in the latter half of the 1980s. Initially, this flew leased IAI F-21A Kfirs but these were returned to Israel in 1989 when VMFT-401 converted to the F-5E, its dozen or so single-seat Tiger IIs being augmented by one F-5F. As with the Navy, DACT support extends to virtually all USMC fighter and attack units since these routinely visit VMFT-401's home base at Yuma, Arizona, in

order to use the extensive range facilities that are located nearby, facilities that extend to a fully instrumented air combat range. In addition, VMFT-401's services are regularly employed by the 'Sharpshooters' of VMFAT-101. The latter squadron often operates from Yuma and functions as a fleet replenishment squadron for Marine Corps F/A-18 Hornet-equipped fighter-attack units – in consequence, the training syllabus devotes some attention to the art of air-to-air combat, normal Tiger II 'rig' when using the range consisting of an inert Sidewinder acquisition round and an Air Combat Maneuvering Instrumentation pod.

The US Navy's VFA-127 'Cylons' at Fallon has now traded its F-5Es for early model F/A-18s which it uses to provide dissimilar air combat training to Pacific Fleet carrier air wings using the Fallon ranges.

MISSION PROFILE

The F-5E is used only as an adversary aircraft, flying profiles designed to simulate the MiG-17 and MiG-21, and other lightweight maneuverable threat aircraft. Inert missile acquisition rounds and ACMI/TACTS pods are sometimes carried on the wingtips.

VARIANTS AND SERIALS

F-5E: Acquisition of Northrop's Tiger II began with an initial batch of five aircraft for service with the Fighter Weapons School and others followed in due course as the aggressor training program expanded. More recently, a number of former USAF F-5Es have been added to the aggressor fleet.
159878 to 159882; 160792 to 160796; 162307; 721387; 730855; 730879; 730881; 730885; 731635; 741519; 741528 to 741531; 741537; 741539 to 741541; 741544; 741545; 741547; 741554; 741556; 741563; 741568; 741570; 741572

F-5F: Three examples of the two-seat derivative of the Tiger II were obtained for transition training with aggressor outfits.
160964 to 160966

Below: After operating the IAI F-21A Kfir for a few years, the Marine Corps aggressor outfit at Yuma was re-equipped with the F-5E Tiger II in the course of 1989. VMFT-401 also includes one example of the two-seat F-5F model in its fleet.

Bottom: Single- and two-seat examples of the F-5 Tiger II are assigned to VF-43 at Oceana, both sub-types being portrayed here. Data relay pods are carried by these two aircraft.

Above: Resident at Fallon, NV, the 'Cylons' of VFA-127 also operated the F-5E and F-5F. This is one of the latter, which was mostly employed for transition training and check rides.

SPECIFICATION

Northrop F-5E
Wing: span over missile rails 26 ft 8 in (8.13 m) and over wingtip missiles 27 ft 11.875 in (8.53 m); aspect ratio 3.82; area 186.0 sq ft (17.28 m²)
Fuselage and tail: length 48 ft 3.75 in (14.73 m); height 13 ft 4.5 in (4.08 m); tailplane span 14 ft 1.5 in (4.31 m); wheel base 16 ft 11.5 in (5.17 m)
Powerplant: two General Electric J85-GE-21B rated at 3,500 lb (15.5 kN) military and 5,000 lb (22.2 kN) afterburning thrusts
Weights: empty 9,558 lb (4349 kg); maximum take-off 24,664 lb (11187 kg)
Fuel and load: internal fuel 677 US gal (2563 liters); external fuel up to three 275-US gal (1040-liter) drop tanks; maximum ordnance 7,000 lb (3175 kg)
Speed: maximum level speed 'clean' at 36,000 ft (10975 m) 1056 mph (1700 km/h); cruising speed at 36,000 ft (10975 m) 647 mph (1041 km/h)
Range: ferry range 2,314 miles (3720 km) with empty tanks dropped or 1,974 miles (3175 km) with empty tanks retained; combat radius with two AIM-9 Sidewinders 875 miles (1405 km)
Performance: maximum rate of climb at sea level 34,300 ft (10455 m) per minute; service ceiling 51,800 ft (15590 m); take-off run 2,000 ft (610 m); take-off distance to 50 ft (15 m) 2,800 ft (853 m) at normal interception take-off weight; landing run 2,450 ft (747 m) with braking parachute; landing distance from 50 ft (15 m) 3,900 ft (1189 m) at 11,340-lb (5143-kg) weight

Northrop F-5F
generally similar to the F-5E except in the following particulars:
Fuselage and tail: length 51 ft 7 in (15.72 m); height 13 ft 1.75 in (4.01 m)
Weights: empty 10,567 lb (4793 kg); maximum take-off 25,147 lb (11406 kg)
Speed: maximum level speed 'clean' at 36,090 ft (11000 m) 1,030 mph (1658 km/h)
Range: ferry range 1,462 miles (2353 km); combat radius with two AIM-9 Sidewinders and two 530-lb (240-kg) bombs 518 miles (834 km)
Performance: maximum rate of climb at sea level 32,700 ft (9966 m) per minute; service ceiling 50,800 ft (15485 m); take-off run 2,200 ft (671 m); take-off distance to 50 ft (15 m) 3,200 ft (975 m) at normal interception take-off weight; landing run 2,600 ft (792 m) with braking parachute; landing distance from 50 ft (15 m) 5,000 ft (1524 m) at 12,245-lb (5544-kg) weight

OPERATORS

US Navy (USN)

VF-43	Oceana, VA	F-5E, F-5F
VF-45	Key West, FL	F-5E, F-5F

US Marine Corps (USMC)

VMFT-401	Yuma, AZ	F-5E, F-5F

Northrop F-5E Tiger II

Looking for a high-performing yet small and nimble aircraft to simulate supersonic fighters such as the MiG-21, the US Navy chose the F-5E for its adversary units to augment the subsonic A-4 Skyhawk. Although the F-5 is still outnumbered by the A-4, and overshadowed by more recent adversary types such as the F-14, F-16 and F/A-18, it still plays an important part in the instruction of air combat to Naval and Marine aviators.

Wing roots
A distinctive feature of the F-5E is the extended root fillet next to the engine intake. This vastly improves airflow at high angles of attack.

Markings
Navy adversary aircraft wear a massive variety of camouflage schemes to represent different threat aircraft, this F-5 displaying a fairly muted three-tone air defense scheme. The traditional aggressor's red star on the fin signifies VF-126, which no longer flies the type. Note the Soviet-style two-digit code.

Missile rails
This aircraft is depicted carrying two blue Sidewinder training rounds. A more normal DACT load is one Sidewinder acquisition round and one AIS pod.

Powerplant
Thrust for the lightweight fighter comes from a pair of General Electric J85-GE-21B turbojets, each rated at 3,500 lb (15 kN) thrust dry and 5,000 lb (22 kN) thrust with afterburning.

Radar
A small radar (APQ-153) is mounted in the nose to provide search and ranging information. Behind it are the barrels for the two Pontiac M39 20-mm cannon.

Service
Three US Navy units continue to operate the Tiger II, these being VF-43 at Oceana, VF-45 at Key West and VFA-127 at Fallon. The single Marine adversary unit, VMFT-401, is totally equipped with the type.

Grumman
F-14 Tomcat

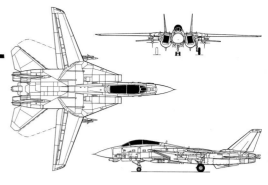

Entering service with training squadron VF-124 almost 20 years ago, **Grumman's F-14 Tomcat** is still the Navy's premier fleet fighter and seems set to remain so for a good few years yet. Currently operating in three basic versions with 22 deployable front-line squadrons, two training units and four second-line outfits of the Navy Reserve, the Tomcat is more familiarly known as the 'Turkey', but this unflattering epithet – an allusion to its ungainly appearance when configured for landing – is not intended as a slur on its capability since the F-14 is able to engage and destroy targets at ranges that vary from just a few hundred feet to more than 100 miles. That capability has existed from the outset and is still unique by virtue of being unmatched by any of its contemporaries or, for that matter, by newer generations of fighter.

The F-14's mission is fundamentally that of conducting air-to-air operations of both an offensive and defensive nature by day or night so as to secure local air superiority and, in the process, provide effective protection of fleet assets. That objective may be accomplished in a variety of ways but the classic application entails mounting combat air patrols (CAPs) at considerable distance from the parent carrier.

Working in concert with the E-2C Hawkeye airborne early warning radar 'picket' and fighter control platform, F-14s establish a defensive screen or 'barrier' well beyond the outer perimeter of that portion of sea that is occupied by the battle group, hence the term 'Barrier CAP' (BarCAP). Anything attempting to cross that unseen line, which is typically some 300 to 400 miles (480 to 650 km) from the

carrier, will be intercepted and, if necessary, engaged, preferably at distances well beyond visual range.

Current tactical doctrine requires F-14s to operate in pairs and since each carrier routinely deploys with two Tomcat squadrons (20 or 24 aircraft) it follows that several pairs may be airborne at any given time, with these normally being positioned along the perceived threat axis. Ideally, an engagement will be initiated at the moment that is most advantageous to a Tomcat pair, one F-14 being a 'shooter' and the other providing mutual support. However, such is the nature of the air battle that the 'lead' can quickly shift and it is not unknown for F-14 pairs to split and pursue individual targets in instances where opposition formation 'integrity' has broken down.

Other kinds of CAP mission can be undertaken. These include the so-called 'Force CAP' (ForCAP) and 'Target CAP' (TarCAP). The former relates to the provision of interceptor air cover for a task force whereby F-14s patrol an inner zone that is much closer to the carrier and its associated battle group. This is, perhaps, less effective than BarCAP and probably stems mainly from peacetime requirements and the need to avoid potentially provocative airspace violations when operating in confined waters such as parts of the Gulf during Desert Shield. TarCAPs, which were widely undertaken during Desert Storm, entails the escort of strike aircraft packages heading for targets located in hostile airspace. As with BarCAP, both of these missions utilize the pair as the basic tactical formation.

While mainly known for its capabilities as an interceptor, the Tomcat is able to perform other missions. One such mission is reconnaissance, it being usual for one of the two Tomcat squadrons within a carrier air wing to employ a small number of aircraft – usually

three – which are compatible with the TARPS (Tactical Air Reconnaissance Pod System) sensor package. Controls for TARPS are sited in the RIO's (Radar Intercept Officer's) cockpit and the pod itself contains a KS-87 frame camera, a KA-99 panoramic camera and an AAD-5 infra-red line-scanner.

Additionally, all versions of the Tomcat are theoretically capable of functioning as 'mudmovers', although the latent air-to-ground capability of the **F-14A** has never been employed by operational units. The advent of the **F-14B** (formerly **F-14A+**) and the **F-14D** has brought about significant change, since they do incorporate software for air-ground weapons delivery. As a consequence, the limited number of squadrons that are equipped with these versions do now train for this role, although there is no evidence of Tomcats being used as 'bombers' during the Gulf War.

Three basic versions have been developed for service with the US Navy. First was the F-14A, the 557 examples built for the Navy making it by far the most numerous sub-type. This model was introduced to Fleet service by VF-1 and VF-2 in September 1974 when these two squadrons deployed to the Western Pacific aboard the USS *Enterprise*. That maiden cruise also included the F-14's combat debut, for

Below: With its afterburners burning bright and evening sunlight glinting on the nose section, a Tomcat of VF-114 gets airborne from the USS Lincoln in spectacular style.

Aircraft

F-14 Tomcat (continued)

some Tomcats were tasked with provision of top cover during the evacuation of Saigon in April 1975.

At peak strength, attained in 1987, the F-14A operated with a total of 30 fighter squadrons. These were distributed equally between the Atlantic and Pacific Fleets, with the 15 squadrons allocated to each Fleet comprising 12 front-line deployable units in six carrier air wings (CVWs), a pair of second-line squadrons assigned to a Reserve CVW and a fleet replenishment squadron (FRS).

That level was maintained only briefly, with two Pacific Fleet squadrons (VF-191 and -194) being disestablished in April 1988. Towards the end of that same year, the F-14B began to enter service with the Atlantic Fleet FRS (VF-101), paving the way for this version to reach operational elements in 1989. Today, four Atlantic Fleet squadrons (VF-74, -103, -142 and -143) use the F-14B. New-build machines account for 38 aircraft, with a further 32 being 'produced' by means of modification of existing F-14As.

The most recent version is the F-14D, with deliveries to the West Coast FRS (VF-124) starting in November 1990. The first two operational squadrons (VF-11 and -31) began converting from F-14As in the spring of 1991. At one time, it looked as though the F-14D would become the definitive Tomcat, since Navy procurement plans anticipated the remanufacture of more than 400 F-14As. That idea has now been abandoned and the rebuild effort may involve no more than 18 airframes. In conjunction with 37 new examples, this will give the Navy sufficient F-14Ds for a small training element and no more than four front-line squadrons, all of which are earmarked for the Pacific Fleet.

At the heart of the Tomcat's capability as an interceptor is the Hughes AWG-9 weapon control system, a package that ties together sensors such as radar and a television camera system (TCS) as well as displays, secure datalink facilities and computers to process all of the relevant data. A key element of this is, of course, the planar-array radar scanner. This is a multimode system with a range of about 150 miles (240 km) and the ability to display information on a total of 24 targets to the RIO in the rear cockpit. Computers associated with the system are able to prioritize targets on a closure-rate basis with cues on the displays alerting the RIO to those which pose the most serious threat. In

addition, it can also assign weapons to targets and advise the crew of the optimum moment to launch those weapons.

It is one of those weapons that gives Tomcat its capacity to engage targets at extreme range, but the F-14's arsenal also includes short- and medium-range missiles as well as a single Vulcan M61A1 20-mm cannon. 'Mixing-and-matching' allows the F-14 to be configured to counter threats across the entire spectrum, with a typical 'BarCAP' missile combination consisting of four Phoenix, two Sparrows and two Sidewinders.

The premier weapon is the Hughes AIM-54 Phoenix, which has demonstrated the ability to seek out and destroy multiple targets at extreme ranges on several occasions, although it has never been fired in anger. Like its parent aircraft, Phoenix has been improved over the years and the current AIM-54C model features solid-state technology as well as a more powerful rocket motor and an improved warhead and fuzing system. In this form, it can cope with virtually all types of target likely to be encountered, including high- and low-flying bombers and cruise missiles.

For medium-range engagements, Tomcat has relied on the AIM-7 Sparrow, a semi-active radar-homing missile which, in its current AIM-7M version, is an improvement over earlier models. It does, nevertheless, have the drawback of requiring the target to be continuously 'illuminated' by radar as it homes in. This shortcoming should be overcome by a new medium-range 'fire-and-forget' missile. This is the AIM-120A, but it has suffered more than its fair share of developmental problems which in turn have brought about lengthy delays – when it reaches the Fleet, though, it will permit multiple targets to be engaged.

Best-known and most deadly of the current weapons is the trusty Sidewinder. This has demonstrated its effectiveness on several occasions over the past decade and was widely used during the recent Gulf conflict. The AIM-9M

Above: Contrasting low- and high-visibility unit markings are evident on this pair of Tomcats of VF-1 aboard the USS Ranger during the course of operations to liberate Kuwait.

model is now the major version used by the Tomcat but work on a new solid-state version (the AIM-9R) with an improved seeker head and a longer-range rocket motor is forging ahead.

Returning to the radar, in the case of long-range engagements with Phoenix it operates in a pulse-Doppler mode, while for medium-range encounters with Sparrow it uses a conventional pulse mode which satisfies this weapon's need for a target to be continuously 'painted' if it is to home accurately.

Additional AWG-9 functions include navigation, gun direction and air-to-ground weapons delivery, although, as noted earlier, the latter facility was never employed by the F-14A.

If the avionics systems were good – and there is every indication that they were rather

Above: One of the most eye-catching Tomcats in Navy service must surely be the all-black F-14A which flies with VX-4 from Point Mugu.

more than that – the situation regarding Tomcat's powerplant was much less satisfactory and it was specifically to address failings in this area that newer models evolved.

Throughout the F-14A's operational career, there has been grave concern over the Pratt & Whitney TF30 turbofan. Efforts at eradicating the more serious problems culminated in adoption of the TF30-P-414A which now powers all remaining F-14As. It is, nevertheless, still far from ideal, since pilots have to exercise care when manipulating the throttles so as to avoid bringing about a compressor stall and, possibly, a departure from controlled flight.

Attempts at finding a new engine in fact date back to the earliest days but have only recently borne fruit, with the General Electric F110-GE-400 being selected to power both the F-14B and the F-14D. Not only does this offer considerable thrust benefits in both the 'wet'

Below: One of the Tomcat's principal weapons is the AIM-54 Phoenix, shown here on launch from a VF-211 machine. Thus far, it has never been put to the test in combat, but has demonstrated its potential in realistic trials.

Above: Deck crew on the USS Nimitz look on as a Tomcat of VF-84 powers its way down the flight deck at the start of a mission during routine peacetime operations with the 6th Fleet.

(afterburning) and 'dry' (non-afterburning) regimes, but it is also highly resistant to compressor stall and has the advantage of allowing 'carefree' power management throughout the engine envelope. That, in turn, permits the Tomcat pilot to handle his machine more confidently and aggressively, especially in a close-in and furious combat situation.

In the case of the F-14D, improvement initiatives went far beyond the addition of a new engine, for this model also has a new suite of avionics, embodying all-digital technology. At the core is the Hughes APG-71 radar which offers enhanced detection and tracking range as well as a greater degree of 'hardening' against hostile ECM. Upgraded jammers and threat warning systems are also provided, along with JTIDS and dual TCS/Infra-Red Search-and-Track (IRST) sensor capability.

As far as combat opportunities are concerned, the Tomcat has had its fair share of exciting moments during the past decade and has also emerged victorious in the few instances where it has been called upon to employ weapons 'for real'. The first such chance came in August 1981 and was eagerly seized by the crews of two VF-41 Tomcats which used AIM-9L Sidewinders to each destroy a Libyan Su-22 'Fitter-J' in a brief but decisive engagement over the Gulf of Sidra.

Even more remarkable was the October 1985 incident in which Tomcats of VF-74 and VF-103 launched from the USS *Saratoga* to intercept an EgyptAir Boeing 737 which was known to be carrying the four Arab terrorists who were responsible for seizing the Italian cruise liner *Achille Lauro*. Accomplished under cover of darkness and in strict radio silence, the intercept was superbly executed and the 737 was subsequently escorted to Sigonella, Sicily, where local Italian authorities arrested those on board.

Further disagreements with Libya saw F-14s claim more victims. The Tomcat was also in the air when American F-111s and carrierborne strike aircraft bombed a number of Libyan facilities in Operation El Dorado Canyon, but the most recent opportunity to seek combat came during the Gulf War. The F-14D arrived too late to play a part in that conflict but the F-14A was certainly present and in the thick of

Right: Sparrow and Sidewinder guided missiles provide the 'bite' of this TARPS-toting Tomcat of VF-32 during Desert Storm. Phoenix is not carried and one of the stores stations has been taken by an ALQ-167 ECM pod.

things, seeing combat with eight squadrons (VF-1, -2, -14, -32, -33, -41, -84 and -102) aboard four carriers. There were also two F-14B squadrons (VF-74 and -103) on another 'flat-top', both of which saw action. As already noted, operations were primarily of an escort nature, offering little or no opportunity to tangle with Iraqi fighters, much to the chagrin of the Navy pilots who were forced to watch their Air Force counterparts compile a fairly impressive tally.

As far as Desert Storm is concerned, the memories of one crew from VF-103 must have been mixed, since they were unfortunate enough to fly the only Tomcat to be lost during the war. This incident occurred on 21 January 1991, when their F-14B was reportedly struck by an SA-2 'Guideline' missile during a reconnaissance mission. Happily, both crew members survived, but their paths diverged for a while. Pilot Lieutenant Devon Jones was picked up by helicopter and soon returned to the fray while his 'back-seater', Lieutenant Laurence Slade, was taken prisoner and endured several weeks of captivity before being released with other POWs.

On a more positive note, that loss was to some extent offset by the destruction of an Iraqi helicopter on 6 February 1991. Using a single AIM-9 Sidewinder heat-seeking missile, Lieutenant Stuart Broce and Commander Ron McElraft of VF-1 shot down an Mi-8, the incident turning out to be one of only three aerial victories claimed by the Navy throughout the war.

MISSION PROFILE

Armament options: While the F-14 can carry a number of different weapon combinations in addition to

its built-in 20-mm Vulcan cannon, its normal load appears to be virtually standard. This is one or two AIM-54Cs on the front fuselage pylons, along with two AIM-7Ms and two AIM-9Ms on the wing pylons, plus two 265-US gal (1003-liter) fuel tanks beneath the inlets. Plans to replace the AIM-7M with the AIM-120A have been deferred indefinitely. When carried, the ALQ-167 replaces the AIM-54C on the front right fuselage pylon. The weapons stations between the engine bays do not appear to be often used, probably because of accessibility.

Reconnaissance: The Grumman TARPS is carried by modified F-14A/Bs under the right side of the aircraft, between the engines. For this mission the front Phoenix pylons are retained, with an ALQ-167 ECM pod on the right one, and the left one empty. The rest of the armament and fuel tanks are as per normal. Squadrons known to have operated TARPS aircraft during Desert Storm are VF-2, VF-32, VF-84 and VF-103.

Attack/SEAD: F-14s have an air-to-ground capability but it has seldom been used. Starting in 1990, when elements within the Navy were trying to prevent the termination of F-14 production, some bombs were dropped to demonstrate that it could be done. These included Mk 83 and Mk 84 LDGPs dropped from the front Phoenix pylons. Beginning in 1993, the ability to launch AGM-88 will be incorporated.

Above: Full Iranian markings are displayed by this 'Top Gun' F-14A, confirming this outfit's tendency to employ unusual (and, possibly, unofficial) insignia on its aircraft. Interestingly, one of the Iranian Tomcats was diverted to the Navy.

No fewer than six examples of the Hughes AIM-54 Phoenix missile are visible beneath this F-14B from VF-211. In practice, the Tomcat will more usually operate with a mix of missiles so as to counter threats at various ranges.

VARIANTS AND SERIALS

YF-14A: Tomcat development was undertaken using a batch of 12 aircraft obtained specifically for trials duties with a variety of test organizations of the US Navy.
157980 to 157991

F-14A: The first production version of the Tomcat was the F-14A and no fewer than 546 examples have seen service with the Navy, including one (160378) ordered by but never delivered to Iran. All are powered by the TF30 turbofan.
158612 to 158637; 158978 to 159025; 159421 to 159468; 159588 to 159637; 159825 to 159874; 160378 to 160414; 160652 to 160696; 160887 to 160930; 161133 to 161168; 161270 to 161299; 161416 to 161445; 161597 to 161626; 161850 to 161873; 162588 to 162611; 162688 to 162711

JF-14A: One early production aircraft modified for test duties.
158613

YF-14B: Initial efforts at re-engining the Tomcat resulted in the YF-14B, powered by the Pratt & Whitney F401 turbofan. Two aircraft were set aside for conversion as prototypes but only one was actually modified. This project was abandoned in the 1970s.
157986

F-14B: This was a re-engined version powered by the F110 turbofan but retaining the avionics suite of the F-14A. Originally given the designation F-14A+, production of new-build F-14Bs totalled 38 and others have been obtained by converting existing F-14As.
New build: 162910 to 162927; 163215 to 163229; 163407 to 163411
Conversions: 160922; 161136; 161282; 161416 to 161419; 161421; 161422; 161424 to 161430; 161432 to 161435; 161437; 161438; 161440 to 161442; 161444; 161599; 161601; 161608; 161610; 161615; 161869; 161870; 161871; 161873; 162701

F-14D: In addition to the F110 engine, the F-14D also embodies a modernized avionics package, including AN/APG-71 radar. Manufacture of this model is expected to total 37 examples and others will result from conversion of F-14As. Original plans to revamp more than 400 have been abandoned.
New build: 163412 to 163418; 163893 to 163904; 164340 to 164351; 164599 to 164604

NF-14D: Three aircraft assigned to permanent test duties use this designation, one being the original prototype conversion of a late production F-14A, while the other two were built as F-14Ds.
161867; 163415; 163416

SPECIFICATION

Grumman F-14A
Wing: span 64 ft 1.5 in (19.54 m) unswept, 38 ft 2.5 in (11.65 m) swept and 33 ft 3.5 in (10.15 m) overswept; aspect radius 7.28; area 565.0 sq ft (52.49 m²)
Fuselage and tail: length 62 ft 8 in (19.10 m); height 16 ft 0 in (4.88 m); tailplane span 32 ft 8.5 in (9.97 m); wheel base 23 ft 0.5 in (7.02 m)
Powerplant: two Pratt & Whitney TF30-P-412A/414A rated at 20,900 lb (93.0 kN) afterburning thrust
Weights: empty 40,104 lb (18191 kg) with -414A engines; normal take-off 'clean' 58,715 lb (26632 kg); maximum take-off 59,714 lb (27086 kg) with four Sparrows or 70,764 lb (32098 kg) with six Phoenixes; overload take-off 74,349 lb (33724 kg)
Fuel and load: internal fuel 16,200 lb (7348 kg); external fuel up to 3,800 lb (1724 kg) in two 267-US gal (1011-liter) drop tanks; maximum ordnance 14,500 lb (6577 kg)
Speed: maximum level speed 'clean' at high altitude 1,544 mph (2485 km/h); maximum speed low altitude 912 mph (1468 km/h; cruising speed between 460 and 633 mph (741 and 1019 km/h)
Range: maximum range with internal and external fuel about 2,000 miles (3220 km); radius on a combat air patrol with six AIM-7 Sparrows and four AIM-9 Sidewinders 765 miles (1231 km)
Performance: maximum rate of climb at sea level more than 30,000 ft (9145 m) per minute; service ceiling more than 50,000 ft (15240 m); minimum take-off run 1,400 ft (427 m); minimum landing run 2,900 ft (884 m)

Grumman F-14B
generally similar to the F-14D

Grumman F-14D
generally similar to the F-14A except in the following particulars:
Powerplant: two General Electric F110-GE-400 rated at 14,000 lb (62.3 kN) dry and 23,100 lb (102.75 kN) afterburning thrusts
Range: radius on a combat air patrol with six AIM-7 Sparrows and four AIM-9 Sidewinders 1,239 miles (1994 km)

OPERATORS

US Navy (USN)

Unit	Base	Type
VF-1	Miramar, CA	F-14A
VF-2	Miramar, CA	F-14A
VF-11	Miramar, CA	F-14D
VF-14	Miramar, CA	F-14D
VF-21	Atsugi, Japan	F-14A
VF-24	Miramar, CA	F-14B
VF-31	Miramar, CA	F-14D
VF-32	Oceana, VA	F-14A
VF-33	Oceana, VA	F-14A
VF-41	Oceana, VA	F-14A
VF-51	Miramar, CA	F-14A
VF-74	Oceana, VA	F-14B
VF-84	Oceana, VA	F-14A
VF-101	Oceana, VA	F-14A, F-14B
VF-102	Oceana, VA	F-14A
VF-103	Oceana, VA	F-14B
VF-111	Miramar, CA	F-14A
VF-114	Miramar, CA	F-14A
VF-124	Miramar, CA	F-14A, F-14D
VF-142	Oceana, VA	F-14B
VF-143	Oceana, VA	F-14B
VF-154	Atsugi, Japan	F-14A
VF-201	Dallas, TX	F-14A
VF-202	Dallas, TX	F-14A
VF-211	Miramar, CA	F-14A
VF-213	Miramar, CA	F-14A
VF-301	Miramar, CA	F-14A
VF-302	Miramar, CA	F-14A
VX-4	Point Mugu, CA	F-14A, F-14B, F-14D
NAWC/AD	Patuxent River, MD	F-14A, F-14D
NFWS	Miramar, CA	F-14A
NAWC/WD	Point Mugu, CA	F-14A, NF-14D

Above: The ultimate Tomcat to join the Navy is the F-14D, which features revised engines and a much improved avionics suite. Production should terminate after the delivery of 37 aircraft, but others will result from conversion of F-14As.

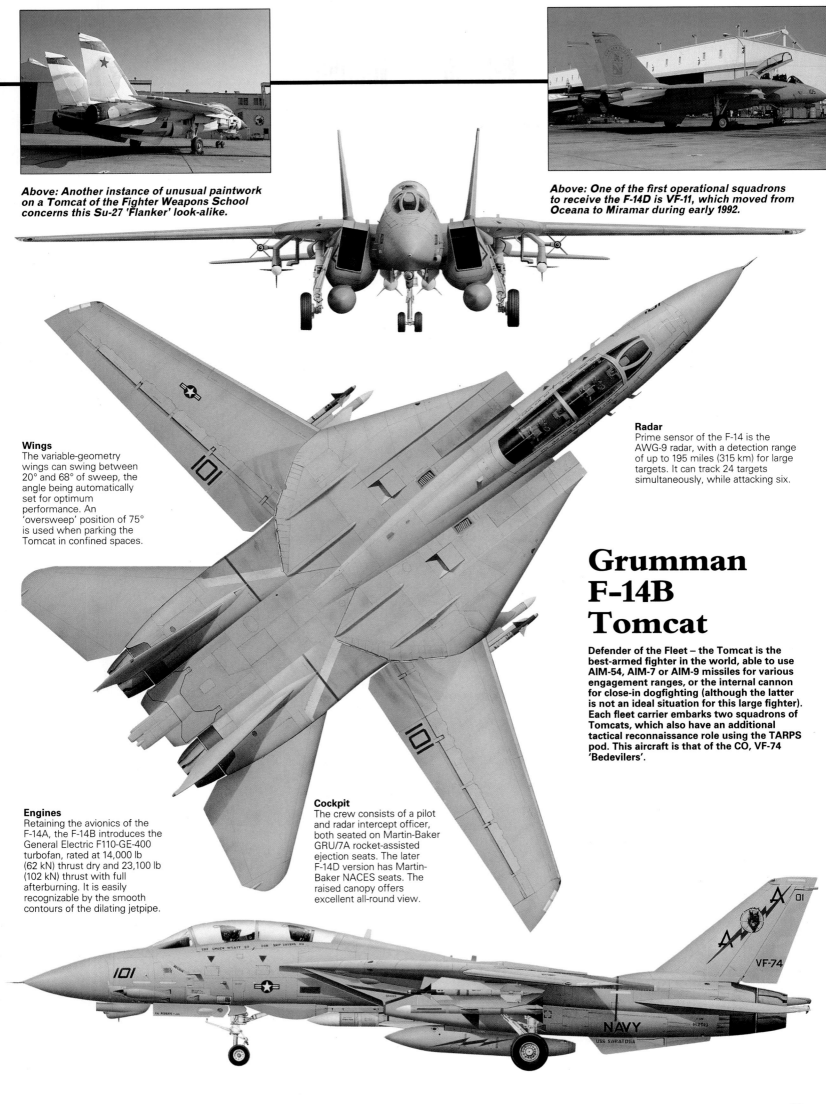

Above: Another instance of unusual paintwork on a Tomcat of the Fighter Weapons School concerns this Su-27 'Flanker' look-alike.

Above: One of the first operational squadrons to receive the F-14D is VF-11, which moved from Oceana to Miramar during early 1992.

Wings
The variable-geometry wings can swing between 20° and 68° of sweep, the angle being automatically set for optimum performance. An 'oversweep' position of 75° is used when parking the Tomcat in confined spaces.

Radar
Prime sensor of the F-14 is the AWG-9 radar, with a detection range of up to 195 miles (315 km) for large targets. It can track 24 targets simultaneously, while attacking six.

Grumman F-14B Tomcat

Defender of the Fleet – the Tomcat is the best-armed fighter in the world, able to use AIM-54, AIM-7 or AIM-9 missiles for various engagement ranges, or the internal cannon for close-in dogfighting (although the latter is not an ideal situation for this large fighter). Each fleet carrier embarks two squadrons of Tomcats, which also have an additional tactical reconnaissance role using the TARPS pod. This aircraft is that of the CO, VF-74 'Bedevilers'.

Engines
Retaining the avionics of the F-14A, the F-14B introduces the General Electric F110-GE-400 turbofan, rated at 14,000 lb (62 kN) thrust dry and 23,100 lb (102 kN) thrust with full afterburning. It is easily recognizable by the smooth contours of the dilating jetpipe.

Cockpit
The crew consists of a pilot and radar intercept officer, both seated on Martin-Baker GRU/7A rocket-assisted ejection seats. The later F-14D version has Martin-Baker NACES seats. The raised canopy offers excellent all-round view.

General Dynamics
F-16 Fighting Falcon

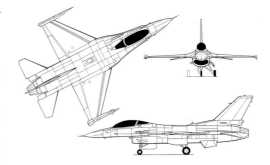

Initial proposals to interest the US Navy in purchasing the **General Dynamics F-16 Fighting Falcon** date back to the mid-1970s and the service's VFAX (fighter-attack experimental) program in which it was pitted against the Northrop YF-17. As is well known, the YF-17 won and provided a basis for the F/A-18 now serving with the Navy and Marine Corps in substantial quantities.

In the meantime, the F-16 has itself also prospered both at home and abroad. It has even found its way into the Navy inventory although it is not – and never will be – designed or intended to operate from aircraft carriers. It will, nevertheless, make a worthwhile contribution to Navy and Marine Corps combat readiness, for the 26 examples that have been purchased are all operated by aggressor outfits in the provision of dissimilar air combat training.

The decision to acquire some Fighting Falcons arose from a desire to more approximately match the expanding capabilities of new-generation Soviet warplanes in the adversary aircraft arena and, by so doing, provide more realistic training opportunities. Several types were considered by the Navy before it settled on the General Dynamics machine, subsequently placing an order for 22 single-seat **F-16N**s and four two-seat **TF-16N**s.

The first example to join the Navy was officially handed over on 6 April 1987 and delivery of all 26 was completed during the course of 1988. Basically similar to the USAF **F-16C**, the Navy F-16Ns are powered by a single General Electric F110-GE-100 turbofan and feature only the minimum of modifications to suit them for the adversary role.

These changes included deletion of the integral Vulcan M61A1 20-mm cannon as well as underwing stores stations, although the wingtip rails have been retained and are used to carry inert target-acquisition AIM-9 Sidewinders and Air Combat Maneuvering Instrumentation (ACMI) data relay pods. Airborne self-protection jammers and Navstar global positioning system equipment are also omitted, while the Navy aircraft are fitted with the lighter and less sophisticated APG-66 radar of the **F-16A** model as well as a chaff/flare dispensing system and a radar warning receiver. With the exception of these alterations, the TF-16N two-seaters are comparable to the F-16D and are mainly used to check out pilots transitioning to the Fighting Falcon, as well as some instructional aspects.

In US Navy service, the 26 aircraft are distributed fairly evenly among four units. Foremost among these is the Naval Fighter Weapons School at Miramar, California. Universally known simply as 'Top Gun', NFWS can properly be described as the 'adversary university', for it devotes a considerable amount of effort to academic studies of the art and techniques of air combat as well as providing more practical tuition courtesy of the F-16 and other types. Most, if not all, Navy and Marine Corps fighter squadrons will include a 'Top Gun' graduate among their executive officer staff. NFWS is also intimately involved in spreading the air combat 'gospel' by training instructors for other aggressor outfits.

There are now several of these outfits, but only three have Fighting Falcons. VF-43 at Oceana, Virginia, and VF-45 at Key West, Florida, operate primarily in support of Atlantic Fleet units stationed on the East Coast while VF-126, also at Miramar, is tasked to provide DACT for the Pacific Fleet fighter squadrons that call this major naval air base home when not deployed at sea.

Operating experience in the early years of service revealed the Fighting Falcon to be an ideal vehicle for the task of DACT in many ways, but all has not been quite such plain sailing in recent times. Repeated exposure to the high-*g* environment that is typically associated with DACT has resulted in unforeseen fatigue-induced problems. These are of a sufficiently serious nature to have resulted in the entire F-16N fleet being grounded towards the end of 1991 while the Navy seeks a remedy for cracks in the wing structure.

Desert camouflage adorns an F-16N from the Fighter Weapons School at Miramar, one of a batch of 16 single-seaters obtained by the Navy primarily for the aggressor role in air combat maneuvering instruction. Problems with fatigue necessitated grounding in late 1991.

MISSION PROFILE

The Navy's F-16Ns serve only in the adversary training role, flying an almost unlimited number of profiles to simulate potential threat aircraft. Weapons are not carried, although inert missile acquisition rounds and ACMI/TACTS pods are sometimes carried on the wingtips.

VARIANTS AND SERIALS

F-16N: This Fighting Falcon derivative was acquired specifically for use as an aggressor aircraft. Cannon armament has been deleted along with other equipment. Navy procurement of this simplified model totals 22.
163268 to 163277; 163566 to 163577

TF-16N: Four two-seaters were obtained for transition training with the Navy aggressor units.
163278 to 163281

SPECIFICATION

General Dynamics F-16N
Wing: over missile launchers 31 ft 0 in (9.45 m) and over wingtip missiles 32 ft 9.75 in (10.00 m); aspect ratio 3.0; area 300.0 sq ft (27.87 m²)
Fuselage and tail: length 49 ft 4 in (15.03 m); height 16 ft 8.5 in (5.09 m); tailplane span 18 ft 3.75 in (5.58 m); wheel base 13 ft 1.5 in (4.00 m)
Powerplant: one General Electric F110-GE-100 rated at 27,600 lb (122.8 kN) afterburning thrust
Weight: maximum take-off 25,071 lb (11372 kg) in typical air-to-air configuration
Fuel and load: internal fuel 6,972 lb (3162 kg); external fuel up to 6,760 lb (3066 kg) in drop tanks of up to 600-US gal (2271-liter) capacity; maximum ordnance (seldom carried) 12,000 lb (5443 kg)
Speed: maximum level speed 'clean' at 40,000 ft (12190 m) more than 1,320 mph (2125 km/h)
Range: ferry range more than 2,415 miles (3890 km); combat radius more than 575 miles (925 km)
Performance: maximum rate of climb at sea level more than 50,000 ft (15240 m) per minute; service ceiling more than 50,000 ft (15240 m)

OPERATORS

US Navy (USN)

VF-43	Oceana, VA	F-16N, TF-16N
VF-45	Key West, FL	F-16N, TF-16N
VF-126	Miramar, CA	F-16N
NFWS	Miramar, CA	F-16N, TF-16N

A quartet of two-seat TF-16Ns was also obtained for the purpose of training instructor pilots for service with aggressor units.

As with most other NFWS hardware, one of the Fighting Falcons at Miramar displays Marine Corps inscriptions.

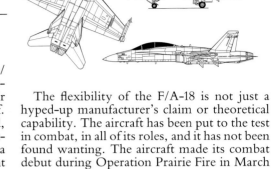

McDonnell Douglas
F/A-18 Hornet

During the early 1970s it had been intended that the US Navy would procure a version of the USAF's winning LWF (LightWeight Fighter) contender as a low-cost supplement to the F-14 and as an A-7 replacement. The Navy however, was implacably hostile to the winning single-engined YF-16, and decided to adopt an aircraft developed from the losing Northrop YF-17. McDonnell Douglas was brought in as prime contractor and the **F/A-18 Hornet** was born, eventually to become the most versatile strike fighter in US Navy history, and perhaps the most important single type in service today.

The keys to the amazing success of the F/A-18 lie in sound aerodynamic design (conferring superb high α performance and great agility) and in the excellent Hughes AN/APG-65 multi-mode pulse-Doppler radar, which was developed specifically for the F/A-18, but which has since come to be regarded as one of the best fighter radars in service today. The AN/APG-65 has been copied by the Soviets for their MiG-29 and has been used to upgrade various older fighters. Updated versions of the same basic radar have been considered for many much newer fighters, including the Eurofighter.

The remarkable APG-65 is an excellent air-to-air radar, with various modes including velocity search (detecting fighter-sized targets at over 80 nm) and track-while-scan (tracking 10 targets simultaneously). It is also an unbeatable air-to-ground radar, again with multiple modes which include ground mapping, ranging and auto-attack functions. Night/all-weather attack performance can be further enhanced by using a Ford Aerospace AN/AAS-38 FLIR and/or a Martin Marietta AN/ASQ-173 laser spot tracker.

Perhaps one of the greatest advantages enjoyed by the F/A-18 pilot is that all information is presented to him with great clarity in what marked the first truly modern fighter cockpit. The excellent HUD is backed up by three large CRT multi-function displays, with up front controls above knee level. All vital flight and weaponeering controls are clustered on throttle and stick giving true HOTAS (Hands On Throttle and Stick) capability. The advantage in not having to interpret hundreds of tiny analogue instruments, nor to look down into the cockpit to make switch selections, is incalculable.

In US Navy service the F/A-18 has now completely replaced the A-7 Corsair, and its prime role is light strike. Similarly, in USMC service, the aircraft has replaced the F-4 Phantom, and, in its F/A-18D form, is replacing the A-6 Intruder. The aircraft is, however, much more than a straight A-7/F-4 attack aircraft replacement, as is indicated by the redesignation of VA (heavier than air attack) A-7 units into VFA (heavier than air fighter/attack) Hornet units. Even when carrying out traditional bomber duties, the F/A-18 can carry AIM-9 Sidewinders and AIM-7 Sparrows (to be replaced by AIM-120 AMRAAMs) with little

penalty, allowing an unparalleled self-defense/self-escort capability, and allowing every mission the chance of becoming a counter air sweep once the iron has been pickled off. Lightly loaded, and especially at slow speed, the Hornet is a superb turn-fighter, able to out-turn virtually any other US fighter. In a close-in fight, the Hornet can use its excellent M61A1 20-mm cannon, which is mounted on the centerline (for minimum aiming errors) in an unbelievably effective vibration damping mount which allows the radar to continue functioning even when the gun is fired.

In its primary role, the F/A-18 can carry virtually the full range of US Navy air-to-ground ordnance, guided and unguided, ranging from slick, laser-guided and retarded bombs of up to 2,000 lb through a range of guided missiles which include AGM-88 HARM, AGM-65 Maverick and AGM-84 Harpoon, to nuclear bombs and depth charges. Thus the Hornet is simultaneously fighter, bomber, defense suppressor and ship-killer, all without requiring any hardware or software change and depending only on what is loaded onto the aircraft's pylons.

The flexibility of the Hornet is such that a carrier air wing commander with two squadrons of Hornets can quite literally have two extra squadrons of fighters to augment his F-14 Tomcat interceptors, or two extra squadrons of all-weather attack aircraft to augment his A-6 Intruders. The flexibility of the aircraft was exploited most effectively by Air Wing Five aboard the USS *Independence*, which had three F/A-18 squadrons and no F-14s. An experimental air wing with four Hornet units was also deployed on the USS *Coral Sea*.

The flexibility of the F/A-18 is not just a hyped-up manufacturer's claim or theoretical capability. The aircraft has been put to the test in combat, in all of its roles, and it has not been found wanting. The aircraft made its combat debut during Operation Prairie Fire in March 1986, knocking out Libyan SAM sites with the AGM-88. The same aircraft/weapons combination was used by Hornets operating in the defense suppression role during Operation El Dorado Canyon in April 1986.

Most recently, the F/A-18 was heavily committed to Operation Desert Storm, with nine carrier-based US Navy (VFA-15, -81, -82, -83, -86, -87, -151, -192, and -195) and seven land-based US Marine (VMFA-232, -235, -312, -314, -333, -451 and VMFA(AW)-121) squadrons. The 190 aircraft committed performed fleet air defense, escort, defensive counter-air, interdiction, close-air support and defense suppression missions. A pair of bomb-laden F/A-18Cs of VFA-81 scored the US Navy's only fast-jet kills of the war, dispatching a pair of Shenyang F-7s (or MiG-21s) with AIM-9 Sidewinders before going on to bomb an Iraqi airfield. Only one Hornet was lost to hostile action, this aircraft falling to an Iraqi SA-6.

No aircraft is perfect, and the Hornet does have its faults, although these have often been exaggerated. The F/A-18 has picked up a reputation for being short-legged, and this has raised particular anxieties when the vexed

Sparrow and Sidewinder missiles form the armament of this pair of F/A-18C Hornets. Both are assigned to VFA-81, which was recently based aboard the USS America when deployed.

Above: An early production example of the two-seat F/A-18B Hornet displays Test Pilot's School titles over a basically white color scheme.

Left: Resident at Yuma, VMFAT-101 functions as the Marines' FRS and recently featured examples of all four Hornet sub-types.

F/A-18 Hornet (continued)

question of replacing the A-6 has arisen. While it is true that current production versions of the F/A-18 certainly cannot match the range of the A-6, the range deficiency is being addressed in versions now being designed, and the range of the current F/A-18C needs to be put in perspective. A clean Hornet can exceed the range of a clean Phantom, and with tanks can still carry a slightly greater bombload than a clean A-7 over the same range. Moreover, the Hornet's bombing accuracy means that it can achieve more over the target on less fuel. In the air combat role, the F/A-18's generous dry power rating allows it to outstay aircraft like the F-14. Hornet pilots seldom 'bingo' (break off an engagement due to fuel limitations) first.

The F/A-18 has been significantly improved since it first entered service. By comparison with the prototypes, production F/A-18As incorporated a host of aerodynamic refinements, improving take-off and turn performance. The baseline single-seat **F/A-18A** gave way on the production line to the improved **F/A-18C** during 1986. This introduced a plethora of flight instrument and avionics upgrades, including an enhanced defensive EW suite and AGM-65/AIM-120 compatibility. Later F/A-18Cs incorporate enhanced night attack

Below: Hooked-up and hot to trot, an F/A-18 of VFA-136 holds full power as its pilot waits for the catapult control officer to signal that he is satisfied and that launch can take place.

capability, with an NVG-compatible cockpit, FLIR and a color digital map display. The US Marine Corps has taken the night attack Hornet concept a step further, procuring a dedicated night-attack two-seater (the **F/A-18D**) to replace its A-6 Intruders, sacrificing range for accuracy and survivability. At least 48 are on order, and the Corps hope to take delivery of an eventual 80.

One role widely touted by McDonnell Douglas for the F/A-18 since the beginning has been reconnaissance, and a mock-up camera installation (designed to be interchangeable with the gun pack) was flown on an early FSD airframe. The US Marine Corps has a requirement for a two-seat all-weather recce aircraft based on the F/A-18D and designated **F/A-18D(CR)**. This will replace the RF-4B with VMFP-3, which will redesignate VMFA(AW)-225 'Vagabonds'.

The F/A-18 Hornet looks set to enjoy a long and continuing success. Variants are already on the drawing board which will completely revolutionize the aircraft's capabilities, and fit it for service well into the next century. The demise of the A-12 has left an urgent need for an A-6 Intruder replacement, and the **F/A-18E** and **F/A-18F** have been designed to fill this gap. The alternative would be one of the many proposed strikefighter derivatives of the F-14 Tomcat, but such an aircraft offers little apart from (irrelevant) Mach 2 performance.

Both the F/A-18E (single seat) and F/A-18F

(two seat) feature a stretched fuselage (through insertion of a 34-in/86-cm plug in the center section) and an enlarged wing (with 100 sq ft/9 m² of extra area). Extra internal fuel (3,000 lb/1360 kg), two extra weapons pylons and a new non-afterburning powerplant developed from the GE F412 give extra warload and considerable extra range/endurance. R&D funding of $435 million has been requested and a first flight is tentatively planned for 1996.

The Hornet entered regular service during 1981, when the joint USMC/USN fleet replenishment squadron received its first aircraft, having formed in November 1980. The first students arrived in 1982, from the US Marines VMFA-314 'Black Knights', who gained the distinction of becoming the first F/A-18 squadron. Two more USMC units, VMFA-323 and VMFA-531, followed, before the first US Navy squadron, VFA-113, converted. The squadron completed carquals in mid-October 1983, and in February 1985 the unit began its first operational deployment (alongside VFA-25) aboard the USS *Constellation* as part of CVW-14. The second deployment was aboard the *Coral Sea*, which embarked the first two USMC squadrons and VFA-131 and VFA-132 for a Sixth Fleet cruise.

The F/A-18 is now in service in huge numbers. The US Marine Corps has 14 regular squadrons, plus two F/A-18D units, and four more are due to form. A fifth squadron will operate the recce version of the F/A-18D, and four Reserve units are scheduled to convert to single-seat Hornets between 1992 and 1995. The US Navy has 24 regular squadrons, and four Reserve units. Even USS *Ranger*, due for retirement in 1992, has now received two F/A-18 units, and the type is entering service in the aggressor and electronic aggressor roles.

MISSION PROFILE

Armament options: The Hornet has a built-in 20-mm Vulcan cannon plus a total of nine weapon stations, comprised of two wingtip AIM-9L/M launcher rails, two fuselage stations for AIM-7F/Ms or sensor pods, a centerline and four underwing pylons. AIM-9s are virtually standard on the wingtip stations in combat, but during peacetime exercises AIS pods are often fitted to one side. When AIM-7s are not carried, the fuselage stations can be fitted with one of three sensors: the ASQ-173 LST/SCAM, AAS-38 FLIR or AAR-50 TINS. AIM-120As will eventually replace the AIM-7F/Ms.

Surface attack: Many different weapon combinations were seen on F/A-18s during Desert Storm. Extremely range limited, carriage of at least one 330-US gal (1250-liter) fuel tank was almost a certainty. Any Mk 80 series fin can be used with the F/A-18.

Single weapons are carried mounted to the pylon (or LAU-118 for AGM-45/88); double weapons are mounted to vertical ejector racks (VERs). The heaviest load seen during the 1991 Gulf War was six Mk 83s, but loads as small as two Mk 82s were also seen. The norm lay between. Towards the end of the war, Marine aircraft began to carry a load of one AGM-65E, and up to three Mk 83s.

Precision attack/anti-ship/nuclear: AGM-62 Walleyes, AGM-84 Harpoon, AGM-88 HARM and nuclear weapons can only be carried on outboard wing stations. AAW-9 Walleye datalink pods can only be carried on the centerline station. GBU-10, -12, and -16 LGBs can be carried on any station, but are very rarely seen on F/A-18s.

SEAD: Up to four AGM-88 HARMs were often carried during Desert Storm. For decoy missions, up to eight ADM-141 TALDs can be carried, although this was not often done because this load required extensive refueling, while A-6Es could carry more TALDs unrefueled.

Fast forward air control: During Desert Storm F/A-18D fast FACs carried two LAU-10s on outboard VERs, a TINS pod, and an AIM-7M. They located targets for more heavily-loaded attack aircraft, marking them with 5-in rockets.

Combat air patrol: In addition to its normal complement of two Sidewinders and Sparrows, on CAP missions Hornets carry three fuel tanks and either two additional AIM-7Ms or four more AIM-9Ms on the outboard wing pylons.

VARIANTS AND SERIALS

YF/A-18A: Following selection of the YF-17 to provide a basis for the Hornet, a batch of 11 RDT&E airframes was ordered, nine of which were completed as single-seaters.
160775 to 160780; 160782; 160783; 160785

YF/A-18B: Two of the 11 RDT&E aircraft were completed in two-seat form for trials work.
160781; 160784

F/A-18A: The first version of the Hornet to enter production and operational service was the F/A-18A, some 371 examples being completed for Navy and Marine Corps units before manufacture switched to the improved F/A-18C.
161213 to 161216; 161248; 161250; 161251; 161353; 161358; 161359; 161361 to 161367; 161519 to 161529; 161702; 161703; 161705; 161706; 161708 to 161710; 161712; 161713; 161715 to 161718; 161720 to 161722; 161724 to 161726; 161728 to 161732; 161734 to 161739; 161741 to 161745; 161747 to 161761; 161925 to 161931; 161933 to 161937; 161939 to 161942; 161944 to 161946; 161948 to 161987; 162394 to 162401; 162403 to 162407; 162409 to 162412; 162414 to 162418; 162420 to 162426; 162428 to 162477; 162826 to 162835; 162837 to 162841; 162843; 162845; 162847 to 162849; 162851 to 162856; 162858 to 162863; 162865 to 162869; 162871 to 162875; 162877 to 162884; 162886 to 162909; 163092 to 163103; 163105 to 163109; 163111 to 163114; 163116 to 163122; 163124 to 163175

RF-18A: The second production F/A-18A was modified to serve as a prototype for a reconnaissance model of the Hornet. Current plans anticipate Marine Corps use of a version of the F/A-18D.
161214

F/A-18B: The two-seat counterpart of the F/A-18A was the F/A-18B (originally TF-18A), some 40 examples being completed for service with fleet replenishment squadrons of the Navy and Marine Corps.
161217; 161249; 161354 to 161357; 161360; 161704; 161707; 161711; 161714; 161719; 161723; 161727; 161733; 161740; 161746; 161924; 161932; 161938; 161943; 161947; 162402; 162408; 162413; 162419; 162427; 162836; 162842; 162846; 162850; 162857; 162864; 162870; 162876; 162885; 163104; 163110; 163115; 163123

F/A-18C: Efforts to improve the Hornet led to the advent of the F/A-18C featuring revised avionics and other enhancements, as well as compatibility with AIM-120 and IR Maverick missiles. A total of 355 aircraft

has been ordered to date.
163427 to 163433; 163435; 163437 to 163440; 163442 to 163444; 163446; 163448 to 163451; 163453; 163455; 163456; 163458; 163459; 163461 to 163463; 163465 to 163467; 163469 to 163471; 163473; 163475 to 163478; 163480; 163481; 163483 to 163485; 163487; 163489 to 163491; 163493 to 163496; 163498; 163499; 163502 to 163506; 163508; 163509; 163699; 163701 to 163706; 163708 to 163719; 163721 to 163733; 163735 to 163748; 163750 to 163762; 163764 to 163770; 163772 to 163777; 163779 to 163782; 163985; 163987; 163988; 163990; 163992; 163993; 163995; 163998 to 164000; 164002 to 164004; 164006 to 164008; 164010; 164012; 164013; 164015; 164016; 164018; 164020; 164021; 164023; 164025; 164027; 164029 to 164031; 164033; 164034; 164036; 164037; 164039; 164041; 164042; 164044; 164045; 164047; 164048; 164050; 164052; 164054; 164055; 164057; 164059; 164060; 164062; 164063; 164065 to 164067; 164197; 164199 to 164202; 164204 to 164206; 164208 to 164210; 164212 to 164215; 164217; 164218; 164220 to 164223; 164225 to 164227; 164229 to 164232; 164234 to 164236; 164238 to 164240; 164242 to 164244; 164246 to 164248; 164250 to 164253; 164255 to 164256; 164258; 164260 to 164262; 164264 to 164265; 164267 to 164271; 164273 to 164278; 164280; 164627 to 164672; 164693 to 164746

Unarmed save for a pair of heat-seeking Sidewinders, two F/A-18C Hornets of VFA-15 take time out from more serious business to pose for the photographer. The distinctive LERX are all too apparent in this view.

F/A-18D: Navy and Marine Corps training units operate the two-seat counterpart of the F/A-18C, this model also assuming responsibility for night/all-weather attack duties with those Marine Corps units that utilize the A-6E Intruder. To date, procurement for both services totals approximately 115 aircraft.
163434; 163436; 163441; 163445; 163447; 163452; 163454; 163457; 163460; 163464; 163468; 163472; 163474; 163479; 163482; 163486; 163488; 163492; 163497; 163500; 163501; 163507; 163510; 163700; 163707; 163720; 163734; 163749; 163763; 163771; 163778; 163986; 163989; 163991; 163994; 163997; 164001; 164005; 164009; 164011; 164014; 164017; 164019; 164022; 164024; 164026; 164028; 164032; 164035; 164038; 164040; 164043; 164046; 164049; 164051; 164053; 164056; 164058; 164061; 164064; 164068; 164196; 164198; 164203; 164207; 164211; 164216; 164219; 164224; 164228; 164233; 164237; 164241; 164245; 164249; 164254; 164257; 164259; 164263; 164266; 164272; 164279; 164281?; 164673 to 164692; 164747 to 164758

Above: The handsome blue and gold color scheme of the Navy's aerobatic display team appears to be particularly well suited to the Hornet. The 'Blue Angels' here hold immaculate formation while en route to another performance somewhere in the United States.

Aircraft

Below: A recent addition to the aggressor pool, the F/A-18A is now assigned to VFA-127 'Cylons' at Fallon. This unit adorned its first Hornet with Iraqi insignia and 'MiG-29' fintips over a basically desert-camouflaged color scheme of brown and tan.

Bottom: AGM-65 Maverick and AGM-88 HARM weapons are carried by an F/A-18C of VMFA-312 of the US Marine Corps at Beaufort, SC. Other Marine outfits which utilize the Hornet include the specialist all-weather attack squadrons.

SPECIFICATION

McDonnell Douglas F/A-18C
Wing: span over missile rails 36 ft 6 in (11.43 m) and over wingtip missiles 40 ft 4.75 in (12.31 m); aspect ratio 3.5; area 400.0 sq ft (37.16 m^2)
Fuselage and tail: length 56 ft 0 in (17.07 m); height 15 ft 3.5 in (4.66 m); tailplane span 21 ft 7.25 in (6.58 m); wheel base 17 ft 9.5 in (5.42 m)
Powerplant: two General Electric F404-GE-400 rated at about 16,000 lb (71.2 kN) afterburning thrusts

Weights: empty 23,050 lb (10455 kg); normal take-off 36,710 lb (16652 kg) for a fighter mission; maximum take-off 49,224 lb (22328 kg) for an attack mission
Fuel and load: internal fuel 10,860 lb (4926 kg); external fuel up to 6,732 lb (3053 kg) in three 330-US gal (1250-liter) drop tanks; maximum ordnance 17,000 lb (7711 kg)
Speed: maximum level speed 'clean' at high altitude more than 1,190 mph (1915 km/h)
Range: ferry range with internal and external fuel more than 2,303 miles (3706 km); combat radius more than 460 miles (740 km) on a fighter mission, or 662 miles (1065 km) on an attack mission
Performance: maximum rate of climb at sea level 45,000 ft (13715 m) per minute; combat ceiling about 50,000 ft (15240 m); take-off run less than 1,400 ft (427 m)

McDonnell Douglas F/A-18A
generally similar to the F/A-18C except in the following particulars:
Weights: normal take-off 33,585 lb (15234 kg) for a fighter mission; maximum take-off 48,253 lb (21888 kg) for an attack mission

McDonnell Douglas F/A-18B
generally similar to the F/A-18A except in the following particulars:
Weights: normal take-off 33,585 lb (15234 kg) for a fighter mission; maximum take-off 47,000 lb (21319 kg) for at attack mission
Fuel and load: internal fuel reduced by less than 6 per cent to provide volume for the accommodation of the second seat
Range: ferry range with internal and external fuel 2,187 miles (3520 km); combat radius 634 miles (1020 km) on an attack mission

McDonnell Douglas F/A-18D
generally similar to the F/A-18B

OPERATORS

US Navy (USN)

VFA-15	Cecil Field, FL	F/A-18C
VFA-22	Lemoore, CA	F/A-18C
VFA-25	Lemoore, CA	F/A-18C
VFA-27	Lemoore, CA	F/A-18C

Below: A Zuni rocket departs in a hurry from an F/A-18D of the Yuma-based Marine Corps training unit during weapons instruction over one of the ranges close to this large facility.

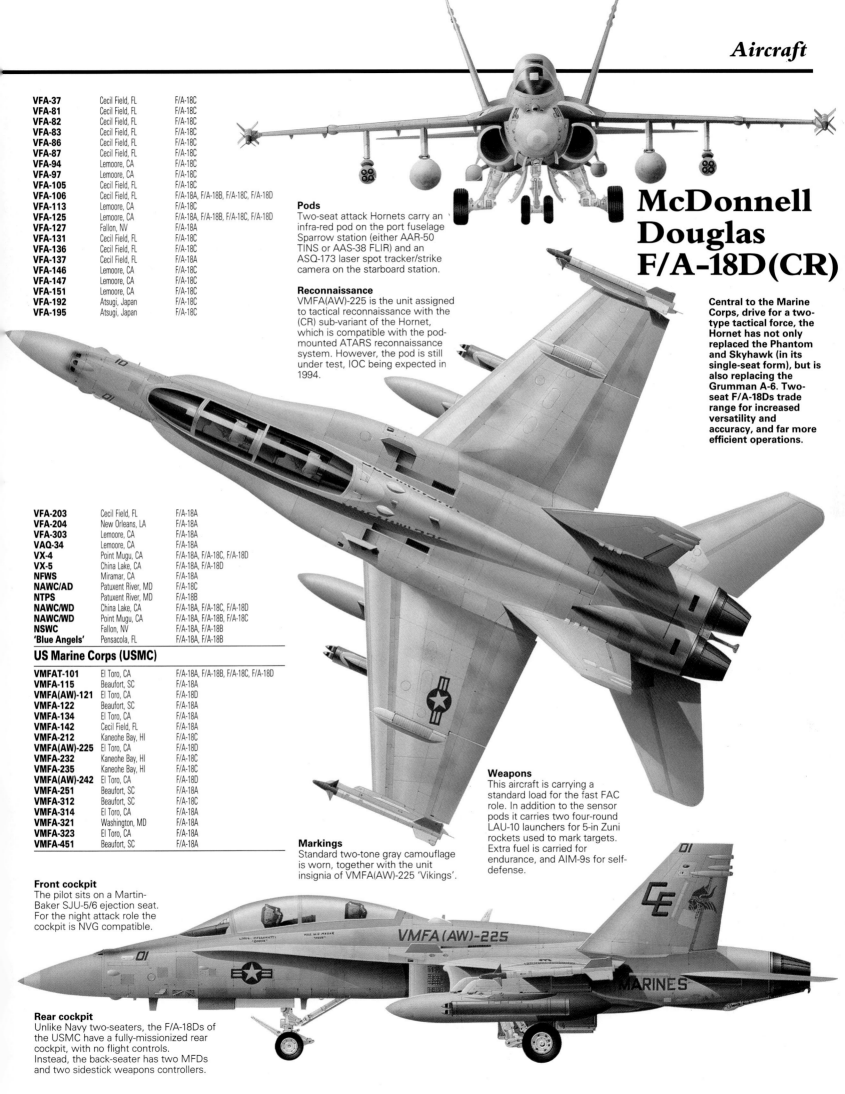

VFA-37	Cecil Field, FL	F/A-18C
VFA-81	Cecil Field, FL	F/A-18C
VFA-82	Cecil Field, FL	F/A-18C
VFA-83	Cecil Field, FL	F/A-18C
VFA-86	Cecil Field, FL	F/A-18C
VFA-87	Cecil Field, FL	F/A-18C
VFA-94	Lemoore, CA	F/A-18C
VFA-97	Lemoore, CA	F/A-18C
VFA-105	Cecil Field, FL	F/A-18C
VFA-106	Cecil Field, FL	F/A-18A, F/A-18B, F/A-18C, F/A-18D
VFA-113	Lemoore, CA	F/A-18C
VFA-125	Lemoore, CA	F/A-18A, F/A-18B, F/A-18C, F/A-18D
VFA-127	Fallon, NV	F/A-18A
VFA-131	Cecil Field, FL	F/A-18C
VFA-136	Cecil Field, FL	F/A-18C
VFA-137	Cecil Field, FL	F/A-18A
VFA-146	Lemoore, CA	F/A-18C
VFA-147	Lemoore, CA	F/A-18C
VFA-151	Lemoore, CA	F/A-18C
VFA-192	Atsugi, Japan	F/A-18C
VFA-195	Atsugi, Japan	F/A-18C

McDonnell Douglas F/A-18D(CR)

Pods
Two-seat attack Hornets carry an infra-red pod on the port fuselage Sparrow station (either AAR-50 TINS or AAS-38 FLIR) and an ASQ-173 laser spot tracker/strike camera on the starboard station.

Reconnaissance
VMFA(AW)-225 is the unit assigned to tactical reconnaissance with the (CR) sub-variant of the Hornet, which is compatible with the pod-mounted ATARS reconnaissance system. However, the pod is still under test, IOC being expected in 1994.

Central to the Marine Corps, drive for a two-type tactical force, the Hornet has not only replaced the Phantom and Skyhawk (in its single-seat form), but is also replacing the Grumman A-6. Two-seat F/A-18Ds trade range for increased versatility and accuracy, and far more efficient operations.

VFA-203	Cecil Field, FL	F/A-18A
VFA-204	New Orleans, LA	F/A-18A
VFA-303	Lemoore, CA	F/A-18A
VAQ-34	Lemoore, CA	F/A-18A
VX-4	Point Mugu, CA	F/A-18A, F/A-18C, F/A-18D
VX-5	China Lake, CA	F/A-18A, F/A-18D
NFWS	Miramar, CA	F/A-18A
NAWC/AD	Patuxent River, MD	F/A-18C
NTPS	Patuxent River, MD	F/A-18B
NAWC/WD	China Lake, CA	F/A-18A, F/A-18C, F/A-18D
NAWC/WD	Point Mugu, CA	F/A-18A, F/A-18B, F/A-18C
NSWC	Fallon, NV	F/A-18A, F/A-18B
'Blue Angels'	Pensacola, FL	F/A-18A, F/A-18B

US Marine Corps (USMC)

VMFAT-101	El Toro, CA	F/A-18A, F/A-18B, F/A-18C, F/A-18D
VMFA-115	Beaufort, SC	F/A-18A
VMFA(AW)-121	El Toro, CA	F/A-18D
VMFA-122	Beaufort, SC	F/A-18A
VMFA-134	El Toro, CA	F/A-18A
VMFA-142	Cecil Field, FL	F/A-18A
VMFA-212	Kaneohe Bay, HI	F/A-18C
VMFA(AW)-225	El Toro, CA	F/A-18D
VMFA-232	Kaneohe Bay, HI	F/A-18C
VMFA-235	Kaneohe Bay, HI	F/A-18C
VMFA(AW)-242	El Toro, CA	F/A-18D
VMFA-251	Beaufort, SC	F/A-18A
VMFA-312	Beaufort, SC	F/A-18C
VMFA-314	El Toro, CA	F/A-18A
VMFA-321	Washington, MD	F/A-18A
VMFA-323	El Toro, CA	F/A-18A
VMFA-451	Beaufort, SC	F/A-18A

Weapons
This aircraft is carrying a standard load for the fast FAC role. In addition to the sensor pods it carries two four-round LAU-10 launchers for 5-in Zuni rockets used to mark targets. Extra fuel is carried for endurance, and AIM-9s for self-defense.

Markings
Standard two-tone gray camouflage is worn, together with the unit insignia of VMFA(AW)-225 'Vikings'.

Front cockpit
The pilot sits on a Martin-Baker SJU-5/6 ejection seat. For the night attack role the cockpit is NVG compatible.

Rear cockpit
Unlike Navy two-seaters, the F/A-18Ds of the USMC have a fully-missionized rear cockpit, with no flight controls. Instead, the back-seater has two MFDs and two sidestick weapons controllers.

North American
F-86 Sabre

Undeniably one of the greatest fighters ever built, the **North American Sabre** was never employed operationally by the Navy, but did provide a basis for the improved FJ Fury which saw extensive service with both the Navy and Marine Corps during the 1950s and early 1960s. Today, the Fury is long gone from the first- and second-line inventories but some examples of the Sabre do fly in Navy colors. These aircraft made a modest but valuable contribution to the development of air-to-air missiles for use by later generations of Navy fighter aircraft.

Operating with the Naval Air Warfare Center Weapons Divisions at China Lake and Point Mugu, California, the Sabre has been one of the main pilotless drone targets for live firing trials involving air-to-air missiles for many years now. Initially, redundant Air National Guard **F-86H**s were fitted with telemetry and remote control equipment and employed as **QF-86H** targets, but stocks of that model ran out some time ago. Drone operations are currently conducted with the **QF-86F**, using former Japanese Air Self Defense Force (JASDF) aircraft. Modification to drone configuration is accomplished at the NAWC/WD which holds a sizable stock of re-dundant JASDF Sabres. There is every reason to expect that these will continue to be used as expendable targets by the NAWCs for a good many years to come.

MISSION PROFILE

The F-86 is now used by the US Navy only as an unmanned target drone, and as a drone chase and range safety aircraft.

VARIANTS AND SERIALS

QF-86F: Substantial stocks of ex-RoKAF and JASDF F-86Fs are held in store at China Lake while they await conversion as unmanned drone targets. This long-running program has already witnessed the destruction of many other aircraft. The following examples have all been noted in service recently.
524450; 524647; 553822; 553838; 553878; 553898; 553905; 553913; 553942; 553945; 562782; 562818; 562875; 576363; 576445
(aircraft identities are based on original USAF serial number)

SPECIFICATION

Sperry (North American) QF-86F
Wing: span 38 ft 9.5 in (11.82 m); area 313.4 sq ft (29.12 m²)
Fuselage and tail: length 37 ft 6 in (11.43 m); height 14 ft 8.75 in (4.49 m)
Powerplant: one General Electric J47-GE-27 rated at 5,970 lb (26.56 kN) dry thrust thrust
Weights: (F-86F) empty 11,125 lb (5046 kg); normal take-off 15,198 lb (6893 kg)
Speed: maximum level speed at sea level 678 mph (1091 km/h)
Performance: maximum rate of climb at sea level 9,800 ft (2987 m) per minute; service ceiling 49,600 ft (15120 m)

Above: In addition to the Phantom, the Navy has made extensive use of retired Sabres for its unmanned target drone program. Redundant Air National Guard QF-86Hs were used for a number of years but the current 'Sabre-drone' is the QF-86F. Large stocks of former Japanese and Korean machines are held in reserve.

North American QF-86H
generally similar to the QF-86F except in the following particulars:
Wing: span 39 ft 1 in (11.91 m); area 313.4 sq ft (29.12 m²)
Fuselage and tail: length 38 ft 8 in (11.79 m); height 15 ft 0 in (4.57 m)
Powerplant: one General Electric J73-GE-3E rated at 8,920 lb (36.4 kN) dry thrust
Weights: (F-86H) empty 13,826 lb (6276 kg); maximum take-off 21,852 lb (9912 kg)
Speed: maximum level speed at sea level 692 mph (1114 km/h)
Performance: maximum rate of climb at sea level 12,900 ft (3932 m) per minute; service ceiling 49,000 ft (14935 m)

OPERATORS

US Navy (USN)

NAWC/WD	China Lake, CA	QF-86F
NAWC/WD	Point Mugu, CA	QF-86F

Below: A QF-86F is captured by the camera just milliseconds before meeting a fiery fate as an AIM-9 Sidewinder homes in for the kill. Not all of the tests result in destruction of the Sabre targets, since drones are by no means cheap.

North American QF-86F Sabre

Aircraft used as subsonic targets only

One 8,920-lb (36-kN) General Electric J73-GE-3E turbojet

Forward-looking TV system in nose

Propane burners fitted to increase IR signature

Some aircraft retain cockpit instrumentation and controls

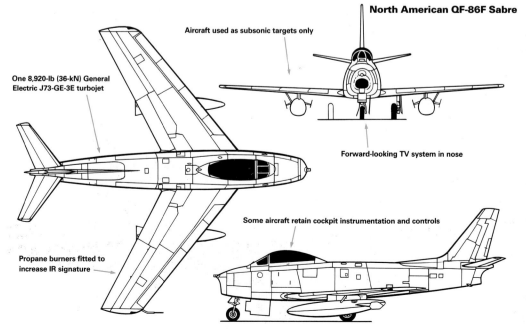

Schweizer
RG-8A Condor

Employed on covert surveillance operations by the US Coast Guard, the **RG-8A Condor** arose out of modification of Schweizer's SGM 2-37 motorized glider, differences centering around a greater wing span incorporating leading edge modifications to bestow enhanced stall characteristics. Power is furnished by a single Textron Lycoming 10-540-W3A5D engine driving a three-bladed constant-speed propeller and also featuring muffler devices intended to reduce noise 'footprint'. Fuel capacity was also greatly increased and there are reports that mission duration can run as long as eight hours.

Full IFR capability is provided, permitting operation around the clock, other avionics equipment allegedly including a Litton INS as well as a Bendix/King avionics suite. Optional equipment includes a radar altimeter and 'LORAN.

Flying in prototype form during the course of 1986, an initial batch of two RG-8As was purchased by the US Army, which has long been actively exploring the merits and demerits of quiet and ultra-quiet surveillance aircraft. One of the original pair was destroyed in an accident and a third example was obtained as a replacement, with both of the survivors being subsequently transferred to the Coast Guard facility at Opa Locka, Florida.

It is from there that they are still operated as part of the steadily expanding effort to counter the influx of drugs through the southeastern portion of the USA. Carrying a two-man crew, seated side by side, they are understood to perform long-duration patrol missions along the Florida coastline and evidently feature a 65-cu ft (1.85-m^3) payload bay behind the cockpit able to hold a variety of sensor pallets. Surveillance equipment in use is understood to include LLLTV, IR imaging systems and conventional cameras, while the RG-8A is also compatible with night vision goggles. A complex array of communications equipment is also carried, enabling crew members to call for assistance with the tracking of inbound traffic and also to alert law enforcement agencies to smuggling activities.

MISSION PROFILE

Sensor and avionics fit: The cockpit is fully NVG compatible, and NVGs are often used as the primary search aid. A Texas Instruments AAQ-15 FLIR is fitted, with images being recorded on VHS video tape, along with voice annotation of time, position and activity by either pilot or SSO. A Sperry WX-11 Stormscope is used for weather avoidance. The avionics suite includes VOR, DME, and RNAV, and the modified TRACOR Omega has a DAC GPS board which gives accuracies within 100 ft (30 m). Communications equipment includes VHF-AM, secure UHF and HF and protected VHF-FM. Geostar satellite communications are being incorporated.

Surveillance: The Condor is used for long-endurance surveillance missions, operating by day and night against drug smugglers, illegal immigrants, illegal fishing boats and pollution. The aircraft is flown by a single pilot in the left-hand seat, assisted by an SSO. The aircraft usually operate singly, supported by a cutter or other surface vessel, flying a search pattern with a track of some 500 miles (800 km). On detection of a target the aircraft enters its 'quiet' mode, using a very low power setting, and descending to low level to allow the SSO to identify, classify and record the target using the FLIR. For safety reasons operations are not undertaken when seas are greater than 6 ft (1.8 m), or when water temperature drops below 60° F (16° C).

VARIANTS AND SERIALS

RG-8A: Two examples of this ultra-quiet, long-duration machine have been obtained by the Coast Guard for use as surveillance platforms in the effort to eradicate drug-smuggling activity in the vicinity of Florida. 8101 to 8102

SPECIFICATION

Schweizer RG-8A
Wing: span 59 ft 6 in (18.14 m); aspect ratio 18.1; area 195.71 sq ft (18.18 m^2)
Fuselage and tail: length 27 ft 5 in (8.36 m); height 7 ft 9.5 in (2.37 m); wheel track 9 ft 2 in (2.79 m); wheel base 18 ft 10 in (5.74 m)
Powerplant: one Textron (Avco) Lycoming IO-540-W3A5D rated at 235 hp (175 kW)
Range: endurance 8+ hours

OPERATORS

US Coast Guard (USCG)

CGAS	Miami, FL	RG-8A

One 235-hp (175-kW) Textron-Lycoming IO-35-W3A5D flat-six piston engine driving a McCauley three-bladed constant-speed low-noise propeller

Exhaust silencers

Removable underfuselage hatches

Modification of Schweizer SGM 2-37 sailplane

Fuselage bay can accommodate LLTV, FLIR or camera packages

Optional seat armor available

Certified for night IFR (Instrument Flight Rules) flying

Litton INS

Cockpit seats two side by side with dual controls, under a hinged canopy

Schweizer RG-8A

Left: The battle to eradicate drug smuggling is the raison d'être *behind Coast Guard operation of the RG-8A Condor, this ultra-quiet machine being used for the surveillance of infiltration routes by day and night. An extensive array of communications equipment is used to notify law enforcement agencies of smuggling activity.*

Bell

AH-1 SeaCobra/SuperCobra

Development of the **AH-1G HueyCobra** gunship for the US Army prompted the Marines to look more closely at the concept of acquiring specialized attack helicopters to take over from the UH-1E Iroquois. That early interest soon resulted in a loan agreement under which a batch of 38 AH-1Gs was obtained from the Army and were soon committed to combat in Southeast Asia, where they generally performed well with the Marines.

Combat experience revealed a number of shortcomings, however, not least of which was the fact that the AH-1G was single-engined and also lacked a rotor brake. Since Marine operating doctrine was mainly predicated upon operation from amphibious assault ships, these two factors were addressed when the service got around to obtaining its own version of the 'Cobra, the **AH-1J**.

Optimized for the Marines, this utilized a United Aircraft of Canada (later Pratt & Whitney Canada) T400-CP-400 coupled turboshaft which neatly circumvented the desire for twin-engined safety. A rotor brake was also provided and the resulting SeaCobra was 'upgunned', using a General Electric M197 three-barrelled 20-mm cannon as the prime gun system. Other ordnance could be carried on the stub wings up to a maximum of around 2,200 lb (1000 kg), loads available including four 19-shot LAU-68 2.75-in (7-cm) rocket pods.

Delivery of the AH-1J began in April 1971 when the first four examples reached an activation cadre at New River, North Carolina. Within a couple of months this formed the

TOW missile launchers are carried under the stub wings of this rather shabby-looking USMC AH-1T SeaCobra. Unit inscriptions indicate assignment to a composite squadron.

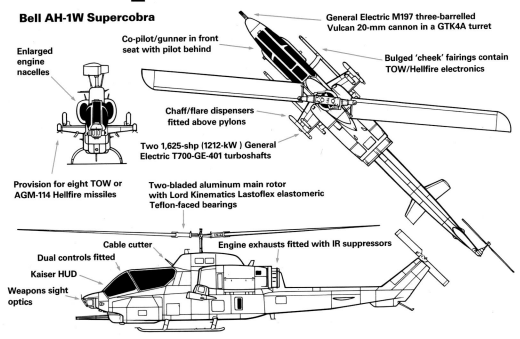

Bell AH-1W Supercobra

Enlarged engine nacelles

Co-pilot/gunner in front seat with pilot behind

General Electric M197 three-barrelled Vulcan 20-mm cannon in a GTK4A turret

Bulged 'cheek' fairings contain TOW/Hellfire electronics

Chaff/flare dispensers fitted above pylons

Two 1,625-shp (1212-kW) General Electric T700-GE-401 turboshafts

Provision for eight TOW or AGM-114 Hellfire missiles

Two-bladed aluminum main rotor with Lord Kinematics Lastoflex elastomeric Teflon-faced bearings

Cable cutter

Engine exhausts fitted with IR suppressors

Dual controls fitted

Kaiser HUD

Weapons sight optics

basis of Attack Helicopter Squadron HMA-269, the first of three similar units to be established within the Marine Corps. Missions undertaken included reconnaissance by fire, escort support of troop-carrying 'slick' helicopters, suppression of landing zones prior to insertion and interdiction of supply lines. Most of these tasks are still performed today, but newer versions of the gunship have brought additional weapons capability and extra tasks in their wake.

An initial batch of 49 AH-1Js was supplemented by a follow-on order for 20 more, although the last two were actually completed

as **AH-1T**s, with the first of these making its maiden flight in May 1976. Changes incorporated in this model were aimed at enhancing payload and performance, power being furnished by a Pratt & Whitney Canada T400-WV-402 turboshaft driving a revised transmission able to deliver full rated power of 1,970 shp. Extra fuel capacity resulted from a decision to 'stretch' the AH-1T by some 3 ft 7 in (1.1 m) and it was further modified to allow it to engage in 'tank-busting' tasks with the Hughes TOW anti-armor missile. Production eventually totalled some 55 aircraft, of which the last one served as the **AH-1T+** (later

AIM-9L, AGM-114 and AGM-122. The AH-1W is capable of carrying both TOW and Hellfire at the same time. All surviving AH-1J/Ts are gradually being converted to AH-1Ws.

Anti-tank/close air support: During Desert Storm AH-1Ws usually mounted LAU-68 rocket pods on their inboard pylons, with BGM-71s and/or AGM-114s outboard. Other weapons included CBU-55 for clearing minefields and AGM-122 for SEAD, with the latter replacing one set of anti-tank missiles.

VARIANTS AND SERIALS

AH-1J: Operational experience with loaned AH-1Gs paved the way for the AH-1J. This model was developed specifically for the Marines, procurement totaling some 69 examples. Acquisition of more modern versions has resulted in remaining AH-1Js being relegated to Reserve force units.
157757 to 157805; 159210 to 159229

AH-1T: Improvement of the AH-1J resulted in the AH-1T, which featured an extended fuselage and additional fuel capacity as well as a more powerful engine installation. Modification of the last two AH-1Js (159228 and 159229) as prototype AH-1Ts paved the way for procurement of 55 production AH-1Ts for Marine Corps usage, but virtually all have now been upgraded to AH-1Ws.
160105 to 160114; 160742 to 160748; 160797 to 160826; 161015 to 161022

AH-1W: The ultimate gunship helicopter in Marine Corps service, the AH-1W (originally AH-1T+) embodies a new engine package as well as improvements to armament capability and is now the standard model in the front-line inventory. The last AH-1T (161022) served as a prototype. Subsequent manufacture of at least 96 new-build airframes has been accompanied by a rework program involving the AH-1T. About 140 examples are thought to be in use.
New build: 162532 to 162575; 163921 to 163954; 164572 to 164578; 164586 to 164596
Conversions: 159228; 160107; 160113; 160743; 160747; 160800; 160801; 160803; 160806; 160813 to 160815; 160820 to 160822; 160825; 160826; 161016; 161017; 161019; 161020; 161022

The ultimate Marine Corps Cobra is the AH-1W, four examples of which are depicted here as they get airborne for a training exercise in the western United States.

AH-1W) SuperCobra prototype.

The principal difference on the AH-1W again relates to powerplant, the prototype using a pair of General Electric T700-GE-700 turboshaft engines, although production specimens have the T700-GE-401 with a combined output of 3,250 shp. Flown in prototype form for the first time in November 1983, the AH-1W began to enter service in early 1986. It is now the principal gunship with front-line light attack helicopter (HMLA) units of the Marine Corps. Procurement of new-build examples looks set to top the 100 mark and modification of the older AH-1T is also under way, at least 20 having been updated to full AH-1W standard with more expected to follow. In addition to the revised engine installation, the AH-1W also introduced new weaponry, which included AIM-9L Sidewinder heat-seeking air-to-air missiles so as to provide a measure of defensive capability in the event of encountering hostile helicopters or fighters.

Acquisition of new and modified machines has allowed the service to standardize on the AH-1W, at least as far as front-line echelons are concerned. It currently serves with six operational squadrons – four at Camp Pendleton, California, and two at New River, North Carolina – as well as a training unit at the former location. In addition, two Reserve outfits are still operating the original AH-1J derivative, although this has benefited from upgrades in regard to weaponry. Eventually, both of the Reserve units will probably also obtain the AH-1W.

Examples of both versions were committed to combat during the recent Gulf War. AH-1Ws were flown by four front-line squadrons (HMLA-169, -269, -367 and -369) that were sent to the region, these being ably supported by AH-1Js flown by the two second-line units (HMA-773 and -775), both of which were mobilized for active duty.

Operating from land bases in Saudi Arabia and amphibious assault ships in Gulf waters, they undertook armed escort duty during Desert Shield, riding 'shotgun' on vehicle convoys, and acting as 'slick' helicopters moving men and material around the Saudi Arabian desert during the build-up. Once Desert Storm kicked off, the 'Cobras took on a more offensive role and there is little doubt that they

claimed their share of enemy armor, being active during the battle for Khafji when they joined Marine AV-8Bs and warplanes in a concerted effort to blunt an Iraqi advance.

Rocket and gun armament probably featured heavily in the fighting around Khafji, with the 'Cobra performing in traditional fashion in support of coalition ground troops that included Marines. TOW and Hellfire anti-armor missiles may also have been expended then, since the Iraqi force did evidently include some armored fighting vehicles. Later, during the 100-hour ground battle to liberate Kuwait, the Hellfire weapons were certainly employed in considerable numbers and there is every reason to assume that the Marines were responsible for a proportion of those weapons.

MISSION PROFILE

Armament options: In addition to the standard GTK4A M197 turret cannon, Marine Cobras have a total of four weapon pylons on their stub wings. As the helicopter has gone through its various transformations, the types of weapons it can employ have increased. The AH-1J could carry rocket and gun pods. The AH-1T added to these with the 100-US gal (380-liter) fuel tank, CBU-55 FAE, M118 grenade launcher, SUU-44 flare dispenser and BGM-71 TOW. The AH-1W added the

Although possibly overshadowed by the US Army AH-64A Apache, the AH-1W SuperCobra played its part in Desert Storm operations.

SPECIFICATION

Bell AH-1W

Rotor system: main rotor diameter 48 ft 0 in (14.63 m); tail rotor diameter 9 ft 9 in (2.97 m); main rotor disc 1,809.56 sq ft (168.11 m²); tail rotor disc area 74.70 sq ft (6.94 m²)

Wing: span 10 ft 7 in (3.23 m); aspect ratio 3.74

Fuselage and tail: length overall, rotors turning 58 ft 0 in (17.68 m) and fuselage 45 ft 6 in (13.87 m); height overall 14 ft 2 in (4.32 m) and to top of rotor head 13 ft 6 in (4.11 m); tailplane span 6 ft 11 in (2.11 m)

Powerplant: two General Electric T700-GE-401 rated at 1,690 shp (1260 kW)

Weights: empty 10,200 lb (4627 kg); maximum take-off 14,750 lb (6690 kg)

Fuel and load: internal fuel 304.5 US gal (1153 liters); external fuel up to four 77-US gal (291-liter) or two 100-US gal (378-liter) external tanks; maximum ordnance 2,466 lb (1119 kg)

Speed: never exceed 219 mph (352 km/h); maximum level speed 'clean' at sea level 175 mph (282 km/h); cruising speed at optimum altitude 173 mph (278 km/h)

Range: range at sea level with standard fuel 395 miles (635 km)

Performance: maximum rate of climb at sea level, one engine out 800 ft (244 m) per minute; service ceiling more than 12,000 ft (3660 m); hovering ceiling 14,750 ft (4495 m) in ground effect

Bell AH-1J

generally similar to the AH-1W except in the following particulars:

Rotor system: main rotor diameter 44 ft 0 in (13.41 m); tail rotor diameter 8 ft 6 in (2.59 m); main rotor disc 1,520.4 sq ft (141.25 m²); tail rotor disc area 56.74 sq ft (5.27 m²)

Wing: span 10 ft 4 in (3.15 m)

Fuselage and tail: length overall, rotors turning 53 ft 4 in (16.26 m) and fuselage 44 ft 7 in (13.59 m); height overall 18 ft 8 in (4.15 m)

Powerplant: one Pratt & Whitney Canada T400-CP-400 rated at 1,800 shp (1342 kW) but flat-rated to 1,250 shp (932 kW) for take-off and 1,100 shp (820 kW) for continuous running

Weights: operating empty 7,261 lb (3294 kg); basic combat 9,972 lb (4523 kg); maximum take-off 10,000 lb (4535 kg)

Fuel and load: internal fuel 268 US gal (1014 liters); maximum ordnance 2,200 lb (998 kg)

Speed: never exceed and maximum level speed 'clean' at sea level 207 mph (333 km/h)

Range: range at sea level 359 miles (577 km)

Performance: maximum rate of climb at sea level 1,090 ft (332 m) per minute; service ceiling 10,550 ft (3215 m); hovering ceiling 12,450 ft (3795 m)

Bell AH-1T

generally similar to the AH-1W except in the following particulars:

Early morning light casts a glow over a pair of HMM-365 AH-1T SeaCobras as they prepare to lift off for the first mission of the day. A long-time Cobra operator, the Marine Corps has used four major sub-types since the late 1960s.

Rotor system: tail rotor diameter 9 ft 8.5 in (2.96 m); tail rotor disc area 74.02 sq ft (6.88 m²)

Wing: span 10 ft 4 in (3.15 m)

Fuselage and tail: length overall, rotors turning 56 ft 11 in (17.35 m) and fuselage 45 ft 6 in (14.68 m); height overall 13 ft 6.25 in (4.12 m)

Powerplant: one Pratt & Whitney Canada T400-WV-402 rated at 1,970 shp 1469 kW)

Weights: empty 8,014 lb (3635 kg); operating empty 8,608 lb (3904 kg); maximum take-off 14,0000 lb (6350 kg)

Fuel and load: internal fuel 304.5 US gal (1153 liters); external fuel up to four 77-US gal (291-liter) or two 100-US gal (378-liter) external tanks; maximum useful load (fuel and ordnance) 5,392 lb (2445 kg)

Speed: never exceed 207 mph (333 km/h); maximum level speed 'clean' at sea level 172 mph (277 km/h)

Range: maximum range 359 miles (577 km)

Performance: maximum rate of climb at sea level 1,785 ft (544 m) per minute; service ceiling 7,500 ft (2255 m)

OPERATORS

Left: Responsibility for the training of pilots and gunners for SeaCobra and SuperCobra units is entrusted to HMT-303 at Camp Pendleton. This AH-1W is typical of the gunships used and wears a distinctive camouflage pattern.

Bell
H-1 Iroquois

Although the development initiative that culminated in the **H-1 Iroquois** lay with the US Army, both the Navy and the Marine Corps have been major customers, buying in excess of 500 examples of this versatile but utilitarian helicopter for a variety of duties that include observation, assault support, light attack, Antarctic exploration and more general transport tasks.

Bulk procurement began in the early 1960s and centered around a navalized derivative of the Army's **UH-1B** incorporating such changes as a rotor brake, additional fuel capacity and revised avionics. Given the designation **UH-1E**, delivery of this model got under way in February 1964. A total of 209 examples was eventually delivered for service with Marine Corps observation squadrons.

Other versions followed in due course but these were all fundamentally similar to the UH-1E, comprising 20 **TH-1E**s and 45 **TH-1L**s for Navy pilot training, 27 **HH-1K**s for search and rescue tasks and eight **UH-1L**s for dual utility/training functions. A number of **UH-1B**s and **UH-1D**s were also obtained on loan from the US Army, the former being employed in Vietnam by HAL-3 which was engaged in riverine operations, while the latter were used to augment Navy training units. Apart from a very small number of TH-1Ls assigned to test organizations, none of these versions remains in service today.

The Iroquois is still widely used by both the Navy and the Marines, but the principal version is now the **HH-1N**. Development of this sub-type arose in response to a Canadian government request for a general-purpose derivative powered by a Pratt & Whitney Canada PT6T-3 Turbo Twin-Pac flat-rated to 1,290 shp (960 kW). Selection of this power-plant offered significant safety benefits since it uses a pair of PT6 engines with a combining gearbox – so, in the event of one PT6 failing, the other will still provide power to drive the rotor blades.

For the Marines, which routinely operated the 'Huey' from the flight decks of amphibious assault vessels, this single feature more than justified adoption of the **UH-1N**. However, there were other benefits, not least of which was much improved performance in 'hot-and-high' conditions; that, too, was welcomed by the Marines as well as the Navy, which received its fair share of the 205 examples that were eventually delivered. In addition, half a dozen VIP-configured **VH-1N**s were acquired for use as staff transports with HMX-1 at Quantico, although it appears that these have all now been withdrawn from service.

As far as operational use is concerned, most of the Navy-owned machines are assigned to base flight elements for local utility/SAR duties. About half a dozen serve with VXE-6 on Antarctic exploration, and a similar number

are flown by HC-16 at Pensacola on SAR and training tasks. By far the majority are used by the Marines which has reorganized part of its large rotary-winged force in fairly recent times, amalgamating the once separate light (HML) and attack (HMA) helicopter squadrons into combined light/attack (HMLA) units which operate UH-1Ns as well as AH-1 Sea-Cobras. 'Huey' missions still include conventional communications and liaison duties but also extend to encompass direct support of attack elements.

Currently, six front-line HMLA units exist, with a definite preponderance of assets assigned to the Fleet Marine Force Pacific (FMFPac), which has four squadrons (HMLA-169, -267, -367 and -369) at Camp Pendleton, California, as well as a specialist training outfit (HMT-303). Its East Coast counterpart, Fleet Marine Force Atlantic (FMFLant), has only two squadrons

(HMLA-167 and -269), both of which reside at New River, North Carolina. One other regular Marine unit which operates the UH-1N is HMH-463 at Kaneohe Bay, Hawaii, which has a few examples for use in support of 1st Marine Expeditionary Brigade activities.

In addition, a few base flights at Marine Corps air stations use some U/HH-1Ns, and it is usual practice to assign one 'Huey' to each of the 'large-deck' amphibious assault vessels for general duties. When at sea, these ships generally deploy with a composite squadron which typically will include three UH-1Ns, 12 CH-46s, four CH-53s, six AH-1s and six AV-8Bs. However, these quantities can be adjusted to meet changing circumstances.

Finally, three Marine Corps Reserve Force light helicopter squadrons also use the UH-1N in modest quantities, these being located at New Orleans, Louisiana; Glenview, Illinois; and South Weymouth, Massachusetts.

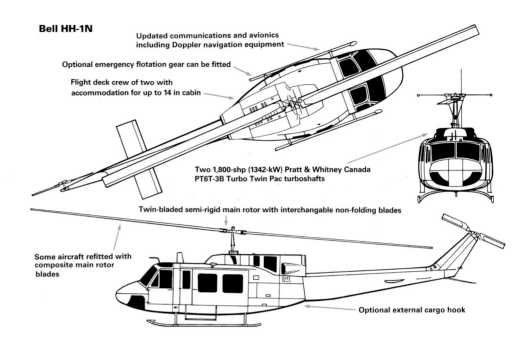

Bell HH-1N

Updated communications and avionics including Doppler navigation equipment

Optional emergency flotation gear can be fitted

Flight deck crew of two with accommodation for up to 14 in cabin

Two 1,800-shp (1342-kW) Pratt & Whitney Canada PT6T-3B Turbo Twin Pac turboshafts

Twin-bladed semi-rigid main rotor with interchangable non-folding blades

Some aircraft refitted with composite main rotor blades

Optional external cargo hook

Right: Low-visibility colors provide a strong contrast to the sea as a HMM-365 UH-1N heads off from its parent amphibious assault ship.

H-1 Iroquois (continued)

MISSION PROFILE

Configuration options: The H-1 is employed in a wide range of missions by the USN and USMC. Provision exists for most versions to be armed with door-mounted .50-in caliber or 7.62-mm M60 machine guns for self-protection. Front-line USMC UH-1Ns have chaff/flare dispensers and IR decoys for battlefield operations. Antarctic development aircraft are configured with skis to assist snow landings.

Light attack/forward air control (airborne): USMC UH-1Ns now serve almost exclusively in this role supporting AH-1 Cobra attack helicopters. Some are fitted with FLIR and laser designators to locate and mark targets for Hellfire missiles fired from AH-1Ws. UH-1Ns deployed on amphibious assault ships also carry out general transport and liaison tasks.

Rescue/utility/Antarctic development: US Navy UH/HH-1Ns serve in a handful of units. They have a maximum range of 374 miles (600 km) with an external load of 4,000 lb (1800 kg).

VARIANTS AND SERIALS

HH-1K: A very small number of HH-1Ks remain in use from the 27 machines that were obtained for rescue tasks and, later, in light attack duties with the Navy Reserve.
157177 to 157203

TH-1L: Some 45 examples of this Iroquois version were used for pilot training for many years. Most have now been disposed of following replacement by the TH-57 but a few are still active at test establishments.
157806 to 157850

HH-1N: A total of 38 UH-1Ns and six VH-1Ns was redesignated as HH-1Ns, although it appears doubtful if the change in designation was accompanied by any physical modification. Most are assigned to local base rescue flights but one example is usually allocated to

Most of the Iroquois that are flown by the Navy are primarily employed for search and rescue tasks, a mission that prompted a recent decision to redesignate virtually all of them from UH-1Ns to HH-1Ns.

act as ship's flights aboard amphibious assault vessels when deployed at sea.
158230; 158231; 158233 to 158235; 158238; 158240; 158242; 158244 to 158246; 158248 to 158250; 158252; 158253; 158256 to 158258; 158264; 158272; 158275; 158278; 158283; 158290; 158551 to 158554; 158556; 158557; 158762 to 158764; 158766; 158770; 158771; 160827; 160829; 160830; 160832; 160834; 160836; 160838

UH-1N: Procurement of this version totalled 205, most of which were destined for service with the Marine Corps. The UH-1N is still in widespread service today on a variety of tasks.
158230 to 158291; 158548 to 158550; 158555; 158558 to 158562; 158762 to 158785; 159186 to 159209; 159565; 159680 to 159703; 159774 to 159777; 160165 to 160179; 160438 to 160461; 160619 to 160624; 160827 to 160838

VH-1N: Six examples of the Iroquois were diverted from a UH-1N contract and completed as VH-1Ns for VIP transportation duties, a task they fulfilled until replaced by the VH-60N. All have since been redesignated as HH-1Ns but most, if not all, are now in storage.
158551 to 158554; 158556; 158557

SPECIFICATION

Bell UH-1N
Rotor system: main rotor diameter with tracking tips 48 ft 2.25 in (14.69 m); tail rotor diameter 8 ft 6 in (2.59 m); main rotor disc area 1,823.72 sq ft (169.42 m²); tail rotor disc area 56.74 sq ft (5.27 m²)
Fuselage and tail: length overall, rotors turning 57 ft 3.25 in (17.46 m) and fuselage 42 ft 4.75 in (12.92 m); height 14 ft 4.75 in (4.39 m); tailplane span 9 ft 4.5 in (2.86 m)
Powerplant: one Pratt & Whitney Canada T400-CP-400 rated at 1,800 shp (1342 kW) but flat rated to 1,290 shp (962 kW) for take-off and 1,100 shp (820 kW) for continuous running
Weights: empty 6,196 lb (2798 kg); normal take-off 10,500 lb (4762 kg); maximum take-off 11,200 lb (5080 kg)
Fuel and load: internal fuel 215 US gal (814 liters); maximum payload 3,383 lb (1534 kg)
Speed: maximum level speed at sea level 126 mph (203 km/h)
Range: maximum range 248 miles (400 m)
Performance: maximum rate of climb at sea level 1,745 ft (532 m) per minute; service ceiling 15,000 ft (4570 m); hovering ceiling 12,900 ft 3930 m) in ground effect and 4,900 ft (1495 m) out of ground effect

Bell UH-1E
generally similar to the UN-1N except in the following particulars:
Rotor system: main rotor diameter 44 ft 0 in (13.41 m); tail rotor diameter 8 ft 6 in (2.59 m); main rotor disc area 1,520.5 sq ft (141.26 m²); tail rotor disc area 56.74 sq ft (5.72 m²)
Fuselage and tail: length overall, rotors turning 53 ft 0 in (16.15 m) and fuselage 42 ft 7 in (12.98 m); height 12 ft 7.25 in (3.84 m); tailplane span 9 ft 4 in (2.84 m)
Powerplant: one Avco Lycoming T53-L-11 rated at

Quite a few examples of the Iroquois are assigned to base flights for local rescue work. Most have been redesignated as HH-1Ns, but this Marine machine from Yuma is still a UH-1N.

1,100 shp (820 kW)
Weights: empty 5,055 lb (2292 kg); maximum take-off 9,500 lb (4309 kg)
Fuel and load: internal fuel 243 US gal (920 liters); maximum payload 4,000 lb (1814 kg)
Speed: maximum level speed at sea level 161 mph (259 km/h); maximum cruising speed at sea level 138 mph (222 km/h)
Range: range with maximum fuel 286 miles (460 km)
Performance: maximum rate of climb at sea level 1,849 ft (563 m) per minute; service ceiling 21,000 ft (6400 m); hovering ceiling 15,800 ft (4815 m) in ground effect and 11,800 (3595 m) out of ground effect

Bell HH-1K
generally similar to the UH-1E except in the following particulars:
Powerplant: one Avco Lycoming T53-L-13 rated at 1,400 shp (1044 kW)

Bell TH-1L
generally similar to the UH-1E except in the following particulars:
Powerplant: one Avco Lycoming T53-L-13 rated at 1,400 shp (1044 kW) derated to 1,100 shp (820 kW)

Marine helicopter attack squadrons also operate the UH-1N in support of the AH-1.

OPERATORS

US Navy (USN)

HC-16	Pensacola, FL	HH-1N
TW-1	Meridian, MS	HH-1N
TW-4	Corpus Christi, TX	HH-1N
VXE-6	Point Mugu, CA	HH-1N, UH-1N
NAWC/AD	Patuxent River, MD	TH-1L
NAWC/WD	China Lake, CA	HH-1K, TH-1L, HH-1N
LHA-1	USS Tarawa	HH-1N
LHA-2	USS Saipan	HH-1N
LHA-3	USS Belleau Wood	HH-1N
LHA-4	USS Nassau	HH-1N
LHA-5	USS Peleliu	HH-1N
LHD-1	USS Wasp	HH-1N
LPH-2	USS Iwo Jima	HH-1N
LPH-3	USS Okinawa	HH-1N
LPH-7	USS Guadalcanal	HH-1N
LPH-9	USS Guam	HH-1N
LPH-10	USS Tripoli	HH-1N
LPH-11	USS New Orleans	HH-1N
LPH-12	USS Inchon	HH-1N
NAS	Bermuda	HH-1N
NAS	Brunswick, ME	HH-1N
NAS	Fallon, NV	HH-1N
NAS	Lemoore, CA	HH-1N

US Marine Corps (USMC)

HMLA-167	New River, NC	UH-1N
HMLA-169	Camp Pendleton, CA	UH-1N
HMLA-267	Camp Pendleton, CA	UH-1N
HMLA-269	New River, NC	UH-1N
HMT-303	Camp Pendleton, CA	UH-1N
HMLA-367	Camp Pendleton, CA	UH-1N
HMLA-369	Camp Pendleton, CA	UH-1N
HML-767	New Orleans, LA	UH-1N
HML-771	South Weymouth, MA	UH-1N
HML-776	Glenview, IL	UH-1N
MCAS	El Toro, CA	UH-1N
MCAS	Yuma, AZ	UH-1N

Kaman
SH-2 Seasprite

Another of the growing number of US Navy types that has been reinstated in production, the **Kaman Seasprite** initially entered service as a single-engined design in response to a 1956 Navy request for a new search and rescue helicopter with secondary liaison and communications roles. Since those early days, it has demonstrated a fair degree of versatility, with suitably modified versions being called upon to undertake armed combat, SAR and antisubmarine warfare; there were even proposals for the Army to use it as a gunship. Changing roles have been accompanied by changes in appearance and the contemporary Seasprite is indeed a very different beast from that which began its US Navy career with Helicopter Utility Squadron Two (HU-2) at Lakehurst, New Jersey, in December 1962.

Original production totalled just 190 machines, a quartet of **YHU2K-1** (**YUH-2A** post-1962) prototypes being followed along the line by 84 **HU2K-1**s (**UH-2A**s) and 102 **HU2K-1U**s (**UH-2B**s). Differences were mainly concerned with the avionics kit, shortages of government-furnished equipment resulting in the UH-2B version being initially configured for purely day VFR operation, although it subsequently acquired full IFR capability. Power was provided by a single General Electric T58-GE-8 turboshaft engine, driving a four-bladed main rotor and a three-bladed anti-torque tail rotor.

For operations over land, this was perfectly adequate. Over sea, however, it was a different matter entirely, and it was the desire for additional safety that lay at the heart of the first major modification project. Company trials of a twin-engined Seasprite began as early as March 1965, this using two T58-GE-8B turboshafts offering a combined maximum power output of 1,685 shp. Navy interest soon brought an order for two prototype **UH-2C** conversions. Testing of these in 1966 led, in turn, to a go-ahead for production conversions

in August of that year, with deliveries following almost exactly 12 months later.

Subsequent developments saw the appearance of the armed and armored **HH-2C** for combat SAR and of the **HH-2D**, which was similar although it lacked armament and armor. Both models used the more powerful T58-GE-8F engine, other alterations being the adoption of a four-bladed tail rotor and twin-wheel main undercarriage units, these being an essential stepping stone in development of the LAMPS (Light Airborne Multi-Purpose System) derivatives which were optimized for antisubmarine warfare (ASW) and anti-ship missile defense (ASMD) missions.

The Kaman helicopter was initially viewed as merely an interim solution to the desire to increase the ASW capability of surface combatants such as destroyers and frigates, but has actually proved to be more enduring and is set to be around until well into the next century. First to appear was the **SH-2D**, only 20 examples being converted before the definitive **SH-2F** made its debut in the early 1970s. This incorporates Kaman's '101' advanced rotor as well as Marconi LN66HP surface-search radar, a tactical navigation/communications system, an AN/ASQ-81(V)2 towed MAD bird, capacity for up to 15 SSQ-41 passive or SSQ-47 active sonobuoys in a launch rack on the port fuselage side and two torpedoes with which to engage sub-surface threats. In addition, a notable external difference concerned the tailwheel which was shifted forward by some 6 ft (1.8 m) so as to provide greater deck-edge clearance when operating from landing platforms aboard smaller warships.

Approximately 100 existing Seasprites – UH-2As, UH-2Bs, UH-2Cs and SH-2Ds – were subjected to the modification program and reconfigured as SH-2Fs, with US Navy resources being boosted by the 1981 decision to re-open the production line with an initial order for 18 brand-new Seasprites. Further

Even though it is configured for ASW and ASMD roles, the SH-2F Seasprite is a versatile machine and may well be called upon to fulfil other tasks, including SAR and insertion and recovery of covert forces.

contracts followed and over 60 were eventually built, raising total production to slightly over the 250 mark. Most of the survivors are expected to be further modified as **SH-2Gs**, featuring the more powerful General Electric T700-GE-401 turboshaft. First flown on the **YSH-2G** prototype in late 1984, this fuel-efficient engine offers range and reliability benefits and is presently scheduled to be installed on roughly 100 Seasprites.

In service, the Seasprite is principally concerned with extending the area of protection provided by the outer defensive screen to a carrier battle group. It usually deploys aboard compatible surface warships in detachments of one or two helicopters provided by squadrons sited conveniently close to the major Navy port installations. Main shore bases operating in support of Atlantic Fleet elements are located at Norfolk, Virginia, which has two deployable squadrons (HSL-32 and HSL-34) and Mayport, Florida, which has one (HSL-36). In addition, Norfolk also has a training unit (HSL-30). Pacific Fleet equivalents are HSL-31 (training), HSL-33 and HSL-35 all at North Island, California, and HSL-37 at Barbers Point, Hawaii.

Finally, three Navy Reserve squadrons also operate the SH-2F but all three are due to obtain SH-2Gs in the near future, if they have not begun to do so already. These units comprise HSL-74 at South Weymouth, Massachusetts; HSL-84 at North Island, California; and HSL-94 at Willow Grove, Pennsylvania. In the normal course of events they do not deploy, although active-duty training obligations do involve brief periods of sea duty so as to remain current in the techniques and skills of operating helicopters at sea.

The MAD bird and surface-search radar of the SH-2F version are clearly visible on this low-visibility example from HSL-32.

Kaman SH-2F Seasprite Mk 1 LAMPS

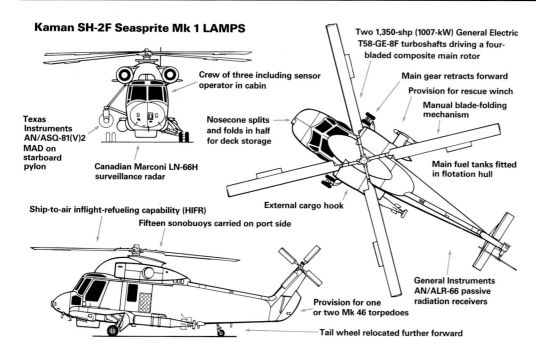

Crew of three including sensor operator in cabin

Two 1,350-shp (1007-kW) General Electric T58-GE-8F turboshafts driving a four-bladed composite main rotor

Main gear retracts forward

Provision for rescue winch

Manual blade-folding mechanism

Texas Instruments AN/ASQ-81(V)2 MAD on starboard pylon

Nosecone splits and folds in half for deck storage

Canadian Marconi LN-66H surveillance radar

Main fuel tanks fitted in flotation hull

Ship-to-air inflight-refueling capability (HIFR)

External cargo hook

Fifteen sonobuoys carried on port side

General Instruments AN/ALR-66 passive radiation receivers

Provision for one or two Mk 46 torpedoes

Tail wheel relocated further forward

SH-2 Seasprite (continued)

MISSION PROFILE

Armament options: The SH-2F is limited to two store stations which can carry either 100-US gal (380-liter) fuel tanks, Mk 46 or Mk 50 torpedoes.

ASW: Dating from 1960 and created as one of those famous interim requirements (like the B-52), the Seasprite came from the light airborne multi-purpose system (LAMPS). It has evolved into an ASW platform, typically deployed in detachments of one or two aircraft aboard destroyers, frigates and guided missile cruisers.

SPECIFICATION

Kaman SH-2G

Rotor system: main rotor diameter 44 ft 4 in (13.51 m); tail rotor diameter 8 ft 1 in (2.46 m); main rotor disc area 1,543.66 sq ft (143.41 m²); tail rotor disc area 51.32 sq ft (4.77 m²)

Despite the age of the basic design, the Seasprite continues to fulfil an important role and is unlikely to disappear from the inventory in the immediate future. Efforts to upgrade its capability still further have resulted in the SH-2G, which relies on the General Electric T700 turboshaft engine for power, giving much better range and reliability. Flown in prototype form in the mid-1980s, the SH-2G is expected to see service with Fleet units.

Fuselage and tail: length overall, rotors turning 52 ft 9 in (16.08 m), fuselage excluding tail rotor 40 ft 0 in (12.19 m), and fuselage with nose and blades folded 38 ft 4 in (11.68 m); height overall with rotors turning 15 ft 0.5 in (4.58 m) and overall with blades folded 13 ft 7 in (4.14 m); tailplane span 9 ft 9 in (2.97 m); wheel base 16 ft 10 in (5.13 m)

Powerplant: two General Electric T700-GE-401 rated at 1,723 shp (1285 kW)

Weights: empty 7,680 lb (3483 kg); maximum take-off 13,500 lb (6123 kg)

Fuel and load: internal fuel 276 US gal (1045 liters); external fuel up to two 100-US gal (379-liter) external auxiliary tanks; maximum payload 4,000 lb (1814 kg)

Speed: maximum level speed 'clean' at sea level 150 mph (241 km/h); normal cruising speed 138 mph (222 km/h)

Range: maximum range 506 miles (815 km); time on station 40 mile (65 km) radius 2 hours 10 minutes with one torpedo or 1 hour 30 minutes with two torpedoes

Performance: maximum rate of climb at sea level 1,550 ft (472 m) per minute; service ceiling 16,700 ft (5090 m); hovering ceiling 1,4400 ft (4390 m) in ground effect and 10,900 ft (3320 m) out of ground effect

Kaman SH-2F

generally similar to the SH-2G except in the following particulars:

Rotor system: main rotor diameter 44 ft 0 in (13.41 m); tail rotor diameter 8 ft 2 in (2.49 m); main rotor disc area 1,520.53 sq ft (141.26 m²); tail rotor disc area 52.38 sq ft (4.87 m²)

Fuselage and tail: length overall, rotors turning 52 ft 7 in (16.03 m); height overall with rotors turning 15 ft 6 in (4.72 m) and to top of rotor head 13 ft 5 in (4.09 m);

wheel base 16 ft 9 in (5.11 m)

Powerplant: two General Electric T58-GE-8F rated at 1,350 shp (1007 kW)

Weights: empty 7,040 lb (3193 kg); maximum take-off 12,800 lb (5805 kg) overload take-off 13,300 lb (6033 kg)

Fuel and load: external fuel up to two 60-US gal (227-liter) external auxiliary tanks; maximum ordnance 1,200 lb (544 kg)

Speed: maximum level speed 'clean' at sea level 165 mph (265 km/h); normal cruising speed 150 mph (241 km/h)

Range: maximum range 422 miles (679 km)

Performance: maximum rate of climb at sea level 2,440 ft (774 m) per minute; service ceiling 22,500 ft (6860 m); hovering ceiling 18,600 ft (5670 m) in ground effect and 15,400 ft (4695 m) out of ground effect

VARIANTS AND SERIALS

YUH-2A: Four prototypes of the Seasprite were obtained for test and trials work but none remain active. 147202 to 147205

UH-2A: The initial production version of the Seasprite was the single-engined UH-2A, some 84 examples of which were purchased for the utility role. None remain in service in original form, but many are still operational as SH-2Fs. 147972 to 147983; 149013 to 149036; 149739 to 149786

UH-2B: Development of Kaman's versatile helicopter led to the twin-engined UH-2B and manufacture of this model eventually terminated after 104 had been completed. As with the UH-2A, none survive in their original form but many were brought to SH-2F standard. 150139 to 150186; 151300 to 151335; 152189 to 152206

SH-2F: Obtained to satisfy the Navy's interim LAMPS requirement, the first SH-2Fs were acquired by virtue of a CILOP program which resulted in approximately 100 existing airframes being modified. Subsequently, a shortage of airframes led to the Seasprite being reinstated in production, and some 66 new-build examples were obtained.
New build: 161641 to 161658; 161898 to 161915; 162576 to 162587; 163209 to 163214; 163541 to 163552
Conversions: 147980; 149013; 149015; 149017; 149019; 149021 to 149024; 149026; 149030; 149031; 149033; 149035; 149036; 149744; 149747; 149748; 149750; 149753; 149755; 149758; 149761; 149765; 149766; 149768 to 149773; 149779; 149780; 150139 to 150141; 150143; 150146; 150148; 150150; 150152; 150154 to 150160; 150163 to 150167; 150169; 150171; 150173 to 150175; 150178; 150179; 150181; 150185; 151300; 151303; 151304 to 151306; 151308 to 151314; 151316; 151319; 151321; 151323; 151325 to 151327; 151329 to 151335; 152189 to 152192; 152199 to 152201; 152203 to 152206

SH-2G: Incorporating a new T700 turboshaft engine installation, the SH-2G possesses greater range and reliability characteristics and was first flown in prototype form during the mid-1980s. Plans exist to update approximately 100 SH-2Fs to this standard, but the program has been affected by budgetary concerns and its extent may be curtailed. 161653

OPERATORS

US Navy (USN)

HSL-30	Norfolk, VA	SH-2F
HSL-31	North Island, CA	SH-2F
HSL-32	Norfolk, VA	SH-2F
HSL-33	North Island, CA	SH-2F
HSL-34	Norfolk, VA	SH-2F
HSL-35	North Island, CA	SH-2F
HSL-36	Mayport, FL	SH-2F
HSL-37	Barbers Point, HI	SH-2F
HSL-74	South Weymouth, MA	SH-2F
HSL-84	North Island, CA	SH-2F
HSL-94	Willow Grove, PA	SH-2F
VX-1	Patuxent River, MD	SH-2F
NAWC/AD	Patuxent River, MD	SH-2F

Sikorsky
SH-3 Sea King

Now in the process of being replaced by the SH-60F, Sikorsky's sub-hunting **Sea King** began life as the **HSS-2** during the late 1950s and has functioned as the Navy's premier sea-going anti-submarine warfare helicopter since entering operational service with HS-3 in 1961. In addition, it is also used by the Marine Corps as a VIP transport and a specially configured variant serves with the US Coast Guard on search and rescue duties.

Following the successful testing of 10 **YSH-3A** development specimens, production of ASW-configured Sea Kings for the US Navy eventually totalled 318, composed of 245 **SH-3A**s, one **YSH-3D** prototype and 72 **SH-3D**s. However, post-production modification programs mean that very few remain active in their original form, although HC-16 at Pensacola does still use a handful of SH-3Ds even though there probably isn't too much call for submarine hunting in the Gulf of Mexico.

As a result of these conversion programs, the principal versions with the Navy are now the **SH-3G** and **SH-3H**. In the case of the SH-3G, the designation is actually quite mis-leading and it should more properly be considered as a utility helicopter, since conversion entailed removal of mission-related ASW avionics with the space vacated being used to fit rudimentary seating for up to 15 passengers and additional fuel tanks. Just over 100 Sea Kings were modified to SH-3G standard with many subsequently being reconfigured as SH-3Hs, and it is doubtful if more than a

Now in the process of giving way to the SH-60F, the veteran SH-3H Sea King has been the only anti-submarine warfare helicopter to serve aboard Navy aircraft carriers for many years, and its retirement is long overdue.

couple of dozen remain in use. Principal operators of the SH-3G are HC-1 at North Island and HC-2 at Norfolk, with the latter parenting a Bahrain-based detachment that flies three or four examples in support of Commander Middle East Forces (ComMidEastFor). Other SH-3Gs are assigned to VC-5 at Cubi Point and VC-8 at Roosevelt Roads, with one of their most important tasks being the recovery of Firebee drones from the sea.

The SH-3H, on the other hand, is very much concerned with ASW and arose out of a Navy desire to give the Sea King enhanced capability in the ASW and ASMD roles, so that it might

more effectively counter sub-surface and aerial threats like low-flying missiles. New equipment for ASMD included electronic surveillance measurement (ESM) gear and Marconi Canada LN66HP radar, while detection of sub-surface threats was improved through provision of AQS-13B dunking sonar and an ASQ-81 towed MAD, which could be streamed from the starboard undercarriage sponson. Eventually, the ESM and LN66HP were deleted in favor of a tactical navigation system and improved sonobuoy-processing capability, with well over 100 SH-3As, SH-3Ds and SH-3Gs being brought up to SH-3H standard during 1972-80.

In recent times, deployment practice has been based on assigning one six-aircraft SH-3H squadron to each carrier air wing. When operating at sea, these are principally

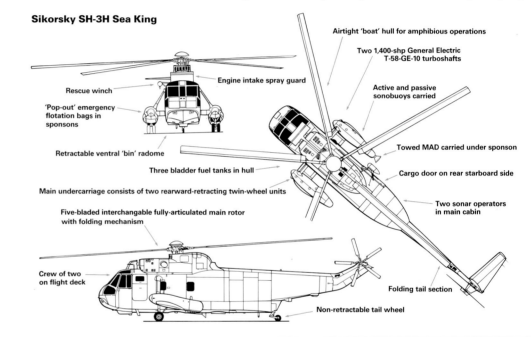

Sikorsky SH-3H Sea King

Although configured for ASW duties, Navy SH-3Hs were also tasked with plane guard, and a helicopter of this type was never far away when fixed-wing flight operations were in progress. With the impending demise of the Sea King, this job will fall to the HH-60H.

SH-3 Sea King (continued)

concerned with inner-zone defense against submarines, although they are fitted with rescue hoists and do, as a matter of routine, fulfil plane-guard functions during launch and recovery periods.

However, as already noted, the SH-60F is now beginning to replace the veteran Sea King, at least four squadrons having converted to the newer Sikorsky type. For the moment, that leaves three front-line SH-3H squadrons with the Pacific Fleet (HS-8 and -14 at North Island, plus HS-12 at Atsugi) and five with the Atlantic Fleet at Jacksonville (HS-5, -7, -9, -11 and -15), each of these two 'communities' also having a training squadron in its line-up. Other units with SH-3Hs comprise development squadron VX-1 at Patuxent River and a couple of squadrons with the Helicopter Wing Reserve, specifically HS-75 at Jacksonville and HS-85 at Alameda. Some are also flown by test organizations.

Marine Corps use of the Sea King has been confined to the VIP airlift role, a task which is performed by the Executive Flight Detachment of HMX-1 from Quantico. Initial equipment consisted of eight **VH-3A**s ordered as long ago as 1961, but these were eventually replaced in 1976 by a batch of 11 **VH-3D**s, still operated. Used to carry senior government officials and foreign dignitaries, the radio call sign 'Marine One' is used whenever the President is aboard one of these handsomely appointed helicopters.

Retaining the generic S-61 company designation, the Coast Guard **HH-3F** differs significantly in terms of physical appearance and also bears a different name, being known as the **Pelican**. Some 40 examples were acquired from 1968 onwards, these being basically similar to the Air Force **HH-3E**, although they lack armor plate and other combat SAR-related equipment. Search radar is contained in a bulbous nose fairing and the cabin is able to accommodate as many as 15 stretchers. Today, these aircraft operate from around half a dozen locations. The Coast Guard has obtained nine surplus USAF CH-3Es for use as a spares source, although at least one has since been restored to active duty as an HH-3F and it is possible that one or two more might follow.

Known by the Coast Guard as the Pelican, the HH-3F is used in fairly modest numbers for search and rescue work and presently operates from a total of eight air stations.

MISSION PROFILE

Armament options: For the ASW mission the SH-3H can carry 840 lb (380 kg) of stores, usually Mk 46 or Mk 50 torpedoes.

Plane guard and ASW: Sea Kings are based on attack carriers and tasked with plane guard and ASW missions. The plane guard mission is a vital part of every carrier evolution, standing by to rescue any aircrew who might end up in the water.

VARIANTS AND SERIALS

YSH-3A: A total of 10 development examples of the Sea King was obtained for trials duties, later being redesignated as SH-3As. None remain in original form but a few are still used on utility tasks as the UH-3A.
147137 to 147146

SH-3A: The initial production version of the Sea King was built in considerable quantity, some 245 being acquired for ASW duties with the Navy. Subsequent modification to SH-3G and SH-3H standard has resulted in this model disappearing from the Fleet.
148033 to 148052; 148964 to 149012; 149679 to 149738; 149893 to 149934; 150618 to 150620; 151522 to 151557; 152104 to 152138

UH-3A: At least seven development and early production Sea Kings have been stripped of mission equipment and assigned to utility transport duties.
147140 to 147142; 147146; 148038; 148040; 148041

VH-3A: Eight VIP-configured Sea Kings were purchased for service with Marine Corps squadron HMX-1. These were eventually replaced by VH-3Ds and the survivors are now employed on utility transport duties. Although they have probably been stripped of their VIP interiors, they retain the original designation.
150610 to 150617

YSH-3D: The final aircraft on the last SH-3A contract was actually completed as the prototype of a new ASW-dedicated version. Following the end of its test career, it was modified to SH-3H standard and issued to the Fleet.
152139

SH-3D: Testing of the SH-3D paved the way for full-scale production and a total of 72 examples was completed, these featuring a more powerful engine installation, improved sonar and additional fuel capacity. Most have since been updated to SH-3H standard.
152690 to 152713; 154100 to 154123; 156483 to 156506

VH-3D: The second VIP-configured version was the VH-3D, 11 examples being acquired to replace the VH-3A with HMX-1 on executive transport tasks.
159350 to 159360

CH-3E/HH-3E: At least nine former USAF machines have been transferred to the US Coast Guard, primarily as a source of spare parts. Three are known to have adopted USCG identities, which indicates that they were placed in service.

USCG identity assigned: 2791 (65-12791); 2793 (65-12793); 9691 (63-9691)
Spares/instructional: 62-12578; 63-9679; 64-14234; 65-12788 to 65-12790

HH-3F: A total of 40 examples of the HH-3F was obtained for use by the US Coast Guard in the search and rescue role. Fitted with nose-mounted radar, they are fully amphibious and can accommodate up to 15 stretcher patients.
1430 to 1438; 1467 to 1497

SH-3G: Removal of certain ASW mission avionics equipment resulted in the SH-3G utility version. Approximately 100 SH-3As were brought to this standard, but many were subsequently converted to SH-3H configuration. The following listing is incomplete.
148034; 148035; 148037; 148039; 148044 to 148048; 148050 to 148052; 148970; 148971; 148973; 148974; 148979; 148987; 148989; 148996; 149000; 149003; 149006; 149679; 149683; 149688; 149694 to 149700; 149702; 149710; 149720; 149722; 149724; 149729 to 149731; 149733; 149737; 149893; 149897; 149914; 149915; 149919; 149923; 149925; 149930; 149932; 150620; 151527; 151529; 151532; 151533; 151536; 151539; 151544; 151545; 151547; 151554; 151555

SH-3H: An improved ASW-dedicated version, incorporating Canadian Marconi LN66HP radar and updated electronics equipment. Roughly 150 SH-3A, SH-3D and SH-3G airframes were modified to SH-3H standard, the rework program also including a pair of former USAF CH-3Bs.
148035; 148036; 148039; 148042; 148043; 148045; 148048 to 148050; 148052; 148964 to 148968; 148969; 148971; 148972; 148974; 148976; 148977; 148980; 148981; 148983; 148984; 148986 to 148988; 148990; 148992; 148995 to 148999; 149005; 149006; 149010; 149684; 149687; 149688; 149690; 149693; 149701 to 149703; 149705; 149706; 149708; 149711 to 149713; 149717 to 149719; 149722; 149724 to 149728; 149730; 149735; 149736; 149738; 149894; 149897 to 149900; 149902; 149904 to 149906; 149910; 149913; 149917; 149918; 149921; 149923; 149927; 149929; 149931; 149934; 151524 to 151526; 151528; 151535; 151541; 151543; 151544; 151546; 151549 to 151551; 152104; 152107 to 152110; 152112; 152113; 152115; 152116; 152119; 152121 to 152125; 152128 to 152139; 152694; 152700 to 152704; 152707; 152709; 154101 to 154103; 154106; 154119; 154121; 154122; 156483; 156484; 156491; 156495; 156498; 156501; 156505; 156506; 212574 (ex-USAF); 212575 (ex-USAF)

SPECIFICATION

Sikorsky SH-3H

Rotor system: main rotor diameter 62 ft 0 in (18.90 m); tail rotor diameter 10 ft 7 in (3.23 m); main rotor disc area 3,019.0 sq ft (280.47 m²); tail rotor disc area 87.97 sq ft (8.17 m²)

Fuselage and tail: length overall, rotors turning 72 ft 8 in (22.15 m), fuselage 54 ft 9 in (16.69 m) and with tail pylon folded 47 ft 3 in (14.40 m); height overall 16 ft 10 in (5.13 m) and to top of rotor head 15 ft 6 in (4.72 m); wheel base 23 ft 1.5 in (7.18 m)

Powerplant: two General Electric T58-GE-10 rated at

Marine Corps operation of the Sea King is limited to a small number which fulfil VVIP airlift tasks from Quantico, VA. Known as VH-3Ds, these are flown by HMX-1 and the radio call sign 'Marine One' is used whenever the US President is aboard.

1,400 shp (1044 kW)
Weights: empty 12,350 lb (5601 kg); maximum take-off 21,000 lb (9525 kg)
Fuel and load: internal fuel 840 US gal (3180 liters); maximum ordnance 840 lb (381 kg)
Speed: maximum level speed 'clean' at optimum altitude 166 mph (267 km/h); cruising speed for maximum range 136 mph (219 km/h)
Range: maximum range 625 miles (1005 m)
Performance: maximum rate of climb at sea level 2,200 ft (670 m) per minute; service ceiling 14,700 ft (4480 m); hovering ceiling 10,500 ft (3200 m) in ground effect and 8,200 ft (2500 m) out of ground effect

OPERATORS

US Navy (USN)

HC-1	North Island, CA	SH-3D, SH-3G, SH-3H
HC-2	Norfolk, VA	VH-3A, SH-3G, SH-3H

HC-16	Pensacola, FL	SH-3D, SH-3H
HS-1	Jacksonville, FL	SH-3G, SH-3H
HS-5	Jacksonville, FL	SH-3H
HS-7	Jacksonville, FL	SH-3H
HS-11	Jacksonville, FL	SH-3H
HS-12	Atsugi, Japan	SH-3H
HS-14	North Island, CA	SH-3H
HS-75	Jacksonville, FL	SH-3H
HS-85	Alameda, CA	SH-3H
VC-5	Cubi Point, RP	SH-3G
VC-8	Roosevelt Roads, PR	SH-3G, SH-3H
VX-1	Patuxent River, MD	SH-3H
NAWC/AD	Patuxent River, MD	SH-3H, VH-3A
PMRF	Barking Sands, HI	UH-3A
AUTEC det	Andros Island, Bahamas	UH-3A, SH-3G
NSWC	Fallon, NV	SH-3D, SH-3H
NAS	Jacksonville, FL	SH-3H

NAS	Key West, FL	SH-3D
NAS	Oceana, VA	SH-3G
NAS	Patuxent River, MD	SH-3D
NAS	Whidbey Island, WA	SH-3D

US Marine Corps (USMC)

HMX-1	Quantico, VA	VH-3D

US Coast Guard (USCG)

CGAS	Cape Cod, MA	HH-3F
CGAS	Clearwater, FL	HH-3F
CGAS	Elizabeth City, NC	HH-3F, CH/HH-3E
CGAS	Kodiak, AK	HH-3F
CGAS	Mobile, AL	HH-3F
CGAS	San Francisco, CA	HH-3F
CGAS	Sitka, AK	HH-3F
CGAS	Traverse City, MI	HH-3F, HH-3E

Hughes

OH-6A Cayuse

One of three contenders for the US Army's Light Observation Helicopter (LOH) competition which took place in the first half of the 1960s, the **OH-6A Cayuse** was flown for the first time on 27 February 1963. Evaluation of the Cayuse against the Bell OH-4 and the Fairchild-Hiller OH-5 followed soon afterwards and in May 1965 the Hughes machine emerged victorious, with just over 1,400 examples being built before production terminated.

Powered by a single Allison T63-A-5A turboshaft engine de-rated to 252 shp, the OH-6A saw extensive combat action in Vietnam and paved the way for the highly successful Hughes 500 family, which includes the well-armed Defender.

US Navy operation of the OH-6A is limited to a few examples which form part of the diverse fleet that is assigned to the Naval Test Pilot's School at Patuxent River, Maryland. These machines are among a number of aircraft and helicopters that have been loaned from the US Army, and its lively performance probably makes it popular with students.

MISSION PROFILE

A few OH-6As are used for the training of rotary wing test pilots by the USN Test Pilot's School at Patuxent River.

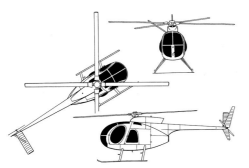

VARIANTS AND SERIALS

OH-6A: Four former US Army Cayuse light observation helicopters have been transferred to the Navy for service with the Test Pilot's School at Patuxent River. 12967 (65-12967); 16041 (67-16041); 696040 (69-6040) plus one

SPECIFICATION

McDonnell Douglas Helicopters OH-6A
Rotor system: main rotor diameter 26 ft 4 in (8.03 m); tail rotor diameter 4 ft 3 in (1.30 m); main rotor disc area 544.63 sq ft (50.60 m²); tail rotor disc area 14.19 sq ft (1.32 m²)
Fuselage and tail: length overall, rotors turning 30 ft 3.75 in (9.24 m) and fuselage 23 ft 0 in (7.01 m); height to top of rotor head 8 ft 1.4 in (2.48 m)
Powerplant: one Allison T63-A-5A rated at 317 shp (236.5 kW) but derated to 252.5 shp (188 kW) for take-off and 214.5 shp (160 kW) for continuous running
Weights: empty equipped 1,229 lb (557 kg); maximum take-off 2,400 lb (1090 kg); overload take-off 2,700 lb (1225 kg)
Fuel and load: internal fuel 61.5 US gal (232 liters)
Speed: never exceed 150 mph (241 km/h); maximum level speed at sea level 150 mph (241 km/h); cruising speed for maximum range at sea level 134 mph (216 km/h)
Range: ferry range 1,560 miles (2510 km); normal range at 5,000 ft (1525 m) 380 miles (611 km)
Performance: maximum rate of climb at sea level 1,250 ft (381 m) per minute; service ceiling 15,800 ft (4815 m); hovering ceiling 11,800 ft (3595 m) in ground effect and 7,300 ft (2225 m) out of ground effect

OPERATORS

US Navy (USN)

NTPS	Patuxent River, MD	OH-6A

A fairly recent addition to the fleet of aircraft and helicopters flown by the Navy Test Pilot's School at Patuxent River, at least four examples of the OH-6A Cayuse have been obtained on loan from the US Army.

Aircraft

Boeing Vertol
H-46 Sea Knight

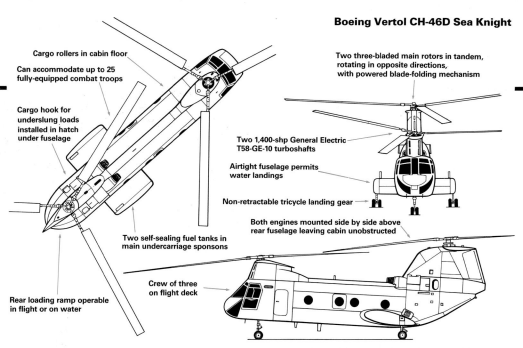

- Cargo rollers in cabin floor
- Can accommodate up to 25 fully-equipped combat troops
- Cargo hook for underslung loads installed in hatch under fuselage
- Two self-sealing fuel tanks in main undercarriage sponsons
- Rear loading ramp operable in flight or on water
- Crew of three on flight deck
- Two three-bladed main rotors in tandem, rotating in opposite directions, with powered blade-folding mechanism
- Two 1,400-shp General Electric T58-GE-10 turboshafts
- Airtight fuselage permits water landings
- Non-retractable tricycle landing gear
- Both engines mounted side by side above rear fuselage leaving cabin unobstructed

Evolving from the commercial Boeing Vertol Model 107 which made its maiden flight in April 1958, three **YHC-1A**s were ordered for evaluation purposes by the US Army, which ended up buying the larger Chinook. Further interest in the tandem-rotor Model 107 was expressed by the Marine Corps, which was at that point anxious to obtain a turbine-powered machine to replace the Sikorsky HUS-1 (UH-34 post-1962) Seahorse in the large number of Medium Helicopter (HMM) squadrons. This eventually secured substantial orders, initially of the **HRB-1**, subsequently redesignated as the **CH-46A** when it began to enter service with HMM-265 at New River, North Carolina, in June 1964.

Production of the CH-46A model for the Marines totalled 160, with a further 14 examples being acquired by the Navy as **UH-46A**s. The latter model was assigned to Helicopter Combat Support (HC) squadrons and was mainly intended for service in the VertRep (vertical replenishment) task, although it could also undertake other utility duties. In normal practice, detachments (usually of two helicopters) were assigned to the ships that provided supply back-up to carrier battle groups.

The next major version was the **CH/UH-46D**, quantities built as such being 266 and 10 respectively. Notable differences related to the adoption of cambered rotor blades and the more powerful General Electric T58-GE-10 turboshaft engine. Manufacture of new-build Sea Knights terminated with the **CH-46F**, this variant being basically similar to the CH-46D although with improved avionics and a number of other detail design changes. A total of 174 CH-46Fs was built and delivered to the Marines between July 1968 and February 1971.

Today, the principal model in Marine Corps service is the **CH-46E**, which came about as a result of a CILOP project launched in the 1970s. Perhaps the most important difference concerned the powerplant, the T58-GE-16 being adopted along with glassfiber rotor blades and a number of other features designed to offer increased crashworthiness and greater battle damage tolerance. Two Sea Knights were modified to serve as prototypes, clearing the way for a 1977 decision to go ahead with the

conversion of well over 250 CH-46Ds and CH-46Fs to this standard.

Presently in use with 15 front-line units, two training squadrons and a couple of Reserve outfits, the CH-46E is currently the subject of another improvement program aimed at enhancing its capability still further. This is being accomplished by greatly enlarging the size of the fuselage sponsons, an action which reportedly doubles the fuel capacity. Modified aircraft are referred to as **CH-46E 'Bullfrogs'** and this derivative began to enter service with Tustin-based squadrons HMM-163 and HMM-166 in 1991. Other units are certain to follow.

Operationally, a Sea Knight-equipped HMM unit usually forms the core of a composite squadron aboard an amphibious assault ship of the 'Wasp', 'Tarawa' or 'Iwo Jima' classes. This will typically include a dozen CH-46s in its line-up, these providing the backbone of airborne assault potential during initial phases of a landing by allowing troops to move rapidly to secure key targets. Once the beach-head has been secured, they may continue to assist in troop movement so as to consolidate the position, or they can switch to the logistics support role, transferring vital supplies from ship to shore.

With the Navy, the Sea Knight continues to undertake resupply tasks and is presently in service with four squadrons, specifically HC-6 and HC-8 at Norfolk, Virginia, as well as HC-3 and HC-11 at North Island, California. These are equipped with a mixture of CH-46Ds and UH-46Ds as well as some **HH-46D**s, the latter being yet another instance of a conversion program. Configured with a winch, it is thus able to perform SAR duties as well as the VertRep task. HH-46Ds also fulfill local rescue needs at a number of air bases, and a few examples of the similar but somewhat older **HH-46A** may still be active.

MISSION PROFILE

Configuration options: Provision exists for H-46 derivatives to be armed with .50-in caliber machine guns in front side doors. USMC CH-46s have flare/chaff dispensers. HH-46As are configured with a winch for rescue missions.

Air assault and logistic support: USMC CH-46Es are employed to bring troops ashore during amphibious landings or to reposition them once ashore. Some 17 troops or 15 casualty litters can be carried. Logistic support is a major task with either internal or underslung loads.

Special operations: Marine Expeditionary Units (Special Operations Capable) employ the CH-46 to evacuate civilians and US government personnel from civil war situations. By parachuting out of the CH-46 rear ramps Marine reconnaissance teams can be covertly inserted behind enemy lines.

VertRep/SAR: USN UH-46s are employed primarily to resupply ships at sea. They are normally embarked on underway replenishment ships and then move supplies to warships. Large items such as ordnance are underslung on specially prepared pallets. HH-46s serve in a similar role but have an additional search and rescue mission because of their winch.

VARIANTS AND SERIALS

CH-46A: This original production model of the Sea King was operated by US Marine Corps medium helicopter squadrons. Production totalled 160 but the few survivors have been updated and none now remain active in their original form.
150265 to 150278; 150933 to 150964; 151906 to 151961; 152496 to 152553

UH-46A: Utility transport model delivered to US Navy units in limited quantities. A total of 14 was obtained but none survive in original form.
150965 to 150968; 151902 to 151905; 152490 to 152495

CH-46D: Second major derivative for US Marine Corps, with a total of 266 being obtained from the manufacturer and about a dozen others resulting from conversion of CH/UH-46As. No longer a part of the operational inventory, surviving airframes have been modified to a variety of configurations.
New build: 152554 to 152579; 153314 to 153403; 153951 to 154044; 154789 to 154844
Conversions: 150276; 150942; 150952; 150956; 150957; 150966; 150968; 151904; 151907; 151941; 151957; 152493

HH-46D: Dedicated search and rescue version, approximately 38 Sea Knights have been modified to

Originally manufacturered as a CH-46F, the Sea Knight portrayed here in service with USMC squadron HMM-365, is one of a large number that have been updated to CH-46E standard with more powerful T58 turboshaft engines.

Above: *The only naval air station known to be operating the rescue-dedicated HH-46D version is Point Mugu, CA, which has a handful that are employed on utility and SAR tasks. In addition, examples of the HH-46D also equip base flights at four USMC air stations.*

Above right: *Unlike most SAR helicopters, this HH-46D from HC-8 at Norfolk, VA, features a low-visibility color scheme, indicative of use in the vertical replenishment mission from Navy resupply vessels at sea.*

this standard.
150941; 150954; 150958; 150963; 150964; 151903; 151908; 151910; 151912; 151914; 151915; 151918; 151921; 151924; 151927; 151933; 151934; 151937; 151939; 151948 to 151951; 151953; 151955; 152495; 151948 to 151951; 152496; 152498; 152501; 152512; 152520; 12522; 152535; 152538; 152539; 152553; 153408; 153409

UH-46D: Utility transport variant of the CH-46D, 10 UH-46Ds were acquired for the Navy as new-build airframes, while at least five CH/UH-46As were updated to this standard.
New build: 153404 to 153413
Conversions: 151902; 151905; 151942; 151952; 152491

CH-46E: In excess of 250 Sea Knights of all basic variants have been brought to CH-46E standard, the rework process including re-engining with more powerful T58 turboshafts and provision of increased crashworthiness. CH-46Es serve only with the Marines.
152531; 152574; 152578; 152579; 153316; 153318; 153321; 153322; 153328; 153330; 153331; 153333; 153346; 153347; 153350; 153353; 153355 to 153358; 153362; 153363; 153365; 153366; 153369; 153372; 153373; 153377; 153380; 153382; 153385; 153388; 153389; 153391 to 153393; 153395; 153398; 153400; 153402; 153952; 153953; 153956 to 153960; 153962; 153965; 153968; 153969; 153973 to 153975; 153977; 153979 to 153981; 153983; 153989; 153992 to 153994; 153998 to 154001; 154003 to 154005; 154009 to 154012; 154014 to 154016; 154020; 154023; 154027; 154031; 154033; 154034; 154036 to 154040; 154789; 154790; 154792; 154798; 154799; 154801; 154803; 154805; 154807; 154808; 154810; 154812; 154815 to 154817; 154819; 154821; 154822; 154825; 154827 to 154829; 154831 to 154834; 154838; 154844 to 154851; 154853 to 154857; 154860; 155301 to 155313; 155315 to 155318; 156418 to 156424; 156426; 156427; 156431 to 156445; 156447 to 156474; 156476; 156477; 157649; 157651 to 157656; 157659 to 157665; 157667 to 157670; 157672 to 157675; 157678; 157685 to 157694; 157696 to 157699; 157701 to 157706; 157708; 157710; 157712 to 157716; 157718; 157720 to 157726

CH-46F: Final production model, of which 174 examples were built for use by Marine Corps medium helicopter squadrons. Most have since been updated to CH-46E standard.
154845 to 154862; 155301 to 155318; 156418 to 156477; 157649 to 157726

VH-46F: VIP-configured version of the final production model of the Sea Knight, developed for executive transportation missions with helicopter squadron HMX-1.
157680 to 157684.

SPECIFICATION

Boeing Vertol UH-46A
Rotor system: rotor diameter, each 50 ft 0 in (15.24 m); rotor disc area, total 3,926.99 sq ft (364.82 m²)
Fuselage and tail: length overall, rotors turning 84 ft 4 in (25.40 m) and fuselage 44 ft 10 in (13.66 m); height to top of the rear rotor hub 16 ft 8.5 in (5.09 m); wheel base 24 ft 10 in (7.57 m)
Powerplant: two General Electric T58-GE-8B rated at 1,250 shp (932 kW)
Weights: empty equipped 12,406 lb (5627 kg); maximum take-off 21,400 lb (9706 kg)
Fuel and load: internal fuel 380 US gal (1438 liters); maximum payload 4,000 lb (1814 kg)
Speed: maximum cruising speed at optimum altitude 155 mph (249 km/h); economical cruising speed at optimum altitude 151 mph (243 km/h)
Range: range with a 6,070-lb (2753-kg) payload 230 miles (370 km)
Performance: maximum rate of climb at sea level 1,440 ft (439 m) per minute; service ceiling 14,000 ft (4265 m); hovering ceiling 9,070 ft (2765 m) in ground effect and 5,600 ft (1707 m) out of ground effect

Boeing Vertol CH-46E
generally similar to the UH-46A except in the following particulars:
Powerplant: two General Electric T58-GE-16 rated at 1,870 shp (1394 kW)
Weights: empty 11,585 lb (5255 kg); maximum take-off 24,300 lb (11022 kg)
Fuel and load: internal fuel 350 US gal (1323 liters); maximum payload 7,000 lb (3175 kg)
Speed: maximum speed at sea level 166 mph (267 km/h); maximum cruising speed at sea level 165 mph (266 km/h)
Range: ferry range 690 miles (1110 km); range with a 2,400-lb (1088-kg) payload 633 miles (1019 km)
Performance: maximum rate of climb at sea level 1,715 ft (523 m) per minute; service ceiling 9,400 ft (2865 m); hovering ceiling 9,500 ft (2895 m) in ground effect and 5,750 ft (1753 m) out of ground effect

Above: *Marine Corps operation of the Boeing Vertol Sea Knight far outstrips that of the US Navy, with the remanufactured CH-46E now being the principal version used in assault/logistic support taskings. It presently equips a total of 14 front-line squadrons plus a small number of training and Reserve outfits.*

OPERATORS

US Navy (USN)

HC-3	North Island, CA	CH-46D, HH-46D
HC-5	Agana, Guam	CH-46D
HC-6	Norfolk, VA	CH-46D
HC-8	Norfolk, VA	CH-46D, HH-46D, UH-46D
HC-11	North Island, CA	CH-46D, HH-46D, UH-46D
NAS	Point Mugu, CA	HH-46D, UH-46D

US Marine Corps (USMC)

HMX-1	Quantico, VA	CH-46E, VH-46F
HMM-161	Tustin, CA	CH-46E
HMM-162	New River, NC	CH-46E
HMM-163	Tustin, CA	CH-46E
HMM-164	Tustin, CA	CH-46E
HMM-165	Kaneohe Bay, HI	CH-46E
HMM-166	Tustin, CA	CH-46E
HMM-204	New River, NC	CH-46E
HMM-261	New River, NC	CH-46E
HMM-263	New River, NC	CH-46E
HMM-264	New River, NC	CH-46E
HMM-265	Kaneohe Bay, HI	CH-46E
HMM-266	New River, NC	CH-46E
HMM-268	Tustin, CA	CH-46E
HMT-301	Tustin, CA	CH-46E
HMM-364	Kaneohe Bay, HI	CH-46E
HMM-365	New River, NC	CH-46E
HMM-764	El Toro, CA	CH-46E
HMM-774	Norfolk, VA	CH-46E
MCAS	Beaufort, SC	HH-46D
MCAS	Cherry Point, NC	HH-46D
MCAS	Iwakuni, Japan	HH-46D
MCAS	Kaneohe Bay, HI	HH-46D

Sikorsky
H-53 Sea Stallion

Known by the manufacturer as the **S-65**, development of this impressively large machine was initiated in the early 1960s in response to a US Navy requirement for a modern, turbine-powered type that could replace the old and rapidly obsolescing CH-37 Mojave, then the principal heavy-lift helicopter in US Marine Corps service. After studying a number of proposals, Sikorsky's candidate was selected in August 1962 and given the designation **CH-53A**, with a couple of prototypes being ordered for trials as a preliminary to full-scale manufacture.

Production examples began to enter service with the Marines in autumn 1966 when HMH-463 at Santa Ana received its first **Sea Stallion**. No time was wasted in introducing the type to the hazards of war, four CH-53As being dispatched to Vietnam where they began operations in January 1967. Initially, they were mainly concerned with recovery tasks and by May of that year they had retrieved no fewer than 100 downed helicopters and a couple of fixed-wing aircraft. Subsequently, the arrival of the rest of the squadron allowed the scope of activity to expand and the Sea Stallion thereafter engaged in all sorts of combat tasks, including the movement of troops and artillery pieces around the battlefield.

Inevitable efforts at improvement led to the CH-53A being supplanted in production by the **CH-53D** after the completion of 139 examples. This new version for the Marines differed in having more powerful T64-GE-413 engines which allowed it to lift heavier loads

Although it is less capable than the CH-53E version, the CH-53D is still in service with a number of Marine Corps heavy helicopter squadrons. The example depicted here in desert camouflage is assigned to HMH-462, based at Tustin, CA.

and it, too, was soon dispatched to Vietnam. A total of 126 CH-53Ds was eventually completed by the spring of 1972, at which time attention turned to 30 examples of the specially configured **RH-53D** airborne mine countermeasures platform.

The latter derivative was basically similar to the CH-53D but had even more powerful engines. Flown for the first time in October 1972, it employed towed sledges in the clearance role and soon showed that it was equally adept at dealing with acoustic, magnetic and mechanical types of mine, playing a major role in the clearance of the Suez Canal during 1974. RH-53Ds were also involved in the disastrously unsuccessful attempt at rescuing American hostages from Tehran in April 1980, which resulted in several of these valuable helicopters being abandoned at the Desert One landing strip.

Today, the RH-53D is still to be found in the inventory but is only flown by Reserve units, mine countermeasures squadrons at Norfolk, Virginia, and Alameda, California, operating the type, as does a Marine Corps unit. In fact,

some RH-53Ds from the latter outfit – HMH-772 detachment 'A' at Alameda – were deployed to Jubail in Saudi Arabia during the recent Gulf War, but it is not known whether they operated in the mine countermeasures role or were assigned to more conventional heavy-lift tasks.

A few CH-53As are also operated by both the Navy and Marine Corps. Navy use is limited to a trio of machines that undertakes drone recovery duties with VC-1 at Barbers Point. Those with the Marines equip second-line elements of the Reserve, although one or two may still have a training function to fulfill. Increasing availability of CH-53Ds displaced by brand-new CH-53Es does, however, mean that the A model is unlikely to be around for too much longer.

As for the CH-53D, this is still very much an important asset and it continues to make a valuable contribution to front-line resources, serving with Marine Corps squadrons of both FMFLant and FMFPac. It was also heavily committed to Operations Desert Shield and Desert Storm, being employed to move troops, equipment and supplies around the various locations occupied by Marine troops and other forces of the coalition.

A couple of somewhat more plushly outfitted CH/VH-53Ds are also still on the strength of HMX-1 at Quantico, Virginia, these Marine-owned and -operated machines forming part of the fleet of VIP-tasked helicopters that is used to transport official visitors and holders of high government office in and around the Washington area.

MISSION PROFILE

Configuration options: The H-53 can be configured for many roles including air assault, logistic support, mine countermeasures, special operations, VIP transport, aircraft recovery or a combination of these missions. Underslung loads up to 20,000 lb (9070 kg) can be carried on a single-point cargo hook. Some versions have inflight-refueling probes. USMC versions have .50-in caliber machine guns and chaff/flare dispensers for self-defense. A hoist can be fitted for rescue work.

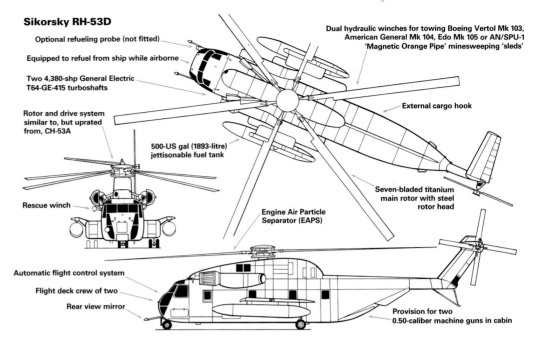

Sikorsky RH-53D

Optional refueling probe (not fitted)

Equipped to refuel from ship while airborne

Two 4,380-shp General Electric T64-GE-415 turboshafts

Rotor and drive system similar to, but uprated from, CH-53A

Rescue winch

500-US gal (1893-litre) jettisonable fuel tank

Automatic flight control system

Flight deck crew of two

Rear view mirror

Dual hydraulic winches for towing Boeing Vertol Mk 103, American General Mk 104, Edo Mk 105 or AN/SPU-1 'Magnetic Orange Pipe' minesweeping 'sleds'

External cargo hook

Seven-bladed titanium main rotor with steel rotor head

Engine Air Particle Separator (EAPS)

Provision for two 0.50-caliber machine guns in cabin

Above: Two CH-53Ds (at left) lead a gaggle of CH-53Es into the air from the major helicopter base at Tustin in a scene that is reminiscent of Gulf War operations.

Air assault and logistic support: USMC CH-53s are used for these missions, with the emphasis on logistic support because of the helicopter's load-carrying capability. Ordnance resupply and other logistic support is provided for USMC attack helicopters and AV-8B forward operating bases. Up to 38 troops or 24 casualty litters can be carried in the CH-53A or 55 in the CH-53D. Some 8,000 lb (3600 kg) of cargo can be carried internally. Two USMC VH-53Ds are employed on executive flight duties with interiors extensively modified to VIP standard. The cargo hook is used to recover aircraft and helicopter air frames from inaccessible terrain.

Airborne mine countermeasures (AMCM): The RH-53D is the USN's main mine countermeasures system. It uses AQS-14 dipping/towed sonar to detect mines then deploys a variety of sleds to bring mines to the surface, where .50-in caliber twin machine guns are used to detonate them. The Mk 103 sled cuts loose contact mines, the Mk 104 sled counters acoustic mines, the Mk 105 hydrofoil sled counters magnetic mines, the Mk 106 sled has acoustic sweep equipment and the SPU-1 Magnetic Orange Pipe counters shallow water mines. Inflight-refueling probes are fitted to extend endurance on station.

Special operations: Marine Expeditionary Units (Special Operations Capable) employ the CH-53A/D in rescue scenarios where civilians and US government personnel are threatened by civil war situations. RH-53Ds have also been used for long-range special operations missions because of their enhanced performance.

VARIANTS AND SERIALS

YCH-53A: Two pre-production prototypes of the Sea Stallion heavy-lift helicopter developed for service with the Marine Corps.
151613; 151614

CH-53A: Initial production model for Marine Corps heavy-lift helicopter squadrons. A total of 139 examples was completed but none are thought to remain in operational service.
151686 to 151701; 152392 to 152415; 153274 to 153313; 153705 to 153739; 154863 to 154884; 154887; 154888

NCH-53A: Two early production CH-53As modified for special test duties with the Naval Air Warfare Center Aircraft Division at Warminster. It is possible that these are still active with the NAWC.
151686; 152399

CH-53D: Enhanced version of CH-53A for Marine Corps service. Features more powerful T64 turboshaft engines and other detail improvements such as automatic rotor blade folding. A total of 126 examples was produced.
156654 to 156677; 156951 to 156970; 157127 to 157176; 157727 to 157756; 157930; 157931

RH-53D: Airborne mine countermeasures derivative using towed sleds for clearance tasks. Also embodied inflight-refueling capability. Production for the Navy totalled 30.
158682 to 158693; 158744 to 158761

VH-53D: Two CH-53Ds fitted out with VIP interiors for service with the executive flight detachment of Marine helicopter squadron HMX-1.
157754; 157755

SPECIFICATION

Sikorsky RH-53D
Rotor system: main rotor diameter 72 ft 3 in (22.02 m); tail rotor diameter 16 ft 0 in (4.88 m); main rotor disc area (4,070.0 sq ft (378.10 m^2); tail rotor disc area 201.0 sq ft (18.67 m^2)
Fuselage and tail: length overall, rotors turning 88 ft 3 in (26.90 m) and fuselage without probe 67 ft 2 in (20.47 m); height overall, rotors turning 24 ft 11 in (7.60 m) and to top of rotor head 17 ft 1.5 in (5.22 m); wheel base 27 ft 0 in (8.23 m)
Powerplant: two General Electric T64-GE-415 rated at 4,380 shp (3266 kW)
Weights: empty 22,444 lb (10180 kg); normal take-off 42,000 lb (19050 kg); maximum take-off 50,000 lb (22680 kg)
Fuel and load: internal fuel 622 US gal (2354 liters); external fuel up to two 550-US gal (2082-liter) drop tanks
Speed: maximum level speed 'clean' at sea level 196 mph (315 km/h); cruising speed at sea level 173 mph (278 km/h)
Range: range 257 miles (413 km); endurance more than 4 hours 0 minutes
Performance: maximum rate of climb at sea level 2,180 ft (664 m) per minute; service ceiling 21,000 ft (6400 m); hovering ceiling 13,400 ft (4080 m) in ground effect and 6,500 ft (1980 m) out of ground effect

Sikorsky CH-53A
generally similar to the RH-53D except in the following particulars:
Powerplant: two General Electric T64-GE-16 rated at 3,435 shp (2562 kW)
Weights: normal take-off 35,000 lb (15875 kg)
Fuel and load: internal fuel 630 US gal (2384 liters); maximum payload 8,000 lb (3629 kg) as an internal load

Above: A reorganization of Reserve forces has led to heavylift resources being concentrated with HMH-772, which has elements at three air bases. This quartet of CH-53Ds is resident at the unit's Willow Grove headquarters.

or 13,000 lb (5897 kg) as a slung load
Speed: maximum level speed 'clean' at sea level 195 mph (314 km/h); cruising speed at sea level 172 mph (277 km/h)
Range: range 257 miles (413 km); endurance more than 4 hours 0 minutes
Performance: maximum rate of climb at sea level 2,240 ft (683 m) per minute; service ceiling 18,550 ft (5,655 m)

Sikorsky CH-53D
generally similar to the RH-53D except in the following particulars:
Powerplant: two General Electric T64-GE-413 rated at 3,925 shp (2927 kW)
Weights: empty 23,485 lb (10653 kg); mission take-off 36,400 lb (16510 kg); maximum take-off 42,000 lb (19050 kg)
Fuel and load: internal fuel 630 US gal (2384 liters); maximum payload 8,000 lb (3629 kg) as an internal load or 13,000 lb (5897 kg) as a slung load

OPERATORS

US Navy (USN)

HM-18	Norfolk, VA	RH-53D
HM-19	Alameda, CA	RH-53D
NAWC/AD	Warminster, PA	NCH-53A
NCSC	Panama City, FL	RH-53D

US Marine Corps (USMC)

HMX-1	Quantico, VA	CH-53D, VH-53D
HMT-204	New River, NC	CH-53D
HMT-302	Tustin, CA	CH-53D
HMH-362	New River, NC	CH-53D
HMH-363	Tustin, CA	CH-53D
HMH-462	Tustin, CA	CH-53D
HMH-463	Kaneohe Bay, HI	CH-53D
HMH-772	Willow Grove, PA	CH-53D
HMH-772 det A	Alameda, CA	RH-53D
HMH-772 det B	Dallas, TX	CH-53D

Sikorsky
H-53 Super Stallion/ Sea Dragon

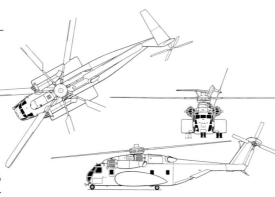

Differing sufficiently from the earlier H-53 versions to merit allocation of a new manufacturer's designation as the **S-80**, the **Super Stallion** and **Sea Dragon** are both currently in quantity production for the Marine Corps and Navy respectively. Present plans anticipate procurement of more than 200 **CH-53E**s, most of which are earmarked for the Marines, while a Navy requirement exists for over 50 examples of the specialist **MH-53E**, now the Navy's premier mine clearance system.

Super Stallion development can be traced back to the late 1960s when Sikorsky first con-

Below: The principal task of the Navy's CH-53E Super Stallion is vertical replenishment. The type is used by three squadrons, including HC-4 at Sigonella, Sicily.

sidered a three-engined version of the Sea Stallion. The Navy remained fairly lukewarm until 1973, when it authorized the manufacturer to press ahead with design and construction of two prototype **YCH-53E**s. The maiden flight took place in March 1974 but the test program was not without its bad moments, the first prototype being destroyed in a ground accident. Nevertheless, in 1978, the first production order was placed and subsequent contracts have increased the total purchase to 201, with more in sight.

Design changes are by no means confined to the installation of a third General Electric T64 engine, for the CH-53E also features an

uprated transmission driving a seven-bladed main rotor (older models have a six-bladed rotor), and the tail pylon has been canted to port by some 20°. In addition, the CH-53E has a longer fuselage, allowing it to carry a maximum of 55 fully-equipped troops, wheeled vehicles or palletized cargo. Extra range is provided courtesy of a retractable inflight-refueling probe located on the starboard side of the nose which, in theory at least, allows it to 'self-deploy' over considerable distances.

In Marine Corps service, the CH-53E attained operational status during June 1981 and now equips at least five first-line squadrons as well as a couple of training units. Missions vary from support of amphibious assault landing operations through aircraft and helicopter recovery to the transportation of men and material in and around the battlefield. The advent of the Super Stallion has greatly enhanced Marine capability in all of those areas. When operating as part of a Marine Amphibious Unit, a composite squadron will typically include four CH-53Es to satisfy heavy-lift requirements.

Some Super Stallions are also operated by Navy helicopter combat support (HC) squadrons, this service being quick to recognize that the CH-53E's impressive external lift ability made it an ideal vehicle for vertical offshore delivery tasks. In the USA, HC-1 at North Island, California, and HC-2 at Norfolk, Virginia, both utilize limited numbers on VertRep tasks, as does HC-4 which operates from Sigonella, Sicily, in support of 6th Fleet activities in the Mediterranean Sea. A few are also assigned to mine countermeasures (HM) units, HM-14 using at least a dozen in 1990-91, conceivably as a 'stepping stone' in readiness for conversion to the MH-53E.

Broadly similar to the Super Stallion, the MH-53E Sea Dragon does feature a number of significant differences, arising out of the peculiar requirements of its mine clearance task. The most obvious of these differences concerns the sponsons on the fuselage sides – these are much bigger and embody composite materials, each holding additional fuel so as to allow the MH-53E to remain airborne for extended periods. Mission duration on just internal fuel may run as long as four hours and this version can be refueled in flight. As was the case with the earlier RH-53D, mechanical, acoustic and magnetic mines can be dealt with using equipment mounted on towed sleds.

Including a single **JMH-53E** test specimen, procurement of 37 Sea Dragons has so far been authorized. The target figure, now set at 56, appears to be sufficient to allow four squadrons to form, each with a unit establishment of about a dozen helicopters. Today, the MH-53E is in service with elements of the Atlantic and Pacific Fleets. At Norfolk HM-12 and HM-14 have equipped. On the West Coast, HM-15 at Alameda, California, also has MH-53Es and this will probably be joined by an extra squadron (HM-17?).

Left: Desert camouflage was hastily applied to most of the Marine Corps' CH-53Es, which played a key role in operations to free Kuwait. Some also acquired unofficial nicknames along with nose art while based in the Gulf region.

MISSION PROFILE

Configuration options: The three-engined H-53E features retractable inflight-refueling probe as standard, twin- or single-point cargo hooks and rescue winch. The AMCM MH-53E Sea Dragon features more modern mine countermeasures equipment.

Air assault, logistic support and special operations: The CH-53E flies similar missions to the old CH-53A/D in support of USMC amphibious assault, logistic and special operations. Some 30,000 lb (13600 kg) of cargo can be carried internally or 36,000 lb (16300 kg) underslung. As with the CH-53D, 55 troops can be carried in a high-density arrangement.

Airborne mine countermeasures (AMCM): All the MCM systems available to the RH-53D can be utilized by the MH-53E. New equipment includes 30,000-lb (13600-kg) tension tow boom and hydraulic winch with 450 ft (140 m) of steel cable to tow MCM sleds. The ALQ-160 acoustic countermeasures system and ALQ-166 magnetic minesweeping hydrofoil sleds can be deployed.

Vertical onboard delivery (VOD): The USN employs the CH-53E for VOD in support of naval forces at sea. Operating from shore bases they lift large cargo items, including nuclear weapons, to and from ships. This often involves operating from forward bases or the use of inflight refueling. Damaged airframes can be recovered from the decks of aircraft carriers.

Sponsons
The grossly enlarged sponsons on the fuselage side contain fuel, raising the internal capacity from 1,017 US gal (3850 liters) for the CH-53E to 3,200 US gal (12100 liters), enough for a four-hour mine-sweeping mission 30 minutes from base. The MH-53E can still be refueled in flight.

Mirrors
Mounted low on the fuselage sides forward of the cockpit are rear-view mirrors so that the flight crew can monitor the sled as it is pulled through the water.

Rotor
In order to absorb the power of the extra engine compared to earlier variants, the H-53E added a seventh blade to the main rotor, while the diameter and blade chord were significantly increased.

Sikorsky MH-53E

By combining the power of the three-engined CH-53E with the minesweeping capabilities of the RH-53D, Sikorsky produced a far more capable minehunter that can pull heavy sleds through much rougher seas than was possible with the earlier machine, an advance matched by improved adverse weather avionics.

Tail
An unusual feature of the H-53E is the tail canted to port, which mounts a large four-bladed tail rotor. To offset the cant of the fin, the tailplane is of gull-wing configuration.

Crew
The MH-53E has a flight crew of three, and three-to-five enlisted crew who operate the minehunting equipment and man the two 0.50-in machine guns that are used to explode surfaced mines.

Minehunting equipment
The MH-53E has a 30,000-lb (13600-kg) tension tow boom and a hydraulic winch for the deployment of various types of minesweeping sleds. Moored mines can be detected by an internal pod system.

VARIANTS AND SERIALS

YCH-53E: Two prototypes of extensively redesigned three-engined version known as Super Stallion in recognition of major changes. Features seven-bladed main rotor assembly and a revised tail unit with a canted tail rotor pylon.
159121; 159122

CH-53E: Production-configured Super Stallion for service with Navy and Marine Corps. At least 182 examples have been ordered, with production continuing for both services.
159876; 159877; 161179 to 161184; 161252 to 161265; 161381 to 161395; 161532 to 161545; 161988 to 162012; 162478 to 162496; 162517 to 162531; 162687; 162718 to 162720; 163059 to 163064; 163071 to 163089; 164358 to 164367; 164470 to 164482; 164536 to 164539; 164776 to 164791

JMH-53E: Prototype of specialist mine countermeasures version of Sea Stallion known as the Sea Dragon. Uses similar towed sled devices to RH-53D for mine clearance task.
162497

MH-53E: Production version of Sea Dragon for service with US Navy mine countermeasures units. At least 53 examples are on order.
162498 to 162516; 163051 to 163058; 163065 to 163070; 164368 to 164371; 164764 to 164775; 164792 to 164795

Two CH-53Es from HMH-464 at New River, NC, maintain close formation while flying over unfamiliar, snow-covered terrain during a NATO exercise in Norway. The Super Stallion serves with five USMC squadrons and a training unit, but more are likely to get this type since procurement is continuing.

SPECIFICATION

Sikorsky CH-53E
Rotor system: main rotor diameter 79 ft 0 in (24.08 m); tail rotor diameter 20 ft 0 in (6.10 m); main rotor disc area 4,901.7 sq ft (455.38 m²); tail rotor disc area 314.2 sq ft (29.19 m²)
Fuselage and tail: length overall, rotors turning 99 ft 0.5 in (30.19 m), fuselage 73 ft 4 in (22.35 m), and overall with rotor and tail pylon folded 60 ft 6 in (18.44 m); height overall, rotors turning 29 ft 5 in (8.97 m), to top of rotor head 17 ft 5.5 in (5.32 m), and overall with rotor and tail pylon folded 18 ft 7 in (5.66 m); wheel base 27 ft 3 in (8.31 m)
Powerplant: three General Electric T64-GE-416 rated at 4,380 shp (3266 kW) for 10 minutes, 4,145 shp (3091 kW) for 30 minutes and 3,696 shp (2756 kW) for continuous running
Weights: empty 33,228 lb (15072 kg); maximum take-off 69,750 lb (31640 kg) with an internal payload or 73,500 lb (33340 kg) with an external payload
Fuel and load: internal fuel 1,017 US gal (3849 liters); external fuel up to two 650-US gal (2461-liter) drop tanks; maximum payload 36,000 lb (16330 kg), or 30,000 lb (13607 kg) carried internally over a 115-mile (185-km) radius or 32,000 lb (14515 kg) carried externally over 57.5-mile (92.5-km) radius
Speed: maximum level speed 'clean' at sea level 196 mph (315 km/h); cruising speed at sea level 173 mph (278 km/h)
Range: ferry range without aerial refueling 1,290 miles (2075 km); radius 575 miles (925 km) with a 20,000-lb (9072-kg) external payload or 57.5 miles (92.5 km) with a 32,000-lb (14515-kg) external payload
Performance: maximum rate of climb at sea level with an 25,000 lb (11340 kg) payload 2,500 ft (762 m) per minute; service ceiling 18,500 ft (5640 m); hovering ceiling 11,550 ft (3520 m) in ground effect and 9,500 ft (2895 m) out of ground effect

Sikorsky MH-53E
generally similar to the CH-53E except in the following particulars:
Weights: empty 36,336 lb (16482 kg); maximum take-off 69,750 lb (31640 kg) with an internal payload or 73,500 lb (33340 kg) with an external payload
Fuel and load: internal fuel 3,200 US gal (12113 liters); auxilliary fuel up to seven internal tanks carrying a total of 2,100 US gal (7949 liters); useful load for influence sweep mission 26,000 lb (11793 kg)

OPERATORS

US Navy (USN)

HC-1	North Island, CA	CH-53E
HC-2	Norfolk, VA	CH-53E
HC-4	Sigonella, Sicily	CH-53E
HM-12	Norfolk, VA	MH-53E
HM-14	Norfolk, VA	MH-53E
HM-15	Alameda, CA	MH-53E
NAWC/AD	Patuxent River, MD	CH-53E

US Marine Corps (USMC)

HMT-302	Tustin, CA	CH-53E
HMH-361	Tustin, CA	CH-53E
HMH-461	New River, NC	CH-53E
HMH-464	New River, NC	CH-53E
HMH-465	Tustin, CA	CH-53E
HMH-466	Tustin, CA	CH-53E

The bulbous side sponsons provide clear evidence that this is an MH-53E Sea Dragon of the US Navy. This specialist mine clearance model is now deployed with operational units located on both the East and West Coasts of the United States.

Bell
TH-57 SeaRanger

Fundamentally a militarized version of the Bell 206A JetRanger, the **TH-57A** represented a rapid solution to the Navy's requirement for a new turbine-powered light helicopter trainer and differed only in having Navy-standard avionics equipment and dual controls. In this guise and known as the **SeaRanger**, it entered US Navy service in 1968 when helicopter training squadron HT-8 at Whiting Field, Florida, took delivery of a batch of 40 TH-57As. Utilized for the transition phase of helicopter training, the TH-57A served as a stepping stone to the Iroquois which was used for advanced tuition until the 1980s, when additional SeaRangers were purchased.

Today, almost all of the TH-57As have been retired. The type is now only flown by the Naval Air Warfare Center Aircraft Division at Patuxent River, where a couple of examples are in use. However, SeaRangers continue to play a vital role in the task of producing qualified helicopter pilots for the Navy, Training Wing Five's two subordinate rotary-wing squadrons having standardized on this type.

Two new variants were at the heart of that standardization, the **TH-57B** and the **TH-57C**. The former was initially obtained to augment the TH-57A in the transition training task but has now completely replaced it, with a total of 51 examples having been delivered. Retaining dual controls, the B models are assigned to HT-8. Student pilots who have successfully completed primary and intermediate helicopter training courses will typically log about 39 hours during six weeks with this squadron before joining HT-18 for a 13-week advanced phase that will see them accumulate an additional 66 flying hours.

These additional hours are accomplished on the TH-57C. The first contract for this version was placed in January 1982, subsequent orders raising the number obtained to 89. These are somewhat more sophisticated machines and feature full IFR instrumentation, thus allowing students to master more complex skills in anticipation of moving on to operational-type helicopters like the Navy SH-60B Seahawk or the Marine Corps AH-1 SeaCobra.

TH-57B: A total of 51 TH-57B SeaRangers was purchased by the Navy as replacements for TH-57A and TH-1 helicopters with training units located at Whiting Field, Florida.
161695 to 161701; 162803 to 162810; 163312 to 163347

TH-57C: Coincident with acquisition of the TH-57B, some 89 TH-57C SeaRangers were also obtained for the helicopter pilot training role at Whiting Field.
162013 to 162067; 162666 to 162686; 162811 to 162823

Initial helicopter training for both US Navy and Marine Corps aircrew is accomplished on the Bell TH-57 SeaRangers of Training Wing Five at Whiting Field, FL. Two sub-types are used, with advanced instruction undertaken on the more sophisticated TH-57C.

SPECIFICATION

Bell TH-57C
Rotor system: main rotor diameter 33 ft 4 in (10.16 m); tail rotor diameter 5 ft 2 in (1.57 m); main rotor disc area 873.0 sq ft (81.10 m^2); tail rotor disc area 20.97 sq ft (1.95 m^2)
Fuselage and tail: length overall, rotors turning 38 ft 9.5 in (11.82 m) and fuselage 31 ft 2 in (2.91 m); tailplane span 6 ft 5.25 in (1.96 m)
Powerplant: one Allison 250-C20J rated at 420 shp (313 kW) but flat-rated to 317 shp (236 kW)
Weights: empty 1,852 lb (840 kg); maximum take-off 3,350 lb (1520 kg)
Fuel and load: internal fuel 76 US gal (288 liters)
Speed: never exceed 140 mph (225 km/h); maximum and economical cruising speed at sea level 133 mph (214 km/h)
Range: range at 10,000 ft (3050 m) 527 miles (848 km)
Performance: maximum rate of climb at sea level 1,540 ft (469 m) per minute; service ceiling more than 20,000 ft (6095 m); hovering ceiling 12,700 ft (3870 m) in ground effect and 6,000 ft (1830 m) out of ground effect

MISSION PROFILE

Configuration options: This dual-control helicopter allows one pilot with one to four students to conduct primary and intermediate helicopter pilot training.

Training: A full range of basic helicopter mission profiles can be simulated by the TH-57 to prepare USN helicopter pilots to progress to fly more advanced machines.

VARIANTS AND SERIALS

TH-57A: Initial version of Bell JetRanger for primary training of helicopter pilots for both services. A total of 40 examples was obtained but these have been replaced by the TH-57B and TH-57C. One or two TH-57As are, however, still active on test work.
157355 to 157394

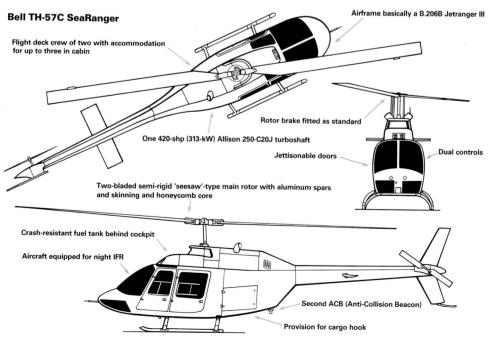

Bell TH-57C SeaRanger

Airframe basically a B.206B Jetranger III

Flight deck crew of two with accommodation for up to three in cabin

Rotor brake fitted as standard

One 420-shp (313-kW) Allison 250-C20J turboshaft

Jettisonable doors

Dual controls

Two-bladed semi-rigid 'seesaw'-type main rotor with aluminum spars and skinning and honeycomb core

Crash-resistant fuel tank behind cockpit

Aircraft equipped for night IFR

Second ACB (Anti-Collision Beacon)

Provision for cargo hook

Bell TH-57A
generally similar to the TH-57C except in the following particulars:
Fuselage and tail: length overall, rotors turning 39 ft 1 in (11.91 m)
Powerplant: one Allison T63-A-700 (250-C18A) rated at 317 shp (236 kW)
Weights: empty 1,407 lb (638 kg); maximum take-off 3,000 lb (1361 kg)
Fuel and load: internal fuel 76 US gal (288 liters); maximum payload 1,200 lb (545 kg)
Speed: maximum and economical cruising speed at sea level 142 mph (229km/h)
Range: range at 5,000 ft (1525 m) 449 miles (722 km)
Performance: at 2,000 lb (907 kg) maximum rate of climb at sea level 2,830 ft (863 m) per minute; service ceiling more than 20,000 ft (6095 m); hovering ceiling 21,000 ft (6400 m) in ground effect and 17,000 ft (5180 m) out of ground effect

Among the skills mastered by students on the TH-57 are those required when operating from landing platforms of ships at sea. Here a TH-57C hovers above a training vessel.

Bell TH-57B
generally similar to the TH-57C except in the following particulars:
Powerplant: one Allison 250-C20 rated at 400 shp (298 kW)
Weights: empty 1,455 lb (660 kg); maximum take-off 3,200 lb (1451 kg)
Speed: maximum and economical cruising speed at sea level 140 mph (225 km/h)
Performance: maximum rate of climb at sea level 1,260 ft (384 m) per minute; service ceiling more than 20,000 ft (6095 m); hovering ceiling 11,300 ft (3445 m) in ground effect and 5,800 ft (1770 m) out of ground effect

OPERATORS

US Navy (USN)

HT-8	Whiting Field, FL	TH-57B, TH-57C
HT-18	Whiting Field, FL	TH-57B, TH-57C
NAWC/AD	Patuxent River, MD	TH-57A

Bell
OH-58A Kiowa

Based on the Model 206 JetRanger, the **OH-58A Kiowa** was chosen to satisfy an Army requirement for a light observation helicopter in the spring of 1968. Contracts for some 2,200 machines were subsequently placed, these differing from the commercially-available Model 206A in having a larger-diameter main rotor blade assembly, plus military-standard avionics equipment and a few other minor alterations. Many of these are still in service today with US Army units around the world while others have been subjected to modernization as the **OH-58C** and **OH-58D**.

US Navy operation of the Kiowa is extremely limited, with the Test Pilot's School at Patuxent River, Maryland, having included two or three loaned US Army examples in its complement since at least the mid-1970s. These have invariably been standard OH-58As.

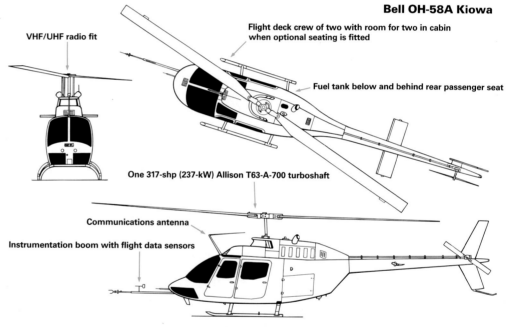

Bell OH-58A Kiowa

VHF/UHF radio fit

Flight deck crew of two with room for two in cabin when optional seating is fitted

Fuel tank below and behind rear passenger seat

One 317-shp (237-kW) Allison T63-A-700 turboshaft

Communications antenna

Instrumentation boom with flight data sensors

MISSION PROFILE

If any examples of the OH-58A Kiowa remain in use, they serve in the rotary wing test pilot training role with the USN Test Pilot's School at Patuxent River.

VARIANTS AND SERIALS

OH-58A: A limited number of OH-58A Kiowa light helicopters have been obtained for service with the Naval Test Pilot's School. At least four have been reported in use.
710554 (71-20554); 710799 (71-20799); 221253 (72-21253); 721193 (72-21193); 816695 (68-16695)

SPECIFICATION

Bell OH-58A
Rotor system: main rotor diameter 35 ft 4 in (10.77 m); tail rotor diameter 5 ft 2 in (1.57 m); main rotor disc area 978.8 sq ft (90.93 m²); tail rotor disc area 20.97 sq ft (1.95 m²)
Fuselage and tail: length overall, rotors turning 40 ft 11.75 in (12.49 m) and fuselage 32 ft 3.5 in (9.84 m); height 9 ft 6.5 in (2.91 m); tailplane span 6 ft 5.25 in (1.96 m)

Powerplant: one Allison T63-A-700 rated at 317 shp (236.5 kW)
Weights: empty equipped 1,583 lb (718 kg); maximum take-off 3,000 lb (1361 kg)
Fuel and load: internal fuel 73 US gal (276 liters)
Speed: maximum level speed at sea level 150 mph (241 km/h); cruising speed for maximum range at sea level 117 mph (188 km/h)
Range: normal range at sea level 299 miles (481 km)
Performance: maximum rate of climb at sea level 1,780 ft (543 m) per minute; service ceiling 19,000 ft (5790 m); hovering ceiling 13,750 ft (4190 m) in ground effect and 9,000 ft (2745 m) out of ground effect

OPERATORS

US Navy (USN)

NTPS	Patuxent River, MD	OH-58A

A handful of OH-58A Kiowa helicopters is used by the Test Pilot's School at Patuxent River, MD, under the terms of a loan arrangement concluded with the US Army.

Sikorsky
H-60 Seahawk/Ocean Hawk/Jayhawk

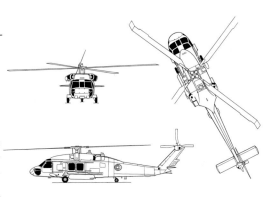

Developed from the UH-60A Black Hawk which won the US Army's Utility Tactical Transport Aircraft System design competition, the **SH-60B Seahawk** was the first version to attain operational service with the US Navy. It has since been joined in the inventory by other models such as the **SH-60F Ocean Hawk** and the **HH-60H**. In addition, the US Marine Corps has a few suitably modified machines for VIP transportation duties and yet another derivative flies with the Coast Guard.

Likely to remain the principal maritime model, the SH-60B was conceived to satisfy a Navy requirement for a LAMPS Mk III shipboard helicopter capable of operation from landing platforms on cruisers, frigates and destroyers, and it was duly selected for further development during 1977. At that time, five prototypes were ordered, the first of these making its initial flight on 12 December 1979. Testing of this and the other prototypes was largely accomplished at Patuxent River, Maryland, and the initial production contract was awarded to Sikorsky in Fiscal Year 1982. At that time, procurement was expected to just exceed the 200 mark; this has now risen to around 260 and may yet go higher still.

Modification of the basic UH-60A airframe for the specialist ASW/ASMD roles required extensive changes to airframe and systems. One of the most visible manifestations of change – apart from the low-visibility, overall-gray tactical color scheme - related to the tailwheel, which was moved forward several feet so as to shorten the wheelbase and allow sufficient deck edge clearance when flying from

landing platforms. In addition, automatic rotor and tail folding mechanisms were incorporated along with more powerful General Electric T700-GE-401 turboshaft engines, extra fuel capacity and the 'High Drink' inflight-refueling system which allows the SH-60B to replenish its fuel tanks while in the hover.

Mission-related equipment includes AN/APS-124 search radar for surveillance and launch tubes for a maximum of 25 sonobuoys in the port side of the fuselage, as well as internal storage for up to four full sets of reloads and an ASQ-81(V)2 towed MAD sensor to starboard. Armament options encompass the Mk 46 torpedo and, on the latest production examples, compatibility with the Norwegian AGM-119 Penguin anti-ship attack missile. During the Gulf War it was also usual to have a single 7.62-mm machine gun mounted in the cabin doorway.

In the ASW/ASMD roles, the SH-60B usually carries a crew of three, comprising a pilot and co-pilot on the flight deck and a sensor operator in the cabin, which features an additional passenger seat at the rear. Datalink equipment allows information to be transferred to and from the parent ship as well as other elements of the battle group but fully independent operation is also possible, using the sensors and weapons. Another sensor that was hurriedly pressed into use on seven Seahawks during Desert Shield and Desert Storm was a Ford Aerospace AN/AAS-38 FLIR – carried on the port weapons pylon, this provided real-time imagery to the parent ship and proved

particularly useful in enforcing the naval blockade during the build-up to war.

Although dealing with surface and sub-surface threats is the primary mission performed by the SH-60B, it may also undertake a number of utility taskings. These include routine communications and liaison, search and rescue, vertical replenishment (up to 6,000 lb; 2700 kg of cargo can be slung externally), communications relay and casualty evacuation.

At present, the SH-60B force is concentrated at two main shore facilities: Mayport, Florida, and North Island, California. Each has five HSL squadrons assigned, comprising one training unit and four operational outfits. As far as the latter are concerned, the primary method of deployment entails the use of detachments (of one or two helicopters) which are assigned to surface combatants for the duration of a cruise. In addition, a new squadron has recently been established at Atsugi, Japan, tasked with providing detachments to elements of the 7th Fleet operating in the Western Pacific.

Antisubmarine warfare is also the principal task allocated to the SH-60F Ocean Hawk

Seen flying near its home base at North Island, this SH-60B is assigned to the Pacific Fleet training unit HSL-41.

Left: Optimized for combat search and rescue, the HH-60H first entered service with Reserve units at Norfolk and Point Mugu. It is now in the process of augmenting SH-60Fs in carrierborne antisubmarine warfare squadrons.

Below: The lastest addition to the Coast Guard fleet is the HH-60J Jayhawk, which is tasked in the medium-range rescue and recovery role. The initial order was for 35 helicopters.

H-60 Seahawk (continued)

which is now in the process of replacing the long-serving SH-3 Sea King aboard aircraft carriers. In this case, however, it has responsibility for inner zone protection of the battle group and is accordingly fitted with a different sensor suite, which has been installed in place of the specialized LAMPS avionics. One of the prime detection systems is the Allied Signal (Bendix Oceanics) AN/AQS-13F dunking sonar. It also features an extra weapons station, allowing it to operate with up to three Mk 50 torpedoes.

Additional missions include plane guard and the closely allied search and rescue, with Navy procurement plans calling for a total of 175 examples to equip 14 squadrons split equally between the two major Fleet organizations. Shore bases are North Island, California, (Pacific) and Jacksonville, Florida, (Atlantic) and one of the seven squadrons in each community will be tasked solely with training – the other six will be deployable units, with one being assigned to each CVW. As with the Sea King, deployed complement is expected to consist of six SH-60Fs.

Examples of the SH-60F began to reach the Fleet in 1989, with initial deliveries going to North Island. This base is now home to at least four squadrons, of which HS-2 was the first to deploy when it embarked aboard USS Nimitz in 1991. The process of transition is also under way at Jacksonville, with HS-3 being the first Atlantic Fleet Ocean Hawk unit in 1991.

The last version in Navy service is the HH-60H, which is a specialized model for combat search and rescue and support of covert operations. Entering the inventory in 1990, this

equips only a pair of Reserve units, specifically HCS-4 at Norfolk, Virginia, and HCS-5 at Point Mugu, California. Both squadrons were called upon to support combat operations in the Gulf War, each providing two helicopters which flew from bases in Saudi Arabia. Procurement was initially limited to 18 examples but more are now on order. The HH-60H is expected to augment the SH-60F aboard aircraft carriers, with current planning calling for two examples to be assigned to each embarked HS outfit when deployed.

The different demands of the missions assigned to the HH-60H inevitably dictate a very different configuration. It lacks the ASW kit of other Navy models, instead being fitted with a variety of threat-warning systems and countermeasures, as well as a pair of cabin-mounted M60 7.62-mm machine guns. Fully compatible with night vision goggles, it has the ability to retrieve up to four personnel at ranges of the order of 250 nm (280 miles; 450 km) or to insert a team of eight SEALs (Navy covert warfare specialists) by parachute at distances of up to 200 nm (230 miles; 370 km).

Marine Corps operation of the Sikorsky helicopter is confined to a total of nine **VH-60Ns** which are all assigned to HMX-1 squadron at Quantico, Virginia. More luxuriously appointed than the utilitarian UH/SH-60s, they are used for VIP and VVIP transportation tasks, carrying the President and other members of his administration as well as visiting heads of state and important dignitaries.

Search and rescue is also the principal job performed by the **HH-60J Jayhawk** which began to enter service with the Coast Guard in 1990. Optimized for the medium-range re-

covery role, a total of 35 has so far been ordered and all of these should be in service by the end of 1993. As with other USCG equipment, Jayhawk may also be employed in a variety of other roles, including interdiction of drug supply routes, investigation of other types of smuggling activity, environmental surveillance and protection and general law enforcement tasks in concert with other agencies.

In maximum range configuration with three 120-US gal (450-liter) auxiliary fuel tanks, the HH-60J has a range of 300 nm (345 miles; 550 km) when carrying a four-man crew consisting of two pilots and a winch operator and diver, both of whom will have some medical skills. Once on station, it can then loiter for three-quarters of an hour before returning to base with six survivors. It is also fully configured to operate from landing platforms on 'Hamilton'- and 'Bear'-class cutters of the Coast Guard, and could use these to deposit survivors and then refuel in major rescue operations.

Specialized equipment consists of Bendix/King RDR-1300 search and weather radar and a complex array of navaids. It is also fully compatible with night vision goggles and possesses secure communications systems, which facilitate use in covert surveillance operations such as during anti-drug smuggling.

Initial Jayhawk deliveries were made to the Coast Guard air station at Mobile, Alabama, during October 1990. Since then, it has also been assigned to facilities at Elizabeth City, North Carolina, and Traverse City, Michigan, but other bases are expected to operate the HH-60J in due course.

MISSION PROFILE

Configuration options: The H-60 is now the USN's main embarked helicopter with versions fulfilling anti-submarine, surface surveillance, strike rescue and utility missions. The USCG has its own version. The USMC has a specialized executive flight version.

Light airborne multi-purpose system (LAMPS): The primary mission of the SH-60B LAMPS III is ASW from USN frigates and destroyers. Two Mk 60 torpedoes are the main ASW weapons, which are fired after enemy submarines are detected by MAD or sonobuoys, or target information has been passed by automatic datalinks from ships or maritime patrol aircraft. The SH-60B is part of an integrated ASW team, weaving an electronic and sound web to trap and destroy enemy submarines. Secondary missions include surface ship surveillance and targeting with radar and electronic sensors to detect enemy radar emissions. Target information is then passed to strike aircraft, attack helicopters and surface ships. Seahawks also have to perform general utility missions for their parent ships, such as medical evacuation, VertRep and rescue.

CV inner zone ASW: The SH-60F provides quick-reaction inner zone ASW protection for USN battle groups, flying from aircraft carriers. An AN/AQS-13F dunking sonar is the main sensor. Mk 46 or Mk 50 torpedoes are carried. In addition, its sonar can be used to drive submarines into designated kill zones by generating sub-surface noise. Datalinks allow the

Folding
To take up the minimum amount of space on the carrier deck or hangar, the SH-60F has folding tail, tailplane and rotors. The main blades fold back to lie above the rear fuselage.

Blades
The four main rotor blades feature swept-back tips, known as 'tip caps', which improve speed and reduce rotor noise. Each blade is formed around an oval titanium spar with Nomex core. The leading edge is titanium, while the tip is Kevlar.

Crew
The SH-60F is operated on the ASW mission by three crew members: a pilot, an air tactical officer and the sensor operator. The latter sits at a station in the cabin and operates the sonar. Large MFD screens present tactical information both here and on the flight deck.

Sikorsky SH-60F
Ocean Hawk

Based on the successful SH-60B Seahawk LAMPS III helicopter employed on smaller US Navy ships, the SH-60F is a dedicated carrier helicopter (CV-Helo). Its primary role is the inner zone antisubmarine defense of the carrier battle group, but it also has a secondary rescue/plane-guard function, although this is better filled by the HH-60H. Carrier deployment envisages six SH-60Fs in each wing, with two HH-60Hs.

Flight control
The Automatic Flight Control System receives data from several sources and then computes control inputs under direction from the pilot.

Sonar
The main antisubmarine sensor of the SH-60F is the AQS-13F dunking sonar, winched out from the main cabin through a port in the lower fuselage. The cable can be lowered 1,500 ft (460 m), allowing the sensor to penetrate several temperature layers in the sea. Eight sonobuoys are also carried, manually loaded into a single dropping tube.

Markings
This Ocean Hawk wears the markings of HS-3 'Tridents', the first SH-60F unit in the Atlantic Fleet. They are deployed in *Theodore Roosevelt*.

Powerplant
The T700-GE-401C engines are fully navalized and have proved very reliable. The high power output provides a wide margin of safety, including single-engined hover.

Weapons
Up to three torpedoes can be carried, either the Mk 46 or Mk 50. Two can be carried on the extended port side pylon, although in practice the inboard station is usually occupied by a fuel tank.

Above: A VIP-type color scheme has been given to the nine VH-60Ns obtained for service with HMX-1 at Quantico, VA. Duties are mainly executive airlift.

Above right: At least three examples of the standard Army UH-60A Black Hawk serve with the Test Pilot's School at Patuxent River. As with the Kiowa and U-21 Ute, these are operated on a loan basis.

H-60 Seahawk (continued)

SH-60F to coordinate combined ASW operations with surface ships or maritime patrol aircraft. In addition, they fly VertRep, plane guard and other utility missions.

Medium-range recovery: Operating from shore bases and USCG ships the SH-60J are a key part of the US search and rescue network, often working in cooperation with fixed-wing patrol aircraft. They also perform law enforcement, drug interdiction, maritime safety, environmental protection and other utility work.

Naval special warfare support/strike rescue: HH-60Hs provide strike rescue support for USN aircrews downed up to 200 miles (320 km) behind enemy lines. Using ANVIS night vision goggles they have a 24-hour capability. Self-defense systems include 7.62-mm door guns, ALQ-44 IR decoys, APR-39 radar warning receivers and ALE-39 chaff/flare dispensers. Strike rescue missions are coordinated by an E-2C and strike aircraft suppress enemy air defenses during the recovery phase of the rescue operation. Navy SEAL special forces teams can be inserted and extracted behind enemy lines by rappeling, fastrope or paradrop.

Executive flight duties: USMC VH-60Ns are kept on 24-hour alert in the Washington DC area to provide airborne transportation to the President and other high-ranking government officials. They have secure communications, VIP-standard interiors and extensive self-defense systems.

Below: Deployment of the SH-60F as a Sea King replacement with the Atlantic Fleet began with HS-3 at Jacksonville in 1991.

VARIANTS AND SERIALS

UH-60A: Three examples of the UH-60 Black Hawk have been acquired from the US Army for the NTPS.
22716 (77-22716); 22725 (77-22725); 23507 (80-23507)

YSH-60B: Five prototypes of the navalized version of the UH-60A were ordered to undertake test duties.
161169 to 161173

SH-60B: The first Seahawk version to enter operational service with the Navy was the SH-60B and at least 168 have so far been ordered for service with light helicopter ASW units.
161553 to 161570; 162092 to 162139; 162326 to 162349; 162974 to 162997; 163038 to 163043; 163233 to 163256; 163593 to 163598; 163905 to 163910; 164174 to 164179; 164461 to 164466

UH-60B: Two utility examples of the Sikorsky helicopter have been purchased for an unknown operator.
163257; 163258

SH-60F: Obtained as a replacement for the SH-3 Sea King on inner zone ASW duties, the SH-60F is currently in quantity production for the Navy, which has so far ordered a total of 73 examples.
163282 to 163288; 164069 to 164104; 164443 to 164460; 164609 to 164620

HH-60H: Optimized for combat search and rescue duties and covert operations, 18 HH-60Hs were ordered for Reserve units. The helicopter has recently also been deployed alongside the SH-60F aboard Navy carriers to fulfil the plane-guard function.
163783 to 163800

HH-60J: Acquisition of 35 examples of the Jayhawk rescue model is presently under way for the US Coast Guard, which employs this version on medium-range recovery missions.
6001 to 6035

VH-60N: A total of nine VIP-configured VH-60Ns has been acquired for service with Marine helicopter squadron HMX-1 on executive airlift tasks.
163259 to 163267

OPERATORS

US Navy (USN)

HCS-4	Norfolk, VA	HH-60H
HCS-5	Point Mugu, CA	HH-60H
HS-2	North Island, CA	SH-60F, HH-60H
HS-3	Jacksonville, FL	SH-60F, HH-60H
HS-4	North Island, CA	SH-60F
HS-6	North Island, CA	SH-60F, HH-60H
HS-8	North Island, CA	SH-60F, HH-60H
HS-9	Jacksonville, FL	SH-60F, HH-60H
HS-10	North Island, CA	SH-60F
HS-15	Jacksonville, FL	SH-60F, HH-60H
HSL-40	Mayport, FL	SH-60B
HSL-41	North Island, CA	SH-60B
HSL-42	Mayport, FL	SH-60B
HSL-43	North Island, CA	SH-60B
HSL-44	Mayport, FL	SH-60B
HSL-45	North Island, CA	SH-60B
HSL-46	Mayport, FL	SH-60B
HSL-47	North Island, CA	SH-60B
HSL-48	Mayport, FL	SH-60B
HSL-49	North Island, CA	SH-60B
HSL-51	Atsugi, Japan	SH-60B
VX-1	Patuxent River, MD	SH-60B
NAWC/AD	Patuxent River, MD	SH-60B, SH-60F, HH-60J
NTPS	Patuxent River, MD	UH-60A

US Marine Corps (USMC)

HMX-1	Quantico, VA	VH-60N

US Coast Guard (USCG)

CGAS	Elizabeth City, NC	HH-60J
CGAS	Mobile, AL	HH-60J
CGAS	San Francisco, CA	HH-60J
CGAS	Traverse City, MI	HH-60J

SPECIFICATION

Sikorsky SH-60B
Rotor system: main rotor diameter 53 ft 8 in (16.36 m); tail rotor diameter 11 ft 0 in (3.35 m); main rotor disc area 2,261.0 sq ft (210.05 m²); tail rotor disc area 95.0 sq ft (8.83 m²)
Fuselage and tail: length overall, rotors turning 64 ft 10 in (19.76 m)' fuselage 50 ft 0.75 in (15.26 m), and overall with rotor and tail pylon folded 40 ft 11 in (12.47 m); height overall with tail rotor turning 17 ft 0 in (5.18 m), to top of rotor head 11 ft 11 in (3.63 m), and with tail pylon folded 13 ft 3.25 in (4.04 m); tailplane span 14 ft 4.5 in (4.38 m); wheel base 15 ft 10 in (4.83 m)
Powerplant: two General Electric T700-GE-401 rated at 1,690 shp (1260 kW) in early helicopters and two General Electric T700-GE-401C rated at 1,900 shp (1417 kW) in helicopters delivered from 1988
Weights: empty 13,648 lb (6191 kg) for the ASW mission; mission take-off 20,244 lb (9182 kg) for the ASW mission or 18,373 lb (8334 kg) for the ASST mission; maximum take-off 21,884 lb (9926 kg) for the utility mission
Fuel and load: internal fuel 590 US gal (2233 liters); maximum payload 8,000 lb (3629 kg)
Speed: dash speed at 5,000 ft (1525 m) 145 mph (234 km/h)
Range: radius with a 3-hour loiter 57.5 miles (92.5 km) or with a 1-hour loiter 173 miles (278 km)
Performance: maximum vertical rate of climb at sea level 700 ft (213 m) per minute

Sikorsky SH-60F
generally similar to the SH-60B except in the following particulars:
Weights: maximum take-off 23,500 lb (10659 kg)

Left: An SH-60B of HSL-46 winds up to full power in anticipation of getting airborne from the USS Doyle somewhere in the Atlantic Ocean.

Aérospatiale
HH-65A Dolphin

Development of this Aérospatiale helicopter was launched in the early 1970s with the objective of producing a replacement for the highly successful Alouette III. The resulting **SA 360** prototype flew for the first time on 2 June 1972 and was a single-engined design, powered by a Turboméca Astazou XVI turboshaft. That engine soon gave way to the more powerful Astazou XVIIIA, but it quickly became apparent that the most promising avenue to explore lay with a twin-engined design. Powered by a pair of Turboméca Arriel turboshafts, the new version was given the designation **SA 365C** and made a successful maiden flight on 24 January 1975. Coast Guard interest in the Dauphin II came later and was conditional upon yet another re-engining exercise although, as it turned out, this may not have been an altogether wise move.

The subject of a major order from the US Coast Guard, delivery of Aérospatiale's Dauphin II – or **HH-65A Dolphin**, as it is known in Coast Guard service – began in 1983, initially to supplant and eventually to replace entirely the Sikorsky HH-52A Seaguard. Today, most of the 96 examples involved in this contract serve from about 15 different locations in the USA. In addition, some Dolphins are deployed aboard Coast Guard vessels and a couple have been assigned to the Navy's Test Pilot's School at Patuxent River.

Employed primarily for short-range search and rescue tasks, the Dolphin has recently come in for heavy criticism. Part of that criticism stems from a lack of 'puff', which imposes hover limitations that in turn seriously compromise its value as a SAR platform. In addition to a lack of power, the helicopter is also overweight, although much of the responsibility for the latter inadequacy could well be levelled at the Coast Guard itself, since the service has apparently added equipment weighing hundreds of pounds over the years that have elapsed since the Dolphin joined the inventory. Whatever their origins, both of these shortcomings were highlighted by a fraught rescue operation in April 1991 which culminated in one HH-65A being damaged when it was forced to make a 'run-on' landing while a second was only able to hoist casualties after dumping fuel.

In view of that, it is perhaps surprising to report that yet another re-engining exercise appears to have been abandoned. Trials with a modified machine, utilizing more powerful Allison/Garrett LHTEC T-800s in place of the HH-65A's standard Lycoming LTS101s, were started but have apparently been curtailed, rather ironically because the original powerplant was said to be functioning adequately. It is, however, quite possible that this project

will be resurrected at some future date, if efforts at weight reduction fail to eradicate the problems that are now being experienced.

MISSION PROFILE

Configuration options: A winch is standard to the HH-65A and provides its main means of rescue.

Short-range recovery: The HH-65A provides shore- and ship-based rescue coverage for the USCG. They have four hours of endurance which includes 15 minutes of hover in the rescue area. The short range of the HH-65A means it is heavily committed to inshore work, particularly off beach resorts.

VARIANTS AND SERIALS

HH-65A: Procurement of 96 examples of the HH-65A Dolphin was undertaken for the US Coast Guard, which utilizes it on short- to medium-range rescue and recovery duties. Two Dolphins are also operated by the Naval Test Pilot's School on a loan basis.
6501 to 6596

SPECIFICATION

Aérospatiale HH-65A
Rotor system: main rotor diameter 39 ft 2 in (11.94 m); 'fenestron' diameter 3 ft 7.25 in (1.10 m); main rotor disc 1,204.5 sq ft (111.90 m²); 'fenestron' disc area 10.23 sq ft (0.95 m²)
Fuselage and tail: length overall, rotors turning 45 ft 6.5 in (13.88 m) and fuselage 38 ft 1.875 in (11.63 m); height overall 13 ft 0.75 in (3.98 m) and to top of rotor head 11 ft 6.5 in (3.52 m); wheel base 11 ft 10.25 in (3.61 m)
Powerplant: two Textron Lycoming LTS101-750A-1 rated at 680 shp (507 kW)
Weights: empty equipped 5,992 lb (2718 kg); maximum take-off 8,928 lb (4050 kg)
Fuel and load: internal fuel 300 US gal (1135 liters); auxiliary fuel up to 47.5 US gal (180 liters) in one optional baggage compartment tank or 125.5 US gal (475 liters) of ferry fuel in an optional tank replacing the rear seats

Speed: never exceed 201 mph (324 km/h); maximum cruising speed at sea level 160 mph (257 km/h)
Range: range with maximum fuel 461 miles (760 km); range with maximum passenger payload 248 miles (400 km); rescue range 191 miles (307 km); endurance with maximum fuel 4 hours 0 minutes
Performance: hovering ceiling 7,510 ft (2290 m) in ground effect and 5,340 ft (1627 m) out of ground effect

OPERATORS

US Navy (USN)

NTPS	Patuxent River, MD	HH-65A

US Coast Guard (USCG)

CGAS	Astoria, OR	HH-65A
CGAS	Borinquen, PR	HH-65A
CGAS	Brooklyn, NY	HH-65A
CGAS	Cape Cod, MA	HH-65A
CGAS	Cape May, NJ	HH-65A
CGAS	Chicago, IL	HH-65A
CGAS	Corpus Christi, TX	HH-65A
CGAS	Detroit, MI	HH-65A
CGAS	Elizabeth City, NC	HH-65A
CGAS	Houston, TX	HH-65A
CGAS	Los Angeles, CA	HH-65A
CGAS	Miami, FL	HH-65A
CGAS	Mobile, AL	HH-65A
CGAS	New Orleans, LA	HH-65A
CGAS	North Bend, OR	HH-65A
CGAS	Port Angeles, WA	HH-65A
CGAS	Sacramento, CA	HH-65A
CGAS	San Diego, CA	HH-65A
CGAS	Savannah, GA	HH-65A

Right: No fewer than 96 examples of the HH-65A Dolphin have been purchased by the Coast Guard for short-range recovery, but some users have expressed dissatisfaction with the lack of available power and recommend a switch to a new engine.

Lockheed
P-3 Orion

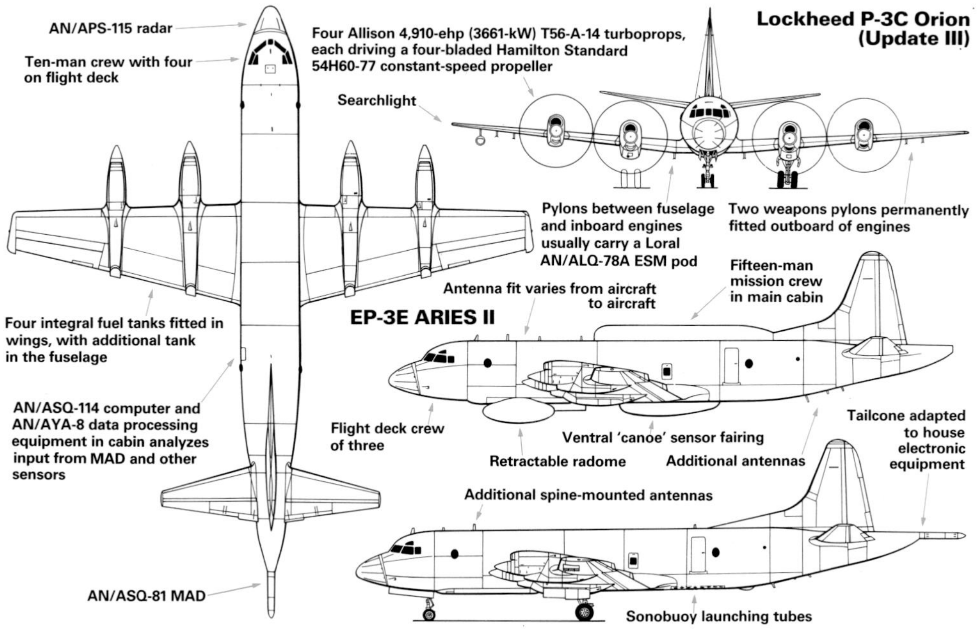

Development of the **P3V** (later **P-3**) **Orion** began in the summer of 1957 when the US Navy issued a request for proposals for a new advanced ASW and maritime patrol aircraft, adding the rider that it would look favorably upon a variation of a type that was already in production. Although it had yet to make its maiden flight, Lockheed had such a type in the L-188 Electra commercial airliner and was also well versed in this air warfare speciality, for the company was responsible for the P2V Neptune which was then in widespread service with the Navy's large force of land-based patrol squadrons.

As a consequence, Lockheed quickly advised the Navy that the Electra could be adapted for the role without too much difficulty and in April 1958 – barely four months after the Electra flew for the first time – the Navy selected it, following up a few weeks later with a development contract for the P3V. With a number of Electra prototypes now flying, Lockheed chose to speed the pace of development by modifying the third example to serve as an aerodynamic testbed. In this form, it got airborne for the first time on 19 August 1958, new features comprising a bulged forward fuselage cross-section to represent the weapons bay and the now-familiar tail 'stinger' which houses a MAD sensor. Subsequently, the aerodynamic prototype was further modified to serve as the **YP3V-1** (later **YP-3A**) prototype.

This made its first flight during November 1959, with production standard **P3V-1s** (**P-3A**s) following suit from April 1961. Testing of these and the YP3V-1 cleared the way for entry into service with patrol squadrons VP-8 and VP-44 at Patuxent River, Maryland, in August 1962. Within weeks of entering the Navy inventory, these early Orions were called upon to assist with the air and sea blockade of Cuba during the missile crisis of October and November 1962, when the world hovered on the brink of full-scale nuclear war.

Known in company parlance as the Model 185, the P-3A also relied on the Allison T56 turboprop engine for power but differed from the Electra in a number of ways. Not least of these was the fact that it had a forward fuselage that was shortened by some 7 ft (2.1 m) – paradoxically, though, the addition of the MAD boom actually meant it was just over 12 ft (3.7 m) longer. As already mentioned, a weapons bay was located in the lower forward fuselage, other changes including provision of 10 hardpoints for external stores beneath the outer wing panels as well as much increased fuel capacity, a strengthened airframe structure which embodied treatment to minimize anti-salt water corrosion and an impressive array of mission avionics equipment in the cabin.

Apart from a switch to a more powerful version of the Allison turboprop and some structural 'beefing up', most of the changes made since the Orion entered service have concerned the mission avionics suite, which is infinitely more sophisticated and possessed of vastly im-

proved detection and tracking ability. Armament options have also been upgraded along the way but these improvements have not resulted in an increase in personnel needed to ensure efficient operation, and the standard patrol aircraft crew numbers 10. They are led by a command pilot, with other crew members comprising two pilots, a navigator, a radio operator, a tactical coordinator and three systems operators. To provide extra eyes, or to share the workload during missions which can run as long as 16 hours, two additional observers may be carried.

Production of the Orion was expected to have ended recently in readiness for a switch to the P-7A. However, the latter type was cancelled and an order for eight Orions from South Korea does mean that new-build aircraft will continue to appear until at least 1995. This leaves the door open for further orders from the US Navy, although the recent decision to disestablish four regular squadrons and to cut patrol squadron strength from nine to eight aircraft appears to confirm that Navy procurement has terminated for good. That procurement eventually surpassed the 550 total for the three main production models, namely the P-3A, **P-3B** and **P-3C**.

Almost exactly half of that total relates to the P-3C, all front-line patrol squadrons now being equipped with 'Charlie' models of the Orion. As to Reserve Force assets, unit estab-

lishment is also to be cut (from nine to six aircraft) and despite the recent assignment of some P-3Cs, it is the older P-3B which is the most numerous version in second-line service.

Front-line elements are distributed between four major bases, with the Atlantic and Pacific Fleet patrol communities each having 11 squadrons including a non-deployable training unit. With the Atlantic Fleet, these are concentrated within Patrol Wing Five (PW-5) at Brunswick, Maine, and PW-11 at Jacksonville, Florida, while their Pacific Fleet counterparts can be found at Barbers Point, Hawaii, (PW-2) and Moffett Field, California (PW-10). Both organizations rely heavily on deployments to extend their 'reach', tours of overseas duty generally lasting for about six months. Deployment bases used by Atlantic Fleet units include Sigonella, Sicily and Keflavik, Iceland; Pacific Fleet units use locations like Misawa, Japan, and Adak, Alaska.

Turning to the Reserve, this also has patrol wing organizations for each Fleet, although assigned units are much less concentrated. With the Atlantic, this consists of seven squadrons at six bases, while the Pacific has six squadrons at five bases. P-3Cs equip five of these units and P-3Bs the remaining eight.

Although it is the submarine force which constitutes the greatest threat, patrol units should more correctly be perceived as being concerned with sea surveillance and may well be called into action against all sorts of vessels should the need arise. As a consequence, sensors that can be used include active ('pinging') and passive (listening) sonobuoys and the MAD for submersibles, as well as radar for surface contacts. Data generated by these and other detection systems is processed by computer for display to crew members on cathode ray tubes. A datalink facility also exists whereby information can be electronically transferred between aircraft during a 'handover' or from aircraft to friendly warships engaged in 'prosecuting' a contact.

In the event of having to attack a contact, various weapons options are available. For submerged vessels, torpedoes may be

Diagram labels

AN/APS-115 radar

Ten-man crew with four on flight deck

Searchlight

Four Allison 4,910-ehp (3661-kW) T56-A-14 turboprops, each driving a four-bladed Hamilton Standard 54H60-77 constant-speed propeller

Lockheed P-3C Orion (Update III)

Four integral fuel tanks fitted in wings, with additional tank in the fuselage

EP-3E ARIES II

AN/ASQ-114 computer and AN/AYA-8 data processing equipment in cabin analyzes input from MAD and other sensors

AN/ASQ-81 MAD

Pylons between fuselage and inboard engines usually carry a Loral AN/ALQ-78A ESM pod

Two weapons pylons permanently fitted outboard of engines

Antenna fit varies from aircraft to aircraft

Fifteen-man mission crew in main cabin

Flight deck crew of three

Ventral 'canoe' sensor fairing

Retractable radome

Additional antennas

Tailcone adapted to house electronic equipment

Additional spine-mounted antennas

Sonobuoy launching tubes

Front-line patrol squadrons of the Navy are now entirely equipped with variations on the P-3C theme and are represented here by an Orion from VP-40 at Moffett Field.

Above: The once-colorful scheme and insignia applied to Orions of the Navy's substantial patrol force has given way to the drabber, low-visibility tactical finish portrayed here on a P-3C from VP-16 at Jacksonville.

Right: After years of operating less-capable P-3A models, the Reserve force has benefited from deployment of P-3B and P-3C versions over the past few years. Among the squadrons that use the 'Charlie' Orion is VP-65.

employed as well as conventional and nuclear depth charges. For dealing with larger surface ships, the Harpoon missile is probably now the weapon of choice but 5-in (12.7-cm) rockets can also be carried, these being far more suitable for use against smaller craft.

Although the Orion is best known for its maritime applications, ASW/patrol is by no means the only task that it undertakes, for a number of specialized versions are also in service with operational and non-operational elements of the US Navy. With the exception of a solitary **RP-3D** that was built as such, these are all conversions of existing airframes and their configurations differ substantially depending upon the nature of the role that is undertaken.

Starting with the P-3A, most of these long-serving machines have now been retired from service, but examples of the **EP-3A**, **RP-3A**, **TP-3A**, **UP-3A** and **VP-3A** are still active. The first version is used by the Naval Air Warfare Center Aircraft Division at Point Mugu, California, and at least two different derivatives are known to exist, namely the **EP-3A (EATS)** and the **EP-3A (SMILS)**. Expanded Area Test System (EATS) airborne instrumentation aircraft are identifiable by virtue of a huge extension to the vertical tail which houses a phased array antenna; modifications to Sonobuoy Missile Impact Locating System (SMILS) aircraft are less apparent but these are engaged in monitoring impact points and determining the degree of accuracy (or otherwise) of SLBM warheads.

Some RP-3As also serve with the NAWC on duties connected with missile testing, but the distinctive red and white RP-3As that were

Right: Fitted out as 'Admiral's Barges', half a dozen early production Orions are now known as VP-3As. The machine shown here is typical and is flown by VC-1 on behalf of the Pacific Fleet Commander-in-Chief.

once flown by VXN-8 on oceanographic research tasks have given way to a few P-3Bs (which may be known as **RP-3Bs**) and the original YP-3C prototype which is now designated **RP-3D**. Tasks assigned to these machines vary, but two particularly long-running activities relate to monitoring acoustic and thermal patterns of the world's oceans (Project Outpost Seascan) and to the collation of data on polar ice (Project Birdseye).

The three other P-3A versions mentioned earlier all lack ASW avionics, with the TP-3A serving as a 'bounce bird' for use by fleet replenishment squadrons VP-30 and VP-31 in pilot training. Modification of the 12 aircraft involved included bringing the cockpit layout up to late-model P-3C standard. Both the UP-3A and the VP-3A are primarily concerned with transport duties, the former being a somewhat utilitarian conversion with the ability to carry some cargo in the weapons bay area, while the latter is more luxuriously appointed as an 'Admiral's Barge'. The few UP-3As that still appear on Navy rolls are mostly assigned as station 'hacks', unlike the VP-3As which are used by officers of flag rank such as the Chief of

Naval Operations and the Commanders-in-Chief of the Atlantic Fleet and the Pacific Fleet.

Orions also undertake electronic warfare duties, primarily with fleet air reconnaissance squadrons VQ-1 and VQ-2 from Agana, Guam, and Rota, Spain, respectively. These units acquired between them a dozen suitably-modified aircraft in the early 1970s as replacements for the EC-121s that were previously assigned. The original batch of aircraft were all heavily-modified P-3As but these have recently given way to a second group of conversions based on the P-3C, which are, for the most part, fitted with equipment removed from the first group of aircraft. Regardless of origin, the designation **EP-3E** applies and these machines are instantly recognizable by virtue of prominent ventral and dorsal canoe fairings, as well as a large radome protruding from the area of the weapons bay.

Used for the acquisition of electronic intelli-

P-3 Orion (continued)

gence, they feature the so-called 'Aries' suite, this being a sophisticated package of equipment that includes direction-finding gear, radar signal analyzers, frequency measuring equipment, communications intercept/recording apparatus, automatic electronic surveillance systems and noise jammers.

Crew strength exceeds that of the standard patrol aircraft and typically numbers around 15, including officers designated as the Electronic Warfare (EW) Aircraft Commander, Mission Commander, EW Tactical Evaluator and EW Navigator. Enlisted personnel also feature, with much of their work relating to the operation of kit used to build up a picture of a potential enemy's electronic order of battle. It was in precisely this role that some of the original EP-3Es were active during the Gulf War, aircraft from VQ-1 and VQ-2 operating alongside standard P-3Cs throughout Desert Shield and Desert Storm.

Conventional patrol aircraft were mostly concerned with enforcing the blockade and were responsible for the majority of the 900 sorties and 9,500 flying hours accumulated during the build-up and the war. Throughout much of that interval, they played a key role in the interception of more than 6,000 ships, often directing coalition warships to interesting contacts. Once the fighting began, surveillance emphasis shifted its focus and the main area of interest was now in forestalling enemy action and the targeting of hostile vessels. In six weeks of war, US patrol forces were involved in 31 engagements and they can certainly claim much of the credit for decimating Iraq's naval capability.

One other new-build version of the Orion continues to form part of the Navy inventory, specifically the **RP-3D**. As already mentioned, only one aircraft was produced as such and it was essentially based on the P-3C, although it lacks ASW equipment. Construction involved fitment of an additional fuel tank in the

Orions are only rarely seen carrying underwing stores but this EP-3B of the Naval Research Laboratory appears to be fitted with several auxiliary fuel tanks. It also features a truncated MAD boom and is one of a number of 'one-off' machines that have served with the NRL on projects of an unspecified nature.

weapons bay area, the extra capacity allowing the RP-3D to set a world record for distance in a closed circuit in November 1972 when it covered 5,445.6 nm (6,266.9 miles; 10085.25 km) in 16 hours 30 minutes, a record that still stands. This machine continues in service with VXN-8 on atmospheric survey and magnetic research duties from Patuxent River. In accomplishing tasks related to Project Magnet, it has operated on a global basis and it certainly lives up to the squadron's nickname 'World Travelers'.

MISSION PROFILE

Armament options: The P-3C internal weapons bay has eight hardpoints on which weapons can be mounted. Authorized internal weapons include torpedoes, depth bombs, underwater mines, general-purpose bombs, Destructor mines and nuclear depth bombs. External stores are carried on 10 stations, three outboard of the engines on each wing and two inboard. Authorized external weapons include depth bombs, underwater mines, Captor mines, general-purpose bombs, Destructor mines, rocket pods, flare dispensers, Harpoon and Sidewinder missiles. In addition, internally it can carry nearly 200 sonobuoys and sound signals, as well as a number of marine markers and parachute flares, to assist in locating and tracking their quarry.

ASW: The majority of Orions are dedicated to ASW. These aircraft can spend three hours on station 1,350 nm (1,550 miles; 2500 km) from home, or travel up to 2,000 nm (2,300 miles; 3700 km) to prosecute a target and still return to base.

ESM: The other P-3 mission is ESM and jamming, which is performed by the EP-3E. This version is unarmed.

VARIANTS AND SERIALS

YP-3A: A converted L-188 Electra, the YP-3A served as an aerodynamic prototype for the Orion series and was eventually transferred to NASA as an NP-3A. 148276

P-3A: Some 157 examples of the initial P-3A production version of the Orion were eventually delivered to the US Navy. This version is no longer operated by Fleet units, although a number of conversions are still active in various roles.
148883 to 148889; 149667 to 149678; 150494 to 150529; 150604 to 150609; 151349 to 151396; 152140 to 152187

EP-3A: At least four P-3A Orions have received electronic modifications for special duties with a variety of different units.
149671; 149674; 150529; 151368

RP-3A: Although the designator prefix ostensibly indicates a reconnaissance function, RP-3As do actually undertake a variety of tasks which include relaying telemetry data. At least nine early production machines have used this designation.
149670; 150499; 150500; 150512; 150520 to 150522; 150524; 150525

TP-3A: A dozen P-3As were stripped of mission avionics and assigned to pilot training duties as 'bounce birds' with regular and Reserve force squadrons.
151352; 151357; 151364; 151367; 151370; 151371; 151375; 151376; 151379; 151382; 151392; 151394

UP-3A: At least 19 P-3As have been redesignated as UP-3As for utility transport duties, modification basically involving the removal of specialized ASW equipment. Some feature changes to the weapons bay area permitting carriage of cargo.
148883; 148885; 148889; 149673; 149677; 150495; 150504; 150518; 150519; 150526 to 150528; 150607; 151354; 151367; 151384; 152141; 152150; 152169

VP-3A: Six early production Orions have been fitted with VIP interiors for use as 'Admiral's Barges'.
149675; 149676; 150496; 150511; 150515; 150605

P-3B: Detail improvements and provision of AGM-12 Bullpup ASM capability were the main differences embodied on the P-3B. Production for the US Navy totalled 125 aircraft, of which one (154605) was diverted to Australia to replace a crashed airframe.
152718 to 152765; 153414 to 153458; 154574 to 154605

P-3B(Mod): Four aircraft have been identified as being involved in an unspecified project which occasionally requires them to adopt bogus squadron markings and identities and masquerade as P-3Cs. Use of the designation P-3B(Mod) is not officially sanctioned but

Right: Artwork and mission symbols adorn the nose section of a VQ-2 EP-3E from Rota, Spain. Among the most secretive versions, the EP-3E is used as an intelligence gatherer.

study of these aircraft does reveal subtle differences when compared with standard P-3Bs.
153450; 154575; 154584; 154585

EP-3B: Various configurations of EP-3B are known to exist, with the first use of this designation relating to a pair of aircraft (149669 and 149678) that was flown by VQ-1 for the acquisition of electronic intelligence. Both of those machines may have been subsequently updated to EP-3E standard.
149669 (wfu?*); 149678 (wfu?); 152719(?); 152753(?); 153442; 154589(?)
(*wfu = withdrawn from use)

NP-3B: Designation applied to a much-modified P-3B that is permanently assigned to test duties.
152739

YP-3C: One P-3B aircraft was completed with revised avionics to serve as a prototype for the P-3C series.
153443

P-3C: The definitive version of the Orion was in production longest. Various improvements were incorporated during the course of manufacture, resulting in at least four different sub-types joining Fleet units. Retrospective modification programs have brought older aircraft to later standards and plans exist to continue this process through fitment of Update-IV avionics to a substantial number of existing Orions. Production of the P-3C for US Navy use totalled 279.
156507 to 156530; 157310 to 157332; 158204 to 158226; 158563 to 158574; 158912 to 158935; 159318 to 159329; 159503 to 159514; 159883 to 159894; 160283 to 160293; 160610 to 160612; 160761 to 160770; 160999 to 161014; 161121 to 161132; 161329 to 161340; 161404 to 161415; 161585 to 161596; 161762 to 161767; 162314 to 162318; 162770 to 162778; 162998 to 163006; 163289 to 163295; 163578 to 163590

RP-3D: One aircraft was specially configured as an RP-3D by Lockheed for oceanographic survey tasks, while three P-3Bs and the original YP-3C have been modified to a similar standard.
New build: 158227
Conversions: 152738; 153443; 154587; 154600

EP-3E: At least 22 (and possibly 24) Orions have used this designation, all of them being operated on electronic intelligence gathering tasks using Aries equipment. The original machines were all modified P-3As but those are now being replaced by newly-modified aircraft based on the P-3C airframe.
148887; 148888; 149668; 150494; 150497; 150498; 150501 to 150503; 150505; 156507; 156511; 156514; 156517; 156519; 156528; 156529; 157316; 157318; 157320; 157325; 157326

SPECIFICATION

Lockheed P-3C
Wing: span 99 ft 8 in (30.37 m); aspect ratio 7.5; area 1,300.0 sq ft (120.77 m²)
Fuselage and tail: length 116 ft 10 in (35.61 m); height 33 ft 8.5 in (10.27 m); tailplane span 42 ft 10 in (13.06 m); wheel base 29 ft 9 in (9.07 m)
Powerplant: four Allison T56-A-14 rated at 4,910 ehp (3661 kW)
Weights: empty 61,491 lb (27890 kg); normal take-off 135,000 lb (61235 kg); maximum take-off 142,000 lb (64410 kg)
Fuel and load: internal fuel 62,500 lb (28350 kg); maximum expendable load 20,000 lb (9072 kg)
Speed: maximum level speed 'clean' at 15,000 ft (4575 m) 473 mph (761 km/h); economical cruising speed at 25,000 ft (7620 m) 378 mph (608 km/h); patrol speed at 1,500 ft (457 m) 237 mph (381 km/h)
Range: mission radius with no time on station 2,383 miles (3835 km); mission radius with 3 hours on station 1,550 miles (2494 km)
Performance: maximum rate of climb at 1,500 ft

(457 m) 1,950 ft (594 m) per minute; service ceiling 28,300 ft (8625 m); take-off run 4,240 ft (1290 m) at maximum take-off weight; take-off distance to 50 ft (15 m) 5,490 ft (1673 m)

Lockheed P-3B
generally similar to the P-3C Orion except in the following particulars:
Weights: empty 60,000 lb (27216 kg); normal take-off 127,200 lb (57697 kg); maximum take-off 134,000 lb (60780 kg)
Fuel and load: internal fuel 9,200 US gal (34826 liters); maximum expendable load 15,000 lb (6804 kg) as 7,252 lb (3290 kg) in the weapon bay and 7,784 lb (3514 kg) under the wings
Speed: maximum level speed 'clean' at 15,000 ft (4575 m) 476 mph (766 km/h); economical cruising speed at 25,000 ft (7620 m) 397 mph (639 km/h); patrol speed at 1,500 ft (457 m) 230 mph (371 km/h)
Range: mission radius with no time on station 2,530 miles (4075 km), or with 3 hours on station 1,935 miles (3114 km); endurance at 1,500 ft (457 m) 12 hours 54 minutes on four engines, or 17 hours 0 minutes on two engines
Performance: maximum rate of climb at sea level 3,270 ft (997 m) per minute; take-off run 3,700 ft (1128 m) at maximum take-off weight; take-off distance to 50 ft (15 m) 4,900 ft (1495 m); landing distance from 50 ft (15 m) 2,420 ft (738 m) at design landing weight

Lockheed EP-3E
generally similar to the P-3C except in the following particulars:
Speed: maximum level speed at 15,000 ft (4575 m) 437 mph (703 km/h); patrol speed at 207 mph (333 km/h)
Range: mission radius with no time on station 2,532 miles (4075 km)
Performance: maximum rate of climb at sea level 2,175 ft (663 m) per minute; service ceiling 28,000 ft (8535 m)

OPERATORS

US Navy (USN)

VP-1	Barbers Point, HI	P-3C
VP-4	Barbers Point, HI	P-3C
VP-5	Jacksonville, FL	P-3C

Above: Augmenting a purpose-built machine, the RP-3D shown here is one of four Orions that have been updated for oceanographic research tasks. All of these colorful aircraft operate with VXN-8 at Patuxent River, MD.

VP-6	Barbers Point, HI	P-3C
VP-8	Brunswick, ME	P-3C
VP-9	Moffett Field, CA	P-3C
VP-10	Brunswick, ME	P-3C
VP-11	Brunswick, ME	P-3C
VP-16	Jacksonville, FL	P-3C
VP-17	Barbers Point, HI	P-3C
VP-22	Barbers Point, HI	P-3C
VP-23	Brunswick, ME	P-3C
VP-24	Jacksonville, FL	P-3C
VP-26	Brunswick, ME	P-3C
VP-30	Jacksonville, FL	TP-3A, UP-3A, VP-3A, P-3C
VP-31	Moffett Field, CA	TP-3A, UP-3A, P-3C
VP-40	Moffett Field, CA	P-3C
VP-45	Jacksonville, FL	P-3C
VP-46	Moffett Field, CA	P-3C
VP-47	Moffett Field, CA	P-3C
VP-49	Jacksonville, FL	P-3C
VP-50	Moffett Field, CA	P-3C
VP-60	Glenview, IL	P-3B
VP-62	Jacksonville, FL	P-3C
VP-64	Willow Grove, PA	P-3B
VP-65	Point Mugu, CA	P-3C
VP-66	Willow Grove, PA	P-3B
VP-67	Memphis, TN	P-3C
VP-68	Washington/Andrews, MD	P-3B
VP-69	Whidbey Island, WA	P-3B
VP-90	Glenview, IL	P-3B
VP-91	Moffett Field, CA	P-3C
VP-92	South Weymouth, MA	P-3C
VP-93	Detroit, MI	P-3B
VP-94	New Orleans, LA	P-3B
VPU-1	Brunswick, ME	P-3B(Mod)
VPU-2	Barbers Point, HI	P-3B(Mod)
VAQ-33	Key West, FL	P-3B
VQ-1	Agana, Guam	UP-3A, P-3B, EP-3E
VQ-2	Rota, Spain	EP-3E
VX-1	Patuxent River, MD	P-3C
VXN-8	Patuxent River, MD	P-3B, RP-3D
NAWC/AD	Warminster, PA	UP-3A, P-3C
NRL	Patuxent River, MD	EP-3A, EP-3B
NAWC/WD	Point Mugu, CA	RP-3A
CinCAFSE	Naples, Italy	VP-3A
CinCPac	Barbers Point, HI	VP-3A
NS	Keflavik, Iceland	UP-3A

Lockheed
S-3 Viking

Evolution of the **Lockheed S-3 Viking** dates back to the winter of 1966 when the US Navy issued a Specific Operational Requirement for a replacement for the Grumman S-2 Tracker carrier-based ASW aircraft. Numerous responses were received by the spring of 1968, and in August 1969 the Lockheed contender was selected as the most suitable candidate, the company soon being rewarded with a contract covering eight development examples of the **YS-3A**. The first of these made a successful maiden flight from Lockheed's Palmdale facility on 21 January 1972.

Within three months, the first production order was placed, this covering just 13 aircraft; subsequent procurement eventually raised the Navy purchase to a total of 179 **S-3A**s, all of which were delivered to Fleet units between February 1974 and August 1978. At that time, the tooling was placed in storage against the possibility of further contracts, but these never materialized.

Representing a quantum leap over the Tracker in terms of performance and capability, the S-3A made its initial deployment in the latter half of 1975 when VS-21 embarked aboard the USS *John F. Kennedy* (CVN-67) for a Mediterranean cruise. Since then, it has become a familiar sight above the world's oceans and it remains in use as the prime carrier-borne ASW platform today, presently serving with 14 squadrons, all but two of which are fully-operational deployable units.

Availability of the Viking coincided closely with a switch in Navy philosophy from one that was based on specialist sea-going ASW task groups aboard 'Essex'-class carriers to one in which ASW assets became an organic element of the carrier air wing on larger ships. At the same time, increased productivity allowed

fewer aircraft and helicopters to be assigned to this task. A typical all-purpose CVW initially included 10 S-3As and eight SH-3 Sea Kings, quantities that were later further reduced to eight and six respectively. In service, the Viking is usually tasked to undertake surveillance of that portion of sea beyond the outer defensive screen of surface combatants.

Although the primary mission is that of locating, tracking and, in times of war, eliminating sub-surface threats to the battle group, the Viking is well able to perform other duties, as was demonstrated emphatically during the battle to liberate Kuwait. Then, with the submarine threat effectively non-existent, the Viking took on additional taskings that included searching for mines, sea surveillance, surface combat air patrol (normally with Rockeye cluster-bomb units or 5-in; 12.7-cm Zuni rockets), inflight-refueling support of other CVW elements using 'buddy' pods, scout reconnaissance, suppression of enemy air defenses by delivery of Tactical Air-Launched Decoys (TALDs) and even, on a few occasions, assisting with the bombing effort.

In the normal course of events, though, the name of the Viking game is very much anti-submarine warfare and that is certainly what it is best at. As delivered, the S-3A relied on a package of sensors that included sonobuoys (a maximum of 60 can be housed in externally loaded racks beneath the aft fuselage), a retractable AN/ASQ-81 MAD, AN/APS-116 radar and an OR-89 FLIR scanner. Processing capability rested with a Univac AN/AYK-10 digital computer, with information presented to the tactical coordinator and the sensor operator who are located directly aft of the pilot and co-pilot, all four crew members having McDonnell Douglas ejection seats.

Offensive stores can be housed in a ventral bomb bay that is able to accommodate up to 2,000 lb (900 kg) of torpedoes, depth charges, bombs or mines, while additional weaponry including Zuni rockets may be carried on two underwing stores stations located just out-

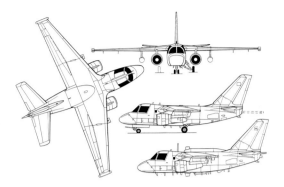

Above: The original production model of the Viking was the S-3A, seen here in the markings of VS-32 aboard the USS America some time ago. If current plans are implemented in their entirety, most Vikings will be brought to S-3B standard.

board of the podded General Electric TF34-GE-400A turbofan engines. Alternatively, 300-US gal (1136-liter) auxiliary fuel tanks may be fitted to extend range and/or duration. A retractable inflight-refueling probe is located above the cockpit.

Efforts to improve the Viking's capability in the ASW arena have resulted in the appearance of the **S-3B**, which incorporates enhanced radar and acoustic processing as well as upgraded electronic support measures, a new

Below: Delivery of modified aircraft to units of the Atlantic Fleet has now been completed. All six deployable squadrons are equipped with the S-3B, which introduced improved radar and acoustic processing capability.

Above: In addition to its primary task of ASW, the S-3B Viking may also be used for several other missions, including inflight refueling as shown here by a 'buddy'-configured aircraft transferring fuel to an F-14B of VF-211.

Right: Apart from a few examples modified for airlift tasks, the first Vikings to be based overseas on a permanent basis were the S-3Bs of VS-21. These now use Atsugi as a shore base when not embarked aboard the USS Independence.

sonobuoy reference system and compatibility with the AGM-84 Harpoon air-to-surface anti-ship attack missile. Work on this project began in the early 1980s and resulted in Lockheed being awarded a $14.5-million contract to modify two existing aircraft as S-3B prototypes during 1984-85.

Testing of these machines revealed significant benefits. The Navy duly opted to obtain a further 40 conversions under the Viking Weapon System Improvement Program (WSIP), with delivery of the first 'production' S-3B taking place shortly before the end of 1987. If all goes well, as many as 140 Vikings may ultimately be brought to this configuration.

So far, the bulk of the S-3B conversions have been allocated to Atlantic Fleet units which are shore-based at Cecil Field, Florida, during the often lengthy intervals between periods of sea duty. Apart from one S-3B squadron that is forward-deployed to Atsugi in Japan as part of CVW-5, Pacific Fleet units continue to fly the unmodified S-3A and are concentrated at North Island, California. Each of these two 'communities' has a total of seven squadrons, including a permanently shore-based training outfit tasked with ensuring a steady flow of suitably qualified air and ground crew to operational forces.

In addition to the ASW-dedicated versions of the Viking, at least three other models have existed, all arising from conversion programs.

Two of these models are currently either in or being introduced to service, of which easily the most significant is the **ES-3A**. Intended to replace the long-serving EA-3B Skywarrior in the electronic reconnaissance role, a total of 16 ES-3As is to be obtained at a cost of approximately $500 million.

First flown in September 1989, initial trials of the ES-3A were purely aerodynamic in nature (no equipment was fitted) and were aimed at verifying that the numerous fairings, protuberances and antenna arrangements do not seriously affect handling qualities. Testing of a fully converted example began not long after, this having had its ASW avionics removed and replaced by an entirely different suite of equipment which is collectively known as the Tactical Airborne Signals Exploitation System (TASES).

In service, the 16 'Queer Vikings' are to be distributed evenly between VQ-5 at Agana, Guam, and VQ-6 at Cecil Field, Florida, and both units will routinely deploy small detachments (normally of just one aircraft) aboard carriers bound for operations in areas of prime interest. In so doing, they will expand the parent vessel's intelligence-gathering potential and will also allow greater flexibility by easing

the workload of the EP-3Es, which have largely shouldered this burden since the 'Queer Whale' ceased flying from carrier decks in November 1987.

Another variation on the Viking theme is the **US-3A** which specializes in COD duties. This evolved out of a Lockheed proposal to replace the Grumman C-1A Trader with a version of the Viking that was stretched by almost 6 ft (1.8 m) which would have allowed it to carry up to 11 passengers or cargo. As it transpired, the Navy elected to reinstate the C-2 Greyhound in production, but the seventh Viking development airframe was subjected to modification for use as a utility transport aircraft and was given the designation US-3A. Flown for the first time in July 1976, it lacked ASW mission avionics and was able to carry up to 3,750 lb (2600 kg) of cargo in the weapons bay and in two 90-cu ft (2.5-m³) underwing pods.

Three more Vikings were subsequently modified to US-3A standard and all four were eventually assigned to VRC-50 at Cubi Point. Three survivors still fly from there today, alongside two minimally-modified development S-3As in the COD role, furnishing support to 7th Fleet carriers operating in the western Pacific.

Left: With its hook dangling, an S-3B of VS-32 returns to its sea-going home aboard the USS America. Fitment of a 'buddy' refueling store indicates that this particular Viking was used as a tanker while airborne.

S-3 Viking (continued)

One other Lockheed proposal concerned the Viking's suitability for the inflight-refueling role as the **KS-3A**. Again, the manufacturer went so far as to modify a development aircraft (the fifth) to demonstrate this concept by fitting hose-and-reel refueling equipment in the weapons bay – again, the Navy chose not to invest, which is perhaps ironic when one recalls that inflight refueling was among the Desert Storm missions.

MISSION PROFILE

Armament options: The S-3 has two internal weapons bays on the 'corners' of its square fuselage. Authorized internal weapons include torpedoes, general-purpose bombs, Destructor mines and nuclear depth bombs, although the latter have been removed from aircraft carriers. Viking external stores are carried on single stations located outboard of the engines on each wing. Authorized external weapons include underwater mines, Captor mines, general-purpose bombs, Destructor mines, rocket pods, flare dispensers, decoys and Harpoon missiles. Where more than two weapons are carried, they are mounted to triple ejector racks.

ASW: For the ASW mission, these Vikings carry 60 sonobuoys to assist in locating and tracking their quarry. For this mission, the Viking is capable of remaining on station for two carrier event cycles – more than three hours.

Anti-ship/surface attack: In addition to an improved ASW avionics suite, the S-3B has enhanced anti-ship and surface attack capabilities with the addition of the ability to employ the AGM-84 Harpoon and SLAM. Most S-3s used during Desert Storm were S-3Bs and some of these were seen to carry AGM-84Es, although there is no indication any were actually employed. However, S-3s did participate in combat missions by launching ADM-141s and attacking patrol boats (and at least one AAA site) with Mk 82 LDGPs, all dropped from TERs mounted on the underwing pylons. Some S-3s were also seen to carry Mk 20s there.

Air refueling: Both S-3As and Bs can perform the buddy refueling mission when fitted with the D-704 air refueling tank on the left wing and a 300-US gal (1135-liter) fuel tank on the right.

ESM: This mission is performed by the new ES-3A, armed only with its battle group passive horizon extension system for long-range signals monitoring.

VARIANTS AND SERIALS

YS-3A: Eight pre-production aircraft were acquired for test and development work in connection with the Viking project, most having subsequently been modified for special duties such as COD or for follow-on development tasks.
157992 to 157999

S-3A: Contracts for 179 production S-3As were eventually placed by the US Navy, but these are now being updated to S-3B standard under an ongoing CILOP project.
158861 to 158873; 159386 to 159420; 159278 to 159772; 160120 to 160164; 160567 to 160607

ES-3A: Intended to assume responsibility for the tactical airborne signals exploitation task from the now-retired EA-3B Skywarrior, the ES-3A is a vastly modified machine. The aerodynamic prototype (157993) first flew in September 1989. A total of 16 full-system aircraft is to be obtained for service with two Fleet squadrons through conversion of existing S-3As.
157993; 158862; 159401; 159404; 159420 (plus 12 others)

US-3A: Three of the development aircraft and an early production S-3A were modified for COD tasks as US-3As, using underwing pods for carriage of mail and small high priority items of cargo. Two other trials airframes are also used for COD duties, retaining the original designation.
US-3A: 157994; 157996; 157998; 158868
S-3A (COD): 157995; 157997

S-3B: Updating of production S-3As to S-3B standard continues steadily, with at least 56 Vikings now having been brought to the revised standard. These incorporate enhanced acoustic and radar processing capability as well as expanded ESM cover and a new sonobuoy reference system. Compatibility with the Harpoon ASM is also a feature of the rework program.
158861; 158864; 158865; 159389; 159390; 159402; 159413; 159418; 159729; 159732; 159733; 159741 to 159744; 159747; 159751; 159753; 159755; 159758; 159760 to 159768; 159770; 160121; 160122; 160125; 160129 to 160132; 160138; 160140 to 160142; 160144; 160145; 160149; 160151 to 160153; 160159; 160160; 160581; 160588; 160600; 160601; 160603; 160604; 160606

SPECIFICATION

Lockheed S-3A
Wing: span 68 ft 8 in (20.93 m); width folded 29 ft 6 in (8.99 m); area 598.0 sq ft (55.56 m^2)
Fuselage and tail: length overall 53 ft 4 in (16.26 m) and with tail folded 49 ft 5 in (15.06 m); height overall 22 ft 9 in (6.93 m) and with tail folded 15 ft 3 in (4.65 m); tailplane span 27 ft 0 in (8.23 m)
Powerplant: two General Electric TF34-GE-2 rated at 9,275 lb (41.2 kN) dry thrust
Weights: empty 26,650 lb (12088 kg); normal take-off 42,500 lb (19277 kg); maximum take-off 52,540 lb (23832 kg)
Fuel and load: internal fuel 12,863 lb (5753 kg); external fuel up to two 300-US gal (1136-liter) drop tanks; maximum ordnance 7,000 lb (3175 kg) including 4,000 lb (1814 kg) carried internally

Above: The distinctive basically-white color scheme of this Viking confirms that it is one of four that were stripped of ASW avionics and redesignated as US-3As. All four are assigned to VRC-50 at Cubi Point, which operates them on carrier onboard delivery duties in support of the 7th Fleet in the western Pacific.

Left: Highly distinctive bumps and bulges, as well as an extensive array of antennas, confirm that this is one of 16 planned conversions to ES-3A standard. Earmarked for service with two units, the ES-3A is to inherit responsibility for the tactical airborne signals exploitation mission. It will ultimately be deployed aboard aircraft carriers in small quantities, typical detachment size being unlikely to ever exceed two aircraft and four crews.

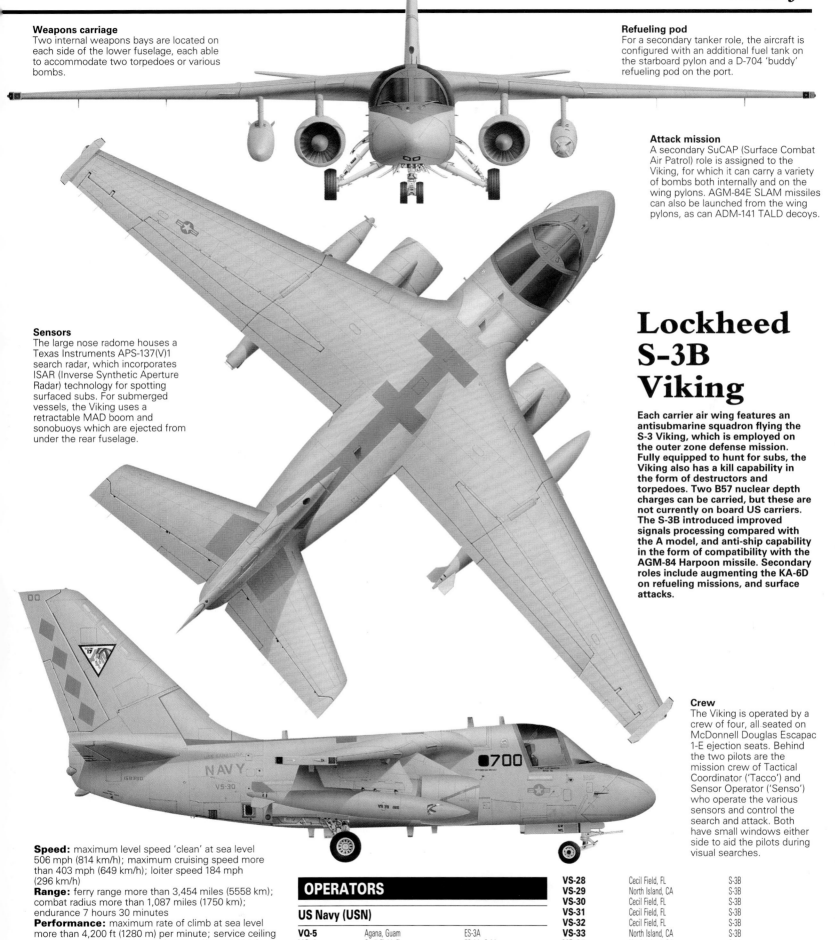

Weapons carriage
Two internal weapons bays are located on each side of the lower fuselage, each able to accommodate two torpedoes or various bombs.

Refueling pod
For a secondary tanker role, the aircraft is configured with an additional fuel tank on the starboard pylon and a D-704 'buddy' refueling pod on the port.

Attack mission
A secondary SuCAP (Surface Combat Air Patrol) role is assigned to the Viking, for which it can carry a variety of bombs both internally and on the wing pylons. AGM-84E SLAM missiles can also be launched from the wing pylons, as can ADM-141 TALD decoys.

Sensors
The large nose radome houses a Texas Instruments APS-137(V)1 search radar, which incorporates ISAR (Inverse Synthetic Aperture Radar) technology for spotting surfaced subs. For submerged vessels, the Viking uses a retractable MAD boom and sonobuoys which are ejected from under the rear fuselage.

Lockheed S-3B Viking

Each carrier air wing features an antisubmarine squadron flying the S-3 Viking, which is employed on the outer zone defense mission. Fully equipped to hunt for subs, the Viking also has a kill capability in the form of destructors and torpedoes. Two B57 nuclear depth charges can be carried, but these are not currently on board US carriers. The S-3B introduced improved signals processing compared with the A model, and anti-ship capability in the form of compatibility with the AGM-84 Harpoon missile. Secondary roles include augmenting the KA-6D on refueling missions, and surface attacks.

Crew
The Viking is operated by a crew of four, all seated on McDonnell Douglas Escapac 1-E ejection seats. Behind the two pilots are the mission crew of Tactical Coordinator ('Tacco') and Sensor Operator ('Senso') who operate the various sensors and control the search and attack. Both have small windows either side to aid the pilots during visual searches.

Speed: maximum level speed 'clean' at sea level 506 mph (814 km/h); maximum cruising speed more than 403 mph (649 km/h); loiter speed 184 mph (296 km/h)
Range: ferry range more than 3,454 miles (5558 km); combat radius more than 1,087 miles (1750 km); endurance 7 hours 30 minutes
Performance: maximum rate of climb at sea level more than 4,200 ft (1280 m) per minute; service ceiling more than 35,000 ft (10670 m); take-off run 2,200 ft (670 m) at maximum take-off weight; landing run 1,600 ft (488 m) at 36,500 lb (16556 kg)

Lockheed S-3B
generally similar to the S-3A

OPERATORS

US Navy (USN)

VQ-5	Agana, Guam	ES-3A
VQ-6	Cecil Field, FL	ES-3A, S-3A
VRC-50	Cubi Point, RP	US-3A, S-3A(COD)
VS-21	Atsugi, Japan	S-3B
VS-22	Cecil Field, FL	S-3B
VS-24	Cecil Field, FL	S-3B
VS-27	Cecil Field, FL	S-3A, S-3B
VS-28	Cecil Field, FL	S-3B
VS-29	North Island, CA	S-3B
VS-30	Cecil Field, FL	S-3B
VS-31	Cecil Field, FL	S-3B
VS-32	Cecil Field, FL	S-3B
VS-33	North Island, CA	S-3B
VS-35	North Island, CA	S-3A
VS-37	North Island, CA	S-3A
VS-38	North Island, CA	S-3A
VS-41	North Island, CA	S-3A, S-3B
VX-1	Patuxent River, MD	S-3B
NAWC/AD	Patuxent River, MD	S-3B

Rockwell International
T-2 Buckeye

The first jet type to be encountered by pilots who have earned selection for the much sought after 'strike' stream will be the **T-2 Buckeye**. Like the T-34, this is another stalwart of the training program, having originally entered service more than 30 years ago, in 1959.

Development of the original **T2J-1** (later **T-2A**) began in the mid-1950s and North American eventually produced a total of 216 aircraft, including half a dozen **YT2J-1** test specimens. In external appearance, these were fundamentally similar to succeeding versions but beneath the surface there were significant differences, not least of which was the fact that the original model was single-engined, relying on a Westinghouse J34-WE-36 turbojet rated at 3,400 lb (15 kN) thrust for propulsion. Deliveries to Basic Training Group Seven (BTG-7) at Memphis, Tennessee, and BTG-9 at Pensacola, Florida, got under way in the summer of 1959. This version remained in use until the end of February 1973 when VT-9 at Meridian, Mississippi, formally retired the last example.

By then, improvement initiatives had resulted in the appearance of two other versions which, in addition to being twin-engined, remarkably each used different types of engine. First was the **T2J-2** (later **T-2B**) which was fitted with a pair of Pratt & Whitney J60-P-6 turbojets, each of which was rated at 3,000 lb (13 kN) thrust. Flown in prototype form on 30 August 1962, flight testing was fairly prolonged and production examples did not begin to reach Navy training units until shortly before the end of 1965. Some 97 T-2Bs were eventually completed, and about a dozen were recently retired from service with VT-4.

The final version for the US Navy arose when a T-2B was re-engined with two General Electric J85-GE-4 turbojets to serve as a prototype for the **T-2C**. This ultimately became the most numerous version of the Buckeye, with the first of a total of 231 aircraft being delivered to Naval Air Training Command on 30 April 1969. Most of those remain in use today, serving in the intermediate strike training role with VT-19 at Meridian, Mississippi, VT-23 at Kingsville, Texas, and VT-26 at Chase Field, Texas, while some are also used in the Naval Flight Officer syllabus, operating with VT-10 from Pensacola.

Trainee strike pilots eventually accumulate about 100 hours of dual and solo flight time in the Buckeye as they progress through the intermediate stage of instruction. This embraces such aspects as high- and low-level flight, formation work, aerobatics, and visual and instrument navigation. All of these are a fairly normal part of any pilot training program, as indeed is weapons training, for students are expected to demonstrate pro-

For more than three decades, Rockwell's T-2 Buckeye has been the first jet aircraft to be encountered by Navy and Marine Corps pilots as they work their way through the demanding training course.

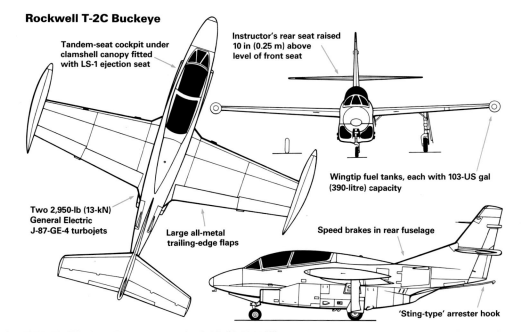

Rockwell T-2C Buckeye

Tandem-seat cockpit under clamshell canopy fitted with LS-1 ejection seat

Instructor's rear seat raised 10 in (0.25 m) above level of front seat

Two 2,950-lb (13-kN) General Electric J-87-GE-4 turbojets

Large all-metal trailing-edge flaps

Wingtip fuel tanks, each with 103-US gal (390-litre) capacity

Speed brakes in rear fuselage

'Sting-type' arrester hook

Right: A Buckeye pilot waits for the 'rush' as a catapult officer aboard USS Lexington gives the signal to launch. All naval aviators get their first experience of flying to and from a carrier in the Buckeye.

ficiency in gunnery by firing at a towed banner target. There is, however, one aspect of the program that is very different, for the students must also undergo the rigours of carrier qualification (carqual) training.

Carqual is a vitally important obstacle to be negotiated and the Buckeye is an admirable tool for this first exposure to the very demanding skills of operating from ships at sea. Preparatory actions include field carrier-landing practice at the home airfield as well as lectures so that when the time comes to make the first 'trap' (arrested landing), the student is as ready as he is ever likely to be. Carqual training is almost invariably conducted in the Gulf of Mexico – until recently aboard the USS *Lexington* and now on the USS *Forrestal* – and requires the student to complete two touch-and-go approaches, four arrested landings and four catapult launches. It is also one of the final hurdles to be cleared before moving on to the TA-4J Skyhawk (soon to be replaced by the T-45 Goshawk) for advanced strike training.

NFO (Naval Flight Officer) instruction involves rather less in the way of flying and begins with a basic course lasting 15 weeks. Placing heavy emphasis on academics, this does also include introductory flights in the T-34C and the T-2C, students getting about 90 minutes or so in the latter type before they are streamed for specialized training. In most instances, subsequent tuition includes an intermediate course of seven weeks' duration that will add another 12 hours of Buckeye flight time, with emphasis on airways navigation, low-level navigation and instrument landings.

Other units which operate a few examples of the T-2C are the Test Pilot's School at Patuxent River, Maryland, as well as the aggressor training outfits VF-43 at Oceana, Virginia, and VF-126 at Miramar, California.

Right: Retaining standard Navy training colors, this T-2C is used by VF-43 from Oceana as a means of imparting knowledge of procedures used in recovery from a spin. The docile nature of the Buckeye makes it almost ideal for this important duty.

Below: Prospective candidates for the world of research and development flying duty master some aspects of the discipline in a handful of T-2C Buckeyes that are assigned to the NTPS.

MISSION PROFILE

Configuration options: The T-2C is a two-seat training aircraft, configured with a tandem cockpit and arrester hook gear for carrier deck operations. Wingtip fuel tanks are normally fitted. Wing pylons allow for up to 640 lb (290 kg) of bombs or rockets to be carried.

Intermediate strike training: Current mission profiles for student naval aviators (SNAs) includes familiarization, basic and radio instruments, two- and four-plane formations, air combat maneuvering, airway navigation, night and air-to-air gunnery and daytime carrier operations. Carrier training includes 10 mock carrier landings on a simulated deck ashore, two real 'touch and goes' on a carrier and four arrested landings. In total, students fly 89 flight and 45 simulator hours over 22 weeks on the intermediate jet flight training course. A 90-minute familiarization flight is part of the primary flight training course. F-14 radar intercept officer (backseaters) also receive training on the T-2C.

VARIANTS AND SERIALS

T-2B: The second production version of the Buckeye trainer was the first model to offer twin-engined safety. A total of 97 was obtained and the last examples were only recently retired.
152382 to 152391; 152440 to 152475; 153538 to 153555; 155206 to 155238

YT-2C: The initial T-2B was later re-engined with two General Electric J85 turbojets to serve as the prototype for the T-2C version. Subsequently redesignated as a T-2C, it was last noted in use with the NTPS at Patuxent River.
152382

T-2C: Successful evaluation of the YT-2C prototype paved the way for large-scale procurement of the T-2C model. An eventual total of 231 machines was obtained for the basic jet training task. This is now the only Buckeye version in Navy service.
155239 to 155241; 156686 to 156733; 157030 to 157065; 158310 to 158333; 158575 to 158610; 158876 to 158911; 159150 to 159173; 159704 to 159727

SPECIFICATION

Rockwell T-2C
Wing: span over tip tanks 38 ft 1.5 in (11.62 m); area 255.0 sq ft (23.69 m²)
Fuselage and tail: length 38 ft 3.5 in (11.67 m); height 14 ft 9.5 in (4.51 m); tailplane span 17 ft 11 in (5.46 m)
Powerplant: two General Electric J85-GE-4 rated at 2.950 lb (13.1 kN) dry thrust
Weights: empty 8,115 lb (3680 kg); maximum take-off 13,179 lb (5977 kg)
Fuel and load: internal fuel 691 US gal (2616 liters); maximum ordnance 640 lb (290 kg)
Speed: maximum level speed 'clean' at 25,000 ft (7620 m) 522 mph (840 km/h)
Range: range 1,047 miles (1685 km)
Performance: maximum rate of climb at sea level 6,200 ft (1890 m) per minute; service ceiling 40,415 ft (12320 m)

Rockwell T-2B
generally similar to the T-2C except in the following particulars:
Powerplant: two Pratt & Whitney J60-P-6 rated at 3,000 lb (13.34 kN) dry thrust

OPERATORS

US Navy (USN)

VF-43	Oceana, VA	T-2C
VF-126	Miramar, CA	T-2C
VT-4	Pensacola, FL	T-2C
VT-19	Meridian, MS	T-2C
VT-23	Kingsville, TX	T-2C
VT-26	Chase Field, TX	T-2C
VT-86	Pensacola, FL	T-2C
NTPS	Patuxent River, MD	T-2C

Beech

T-34 Mentor/Turbo-Mentor

A cornerstone of US Navy and Marine Corps pilot training since the 1950s, current generations of aspiring aircrew continue to 'cut their teeth' on this Beech product, although today's **T-34C** is a much improved machine when compared with the original **T-34B** model. The benefits stem mostly from turbine power, for the T-34C is fitted with a single Pratt & Whitney Canada PT6A-25 turboprop which is torque-limited to 400 shp. The familiar tandem two-seat layout was retained but improvements were made to the cockpit area, including a revised canopy that offers much improved visibility, and air conditioning, which is especially welcome in the steamy south where the Navy has its main training bases.

Initial procurement during the 1950s saw the Navy obtain more than 400 T-34B **Mentors**, some of which are still in service today, being mostly used as 'hacks' by Navy officers responsible for recruiting new personnel. Apart from the fact that they still rely on a piston engine as a means of propulsion, these machines are perhaps most easily identified by virtue of an attractive blue overall color scheme which incorporates the 'Wings of Gold' and a 'Fly Navy' legend.

When the time eventually came for the Navy to find a T-34B replacement in the 1970s, Beech came up with a proposal for a turbine-powered version of the Mentor. This evidently found favor, since the Navy awarded a contract covering the conversion of two T-34Bs to **YT-34C** standard for evaluation. Flown for the first time on 21 September 1973, the test program paved the way for major contracts and the Navy subsequently received no fewer than 352 T-34C **Turbo-Mentors**.

Unflatteringly referred to as the 'Tormentor', the T-34C is still the principal basic trainer

Right: Assigned to Light Attack Wing One at Cecil Field, this T-34C is used as an airborne range control platform.

Below: A four-ship of Turbo-Mentors from VT-27 at Corpus Christi maintains tight formation as it overflies home base at the conclusion of a routine training sortie.

and the first machine to be mastered by aspiring pilots. Regardless of the type they will eventually fly, all students accumulate at least 66 hours in the T-34C, with the all-important 'solo' usually being accomplished on about the 13th trip aloft. Most students undergo their primary training at Whiting Field, Florida, with one of Training Wing Five's three squadrons: specifically, VT-2, VT-3 and VT-6. Between them, they share approximately 200 T-34Cs. The other base which offers primary training is at Corpus Christi, Texas, but Training Wing Four's T-34C fleet is much smaller and numbers only about 70 aircraft, all of which are assigned to VT-27.

NFOs also receive some instruction in the T-34C but this is limited to just 20 hours, which is provided by Training Wing Six at Pensacola, Florida. One squadron (VT-10) operates an assortment of equipment which includes about 20 examples of the T-34C.

As far as fleet units are concerned, the Turbo-Mentor is operated in very limited numbers but has been noted in use with several fleet replacement training squadrons during the past couple of years. Light Attack Wing One at Cecil Field, Florida, has a couple which undertake FAC (Forward Air Control) duties at weapons ranges, similar tasks almost certainly being performed by VA-42's small number of T-34Cs. Also resident at Oceana, Virginia, VF-43 has at least three 'Tormentors' which are used to demonstrate recovery procedures during spin training as a lead-in to this unit's air combat maneuvering syllabus.

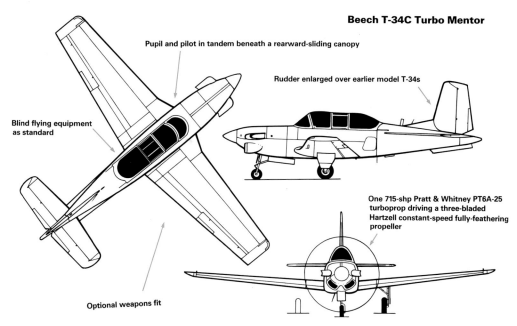

Beech T-34C Turbo Mentor

Pupil and pilot in tandem beneath a rearward-sliding canopy

Rudder enlarged over earlier model T-34s

Blind flying equipment as standard

One 715-shp Pratt & Whitney PT6A-25 turboprop driving a three-bladed Hartzell constant-speed fully-feathering propeller

Optional weapons fit

Above: Another regular Fleet squadron which is known to operate a small number of T-34Cs is VF-124 at Miramar, CA. For the most part, though, the Turbo-Mentor is employed for primary training duties with units at Whiting Field, Pensacola and Corpus Christi.

Northrop
T-38A Talon

One of the evolutionary strands taken by Northrop's private venture N-156 light fighter resulted in the **T-38A Talon**, which has served as the US Air Force's principal advanced jet trainer since the early 1960s and which looks set to remain in service for some time to come.

As far as the US Navy was concerned, the Talon was never a contender to satisfy its own training needs, primarily because the rather different demands of carrier aviation dictated that it needed a carrier-compatible aircraft. While the T-38A may be many things, it is most emphatically not designed to cope with the rigors of sea operation. Nevertheless, the US Navy has operated the Talon in modest quantities and even went so far as to acquire some on loan for training duties of a highly specialized nature.

The initial transfer of aircraft from the USAF was, in fact, a permanent one, a total of five machines being obtained specifically for service with the Test Pilot's School at Patuxent River. At least three of these remain in use today. Other examples followed – usually on a temporary loan basis – and Navy operation of the Talon probably reached its peak in the 1970s, when the aircraft flew regularly from a number of locations. Undoubtedly the most important in terms of assisting operational readiness were the dozen or so 'aggressors' that fulfilled dissimilar air combat training duties with VF-43 at Oceana and the Fighter Weapons School ('Top Gun') at Miramar. Each of these two outfits had a handful of T-38As which lingered in this role until more suitable equipment became available.

Elsewhere, the loss of two Test Pilot's School Talons resulted in further examples being obtained on loan (including at least one that came from NASA), and some of these may still be used by the school. In addition, the NAWC Weapons Division at China Lake also

Right: Although once in fairly widespread use as an aggressor aircraft, the T-38A Talon now serves only with the Test Pilot's School. One of their aircraft is portrayed here.

acquired some very early production examples in the mid-1970s for use in connection with drone aircraft programs, but this project does not appear to have come to fruition and it is doubtful if any still fly with the NAWC.

MISSION PROFILE

The Navy's few remaining T-38s serve only with the USN TPS, for test pilot training.

VARIANTS AND SERIALS

T-38A: Navy acquisition of the Talon began with an initial batch of five aircraft that was diverted from USAF contracts for service with the Test Pilot's School. During the 1970s, others were obtained from the USAF for use as aggressor aircraft and in connection with drone operations from China Lake, both operations that no longer rely on the T-38 which now serves only with the NTPS.
158197 to 158201; 510327 (USAF 65-10327) 591604 (59-1604); 600582 (60-582)

SPECIFICATION

Northrop T-38A
Wing: span 25 ft 3 in (7.70 m); area 170.0 sq ft (15.79 m²)
Fuselage and tail: length 46 ft 4.5 in (14.14 m); height 12 ft 10.5 in (3.92 m); tailplane span 14 ft 1.5 in

(4.31 m); wheel base 16 ft 11.5 in (5.17 m)
Powerplant: two General Electric J85-GE-5 rated at 2,680 lb (11.9 kN) dry and 3,850 lb (17.1 kN) afterburning thrusts
Weights: empty 7,174 lb (3254 kg); maximum take-off 12,050 lb (5465 kg)
Fuel and load: internal fuel 583 US gal (2206 liters)
Speed: maximum level speed at 36,000 ft (10975 m) 858 mph (1381 km/h); maximum cruising speed at 40,000 ft (12190 m) 578 mph (930 km/h)
Range: ferry range 1,093 miles (1759 km); typical range 860 miles (1384 km)
Performance: maximum rate of climb at sea level 33,600 ft (10241 m) per minute; service ceiling 53,600 ft (16335 m); take-off distance 2,500 ft (762 m) at maximum take-off weight; landing distance 3,000 ft (914 m) at maximum weight

OPERATORS

US Navy (USN)

NTPS	Patuxent River, MD	T-38A

Rockwell
T-39 Sabreliner

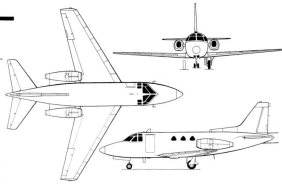

First introduced to US Navy service in the early 1960s, the **Rockwell** (formerly North American) **Sabreliner** was initially used to provide radar training instruction for NFOs from Pensacola, Florida. In all, some 42 **T3J-1**s (later **T-39D**s) were obtained. Most of these remained in service until they were replaced by a much smaller quantity of T-47A Citations in the 1980s. Today, one or two of the original aircraft are still active with test organizations such as the NAWC Weapons Division at China Lake.

Radar instruction of NFOs is once again being undertaken with the Sabreliner, Training Wing Six receiving the first of a batch of **T-39N**s in the closing months of 1991 as the T-47A contract ended. Contractual irregularities which resulted in an unsuccessful bidder resorting to legal action will, however, mean that these modified Sabreliners are only to be operated for some 18 months, until such time as another company, Flight International, is able to assume responsibility for NFO instruction with a fleet of suitably-configured Lear 35s.

The remainder of the Sabreliner fleet is concerned with transport duties, using more modern versions, two different sub-types having been acquired for the high-speed, high-priority airlift task. The first of these is the **CT-39E**, a total of seven examples being purchased. Basically nothing more than a Sabreliner 40, some of these minimally-modified aircraft are known to have begun their Navy service careers with civil registration marks. At least two have been destroyed and the remaining examples are spread thinly between VRC-30, VRC-40 and VRC-50 of the US Navy, while one is believed to be assigned to the Marines, serving with the Station Operations and Engineering Squadron (SOES) at Cherry Point, North Carolina.

Subsequent purchases saw the acquisition of 13 examples of the **CT-39G**, a version based on the commercial Sabreliner 60. Like the CT-39E, it normally has a crew of three and

cabin accommodation for up to seven passengers. Again, this model is spread thinly, Navy operators including VR-24 at Sigonella, Sicily, and the Chief of the Naval Reserve (CNavRes) at New Orleans, Louisiana. Marine Corps examples are known to be active with the SOES and with Marine Wing Headquarters Squadron One (MWHS-1) at Iwakuni, Okinawa.

MISSION PROFILE

Configuration options: For radar training, an APQ-94 radar is fitted to T-39Ds. Transport T-39E/Gs are configured to executive travel standard for up to seven passengers.

Fleet logistic support: The rapid movement of high-priority personnel or supplies to naval units and ships around the world is the T-39's primary mission. T-39s work in coordination with COD C-2As to ensure the rapid transit of cargo or personnel to and from aircraft carriers at sea.

Radar training: A pilot, plus a pilot/instructor and four students, are carried during radar training missions. Bombardier/navigators and radar intercept officers can also be carried.

VARIANTS AND SERIALS

T-39D: Training of certain categories of Naval Flight Officer in the intricacies of navigation was for many years undertaken in 42 Sabreliners. Responsibility for this task was eventually contracted out and most of the T-39Ds were retired. Today, a few are still flown on communications and test duties.
150542 to 150551; 150969 to 150992; 151336 to 151343

CT-39E: Seven examples of the Sabre 40 executive jet were bought for high-speed communications and light transport duties, these originally being given the designation VT-39E.
157352 to 157354; 158380 to 158383

CT-39G: Acquisition of additional examples of the Rockwell executive jet involved a total of 13 Sabre 60s, which are operated as the CT-39G on similar duties to the CT-39E.
158843; 158844; 159361 to 159365; 160053 to 160058

T-39N: NFO navigation training is currently undertaken on a contract basis by a civil company which uses

civilian-registered T-39N Sabreliners from Pensacola. Due to irregularities in the award of this contract, these machines are expected to fulfil this duty for no more than 18 months.
N301NT to N308NT, N310NT (plus others)

SPECIFICATION

Rockwell CT-39E
Wing: span 44 ft 5.25 in (13.54 m); area 342.05 sq ft (31.78 m²)
Fuselage and tail: length 43 ft 9 in (13.34 m); height 16 ft 0 in (4.88 m); tailplane span 17 ft 6.5 in (5.35 m); wheel base 14 ft 6 in (4.42 m)
Powerplant: two Pratt & Whitney JT12A-8 rated at 3,300 lb (14.6 kN) dry thrust
Weights: operating empty 9,845 lb (4488 kg); maximum take-off 18,650 lb (8498 kg)
Fuel and load: internal fuel 1,063 US gal (4024 liters); maximum payload including crew 2,000 lb (907 kg)
Speed: maximum level speed at 21,500 ft (6550 m) 563 mph (906 km/h); economical cruising speed at between 39,000 and 45,000 ft (11885 and 13715 m) 495 mph (797 km/h)
Range: range with four passengers 2,118 miles (3408 km)
Performance: maximum rate of climb at sea level 4,800 ft (1463 m) per minute; operational ceiling 40,000 ft (13715 m); take-off balanced field length 4,800 ft (1463 m) at maximum take-off weight; landing run 2,200 ft (671 m) at maximum landing weight with four passengers

Rockwell T-39D
generally similar to the CT-39E except in the following particulars:
Powerplant: two Pratt & Whitney J60-P-3A rated at 3,000 lb (13.3 kN) dry thrust
Weights: maximum take-off 17,760 lb (8056 kg)
Speed: maximum level speed at 20,000 ft (6095 m) 540 mph (869 km/h); economical cruising speed at between 39,000 and 45,000 ft (11885 and 13715 m) 406 mph (702 km/h)
Range: ferry range 1,735 miles (2792 km); typical range 1,375 miles (2213 km)
Performance: service ceiling 42,000 ft (12800 m)

OPERATORS

US Navy (USN)

VT-10	Pensacola, FL	T-39N
VT-86	Pensacola, FL	T-39N
TW-6	Pensacola, FL	T-39D
VR-24	Sigonella, Sicily	CT-39G
VRC-30	North Island, CA	CT-39E
VRC-50	Cubi Point, RP	CT-39E
NTPS	Patuxent River, MD	T-39D
NAWC/WD	China Lake, CA	T-39D
CFLSW det	Washington/Andrews, MD	CT-39G
CNR	New Orleans, LA	CT-39G

US Marine Corps (USMC)

MWHS-1	Iwakuni, Japan	CT-39G
SOES	Cherry Point, NC	CT-39G
SOMS	El Toro, CA	CT-39G

Naval Flight Officer navigation training is presently undertaken aboard civil-owned and -operated T-39N Sabreliners on a contract basis from Pensacola, unlike the Navy's own fleet of CT-39s which is mainly employed on high-speed transport and communications duties. One or two T-39Ds also fulfil test functions.

Beech
T-44A Pegasus

Virtually identical to the commercial Beech King Air 90 executive twin, the **T-44A Pegasus** began to replace the Grumman TS-2A Tracker in the advanced training role in 1977. Some 61 aircraft had been delivered by the time procurement terminated in 1980. Most of these remain in use today, but five **T-44Bs** have recently been purchased as attrition replacements.

Powered by a pair of Pratt & Whitney Canada PT6A-34B turboprops, they continue to give good service with Training Wing Four at NAS Corpus Christi, Texas, this organization parenting two subordinate squadrons, specifically VT-28 and VT-31. The primary task of these two squadrons is that of advanced maritime training, and students who have completed the basic and intermediate phases of instruction will typically accumulate 88 hours of flight time in the T-44A, plus about 30 hours of simulator time during an 18-week course. Aspects of the syllabus include single-engine operation, instrument flight, airways procedures, night flying and use of navigation aids. Students who complete the course most commonly move on to the P-3 Orion, but the lessons taught at Corpus Christi are equally applicable to other large multi-engine types such as the C-130 Hercules.

In addition, the T-44A is used as one element of a special training program designed to produce aircrew for the E-2C Hawkeye and C-2A Greyhound communities. Following primary and instrument training on the T-34, students undergo an intermediate course at Meridian, Mississippi, which is based upon almost 95 hours of T-2C time, including the all-important carqual phase. Finally, multi-engine flying skills are imparted during an abbreviated 16.5-hour advanced course on the Pegasus with either VT-28 or VT-31.

MISSION PROFILE

Configuration options: The T-44A is an intermediate training aircraft. In the training role, it is configured to carry one pilot and two students. It can be configured for utility missions carrying two aircrew and three passengers.

Training: Multi-engined aircraft training is the primary mission of the T-44A. The intermediate prop course includes instrument flying, night flying and use of instrument aids over 88 flight hours and 30 simulator hours.

VARIANTS AND SERIALS

T-44A: A total of 61 T-44A King Airs was obtained by the Navy for the multi-engine pilot training role during the late 1970s. They are still operated from Corpus Christi today.
160839 to 160856; 160967 to 160986; 161057 to 161079

Over 60 examples of the Beech T-44A are operated on multi-engine pilot training tasks from Corpus Christi with VT-28 and VT-31. Most students eventually progress to the maritime community and the P-3 Orion, but some will move on to fly the C-2A Greyhound, E-2C Hawkeye and C-130 Hercules.

T-44B: A batch of five T-44B King Airs was purchased recently to make good the attrition experienced during some 15 years of operation by the T-44A fleet.
164579 to 164583

SPECIFICATION

Beech T-44A
Wing: span 50 ft 3 in (15.32 m); aspect ratio 8.57; area 293.94 sq ft (27.31 m²)
Fuselage and tail: length 35 ft 6 in (10.82 m); height 14 ft 2.5 in (4.33 m); tailplane span 17 ft 2.5 in (5.25 m); wheel base 12 ft 3.5 in (3.75 m)
Powerplant: two Pratt & Whitney Canada PT6A-34B rated at 680 shp (507 kW) flat-rated to 550 shp (410 kW)

Weights: empty 6,326 lb (2869 kg); maximum take-off 9,650 lb (4377 kg)
Fuel and load: internal fuel 474 US gal (1794 liters)
Speed: maximum cruising speed at 12,000 ft (3660 m) 287 mph (462 km/h); cruising speed for maximum range 227 mph (365 km/h)
Range: typical range 1,457 miles (2345 km)
Performance: maximum rate of climb at sea level 1,870 ft (570 m) per minute; service ceiling 27,620 ft (8420 m); take-off run 1,553 ft (473 m) at maximum take-off weight; take-off distance to 50 ft (15 m) 2,024 ft (617 m) at maximum take-off weight; landing run 1,030 ft (314 m) at maximum landing weight; landing distance from 50 ft (15 m) 2,110 ft (643 m) at maximum landing weight

OPERATORS

US Navy (USN)

VT-28	Corpus Christi, TX	T-44A, T-44B
VT-31	Corpus Christi, TX	T-44A, T-44B

Beech T-44A

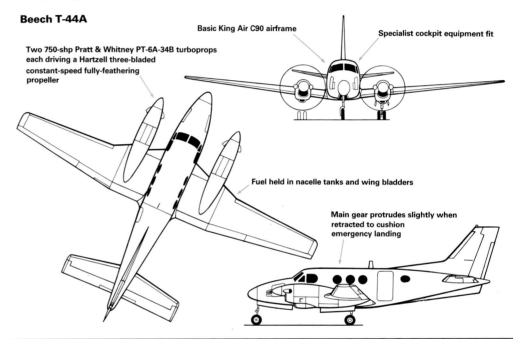

Basic King Air C90 airframe

Specialist cockpit equipment fit

Two 750-shp Pratt & Whitney PT-6A-34B turboprops each driving a Hartzell three-bladed constant-speed fully-feathering propeller

Fuel held in nacelle tanks and wing bladders

Main gear protrudes slightly when retracted to cushion emergency landing

McDonnell Douglas/British Aerospace
T-45 Goshawk

Announced as the winning contender for the Navy's VTXTS competition in November 1981, the **British Aerospace Hawk** should soon begin to assume an ever-increasing share of responsibility for undergraduate pilot training tasks on behalf of both the Navy and Marine Corps. Intended to replace the T-2C Buckeye and the TA-4J Skyhawk, production plans anticipate the manufacture of 302 Goshawks by McDonnell Douglas, this figure including a pair of Full-Scale Development (FSD) prototypes. Deliveries to the Naval Air Training Command are set to begin from St Louis, Missouri, during 1992.

Initial intentions called for the service to obtain a batch of 54 'dry' (i.e., land-based) examples of the **T-45B**, which would have been virtually identical to the standard British-built Hawk. They were to be followed by 253 'wet' (carrier compatible) **T-45A**s but this plan was changed in the mid-1980s when the Navy opted to purchase only the 'wet' model.

Work on manufacturing the pair of FSD aircraft began in February 1986 and these made successful maiden flights in April and November 1988. By then, the initial contract for a dozen T-45As had been awarded, but the October 1989 target date for delivery of production-configured examples has suffered serious slippage. It is probably fair to say that transforming the Hawk into the Goshawk has at times been a painful business.

Certainly, the program has suffered from its share of problems, most notably with regard to handling and performance qualities which have caused the Navy to request additional airframe and engine modifications to the FSD and subsequent aircraft. In modified form, the FSD prototypes returned to flight status in September and October 1990. The first true produc-

Currently in the process of joining the Naval Air Training Command, the T-45A Goshawk is destined to replace the T-2 Buckeye and the TA-4 Skyhawk. Initial deliveries were made to VT-21 at Kingsville, TX.

tion examples also became available for flight test duty during 1990, two of these being handed over to the Naval Air Test Center at Patuxent River, Maryland, in October and November 1990 for service evaluation.

Differences between the Goshawk and the basic Hawk relate mainly to the need for carrier compatibility. As a consequence, a substantial amount of airframe strengthening was necessary in order to cope with the stresses and strains of operating at sea. In addition, the undercarriage was entirely redesigned, perhaps the most visible evidence of this being provided by the twin-wheel nose unit which incorporates the standard nose-tow catapult launch attachment as well as a 'holdback' bar.

An arrester hook was also fitted and the ventral air brake of the Hawk was replaced by two fuselage-side air brakes, other design changes seeing the elimination of the twin ventral fins in favor of a single ventral fin. Further revisions concern the fin, which is taller; tailplane span, which is greater; and the wingtips, which have been squared off. Manufacture of the Goshawk is a joint effort, with BAe responsible for wings, center and rear fuselage sections, fin and tailplane assemblies, windscreen, canopy and flight control systems.

Entry into service in the pilot training role is expected to begin imminently, initially with Training Wing Two (TW-2) at Kingsville, Texas. In addition to the Goshawk itself, the T45TS package also includes 32 Hughes Flight Systems simulators, 49 computer-aided instructional devices, four training integration system mainframes and 200 terminals, as well as academic material. Logistical support for operations from the training bases is also to be furnished by the contractor.

Other training bases that are earmarked to operate the Goshawk are Chase Field, Texas, (TW-3) and Meridian, Mississippi, (TW-1) while some aircraft may also eventually go to elements of TW-6 at Pensacola, Florida, for NFO instruction. Availability of the T-45A is

expected to offer significant benefits, many of which center around replacement of the existing T-2C and TA-4J pairing by a single type. This should result in pilot training needs being satisfied by 42 per cent fewer aircraft and 25 per cent fewer flying hours. In addition, current estimates expect the training task to be accomplished with 46 per cent fewer personnel, offering the prospect of substantial financial gains at a time when all elements of the armed forces are facing deep budget cuts.

MISSION PROFILE

Configuration options: The T-45 is a two-seat intermediate and advanced training aircraft, configured with a tandem cockpit, arrester hook and improved landing gear for aircraft carrier operations. Underwing stores include AIM-9 Sidewinder air-to-air missiles, rockets, bombs and gun pods.

Training: When in service, the T-45 will fly all the intermediate strike training missions currently flown by the T-2C and the advanced (fast jet) training missions flown by the TA-4J. The latter involves firing a wide range of live ordnance, air combat maneuvering and carrier operations.

VARIANTS AND SERIALS

T-45A: Now in the process of entering service with the Navy's training organization, the T-45A Goshawk is set to replace TA-4J Skyhawks in the advanced training role and has been extensively modified to suit it for the carrier qualification task, which is an important part of the syllabus. Two development machines are expected to be followed by 300 production examples, but procurement rates have been slowed and it is possible that the eventual purchase will be curtailed. 162787; 162788; 163599 to 163658 (plus up to 240 more)

SPECIFICATION

McDonnell Douglas/British Aerospace T-45A
Wing: span 30 ft 9.75 in (9.39 m); aspect ratio 5.3; area 176.9 sq ft (16.69 m²)
Fuselage and tail: length including probe 39 ft 3.125 in (11.97 m); height 13 ft 11 in (4.24 m); tailplane span 15 ft 0.75 in (4.59 m); wheel base 14 ft 1 in (4.29 m)
Powerplant: one Rolls-Royce/Turboméca F405-RR-401 rated at 5,840 lb (25.9 kN) dry thrust
Weights: empty 9,394 lb (4261 kg); maximum take-off 12,758 lb (5787 kg)

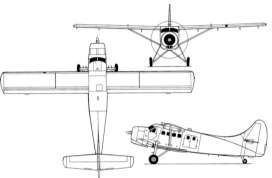

Full-span wing leading-edge slats

OBOGS (On-Board Oxygen-Generating System)

One 5,845-lb (26-kN) Rolls-Royce/Turboméca F405-RR-401 turbofan (production aircraft)

Cockpit equipped with two Martin Baker Mk 14 NACES (Naval Aircrew Common Ejection Seat)

Vortex generators on wing

Arrester hook

Provision for weapons underwing

SMURFs (Side-Mounted Unit horizontal Root tailFins)

Undercarriage stressed for carrier operations

Forward fuselage longer and deeper than Hawk

Nose-mounted pitot and instrumentation boom

Nose gear tow and catapult launch bar

Fuel and load: internal fuel 2,893 lb (1312 kg); external fuel up to two 156-US gal (591-liter) drop tanks
Speed: maximum level speed 'clean' at 8,000 ft (2440 m) 620 mph (997 km/h)
Range: ferry range on internal fuel 1,150 miles (1850 km)
Performance: maximum rate of climb at sea level 6,982 ft (2128 m) per minute; service ceiling 42,250 ft (12875 m); take-off distance to 50 ft (15 m) 3,744 ft (1189 m) at maximum take-off weight; landing distance from 50 ft (15 m) 3,900 ft (1189 m) at maximum landing weight

OPERATORS

US Navy (USN)

| VT-21 | Kingsville, TX | T-45A |
| NAWC/AD | Patuxent River, MD | T-45A |

de Havilland Canada
U-1 Otter

The first of a succession of STOL aircraft to appear from de Havilland Canada, the Otter made its maiden flight in December 1951. Powered by a single Pratt & Whitney R-1340 Twin Wasp air-cooled radial piston engine rated at 600 hp (448 kW), it bore a strong resemblance to the same company's Beaver but had roughly twice the capacity of that type, being able to accommodate a maximum of 14 occupants. Just under 500 examples had been built when production came to a close during 1968, with most of them going to military customers.

One of those customers was the US Navy which ultimately obtained 16 examples, initially as the **UC-1** and, from 1962 onwards, as the **U-1B**. In fact, not all 16 aircraft were destined for the service's own use, since it was responsible for obtaining two that were supplied to the Philippine Air Force under the terms of the Military Assistance Program.

In US Navy service, most U-1Bs were originally assigned to Operation Deep Freeze, for the Navy was intimately involved in supporting the Antarctic exploration project. Operating with VXE-6 from 1955 until 1966 while this unit was stationed at Patuxent River, Maryland, and Quonset Point, Rhode Island, the Otter's utilitarian nature was well-suited to the demands of this mission. In practice, much of the time was spent with the detachment that was stationed at McMurdo Sound during the months of the Antarctic 'summer', and the hazardous nature of operations on the ice resulted in several being destroyed.

Retirement from Deep Freeze resulted in other tasks being found for the Otter. By the early 1970s the three or four survivors were allocated to test agencies, two aircraft being on the strength of the Test Pilot's School at Patuxent River while another one served with the Naval Air Test Facility at El Centro. Today, only one of that quartet is still active, continuing to give good service to the Test Pilot's School. Another surviving example forms part of the US Naval Aviation Museum collection at Pensacola.

MISSION PROFILE

The Navy's sole surviving U-1 serves with the USN Test Pilot's School at Patuxent River for test pilot training.

VARIANTS AND SERIALS

U-1B: A total of 14 Otters was obtained by the Navy, these being earmarked for Antarctic exploration tasks with VXE-6. Only one is still on Navy charge in flying status.
142424 to 142427; 144259 to 144261; 144669 to 144674; 147574

NU-1B: At least three of the 14 Navy Otters were reassigned to test duties with the designation NU-1B after service with VXE-6.
142425; 144670; 144672

SPECIFICATION

de Havilland Canada U-1B
Wing: span 58 ft 0 in (17.68 m); area 375.0 sq ft (34.84 m²)
Fuselage and tail: length 41 ft 10 in (12.75 m); height 12 ft 7 in (3.84 m)
Powerplant: one Pratt & Whitney R-1340-S1H1-G Wasp rated at 600 m hp (447 kW)
Weights: empty 4,431 lb (2010 kg); maximum take-off 8,000 lb (3629 kg)
Fuel and load: maximum payload 3,000 lb (1361 kg)
Speed: maximum level speed at 5,000 ft (1525 m) 160 mph (257 km/h); cruising speed at 5,000 ft (1525 m) 138 mph (222 km/h)
Range: range with maximum fuel 960 miles (1545 km);

range with a 2,325-lb (1055-kg) payload 882 miles (1419 km) or with a 3,153-lb (1430-kg) payload 200 miles (322 km)
Performance: maximum rate of climb at sea level 1,000 ft (305 m) per minute; service ceiling 17,900 ft (5425 m)

OPERATORS

US Navy (USN)

| NTPS | Patuxent River, MD | NU-1B |

The sole active survivor of more than a dozen Otters obtained for service with the US Navy, this NU-1B continues to give good value for money to the Navy Test Pilot's School at Patuxent River, more than 30 years after the type was purchased specifically for Antarctic exploration duties.

de Havilland Canada
U-6A Beaver

Making its initial flight on 16 August 1947, the **DHC-2 Beaver** light utility transport was produced in substantial numbers for military and civil operators around the world. Its rugged 'go-anywhere' characteristics have ensured that it remains popular today despite its age. One of the major export customers was the USA, which obtained several hundred examples for service with the Army and the Air Force, with whom they were primarily employed on routine communications and liaison duties. The appearance in the 1960s of modern turbine-powered helicopters such as the UH-1 Iroquois effectively signalled the end of the line for the Beaver with the US Army, which was the last element of the armed forces to operate it in any numbers.

Two or three Beavers were transferred from the US Army to the US Navy many years ago and one of these machines is evidently still active at Patuxent River, Maryland. There, it continues to give good service to the Naval Test Pilot's School both as a subject for assessment by students at the school and, probably, for the occasional liaison tasking. Surprisingly, after years of being the only Beaver on TPS charge, it has recently been joined by two more examples obtained secondhand.

MISSION PROFILE

The Navy's three U-6As serve only with the USN Test Pilot's School for test pilot training.

A rather garish yellow and chocolate paint job is still worn by this U-6A Beaver of the Test Pilot's School, one of two obtained from commercial sources in recent times.

VARIANTS AND SERIALS

U-6A: At least five Beavers have been operated by the Navy and three are still active with the NTPS at Patuxent River.
150191; 150192; 151348; 164524; 164525

SPECIFICATION

de Havilland Canada U-6A
Wing: span 48 ft 0 in (14.63 m); area 250.0 sq ft (23.23 m²)
Fuselage and tail: length 30 ft 3 in (9.22 m); height 9 ft 0 in (2.74 m)
Powerplant: one Pratt & Whitney R-985-AN-1/3 Wasp Junior rated at 450 hp (336 kW)
Weights: empty 2,850 lb (1293 kg); maximum take-off 5,100 lb (2313 kg)
Fuel and load: maximum payload 1,500 lb (680 kg)
Speed: maximum level speed at 5,000 ft (1525 m) 153 mph (262 km/h); cruising speed at 5,000 ft (1525 m) 143 mph (230 km/h)
Range: range with maximum fuel 733 miles (1180 km); range with 1,350-lb (613-kg) payload 470 miles (756 km)
Performance: maximum rate of climb at sea level 1,020 ft (311 m) per minute; service ceiling 18,000 ft (5485 m); take-off run 595 ft (181 m) at maximum take-off weight

OPERATORS

US Navy (USN)

NTPS	Patuxent River, MD	U-6A

Beech
U-21 Ute

Originally acquired by the US Army during the latter half of the 1960s, this light utility transport was essentially a marriage of an unpressurized Queen Air 65-80 fuselage with the wings, tail and undercarriage of the King Air 65-90. Powered by a pair of 550-shp UAC PT6A-20 turboprop engines, the result was known in company parlance as the King Air 65-A90-1C and by the Army as the **U-21A Ute**. Procurement of the basic 12-seater model eventually terminated in the early 1970s after 141 examples had been delivered, some of which were subsequently converted for specialized tasks such as electronic reconnaissance.

In US Navy service, the U-21A is flown only by the Naval Test Pilot's School at Patuxent River, Maryland, which presently includes a couple of examples of the Ute in its rather disparate fleet of aircraft and helicopters. Obtained on loan from the Army during the course of 1989, the aircraft were introduced as replacements for some Grumman OV-1B Mohawks which had previously been assigned under a similar Army-Navy arrangement to provide some experience of piloting light twin-engined aircraft to students on courses run by the NTPS.

MISSION PROFILE

The Navy's U-21s serve only with the USN Test Pilot's School for test pilot training.

VARIANTS AND SERIALS

U-21A: Two examples of the Beech Ute have been acquired on loan from the US Army for service with the NTPS, with which they have replaced a similar number of loaned OV-1 Mohawks.
18004 (66-18004); 18096 (67-18096)

Obtained as replacements for the Mohawk, two examples of the U-21A are presently on charge of the Test Pilot's School to provide experience of light twin-engined designs.

Beech U-21A
Wing: span 45 ft 10.5 in (13.98 m); aspect ratio 7.52; area 279.70 sq ft (25.98 m²)
Fuselage and tail: length 35 ft 6 in (10.82 m); height 14 ft 2.5 in (4.33 m); tailplane span 17 ft 2.25 in (5.25 m); wheel track 12 ft 9 in (3.89 m); wheel base 12 ft 3.5 in (3.75 m)
Powerplant: two Pratt & Whitney Canada PT6A-20 each rated at 550 shp (410 kW)
Weights: empty equipped 5,434 lb (2464 kg); operating empty lb (kg); normal take-off lb (kg); maximum take-off 9,650 lb (4377 kg)
Fuel and load: internal fuel 378 US gal (1427 liters);

external fuel none; maximum payload 3,936 lb (1785 kg)
Speed: maximum level sped 'clean' at 10,000 ft (3050 m) 265 mph (426 km/h); maximum cruising speed at 10,000 ft (3050 m) 245 mph (395 km/h); economical cruising speed at 10,000 ft (3050 m) 205 mph (328 km/h)
Range: range 1,676 miles (2697 km) with maximum fuel, or 1,216 miles (1956 km) with maximum payload
Performance: maximum rate of climb at sea level 2,160 ft (658 m) per minute; service ceiling 26,150 ft (7970 m); take-off run 1,618 ft (493 m) at maximum take-off weight; take-off distance to 50 ft (15 m) 1,923 ft (586 m) at maximum take-off weight; landing distance from 50 ft (15 m) 2,453 ft (748 m) at normal landing weight; landing run 1,280 ft (390 m) at normal landing weight

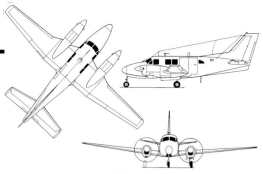

OPERATORS

US Navy (USN)

NTPS	Patuxent River, MD	U-21A

Dassault-Breguet

HU-25 Guardian

First flown in prototype form in May 1963, Dassault-Breguet's Falcon began life as an executive jet and subsequently found favor with a number of military air arms around the world. In most cases, it is used for VIP transport duties but some suitably modified examples also undertake electronic counter-measures, calibration of navigation aids and radar instruction.

In January 1977, the US Coast Guard opted to purchase a total of 41 Falcon 20Gs, these differing from earlier versions in that they were fitted with Garrett AiResearch ATF3-6-2C turbofans which offered the additional power needed to operate effectively at greater weights. Given the designation **HU-25A**, these machines featured a sophisticated array of equipment which included comprehensive navigation and communications gear as well as APS-127 radar so that they could perform overwater search and rescue, maritime surveillance and environmental protection tasks.

Originally, it was intended that deliveries should begin in the summer of 1979 but engine-related problems resulted in a fairly lengthy delay, and it was not until 1981 that the first example was accepted. Replacing the long-serving Grumman HU-16E Albatross, or 'Goat', the HU-25A also incorporated a drop hatch through which rescue supplies could be delivered by parachute. In normal operation, the HU-25A may carry up to 3,200 lb (1450 kg) of supplies internally in addition to the normal crew of two pilots, two observers and a sensor system operator.

Today, quite a few Coast Guard Guardians have been subjected to further modification programs and only just over half remain in the original configuration. These are operated from at least seven Coast Guard stations, including Cape Cod, Massachusetts; Sacramento, California; Corpus Christi, Texas; Miami, Florida; and Mobile, Alabama.

Of the other aircraft, 11 have been updated as **HU-25B**s and seven or eight as **HU-25C Interceptors**. Coast Guard facilities at Miami and Mobile operate both of these sub-types, while the HU-25B model is also flown from

Astoria, Oregon; Elizabeth City, North Carolina; and Cape Cod, Massachusetts.

Differences on the HU-25B are mainly concerned with the fitment of a Motorola AN/APS-131 side-looking airborne radar (SLAR) in a fuselage pod which is slightly offset to starboard; a Texas Instruments RS-18C linescan unit in another pod under the starboard wing; and a laser-illuminated TV under the port wing. In service, they undertake surveillance duties connected with the detection of maritime pollution and the identification of the vessels responsible, while at least two HU-25Bs from Cape Cod were dispatched to Bahrain to undertake environmental assessment tasks in the wake of the Gulf War.

The HU-25C Interceptor arose from the need for a high-performance aircraft for use in interdiction of drug smuggling activity. Fitted with Westinghouse AN/APG-66 radar in the nose and a turret-mounted Texas Instruments WF-360 FLIR sensor, the HU-25C is tasked with pursuit and identification of suspicious air and sea traffic. A complex suite of secure communications equipment is also installed on this version, which entered service with the Coast Guard at the end of May 1988.

Medium-range surveillance is the major task performed by the Coast Guard HU-25A but it may also play a more active part in rescue and recovery missions by virtue of being able to carry and drop rescue packs.

MISSION PROFILE

Configuration options: The HU-25 is a medium-range surveillance aircraft configured by the USCG for drug interdiction work and medium-range search work in search and rescue operations. Specialized search windows are installed. The HU-25A has four fuselage hardpoints to carry rescue packs and four underwing hardpoints for sensor pods. HU-25Bs carry an SLAR pod and an APS-131IR/IV pod on wing hardpoints. The HU-25C has an AN/APG-66 radar installed in the nose and an WF-360 FLIR sensor for night surveillance operations. Secure HF, UHF and VHF-FM communication are carried by the HU-25C.

Medium-range search: In search and rescue operations the speed and endurance of the HU-25 allows it to transit quickly to search areas and then remain on station for long periods. Once survivors are located, rescue equipment is dropped and the HU-25 monitors the scene until ships or helicopters make the actual rescue.

Drug interdiction: This mission requires the HU-25 to adopt a semi-covert approach to maintain surveillance on suspected drug-smuggling ships or aircraft. The AN/APG-66 and FLIR allow targets to be followed at a safe distance. Secure communications is used to coordinate operations with law enforcement agencies.

VARIANTS AND SERIALS

HU-25A: A total of 41 HU-25A Guardians was obtained by the Coast Guard for medium-range, all-weather SAR duties, but subsequent modification has resulted in approximately half of these machines adopting new missions and designations.
2101 to 2141

Aircraft

Above: Unmodified versions of the Guardian are currently flown by eight Coast Guard stations, while specially-configured variants undertake such tasks as drug interdiction.

HU-25B: About 11 Coast Guard Guardians have been fitted with a ventral pod housing SLAR sensor systems. They are now employed on a variety of surveillance tasks.
2101; 2102; 2105; 2111; 2118; 2122; 2125; 2132; 2134 to 2136

HU-25C Interceptor: Modification of nine Guardians with APG-66 radar and an FLIR sensor resulted in the appearance of the HU-25C version, which is used by the Coast Guard on drug interdiction duties.
2104; 2112; 2119; 2131; 2133; 2139; 2141 (plus two)

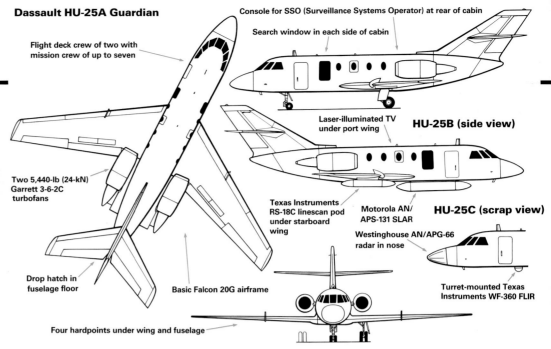

Dassault HU-25A Guardian

Flight deck crew of two with mission crew of up to seven

Two 5,440-lb (24-kN) Garrett 3-6-2C turbofans

Drop hatch in fuselage floor

Basic Falcon 20G airframe

Four hardpoints under wing and fuselage

Console for SSO (Surveillance Systems Operator) at rear of cabin

Search window in each side of cabin

Laser-illuminated TV under port wing — **HU-25B (side view)**

Texas Instruments RS-18C linescan pod under starboard wing

Motorola AN/APS-131 SLAR

HU-25C (scrap view)

Westinghouse AN/APG-66 radar in nose

Turret-mounted Texas Instruments WF-360 FLIR

SPECIFICATION

Dassault-Breguet HU-25A
Wing: span 53 ft 6 in (16.30 m); aspect ratio 7.02; area 450.00 sq ft (41.80 m²)
Fuselage and tail: length 56 ft 3 in (17.15 m); height 17 ft 5 in (5.32 m); tailplane span 22 ft 1 in (6.74 m); wheel track 12 ft 1.25 in (3.69 m); wheel base 18 ft 10 in (5.74 m)
Powerplant: two Garrett ATF3-6-2 each rated at 5,440 lb (24.20 kN) dry thrust

Weights: empty 19,004 lb (8620 kg); operating empty 20,888 lb (9475 kg) with full avionics and five crew; maximum take-off 33,510 lb (15200 kg)
Fuel and load: internal fuel 10,626 lb (4820 kg); external fuel none
Speed: maximum cruising speed at 40,025 ft (12200 m) 531 mph (855 km/h); economical cruising speed at 41,010 ft (12500 m) 475 mph (764 km/h)
Range: range 2,591 miles (4170 km) with six crew
Performance: initial cruising altitude 41,010 ft (12500 m); take-off run 4,052 ft (1235 m) at maximum take-off weight; landing distance from 50 ft (15 m) 00 ft (00 m) at normal landing weight; landing run 2,051 ft (625 m) at normal landing weight

OPERATORS

US Coast Guard(USCG)

CGAS	Astoria, OR	HU-25A, HU-25B
CGAS	Cape Cod, MA	HU-25A, HU-25B
CGAS	Corpus Christi, TX	HU-25A
CGAS	Elizabeth City, NC	HU-25A, HU-25B
CGAS	Miami, FL	HU-25A, HU-25B, HU-25C
CGAS	Mobile, AL	HU-25A, HU-25B, HU-25C
CGAS	Sacramento, CA	HU-25A
CGAS	San Diego, CA	HU-25A, HU-25B

Rockwell
OV-10 Bronco

Having its origins in the tri-service Light Armed Reconnaissance Aircraft program of the early 1960s, the **Rockwell OV-10 Bronco** began life as North American's NA-300 design project, which was announced as the winning contender in August 1964. An initial contract covering seven prototype **YOV-10A**s was placed soon afterwards, the first of these making its maiden flight on 16 July 1965. At that time, it was expected to enter service with the US Army, US Air Force and US Marine Corps but, as it transpired, only the latter two organizations went ahead with procurement plans, receiving 157 and 114 examples respectively.

One of the more unusual designs to attain operational service with the US armed forces, the Bronco looked decidedly odd, with one of its more distinctive features being a plank-like

wing structure. Suspended from this were a pair of Garrett T76 turboprop engines and a central 'pod' which accommodated a pilot and observer sitting in tandem. Aft of the engines, tail booms extended rearwards to terminate in twin fin and rudder assemblies, the upper extremities of which served as suspension points for the horizontal tail surface.

It may have looked strange but it was certainly functional, since the rear section of the fuselage 'pod' was also able to carry a variety of loads. These included cargo and personnel, typical payloads being two stretchers and a medical attendant, or four armed paratroops. In addition, it was also capable of toting a fairly respectable array of weaponry, with production **OV-10A**s carrying pairs of M60C 7.62-mm machine guns buried in sponsons

which extended outwards from the lower fuselage sides, as well as a total of seven hardpoints for external stores. One was located on the fuselage centerline with four more on the sponsons and the remaining two beneath the outer wing sections.

Weapons available for use by the OV-10A included napalm, slick and retarded Mk 82 500-lb (227-kg) bombs, unguided 2.75-in or 5-in rockets and smoke markers, or combinations of these up to the maximum payload of 3,600 lb (1630 kg). Subsequent development of the **OV-10D** added to ordnance options the Hellfire laser-guided anti-armor air-to-surface missile.

Deliveries to the Marines kicked off in February 1968. The type was soon in combat in Southeast Asia, where its superior performance compared with other FAC platforms was most welcome. Maneuverability was also quite outstanding, allowing crews to take full advantage of terrain masking when working a 'hot' target area. In addition to USMC and USAF use, the Navy also borrowed 18 Broncos from the Marines, assigning these to a special light attack unit known as VAL-4 'Black Ponies'. Operating from Binh Thuy during 1969-72, these were used to interdict river traffic in the Mekong Delta.

Further development aimed at providing enhanced night and all-weather capability resulted in two airframes being modified as **YOV-10D NOGS** (Night Observation Gun-

Purpose-built for both the observation and forward air control missions, the Rockwell OV-10A Bronco married excellent visibility and rugged design to produce an effective but odd-looking machine.

Rockwell OV-10D Bronco

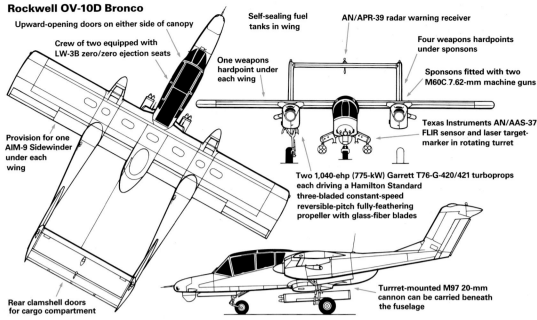

- Upward-opening doors on either side of canopy
- Crew of two equipped with LW-3B zero/zero ejection seats
- Self-sealing fuel tanks in wing
- AN/APR-39 radar warning receiver
- Four weapons hardpoints under sponsons
- One weapons hardpoint under each wing
- Sponsons fitted with two M60C 7.62-mm machine guns
- Provision for one AIM-9 Sidewinder under each wing
- Texas Instruments AN/AAS-37 FLIR sensor and laser target-marker in rotating turret
- Two 1,040-ehp (775-kW) Garrett T76-G-420/421 turboprops each driving a Hamilton Standard three-bladed constant-speed reversible-pitch fully-feathering propeller with glass-fiber blades
- Rear clamshell doors for cargo compartment
- Turrret-mounted M97 20-mm cannon can be carried beneath the fuselage

Above: Two basic models of the Bronco continue in US Marine Corps use at the present time, with the original OV-10A probably being around in greatest numbers.

Below: The other model is the OV-10D, which has special night and all-weather sensors fitted in a much-extended nose section. About 20 Broncos have been converted to this form.

ship System) prototypes. These embodied a FLIR sensor and a laser illuminator in an extended nose section as well as a General Electric M97 20-mm cannon in a turret situated beneath the aft fuselage. Combat evaluation was undertaken but it was to be several years before 'production' OV-10D conversions began to join the Marines. Approximately 20 OV-10As have been retrospectively modified to this configuration. The definitive OV-10D actually lacked the gun package, although it did introduce the AIM-9 Sidewinder air-to-air missile. Other changes included uprated engines, increased fuel capacity through fitment of underwing tanks and infra-red-suppressing exhaust ducts.

More recently, a service-life extension program (SLEP) has been launched at the Cherry Point maintenance facility which, during 1991-93, will update a total of 37 Marine Corps aircraft (23 OV-10As and 14 OV-10Ds) to **OV-10D+** standard. Avionics, navigation and weapons systems are all to be improved, and the work will also encompass structural strengthening to allow the Bronco to operate safely from carrier flight decks. Completion of this project was expected to ensure that some Broncos would remain in the Marine Corps inventory for at least another 15 years. All will now be retired by FY 1994, however.

Today, the Bronco remains active in fairly modest quantities with the Marine Corps, which continues to use both the OV-10A and OV-10D versions. Principally tasked with FAC duties, regular units are assigned to

FMFLant (VMO-1 at New River, North Carolina) and FMFPac (VMO-2 at Camp Pendleton, California) while the Reserve force also has a single squadron (VMO-4 at Atlanta, Georgia). USMC OV-10s from VMO-1 and VMO-2 were certainly in action during Desert Storm, flying from Jubail in support of co-located AV-8Bs and other types operating from other bases in the Gulf. Two examples were shot down, with three of the four crew members involved surviving to be repatriated later.

MISSION PROFILE

Armament options: OV-10A wing sponsons are fitted with four M60 machine guns. While the centerline station commonly carries a 150-US gal (570-liter) fuel tank, the Mk 83 bomb or GPU-2 gun pod are also permissible. Stores the OV-10A can currently carry from its other four sponson pylons include fire and Mk 82 bombs, FAE, rocket and gun pods, or flare dispensers. Only USMC OV-10As are equipped with underwing AIM-9 launcher rails.

The OV-10D is equipped for the night observation system mission and is equipped with the AAS-37 detection, ranging and tracking system in an undernose turret. When it uses the optional M197 20-mm cannon, mounted in an underfuselage turret, the sponsons are removed. OV-10D stores include FAE, rocket pods, or flare dispensers. Also, the OV-10D can carry 100-US gal (380-liter) fuel tanks from its outboard wing pylons.

Forward air control: During Desert Storm OV-10s appeared to travel light, with most carrying a single LAU-10 from the left sponson station and a centerline fuel tank. While up to two AIM-9L/Ms could be carried

on the wing pylons, seeing the launcher rail without the missile was more normal. In all probability, AGM-122 Sidearms were carried rather than Sidewinders. Broncos also reportedly used rocket pods, FAE and CBU-7B Gator. If true, only one of the latter could have been carried from the centerline.

VARIANTS AND SERIALS

YOV-10A: Development and testing of the Bronco forward air control aircraft was undertaken with a batch of seven YOV-10As, all of which have now been stricken from the inventory.
152879 to 152885

OV-10A: Quantity production of the Bronco for service with observation squadrons of the Marine Corps totaled 114, but the number of aircraft in original configuration is steadily declining, with attrition, disposal and remanufacture combining to reduce the size of the OV-10A fleet.
153390 to 155503

OV-10D: Designed to possess night and all-weather capability, the OV-10D embodies an extended nose section housing a FLIR sensor turret on its underside. At least 18 OV-10As have been modified to this configuration but more are due, and the Marine Corps is to receive several former USAF aircraft as attrition replacements. These are also scheduled for conversion to OV-10D standard.
155395; 155396; 155409; 155410; 155436; 155451; 155466; 155468; 155470; 155472; 155473; 155479; 155482; 155489; 155492 to 155494; 155502 (plus others)

SPECIFICATION

Rockwell OV-10A

Wing: span 40 ft 0 in (12.19 m); area 291.0 sq ft (27.03 m²)

Fuselage and tail: length 41 ft 7 in (12.67 m); height 15 ft 2 in (4.62 m); tailplane span 14 ft 7 in (4.45 m)

Powerplant: two Garrett T76-G-416/417 rated at 715 ehp (533 kW)

Weights: empty equipped 6,969 lb (3161 kg); normal take-off 9,908 lb (4494 kg); maximum take-off 14,444 lb (6552 kg)

Fuel and load: internal fuel 578 US gal (976 liters); external fuel up to one 150-US gal (568-liter) drop tank; maximum ordnance 3,600 lb (1633 kg)

Speed: maximum level speed 'clean' at sea level 281 mph (452 km/h)

Range: ferry range 1,428 miles (2298 km); combat radius with maximum warload and no loiter 228 miles (367 km)

Performance: maximum rate of climb at sea level 9,908-lb (4494-²kg) weight 2,650 ft (808 m) per minute; service ceiling 24,000 ft (7315 m); take-off run 740 ft (226 m) at normal take-off weight; take-off distance to 50 ft (15 m) 2,800 ft (853 m) at overload take-off weight; landing run 740 ft (226 m) at normal weight; landing distance from 50 ft (15 m) 1,220 ft (372 m) at normal weight

The lengthened nose of the OV-10D model is most apparent when viewed from the side. An aircraft from VMO-1 is portrayed here about to touch down somewhere in the Gulf.

Rockwell OV-10D

generally similar to the OV-10A except in the following:
Fuselage and tail: length 44 ft 0 in (13.41 m)
Powerplant two Garrett T76-G-420/421 rated at 1,040 ehp (776 kW)
Weights: empty equipped 6,893 lb (3127 kg)
Speed: maximum level speed 'clean' at sea level 288 mph (463 km/h)
Range: combat radius 305 miles (491 km)
Performance: maximum rate of climb at sea level at 12,443-lb (5644-kg) weight 2,665 ft (812 m) per minute; service ceiling 30,000 ft (9145 m); take-off run 1,110 ft (338 m) at 13,284-lb (6025-kg) weight; landing run 800 ft (244 m) at maximum landing weight

Bell/Boeing
V-22 Osprey

Considerable controversy surrounds the **V-22 Osprey** tilt-rotor project, with Secretary of Defense Dick Cheney an ardent advocate of cancellation while the US Congress has persistently voted appropriations to ensure that development work continues. In response, the Bell/Boeing team has initiated a cost-cutting program so as to try and alleviate financial concerns.

Originally conceived to meet the needs of all four US armed services, the most enthusiastic supporter is the Marine Corps, which hopes to obtain no fewer than 552 **MV-22**s for use in assault operations. Another possible operator is the Navy, which planned to buy a total of 300 **SV-22**s for antisubmarine warfare and 50 **HV-22**s for SAR duties, while the Air Force also revealed an intent to obtain just over 50 **CV-22**s for use by Special Operations forces. Army interest has declined and it has deferred its requirement for more than 200 examples due to financial constraints arising out of diminishing budgets. So far, though, only six prototypes and a dozen production standard Ospreys have been funded.

Flying for the first time on 19 March 1989, the Osprey successfully made the transition from helicopter mode flight to airplane mode on 14 September of that year, but the project received a serious setback in 1991 when the fifth prototype was destroyed in an accident. Powered by two Allison T406-AD-400 turboshaft engines, it has already demonstrated a cruising speed of 275 kt and a 'dash' speed of 300 kt, built-in safety factors including a cross-shaft arrangement whereby power is supplied to both rotors in the event of one engine failing.

Apart from the hiatus that followed the crash of the fifth machine, test work has been making steady progress, one highlight occurring in December 1990 when an initial series of ship-board trials was conducted aboard the USS *Wasp* (LHD-1) using Ospreys flying from Patuxent River, Maryland. A total of 15 landings and take-offs was completed during these trials, which also included suitability studies.

In Marine Corps service (if it goes ahead), the MV-22 will primarily be intended to replace the long-serving CH-46 Sea Knight and will be able to carry up to 24 fully-equipped troops in the assault role. At present, however, that day seems to be a long way off and the Osprey is presently only active in very limited numbers with the Naval Air Warfare Center Aircraft Division at Patuxent River.

MISSION PROFILE

Configuration options: The V-22 is intended to be configured for air assault, special operations, anti-submarine warfare, strike rescue and logistic support. Details of weapons fits and equipment modifications for each version have yet to be determined.

Air assault and logistic support: It is intended that the MV-22 should take over the current USMC missions of the CH-46E, flying troops and supplies into combat zones. Some 24 troops can be carried up to a total of 200 miles (320 km), or the aircraft make two 50-mile (80-km) flights from amphibious assault ships without refueling. Up to 15,000 lb (6800 kg) of cargo can be underslung using two cargo hooks, or 10,000 lb (4500 kg) with a single hook.

Naval special warfare support/strike rescue: HV-22s are to take over the missions currently flown by the HH-60H, inserting and extracting USN SEAL teams and rescuing downed aircrew from behind enemy lines.

Anti-submarine warfare/utility: Operating from ships, the SV-22 is to take over the ASW missions of the SH-60B/F.

Fleet logistic support: The V-22 is intended to operate in the VertRep, VOD and COD roles flying from underway replenishment ships or shore bases. Its V/STOL capability will allow it to carry out VOD to ships at a significantly greater range than current fleet logistic support helicopters.

VARIANTS AND SERIALS

YV-22A: Six prototypes of the Bell/Boeing Osprey have been bought for trials work but the future of this project remains very much in doubt, even though a block of serial numbers has been allocated to an initial batch of 12 aircraft. If it goes ahead, plans call for 552 MV-22A assault transports to be delivered to the Marine Corps and 50 HV-22A combat SAR examples to the Navy.
163911 to 163916; 164389 to 164400

SPECIFICATION

Bell/Boeing MV-22A
Wing and rotors: rotor diameter 38 ft 0 in (11.58 m); span including nacelles 50 ft 11 in (15.52 m); width overall, rotors turning 84 ft 6.8 in (25.78 m); aspect ratio 5.52; total rotor disc area 2,268.23 sq ft (210.72 m²)
Fuselage and tail: length, fuselage excluding probe 57 ft 4 in (17.47 m); height over fins 17 ft 7.8 in (5.38 m) and overall with nacelles vertical 20 ft 10 in (6.35 m); tailplane span over fins 18 ft 5 in (5.61 m); wheel base 21 ft 7.5 in (6.59 m)

Above: Development of the remarkable Osprey is continuing despite heated debate over the future of this project. One major setback was the destruction of a prototype.

Left: The tilt-rotor arrangement which bestows VTOL capability on the Osprey can be clearly seen in this study of the first prototype as it transitions to the hover in readiness for a vertical landing.

Powerplant: two Allison T406-AD-400 rated at 6,150 shp (4586 kW) for take-off and 5,890 shp (4392 kW) for continuous running

Weights: empty equipped 31,886 lb (14463 kg); normal mission take-off 47,500 lb (21545 kg) for VTO and 55,000 lb (24947 kg) for STO; maximum take-off 60,500 lb (27442 kg) for STO

Fuel and load: internal fuel 13,700 lb (6215 kg) standard and 30,074 lb (13641 kg) with self-ferry cabin tanks; external fuel none; maximum internal payload 20,000 lb (9072 kg); maximum external payload 10,000 lb (4536 kg) on a single hook or 15,000 lb (6804 kg) on two hooks

Speed: maximum cruising speed at optimum altitude 361 mph (582 km/h) in aeroplane mode; maximum cruising speed at sea level 115 mph (185 km/h) in helicopter mode and 316 mph (509 km/h) in aeroplane mode; maximum forward speed with maximum slung load 230 mph (370 km/h)

Range: ferry range 2,418 miles (3892 km) after STO at 60,500 lb (27442 kg); tactical range 1,382 miles (2224 km) after VTO at 44,619 lb (21146 kg) with a 12,000-lb (5443-kg) payload, or 2,075 miles (3336 km) after STO at 55,000 lb (24947 kg) with a 20,000-lb (9072-kg) payload

Performance: service ceiling 26,000 ft (7925 m); take-off run less than 500 ft (152 m) at normal STO weight

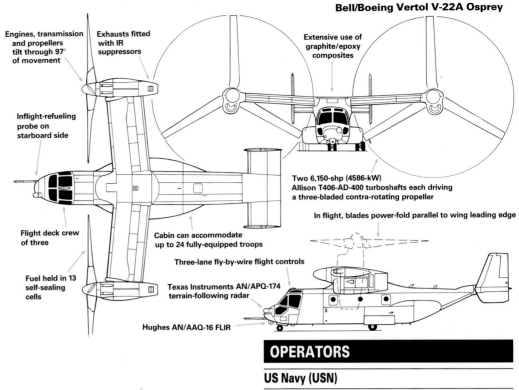

Bell/Boeing Vertol V-22A Osprey

Engines, transmission and propellers tilt through 97° of movement

Exhausts fitted with IR suppressors

Extensive use of graphite/epoxy composites

Inflight-refueling probe on starboard side

Two 6,150-shp (4586-kW) Allison T406-AD-400 turboshafts each driving a three-bladed contra-rotating propeller

In flight, blades power-fold parallel to wing leading edge

Flight deck crew of three

Cabin can accommodate up to 24 fully-equipped troops

Three-lane fly-by-wire flight controls

Fuel held in 13 self-sealing cells

Texas Instruments AN/APQ-174 terrain-following radar

Hughes AN/AAQ-16 FLIR

OPERATORS

US Navy (USN)

NAWC/AD	Patuxent River, MD	YV-22A

Schweizer
X-26

For more than two decades, US Navy use of gliders has been confined to the Naval Test Pilot's School at Patuxent River, Maryland, where they have been used to impart some knowledge of and expertise in dealing with the phenomenon known as yaw/roll coupling. Use of jet aircraft in this project was considered to pose too many dangers. It was therefore decided to obtain gliders, which seemed to offer the advantages of a slow rate of roll and superior recovery characteristics. Schweizer's SGS 2-32 sailplane was duly selected as being the most suitable type and an initial batch of two was obtained under the designation **X-26A**.

Basically identical to the commercially available SGS 2-32, the aircraft featured all-aluminum construction with fiberglass wing panels, and could accommodate up to three occupants beneath a single-piece Plexiglas canopy. Some structural strengthening was undertaken to make them more suitable for the task, but modifications were of a minimal nature.

Introduction to service at Patuxent River occurred in the summer of 1968. Both of the first two machines were ultimately destroyed in accidents in 1971-72, prompting the Navy to purchase a third X-26A as a replacement fairly soon after the second loss. This enjoyed a somewhat longer career with the Test Pilot's School but was itself written off in September 1980. At that time, a fourth example was acquired and this X-26A is still thought to be on charge, although another machine – retaining a USAF identity – was also reported on TPS strength during 1989. Students with the school are understood to experience eight flights in the X-26A, these examining yaw/roll coupling and other facets of aircraft that utilize a high aspect ratio wing.

One other variant of the X-26 has also seen service with the TPS. This was the **X-26B**, which was fundamentally a powered version of the SGS 2-32. Originally developed by Lockheed under a Defense Advanced Research Projects Agency (DARPA) program, the pair of X-26Bs began life as the single-seat QT-1 and evolved into the two-seat QT-2PC, in which guise they were evaluated in Vietnam. Performing covert intelligence-gathering duties, the ultra-quiet QT-2PC paved the way for Lockheed's YO-3A, which also undertook US Army surveillance tasks in Southeast Asia.

Availability of the YO-3A freed the QT-2PCs and they were duly transferred to Patuxent River as X-26Bs, one being flown regularly by the TPS on yaw/roll coupling demonstrations and the other used as a spares source. Powered by a single Continental O-200-A engine rated at 100 hp, the self-launch and recovery facility was particularly welcome. The TPS operated this type from 1969 until 1973 when problems with maintenance brought about its forced withdrawal.

MISSION PROFILE

In USN service, the X-26 is used solely for test pilot training duties, representing an aircraft type with very different performance characteristics to those normally encountered by naval aviators.

Right: *Among the unusual types in the fleet of aircraft and helicopters assigned to the Test Pilot's School is the Schweizer X-26. This aircraft is employed to provide students with experience of yaw/roll coupling.*

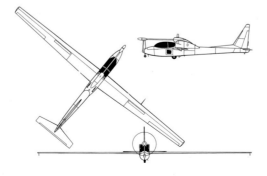

VARIANTS AND SERIALS

X-26A: Four X-26As have been purchased outright by the Navy for service with the NTPS at Patuxent River, but three have been lost in accidents. The sole survivor was recently joined by an ex-USAF aircraft which is believed to be operated on a loan basis.
157932; 157933; 158818; 159260; 760086 (USAF 76-0086)

SPECIFICATION

Schweizer X-26A

Wing: span 57 ft 1 in (17.40 m); area 180.0 sq ft (16.70 m²)

Fuselage and tail: length 26 ft 9 in (8.15 m); height 9 ft 3 in (2.82 m); tailplane span 10 ft 6 in (3.20 m)

Powerplant: none

Weights: empty 857 lb (389 kg); maximum take-off 1,430 lb (649 kg)

Fuel and load: internal fuel none

Speed: maximum aero-tow speed 110 mph (177 km/h); maximum gliding speed 158 mph (254 km/h)

Performance: best glide ratio 34:1 at 59 mph (95 km/h); minimum sinking speed 2.38 ft (0.72 m) per second at 50 mph (80 km/h)

OPERATORS

US Navy (USN)

NTPS	Patuxent River, MD	X-26A

USN/USMC ORDNANCE

This article simplifies weapons designations as much as possible. Most of the prefixes and suffixes which append them have been omitted. For instance, the prefix 'AF/' indicates an item used only by the Air Force while 'AN/' means one used by both the Air Force and Navy. Using the current weapon designation system, a '/B' suffix indicates the device is released from the aircraft to do whatever it is designed to do, while an '/A' indicates that it remains attached to the aircraft. While the original design has just a numerical designation, subsequent models are indicated by a letter following the number (eg., GBU-12/B, -12A/B, etc.). This article uses only enough of a designation to visually distinguish between versions. For example, while a new explosive filler may result in a new bomb version, since the bomb's external appearance is unchanged, it is ignored.

FIRE BOMBS

The only operational fire bomb in the USN/USMC inventory is the Mk 77. The original Mk 77 was a streamlined weapon, dating from 1951. Later, smaller Mk 77s were used extensively during Vietnam. The blunt, unpainted **Mk 77 Mod 5** bomb body is delivered

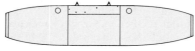

MK 77 Mod 5 fire bomb

with 43 lb (20 kg) of imbiber beads which, when filled with 63 US gal (238 liter) of fuel, form napalm. The

Armorers load Mk 77s on to a Harrier. The napalm bombs are very distinctive due to their blunt ends.

complete bomb weighs about 520 lb (235 kg). During the Gulf War they were used to ignite oil-filled Iraqi trenches in preparation for the ground war.

GENERAL-PURPOSE BOMBS

General-purpose (**GP**) bombs are the most commonly used weapons of aerial warfare. They are inexpensive, easy to produce and have numerous applications, including providing the warhead for most PGMs. The USN inventory includes the 500-lb **Mk 82**, 1,000-lb **Mk 83** and 2,000-lb **Mk 84**. These bombs, with an explosive content of roughly 50 per cent, are based on studies done by Douglas Aircraft in 1946. Production began during the Korean War, although they did not actually see service until Vietnam. All have suspension lugs spaced at 14 in (35 cm), except for the Mk 84s, which are 30 in (76 cm). There was originally a Mk 81 250-lb bomb, but it was found to be ineffective during Vietnam and its use was discontinued. The only bomb body still being produced for the Navy is the Mk 83, which is increasingly becoming their standard GP bomb, especially for the F/A-18.

A number of different fins can be fitted to Mk 80 series GP bombs. The most common is the low-drag, general purpose (**LDGP**) conical fin. The BSU-33 is a new conical tail for the Mk 82 with fins which are slightly canted to improve bomb accuracy by spinning. High-drag fins include both the new Goodyear Aerospace BSU-85 air inflatable retard (**AIR**) used by the Mk 83, as well as two types of Snakeye-type fins for the Mk 82, the Vietnam-era Mk 15 **Snakeye** (**SE**) being slowly replaced by the improved BSU-86. (The 'eye' suffix identifies a weapon developed by the Naval Weapons Center, at China Lake, CA).

An A-6E Intruder drops Mk 82 Snakeye bombs at low level, illustrating the four pop-out retarding fins.

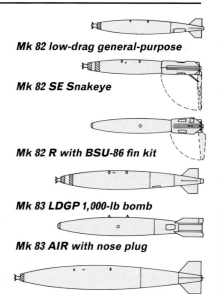

Mk 82 low-drag general-purpose

Mk 82 SE Snakeye

Mk 82 R with BSU-86 fin kit

Mk 83 LDGP 1,000-lb bomb

Mk 83 AIR with nose plug

Mk 84 LDGP 2,000-lb bomb

GENERAL-PURPOSE BOMBS

BOMB	WARHEAD	CLASS	FIN KIT	REMARKS
Mk 82 LDGP	Mk 82	540 lb	Mk 82	conical fin
Mk 82 LDGP	Mk 82	540 lb	BSU-33	conical fin
Mk 82 SE	Mk 82	570 lb	Mk 15	Snakeye retard fin
Mk 82 R	Mk 82	565 lb	BSU-86	Snakeye-type retard fin
Mk 83 LDGP	Mk 83	1,040 lb	Mk 83	conical fin
Mk 83 AIR	Mk 83	1,110 lb	BSU-85	Air Inflatable Retard
Mk 84 LDGP	Mk 84	2,020 lb	Mk 84	conical fin

* **BLU-110** can be substituted for Mk 83, **BLU-111** for Mk 82, and **BLU-112** for Mk 84. These are the same bomb bodies with a new explosive filler.

GENERAL-PURPOSE BOMB FUZE OPTIONS

FUZE	LOCATION	TYPE	REMARKS
M904	nose	instantaneous/short delay	
Mk 43	nose	proximity	high-drag bombs only
Mk 344	tail	impact	electrical
Mk 346	tail	impact	electrical
Mk 347	nose	impact	mechanical
Mk 376	tail	impact	electrical
FMU-117	tail	proximity	
FMU-149	tail	instantaneous/short delay	nose plug for penetration

The visually distinguishing characteristic of naval GP bombs is a very rough ablative coating applied to the warheads (but not fins). Developed after several tragic shipboard fires during the Vietnam War, this makes bombs burn in a fire, rather than exploding. Instead of the single 3-in (8-cm) yellow band found on Air Force bombs, the Navy bombs have two, spaced 3 in (8 cm) apart, to reaffirm from a distance that the bombs have the ablative coating. GP bombs are carried by the A-6E, AV-8B, F-14, F/A-18, OV-10 and S-3.

Many Navy weapons have a fire-resistant coating, denoted by two yellow bands. These are Mk 83 LDGPs.

Often overlooked, the different fuzes used with GP bombs are absolutely crucial to inflicting the desired damage to a given target. While nose fuzes are usually identifiable visually, most tail fuzes are hidden by the fin assembly. Recently, the Navy began using the blunt MXU-735 nose plug on their GP bombs when electrical fuzes are fitted.

PAVEWAY LASER-GUIDED BOMBS (LGB)

The precision avionics vectoring equipment (**PAVE**) was an Air Force effort begun during the Vietnam War which resulted in a number of programs, the most successful of which was Texas Instruments' Paveway laser guidance kit for 'dumb' bombs. The formal designation for this class of weapon is guided bomb unit (**GBU**). **Paveway I** LGBs used during Vietnam had fixed wings (the front fins are called canards, while the rear ones are wings). The so-called 'Long Wing' versions of these bombs are still used occasionally for training. Of all the Paveway I LGBs, only the Mk 82-based **GBU-12**, Mk 83-based **GBU-16** and Mk 84-based **GBU-10** were retained and improved. **Paveway II** bombs are externally distinguishable from Paveway Is by their 'pop-out' wings,

which make handling and carriage easier. Both bombs have 'bang-bang' computer control and guidance (CCG) sections which used full control deflection to alter the bomb's path, thus shortening the range.

A fascinating item from Desert Storm was Navy use of the 'LGB CCG', which is a USN term for the Portsmouth Aviation CPU-123 Paveway II bomb based on the British 1,000-lb bomb. They dropped nearly as

many of these (611) as they did of all US LGBs (623). If true, the most probable explanation is that the British warhead has better penetration characteristics than the American Mk 80-series bombs, making them better for use against hardened aircraft shelters (HAS).

The table identifies the various members of the USN Paveway LGB family still used operationally. When several models have the same external configuration, with the differences being internal to the CCG, they are all shown on the same line.

The A-6 is the principal delivery platform for the USN's LGBs, this bomb being a GBU-16. No Paveway IIIs are in the inventory.

GBU-12 Paveway I short wing

GBU-12A Paveway I long wing

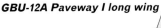

GBU-12B/C/D Paveway II

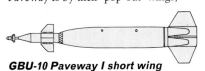

GBU-10 Paveway I short wing

GBU-10A Paveway I long wing

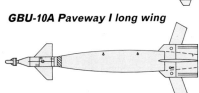

GBU-10C/D/E/F Paveway II

Mk 83 LGB Paveway I

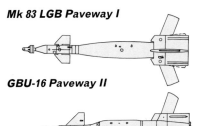

GBU-16 Paveway II

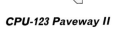

CPU-123 Paveway II

PAVEWAY BOMBS

BOMB	WARHEAD	CLASS	FIN KIT	REMARKS
GBU-10	Mk 84	2,055 lb	MXU-600	Paveway I short wing
GBU-10A	Mk 84	2,062 lb	MXU-600A	Paveway I long wing
GBU-10C/D/E/F	Mk 84*	2,083 lb	MXU-651	Paveway II
GBU-12	Mk 82	614 lb	MXU-602	Paveway I short wing
GBU-12A	Mk 82	619 lb	MXU-602A	Paveway I long wing
GBU-12B/C/D	Mk 82*	611 lb	MXU-650	Paveway II
1,000-lb LGB	Mk 83	1,100 lb	MXU-641	Paveway I long wing
GBU-16A/B	Mk 83*	1,110 lb	MXU-667	Paveway II
LGB CCG	British	1,230 lb	No. 120	Paveway II (CPU-123)

* BLU-110 can be substituted for Mk 83, BLU-111 for Mk 82, and BLU-112 for Mk 84. These are the same bomb bodies with a new explosive filler.

Fuzing for LGBs depends on which Paveway version and warhead is being used:

PAVEWAY FUZE OPTIONS

FUZE	LOCATION	TYPE	REMARKS
M905/ATU-35	tail	short delay	Paveway I
FMU-26	nose or tail	short delay	Paveway I
MU-81	nose or tail	short delay	Paveway II
FMU-124	tail	impact	Paveway II
FMU-139	nose or tail	instantaneous/short delay	Paveway II
No. 947	tail	impact	LGB CCG only

Delivery of LGBs requires laser designation of the target. While ground-based designation is an option, it is an extremely problematical one requiring extensive coordination to

ensure the proper laser codes are used, and that the target is illuminated at the right time and direction. The preferred method is aerial designation from the delivery aircraft, if at all possible.

CLUSTER BOMBS

While structures and other 'hard' targets are best dealt with by classical bombs, area targets such as troop and armor

concentrations, truck parks and artillery batteries are more susceptible to cluster munitions. Cluster-bomb dispensers have 14-in (36-cm) suspension lug spacing and are employed by all tactical fighters. All work basically the same way: once released from the aircraft, the

dispenser shell breaks apart, scattering the bomblets.

All versions of ISC Technologies' **Mk 7** dispenser use the Mk 339 time-delay nose fuze, which is set before take-off and requires bomb release at a specific altitude and airspeed to produce

optimum bomblet dispersion. Mods (versions) prior to Mod 6 had a single yellow band, while Mod 6 and later have two yellow bands to indicate their thermal protective coating.

The **Mk 20 Rockeye II** is the most widely used version of the Mk 7

Unlike the USAF, the USN/USMC handle all their cluster bomb requirements with the Mk 7 dispenser.

dispenser. This anti-armor weapon, developed by the Naval Weapons Center (and adopted by the Air Force), first entered service in 1968 and was used extensively in both Vietnam and Iraq. Its shaped-charge bomblets look very much like throwing darts and are effective against both tanks and ships. This is the *only* cluster bomb to bear the title Rockeye II. The Mk 12 Rockeye I was a 1960s development program

which resulted in a 750-lb dispenser containing 96 anti-armor bomblets; it was not produced. Often mistakenly identified as Rockeye II, the USAF's CBU-87 combined effects munition (CEM) is a completely different cluster bomb.

The **CBU-59** anti-personnel, anti-material (**APAM**) munition is effective against concentrations of thin-skinned vehicles and personnel. It, too, uses the Mk 7 dispenser, and can be distinguished from other Mk 7 versions by stenciling on the side of the dispenser stating "Contents: (Live loaded) BLU-77/B."

The **CBU-78 'Gator'** uses the Mk 7 to deliver a combination of the same APAM mines used by the Air Force version of 'Gator', but in a different

dispenser. It can be identified by the word 'Gator' stenciled on the side of the dispenser. The BLU-91 deploys tripwires that detonate the mine when they are disturbed. The BLU-92 senses magnetic disturbances as a tank passes nearby and fires a self-forging warhead. Both mines eventually self destruct.

The **ISCB-1** is a proposed area denial cluster weapon based on the Mk 7

dispenser. In addition to 65 dummy mines, it would contain 160 fragmentation mines which can be electrically timed to explode from impact up to 24 hours later.

Mk 7 cluster bomb dispenser

CLUSTER BOMB SUMMARY

BOMB	DISPENSER	SUBMUNITIONS	TYPE	WEIGHT
Mk 20	Mk 7	247 Mk 118	Rockeye II anti-armor	511 lb
CBU-59	Mk 7	717 BLU-77	APAM	760 lb
CBU-78	Mk 7	26 BLU-91	anti-personnel mines plus	
		38 BLU-92	Gator anti-tank mines	
ISCB-1	Mk 7	160 BLU-??	fragmentation mines plus	
		65 BDU-??	dummy mines	

FUEL-AIR EXPLOSIVES

Fuel-Air Explosives (**FAE**) were developed for use against underground bunker complexes during Vietnam and saw limited use both then and in the Gulf War. Using as a kill mechanism three BLU-73 bomblets which explode with a force of about 10 atmospheric pressures, the FAE-1 family is also useful for clearing many types of minefields. This type of bomb was only used by Marine aircraft during the Gulf War. A follow-on program, called FAE-2, to develop the 500-lb BLU-95 and 2,000-lb BLU-96 unitary was cancelled prior to production.

All operational FAEs use the SUU-49 dispenser, a cylinder with a rounded

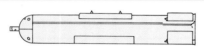

CBU-55 fuel-air explosive

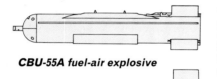

CBU-55A fuel-air explosive

CBU-72 FAE for high-speed carriage.

nose and a flat end-plate, which is jettisoned to allow the parachute-retarded bomblets to be ejected. Its four

fins are folded to the side of the dispenser for storage and handling, but are manually unfolded prior to flight. The original **CBU-55** used the SUU-49 with an FMU-83 dispenser fuze and was dropped from helicopters or low-performance aircraft (such as the AH-1 or OV-10). The **CBU-55A** is an improved version of the same weapon identifiable by the addition of an external hardback allowing it to be carried by higher-performance aircraft (such as the AV-8B). The **CBU-72** is a

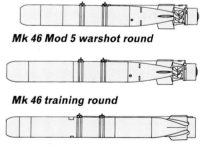

CBU-72s loaded on a wing MER of a USMC A-6 during Desert Storm.

CBU-55A equipped with the same Mk 339 fuze used by the Mk 7.

FAE BOMB SUMMARY

BOMB	DISPENSER	SUBMUNITIONS	TYPE	WEIGHT
CBU-55	SUU-49	3 BLU-73	FAE	512 lb
CBU-55A	SUU-49A	3 BLU-73	FAE with strongback	520 lb
CBU-72	SUU-49A	3 BLU-73	CBU-55A with Mk 339 fuze	522 lb

TORPEDOES

The Aerojet **Mk 46** is a deep-diving, high-speed, lightweight torpedo which features active/passive acoustic homing. Designed with modular construction to facilitate maintainability, it began development in 1960, entered service in 1965 and began replacing the earlier Mk 44 in 1967. The original **Mod 0** weighed about 570 lb and had a solid propellant motor. Maintenance problems led to the development of the liquid-powered **Mods 1** and **2**, which only weighed about 540 lb. All Mod 0s were converted to Mod 1 standard by 1975. Introduction of anechoic coatings on Soviet submarines led to the near-term improvement program (NearTIP), which resulted in the current **Mk 46 Mod 5**. In addition to new production, Mod 1s were modified to the Mod 5

standard. The Mk 46 has a speed of about 40 kt (46 mph; 73 km/h), uses a helical search pattern for target acquisition and is capable of multiple re-attacks if it misses the target. Over

A Mk 46 torpedo nestles alongside the fuselage of an SH-3.

6,000 have been built, with many having been exported. Equipped with a 100-lb warhead, the Mk 46 can be launched from surface ships as well as being carried internally by the P-3C and S-3A/B, and externally by the SH-2F and SH-3H.

The Honeywell **Mk 50 Barracuda** advanced lightweight torpedo (ALWT) was selected for development in 1981 over the rival Mk 51 to replace the Mk 46. Weighing 770 lb, it entered production in 1987. Compared to the Mk 46, it has greater speed, operating depth and endurance, as well as improved terminal homing. The latter is essential for use of its shaped-charge warhead. In addition to fast, deep submarines, Barracuda has good capability against slow, shallow

Mk 46 Mod 5 warshot round

Mk 46 training round

Mk 50 Barracuda warshot round

'boomers' and surface vessels. It is propelled by a chemical reaction which supplies a closed-cycle steam turbine. The Mk 50 can be launched from submarines and surface ships, as well as being carried internally by the P-3C and S-3A/B, and externally by the SH-2F and SH-3H.

UNDERWATER MINES AND DEPTH BOMBS

The Mk 36, Mk 40 and Mk 41 **Destructors** (**DST**s) are standard Mk 80 series GP bombs with Mk 75 DST acoustic/magnetic influence fuzing. Since they differ only in fuzing, they can be delivered by any aircraft that can drop

the basic bomb being used. Developed during the Vietnam War, they are intended primarily for use as shallow underwater mines against surface ships, but also have capabilities against overland targets. Although technically cleared for use with standard conical fins, given GP bombs' propensity for exploding when they hit the water at high speeds it is doubtful that they would ever be used with anything but

Snakeye-type fins. Although developed, the Mk 84-based Mk 41 does not appear to have been deployed.

The **Mk 52** is an air-delivered ground mine which introduced modular construction, allowing the firing assembly to be stored separately from the mine case. All versions contain a 625-lb (284-kg) warhead within a common 18.2-in × 70.2-in (47-cm × 178-cm) mine case. It is carried both

internally and externally by the P-3C and externally by the S-3A/B. The **Mk 54** is a 350-lb (160-kg) depth bomb which contains 250 lb (113 kg) of explosives. It can be carried both internally and externally by the P-3C and internally by the S-3A. The **Mk 55** is an air-delivered bottom mine. Although effective against surface ships, its primary use is as an anti-submarine weapon. It is carried externally by the

A-6E and S-3A/B and either internally or externally by the P-3C and HSAB-equipped B-52Gs. The **Mk 56** is an air-delivered moored mine designed for use

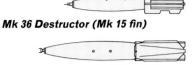

Mk 36 Destructor (Mk 15 fin)

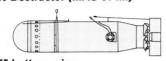

Mk 40 Destructor (MAU-91 fin)

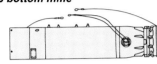

Mk 55 bottom mine

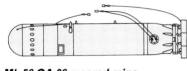

Mk 56 OA 05 moored mine

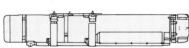

Mk 56 OA 06 moored mine

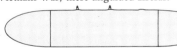

Mk 60 Captor torpedo mine

against either surface ships or submarines. It is carried externally by the A-6E and S-3A/B and either internally or externally by the P-3C and HSAB-equipped B-52Gs. The **Mk 57** depth bomb is another term for the B57 nuclear bomb. It was carried internally by the P-3C and S-3A/B until the change in US policy in September 1991.

The Loral **Mk 60 Captor** is a mine casing which contains a Mk 46 torpedo. Used as an anti-submarine weapon, its detection and control unit (DCU) is capable of discriminating between

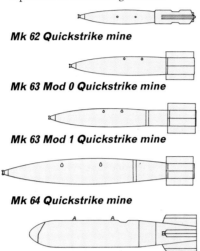

Mk 62 Quickstrike mine

Mk 63 Mod 0 Quickstrike mine

Mk 63 Mod 1 Quickstrike mine

Mk 64 Quickstrike mine

Mk 65 Quickstrike mine

surface ships and submarines, but not between friendly and enemy submarines. Deployed by ships, submarines or aircraft, it initially operates in a passive mode, listening for submarines. Once a target is detected and judged to be within 3,280 ft (1000 m), Captor will shift to an active mode, determining the optimum time to release the torpedo. It has been operational since 1979, and can be carried externally by the A-6E, P-3C and S-3A/B and either internally or

externally by HSAB-equipped B-52Gs.

The **Quickstrike** mine family is parachute-retarded (except for the Mk 62 which uses the Snakeye fin), influence-fuzed bottom mines. This type is useful to depths of about 300 ft (90 m), but require the target to be relatively close to function. Successors to the Destructors, and carried by the same aircraft, their name comes from the short amount of time needed for assembly.

UNDERWATER MINES

MINE	WARHEAD	WEIGHT	FIN KIT	REMARKS
Mk 36	Mk 82	560 lb	Mk 15	acoustic/magnetic, 300 ft
Mk 40	Mk 83	1,060 lb	MAU-91	acoustic/magnetic, 300 ft
Mk 41	Mk 84	2,000 lb	unknown	acoustic/magnetic, 300 ft
Mk 52 Mod 1		1,130 lb	n/a	acoustic
Mod 2		1,170 lb	n/a	magnetic
Mod 3		1,190 lb	n/a	pressure/magnetic
Mod 5		1,200 lb	n/a	acoustic/magnetic
Mod 6		1,235 lb	n/a	pressure/acoustic/magnetic
Mk 53		500 lb		
Mk 55 Mod 2		2,160 lb	n/a	magnetic, 600 ft
Mod 3		2,180 lb	n/a	pressure/magnetic, 150 ft
Mod 5		2,180 lb	n/a	acoustic/magnetic, 150 ft
Mod 6		2,190 lb	n/a	pressure/acoustic/magnetic, 150 ft
Mod 7		2,190 lb	n/a	dual-channel magnetic, 600 ft
Mk 56 OA 05		2,150 lb	n/a	dual-channel magnetic, 1,200 ft
OA 06		2,215 lb	n/a	faired nose
Mk 60	Mk 46	2,360 lb	n/a	Captor anti-submarine torpedo
Mk 62	Mk 82	580 lb	Mk 15	Quickstrike, 300 ft
Mk 63 Mod 0	Mk 83	1,020 lb	EX 9	Quickstrike, 300 ft
Mod 1	Mk 83	1,080 lb	EX 126/9	Quickstrike, 300 ft
Mk 64 OA 1/2	Mk 84	2,130 lb	EX 127/9	Quickstrike, 300 ft
OA 3	Mk 84	2,145 lb	EX 128/9	Quickstrike, 300 ft
Mk 65		2,360 lb	EX 7	Quickstrike, 300 ft

2.75-in UNGUIDED ROCKETS

Developed under the 'Mighty Mouse' program and widely used during the Vietnam War, these unguided aircraft

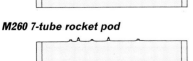

LAU-3/60 19-tube rocket pod

LAU-61 19-tube rocket pod

LAU-69 19-tube rocket pod

LAU-68/131 7-tube rocket pod

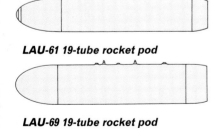

M260 7-tube rocket pod

M261 19-tube rocket pod

rockets are used mainly by helicopters in today's US Navy and Marine Corps. There are three types of 2.75-in (70-mm) rocket motors, 20 warheads and numerous rocket pods which have been used over the years. The older **Mk 4** (high speed) and **Mk 40** (low speed) **FFAR** motors are 39.4 in (100 cm) long and weigh 11.4 lb (5 kg). The Mk 40 differs in its nozzle design, which spin-stabilizes the rocket when launched from low speed platforms (i.e. helicopters and propeller-driven aircraft). The modern **Mk 66 WAFAR** motors form the basis of the **Hydra 70** family and are 41.7 in (106 cm) long and weigh 13.6 lb (6 kg). WAFARs create less smoke, and have about 40 per cent more range than FFARs because the fin configuration allows carriage of more propellant in the same overall motor length.

Warhead types include: high-explosive (HE); high-explosive anti-tank (HEAT) with a shaped charge; target practice (TP) and warhead training units (WTU); high explosive fragmentation (HE Frag), sometimes called pearlite malleable iron (PMI); white phosphorus (WP) for target marking; red phosphorus (RP) for creating smoke screens; flechette with hundreds of anti-personnel darts; multi-purpose submunition (MPSM) with nine shaped-charge bomblets; flare, which provides 1 million candlepower for two minutes; and a developmental kinetic energy warhead with 14 mini-rockets which deploy from the main warhead. Combat warheads are olive drab with yellow nose bands, WP and smoke are green with white letters, and

TP heads are blue with white lettering.

While most older warheads used impact-type fuzes (except for the WDU-4, with a built-in fuze which sensed deceleration before firing its flechettes), many newer ones are more sophisticated. Newer fuzes use proximity, selectable delay penetration, and motor burnout to determine when to function and are often integral with the warhead.

Rocket pods are made of treated paper with a thin aluminum outer skin. They have optional paper front fairings which shatter upon rocket impact. While some older pods used paper aft fairings which shattered to form a

funnel, protecting the underside of the launching aircraft's wing from rocket debris, many now have metal funnels – if they bother with such niceties at all. All of the pods are retained by the aircraft, most having at least some reusable components. All use 14 in (36-cm) suspension lug spacing.

There have been numerous launcher units (**LAU**) over the years, varying little in external appearance. Loaded 19-tube launchers weigh about 500 lb (227 kg), and have included (current pods underlined) the LAU-3, -50, -51, -60, -61, -69, -91, -94 and -130, as well as the Army's M159,

2.75-in WARHEAD/ROCKET COMBINATIONS

WARHEAD	TYPE	WARHEAD length	WARHEAD weight	WAFARs length	WAFARs weight	REMARKS
Mk 1	HE	6.0 in	5.8 lb	50.8 in	20.0 lb	1a, 2a/b/d/e/f/g
Mk 5	HEAT	6.5 in	5.8 lb	50.3 in	20.2 lb	2c
Mk 61	TP (Mk 1)	8.1 in	6.5 lb	49.8 in	20.1 lb	3a
Mk 64	HE Frag	10.5 in	8.6 lb	55.3 in	22.8 lb	1a, 2d/e/f/g
Mk 67	WP	10.5 in	4.5 lb	55.3 in	18.7 lb	1a, 2d/e/f/g
* M151	HE Frag	10.5 in	8.6 lb	55.3 in	22.8 lb	1a, 2d/e/f/g/h/i/j
M156	WP	10.5 in	10.4 lb	55.3 in	24.6 lb	1a, 2d/e/f/g
M229	HE	23.2 in	15.9 lb	67.7 in	30.1 lb	1a, 2f/g (Mk 40 only)
M230	TP (M151)	10.5 in	8.7 lb	55.3 in	22.9 lb	2k, 3b
* M255	Flechette	26.2 in	12.5 lb	71.0 in	26.1 lb	2l/o 585 or 1,200 flechettes
* M261	MPSM	26.2 in	13.5 lb	71.0 in	27.1 lb	integral fuze
* M262	Flare	26.2 in	10.8 lb	71.0 in	24.4 lb	2l/m/n
* M264	Smoke	26.2 in	8.8 lb	71.0 in	22.4 lb	2l/m/n
* M267	TP (M261)	26.2 in	13.5 lb	71.0 in	27.1 lb	2l/m/n
* M274	TP (M151)	11.7 in	9.3 lb	55.3 in	24.4 lb	flash, bang, smoke
MXXX	Shot Rkt					2i
WDU-4	Flechette	15.5 in	9.1 lb	57.2 in	22.7 lb	2,200 flechettes
WTU-1	TP (M151)	13.6 in	9.4 lb	55.3 in	23.0 lb	3c
WTU-10	TP (Mk 1)	10.5 in	10.1 lb	52.2 in	23.7 lb	3d
WTU-14	TP (Mk 1)	11.9 in	10.1 lb	53.6 in	23.7 lb	3e

* = in production

XM200 and M261 (different than the warhead). Loaded seven-tube launchers weigh about 250 lb (113 kg) and have included (current pods underlined) the LAU-32, -49, -54, -56, -59, -68, -90 and -131, as well as the Army's XM157, M158 and M260.

The chart matches fuzes, warheads and motors. Fuze and warhead lengths are exposed lengths and do not include the screw-in connections. Warhead details do not include the fuze unless specifically stated. WAFAR details are for the fuze specified in the remarks. For an older FFAR, subtract 2.3 in (6 cm) and 2.2 lb (1 kg).

Remarks:
1a) Lengths and weights computed for M427 fuze.

1b) Lengths and weights computed for Mk 176 fuze.
2a) Mk 176 fuze extends 2.1 in (5.3 cm) from the warhead and has a slight delay between impact and detonation. It weighs 0.7 lb (0.32 kg).
2b) Mk 178 is physically identical to the Mk 176, but explodes on impact.
2c) Mk 181 fuze extends 2.1 in (5.3 cm) from the warhead and explodes on impact. It weighs 0.8 lb (0.36 kg).
2d) Mk 352 fuze extends 2.2 in (5.6 cm) from the warhead and explodes on impact. It weighs 0.4 lb (0.18 kg).
2e) FMU-90 is physically identical to the Mk 352, but has a slight delay between impact and detonation.
2f) M423 fuze is used with helicopters. It extends 3.1 in (7.9 cm) from the warhead and explodes on impact. It weighs 0.6 lb (0.27 kg) and is only

used with the Mk 40 FFAR motor.
2g) M427 fuze is used with fixed-wing aircraft. Identical to the M423 in appearance and function, but it can also be used with the Mk 4 FFAR motor.
2h) M429 fuze extends 5 in (13 cm) from the warhead and is a proximity (VT) fuze. It weighs 0.9 lb (0.4 kg) and is only used with the Mk 40 FFAR motor and the M151 warhead.
2i) M432 is a remote set airburst (proximity) fuze.
2j) M433 is a selectable delay penetration fuze.
2k) M435 is an inert M423/M427 fuze.
2l) M439 is an integral remote set (proximity) fuze.
2m) M442 is an integral motor burnout fuze.

2n) M446 is an integral motor burnout fuze.
2o) M466 is an integral motor burnout fuze.
3a) Mk 61 is an inert, cast shape simulating the Mk 1 warhead with a Mk 176 fuze.
3b) M230 is an inert, cast shape simulating the M151 warhead. It is used with the M435 inert fuze.
3c) WTU-1 is an inert, cast shape simulating the M151 warhead with a M423 fuze.
3d) WTU-10 dummy warhead is a Mk 1 casing with a cylindrical, inert plug inserted in it, increasing length by 4.5 in (11.4 cm).
3e) WTU-14 dummy warhead is a Mk 1 casing with a streamlined, inert plug inserted in it, increasing length by 5.9 in (15 cm).

5-in ZUNI UNGUIDED ROCKETS

Widely used during the Vietnam War by both the Navy and Marines, Zuni unguided rockets with WP and HE warheads were used during the Gulf War for target marking by Marines F/A-18D and OV-10 FACs.

There are three types of 5-in (13-cm) rocket motors, nine warheads and two types of rocket pods. The older **Mk 16 FFAR** motors are 76.3 in (194 cm) long and weigh about 65 lb (30 kg). The **Mk 71 Mod 0 WAFAR** motors are 69.7 in (177 cm) long and weigh about 68 lb (31 kg), while the **Mk 71 Mod 1s** are 76.4 in long and weigh about 80 lb (36 kg). The Mod 0 WAFARs use the same basic rocket motor, but are shorter because of their fin configuration; the Mod 1s use this more efficient design feature to increase the amount of propellant in the same motor length as that of the FFAR.

Warheads include the GP, ATAP, practice – sometimes called warhead training unit (WTU) – high explosive fragmentation (HE Frag), flare for target illumination, and smoke for target marking and incendiary missions.

LAU-10 4-tube rocket pod

Combat warheads are olive drab with yellow nose-bands, Smoke are green with white lettering, and practice heads are blue with white lettering. All warheads use impact fuzes except for the flare head, which uses an integral mechanical time delay fuze.

The reusable **LAU-10** rocket pods are made of treated paper with a thin aluminum outer skin. They also have optional (and seldom used) paper front and rear fairings which are interchangeable and shatter upon rocket impact. When used, the aft fairing forms a funnel which protects the underside of the launching aircraft's wing from debris during rocket firing. All versions use 14-in (36-cm) suspension lug spacing and hold four Zuni rockets. The basic pod is 94.9 in (241 cm) long; with fairings this increases to 128.9 in (327 cm). A longer version of the **LAU-10D** has been proposed; sometimes referred to as

During Desert Storm, fast FAC USMC F/A-18Ds used Zuni rockets for marking targets.

LAU-97, it would be 115 in (292 cm) long without fairings and 144.5 in (367 cm) with them. There is no indication that the **LAU-97**, which would enclose the entire length of any 5-in warhead/rocket combination, has entered production. Loaded LAU-10s weigh 650 lb (295 kg), while LAU-97s would be 100 lb (45 kg) heavier.

The chart matches fuzes, warheads and motors. Fuze and warhead lengths

are exposed lengths and do not include the screw-in connections. Warhead details do not include the fuze unless specifically stated. FFAR details are for the complete round with the fuze specified in the remarks. For Mk 71 Mod 0, subtract 6.6 in (16.7 cm) and add 3.0 lb (1.36 kg); for Mk 71 Mod 1 add 0.1 in (0.25 cm) and 15.0 lb (6.8 kg). Source data is very inconsistent – all weights and lengths approximate.

5-in WARHEAD/ROCKET COMBINATIONS

WARHEAD	TYPE	WARHEAD length	weight	Mk 16 FFARs length	weight	REMARKS
Mk 6	Practice	16.0 in	47.1 lb	96.2 in	113.1 lb	1a, 2f/g, 3a
Mk 24/0	GP	16.0 in	44.1 lb	96.1 in	109.5 lb	1b, 2a/b/c/d/f/g
Mk 24/1	GP	15.9 in	45.0 lb	96.0 in	110.4 lb	1b, 2a/b/c/d/f/g
Mk 32	AT/APers	24.0 in	43.3 lb	102.6 in	108.7 lb	1c, 2b/c/d
Mk 33	Flare	33.0 in	45.9 lb	109.3 in	110.9 lb	
Mk 34	Smoke	33.5 in	50.9 lb	112.1 in	116.3 lb	1d, 2b/c/d
Mk 34	Incendiary	32.9 in	50.9 lb	115.4 in	118.5 lb	1e, 2a
Mk 62	Practice	18.8 in	46.8 lb	95.1 in	111.8 lb	3b
M 63	HE Frag	28.2 in	56.4 lb	110.7 in	124.0 lb	1f, 2a/b/c/d/e
WTU-11	Practice	28.7 in	56.4 lb	111.2 in	124.0 lb	1f, 2a/e, 3c

Remarks:
1a) Lengths and weights computed for ogive nose.
1b) Lengths and weights computed for Mk 352 fuze with BBU-15 adapter and 1.5-in (3.8-cm) fuze adapter collar, also used with FMU-90 and Mk 188.
1c) Lengths and weights computed for Mk 352 fuze with BBU-15 adapter.
1d) Lengths and weights computed for Mk 352 fuze with BBU-15 adapter and 2.9-in (7.4-cm) fuze adapter collar.
1e) Lengths and weights computed for Mk 93 nose and 2.3-in (5.8-cm) fuze adapter collar.
1f) Lengths and weights computed for Mk 93 nose.
2a) Mk 93 ogive nose extends 6.2 in (15.7 cm) from the warhead and weighs 2.6 lb (1.2 kg). Used to penetrate targets, it depends on the integral M191 fuze at the back of the warhead for detonation.
2b) Mk 188 fuze extends 2.5 in (6.4 cm)

from the warhead and explodes on impact. It weighs 0.8 lb (0.4 kg).
2c) Mk 352 fuze with the BBU-15 adapter extends 2.3 in (5.8 cm) from the warhead and explodes on impact. It weighs 0.4 lb (0.2 kg).
2d) FMU-90 fuze with the BBU-15 adapter is physically identical to the Mk 352/BBU-15, but has a slight delay between impact and detonation.
2e) M414 is identical to the Mk 93 in appearance and function.
2f) Ogive nose extends 3.9 in (10.0 cm) from the warhead and weighs about 1.0 lb (0.45 kg).
2g) Plug nose extends about 2.0 in (5 cm) from the warhead and weighs about 0.2 lb (0.1 kg).
3a) Mk 6 is a cement-filled inert version of the Mk 24 warhead.
3b) Mk 62 is an inert, cast shape simulating the Mk 24 warhead with an ogive nose.
3c) WTU-11 is a cement-filled inert version of the Mk 63 warhead.

NUCLEAR BOMBS

All US nuclear weapons are thermonuclear (i.e. hydrogen bombs). Delivery options are dependent on the

bomb/aircraft combination and the type of target destruction required. All bombs incorporate parachutes which

can be used to assist in level weapon delivery (and aircraft escape!). With the relatively recent retirement of the older

B43s, the following table presents the currently active aircraft-delivered gravity weapons. While there may be several variants to a given weapon, only the basic designations are presented here. (The term 'Mk' is sometimes seen instead of 'B'.) In line with a change in US policy announced in September 1991, all tactical nuclear weapons were removed from US Navy ships. No one is happier about that than the crews who were charged with their care and delivery.

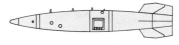

B57 nuclear bomb or depth charge

B61 tactical nuclear weapon

The **B57** was designed as a nuclear depth charge, but was later adopted for use as a low-yield tactical nuclear weapon. Nicknamed the 'Dr Pepper' bomb (after the American soft drink), its delivery options include laydown, and toss (sometimes called loft) with either air or surface burst.

The **B61**, in addition to its strategic use, is the most commonly used weapon by tactical fighters and is nicknamed the 'Silver Bullet' because of its shape and color. Delivery options include free-fall or retarded airburst, laydown, and toss (with either air or surface burst).

USN NUCLEAR BOMBS

BOMB	WEIGHT	YIELD	INVENTORY	SHAPE	USE
B57	500 lb	5-20 kt	about 1,000	BDU-12	tactical and maritime
B61	710 lb	10-500 kt	over 3,000	BDU-38	tactical and strategic

TRAINING WEAPONS AND OTHER STORES

Dropping and firing live weapons is something done infrequently during training. Most of the time training ordnance is used. For missiles this means rounds with working seekers but no rocket motors, warheads or guidance sections. Where a live missile would display black (guidance), yellow (warhead), or brown (rocket motor) bands, training rounds display either blue bands or paint the entire section blue.

The designation of air-to-ground training missiles is **ATM** rather than AGM. Air-to-air missiles are normally referred to as 'captive', for instance, AIM-9L-**CAP**. Full-scale training bombs are normally referred to as 'inert Mk 82' rather than the formal title of bomb, dummy unit (**BDU**) -50. There

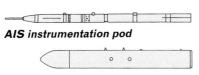

AIS instrumentation pod

SUU-44 flare dispenser

are also **inert Mk 83s** and **inert Mk 84s**, but without a BDU designation. These bombs are usually painted overall blue and are filled with concrete instead of explosives.

The most commonly carried training bombs are referred to as 'blue bombs' and 'beer cans.' The 'blue bombs' are a streamlined 25-lb (11-kg) bomb called **Mk 76**. It simulates the ballistics of a Mk 82 SE. **Mk 106** 'beer cans' are painted Dayglo orange, weigh 10 lb (4.5 kg) and are shaped like a beer can with fins. Its ballistics most closely resemble a retarded nuclear weapon. Both of these bombs can be mounted on specially modified multiple or triple

ejector racks (MERs or TERs).

The air instrumentation pods (**AIS**) are used as part of the air combat maneuvering instrumentation (**ACMI**) and related systems. These systems allow real-time and post-mission evaluation of exercises. ACMI allows the battle to be viewed from any angle, even from the 'cockpits' of opposing aircraft. It also evaluates surface-to-air and air-to-air engagements and recently has begun to include bombing accuracy. AIS pods resemble unfinned Sidewinder missiles with pitot tubes and are mounted to AIM-9 launchers. There are several versions, including the airborne, special type (**ASQ**) **T-11**, **-13**, **-17**, **-20**, **-21** and **-25**. Except for the T-11, which has a ram air scoop on its side, all pod differences are internal.

The **D-704** is a buddy refueling store. Resembling a 300-US gal (1136-liter) fuel tank, it can be carried by the A-6E (on the centerline) and S-3A/B (under the left wing).

The **SUU-25** was a LAU-10 5-in (12.7-cm) rocket pod modified to dispense flares and sonobuoys. It weighed about 500 lb (227 kg) when loaded and carried eight Mk 24, 45 or LUU-2 flares or various sonobuoys. The flares all burned at 2 million candlepower and lasted 3, 3.5 and 5 minutes respectively. The **SUU-40** was similar to the SUU-25, but only weighed about 350 lb (159 kg) when loaded. The **SUU-44** is a purpose-built flare dispenser, similar to the SUU-40; however, the only store it presently dispenses is the Mk 45 flare. It can be carried externally by the A-6E, AH-1T/W, P-3C, S-3A/B and OV-10A/D.

D-704 buddy refueling pod

ELECTRONIC COUNTER-MEASURES (ECM) PODS

Over the years the Navy has generally preferred internal ECM systems. Presently, aside from the ALQ-99 pods carried by the EA-6B, only two pods, the **ALQ-164** and **ALQ-167**, are in use. On AV-8Bs, the ALQ-164 is

carried on the centerline. The ALQ-167 is carried on the front-right Phoenix pylon of F-14s, and on the right inboard wing pylon of the A-6E. These pods use deception techniques to make radars report that the aircraft is in a

slightly different location than where it actually is, causing radar-guided SAMs to detonate just far enough away from their target to allow the aircraft to escape.

GUNS

The US Army-designed **M60** 7.62-mm machine gun uses a disintegrating link feed system and is gas-operated. It fires 600 rpm with a muzzle velocity of 2,800 fps (853 m/s) and a maximum range of 3,500 ft (1070 m). Four of the 25-lb (11-kg) M60s are used in the OV-10, while two are used with the HH-60H.

The General Electric **M61 Vulcan** 20-mm, six-barrelled Gatling gun was developed in the 1950s. It uses a linkless feed system and is externally powered from the aircraft's hydraulic or electrical system. A self-powered variation, the aircrft gun unit (**GAU**)-4, is virtually identical except for being driven by gun gas. Both fire at up to 6,000 rpm with a muzzle velocity of 3,400 fps (1040 m/s). At maximum rate of fire, prolonged bursts can generate nearly 4,000 lb (1810 kg) of reverse thrust! Active Naval aircraft equipped with the 265-lb (120-kg) M61 include the F-14 and F/A-18 (GAU-11).

The General Electric **M197** 20-mm, three-barrelled Gatling gun weighs 145 lb (66 kg) and is used by both the

SUU-11 7.62-mm six-barrelled gun pod

GPU-2 20-mm three-barrelled cannon pod

AH-1J/T/W in its GTK4A universal nose turret, and the OV-10D in its very similar underfuselage turret. The AH-1 turret has a capacity of 750 rounds, uses an integrated feed system and is powered by the helicopter's electrical system, while the OV-10D turret has a capacity of 1,500 rounds. While the gun is capable of firing at up to 3,000 rpm, it fires at either 750 or 1,500 rpm in the OV-10D and 675 rpm in the AH-1. The muzzle velocity is 3,400 fps (1040 m/s).

The General Electric **GAU-2** 7.62-mm six-barrelled Gatling gun is a scaled-down version of the M61 and weighs 67 lb (31 kg). It uses either linkless or belted feed systems and is externally powered from the aircraft's electrical system. It fires up to 6,000 rpm with a muzzle velocity of 2,850 fps

(870 m/s). The GAU-2 forms the basis for the 325-lb (147-kg) **SUU-11** gun pod (sometimes identified by its Army designation **M18**) used by the AH-1J/T/W and OV-10.

The General Electric **GAU-12 Equaliser** 25-mm five-barrelled Gatling gun was developed from the M61 for use with the AV-8B. It uses a linkless feed system from the 300-round magazine in the Harrier's right fuselage pod to the 275-lb (125-kg) gun in the left pod, which is powered from engine bleed air. It fires up to 4,200 rpm, but normally 3,600 rpm, with a muzzle velocity of 3,600 fps (1100 m/s).

The General Electric **GPU-2 Lightweight Gun Pod** uses the M197 gun system and is used by both the AH-1J/T/W and the OV-10. It uses a linkless feed system and is powered by an internal battery capable of firing three 300-round loads without recharge, firing at either 750 or

1,500 rpm. The muzzle velocity is 3,400 fps (1040 m/s).

The McDonnell Douglas **Mk 11** 20-mm cannon was produced for the Navy between 1965 and 1967 for use with the **Mk 4** gun pod. The gun weighed 240 lb (110 kg), while the pod, with 750 rounds of ammunition, weighed 1,390 lb (630 kg). An 'over and under' two-barrelled weapon, ammunition was fed from both sides into an eight-chamber revolving cylinder and fired simultaneously from both barrels at rates of 700 or 4,200 rpm. The only aircraft still in service which might use this weapon is the OV-10.

A new airborne weapon developed from the widespread Vulcan is the GAU-12 Equaliser, a five-barrelled cannon of 25-mm caliber. It is carried externally by the AV-8B.

AIM-7 SPARROW

AIM-7F/M/P Sparrow MRAAM

The Raytheon air intercept missile (**AIM**) **-7 Sparrow** is a 500-lb (227-kg) class, medium-range missile which began as the AAM-N-6 Sparrow III in 1951. Production began in 1951, and it first intercepted a target in December 1953. Early versions were developed to shoot down non-maneuvering targets. When the Vietnam War came, experience proved the **AIM-7E** to be virtually useless against maneuvering, fighter-sized targets, especially at low level. The **AIM-7E-2** 'dogfight' modification, identifiable by the 'L' markings on its wings, was introduced in 1969 to answer these shortcomings. This missile served as the jumping-off

point for both the British Sky Flash and Italian Aspide missiles. Further refinements resulted in the **AIM-7E-3**, **-4** and **-6**, which are no longer operational.

Up to this point, the configuration of AIM-7s had been guidance and control section, wing, warhead and rocket motor. With the advent of the **AIM-7F**, avionics improvements enabled the high explosive, blast-fragmentation warhead to be moved in front of the wing, allowing the rocket

motor to be enlarged and thus improving range. This virtually new missile introduced a Doppler seeker and improved virtually all other components to make it more capable against maneuvering, low-altitude targets. The current front-line version is the **AIM-7M**, which has a monopulse

Hornets and Tomcats carry the Sparrow, used for medium-range BVR engagements.

seeker and numerous other evolutionary improvements to increase reliability and decrease cost.

AIM-9 SIDEWINDER

Development of the 200-lb (90-kg) class Sidewinder missile family began in 1951 at the Naval Ordnance Test Station (NOTS). Forty years and nearly 30 versions later, it is by far the most successful and deadly air-to-air missile in the world, copied by friend and foe

alike. Produced mainly by Ford Aerospace and Raytheon, the **AIM-9** has evolved from a missile which could only be launched at close range from directly behind a non-maneuvering target, to an all-aspect weapon with up to five times the range of the original. It

An AIM-9 launches from an F/A-18A. The Sidewinder is the West's standard short-range IR-homing missile.

has also served as the basis for the MIM-72 Chaparral and AGM-122 Sidearm. Beginning as a Navy missile adopted by the Air Force, requirements soon drove the two services along separate development paths. This persisted throughout the Vietnam War, until costs forced common development of the AIM-9L and subsequent versions. The **AIM-9L/M** is standard armament on all Navy tactical fighters.

Modification of the original **Aero 3B**

AIM-9L/M/R Sidewinder SRAAM

launcher rails to accept the AIM-9L/M/R missiles resulted in the **LAU-105**, while the newest launcher for Sidewinders is the **LAU-114**.

The following list defines just the versions of the AIM-9 family currently active with the Navy and Marines.

AIM-9 SIDEWINDER VARIANTS

VERSION	REMARKS
AIM-9L	About 16,000 built for USN and USAF, 3,500 for Europe. Swedish designation Rb 74.
	25.5 in (65 cm) long AN/DSQ-29 GCS has an indium-antimony (InSb) seeker which gives it an all-aspect capability. BSU-32/B 22-in (56-cm) span 'pointy' fins.
	USAF versions are argon-cooled from a bottle contained in the missile, while USN versions are nitrogen-cooled from a launcher rail bottle.
	6.5 in DSU-15/B active optical target detector (AOTD).
	11.5 in (29 cm) long WDU-17 annular blast-fragmentation (**ABF**) warhead.
	71 in (180 cm) long Mk 36 rocket motor with Mk 1 wings.
AIM-9M	Originally AIM-9L product improvement program (**PIP**). Over 7,000 built.
	Modified with closed cycle cooling, infra-red countermeasures (**IRCM**) and background discrimination.
	Reduced-smoke version of Mk 36 rocket motor.
AIM-9R	AIM-9M with imaging infra-red (**IIR**) GCS which does not require refrigeration

AGM-45 SHRIKE

The air-to-ground missile (**AGM**) **-45** was developed by the Navy during the Vietnam War as the first anti-radiation missile (**ARM**). The original **AGM-45A** had a single-burn motor and became operational in 1965. The

AGM-45B introduced a dual-burn motor, with the initial acceleration thrust followed by a second, sustaining thrust. Altogether, 12 guidance, eight warhead, three control and seven motor sections were developed by the time production of over 13,000 Shrikes ceased in 1978. All versions maintained

the same external configuration, and six guidance sections remain operational. The 400-lb (180-kg) class AGM-45 can be launched from either the **LAU-34** or the newer **LAU-118**, which can also be used to launch the AGM-88. The Shrike in USN/USMC service can be carried by the A-6E and F/A-18.

AGM-45 Shrike ARM

AIM-54 PHOENIX

The Hughes **Phoenix** program began in 1960 as the AAM-N-11. It was actually the result of combining two earlier Hughes efforts: the Navy AAM-N-10 Eagle, which was to have armed the Douglas F6D Missileer; and the Air Force GAR-9, which was first developed for the North American F-108 Rapier and then tested with the Lockheed YF-12A as the AIM-47. Phoenix began flight testing in 1965 and was originally intended for use with the F-111B, which was cancelled in 1967.

With its name now supremely appropriate, the **AIM-54A** finally

entered service in 1973 with the F-14A, the only aircraft to carry it. The key operational features of Phoenix were defined by the Cold War mission of fleet air defense against attacks by Soviet cruise missiles. These features

A test AIM-54C carried by VX-4's black Tomcat, 'Vandy One'.

were its 72.5-nm (83-mile; 135-km) range, 132-lb (60-kg) continuous-rod warhead, and active terminal radar seeker, which gave the launching aircraft a simultaneous multiple-target kill capability. While each F-14 could carry up to six of these weapons, in practice the maximum load was usually two, carried on the forward fuselage station's LAU-93s. This was because each missile weighed 983 lb (446 kg), making recovery with a load of six back aboard a carrier very difficult in some instances. At a cost of over $1 million each, jettisoning them to land is something no one wanted to explain. By the time production ended, in 1981, 2,566 had been built. Alterations to some of the 484 Phoenix supplied to its only export customer, Iran, led to modifications to the AIM-54A, acceleration of the AIM-54C program, and development of the MiG-31's primary armament – the AA-9 'Amos',

which the Russians call 'Phoenix'.

The **AIM-54B** differed from the AIM-54A only in that it featured simplified construction techniques. It entered production in late 1977 and is included in the AIM-54A production numbers.

The 1,025-lb (465-kg) **AIM-54C** entered production in 1982 and service in 1985. It featured a digital guidance

section and solid-state radar to improve both performance and reliability. Its range was increased to 80 nm (92 miles; 148 km), ECCM features improved and a new proximity fuze incorporated. Unlike the original fuze, which had four externally visible target detecting devices (TDDs), the AIM-54C had eight TDDs hidden beneath its skin.

With the end of the Cold War and

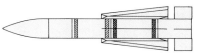

AIM-54C Phoenix long-range AAM

plummeting defense budgets, the proposed replacement for Phoenix, the advanced air-to-air missile (AAAM), was cancelled in early 1992.

AGM-62 WALLEYE

Walleye is an unpowered guided missile developed for the Navy beginning in 1962. Although it has been allocated the designation AGM-62, it is usually referred to as 'Walleye'. There are numerous Marks and Mods of the four basic Walleye versions, denoting various internal differences.

Over 4,500 **Walleye I**s were produced between 1966 and 1970 by Martin Marietta. Equipped with a TV seeker which required lock-on before launch (LOBL), it had an 845-lb (383-kg) linear shaped-charge warhead. Built by Martin, the 1,120-lb (508-kg) missile entered service in 1967 and was used in combat during the Vietnam War by Navy A-4Fs, A-6Es and A-7Es. It also saw limited use by Air Force F-4D/Es and was exported to Israel. (A one-kiloton yield W72 nuclear warhead was fitted to the Walleye I Mk 5 for the USAF. A total of 300 W72s was produced between 1970 and 1972; they were retired in 1979.)

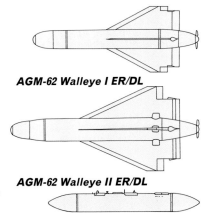

AGM-62 Walleye I ER/DL

AGM-62 Walleye II ER/DL

AWW-7/9 datalink pod

Walleye I ER/DL resulted from a Navy requirement for increased stand-off range. One thousand four hundred of the extended-range/datalink (ER/DL) versions were converted from Walleye Is beginning in late 1972. The 1,200-lb (544-kg) missiles featured

larger wings and incorporated a lock-on after launch (LOAL) capability which used the 168-lb (76-kg) airborne armament fire-control (**AWG**) -16 datalink pod. Although the missile could be guided by the launching aircraft, usually a different aircraft would carry the datalink pod and provide guidance.

Walleye II featured a 2,060-lb (934-kg) linear shaped-charge warhead. Initially known as 'Fat Albert', 529 of the 2,455-lb (1114-kg) missiles were built for the Navy by Hughes, and an additional 1,481 were converted from Walleye Is. 'Conversion' is perhaps too mild a term, the only external similarity being the nose section.

Walleye II ER/DL was developed towards the end of the Vietnam War, with three being used in combat. Weighing 2,490 lb (1130 kg), a total of 2,400 was converted from earlier versions for the Navy. While externally similar to the Walleye II, they had larger wings. Also, the AWG-16 was superseded by the 645-lb (292-kg)

airborne armament remote control (**AWW**) -7 and the externally identical, 690-lb (313-kg) **AWW-9** Walleye datalink pods. In 1977, Hughes was given a contract to develop an imaging infra-red (**IIR**) seeker head which is now used by the AGM-62, AGM-65, GBU-15 and AGM-130.

A total of 131 Walleyes was expended by carrier-based aircraft, primarily A-7Es, during Desert Storm. Most, but not all, were Walleye II ER/DLs.

A Walleye II ER/DL in flight. The missile is usually controlled from a different aircraft.

AGM-65 MAVERICK

Developed during the Vietnam War as a subsonic, launch-and-leave replacement for the AGM-12 Bullpup, the Hughes Maverick has evolved over the years and remains in production. While all the same size, AGM-65s utilize a variety of guidance and warhead sections. The original 125-lb (57-kg) high-explosive, shaped-charge warheads have been replaced in later AGM-65s by 300-lb (136-kg) blast-penetration warheads. All versions use the same rocket motor, with maximum launch range dependent on target size and seeker performance. While maximum aerodynamic range is about 12.5 nm (14 miles; 23 km), a more realistic range is nearer 8 nm (9 miles; 15 km). Mavericks are used by the A-6E, AV-8B and F/A-18; however, during the Gulf War, over 90 per cent of the AGM-65s fired were from A-10s. Maverick is a very workload-intensive weapon which pilots of faster aircraft, such as the F/A-18, found very difficult to employ in combat. Launchers include the three-rail **LAU-88** (for A, B and D versions) and single-rail **LAU-117** (which can be used with any version).

AGM-65A has an electro-optical (television) seeker which the pilot uses to acquire the target. After designating the target and ensuring the missile is locked-on, he fires it and can either select another target or commence escape maneuvers. The **AGM-65B** has the advantage of 'scene magnification',

which enables it to be locked-on to the same target as an AGM-65A from twice the range. Both missiles are white, with clear seeker domes. The AGM-65B has 'SCENE MAG' stenciled on its side.

AGM-65C was a semi-active laser (**SAL**) version developed in the late 1970s, although in 1979 both the USAF and USN decided to forego this seeker in favor of imaging infra-red (IIR). The USMC became the only user of SAL guidance, in the form of the **AGM-65E**, which features the larger warhead. SAL permits ground troops to designate targets for their close air support. During the Gulf War, this capability was used fewer than 10 times. AGM-65Es are gray.

AGM-65D was the first IIR version produced, becoming operational during 1986 with USAF 81st TFW A-10s. The advantage of IIR over EO guidance is its ability to be used at night and in conditions of smoke and haze. For the **AGM-65F**, the Navy modified the IIR seeker's tracking function for anti-ship attacks and incorporated the larger warhead. The **AGM-65G** combines the guidance features of both the 'D' and 'F' with the latter's warhead. The USAF IIR missiles are olive drab, while the USN's are gray. IIR training missiles have yellowish seeker domes, while on

the actual missiles they are silverish.

A turbine-engined variant, called **Longhorn**, has been proposed. It would be equipped with either IIR or millimeter-wave guidance sections and have triple the range of existing versions.

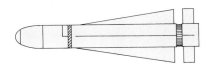

AGM-65 Maverick ASM

AGM-65 MAVERICK VARIANTS

VERSION	GUIDANCE	WEIGHT	WARHEAD	REMARKS
AGM-65A	EO	465 lb	125 lb	
AGM-65B	EO (Scene Mag)	465 lb	125 lb	
AGM-65C	SAL	465 lb	125 lb	not produced
AGM-65D	IIR	485 lb	125 lb	USAF only
AGM-65E	SAL	645 lb	300 lb	USMC only
AGM-65F	IIR (anti-ship)	675 lb	300 lb	USN only
AGM-65G	IIR	675 lb	300 lb	USAF/USN

For anti-armor work the AV-8B would carry the Maverick missile, notably the AGM-65E with semi-active laser guidance. This allows the ground forces to designate the targets for attack.

BGM-71 TOW

The Hughes tube-launched, optically-guided, wire-tracked (**TOW**) missile was first developed during the 1960s, entered service in 1970, and saw service in Vietnam. It is used by US Army AH-1S/P/E/F, Marine AH-1T/W and various foreign attack helicopters. They are delivered to the field in sealed containers which are then attached to the launcher. By 1991, about 360,000 TOWs had been produced.

BGM-71A TOW became operational in 1970. It featured guidance through two wires which unreeled with the missile, had a 9-lb (4-kg) shaped-charge warhead and a range of 9,900 ft (3000 m). **BGM-71B** extended-range TOW (**ER TOW**) became operational in 1975. Equipped with longer wires than the BGM-71A, its range increased to 12,300 ft (3750 m). The **BGM-71C** improved TOW (**ITOW**) became operational in 1981. Its warhead featured

an 11-in (28-cm) nose probe to improve armor penetration. The Israeli SAL-guided MAPATAS, revealed in 1984, is probably a derivative of ITOW. The BGM-71A, B and C all weighed about 42 lb (19 kg). **BGM-71D TOW 2** featured improved guidance, a 13-lb (6-kg) warhead fitted with a 15-in (38-cm) probe to increase lethality and a larger motor to maintain performance. Production of this 47-lb (22-kg) version began in 1983, with both new missiles and modification kits to upgrade BGM-71As to BGM-71D standards. **BGM-71E TOW 2A** entered service in 1988. Externally similar to the TOW 2, it is designed to attack the top of armored targets. TOW 2A is fitted with guidance and fuzing modifications developed by the British for their further improved TOW (**FITOW**). These permit over-the-top attacks on tanks (to defeat reactive armor) while retaining the ability to directly attack

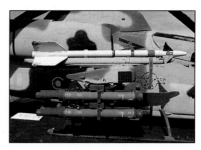

Four TOW tubes mounted on the stub pylon of an AH-1W, together with an experimental AIM-9 Sidewinder fitting above the pylon.

other types of targets. **BGM-71F TOW 2B** is yet a further development, which became operational in late 1991. It introduced a blunt nose, fitted with a dual-mode, passive-IR and active-millimeter wave seeker and dual, explosively-formed penetrator warheads.

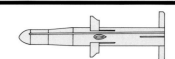

BGM-71A TOW/BGM-71B ER TOW

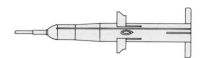

BGM-71C ITOW

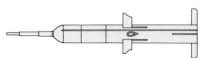

BGM-71D TOW 2/BGM-71E TOW 2A BGM-71F TOW 2B

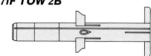

AGM-84 HARPOON

The McDonnell Douglas Harpoon is a 1,200-lb (544-kg) class anti-ship missile which has been operational with the US Navy since the mid-1970s. It can be launched from ships (RGM-84) and submarines (UGM-84), as well as aircraft (AGM-84). The AGM-84A through D are externally identical. All versions of this subsonic missile are turbojet powered, with the NACA inlet located on the bottom of the missile between the wings. Used successfully by the Navy against Libyan patrol boats in 1986, no anti-ship Harpoons were used during the Gulf War. Harpoons are carried by the A-6E, F/A-18, P-3C and S-3B.

The **AGM-84A** uses a radar altimeter to fly at sea-skimming heights. Its inertial guidance section is programmed

AGM-84A/D Harpoon ASM

AGM-84E SLAM

prior to launch to direct it to the target area, where an active radar seeker controls terminal guidance. As it attacks its target, the AGM-84A performs a pop-up maneuver to enhance warhead penetration. The **AGM-84B** has a guidance program which dispenses with the terminal pop-up maneuver. The **AGM-84C** has a refined pop-up maneuver. The **AGM-84D** features an increase in range from 57 to 75 nm (66

This is an ATM-84A training round.

to 86 miles; 106 to 139 km), and the ability to navigate to several turnpoints en route to the target area and then execute one of several terminal attack maneuvers.

The **AGM-84E** stand-off land attack missile (**SLAM**) is a modification to the Harpoon for exactly what its name

The SLAM gives the A-6 and F/A-18 long-range precision capability.

implies. To the basic airframe and engine combination is added an AGM-65D seeker, AGM-62 datalink, and a GPS receiver for updating the inertial guidance section. These add 22.5 in (57 cm) to the missile's length. SLAM has a range of about 55 nm (63 miles; 102 km).

AGM-88 HIGH-SPEED ANTI-RADIATION MISSILE (HARM)

Based on lessons learned in Vietnam, the 800-lb (363-kg) class AGM-88 is fast enough to give SAM operators minimum opportunity to shut down their radar before the HARM does it for them. HARM has three modes of employment: (**1**) In the pre-briefed mode the missile is programmed on the ground for up to three specific missile sites. Upon detecting those sites, it is launched on a ballistic trajectory.

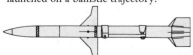

AGM-88 HARM

(Although HARM can be launched in the direction of a target, it guides in azimuth only, not range, thus relying on the target to emit and identify itself.) (**2**) The self-protection mode launches the missile against threats detected by the launching aircraft's radar warning receiver. (**3**) The target of opportunity mode uses the HARM's seeker to help determine when to launch against a

Among the Navy's launch platforms for HARM is the EA-6B.

previously unknown threat. One interesting technique used during the opening stages of the Gulf War was to use multiply-launched drone missile (BQM) -74C targets as decoys, thus enticing the SAM sites into turning on their radars for the incoming HARMs.

There are three versions of the AGM-88, differing mainly in the features of guidance section electronics. The **AGM-88A** requires the seeker to be sent back to a depot in the US to be reprogrammed. The **AGM-88B** allows the seeker to be reprogrammed on the flight line. This version, with Block-3 software, was the main one used during the Gulf War. The **AGM-88C** will incorporate further seeker improvements and replace the steel cubes in the warhead with considerably more lethal tungsten alloy ones. HARMs are launched from the

HARM is not only capable of hitting land-based air defense radars, but can also be used in an anti-ship role.

LAU-118 launch rail, which can also accommodate the older AGM-45. HARM is carried by the improved capability-2 (ICAP-2) EA-6B, SWIP A-6E, F/A-18 and F-14 (after 1993).

AGM-114 HELLFIRE

The Rockwell Hellfire began development in the 1970s, culminating in operational deployment in 1985 with the US Army and Marine Corps. With total production approximately 60,000,

AGM-114s are used by the Marine AH-1W, as well as the Army's OH-58D and AH-64A. A total of 2,876 was fired in Desert Storm. The Army's 101-lb (46-kg) **AGM-114A** is 64 in (163 cm) long, has SAL guidance and can be fired prior to the seeker actually

locking-on to the target. It has a 17.5-lb (8-kg) shaped-charge warhead and is powered by a solid rocket motor which gives it a maximum range of 4.3 nm (4.9 miles; 7.9 km). Although it can be used against any kind of point target, its primary use is anti-armor, which it

AGM-114B Hellfire. The USMC version is available with three guidance systems.

accomplishes by approaching at low level then pitching up before diving into the top of its target. The Marines' 106-lb (48-kg) **AGM-114B** is a slightly longer missile with three guidance options: the 68 in (173 cm) long dual-mode radio frequency/infra-red (RF/IR); the 70 in (178 cm) long IIR system (IRIS); and SAL. It also incorporates a low smoke motor, blast fragmentation

warhead and a safety arming device. The Army's **AGM-114C** is identical to the AGM-114B, except that it lacks the safety arming device. **RBS-17** is a Swedish coastal defense version of Hellfire.

This AH-1W carries AGM-114Bs featuring two guidance systems. The top missile has an IR seeker while the lower has SAL.

AGM-119 PENGUIN

This Norwegian-developed anti-ship missile was selected by the Navy for use with the SH-60B Seahawk in 1984. It is built in the US by Grumman and became operational in 1992. The 820-lb (372-kg) **AGM-119A Penguin 3** has a

range of 21.5 nm (25 miles; 40 km) and is used by fixed-wing aircraft. Operational with Norwegian air force F-16As, the 125 in (318 cm) long missile was evaluated by the USAF.

The 850-lb (389-kg) **AGM-119B Penguin 2 Mod 7** is a 116.5 in (296 cm) long variant, with a range of 16.5 nm

(19 miles; 31 km), which is used by helicopters. Both versions have inertial guidance and can navigate to several turn points en route to their target. A radar altimeter permits flight over land, while passive IR terminal guidance is used to deliver the 265-lb (120-kg) shaped-charge warhead.

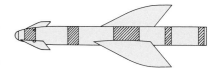

AGM-119B Penguin 2 Mod 7

AIM-120 ADVANCED, MEDIUM-RANGE AIR-TO-AIR MISSILE (AMRAAM)

The Hughes AIM-120 is the replacement for the AIM-7 Sparrow. An extremely controversial weapon, it has had a long and difficult gestation, emerging as a missile far more lethal than the one it replaces.

AMRAAM's most important improvement is the incorporation of an active-radar seeker. Although done

AIM-120 AMRAAM

before with the AIM-54 Phoenix, putting this feature into a Sparrow-sized airframe is a significant achievement. It allows the launching aircraft to simultaneously engage several targets and maneuver 'out of the fight' before the missiles hit their targets. The Sparrow, by comparison, requires the launching aircraft to maintain radar contact with a single target until the missile hits it. The

disadvantage of this was dramatically demonstrated during the famous Aimval/Aceval tests during the mid-1970s. In one engagement, which became known as 'The Towering Inferno', four F-15s engaged four F-5s with simulated AIM-7s. Before they were all 'shot down' by the Sparrows, the F-5s were able to launch simulated AIM-9s which 'destroyed' all the F-15s. AMRAAM would have allowed a single F-15 to target all four F-5s before withdrawing beyond the range of their AIM-9s.

The other main area of emphasis with AMRAAM has been reliability and

maintainability. Getting these features right was one of the main reasons it took so long to get the AIM-120 into full-scale production, which finally happened in early 1992. Virtually all areas of performance have been improved over the AIM-7, including reducing motor smoke, increasing speed and range, improving warhead fuzing and lethality, and improving ECCM performance.

With a weight of only 350 lb (159 kg), the AIM-120 can be rail-launched from stations previously associated only with AIM-9 Sidewinders.

AGM-122A SIDEARM

The Motorola **AGM-122A** uses modified AIM-9C SAR guidance

AGM-122A Sidearm

control units (GCUs) to make a lightweight anti-radiation missile (ARM) suitable for use even by helicopters. A total of 885 GCUs was modified for use by AH-1T/Ws and AV-8Bs. AIM-9D/G/H-type fins are used, along with the AIM-9L's Mk 36 rocket motor. They were carried, but not used, by AH-1Ws (and possibly

OV-10s) during Desert Storm. **AGM-122B**, if pursued, will enter service in the mid-1990s and feature an all-new, passive seeker.

A test Sidearm carried by an AH-1 shows the weapon's similarity to early Sidewinder versions, upon which it is based.

AGM-123 SKIPPER II

Emerson's **AGM-123A Skipper II** is a rocket-powered LGB consisting of a Mk 83 1,000-lb bomb, WCU-10

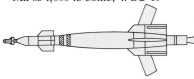

AGM-123A Skipper II

Paveway II seeker head and MXU-737 tail section incorporating the WPU-5 rocket motor used by the AGM-45 Shrike. Although the wings are partially folded (to a 36-in/91-cm span) for ground handling, once the weapon is loaded onto the aircraft they are released to their full (63-in/160-cm) span and the guidance fins attached. As with the USAF's unpowered Paveway III LGB, the low-altitude launch is designed to increase stand-off range.

The Skipper is based on the Mk 83 LGB with Paveway II systems. The A-6E is the prime launch platform.

Skipper II is intended for use by the A-6E and F/A-18.

AGM-137 TRI-SERVICE STAND-OFF ATTACK MISSILE (TSSAM)

TSSAM is a stealthy missile being developed by the USAF for use by itself as well as the Army and Navy. It will have a range of up to 300 nm (345 miles; 550 km) and employ brilliant anti-tank (BAT) autonomously-guided submunitions. The Army's ground-launched version will be designated MGM-137.

ADM-141 TACTICAL, AIR-LAUNCHED DECOY (TALD)

Over 4,000 Brunswick air-launched decoy missile (**ADM**) **-141**s have been built for the US Navy and Marine Corps. It employs chaff, radio frequency (RF) reflectors/amplifiers, and an IR emitter. This unpowered decoy has a radar signature which is difficult to distinguish from that of an actual aircraft, and attracts a lot of attention from SAMs. Weighing

between 200 and 400 lb (90 and 181 kg), it deploys wings and glides on a preset path after launch. A powered version known as improved TALD (**ITALD**) is under development.

A total of 137 was employed by various USN and USMC aircraft during the first three days of Desert Storm. A-6Es could carry as many as 26 of the 92 in (235 cm) long decoys, each worth $15-18,000. However, operationally, a typical load was eight. After TALDs were launched on the first day of the air war, over 200 HARMs were launched by other aircraft at the

ADM-141 Tactical Air-Launched Decoy (TALD). A-6s were used to launch many of these during the first night of Desert Storm.

resulting SAM activity. It was estimated that TALD doubled or tripled HARM effectiveness against an unsuspecting foe, from 10-15 per cent to 25-50 per cent probability of destroying a radar transmitter.

AIRCRAFT ORDNANCE CONFIGURATIONS

A-4 (Douglas Skyhawk)

The A-4 is still used as a threat simulator for air-to-air training by the Navy and Marines. In this role it carries a single **AIS** pod suspended from one or the other underwing pylon by a Sidewinder launcher rail. For ferry purposes it carries up to three 450-US gal (1700-liter) fuel tanks. The TA-4J is the primary jet trainer for Navy and Marine fighter pilots. They are most often seen with two underwing fuel tanks. No American A-4s were used during Desert Storm.

A-6E (Grumman Intruder)

The A-6 has five weapons pylons. They are numbered one through five, from left outboard to right outboard. The airborne, infra-red search and detection (**AAS**) **-33 TRAM** is used by all A-6Es, and is housed in a turret mounted just behind and below the aircraft radome.

Although the centerline station is capable of weapons carriage, it is normally occupied by a 300-US gal (1135-liter) fuel tank or left empty. There is some evidence that this is linked to the size of aircraft carrier being operated from (i.e., aircraft launched from older carriers with weaker catapults might not carry the tank for weight considerations, while an airplane launching from a newer carrier with the same load would). Other fuel tanks can be carried on the wing stations, loaded in many configurations: inboard, outboard, symmetric or asymmetric.

Bombs carried on the four wing stations are either mounted directly from the pylon or suspended from MERs. Because of clearance problems with the main landing gear doors, the front inboard MER stations on the inboard pylons are always left empty.

While up to 22 Mk 82 and Mk 7s can be carried on the wings, 'partial downloads' are common. These MER loads include: five bombs, achieved by leaving empty the front inboard station; four bombs, leaving empty both inboard stations; three bombs, loading the two bottom and aft-outboard stations; two bombs, loading only the two bottom stations; or one bomb, loading only the aft-bottom station. Single bombs can also be mounted directly to the pylon.

Only 10 of the heavier and longer **Mk 83**s can be carried, with three on the front-shoulder and aft-bottom MER stations of the outboard pylons, and two on the front-outboard and aft-bottom MER stations of the inboard pylons. They can also be mounted directly to the pylons.

As many as five pylon-mounted **Mk 77 fire bombs** can be carried; however, these would probably only be used by Marine aircraft.

PGM derivatives of the Mk 83 – the **GBU-16** and **AGM-123** 'Skipper II' –

After many years' service the A-6 Intruder is the Navy's prime weapons platform, able to carry a huge variety of stores. This example has an AGM-84 Harpoon, Mk 7 cluster bomb dispensers and a single GBU-12 LGB.

plus the **Mk 84** and **GBU-10** can only be pylon mounted. Normal 'dumb bomb' and GBU loads are four bombs. While GBU-12s are normally pylon-mounted, they have also been carried on aft-bottom MER stations. The AGM-123 was normally loaded only for the armed surface reconnaissance (ASR) mission during Desert Storm (the smaller *Midway* did not employ the Skipper II).

B57 and B61 (as well as earlier B28EX/RE and B43) tactical **nuclear bombs** were carried on the centerline and centerline pylons. However, since the September 1991 change in US policy, nuclear weapons are no longer carried by aircraft carriers. SWIP is gradually being retrofitted to the A-6E fleet. Among other improvements, it provides the capability to employ the AGM-65, AGM-84E, AGM-88 and AIM-120. **AGM-65 Maverick**s have been tested, but not seen operationally. As many as four anti-ship **AGM-84 Harpoon**s, including the **AGM-84E SLAM** version, can be mounted from the wing pylons. However, a normal load would more likely be just two, in combination with other stores. As many as four **AGM-88 HARM**s were seen loaded on SWIP Intruders during the Gulf War.

AGM-62 Walleyes can be carried on any wing pylon, although their most common placement is on the outboard stations. Although the A-6E can launch AGM-62s and AGM-84Es, it apparently cannot employ the AAW-9

TYPICAL A-6E WEAPON LOADS

Station 1	Station 2	Station 3	Station 4	Station 5	Remarks
Attack					
1 Mk 84	1 Mk 84	fuel tank	1 Mk 84	1 Mk 84	All GP bomb fins
3 Mk 83	2 Mk 83	fuel tank	2 Mk 83	3 Mk 83	can be used.
1 Mk 83	1 Mk 83	fuel tank	1 Mk 83	1 Mk 83	
6 Mk 82	5 Mk 82	fuel tank	5 Mk 82	6 Mk 82	
6 Mk 82	4 Mk 82	fuel tank	4 Mk 82	6 Mk 82	
5 Mk 82	5 Mk 82	fuel tank	5 Mk 82	5 Mk 82	
6 Mk 82	empty	fuel tank	empty	6 Mk 82	
6 Mk 82	fuel tank	empty	fuel tank	6 Mk 82	
fuel tank	5 Mk 82	empty	5 Mk 82	fuel tank	
6 Mk 7	5 Mk 82	empty	5 Mk 82	6 Mk 7	
6 Mk 7	empty	fuel tank	empty	6 Mk 7	
1 Mk 77	1 Mk 77	1 Mk 77	1 Mk 77	1 Mk 77	USMC only
Armed Surface Reconnaissance					
2 Mk 82	AGM-123	fuel tank	fuel tank	2 Mk 20	VA-145
1 Mk 20	empty	AGM-123	empty	1 Mk 20	VA-65/85 (Mk 20s on MER)
GBU-12	AGM-123	fuel tank	empty	GBU-12	VA-85
2 Mk 20	fuel tank	fuel tank	fuel tank	GBU-12	VA-115 (GBU-12 on aft-outboard MER)
3 Mk 83	GBU-12	empty	GBU-12	3 Mk 83	VA-35
1 Mk 20	1 Mk 20	fuel tank	AGM-123	empty	VA-155 (Mk 20s on pylon)
2 Mk 20	fuel tank	fuel tank	fuel tank	1 GBU-12	VA-115 (GBU-12 on MER)
Precision-Guided Munitions					
1 LGB	1 LGB	fuel tank	1 LGB	1 LGB	GBU-10, -12, -16
1 AGM-62	fuel tank	fuel tank	fuel tank	1 AGM-62	
Anti-ship					
1 AIM-9L	1 AGM-84	fuel tank	1 AGM-84	1 AIM-9L	Libya, 1986
1 AGM-84	5 Mk 82	fuel tank	5 Mk 82	1 AGM-84	
1 AGM-84	5 Mk 7	fuel tank	5 Mk 7	1 AGM-84	
Nuclear Weapons					
fuel tank	1 bomb	1 bomb	1 bomb	fuel tank	B57, B61
fuel tank	1 bomb	fuel tank	1 bomb	fuel tank	
fuel tank	fuel tank	1 bomb	fuel tank	fuel tank	
Suppression of Enemy Air Defenses					
1 AGM-88	1 AGM-88	fuel tank	1 AGM-88	1 AGM-88	
6 ADM-141	5 ADM-141	4 ADM-141	5 ADM-141	6 ADM-141	
1 AGM-45	2 Mk 7	fuel tank	2 Mk 7	1 AGM-45	Libya, 1986
Underwater Mining					
1 mine	1 mine	1 mine	1 mine	1 mine	Mk 55, 56, 60, 65
Electronic Countermeasures					
			1 ALQ-167		Used with any load
Air Refueling					
fuel tank	fuel tank	1 D-704	fuel tank	fuel tank	

An impressive display of 'dumb' weapons in front of a Marine Harrier. Conventional bombs, cluster weapons, Mk 77 fire bombs and rocket pod options are shown, along with self-defense AIM-9s.

datalink pod used to guide them. **AIM-9L/M Sidewinder**s can be mounted on any wing pylon from LAU-105 launchers.

A total of five pylon-mounted **underwater mines** can be carried. These include the Mk 55 and Mk 56, the Mk 60 Captor and Mk 65 Quickstrike. The Mk 36 and Mk 40 Destructors, as well as the Mk 62, Mk 63 and Mk 64 Quickstrike mines, are carried in the same manner as their Mk 80 series bomb counterparts.

ALQ-167 ECM pods, when carried, are mounted to the right inboard pylon, with either a fuel tank or bombs carried on the right inboard pylon. The D-704 can be carried on the centerline, usually with extra fuel tanks on the wing stations.

EA-6B (Grumman Prowler)

Virtually all EA-6Bs are now of the improved capability -2 (ICAP-2) variety. The next set of improvements will be incorporated into the advanced capability (ADVCAP) aircraft, which will begin to appear in 1993 and will be externally identifiable by their extra weapons stations. During Desert Storm EA-6Bs showed a wide variety of configurations for its three stores: the AGM-88, ALQ-99 and 300-US gal (1135-liter) fuel tank. These configurations were apparently squadron determined.

AV-8B (McDonnell Douglas/British Aerospace Harrier II)

Despite being capable of mounting weapons from TERs, in practice the weight and drag involved do not make this a viable option. The weapon loads seen during Desert Storm are probably the extent of the AV-8B's capabilities. The **GAU-12** gun system, while not mandatory, appeared to be virtually standard in combat. **ALQ-167**s were seen on the centerline of some aircraft, but were not universal by any means. **AIM-9L**s could be carried on any pylon, but in practice only on the left one, with a launcher rail mounted on the right.

The four inboard pylons carried four of the same kind of weapon on any given sortie; these were primarily **Mk 7** dispensers or Mk 82s. While any fin group could be used with **Mk 82** or **Mk 83** bombs, during the Gulf War most bombs used LDGP conical fins. **Mk 77 Mod 4** fire bombs were used to ignite oil in Iraqi defensive trenches, while **CBU-55/72** FAEs cleared minefields prior to the start of the ground war. Although capable (with the assistance of ground-based laser designator teams) of delivering laser-guided **GBU-12** and **GBU-16** bombs, as well as **AGM-65E**s (from LAU-117s), no LGBs and fewer than 10 Mavericks were reported to have been delivered by AV-8Bs during Desert Storm. **LAU-10**, **-68** and **-69** rocket pods can also be employed. Finally, up to four 300-US gal (1135-liter) fuel tanks can be carried, but are normally used only for ferry flights.

The night attack Harrier II Plus will feature additional pylons in front of the outrigger wheel fairing and has the

capability to employ the **AIM-7F/M**, **AGM-84** and **AIM-120** missiles. A typical mission configuration might be two fuel tanks inboard, then two Harpoons and AIM-9Ls outboard.

F-14A/B (Grumman Tomcat)

While the F-14 can carry a number of different weapon combinations in addition to its built-in 20-mm Vulcan cannon, including up to six **AIM-54C**s, the normal load is substantially less and appears to be virtually standard. This is one or two AIM-54Cs on the front fuselage pylons, along with two **AIM-7M**s and two **AIM-9M**s on the wing pylons, as well as two 265-US gal (1000-liter) fuel tanks beneath the inlets. Plans to replace the AIM-7M with the **AIM-120A** have been deferred indefinitely. When carried (as was common during the first three weeks of Desert Storm), the **ALQ-167** replaces the AIM-54C on the front-right fuselage pylon. The weapons stations between the engine bays initially carried up to two AIM-7F/Ms, but as the war progressed this practice was halted.

The Grumman **TARPS** is carried by modified F-14A/Bs under the right side of the aircraft, between the engines. For this mission the front Phoenix pylons are retained, with an ALQ-167 ECM pod on the right one, and the left one empty. The rest of the armament and fuel tanks are as per normal. Squadrons known to have operated TARPS aircraft during Desert Storm are VF-2, VF-32, VF-84 and VF-103.

Like the USAF's F-15C, the Tomcat has a little-known bomb-dropping capability, as evidenced by this F-14B of VF-24. It carries four Mk 82 Snakeyes on the Phoenix pylons. The AIM-7/AIM-9 configuration is typical for the aircraft.

F-14s have an air-to-ground capability, but it has seldom been used. Starting in 1990, when elements within the Navy were trying to prevent the termination of F-14 production, some bombs were dropped to demonstrate that it could be done. These included **Mk 83** and **Mk 84** LDGPs dropped from the front Phoenix pylons. Beginning in 1993, the ability to launch **AGM-88** will be incorporated.

F/A-18 (McDonnell Douglas Hornet)

The Hornet has replaced the venerable A-7 in the light attack role and, despite its capabilities in the air-to-air arena, the emphasis is definitely on the 'A', not the 'F' in its mission. The aircraft has a built-in 20-mm **GAU-11** Vulcan cannon plus a total of nine weapons stations, comprised of two wingtip **AIM-9L/M** launcher rails, two fuselage stations for **AIM-7F/M**s or sensor pods, a centerline and four underwing pylons. AIM-9s are virtually standard on the wingtip stations in combat, but during peacetime exercises AIS pods are

The Hornet is a highly versatile warplane, capable of performing many tasks. This aircraft has two Harpoons for anti-shipping attack.

USN/USMC Ordnance

TYPICAL EA-6B WEAPON LOADS

Station 1	Station 2	Station 3	Station 4	Station 5	Remarks
ALQ-99	fuel tank	ALQ-99	ALQ-99	AGM-88	VAQ-130
AGM-88	fuel tank	ALQ-99	AGM-88	ALQ-99	VAQ-130 & 136
ALQ-99	AGM-88	fuel tank	fuel tank	ALQ-99	VAQ-132
AGM-88	fuel tank	ALQ-99	ALQ-99	AGM-88	VAQ-131 & 141
AGM-88	fuel tank	ALQ-99	fuel tank	AGM-88	VAQ-141
AGM-88	fuel tank	ALQ-99	fuel tank	ALQ-99	VMAQ-2
ALQ-99	fuel tank	ALQ-99	ALQ-99	ALQ-99	VMAQ-2
ALQ-99	fuel tank	ALQ-99	fuel tank	ALQ-99	VMAQ-2

often fitted to one side. When AIM-7s are not carried, the fuselage stations can be fitted with one of three sensors: the ASQ-173 LST/SCAM, AAS-38 FLIR or AAR-50 TINS. **AIM-120A**s will eventually replace the AIM-7F/Ms.

For simplicity, the table below only reflects the five main weapons stations, from station one on the left outboard to station five on the right outboard. While these loadings are not all-encompassing, they do represent what is practical under typical circumstances. Unless otherwise noted, AIM-7/9s are

TYPICAL F/A-18 WEAPON LOADS

Station 1	Station 2	Station 3	Station 4	Station 5	Remarks
Surface Attack					
1 Mk 7	fuel tank	1 Mk 7	fuel tank	1 Mk 7	LST/SCAM
2 Mk 7	fuel tank	fuel tank	fuel tank	2 Mk 7	
1 Mk 82	fuel tank	fuel tank	fuel tank	1 Mk 82	FLIR, no AIM-7
1 Mk 82	1 Mk 82	fuel tank	1 Mk 82	1 Mk 82	TINS
2 Mk 82	fuel tank	1 Mk 82	fuel tank	2 Mk 82	
1 AGM-65E	fuel tank	fuel tank	fuel tank	2 Mk 7	USMC
1 Mk 83	1 Mk 83	fuel tank	1 Mk 83	1 Mk 83	
2 Mk 83	fuel tank	fuel tank	fuel tank	2 Mk 83	
2 Mk 83	fuel tank	1 Mk 83	fuel tank	2 Mk 83	
1 Mk 83	2 Mk 83	fuel tank	2 Mk 83	1 Mk 83	
1 Mk 84	fuel tank	empty	fuel tank	1 Mk 84	
1 Mk 84	1 Mk 84	fuel tank	1 Mk 84	1 Mk 84	
1 AGM-65E	fuel tank	fuel tank	1 Mk 83	2 Mk 83	USMC
Anti-Ship/SLAM					
1 AGM-84	fuel tank	fuel tank	fuel tank	1 AGM-84	
Nuclear					
1 B61	fuel tank	fuel tank	fuel tank	1 B61	
SEAD/Surface Combat Air Patrol (SuCAP)					
1 AIM-7	fuel tank	1 Mk 7	fuel tank	1 AGM-88	VMFA-323, Libya, 1986
1 Mk 7	fuel tank	fuel tank	fuel tank	1 AGM-88	
1 AGM-88	1 AGM-88	fuel tank	fuel tank	1 AGM-88	
1 AGM-88	1 AGM-88	fuel tank	fuel tank	1 AGM-88	
1 AGM-88	fuel tank	empty	fuel tank	1 AGM-88	
1 AGM-88	1 Mk 84	fuel tank	1 Mk 84	1 AGM-88	
1 AGM-88	fuel tank	Mk 83	fuel tank	1 AGM-65E	USMC (sometimes with FLIR)
2 ADM-141	fuel tank	fuel tank	fuel tank	2 ADM-141	
1 ADM-141	2 ADM-141	fuel tank	2 ADM-141	1 ADM-141	
Precision-Guided Munitions					
1 AGM-62	fuel tank	AWW-9	fuel tank	1 AGM-62	VFA-151, FLIR, no AIM-7, ER/DL-I
1 GBU-12	fuel tank	empty	fuel tank	1 GBU-12	VMFA-323, Libya, 1986, no missiles
Fast Forward Air Control (USMC F/A-18D only)					
1 LAU-10	fuel tank	empty	fuel tank	1 LAU-10	FLIR
1 LAU-10	2 Mk 83	fuel tank	2 Mk 83	1 LAU-10	no AIM-9
Combat Air Patrol					
1 AIM-7	fuel tank	fuel tank	fuel tank	empty	
1 AIM-7	fuel tank	fuel tank	fuel tank	1 AIM-7	
2 AIM-9L	fuel tank	empty	fuel tank	2 AIM-9L	VMFA-323, Libya, 1986, FLIR

fitted to fuselage and wingtip stations. Single weapons are carried mounted to the pylon (or LAU-118 for AGM-45/88); double weapons are mounted to VERs.

Ford's airborne infra-red search and track (**AAS**) **-38 FLIR** is used by the F/A-18. Mounted on the left fuselage station, newer versions of this pod incorporate a laser designator in its nose turret. Some reports indicate AAS-38 performance during the Gulf War was less than satisfactory, generating Navy interest in a system based on the USAF's LANTIRN system.

The airborne infra-red receiving (**AAR**) **-50 TINS**, developed by Hughes, is also used by the F/A-18. Unlike the AAS-38, TINS has a fixed, forward-staring FLIR. While this allows the pilot to see at night, it has no laser designation capability. This system is also mounted on the left fuselage station of the Hornet.

The final podded sensor system used by the F/A-18 is the **ASQ-173 LST/SCAM**. Mounted on the right fuselage station, this McDonnell Douglas pod has a function very similar to that of the Pave Penny pod used by Air Force A-10s: sensing laser energy from a target designated by ground troops or other aircraft, and then displaying a symbol on the HUD to assist the pilot in acquiring it. However, this daytime-only system has no laser designation capability. It also houses a strike camera to aid in bomb damage assessment (BDA).

Many different weapon combinations were seen on F/A-18s during Desert Storm. Extremely range-limited when carrying a bomb load, carriage of at least one 330-US gal (1250-liter) fuel tank was almost a certainty. Because it was primarily a high-altitude war, the Mk 20 proved ineffective due to bomblet dispersion and soon fell from favor. Although most bombs dropped were conical-finned LDGPs, any Mk 80 series fin can be used with the F/A-18, as can any underwater mine based on Mk 80 series bombs.

AGM-122 Sidearm is among the weapons available to the AH-1W. It is fired from a standard Sidewinder rail under the stub pylon.

AGM-62, **AGM-84** and nuclear weapons can only be carried on outboard wing stations. The **AAW-9** Walleye datalink pod can only be carried on the centerline station. **GBU-10**, **-12** and **-16** LGBs can be carried on any station, but are very rarely seen on F/A-18s. During Desert Storm F/A-18D fast FACs carried **LAU-10**s on outboard VER stations.

AH-1J/T/W (Bell Sea Cobra, Improved Sea Cobra and Super Cobra)

In addition to the standard GTK4A M197 turret cannon, Marine Cobras have a total of four weapons pylons on their stub wings. As the helicopter has gone through its various transformations, the types of weapons it can employ has increased. The **AH-1J** could carry the 19-tube LAU-61 or seven-tube LAU-68 rocket pods, as well as the SUU-11 gun pod (sometimes called by its Army designation M18). While these weapons could be carried on any station, only two gun pods could be carried, usually on the inboard stations. The **AH-1T** added to these the 19-tube LAU-69 rocket pod and GPU-2 gun pod, which could be carried on all stations (but only two gun pods), as well as the 100-US gal (380-liter) fuel tank, CBU-55 FAE, M118 grenade launcher, SUU-44 flare dispenser and BGM-71 TOW (four per launcher), which could only be carried on the outboard stations. The **AH-1W** added to the weapons which can be carried on the outboard pylons with the AIM-9L (on LAU-7 rails), AGM-114 (four per launcher) and AGM-122. The AH-1W is capable of carrying both TOW and Hellfire at the same time. All surviving AH-1J/Ts are gradually being converted to AH-1Ws.

During Desert Storm AH-1Ws usually mounted LAU-68 rocket pods on their inboard pylons, with BGM-71s and/or AGM-114s outboard. Other weapons included CBU-55 and AGM-122, with the latter replacing one set of anti-tank missiles.

SH-2F (Kaman Seasprite)

Dating from 1960 and created as one of those famous interim requirements (like the B-52), the Seasprite began as LAMPS but has evolved into an ASW platform. It is typically deployed in detachments of one or two aircraft aboard destroyers, frigates and guided-missile cruisers.

The SH-2F is limited to two stores stations which can carry either 100-US gal (378-liter) fuel tanks, **Mk 46** or **Mk 50** torpedoes.

SH-3H (Sikorsky Sea King)

Sea Kings are based on attack carriers and tasked with plane guard and ASW missions. The plane guard mission is a vital part of every carrier evolution, standing by to rescue any aircrew who might end up in the water. For the ASW mission the SH-3H can carry 840 lb (380 kg) of stores, usually **Mk 46** or **Mk 50** torpedoes.

SH-60B/F, HH-60H (Sikorsky Seahawk/ Ocean Hawk)

Developed from the Army Black Hawk, the SH-60B Seahawk is designed primarily for ASW and anti-ship surveillance and targeting (ASST), with secondary missions of SAR, VertRep, medevac, communications relay and fleet support. The helicopter can carry two 120-US gal (454-liter) fuel tanks or **Mk 50** torpedoes. During the Iran-Iraq war, some SH-60Bs were fitted with the F/A-18's **AAS-38** FLIR pod on their left pylon.

The SH-60F Ocean Hawk will replace the SH-3H. To accomplish its primary mission of close-in ASW protection of the aircraft carrier battle group it has an additional pylon, enabling it to carry three Mk 50 torpedoes.

The HH-60H is a special warfare support and strike-reconnaissance helicopter. Operating from destroyer-sized or larger ships, its basic armament design includes two cabin-mounted M60 machine guns. However, based on the experience of Desert Storm, this will probably be increased.

P-3C (Lockheed Orion)

The P-3 has two major missions, the secondary one being ESM and jamming, in the guise of the EP-3E. This version is unarmed. The majority of Orions are dedicated to anti-submarine warfare and carry nearly 200 sonobuoys and sound signals, as well as a number of marine markers and

parachute flares to assist in locating and tracking their quarry.

The P-3C internal bomb bay has eight hardpoints from which weapons can be mounted. Authorized internal weapons (and maximum load) include: **Mk 46** (eight) or **Mk 50** (six) torpedoes; **Mk 54** (eight) depth bombs; **Mk 52** (three), **Mk 55** (one), **Mk 56** (one) or **Mk 65** (one) underwater mines; **Mk 82/Mk 36/Mk 62** (eight) or **Mk 83/Mk 40/Mk 63** (three) GP bombs and Destructor/Quickstrike mines; and **B57** (three) nuclear depth bombs.

Orion external stores are carried on 10 stations, three outboard of the engines on each wing and two inboard. Authorized external weapons (and maximum load) include: **Mk 54** (10) depth bombs; **Mk 52** (eight), **Mk 55** (six) or **Mk 56** (six) underwater mines; **Mk 60** (six) Captor mines; **Mk 82/Mk 36/Mk 62** (10) or **Mk 83/Mk 40/Mk 63** (eight) GP bombs and Destructor/ Quickstrike mines; **LAU-10, -68** and **-69** (four) rocket pods; **SUU-44** (four) flare dispensers; **AGM-84 Harpoon** (eight) and the **AIM-9L/M** self protection air-to-air missile.

S-3A/B (Lockheed Viking)

The S-3 Viking performs five basic missions: anti-submarine, anti-ship, surface attack, air refueling and electronic support measures . While the latter function will be performed by the new ES-3A, armed only with its battle group passive horizon-extension system for long-range signals monitoring, the remainder of the missions belong to the S-3A/B. For the ASW mission, these Vikings carry 60 sonobuoys to assist in locating and tracking their quarry. In addition to an improved ASW avionics suite, the S-3B has enhanced anti-ship and surface attack capabilities with the addition of the ability to employ the **AGM-84** Harpoon and **SLAM**. Both S-3As and Bs can perform the buddy-refueling mission when fitted with the **D-704** air refueling pod on the left wing and a

300-US gal (1135-liter) fuel tank on the right.

The S-3 has two internal weapons bays on the 'corners' of its square fuselage. Authorized internal weapons (and maximum load) include: **Mk 46** (four) or **Mk 50** (four) torpedoes; **Mk 82/Mk 36/Mk 62** (four) GP bombs and Destructor/Quickstrike mines; and **B57** (two) nuclear depth bombs, although the latter have been removed from aircraft carriers.

Viking external stores are carried on single stations located outboard of the engines on each wing. Authorized external weapons (and maximum load) include: **Mk 52** (two), **Mk 55** (two) or **Mk 56** (two) underwater mines; **Mk 60** (two) Captor mines; **Mk 82/Mk 36/Mk 62** (six) GP bombs and Destructor/ Quickstrike mines; **Mk 7** (six) dispensers; **ADM-141** (six) decoys; **LAU-10, -68** and **-69** (six) rocket pods; **SUU-44** (six) flare dispensers; **AGM-84** (two) Harpoons. Where more than two weapons are carried, they are mounted to TERs.

Most S-3s used during Desert Storm were S-3Bs, some of which carried AGM-84Es, although there is no indication any were actually employed by the Vikings. However, S-3s did participate in combat missions by launching ADM-141s and attacking patrol boats (and at least one AAA site) with Mk 82 LDGPs. Some S-3s were also seen to carry Mk 20s.

OV-10A/D (Rockwell Bronco)

Designed during the Vietnam era as a FAC aircraft, the OV-10 has a limited close air support capability in a benign threat environment. However, with the proliferation of SA-7 'Grails' and FIM-92 Stingers, the few Broncos left have reverted mainly to their original mission.

OV-10A wing sponsons are fitted with four **M60** machine guns. While the centerline station commonly carries a 150-US gal (570-liter) fuel tank, the **Mk 83** bomb or **GPU-2** gun pod are also

With a Mk 46 torpedo on the fuselage side, an SH-2F drops a sonobuoy during ASW operations.

With TERs fitted to the wing pylons, the S-3 can perform a secondary bombing role.

permissible. Stores the OV-10A can currently carry on its other four sponson pylons include the **Mk 77 Mod 5** fire bomb, **Mk 82 bomb, CBU-55 FAE, LAU-10, -68** and **-69** rocket pods, **SUU-11** gun pod or **SUU-44** flare dispenser. Only USMC OV-10s are equipped with underwing **AIM-9** launcher rails.

The **OV-10D** is equipped for the night observation system (NOS) mission and is equipped with the AAS-37 detection, ranging and tracking system (DRTS) in an undernose turret. When it uses the optional **M197** 20-mm cannon, mounted in an underfuselage turret, the sponsons are removed. OV-10D stores include the **CBU-55 FAE, LAU-10, -68** and **-69** rocket pods, or **SUU-44** flare dispenser. Also, the OV-10D can carry 100-US gal (378-liter) fuel tanks from its outboard wing pylons.

During Desert Storm OV-10s appeared to travel light, with most carrying a single **LAU-10** from the left sponson station and a centerline fuel tank. While up to two **AIM-9L/M**s could be carried from LAU-105s on the wing pylons, seeing the launcher rail without the missile was more common. In all probability, during Desert Storm **AGM-122** Sidearms were carried rather than Sidewinders. They also reportedly used **LAU-68** and **-69** rocket pods, **CBU-55** FAE and **CBU-78** Gator. If true, only one of the latter could have been carried from the centerline.

NAVAL, MARINE CORPS AND COAST GUARD AIR STATIONS

Not surprisingly, the bases of the USN, USMC and USCG are mainly located along the American seaboard. Notable exceptions are the bases around the Great Lakes, the basic training establishments in Texas and the test and tactical training bases in the southwestern desert. As befits a global force, the Navy/Marine Corps maintains a sizable base structure outside the United States, particularly in the Mediterranean and Far East.

Left: Returning from a Pacific cruise, the Tomcats of VF-1 and VF-2 overfly NAS Miramar. Thanks to a certain movie this is the Navy's best-known base, and proclaims itself as 'Fightertown, USA'.

US NAVY AIR STATIONS

Adak NAS, AK

Location: on Adak Island in the Aleutian Isles chain
Units assigned: Base Flight – KC-130F

Fleet support air station which periodically has P-3 patrol squadrons detached for temporary duty from the NAS Barbers Point, HI, and NAS Moffett Field, CA. The only aircraft in permanent residence is a KC-130F which was formerly operated by the 'Blue Angels' as their support craft and is now flown from Adak on communications duties. Airfield known as Albert Mitchell Field in honor of Ensign Albert E. Mitchell.

Agana NAS, Guam

Location: on the island of Guam in the Pacific Ocean
Units assigned: HC-5 – HH-46A, CH-46D; VQ-1 – EP-3E, P-3B; VQ-5 – ES-3A; Base Flight – UC-12F

Fleet support station which provides facilities for naval aircraft operating from aircraft carriers within the waters around Guam, and for aircraft in transit to the Far East. Station houses two fleet air reconnaissance squadrons flying the EP-3E and ES-3A, plus a helicopter support squadron which performs vertical replenishment to passing vessels as well as search and rescue in the locality. Facility known as Brewer Field after Naval Commander Charles W. Brewer.

Alameda NAS, CA

Location: two miles west of Alameda
Units assigned: HM-15 – MH-53E; HM-19 – RH-53D; HS-85 – SH-3H; VA-304 – A-6E/KA-6D; VR-55 – C-9B; HMH-772 det C – RH-53D; MALS-42 – TA-4J; VMA-133 – A-4M; Base Flight – UC-12B

Alameda is a major facility for West Coast Navy and Marine Corps Reserve squadrons and pos-

sesses a deep water jetty alongside, which enables the largest of aircraft carriers to dock for maintenance. Among the carriers whose home port is Alameda are CVN-65/USS *Enterprise*, CVN-70/USS *Carl Vinson* and CVN-72/USS *Abraham Lincoln*. In addition, the base houses a Naval Air Depot which conducts major overhauls of A-6 Intruders and P-3 Orions. Station named Nimitz Field in honor of legendary Fleet Admiral Chester W. Nimitz.

Atlanta NAS, GA

Location: 10 miles west of Atlanta
Units assigned: VA-205 – A-6E/KA-6D; VR-46 – C-9B; HMA-773 – AH-1J; VMO-4 – OV-10A/D (to deactivate by 1994); Base Flight – UC-12B

A Naval Air Reserve Station, Atlanta NAS houses two Navy and three Marine Corps Reserve squadrons of fixed-wing and rotary types. Among these is an A-6 Intruder squadron which, unlike its front-line counterparts, is shore-based for the majority of the year with just a short period of carrier time to enable aircrew to remain fully qualified. The station is located on the same site as Dobbins AFB and the Lockheed Aeronautical Service Company facility.

Atsugi NAF, Japan

Location: in Kanagawa Prefecture to the west of Tokyo
Units assigned: HS-12 – SH-3H (CVW-5); HSL-51 – SH-60B; VA-115 – A-6E (CVW-5); VAQ-136 – EA-6B (CVW-5); VAW-115 – E-2C (CVW-5); VF-21 – F-14A (CVW-5); VF-154 – F-14A (CVW-5); VFA-192 – F/A-18C (CVW-5); VFA-195 – F/A-18C (CVW-5); VS-21 – S-3B (CVW-5); Base Flight – UC-12F

The facility has since 1973 been the home station for Carrier Air Wing 5, which was assigned aboard

CV-41/USS *Midway* whose home port was Yokosuka, Japan. The only aircraft carrier and carrier air wing based outside of the USA, the *Midway* was relieved of duty during September 1991 and replaced by CV-62/USS *Independence*. The official exchange of duties was carried out at Pearl Harbor between 22 and 28 August 1991 for the formal swap-over of CVW-5 from *Midway* to *Independence* and CVW-14 from the latter carrier back to the USA aboard *Midway*. All of the squadrons listed above are assigned to CVW-5 with the exception of HSL-51, which was formed in October 1991 to provide detachments aboard 7th Fleet vessels. The Commander Fleet Air Western Pacific has his headquarters at Atsugi with responsibility for activities in the Far East and Indian Ocean. A Naval Air Pacific Repair Activity was formed in May 1990 to take over repair work which was formerly contracted to Nippi Industries at Atsugi.

Barbers Point NAS, HI

Location: 20 miles west of Honolulu
Units assigned: HSL-37 – SH-2F, SH-60B; VC-1 – A-4E, TA-4J; SH-3G, UP-3A; VP-3A; VQ-3 – E-6A; VP-1 – P-3C, VP-4, P-3C, VP-6, P-3C; VP-17 – P-3C; VP-22 – P-3C

The facility is one of two which house the patrol squadrons of the Pacific Fleet, with five P-3 Orion squadrons together forming Patrol Wing Two. At least one squadron is deployed to the Far East as well as detachments to bases in Alaska and other locations in the Western Pacific and Indian Ocean. Fleet Composite Squadron One provides adversary training for carrier air wings on WEST-PAC cruises, while Fleet Air Reconnaissance Squadron Three recently completed conversion from the EC-130Q to the E-6A Hermes. The station also acts as an important staging facility for aircraft on transpacific flights, and houses a Coast Guard facility with fixed-wing and rotary types assigned. Station is named John Rodgers Field in honor of Commander John Rodgers.

Barking Sands NAWC, HI

Location: at Barking Sands in the Hawaiian Islands
Units assigned: Naval Air Warfare Center (NAWC) Range Facility – RC-12F, UH-3A

The Range Facility is a subordinate organization of the Naval Air Warfare Center Weapons Division with headquarters at Point Mugu, CA. The range was formerly run by the Pacific Missile Test Center until January 1992 and provides support for aircraft utilizing the missile range.

Bermuda NAS, Bermuda

Location: on Bermuda International Airport at what was formerly the Air Force base known as Kindley Field
Units assigned: Base Flight – UH-1N

Facility supports P-3 Orion squadrons from stateside installations in temporary residence as a forward operating base to monitor the western Atlantic and the major sea lanes. The UH-1N is operated primarily in the search and rescue and support roles. However, it was announced during 1990 that P-3 deployments would cease and the base close in due course.

Brunswick NAS, ME

Location: three miles east of Brunswick
Units assigned: VP-8 – P-3C; VP-10 – P-3C; VP-11 – P-3C; VP-23 – P-3C; VP-26 – P-3C; VP-44 – P-3C; Base Flight – UC-12B, UH-1N

The station is one of two which operate the P-3 Orion under control of the Commander Patrol Wings Atlantic. The six squadrons stationed at Brunswick form Patrol Wing Five, with squadrons and detachments regularly operating from Bermuda, Lajes and Sigonella.

Cecil Field NAS, FL

Location: 15 miles west of Jacksonville
Units assigned: VFA-15 – F/A-18A (CVW-8); VFA-37 – F/A-18C (CVW-3); VFA-81 – F/A-18C (CVW-17); VFA-82 – F/A-18A (CVW-1); VFA-83 – F/A-18C (CVW-17); VFA-86 – F/A-18A (CVW-1); VFA-87 – F/A-18A (CVW-8); VFA-105 – F/A-18C (CVW-3); VFA-131 – F/A-18C (CVW-7); VFA-132 – F/A-18C (CVW-6) (to disestablish by October 1992); VFA-136 – F/A-18C (CVW-7); VFA-137 – F/A-18A (CVW-6) (to move to Lemoore and convert to F/A-18C); VS-22 – S-3B (CVW-3); VS-24 – S-3A (CVW-8); VS-28 – S-3B (CVW-6) (to disestablish by October 1992); VS-30 – S-3B (CVW-17); VS-31 – S-3B (CVW-7); VS-32 – S-3A (CVW-1); VF-45 det – A-4E, TA-4J, F-16N; VFA-106 – F/A-18A/B/C/D, T-34C (LANTFLT FRS); VFA-203 – F/A-18A; VQ-6 – ES-3A; VS-27 – S-3A (LANTFLT FRS); VMFA-142 – F/A-18A

Cecil Field was created as an auxiliary airfield to NAS Jacksonville in 1941 and did not become a naval air station until 1952. During the late 1940s the base was conducting advanced fighter pilot training and was earmarked for maintenance status in 1950 when the Korean War erupted. Cecil Field, like many other stateside naval air stations, expanded rapidly to become one of the most active facilities. Today Cecil Field is the shore base for Atlantic Fleet light attack and fixed-wing antisubmarine warfare squadrons. Light Attack Wing One is the controlling unit for the F/A-18 Hornet squadrons. Cecil Field has the Fleet Replenishment Squadrons (FRS) for the F/A-18 and S-3 for the Atlantic Fleet. Fleet Air Reconnaissance Squadron Six is to be established to operate the ES-3A to deploy aboard Atlantic Fleet aircraft carriers. Named for Commander Henry B. Cecil, this is one of the few facilities whose airfield and NAS names are the same.

Chase Field NAS, TX

Location: 10 miles north of Alice
Units assigned: VT-24 – TA-4J; VT-25 – TA-4J; VT-26 – T-2C

The facility has Training Wing 3 (TW-3) in residence to conduct intermediate and advanced strike jet training of naval aviators. The station is scheduled to close at the end of 1992 with the flying squadrons relocating to Kingsville, TX, and Meridian, MS, and TW-3 inactivating. Named after Lieutenant Commander Nathan B. Chase, the station is also known as Beeville.

China Lake NAWC, CA

Location: six miles east of Inyokern
Units assigned: Naval Air Warfare Center Weapons Division (NAWC/WD) – A-4M, NTA-4F/J, A-6E, UC-8A, QF-4N, QF-86F, HH-1K, TH-1L, T-39D, AV-8B; VX-5 – A-4M, TA-4J, A-6E, EA-6B, F/A-18D, AV-8B, OV-10D

China Lake encompasses a huge range complex located in a remote part of eastern California and includes a nuclear weapons testing site. The facility was operated by the Naval Weapons Center (NWC) until January 1992 when replaced by the Naval Air Warfare Center Weapons Division. The Center utilizes dozens of surplus aircraft to be expended as ground targets to evaluate the performance and capabilities of various weapons systems. Headquarters NAWC is located at Arlington, VA, while both China Lake and Point Mugu have headquarters of the Weapons Division in residence. Many of these aircraft have spent more years on the China Lake range than they did in operational service, and some have been rescued for display in museums. The airfield is known as Armitage Field in honor of Lieutenant John W. Armitage.

Corpus Christi NAS, TX

Location: three miles west of Corpus Christi
Units assigned: VT-27 – T-34C; VT-28 – T-44A; VT-31 – T-44A

Training Wing Four (TW-4) is the major flying unit which teaches primary and intermediate training on the T-34C and advanced training on the T-44A for pilots destined to fly multi-engined types such as the P-3 Orion. Corpus Christi is headquarters Naval Training with the Command Naval Air Training Command (CNATRA) in residence. The station also houses the Corpus Christi Army Depot (CCAD), which is a major overhaul facility for US Army helicopters, and the Corpus Christi Coast Guard Air Station, operating the HH-65A and HU-25A. The aircraft carrier AVT-16/USS *Lexington* is to be displayed at Corpus Christi following the ship's decommissioning in November 1991.

Cubi Point NAS, Republic of the Philippines

Location: on Luzon Island adjacent to Subic Bay
Units assigned: VC-5 – A-4E, TA-4J, OA-4M, UH-3A, SH-3G, CH-53E; VRC-50 – C-2A, C-130F, US-3A, CT-39E; Base Flight – UC-12B

The base is part of the large naval complex at Subic Bay and, apart from all facilities required to support naval flight operations, has a 1,000-ft long carrier pier to enable all sizes of aircraft carrier to dock. The air station was established in July 1956, although the naval base is considerably older. The field was extremely active during the Vietnam War, providing shore facilities for squadrons and supporting aircraft carriers on Yankee Station. The naval air station is scheduled to close, while the Subic Bay naval complex will be vacated by US forces by the end of December 1992. VRC-50 will move to NAS Agana, Guam, while the fate of VC-5 has yet to be determined. Named Arthur W. Radford Field in honor of Admiral Radford, who was the inspiration behind the airfield being constructed.

Dallas NAS, TX

Location: five miles west of Dallas
Units assigned: VF-201 – F-14A; VF-202 – F-14A; VR-59 – C-9B; VMFA-112 – F/A-18A; NARU Dallas – A-4M; HMH-772 det B – CH-53D; Base Flight – UC-12B

The station is home to a sizable contingent of Navy and Marine Corps Reserve squadrons. The base was the last to operate the F-4 with VMFA-112 finally retiring the type by January 1992. In addition, the base is home to US Army National Guard and Reserve helicopter units and an Air National Guard C-130 squadron. Located across the runway from the naval air station is the huge LTV facility which produced the F-8 Crusader and A-7 Corsair II. Named Hensley Field after USMC Colonel William N. Hensley.

Dallas is a major Reservist base, housing two Navy Tomcat squadrons and a Marine Hornet unit. In order to provide dissimilar air combat for these units the base flight operates some A-4M Skyhawks in adversary colors.

Detroit NAF, MI

Location: 25 miles north of Detroit
Units assigned: VP-93 – P-3B; VR-62 – C-9B

NAF Detroit is located at Selfridge Air National Guard Base with a P-3B and a C-9B squadron. The facility also houses a sizable Air National Guard, Air Force Reserve and Army Reserve presence, along with helicopters of Coast Guard Air Station Detroit.

Diego Garcia NAF, Indian Ocean

Location: on the island of Diego Garcia in the Indian Ocean
Units assigned: nil

The tiny island of Diego Garcia hosts the strategically important staging facility which has Pacific Fleet P-3 Orions in temporary residence to conduct patrols over the Indian Ocean. No aircraft are permanently based, although carrier onboard delivery aircraft from VRC-50 at Cubi Point are detached to Diego Garcia whenever carriers are operating in the Indian Ocean. The base was extremely active during Desert Shield and Desert Storm, with many US Air Force and Navy aircraft movements.

Air Stations

El Centro NAF, CA

Location: six miles west of El Centro
Units assigned: Base Flight – UC-12B

Administered by the Commander Pacific Fleet Fighter Airborne Early Warning Wing, El Centro has a regular detachment of TA-4J Skyhawks from Training Wings One, Two and Three in residence. In addition, front-line and Naval Reserve fighter and attack aircraft deploy in small numbers to conduct air-to-ground operations on the nearby bombing range and for gunnery practice against targets towed behind A-4s. The facility housed the National Parachute Test Range for many years, although this is believed to have been transferred elsewhere.

Fallon NAS, NV

Location: seven miles east of Fallon
Units assigned: Naval Strike Warfare Center (NSWC) – F/A-18A, F/A-18B, SH-3H; VFA-125 det – F/A-18C/D; VFA-127 det – F/A-18A, F-5E/F; Base Flight – UC-12B, UH-1N

The station supports visiting ground attack types from Atlantic and Pacific Fleet carrier air wings to attend the Naval Strike Warfare Center and use the nearby weapons ranges. VFA-125 and VFA-127, both from NAS Lemoore, CA, have a detachment operating a number of F/A-18C/Ds and F-5E/Fs respectively, the latter adding an adversary role during these exercises.

Fallon is a major work-up base for Fleet units. F-5Es from VFA-127 regularly fly from here on adversary missions.

Glenview NAS, IL

Location: 15 miles north of Chicago
Units assigned: VP-60 – P-3B; VP-90 – P-3B; VR-51 – C-9B; HML-776 – UH-1N; VMGR-234 – KC-130T

One of six dedicated Naval Reserve stations with a mixture of Navy and Marine Corps types operated. The base also houses an Army Reserve helicopter unit plus the Chicago US Coast Guard Air Station operating the HH-65A.

Guantanamo Bay NAS, Cuba

Location: at the southeastern end of the Cuban mainland
Units assigned: VC-10 – EA-4F, TA-4J, OA-4M

One of the oldest overseas naval aviation facilities, the site was used in 1913 for an aviation camp by aviators and students to practice detection of submarines and mines and for the indoctrination of Fleet officers into the potentialities of aviation in support of the Fleet. The site became an air station in 1941 and was primarily an antisubmarine warfare seaplane base during World War II. The base was heavily used during the 1962 Cuban missile crisis with large numbers of US aircraft in residence. Guantanamo Bay now serves as a logistics base in the Caribbean, as well as hosting train-ing exercises conducted by a fleet composite squadron. Named McCalla Field after Captain Bowman H. McCalla.

Jacksonville NAS, FL

Location: eight miles south of Jacksonville
Units assigned: HS-3 – SH-60F, HH-60H (CVW-8); HS-5 – SH-3H (CVW-7); HS-7 – SH-3H (CVW-3); HS-9 – SH-3H (CVW-17); HS-11 – SH-3H (CVW-1); HS-15 – SH-3H (CVW-6) (to SH-60F in March 1992); VP-5 – P-3C; VP-16 – P-3C; VP-24 – P-3C; VP-45 – P-3C; VP-49 – P-3C; VP-56 – P-3C; VP-62 – P-3C; VP-30 – TP-3A; VP-3A – P-3C (PACFLT FRS); HS-1 – SH-3H (add SH-60F late 1992); HS-75 – SH-3H; VR-58 – C-9B; Base Flight – UC-12B, SH-3H

This is the second antisubmarine warfare facility, along with NAS Brunswick, operating the P-3 Orion by the Atlantic Fleet within Patrol Wing Eleven. Jacksonville is also the home station for the Commander Sea-Based ASW Wings Atlantic with jurisdiction for helicopter and fixed-wing ASW units at Cecil Field, Norfolk and Mayport. Antisubmarine Helicopter Wing One is located at Jacksonville, with responsibility for Atlantic Fleet SH-3H and SH-60F squadrons while shore-based. In addition, Jacksonville has the Fleet Replenishment Squadrons (FRS) for the P-3 and SH-3 of the Atlantic Fleet. The Naval Air Depot performs major overhaul of various types including F/A-18s, P-3s and T-2s. Named John Towers Field after Admiral John H. Towers.

Kadena NAF, Okinawa

Location: at Kadena Air Base on the island of Okinawa
Units assigned: Base Flight – UC-12B

The small naval facility supports P-3C detachments from Barbers Point and Moffett Field, as well as visiting Navy and Marine Corps aircraft from shore locations and carriers in the Far East.

Keflavik NS, Iceland

Location: to the west of Reykjavik on the west side of Iceland
Units assigned: Base Flight – UP-3A

Keflavik operates P-3 Orion rotations from Atlantic Fleet squadrons to patrol the large expanse of northern Atlantic Ocean and Norwegian Sea.

Key West NAS, FL

Location: 10 miles east of Key West
Units assigned: VF-45 det – A-4E, TA-4J, F-5E/F, F-16N, TF-16N; VAQ-33 – EA-6A, EP-3A, EP-3J; Base Flight – UC-12B, SH-3D

Key West was established during World War II to conduct training of naval aviators prior to them being relocated overseas. Key West has the primary role of evaluating the effectiveness of Atlantic Fleet carrier-based fighter squadrons, and also hosts major Fleet exercises involving Navy, Air Force and other NATO squadrons. VF-45 conducts the adversary role during Fleet exercises, while VAQ-33 performs tactical electronic warfare to add realism for the deployed fighter squadrons.

Kingsville NAS, TX

Location: three miles east of Kingsville
Units assigned: VT-21 – TA-4J to T-45A; VT-22 – TA-4J; VT-23 – T-2C

The facility has Training Wing 3 (TW-3) in residence to conduct intermediate and advanced strike jet training of naval aviators. VT-21 became the first Navy squadron to receive the T-45A Goshawk when it began transition from the TA-4J during January 1992.

Lajes NAF, Azores

Location: on Terceira Island in the Atlantic Ocean, 900 miles west of Portugal
Units assigned: nil

Lajes operates P-3 Orion rotations from Atlantic Fleet squadrons to patrol the large expanse of the eastern Atlantic Ocean. The base is administered by Naval Forces Azores.

Lakehurst NAWC, NJ

Location: three miles north of Lakehurst
Units assigned: Naval Air Warfare Center Aircraft Division (NAWC/AD) – TH-1L

The major unit located at Lakehurst is the Naval Air Warfare Center Aircraft Division, which conducts research and development of all forms of engineering for aircraft launch and recovery systems and landing aids, plus support equipment for aircraft. Surplus airframes are employed for test, including A-3s and F-4s. The Center periodically conducts tests involving the destruction of aircraft in a controlled ground accident to evaluate the volatility of aviation fuel. A Naval Air Technical Training Center (NATTC) at Lakehurst conducts courses to train enlisted personnel in the handling of aviation fuel, and catapult and arrester gear usage and handling. The latter is conducted inside a former airship hangar with a mock-up of an aircraft carrier deck to train personnel in the skill of aircraft movement within a confined area. The NAWC Aircraft Division was established at Lakehurst in January 1992, replacing the Naval Air Engineering Center. Named Maxfield Field after Commander Louis H. Maxfield.

Lemoore NAS, CA

Location: five miles west of Lemoore
Units assigned: VFA-22 – F/A-18C (CVW-11); VFA-25 – F/A-18C (CVW-14); VFA-27 – F/A-18A (CVW-15); VFA-94 – F/A-18C (CVW-11); VFA-97 – F/A-18A (CVW-15); VFA-113 – F/A-18C (CVW-14); VFA-146 – F/A-18C (CVW-9); VFA-147 – F/A-18C (CVW-9); VFA-151 – F/A-18A (CVW-2); VAQ-34 – F/A-18A/B; VFA-127 – F-5E/F; VFA-125 – F/A-18A/B/C/D, T-34C (PACFLT FRS); VFA-303 – F/A-18A; Base Flight – UC-12B, UH-1N

NAS Lemoore was commissioned in July 1961 as the shore base for the Pacific Fleet light attack community located at NAS Moffett Field, the community being the responsibility of the Commander Light Attack Wing Pacific Fleet. The establishment of Lemoore in the wide open spaces of central California went some way towards relieving the pressure of flight operations in the San Francisco Bay area. Lemoore initially housed the A-1 Skyraider and A-4 Skyhawk, until November 1966 when the first A-7 Corsairs were delivered to VA-122. Subsequently the F/A-18 Hornet began entering service in 1980 and has completely replaced the A-7, with nine deploy-

Most base flights have UC-12s for liaison work, and several boast helicopters for rescue and utility duties. This is Key West's SH-3D.

164

able squadrons currently assigned. The squadrons have gradually switched from the A-7 Corsair II to the F/A-18 Hornet, with conversion being completed in 1990. Lemoore has the Pacific Fleet Replenishment Squadrons (FRS) to conduct aircrew training with the F/A-18. Tactical Electronic Warfare Squadron 34 moved to Lemoore from Point Mugu during 1991, but was inactive for a time while the unit transitioned from the EA-7L to the F/A-18A/B.

Mayport NAF, FL

Location: 11 miles east of Arlington
Units assigned: HSL-36 – SH-2F; HSL-40 – SH-60B; HSL-42 – SH-60B; HSL-44 – SH-60B; HSL-46 – SH-60B; HSL-48 – SH-60B; Base Flight – UC-12B

Mayport is the home station for several ASW light helicopter squadrons which are formed into Helicopter Antisubmarine Light Wing One. For many years the only squadron in residence was HSL-36 operating the SH-2F, but it was joined by the five SH-60B squadrons during the latter half of the 1980s. The station is home port for one of the smaller aircraft carriers, CV-60/USS *Saratoga*.

Memphis NAS, TN

Location: three miles south of Millington
Units assigned: VP-67 – P-3B; VR-60 – C-9B; VMA-124 – A-4M, TA-4J; Base Flight – UC-12B

The Naval Air Technical Training Center (NATTC) is located at NAS Memphis to conduct courses to train enlisted personnel in aircraft maintenance and other aviation skills. Among the many courses hosted are those covering all manner of aircraft maintenance, together with ordnance, air traffic control and antisubmarine warfare equipment. Among the ground instructional airframes employed by the Center are examples of the A-4A, A-4C, A-4L, A-6A, A-7A, A-7B, A-7E, E-2B, F-4B, F-4J, UH-1E, CH-46D and AV-8A. Apart from the NATTC, the station houses three Navy and Marine Corps Reserve squadrons.

Meridian NAS, MS

Location: 14 miles north of Meridian
Units assigned: VT-7 – TA-4J; VT-19 – T-2C; Base Flight – UH-1N

NAS Meridian was commissioned in 1959 and opened for operations in mid-1961, to become the Navy's newest and most modern jet training installation. Initially known as McCain Field in honor of Admiral John S. McCain, the base was a naval auxiliary air station until 1968, when it became a naval air station in its own right. Since August 1971 the facility has had Training Wing 1 (TW-1) in residence to conduct intermediate and advanced strike jet training of naval aviators.

Midway Island NAF, Midway Island

Location: on Midway Island in the Pacific Ocean
Units assigned: nil

Midway NAF has no unit in residence and is primarily a support facility for aircraft in transit across the Pacific or those operating from aircraft carriers in the locality. The station is named Henderson Field after Marine Corps Major Lofton R. Henderson.

Mildenhall NAF, England

Location: two miles northwest of Mildenhall
Units assigned: Base Flight – UC-12M

The facility operates a trio of UC-12Ms which perform routine resupply flights within the United Kingdom and parts of northern Europe. Mildenhall also supports a limited amount of visiting Navy and Marine Corps traffic, particularly P-3s and KC-130s.

Miramar NAS, CA

Location: 10 miles north of San Diego
Units assigned: VAW-112 – E-2C (CVW-9); VAW-113 – E-2C (CVW-14); VAW-114 – E-2C (CVW-15); VAW-115 – E-2C (CVW-4); VAW-116 – E-2C (CVW-2); VAW-117 – E-2C (CVW-11); VF-1 – F-14A (CVW-2); VF-2 – F-14A (CVW-2); VF-11 – F-14D; VF-24 – F-14B (CVW-9); VF-31 – F-14D; VF-51 – F-14A (CVW-15); VF-111 – F-14A (CVW-15); VF-114 – F-14A (CVW-11); VF-211 – F-14B (CVW-9); VF-213 – F-14A (CVW-11); VAW-88 – E-2C; VAW-110 – C-2A, E-2C, TE-2C (PACFLT FRS); VF-124 – F-14A/B/D, T-34C (PACFLT FRS); VF-126 – A-4E/F, TA-4J, F-16N, T-2C; VF-301 – F-14A, VF-302, F-14A; VFC-13 – A-4F, TA-4J; Navy Fighter Weapons School (NFWS) – A-4E/F, F-14A, F-16A, TF-16N

Miramar is one of the principal naval stations in the USA with the Commander Fighter Airborne Early Warning Wing Pacific Fleet responsible for deployable E-2 and F-14 squadrons of the Pacific Fleet. The wing also has the Pacific Fleet Replenishment Squadrons (FRS) for the E-2 Hawkeye and F-14 Tomcat, with the former also training crews for the C-2 Greyhound, as the two types have similar flight characteristics. The Navy Fighter Weapons School is located at Miramar to train experienced Navy and Marine Corps fighter aircrew in all aspects of fighter and adversary operation. 'Top Gun', as the NFWS is universally known, conducts six courses annually each lasting five weeks. Four Naval Reserve squadrons are stationed at Miramar performing AEW, fighter and adversary roles alongside their front-line colleagues. The station is named Mitcher Field after Admiral Marc A. Mitcher.

Misawa NAF, Japan

Location: in Aomori Prefecture at the northeastern end of Honshu Island
Units assigned: Base Flight – UC-12B

The facility is a Fleet support air station with P-3 patrol squadrons detached for temporary duty from NAS Barbers Point and NAS Moffett Field.

Moffett Field NAS, CA

Location: 10 miles west of San Jose
Units assigned: VP-9 – P-3C; VP-19 – P-3C; VP-40 – P-3C; VP-46 – P-3C; VP-47 – P-3C; VP-48 – P-3C; VP-50 – P-3C; VP-91 – P-3C; VP-31 – P-3C (PACFLT FRS); Base Flight – UC-12B

Moffett Field was established as an air station in 1933, initially as a facility for dirigibles while also serving as an army air training base. During World War II the base housed Navy blimps before being upgraded to enable jet operations postwar. Today, Moffett Field is the main facility on the West Coast of the USA, housing patrol squadrons of the Pacific Fleet which are combined to form Patrol Wing Ten. The Pacific Fleet Replenishment Squadron (FRS) for the P-3 Orion is also located at the station. Moffett Field also houses the Commander Patrol Wings Pacific Fleet with responsibility for all Pacific-based patrol squadrons. In addition, the Commander has responsibility for the stations at Barbers Point, Moffett Field, Adak and Midway Island. Moffett Field houses an Air National Guard rescue squadron

and a facility operated by ESL to modify RC-12Ks. The station is scheduled to close by 1995 as part of budget cuts, with the resident P-3 squadrons being inactivated or reassigned. The naval air station is named after Rear Admiral William A. Moffett.

Naples NAVSUPACT, Italy

Location: at Naples Airport
Units assigned: nil

The Commander Fleet Air Mediterranean (COMFAIRMED) has his headquarters at Naples and is responsible for a range of shore activities including ship and aircraft support facilities at Rota, Spain; La Maddalena, Sardinia; Naples, Italy; Sigonella, Sicily; and Souda Bay, Crete. In addition, Naples is headquarters for the Commander-in-Chief Allied Forces Southern Europe (CINCSOUTH), which is a NATO post with a VP-3A made available for the Commander, although for maintenance purposes it is assigned to Sigonella. Reconnaissance Wing Atlantic was formed in 1989 with responsibilities for the activities of VQ-2 based at Rota. An SH-3G detached from HC-2 at NAS Norfolk is normally assigned to whichever vessel is acting as flagship of the US Sixth Fleet, as the latter has its headquarters at Gaeta to the north of Naples. Naples is known as a Naval Support Activity rather than a Naval Air Station.

New Orleans NAS, LA

Location: 10 miles south of New Orleans
Units assigned: VMA-204 – F/A-18A; VP-94 – P-3B; VR-54 – C-130T; HML-767 – UH-1N; MWHS-4 – UC-12B, CT-39G; Base Flight – UC-12B

The station is another facility which houses a variety of Navy and Marine Corps Reserve squadrons along with Air Force and Army Reserve and National Guard units. VR-54 was established here during 1991 as the first Naval Reserve squadron to operate the C-130T. Headquarters 4th Marine Air Wing is located at New Orleans and is the controlling element of the Marine Corps Reserve aviation. The station is named Alvin Callender Field after Royal Flying Corps Captain Alvin A. Callender.

Norfolk NAS, VA

Location: in the northwest suburbs of Norfolk
Units assigned: VAW-121 – E-2C (CVW-7); VAW-122 – E-2C (CVW-6) (to disestablish by October 1992); VAW-123 – E-2C (CVW-1); VAW-124 – E-2C (CVW-8); VAW-125 – E-2C (CVW-17); VAW-126 – E-2C (CVW-3); HC-2 – VH-3A, SH-3G, CH-53E; HC-6 – CH-46A/D; HH-46A, VH-3A; HC-8 – CH-46D, HH-46D, UH-46D; HCS-4 – HH-60H; HM-12 – H-53E; HM-14 – MH-53E; HM-18 – RH-53D; HSL-30 – SH-2F; HSL-32 – SH-2F; HSL-34 – SH-2F; VAW-78 – E-2C; VAW-120 – C-2A, E-2C (LANTFLT FRS); VR-56 – C-9B; VRC-40 – C-2A, CT-39E; HMM-774 – CH-46E; Base Flight – UC-12B/M

Norfolk Naval Air Station is located adjacent to the largest naval complex in the western world and has no fewer than 120 ships home-ported, with piers and jetties located at various points on the south, west and north shoreline. Among these are aircraft carriers CV-66/USS *America*, CV-67/USS *John F. Kennedy*, CVN-69/USS *Dwight D. Eisenhower*, CVN-71/USS *Theodore Roosevelt* and, until recently, CV-61/USS *Ranger*. CVN-73/USS *George Washington* will be based at Norfolk following commission on 4 July 1992, with CV-67 moving to Mayport. In addition, amphibious assault ships LHA-2/USS *Saipan*, LHA-4/USS *Nassau*, LPH-2/USS *Iwo Jima*, LPH-7/USS *Guadalcanal*, LPH-9/USS *Guam*, LPH-12/USS *Inchon* have Norfolk as their home port. Norfolk

Air Stations

is home to the Commander Naval Air Force US Atlantic Fleet (COMNAVAFLANTFLT) and the Commanders of Helicopter Tactical Wing One and Tactical Support Wing One. Some two dozen flying units are located at Norfolk including the Atlantic Fleet AEW E-2 Hawkeye squadrons, along with the Atlantic Fleet Replenishment Squadrons (FRS) for the E-2 Hawkeye, which also conducts C-2 Greyhound aircrew training. A variety of support helicopter squadrons are stationed at Norfolk with many one- or two-aircraft detachments deployed aboard vessels for Atlantic and Mediterranean cruises. The station has a huge naval air depot which conducts major overhauls of various types, including the A-6 and F-14. The station is named Chambers Field after Captain Washington I. Chambers.

North Island NAS, CA

Location: two mile north of Coronado
Units assigned: HS-2 – SH-60F/HH-60H (CVW-9); HS-4 – SH-3H (CVW-15); HS-6 – SH-60F, HH-60H (CVW-11); HS-8 – SH-60F, HH-60H (CVW-14); HS-14 – SH-3H (CVW-2); HS-15 – SH-3H (CVW-6); VS-29 – S-3A (CVW-15 to ?); VS-35 – S-3B (CVW-14); VS-33 – S-3A, (CVW-9); VS-37 – S-3B (CVW-15); VS-38 – S-3A (CVW-2); HC-1 – SH-3G, CH-53E; HC-3 – CH-46D, HH-46D (PACFLT FRS); HC-11 – CH-46D, HH-46D, UH-46D; HS-10 – SH-3H, SH-60F (PACFLT FRS); HSL-31 – SH-2F (PACFLT FRS); HSL-33 – SH-2F to SH-2G; HSL-35 – SH-2F; HSL-41 – SH-60B; HSL-43 – SH-60B; HSL-45 – SH-60B; HSL-47 – SH-60B; HSL-49 – SH-60B; HSL-84 – SH-2F to SH-2G; VR-57 – C-9B; VRC-30 – C-2A, UC-12B, CT-39E; VS-41 – S-3A/B (PACFLT FRS); Base Flight – UC-12B

North Island was one of the first sites to operate naval aircraft when a contingent was relocated from Greenbury Point, MD, in January 1912 to conduct fine weather flying. However, the facility was only employed on a temporary basis. From its humble beginnings North Island has subsequently become a huge naval complex accommodating a sizeable contingent of ships which are home-ported to the station. Among these are several aircraft carriers including CV-63/USS *Kitty Hawk*, CV-61/USS *Ranger* and CV-64/USS *Constellation*, plus amphibious assault ships LHA-1/USS *Tarawa*, LHA-3/USS *Belleau Wood*, LPH-3/USS *Okinawa*, LPH-10/USS *Tripoli* and LPH-11/USS *New Orleans*. North Island is home of the Commander Naval Air Force US Pacific Fleet (COMNAVAFPACTFLT) and the Commander Antisubmarine Warfare Wing Pacific Fleet. As with Norfolk, its sister station, North Island has a variety of support helicopter squadrons assigned along with the Pacific Fleet S-3 Viking squadrons. A naval air depot performs major overhaul of F/A-18s. No fewer than five Fleet Replenishment Squadrons (FRS) are in residence, including those for the SH-2, SH-3, CH-46, SH-60 and S-3. The station is named Halsey Field after Admiral William F. Halsey.

Oceana NAS, VA

Location: five miles west of Virginia Beach
Units assigned: VA-34 – A-6E/KA-6D (CVW-7); VA-35 – A-6E/KA-6D (CVW-17); VA-36 – A-6E (CVW-8); VA-65 – A-6E/KA-6D (CVW-8); VA-75 – A-6E/KA-6D (CVW-3); VA-85 – A-6E/KA-6D (CVW-1); VA-176 – A-6E/KA-6D (CVW-6) (to disestablish by October 1992); VF-14 – F-14A (CVW-6) (to disestablish by October 1992); VF-14 – F-14A (CVW-3); VF-32 – F-14A (CVW-3); VF-33 – F-14A (CVW-1); VF-41 – F-14A (CVW-8); VF-74 – F-14B (CVW-17); VF-84 – F-14A (CVW-8); VF-102 – F-14A (CVW-1); VF-103 – F-14B (CVW-17); VF-142 – F-14B (CVW-7); VF-143 – F-14B (CVW-7); VA-42 – A-6E, TC-4C, T-34C (LANTFLT FRS); VF-43 – A-4E/F, TA-4J, F-5E/F, F-16N, T-2C; VF-101 – F-14A/B/D (LANTFLT FRS); VFC-12

– A-4F, TA-4J; Base Flight – UC-12B, SH-3G

The station began life in 1940 as an auxiliary airfield but was expanded during World War II until it had become a naval auxiliary air station by 1943. The introduction of jet aircraft into service resulted in the base being upgraded to a naval air station in 1952, before gaining master jet base status in 1957. Oceana is home of the Commander Tactical Wings, Atlantic, who is ultimately responsible for all deployable attack, fighter and airborne early warning squadrons of the Atlantic Fleet. The station has a large number of attack and fighter squadrons in residence, as it is home base for the Atlantic Fleet A-6 Intruder and F-14 Tomcat units. In addition, the F-14 and A-6 Fleet Replenishment Squadrons (FRS) are based, with the latter unit employing examples of the TC-4C fitted with the Intruder radar suite housed in an extended nose cone. The station is named Appollo Soucek Field after Vice Admiral Appollo Soucek.

Patuxent River NAWC, MD

Location: three miles south of Lexington Park
Units assigned: Naval Air Warfare Center Aircraft Division (NAWC/AD) – A-4M, TA-4J, A-6E, EA-6B, C-2A, UC-880, E-2C, F-14A/D, F/A-18A, F/A-18C, F/A-18D, AH-1J, AH-1W, UH-1N, SH-2F, HH-3A, SH-3G/H, NVH-3A, CH-46E, CH-53A/E, MH-53E, TH-57A, HH-60H, SH-60B, VH-60A, HH-60A, P-3B/C, S-3A/B, NT-34C, T-34C, T-45A, AV-8B, TAV-8B; Test Pilot's School (TPS) – TA-4J, F/A-18B, UC-12B, SH-3G, OH-58A, UH-60A, T-2C, T-38A, T-39D, NU-1B, U-6A, X-26A; Naval Research Laboratory (NRL) – EP-3A, EP-3B, RP-3A, UP-3A; VQ-4 – E-6A; VX-1 – SH-2F, SH-3H, SH-60B/F, P-3C, S-3A/B; VXN-8 – RP-3D, UP-3A

Patuxent River was constructed in 1942 and 1943 to provide a single facility to conduct various kinds of naval aircraft tests. Prior to this time disparate facilities in the Washington area had performed this role, including Anacostia, Dahlgren, Norfolk, Philadelphia and the Washington Navy Yard, which was wholly unsatisfactory. The consolidation of test duties at Patuxent River enabled the process to be streamlined and expanded to include the Naval Test Pilot's School.

The primary unit at Patuxent River is the Naval Air Warfare Center Aircraft Division, which was established in January 1992. Its main duty is to test and evaluate all manner of new and modified aircraft and helicopter designs. Each prototype aircraft or helicopter destined for Navy or Marine Corps service is assigned to NAWC for full evaluation prior to production contracts being placed. This involves close liaison between NAWC and the manufacturer. Prior to the creation of NAWC, the Naval Air Test Center was the main operator at Patuxent River and was divided into three distinct sections consisting of the Strike Aircraft Test Directorate (SATD), Fixed-Wing Aircraft Test Directorate (FWATD) and Rotary Wing Aircraft Test Directorate (RTATD). In addition, NAWC operates the Naval Test Pilot's School to train future test pilots for service with the US Navy and allied nations. Headquarters NAWC is located at Arlington, VA.

The Naval Research Laboratory maintains several complexes in the Washington area and operates a small fleet of highly modified P-3 Orions to conduct electronic and reconnaissance research. Air Test and Evaluation Squadron One is located at Patuxent River to work closely with NATC to develop tactics for employment by Fleet antisubmarine warfare squadrons. Oceanographic Development Squadron Eight has its home base at Patuxent River, although it deploys its P-3 Orions worldwide to perform special projects such as geomagnetic surveys and research work in conjunction with antisubmarine warfare and environment issues.

Pensacola NAS, FL

Location: five miles south of Pensacola
Units assigned: HC-16 – UH-1N, SH-3D/H; VT-4 – TA-4J, T-2C; VT-10 – T-2C; VT-86 – T-34C, T-39N; 'Blue Angels' – F/A-18A/B, KC-130F; Base Flight – UC-12B, T-39D

Pensacola was the first naval flying station with a formal training program, being established in

Above: Oceana is the biggest and busiest fast jet airfield on the East Coast, housing a pair of adversary units, RAGs for the F-14 and A-6, and all Atlantic Fleet Tomcat and Intruder squadrons when these are not deployed. This makes it AIRLANT's equivalent to Miramar.

Above: Informally known as 'Pax River', Patuxent River is home to the Naval Air Warfare Center's Aircraft Division, and houses a bewildering array of aircraft types, most of them non-standard and some of them unique in USN service. These are the T-38s of the NTPS.

January 1914 and the site being designated a naval air station in December 1917. Postwar, Pensacola was expanded to become a permanent training base for naval aviators. Pensacola has Training Wing 6 (TW-6) in residence to conduct intermediate and advanced strike jet training on the TA-4J/T-2C, and basic/intermediate Naval Flight Officer training with the T-2C/T-47A before progressing to the advanced NFO course on the T-47A/TA-4J. HC-16 was formerly under Naval Air Arm Training Command training aircrew to operate HH-46As, but has subsequently re-equipped with the UH-1N and SH-3D and now reports to the Commander Helicopter Tactical Wing One at Norfolk. The 'Blue Angels' demonstration team is housed at Pensacola and spends a considerable amount of time perfecting its routine at home base. Pensacola is composed of the main facility and Chevalier Field which houses the naval air depot. The NAD overhauls helicopters exclusively, with H-3s, H-53s and H-60s among the types which receive major overhaul. Pensacola was home to the training aircraft carrier AVT-16/USS *Lexington* until November 1991, when the ship was retired after 29 years in the role. CV-59/USS *Forrestal* became AVT-59 during February 1992 when the ship was transferred to Pensacola as replacement. The station is named Forrest Sherman Field after Admiral Forrest Sherman.

Point Mugu NAS, CA

Location: five miles south of Oxnard
Units assigned: Naval Air Warfare Center Weapons Division (NAWC/WD) – A-6E, RC-12M, QF-4N, F-14A/D, F/A-18A, F/A-18B, F/A-18C, QF-86F, HH-46D, UH-46D, EP/RP-3A; HCS-5 – HH-60H; VFA-305 – F/A-18A; VP-65 – P-3C; VX-4 – F-14A/B/D, F/A-18A/C; VXE-6 – LC-130F/R, UH-1N; Base Flight – UC-12B

Point Mugu was opened in 1946 as one of the primary missile evaluation centers. The site was selected due to its geographical location adjacent to the Pacific Ocean affording a safe area for test operations, with nearby Laguna Peak providing a convenient elevated position for communications and instrumentation equipment. The organization responsible for missile tests has changed name several times, with the Naval Missile Center (NMC) being in residence for many years, before becoming the Pacific Missile Test Center (PMTC). A reorganization of Naval Air Systems Command has resulted in the latter being retitled.

The Naval Air Warfare Center Weapons Division was formed in January 1992 as the major operator at Point Mugu, replacing the PMTC. The Center is responsible for all types of Navy missile development including compatibility of existing weapons with new aircraft designs. NAWC operates a variety of fighter and attack airframes along with a handful of QF-4 and QF-86 drones. Sorties involving the firing of live weapons are conducted over the large sea test range to the west of Point Mugu. The target drone is flown from Point Mugu to the small airfield at San Nicolas Island where a ground-controlled pilotless take-off is made before the drone is handed over to a DF-4 drone director. If the drone is not destroyed during the test it returns to San Nicolas before being flown back to Point Mugu by a pilot. A number of modified P-3s are flown to extend the range coverage. Air Test and Evaluation Squadron Four works alongside NAWC during missile development with a small number of F-14s and F/A-18s.

Antarctic Development Squadron Six has been stationed at Point Mugu for 20 years with aircraft and helicopters ferried to New Zealand each autumn to perform a host of duties on the Antarctic continent during the austral summer.

Roosevelt Roads NS, PR

Location: on the coast of Puerto Rico Island
Units assigned: VC-8 – TA-4J, SH-3G

The naval station has a fleet composite squadron in residence to conduct adversary training for carrier air wings in the Caribbean and to serve as a logistics base. In addition, the squadron hosts training exercises with shore-based and carrier-borne squadrons. The station is known as Ofstie Field after Vice Admiral Ralph A. Ofstie.

Rota NS, Spain

Location: on the coast of the Gulf of Cadiz to the west of Jerez
Units assigned: VQ-2 – EP-3E; VR-22 – C-130F, KC-130F; Base Flight – UC-12M

Rota is a joint US Navy and Spanish Navy base which houses a fleet air reconnaissance squadron operating the EP-3E 'Aries II' version of the Orion solely since the unit's EA-3B Skywarriors were withdrawn at the end of 1991. The only other unit in residence is VR-22 with approximately six C-130F and KC-130F examples which perform airlift duties within the Sixth Fleet area. Rota has a jetty alongside which provides facilities for submarines to dock for resupply and maintenance.

Sigonella NAS, Sicily

Location: on the coast of the Sicilian mainland
Units assigned: HC-4 – CH-53E; VR-24 – C-2A, CT-39G; Base Flight – UC-12M, VP-3A

Sigonella was opened in 1959 as a naval air facility due to its strategically important position in the central Mediterranean region. Increasing importance of Sixth Fleet operations resulted in Sigonella being upgraded to a naval air station in 1981. The station has a transport squadron in residence which includes approximately eight C-2A Greyhounds for carrier onboard delivery (COD) duties aboard aircraft carriers in the Mediterranean. Land-based antisubmarine operations are conducted from Sigonella by P-3 Orion squadrons which rotate from their stateside bases. The base flight operates a small fleet of communications types together with a VP-3A which is operated on behalf of the Commander-in-Chief Allied Forces Southern Europe (CINCSOUTH), whose headquarters is at Naples.

Souda Bay AB, Crete

Location: on the northwest side of the Island of Crete
Units assigned: nil

Souda Bay has a regular detachment of EP-3Es from Fleet Air Reconnaissance Squadron Two at Rota, Spain. The facility also supports detachments of USAF reconnaissance aircraft along with a Greek air force fighter wing.

South Weymouth NAS, MA

Location: five miles south of Weymouth
Units assigned: HML-771 – UH-1N; HSL-74 – SH-2F to SH-2G; VP-92 – P-3C; VMA-322 – A-4M; Base Flight – UC-12B

South Weymouth is another station which houses only Navy and Marine Corps Reserve squadrons. The station is named Shea Field after Lieutenant Commander John J. Shea.

Stewart ANGB, NY

Location: four miles west of Newburgh
Units assigned: VMGR-452 – KC-130T

The single Marine Corps Reserve Hercules squadron is located at Stewart ANGB along with Air National Guard aircraft in one corner of Stewart International Airport, which was an Air Force base until 1969.

Warminster NAWC, PA

Location: 15 miles west of Philadelphia
Units assigned: Naval Air Warfare Center Aircraft Division (NAWC/AD) – NA-7E, F-14A, NCH-53A, P-3C, UP-3A, T-2C

The Naval Air Warfare Center is primarily concerned with the advancement of technology by enhancing existing weapons systems. The Center is housed in a complex at Warminster and operates a small number of aircraft including the P-3, as NAWC has conducted extensive work improving the detection of submarines. NAWC was established at Warminster in January 1992, having replaced the Naval Air Development Center (NADC) which was the major test organization here previously.

Washington NAF, MD

Location: 15 miles southeast of Washington
Units assigned: VP-68 – P-3C; VAQ-209 – EA-6B; VMFA-321 – F/A-18A; CFLSW – C-20D; HQ USMC Flight – UC-12B; Base Flight – UC-12B

The naval air facility operates from one of the flight lines at Andrews Air Force Base. The Navy and Marine Corps presence is restricted to Reserve squadrons although the Base Flight UC-12s and CFLSW C-20s perform VIP duties. The headquarters of the Marine Corps is also located in Washington with an HQ flight operating a small number of UC-12Bs. The proximity of Andrews AFB/Washington NAF to the seat of government and the Pentagon ensures a large number of visiting aircraft.

Whidbey Island NAS, WA

Location: five miles north of Oak Harbor
Units assigned: VAQ-130 – EA-6B (CVW-3); VAQ-131 – EA-6B (CVW-2); VAQ-132 – EA-6B (CVW-17); VAQ-133 – EA-6B (CVW-6) (to disestablish by October 1992); VAQ-134 – EA-6B (CVW-15); VAQ-135 – EA-6B (CVW-11); VAQ-137 – EA-6B (CVW-1); VAQ-138 – EA-6B (CVW-9); VAQ-139 – EA-6B (CVW-14); VAQ-140 – EA-6B (CVW-7); VAQ-141 – EA-6B (CVW-8); VA-52 – A-6E/KA-6D (CVW-15); VA-95 – A-6E/KA-6D (CVW-11); VA-145 – A-6E/KA-6D (CVW-2); VA-155 – A-6E (CVW-2); VA-165 – A-6E/KA-6D (CVW-9); VA-196 – A-6E/KA-6D (CVW-14); VA-128 – A-6E, KA-6D, TC-4C (PACFLT FRS); VMAQ-4 – EA-6A; VAQ-35 – EA-6B; VAQ-129 – EA-6B (LANTFLT and PACFLT FRS); VAQ-309 – EA-6B; VP-69 – P-3B; VR-61 – C-9B; Base Flight – UC-12B, SH-3D

Whidbey Island is the home station for the Pacific Fleet A-6 Intruder squadrons and home base for both the Pacific and Atlantic Fleet EA-6B Prowler squadrons. The assignment of the latter aircraft from both Fleets is a unique situation in the Navy at present. The A-6 and EA-6B Fleet Replenishment Squadrons (FRS) are stationed at Whidbey Island. The station is named Ault Field after Commander William B. Ault.

Whiting Field NAS, FL

Location: 10 miles west of Pensacola
Units assigned: VT-2 – T-34C; VT-3 – T-34C; VT-6 – T-34C; HT-8 – TH-57B; HT-18 – TH-57B/C

Whidbey Island is unique in being the shore base for an entire community, this being the EA-6B Prowler force, with aircraft detaching to both Pacific and Atlantic Fleets. In addition, the base also houses the Pacific Fleet Intruders.

Whiting Field has the largest number of fixed- and rotary-wing training aircraft at any naval base, with an excess of 400 assigned to the five squadrons of Training Wing Five (TW-5). The three

squadrons of T-34Cs are for primary and intermediate training, while the two TH-57 squadrons are for basic and advanced helicopter pilot training. The number of training sorties launched each day is more than Whiting Field could handle without approximately a dozen outlying fields in the vicinity being employed to relieve the pressure. The station is named after Captain Kenneth Whiting.

Willow Grove NAS, PA

Location: five miles north of Willow Grove
Units assigned: HSL-94 – SH-2F to SH-2G; VP-64 – P-3B; VP-66 – P-3B; VR-52 – C-9B; HMH-772 – CH-53A; VMA-131 – A-4M; Base Flight – UC-12B

The naval air station serves as the major facility for Navy, Air Force, Marine Corps and Army Reserve personnel in the state of Pennsylvania. Situated close to Philadelphia, the station has received modern equipment for its squadrons in recent years.

US MARINE CORPS AIR STATIONS

Beaufort MCAS, SC

Location: five miles west of Beaufort
Units assigned: VMFA-115 – F/A-18A; VMFA-122 – F/A-18A; VMFA-251 – F/A-18A; VMFA-312 – F/A-18C; VMFA-333 – F/A-18A (to deactivate during 1992); VMFA-451 – F/A-18A; MARTD – UC-12B, HH-46D

Beaufort is the main F/A-18 Hornet base for Fleet Marine Force Atlantic (FMFLANT) with six squadrons of aircraft which together form Marine Air Group 31 (MAG-31). Headquarters and Maintenance Squadron 32 (H&MS-32) and latterly Marine Air Logistics Squadron 31 (MALS-31) operated a small number of OA-4Ms, although these were retired and the unit is now without aircraft assigned. Named Merritt Field in September 1975 after Lewis G. Merritt.

Bogue Field, MCALF, SC

Location: two miles east of Bayshore Park near Camp Lejeune
Units assigned: nil

Bogue Field is a training and support site for Marine Corps helicopters and AV-8 operations from MCAS New River and Cherry Point.

Camp Pendleton MCAF, CA

Location: 10 miles south of San Clemente
Units assigned: HMLA-169 – AH-1W, UH-1N; HMLA-267 – AH-1W, UH-1N; HMLA-367 – AH-1W, UH-1N; HMLA-369 – AH-1W, UH-1N; HMT-303 – AH-1W, UH-1N, OV-10A; HMA-775 – AH-1J; VMO-2 – OV-10A/D (to deactivate by 1994)

Marine air bases are located close to or within major camps. Camp Pendleton is home to AH-1 Cobras (illustrated) and OV-10 Broncos.

The air facility is located inside the huge Camp Pendleton training area and forms part of the 3d Marine Air Wing (3d MAW), with Marine Air Group 39 (MAG-39) responsible for a single observation and several helicopter squadrons. Camp Pendleton will assume greater importance, and be upgraded to air station status if it has not already been so, with the closure of Tustin MCAS as several of their squadrons will make greater use of Pendleton. MAG-39 will inactivate, as all front-line helicopter squadrons of FMFPAC based on the US mainland will be assigned to MAG-16.

Cherry Point MCAS, NC

Location: one mile north of Havelock
Units assigned: MALS-14 – TA-4F; VMA-223 – AV-8B; VMA-231 – AV-8B; VMA-331 – AV-8B; VMA-542 – AV-8B; VMAT-203 – AV-8B, TAV-8B; VMA(AW)-224 – A-6E; VMA(AW)-332 – A-6E; VMA(AW)-533 – A-6E; VMAT(AW)-202 – A-6E, TC-4C; VMAQ-2 – EA-6B; VMGR-252 – KC-130F/R; VMGRT-253 – KC-130F; MARTD – UC-12B, HH-46D; SOES – C-9B, CT-39G

MCAS Cherry Point had opened by the time the US entered World War II. The station is one of the major Marine Corps stations of FMFLANT under the 2d Marine Air Wing (2d MAW) with both Marine Air Group 14 and 32 in residence. MAG-14 is responsible for the A-6, EA-6B and KC-130 squadrons while MAG-32 oversees the AV-8 units. Headquarters and Maintenance Squadron 32 was operational flying the OA-4M although MALS-14 is the current unit flying a handful of TA-4F. Cherry Point has three training squadrons for aircrew transitioning to the AV-8B, A-6E and all three versions of the

Yuma is home to four AV-8B squadrons, but is also the main tactical training base, with a large desert range attached.

KC-130. The station was named Cunningham Field in September 1941 in honor of Lieutenant Colonel Alfred A. Cunningham, who was the first Marine Corps aviator.

El Toro MCAS, CA

Location: eight miles south of Santa Ana
Units assigned: HMM-764 – CH-46E; VMFA-134 – F/A-18A; VMFA-314 – F/A-18A; VMFA-323 – F/A-18A; VMFA-531 – F/A-18A (to deactivate during March 1992); VMFAT-101 – F/A-18A/B/C/D; VMFA(AW)-121 – F/A-18D; VMFA(AW)-225 – F/A-18D; VMFA(AW)-242 – F/A-18D; VMGR-352 – KC-130F/R; MARTD – UC-12B, UH-1N

MCAS El Toro opened in July 1942 with the 3d Marine Air Wing being formed five months later. Headquarters 3d MAW is still in residence with responsibility for the Marine bases in the western USA which have been concentrated in Arizona and California as part of FMFPAC. The three F/A-18A squadrons are assigned to Marine Air Group 11 (MAG-11), while the Hercules and night attack Hornet squadrons form MAG-13. El Toro is the main Marine base for the F/A-18 Hornet in the Pacific with three front-line and one Reserve squadrons, plus a further three squadrons dedicated to the night attack role.

Futemma MCAS, Okinawa

Location: on the island of Okinawa
Units assigned: MALS-36 – OV-10A/D; MWHS-1 – CT-39G; VMGR-152 – KC-130F; MARTD – UC-12B

Futemma operates under Marine Air Group 36 with a Hercules tanker/transport squadron in residence to support Marine Corps fighter and attack squadrons which rotate for six months' temporary duty in the western Pacific. Marine Wing Headquarters Squadron One (MWHS-1) is in residence with a CT-39G for VIP duties for the commander of 1st MAW.

Iwakuni MCAS, Japan

Location: in Yamaguchi Prefecture
Units assigned: MARTD – UC-12F, HH-46D

Marine Corps fighter and attack aircraft units deploy here for six-month periods of duty and normally consist of one A-6E, two F/A-18A/C, and one AV-8B squadrons, plus a detachment of EA-6Bs. These squadrons are drawn from all three Marine Corps wings. MAG-12 is located here to coordinate activities, and was assigned a number of OA-4Ms until these were withdrawn during 1990. The only residents are a UC-12F and a pair of HH-46Ds for SAR duties.

Kaneohe Bay MCAS, HI

Location: three miles east of Kaneohe on Oahu Island
Units assigned: HMH-463 – CH-53D; HMM-165 – CH-46E; HMM-265 – CH-46E; HMM-364 – CH-46E; VMFA-212 – F/A-18C; VMFA-232 – F/A-18C; VMFA-235 – F/A-18C

Kaneohe Bay was earmarked to become an air station in 1938 when the Secretary of the Navy identified several Pacific locations to be prepared in case the US was required to go to war. The station is home to the 1st Marine Brigade (1st MARBDE) which reports directly to Head-quarters Fleet Marine Force Pacific. Marine Air Group 24 is responsible for three Hornet and four helicopter squadrons. The disproportionately large Marine Corps presence in Hawaii has an operating area of responsibility extending across the Pacific Ocean, which involves fixed-wing squadrons deploying to Iwakuni and helicopters embarking aboard assault carriers.

New River MCAS, NC

Location: three miles east of Jacksonville
Units assigned: HMH-362 – CH-53D; HMH-461 – CH-53E; HMH-464 – CH53E; HMM-162 – CH-46E; HMM-261 – CH-46E; HMM-263 – CH-46E; HMM-264 – CH-46E; HMM-266 – CH-46E; HMM-365 – CH-46E; HMLA-167 – UH-1N, AH-1W; HMLA-269 – UH-1N, AH-1T; HMT-204 – CH-46E, CH-53A; VMO-1 – OV-10A/D (to deactivate by 1994); MARTD – UC-12B (HH-46D tailcode 5D)

Marine Air Groups 26 and 29 are both stationed at New River with almost a dozen helicopter squadrons, including one dedicated to the training role for Fleet Marine Force Atlantic. New River is close to the huge Camp Lejeune training facility with helicopters frequently involved in large-scale exercises. The facility is known as McCutcheon Field after General Keith B. McCutcheon.

Quantico MCAF, VA

Location: three miles east of Triangle
Units assigned: HMX-1 – VH-3D, CH-53D, VH-60N

Quantico is one of the oldest Marine Corps aviation sites with forces in residence since the end of World War I. The facility was one of the first three to be approved by Congress as a permanent air station (the other two being located in San Diego, CA, and Parris Island, SC). The proximity of Quantico to the Piasecki and Sikorsky helicopter plants in Connecticut, as well as the nation's capital in Washington, resulted in HMX-1 being established in January 1948 primarily for Marine helicopter development. In later years the squadron switched from development to that of providing helicopters for Presidential transportation both at home and overseas. Named Brown Field after Second Lieutenant Walter Brown who was killed at Quantico in an aircraft accident, the field was subsequently renamed Turner Field after Colonel Thomas C. Turner.

Tustin MCAS, CA

Location: two miles east of Santa Ana
Units assigned: HMH-361 – CH-53E; HMH-363 – CH-53D; HMH-462 – CH-53D; HMH-465 – CH-53E; HMH-466 – CH-53E; HMM-161 – CH-46E; HMM-163 –

CH-46E; HMM-164 – CH-46E; HMM-166 – CH-46E; HMM-268 – CH-46E; HMT-301 – CH-46E; HMT-302 – CH-53D/E

Tustin was opened as a lighter-than-air facility in September 1942 and was named MCAS Santa Ana until the 1970s, when it was renamed MCAS Tustin. A large hangar built for airships is still in use to house helicopters. The station is the main medium and heavy-lift helicopter facility for Fleet Marine Force Pacific, with approximately a dozen squadrons assigned to Marine Air Group 16 under the 3d MAW. Included in the squadrons are two devoted to training helicopter aircrew for Pacific-based units. Tustin is earmarked for closure with its squadrons being relocated to Camp Pendleton and a new facility being constructed at the large training site at Twentynine Palms to the southeast of Barstow.

Yuma MCAS, AZ

Location: one mile south of Yuma
Units assigned: VMA-211 – AV-8B; VMA-214 – AV-8B; VMA-311 – AV-8B; VMA-513 – AV-8B; VMFT-401 – F-5E; MARTD – UC-12B, UH-1N

Yuma is the home of Marine Combat Crew Readiness Training Group 10 (MCCRT-10) and regularly hosts large-scale exercises involving all types of aircraft and helicopter in Marine Corps service. A squadron of aggressor F-5s is in residence to provide a realistic threat during exercises. In addition, Marine Corps ground attack squadrons deploy to Yuma to use the nearby gunnery range. For many years the base conducted A-4 and F-4 training for Marine Corps aviators, although the retirement of these two types from service resulted in fighter-attack training being transferred to El Toro with the F/A-18 Hornet.

US COAST GUARD STATIONS

Astoria, OR

The Coast Guard air station is located on the former Tongue Point Naval Air Station, now known as the Port of Astoria Airport, on the outskirts of the city, and was established in August 1964. Currently assigned are the HH-65A and HU-25A which operate over an area extending from the Canadian border to northern California.

Barbers Point, HI

The CGAS was established on the Hawaiian Islands at Kaneohe Bay shortly after World War II, and moved to its present site at the naval air station in 1949. The HC-130H and HH-65A are currently operated. Barbers Point has one of the largest operating areas of any Coast Guard air station, extending southward to American Samoa, eastward to the US mainland, northward to Alaska, and west to Japan.

Borinquen, PR

CGAS Borinquen has been located on the former Ramey Air Force Base near Aquadilla since the early 1970s, and operates the HC-130H and HH-65A. The HU-25A was stationed at Borinquen until 1987 when they were relocated with the arrival of the C-130s. Borinquen also has a large area of responsibility which extends to more than one million square miles of the Caribbean basin.

Brooklyn, NY

The CGAS at Brooklyn was created in April 1938 at Floyd Bennett Field, which later became a naval air station during World War II before being vacated by the Navy. Brooklyn operates the HH-65A, which at present are restricted to the New York area.

Cape Cod, MA

Cape Cod CGAS is located in one corner of Otis Air National Guard Base and was commissioned in August 1970. The HH-65A together with both the HU-25A and B models of the Guardian are in residence, overseeing an area stretching along the coastline from the Canadian border to Connecticut.

Cape May, NJ

Cape May CGAS was one of the first such facilities established during the 1930s. The station is located to the east of the town and has the HH-65A assigned. Apart from conducting routine search and rescue duties, Cape May has the Coast Guard Training Center in residence.

Chicago, IL

CGAS Chicago was established in March 1969 at Naval Air Station Glenview. The HH-65A is at present operated over the southern part of Lake Michigan.

Clearwater, FL

The original Clearwater CGAS was established at Albert Whited Airport in 1934 but moved to St Petersburg/Clearwater International Airport in 1976. The HC-130H is assigned for long-range duties over the Gulf of Mexico and southward towards Central America, while the HH-3Fs operate along the west side of the Florida coastline. The solitary EC-130V is also located at Clearwater.

Corpus Christi, TX

Coast Guard operations began at Corpus Christi Naval Air Station in November 1950. The HH-65A and HU-25A are assigned for duties between Port O'Connor, TX, and the Mexican border.

Detroit, MI

Detroit CGAS began operations from Selfridge AFB (now an Air National Guard base) in 1965 to expand coverage of the Great Lakes. The station operates the HH-65A over an area encompassing Lakes Erie, Ontario and St Clair, plus the southern half of Lake Huron.

Elizabeth City, NC

The Coast Guard Air Station is located to the south of Elizabeth City beside the Pasquotank River and is the largest such base. Opened in August 1940, the station is the only airport-style facility fully manned by the Coast Guard. Apart

Elizabeth City is the Coast Guard's major base, responsible for ground crew training and aircraft overhaul in addition to the regular activities. Here is the USCG's first HC-130H over the North Carolina base.

from performing the full Coast Guard range of duties with the HC-130H, HH-60J, HH-65A, HU-25A and HU-25B, the station also has the Aviation Technical Training Center (ATTC) which opened in August 1978 to train maintenance personnel in the technical skills required to repair and overhaul Coast Guard aircraft and helicopters. A number of airframes are employed including retired HH-52A Seaguards and HH-3F Pelicans, plus HU-25A on loan for this purpose. The Aircraft Repair and Supply Center (ARSC) is also located at Elizabeth City to perform overhaul, repair and modification of the aircraft and helicopters themselves, plus their engines. The VC-4A Gulfstream I is stationed at Elizabeth City for VIP duties.

Houston, TX

The CGAS is situated at Ellington Field, which was formerly Ellington Air Force Base, and was commissioned in December 1963. The station used the HH-65A and is responsible for an area of operations extending from Matagorda Bay to Calcasieu Lake, LA.

Humboldt Bay, CA

Humboldt Bay CGAS is located at Arcata/Eureka Airport in McKinleyville and was opened in June 1977. The station employs the HH-65A with an operating area extending along the northern California and southern Oregon coast.

Kodiak, AK

The air station at Kodiak is located at the former Kodiak Naval Air Station on the island of the same name. The HC-130H and HH-65A are stationed at Kodiak where the latter perform search and rescue duties along with fishery protection inshore, while the long-range Hercules conduct missions over the Gulf of Alaska and the Bering Sea.

Los Angeles, CA

Located on the south side of Los Angeles International Airport since November 1962, the station operates the HH-65A over an area extending from San Clemente north to the estuary of the Santa Maria River.

Miami, FL

Miami has had a Coast Guard air station since June 1932, initially at Dinner Key on Biscayne Bay until November 1965, when it moved to new premises at Opa Locka Airport. The station operates the HH-65A plus all three versions of the Guardian, consisting of the HU-25A, B and C. In addi-

tion the two RG-8As are based at Opa Locka. Miami CGAS is one of the busiest stations as, apart from search and rescue duties associated with commercial shipping and tourism, the Coast Guard has added law enforcement to its role, particularly the detection of drug smuggling from South America. Miami has a large area to protect extending south and east to the Bahamas, Jamaica, Puerto Rico and the Virgin Islands, as well as west into the Gulf of Mexico.

New Orleans, LA

The CGAS was commissioned at New Orleans Naval Air Station in July 1955 and currently operates the HH-65A. The station is responsible for the area extending from the Louisiana/Texas border to Apalachicola, FL.

Norfolk, VA

An air facility was established at Norfolk Naval Air Station in January 1987 to operate a pair of E-2C Hawkeyes on loan from the US Navy for drug smuggling detection. However, E-2 operations were moved to St Augustine in August 1989 and the Coast Guard air facility closed.

North Bend, OR

The CGAS is located at North Bend Municipal Airport and is responsible for the coastline from the California border to Depoe Bay north of Newport with the HH-65A assigned.

Port Angeles, WA

The CGAS is located to the north of Port Angeles facing Vancouver Island across the Strait of Juan de Fuca. The station has the HH-65A assigned to conduct duties extending from the Canadian border along the waterways adjacent to Seattle and Tacoma, and the Washington state coastline of the Pacific Ocean.

St Augustine, FL

The air facility at Norfolk was moved to St Augustine Airport, south of Jacksonville, to operate a total of nine E-2Cs on loan from the Navy. The delivery of the first EC-130V to the Coast Guard at Clearwater enabled the E-2s to be returned to the Navy and the facility at St Augustine to close in November 1991.

Sacramento, CA

The station at Sacramento was formed at McClellan Air Force Base in the northeast suburbs of the city in September 1978. The station operates HC-130Hs, which were moved to Sacramento from San Francisco as the latter facility was unable to adequately support fixed-wing Coast Guard operations due to an increase in commercial traffic and a lack of ramp space. The area of operation for the Sacramento HC-130s includes the eastern Pacific Ocean from the Mexican to the Canadian borders.

San Diego, CA

The station is located across North Harbor Drive

from Lindbergh Field, San Diego and was established in June 1936. The HH-65A and HU-25A are assigned for duties from the Mexican border northward to Oceanside which, although encompassing a coastline of less than 100 miles, performs an important duty including the detection of illegal immigrants from Mexico.

San Francisco, CA

Initially formed at Mills Field close to San Francisco Airport in February 1941, the station operated the HC-130H until September 1978 when the fixed-wing element moved to Sacramento. The station currently operates the HH-60J and HH-65A over an area from northern California to the estuary of the Santa Maria River.

Savannah, GA

The CGAS is located on Hunter Army Air Field to the southwest of Savannah. The station was opened in June 1963 when the site was known as Hunter Air Force Base, and currently operates the HH-65A along the Georgia and South Carolina coastline.

Sitka, AK

The station at Sitka was opened in October 1977 to replace the facility at Annette Island. The HH-65A is assigned for operation over the eastern Alaskan coastline as far as the Canadian border.

Traverse City, MI

Located at Cherry Capitol Airport the CGAS was formed in 1938 as a part-time site for operations during the summer months. The station was upgraded to full-time status in 1946, and currently operates the HH-3F and HH-60J on multi-purpose duties over all four of the Great Lakes.

Washington, DC

Headquarters of the US Coast Guard is located in Washington, DC, with a support unit located at Washington National Airport since February 1952. At present the VIP-configured VC-11A Gulfstream II is stationed at the airport to perform duties for senior personnel, including the Commandant of the Coast Guard and the Secretary of Transportation.

Coast Guard Aviation Training Center, Mobile, AL

The Coast Guard Aviation Training Center was opened in December 1966 on land formerly used as a USAF Reserve facility at Bates Field. The station uses the HH-3F, HH-60J, HH-65A, plus the HU-25A and C models of the Guardian. Apart from providing routine Coast Guard duties for the middle and eastern sectors of the Gulf of Mexico, the Center provides helicopters aboard icebreakers for polar operations. However, the primary duty at Mobile is to train aircrew for Coast Guard aircraft and helicopters. This training encompasses newly designated aviators who have graduated from the US Naval Air Training Command School at Pensacola, FL, as well as those who are transitioning to a different aircraft type.

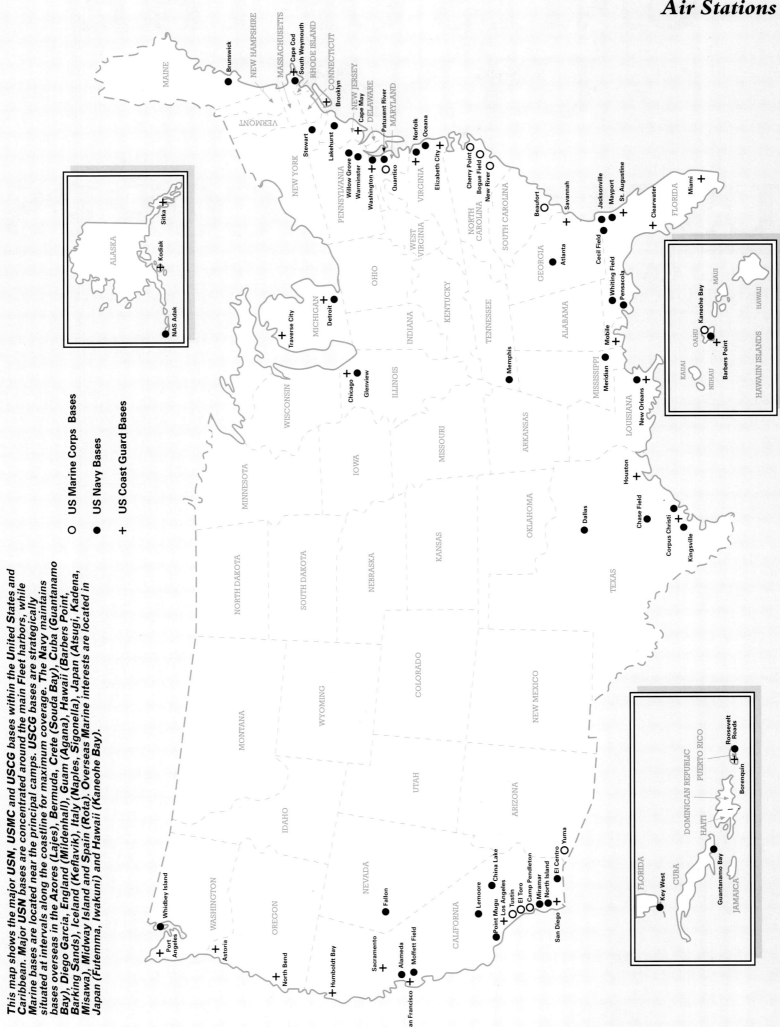

Air Stations

This map shows the major USN, USMC and USCG bases within the United States and Caribbean. Major USN bases are concentrated around the main Fleet harbors, while Marine bases are located near the principal camps. USCG bases are strategically situated at intervals along the coastline for maximum coverage. The Navy maintains bases overseas in the Azores (Lajes), Bermuda, Crete (Souda Bay), Cuba (Guantanamo Bay), Diego Garcia, England (Mildenhall), Guam (Agana), Hawaii (Barbers Point, Barking Sands), Iceland (Keflavik), Italy (Naples, Sigonella), Japan (Atsugi, Kadena, Misawa), Midway Island and Spain (Rota). Overseas Marine interests are located in Japan (Futemma, Iwakuni) and Hawaii (Kaneohe Bay).

○ US Marine Corps Bases

● US Navy Bases

+ US Coast Guard Bases

171

UNITS OF THE US NAVY AND US MARINE CORPS

US Naval Aviation Unit Designations and Codes

US Naval Aviation units are identified by a variety of letter/numeral designations, which indicate the unit's function and equipment. The unit designation can also be presented as an abbreviation (and in Navy squadrons by an acronym). Many also bear a nickname of some description. To make sense of the jumble of letters which comprise a squadron designation, it is helpful to understand what the various letters stand for. The letter **V** (used as the initial letter of a squadron designation, or the second letter of a carrier or carrier air wing, after the letter **C**) stands for heavier than air, and dates from the time that balloon and airship squadrons existed, these being identified by the initial letter **Z**. The letter **H** is used as an initial letter by helicopter units. The second (and third, and sometimes fourth) letter represents the unit's role. Marine units insert a letter **M** between the first and second letters. The letters are followed by a hyphen and a numeral or set of numerals, some of which are duplicated several times. Thus there is no 'Number One Squadron', but there can be a separate VF-1 (Fighter Squadron 1), VA-1 (Attack Squadron One), VP-1 (Patrol Squadron One) etc.

Current/recent squadron prefixes:

HC-	Helicopter Combat Support Squadron (HELSUPPRON)
HCS-	Helicopter Combat Support Special Squadron (HELSUPPSPECRON)
HM-	Helicopter Mine Countermeasures Squadron (HELMINERON)
HS-	Helicopter Antisubmarine Squadron (HELANTISUBRON)
HSL-	Helicopter Antisubmarine Squadron (Light) (No acronym known)
HT-	Helicopter Training Squadron (HELTRARON)
HU-	Helicopter Utility Squadron (no acronym known)
VA-	Attack Squadron (ATKRON)
VAK-	Aerial Refueling Squadron (AEREFRON) Not used
VAQ-	Tactical Electronic Warfare Squadron (TACELRON)
VAW-	Carrier Airborne Early Warning Squadron (CARAEWRON)
VC-	Fleet Composite Squadron (FLECOMPRON)
VF-	Fighter Squadron (FITRON)
VFA-	Strike Fighter Squadron (STRKFITRON)
VFC-	Fighter Squadron Composite (FITRON COMP)
VFP-	Light Photo Reconnaissance Squadron (LIGHTPHOTORON) Not used
VP-	Patrol Squadron (PATRON)
VPU-	Patrol Squadron Special Projects Unit (PATRON SPECPROJ UNIT)
VQ-	Fleet Air Reconnaissance Squadron (FAIRECONRON)
VR-	Fleet Logistics Support Squadron (FLELOGSUPRON)
VRC-	These squadrons use the same name and acronym as VR units, but are assigned to COD duties.
VRF-	Air Ferry Squadron (AIRFERRON)
VS-	Air Antisubmarine Squadron (AIRANTISUBRON)

VT-	Training Squadron (TRARON)
VX-	Air Test and Evaluation Squadron (AIRTEVRON)
VXE-	Antarctic Development Squadron (ANTARCTICDEVRON)
VXN-	Oceanic Development Squadron (OCEANDEVRON)
VMA-	Marine Attack Squadron
VMA(AW)-	Marine All Weather Attack Squadron
VMAQ-	Marine Tactical Electronic Warfare Squadron
VMAT-	Marine Attack Training Squadron
VMFA-	Marine Fighter Attack Squadron
VMFA(AW)-	Marine All-Weather Fighter Attack Squadron
VMFAT-	Marine Fighter Attack Training Squadron
VMF-	Marine Fighter Squadron (Not used)
VMFT-	Marine Fighter Training Squadron
VMFP-	Marine Tactical Reconnaissance Squadron (Not used)
VMGR-	Marine Aerial Refueler Transport Squadron
VMGRT-	Marine Aerial Refueler Transport Training Squadron
VMO-	Marine Observation Squadron
HM-	Marine Helicopter Squadron
HMA-	Marine Attack Helicopter Squadron
HMH-	Marine Heavy Helicopter Squadron
HML-	Marine Light Helicopter Squadron
HMLA-	Marine Light Attack Helicopter Squadron
HMM-	Marine Medium Helicopter Squadron
HMT-	Marine Helicopter Training Squadron
HMX-	Marine Helicopter Squadron
MALS-	Marine Aviation Logistics Squadron
HAMS-	Headquarters and Maintenance Squadron
SOES-	Station Operations and Engineering Squadron

Deployed carrier aircraft belonging to a particular unit will usually have the abbreviated letter/numeral identifier painted onto the aircraft, sometimes with the CVW- designation and even the aircraft carrier name as well. They also carry a three-numeral code (or 'Modex') on the nose, the last two digits of which are sometimes repeated on the tailfin and/or flaps. The first digit of the Modex indicates a squadron's 'status' within a carrier air wing. A uniform set of colors (rarely used in today's toned-down Navy) is also sometimes used to differentiate between squadrons.

Squadron	Modex	Color
First VF Squadron	100-114	Insignia red
Second VF Squadron	200-214	Orange-yellow
First VA Squadron	300-315	Light blue
Second VA Squadron	400-415	International orange
Third VA Squadron	500-512	Light green
Strike tankers	520-524	Light green
VAW Squadron	600-603/4	Insignia blue
VAQ Squadron	604-607 or 620-625	Maroon
HS/HC Squadron	610-617	Magenta
VS Squadron	700-713	Dark green
VFP Detachment	115-117	Black

The changing structure of some air wings has led to many exceptions to the above rule. Some VAQ squadrons have codes commencing 620, while some VAW units have codes ending 605. Where there are four VA squadrons, the fourth will often have codes commencing with 530. When Air Wing Five had no F-14s but three F/A-18 and two A-6 squadrons, the VA units had codes commencing 100, 200, 300, 400 and 500 respectively. The Modex carried by an aircraft is temporary, and may change during a cruise, and will always change if an aircraft is assigned to another squadron, and often if a squadron joins a new air wing. The aircraft's permanent identity is shown by its construction number (stamped or painted onto various internal locations by the manufacturer). Since different manufacturers use different systems, a uniform system of Bureau numbers (BuNos) has been developed. Essentially a sequential inventory number (though there are deliberate gaps in the system) an aircraft's BuNo. is normally painted on or near the rear fuselage, and stays with an aircraft for its whole working life. Unlike the USAF's system of serial numbers, the Bureau numbers include no fiscal year designator.

Shore-based aircraft do not have the CVW- or ships names painted on. Virtually all front-line naval aircraft, however, carry a two-letter tailcode, which provides a clue to Fleet assignment. Units assigned to Air Forces Atlantic Fleet (AIRLANT) use an initial letter between A and M while those assigned to Air Forces Pacific Fleet (AIRPAC) use letters from N to Z. Carrierborne aircraft in each Fleet all use the first assigned letter for that Fleet, A in the Atlantic and N in the Pacific. The letters I and O are not used, to avoid confusion with the numerals 1 and 0. Aircraft assigned to the Chief of Naval Air Training carry a single-letter tailcode between A and F, while air stations, technical training and some Reserve units and overseas support units use a number-letter combination.

US Marine Corps aircraft carry two-letter codes when deployed on US Navy aircraft carriers, but otherwise carry the squadron's own two-letter code, designation and sometimes the Marine Air Group or Marine Air Wing designations. When embarked on LHD, LHA or LPH ships, Marine helicopters and AV-8Bs will normally, but not always, form one composite squadron, usually forming around the HMM squadron and adopting the tailcode of that unit for the cruise. Hence, it is common to see CH-53, AH-1, UH-1 and AV-8B aircraft with codes and designators of the HMM CH-46 squadron. Otherwise, Marine Corps codes follow the overall USN pattern.

HC (Helicopter Combat Support Squadron)

HC-1 'Angels'

NAS North Island, CA: 'UP'
SH-3G/H, CH-53E

HC-1 was established as HU-1 on 1 April 1948 and redesignated HC-1 on 1 July 1965. The squadron operates a mix of Sikorsky helicopters in utility and transport duties.

Det 3 of HC-1 was embarked on the assault ship USS *Tarawa* (LHA-1) during Operation Desert Storm. Returning from the war, *Tarawa* was diverted on 15 May 1991 to assist survivors of a devastating cyclone in Bangladesh in Operation Productive Effort. Helicopters from the squadron participated in this humanitarian effort.

HC-2 'Circuit Riders'

NAS Norfolk, VA: 'HU'
VH-3A, SH-3G/H, CH-53E

HC-2, callsign REDHAWK, is unique among Navy composite squadrons in operating no fewer than four types. The squadron maintains two permanent detachments: det 1 'Ghost Riders' in Naples, Italy, with a single SH-3G (BuNo. 151527) and det 2 'Desert Duck Airlines' in Bahrain with a pair of SH-3Gs (BuNos 148047 and 149733). This squadron knew about the Persian Gulf two decades before most Americans: the 'Ducks' have been flying in Bahrain since 1972.

The VH-3As are former presidential aircraft now used for VIP missions with key Atlantic Fleet officers and for regular runs between Norfolk and the Pentagon. At the outbreak of war, a VH-3A would rush CINCLANT to his Boeing EC-135 airborne command post waiting at Langley AFB 23 miles (37 km) away. The SH-3Hs, stripped of the antisubmarine equipment which came with their original mission, are gradually replacing the SH-3Gs as all-purpose utility and SAR helicopters. The CH-53Es perform a variety of heavy-lift duties.

During Desert Storm, HC-2's SH-3Gs performed fleet logistics, SAR, combat SAR, medical evacuation, executive transport and enemy prisoner of war transport.

HC-3 'Pack Rats'

NAS North Island, CA: 'SA'
CH-46D, HH-46D

HC-3 was established on 1 September 1967. The squadron operates Boeing helicopters to provide utility, transport and SAR support to the Pacific Fleet, and acts as the Pacific Fleet H-46 FRS.

HC-4 'Black Stallions'

NAS Sigonella, Italy: 'HC'
CH-53E

HC-4 was established on 6 May 1983 and is the second squadron in the US Navy to carry the HC-4 designation. The 'Stallions' fly the Sikorsky CH-53E Super Stallion on transport and utility duties in the Mediterranean. In 1991, the squadron was described in a US Navy publication as having been "continuously supporting American efforts in one crisis or another for over a year."

The squadron deployed CH-53Es to Lungi and Freetown, Sierra Leone, for Operation Sharp Edge, the December 1990 evacuation of more than 2,400 citizens of 30 nations from war-torn Liberia in West Africa. Thereafter, HC-4 supported Desert Shield/ Storm and the humanitarian effort which followed, Operation Provide Comfort. Three CH-53Es were dispatched for the latter effort to relieve the plight of Kurdish refugees in western Iraq. Helicopter crews ferried food supplies and performed *ad hoc* humanitarian and rescue missions.

Right: Support for Mediterranean Fleet activities is provided by the 'Black Stallions' of HC-4, based at Sigonella. Flying the CH-53E, this unit has been heavily involved in many overseas activities, including Desert Storm and the Kurdish refugee relief effort.

HC-5 'Providers'

NAS Agana, Guam
HH-46A

HC-5 was established on 3 February 1984 and is the second squadron in the US Navy to carry the HC-5 designation. The squadron provides utility, transport, and SAR support in the region with Boeing H-46 Sea Knight helicopters. A detachment from HC-5 provided VOD support from USS *Niagara Falls* (AFS-3) during Desert Storm.

HC-6 'Chargers'

NAS Norfolk, VA: 'HW'
CH/HH/UH-46D

HC-6 was established 1 September 1967 and is a composite helicopter squadron with Boeing CH-46D, HH-46D and UH-46D Sea Knight helicopters for transport, utility work, and VOD support of US Navy warships. HC-6 supplied a detachment for VOD deliveries during Desert Shield/Storm.

HC-8 'Dragon Whales'

NAS Norfolk, VA: 'BR'
CH/HH/UH-46D

HC-8 was established 3 December 1984. Like HC-6, the 'Whales' have composite helicopter duties with Boeing CH-46D, HH-46D and UH-46D Sea Knights. The 'Dragon Whales' provided VOD support to US Navy warships during the Persian Gulf conflict. HC-8's det 3 was one of the busiest Desert Storm helicopter units, supporting not only US Navy vessels but those of Britain, France, Greece, Portugal, Saudi Arabia and Spain. The detachment also supported explosive ordnance disposal training at Sigonella in December 1990. Det 3 logged 1,100 flight hours in the Gulf region from September 1990 to March 1991.

HC-9

This unit was disestablished 31 July 1990.

Above right: Two of HC-2's 'Desert Ducks' at Bahrain after the Gulf War. The nearest aircraft is named 'Stealth Duck'.

Right: HC-3 is based at North Island to support the Pacific Fleet with HH-46s.

HC-11 'Gunbearers'
NAS North Island, CA: 'VR'
HH-46A/D, CH/HH-46D

HC-11 was established 1 October 1977 and performs transport, utility and SAR duties with a mix of Boeing HH-46A, HH-46D, CH-46D and HH-46D Sea Knight helicopters. Elements of the squadron were deployed to the Persian Gulf region aboard USS *Kiska* (AE-35) during Desert Storm.

A crew from det 4 was involved in a SAR operation with an Omani freighter during Desert Storm. Upon receiving a distress call, a five-person Sea Knight crew searched for and located the vessel. The helicopter hovered over the stricken ship to serve as a locator for rescue ships heading into the area. Sea Knights from the squadron also performed a wide range of other duties including VOD delivery of supplies to US Navy vessels at sea.

HC-8 (above) is at NAS Norfolk for Atlantic Fleet support, while HC-11 (above right) performs the same task from North Island on the West Coast.

HC-16 'Bullfrogs'
NAS Pensacola, FL: 'BF'
SH-3D, HH-1N

HC-16 was established as HCT-16 on 1 November 1974, and redesignated HC-16 on 20 May 1977. The 'Bullfrogs' operate Sikorsky SH-3D Sea King and Bell HH-IN Huey (formerly UH-IN) helicopters in composite duties supporting the Atlantic Fleet.

The 'Bullfrogs' (note tailcode) of HC-16 operate the Bell HH-1N (illustrated) alongside SH-3Ds.

HCS (Helicopter Combat Support Special Squadron)

HCS-4 'Red Wolves'
NAS Norfolk, VA: 'NW'
HH-60H

HCS-4 is a Naval Air Reserve squadron operating the Sikorsky HH-60H Seahawk strike rescue aircraft. The squadron was called to active duty for Operations Desert Shield/Storm and carried out combat rescue and special operations missions. To carry out their strike mission, HCS crews practice extensively using night vision goggles and flying nap-of-the-earth profiles to evade enemy air and ground defenses.

During their three-month detachment to the Persian Gulf, HCS-4 and HCS-5 flew 750 flight hours and were mission-ready 90 per cent of the time, despite difficulties operating the HH-60H in desert conditions.

In mid-1991, 'Red Wolves' HH-60Hs deployed to Texas to support a marijuana eradication program. Accompanied by a detachment of HCS-5 from the West Coast, the helicopter crews operated from Bergstrom AFB, TX, to aid the Texas Department of Public Safety in counter-narcotics efforts. The program involved 240 flight hours.

Right: Both HCS units sent a two-aircraft detachment to the Gulf, this HH-60H being from HCS-5.

HCS-5 'Firehawks'
NAS Point Mugu, CA: 'NW'
HH-60H

HCS-5 is a Naval Air Reserve combat support squadron which was called to active duty during Desert Storm with its Sikorsky

HH-60H Seahawks. The squadron had received its first HH-60H in July 1989, replacing the Vietnam-era Bell HH-IK Huey, and was at full strength when the Persian Gulf crisis began. The 'Firehawks' operated with two aircraft from Tabuk in the western Saudi desert near the Iraqi border.

Above: In addition to the strike rescue role, the HH-60H is also used for general SAR duties.

HM (Helicopter Mine Countermeasures Squadron)

HM-12 'Sea Dragons'
NAS Norfolk, VA: 'DH'
CH/MH-53

HM-12 was established 1 April 1971 and is the FRS squadron for East Coast Sikorsky CH-53/MH-53 Sea Stallion/Super Stallion personnel who operate the large helicopters in minelaying, transport and utility duties.

HM-14 'Sea Stallion'
NAS Norfolk, VA: 'BJ'
MH-53E

HM-14 was established 12 May 1978 and operates the Sikorsky MH-53E Sea Stallion in minesweeping work, and in transport, utility and heavylift duties.

In the aftermath of Desert Storm, where HM-14 performed from several ship decks, the squadron was called upon for mine-clearing duties. USS *La Salle* (AGF-3) provided a deck for HM-14 MH-53Es to operate until the assault ship USS *New Orleans* (LPH-11) arrived to replace USS

Heavily patched during the continual battle against saltwater corrosion, this MH-53E serves with HM-12, the 'Sea Dragons' from Norfolk. This unit acts as the fleet replenishment squadron for the East Coast H-53 community.

Tripoli (LPH-10), which had been damaged by a mine during the war. HM-14 then shifted to *Tripoli* to carry out mine-clearing duties, which neutralized more than 1,000 mines laid by Iraq during the war.

In January 1992, after returning stateside, a squadron helicopter employed AN/AQS-14 side-scanning radar to search successfully for containers of hazardous cargo which had fallen from a merchant vessel during rough weather in the mouth of the Delaware Bay.

HM-15 'Blackhawks'
NAS Alameda, CA: 'TB'
MH-53E

HM-15 was established on 27 October 1978 and operates the Sikorsky MH-53E Super Stallion.

The 'Blackhawks' maintained an MH-53E VOD detachment in the Persian Gulf region during Operations Desert Shield/Storm. Following the conflict, a two-helicopter detachment of HM-15 deployed from Alameda to Bahrain 19 July 1991 to provide VOD services to US Navy ships deployed in the Persian Gulf region after the war.

HM-14's badge is derived from the 'Sea Stallion' name and its role.

HM-18 'Norsemen'
NAS Norfolk, VA: 'NW'
RH-53D

HM-18, a Naval Air Reserve unit, operates the Sikorsky RH-53D Sea Stallion helicopter for minesweeping, utility and transport duties. The HM-18/19 helicopters are the RH-53Ds which proved unsuccessful in the April 1980 attempt to rescue American hostages in Iran.

HM-19 'Golden Bears'
NAS Norfolk, VA: 'NW'
RH-53D

HM-19 shares with HM-18 at Norfolk, VA, the Reserve mission using the RH-53D.

At present there are two active-duty MH-53E squadrons, augmented in the mine-hunting role by two Reserve units flying the less-capable RH-53D. This aircraft is from HM-15.

HS (Helicopter Antisubmarine Squadron)

HS-1 'Sea Horses'
NAS Jacksonville, FL: 'AR'
SH-3G/H

HS-1 was established 3 October 1951 and is currently the Atlantic Fleet FRS squadron for the Sikorsky SH-3G/H Sea King helicopter.

HS-2 'Golden Falcons'
NAS North Island, CA: 'NG'
SH-60F, HH-60H

HS-2 was established on 7 March 1952. The squadron operates the Sikorsky SH-60F Seahawk antisubmarine helicopter and is part of CVW-9 aboard USS *Nimitz* (CVN-68), home-ported at North Island, CA. The squadron was the first in the Fleet to transition to the SH-60F and has since added two HH-60H strike rescue helicopters to its inventory. A 1991 deployment by *Nimitz* to the Indian Ocean marked the first occasion when both SH-60F and HH-60H helicopters had operated from carrier decks during an operational cruise.

HS-3 'Tridents'
NAS Jacksonville, FL: 'AJ'
SH-60F, HH-60H

HS-3 was established on 18 June 1952 and carries out its submarine-hunting duties with the Sikorsky SH-60F Seahawk. A transition which began in April 1991 made HS-3 the first East Coast squadron to replace the Sikorsky SH-3H Sea King helicopter with the SH-60F, and a ceremony marked completion of the process on 27 August 1991.

Members of the 'Tridents' are unperturbed at being graced with the same nickname as HSL-32 and two P-3C Orion squadrons, VP-26 at NAS Brunswick, ME,

Right: This SH-3 belongs to HS-1, and carries the unit's seahorse insignia.

and Reserve squadron VP-65 at Point Mugu, CA.

HS-3 participated in Desert Storm as part of CVW-17 aboard USS *Saratoga* (CV-60). After the Gulf War, squadron personnel traveled to North Island, CA, for training in operation and maintenance of the SH-60F from the Pacific Fleet's SH-60F fleet replenishment squadron, HS-10.

In 1992, HS-3 was scheduled for transfer to CVW-8 aboard USS *Theodore Roosevelt* (CVN-71) and was scheduled to augment its inventory of six SH-60Fs with two HH-60H strike rescue versions of the Seahawk.

HS-4 'Black Knights'
NAS North Island, CA: 'NL'
SH-60F, HH-60H

HS-4, established on 30 June 1952, made the transition from the Sikorsky SH-3H Sea King to the Sikorsky SH-60F Seahawk antisubmarine helicopter in late 1991, becoming the third West Coast squadron to operate the carrier-based version of the Seahawk. HS-4 is part of CVW-15, aboard USS *Kitty Hawk* (CV-63).

HS-5 'Night Dippers'
NAS Jacksonville, FL: 'AG'
SH-3H

HS-5, established on 3 January 1956, operates the Sikorsky SH-3H Sea King as part of CVW-7 aboard USS *Dwight D. Eisenhower* (CV-69). The squadron provided antisubmarine, SAR and utility support when 'Ike' rushed to the Persian Gulf region during Desert Shield.

HS-6 'Indians'
NAS North Island, CA
SH-60F, HH-60H

HS-6 was established on 1 June 1956 and operates the Sikorsky SH-60F Seahawk antisubmarine helicopter with CVW-11 aboard USS *Abraham Lincoln* (CVN-72). The squadron became the US Navy's second deploying SH-60F unit when it received its first Seahawk in September 1990.

HS-3 was the first Atlantic Fleet squadron to exchange its SH-3Hs for SH-60F Ocean Hawks. It currently flies from USS Theodore Roosevelt in the CV-Helo role.

The 'Black Knights' of HS-4 have also made the transition to the SH-60F. The Ocean Hawk dramatically increases ASW capability, especially while sonar dunking.

Above: An SH-3H of HS-9, while on a previous cruise in Nimitz.

Above left: HS-5 still operates the SH-3H on ASW and SAR duties. The unit took part in Desert Shield.

Left: In view of the sonar dunking tactic, HS-7's 'Big Dipper' name is highly appropriate.

King as part of CVW-1 aboard USS *America* (CV-66). *America*'s air wing was in combat in the Persian Gulf, and the 'Dragonslayers' supported the war effort.

HS-12 'Wyverns'
NAS North Island, CA: 'NF'
SH-3H

HS-12 was established 15 July 1977. The squadron, operating the Sikorsky SH-3H Sea King, was long associated with CVW-5 on USS *Midway* (CV-41). The squadron was aboard *Midway* for the carrier's final cruise to provide medical and humanitarian relief as part of Operation Fiery Vigil following the 10 June 1991 eruption of Mount Pinatubo in the Philippines. The squadron's Sea Kings joined CH-53D helicopters of Marine squadron HMH-772 in providing support for the beleaguered naval base at Subic Bay during the volcano disaster.

HS-12 transitioned from *Midway* to USS *Independence* (CV-62) at Pearl Harbor in August 1991, when the former aircraft carrier was en route to the US for retirement and the latter became home-ported with CVW-5 at Yokosuka, Japan.

HS-14 'Chargers'
NAS North Island, CA: 'NE'
SH-3H

HS-14 was established 10 July 1984 and thus ranks as one of the US Navy's most recent squadrons. HS-14 operates the Sikorsky SH-3H Sea King with CVW-2 on USS *Ranger* (CV-61). The squadron participated in combat during Desert Storm.

HS-15 'Red Lions'
NAS Jacksonville, FL: 'AE'
SH-60F, HH-60H

HS-15 was established 29 October 1971 and was part of CVW-6 on USS *Forrestal* (CV-59) until late 1991. The squadron has assigned detachments to other surface warships and logged its 1,000th deck landing for 1991 aboard the cruiser USS *Yorktown* (CG-48). When *Forrestal* changed status in 1992 to become the US Navy's training carrier, HS-15 was scheduled to operate from Jacksonville, FL, and to transition to the Sikorsky SH-60F Seahawk.

HS-16

This unit was disestablished in 1991.

HS-17 'Neptune's Raiders'

This unit was disestablished on 2 July 1991.

SH-60F from HS-6 dropped a two-man EOD team from *Lincoln* into the Persian Gulf to destroy a mine spotted earlier by a Marine helicopter. Naval Aviation squadrons destroyed more than 1,250 mines during the six-month period following the end of the war.

The US Navy has decided to augment HS-6 with two HH-60H strike rescue helicopters in addition to its SH-60Fs.

HS-7 'Big Dippers'
NAS Jacksonville, FL: 'AC'
SH-3H

HS-7 was established 15 December 1969 and is the second US Navy squadron to carry the designation HS-7. The 'Dippers' operate the Sikorsky SH-3H Sea King helicopters part of CVW-3 aboard USS *John F. Kennedy* (CV-67). The squadron provided antisubmarine, SAR and utility support when 'Big John' participated in Desert Shield, followed by combat operations in Desert Storm.

HS-8 'Eight Ballers'
NAS North Island, CA: 'NK'
SH-60F, HH-60H

HS-8 was established 1 November 1969, the second squadron to carry the HS-8 designation. HS-8 commenced transition to the SH-60F Seahawk in September 1991, the fourth North Island-based deploying station to operate the F model of the antisubmarine helicopter. HS-8 also operates the HH-60H strike version when deployed. The squadron forms part of *Vinson*'s CVW-14.

HS-9 'Sea Griffins'
NAS Jacksonville, FL: 'AA'
SH-3H

HS-9 belongs to CVW-17 aboard USS *Saratoga* (CV-60) and operates the Sikorsky SH-3H Sea King antisubmarine helicopter. This is the second US Navy squadron to carry the designation HS-9, and was established on 4 June 1976. The squadron previously formed part of *Roosevelt*'s CVW-17.

Roosevelt's battle group participated in the Persian Gulf conflict. During Desert Storm, one SH-3H belonging to the 'Sea Griffins' was credited with detecting and directing the destruction of 10 Iraqi mines which threatened friendly shipping.

HS-10 'Taskmasters'
NAS North Island, CA: 'RA'
SH-60F

HS-10 was established on 1 July 1960. The squadron is the Pacific Fleet FRS for the Sikorsky SH-60F Seahawk. The squadron trains air crew and maintenance personnel in carrier-based SH-60F operations.

HS-11 'Dragonslayers'
NAS Jacksonville, FL: 'AB'
SH-3H

HS-11 was established 27 June 1957. The squadron operates the Sikorsky SH-3H Sea

The squadron, together with the carrier's air wing, arrived in the Persian Gulf region in the June 1991 in the aftermath of Desert Storm. Although the primary mission of the SH-60F is to fight submarines, the helicopter was used in the Persian Gulf region during explosive ordnance disposal (EOD) operations, including the clearing of mines. This was the activity which caused the largest number of US casualties in the conflict and is deemed by many to be the most dangerous. On 2 August 1991, an

HS-75 'Emerald Knights'
NAS North Island, CA: 'NW'
SH-3H

HS-75 is a Naval Air Reserve operator of the Sikorsky SH-3H Sea King antisubmarine helicopter. The squadron was activated during Desert Shield/Storm and sent detachments to several locations. HS-75 det Alpha rescued three US Air Force crew members from the only B-52 Stratofortress lost during the Gulf conflict. The B-52, callsign HULK 46, with six crew members on board, was forced to ditch 20 miles (33 km) from Diego Garcia on 3 February 1991 after a series of multiple mechanical problems. The 'Emerald Knights' SH-3H Sea King quickly located the three survivors. Some wreckage was still burning and heavy fuel covered an area 300 ft (92 m) across. All three survivors were in rafts inside the wreckage area, with parachutes still attached. At considerable risk, the SH-3H crew brought the survivors to safety.

Above: An HS-11 SH-3H cruises alongside America *in the plane-guard role. Underneath the starboard sponson is the towed* MAD *bird used for submarine detection.*

Right: With rotors and tail fully stowed, an HS-14 SH-3H sits on Ranger's *deck.*

HS-85 'Golden Gaters'
NAS Alameda, CA: 'NW'
SH-3H

HS-85 was established 1 July 1980. This Naval Air Reserve squadron uses the Sikorsky SH-3H Sea King helicopter.

HSL (Helicopter Antisubmarine Squadron Light)

HSL-30 'Scooters'
NAS Norfolk, VA: 'HT'
SH-2F

HSL-30 was established as HU-4 on 1 July 1960, redesignated HC-4 on 1 July 1965, and again given a new designation as HSL-30 on 1 March 1972. The 'Scooters' is the East Coast FRS squadron for the Kaman SH-2F Seasprite LAMPS Mk I antisubmarine helicopter. The squadron trains air crews and other personnel who deploy aboard surface warships in the Seasprite.

HSL-31 'Archangels'
NAS North Island, CA: 'TD'
SH-2F

HSL-31 was established as HC-5 on 1 September 1967, and received its current designation on 1 March 1972. The 'Archangels' are the West Coast FRS squadron for the Kaman SH-2F Seasprite LAMPS Mk I antisubmarine helicopter and provide training for Pacific Fleet SH-2F operators. The squadron is scheduled to disestablish in FY 1992.

HSL-32 'Tridents'
NAS Norfolk, VA: 'HV'
SH-2F

HSL-32 was established 17 August 1973 and operates the Kaman SH-2F Seasprite LAMPS Mk I helicopter. The squadron provides detachments for Atlantic Fleet vessels. The 'Tridents' share their nickname with HS-3, VP-26 and VP-65.

Far right: This SH-2F is from North Island-based HSL-33.

Below: The Atlantic SH-2 fleet is home-based at Norfolk, but regularly deploys on board surface warships.

Above: This SH-2F of HSL-30 displays the previous standard color scheme of the type.

HSL-33 'Sea Snakes'
NAS North Island, CA: 'TF'
SH-2F

HSL-33 was established 31 July 1973. Now at North Island, CA, the squadron operates the Kaman SH-2F Seasprite LAMPS Mk I helicopter and provides detachments to Pacific Fleet warships.

HSL-34 'Gray Checkers'
NAS Norfolk, VA: 'HX'
SH-2F

HSL-34, established 27 September 1974, operates the Kaman SH-2F Seasprite LAMPS Mk I helicopter and is tasked to

Above: The SH-60B has far from ousted the SH-2 from service. This example is from HSL-40.

provide antisubmarine support to US Navy surface ships in the Atlantic Fleet. HSL-34's helicopters wear a yellow/black checkerboard pattern on their tails, and the squadron shares its nickname with training squadron VT-23.

HSL-34 played host to the Australian frigate HMAS *Sydney* (FFG03) during the latter's goodwill visit to Norfolk, VA, in 1990, resulting in some unusual flying formations as its Seasprites flew in company with Australian AS 350B Squirrel helicopters.

HSL-35 'Magicians'
NAS North Island, CA: 'TG'
SH-2F

HSL-35, established 15 January 1974, operates the Kaman SH-2F Seasprite LAMPS Mk I helicopter and provides detachments to Pacific Fleet warships.

HSL-36 'Lamplighters'
NAS Mayport, CA: 'HY'
SH-2F

HSL-36, established 26 September 1975, operates the Kaman SH-2F Seasprite LAMPS Mk I and typically assigns detachments to US Navy warships in the Atlantic Fleet.

HSL-37 'Easy Riders'
NAS Barbers Point, HI: 'TH'
SH-2F

HSL-37, established 3 July 1975, operates Kaman SH-2F Seasprite LAMPS Mk I helicopters, with detachments aboard US Navy surface warships. Detachment 5, deployed aboard the destroyer USS *Ingersoll* (DD-990), played a role in the largest hashish drug bust in American history on 1 July 1991, near Midway Island, when an SH-2F helicopter chased down a smugglers' vessel and guided *Ingersoll* to the intercept. Thousands of bricks of hashish were discovered aboard the smugglers' vessel, *Lucky Star*, whose crew and cargo were escorted back to Pearl Harbor and turned over to the US Customs Service.

HSL-37 was scheduled to transition from the SH-2F to the Sikorsky SH-60B Seahawk following a 6 February 1992 ceremony at Barbers Point, HI. The first SH-2F squadron to transition to the SH-60B, HSL-37 is unique in that it will operate a mix of the two types until older surface warships based at Pearl Harbor, which accommodate the SH-2F, are replaced by vessels able to handle the larger SH-60B.

HSL-40 'Air Wolves'
NAS Mayport, FL: 'HK'
SH-60B

HSL-40, established 4 October 1985 and among the Navy's younger squadrons, is the East Coast FRS squadron for the Sikorsky SH-60B Seahawk LAMPS Mk III helicopter.

Above: An HSL-34 SH-2F in the hover, complete with MAD bird and auxiliary fuel tank.

Left: This HSL-36 SH-2F displays the latest gray paint scheme adopted by most USN aircraft.

HSL-41 'Sea Hawks'
NAS North Island, CA: 'TS'
SH-60B

HSL-41, established 21 January 1983, operates the Sikorsky SH-60B Seahawk LAMPS Mk III helicopter and provides detachments to the Pacific Fleet. The squadron acts as the Pacific Fleet SH-60F FRS.

HSL-42 'Proud Warriors'
NAS Mayport, FL: 'HH'
SH-60B

HSL-42 was established 5 October 1984. The squadron operates the Sikorsky SH-60B Seahawk LAMPS Mk III antisubmarine helicopter and provides detachments for US Navy surface warships.

Large boxes on the nose of the SH-60B house ESM equipment. This example serves with HSL-41.

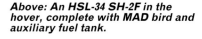

HSL-43 'Battle Cats'
NAS North Island, CA: 'TT'
SH-60B

HSL-43 was established 5 October 1984 and operates the Sikorsky SH-60B Seahawk LAMPS Mk III antisubmarine helicopter and provides detachments for Pacific Fleet warships.

HSL-44 'Swamp Foxes'
NAS Mayport, FL: 'HH'
SH-60B

HSL-44 operates the SH-60B Seahawk LAMPS Mk III antisubmarine aircraft and provides detachments for US Navy surface warships.

During Desert Storm it was an SH-60B crew from HSL-44 detachment 8 aboard the frigate USS *Nicholas* (FFG47) which rescued a US Air Force F-16 pilot from the Gulf on 24 January 1991. The 'Swamp Foxes' also supported Special Operations forces deployed aboard *Nicholas* in action against Iraqi forces on small islands and against Iraqi surface craft. HSL-44 also supported battleship bombardments in the Gulf and performed EOD duties.

HSL-45 'Wolfpack'
NAS North Island, CA: 'TZ'
SH-60B

HSL-45, established 3 October 1986, is one of the Navy's newest helicopter squadrons, operating the Sikorsky SH-60B Seahawk LAMPS Mk III antisubmarine helicopter and providing detachments for Pacific Fleet warships.

HSL-46 'Grandmasters'
NAS Mayport, FL: 'HQ'
SH-60B

HSL-46 operates the Sikorsky SH-60B Seahawk LAMPS Mk III antisubmarine helicopter and assigns detachments to Atlantic Fleet warships.

An HSL-44 SH-60B displays the installation of the MAD bird.

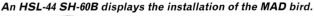

HSL-47 'Saberhawks'
NAS North Island, CA: 'TY'
SH-60B

HSL-45 operates the Sikorsky SH-60B Seahawk LAMPS Mk III antisubmarine helicopter and provides detachments for Pacific Fleet warships.

Below: The 'Demon Elves' of HSL-74 operate the SH-2F as part of the Naval Air Reserve force.

Above: SH-60B of HSL-48.

HSL-48 'Vipers'
NAS Mayport, FL: 'HR'
SH-2F

HSL-48 operates the Sikorsky SH-60B Seahawk LAMPS Mk III antisubmarine helicopter and assigns detachments to Atlantic Fleet warships. A typical deployment to the Gulf region began on 26 March 1992, when the squadron's

detachment 6, 'Spitting Cobras', embarked on USS *Robert G. Bradley* (FFG-49) with its sole SH-60B helicopter (BuNo. 162335, coded HR-506).

HSL-49 'Scorpions'
NAS North Island, CA: 'TX'
SH-60B

HSL-49 operates the Sikorsky SH-60B Seahawk LAMPS Mk III antisubmarine helicopter and provides detachments for Pacific Fleet warships.

HSL-51 'Warlords'
NAF Atsugi, Japan: 'TA'
SH-60B

HSL-51 was established 1 October 1991 at NAF Atsugi, Japan. This new operator of 10 Sikorsky SH-60B Seahawk LAMPS Mk IIIs was formed by consolidating detachments from various West Coast HSL squadrons. The squadron is assigned to deploy aboard carriers and surface warships in the western Pacific.

Above: A pair of HSL-47 SH-60Bs, showing to advantage the 360° undernose search radar.

HSL-74 'Demon Elves'
NAS South Weymouth, MA: 'NW'
SH-2F

HSL-74 is a Naval Air Reserve operator of the Kaman SH-2F Seasprite LAMPS Mk I antisubmarine helicopter. The US Navy planned to disestablish HSL-74 as part of its overall force reduction plan during FY 1993.

HSL-84 'Thunderbolts'
NAS North Island, CA: 'NW'
SH-2F

HSL-84 was established 1 July 1970 as HS-84, and was redesignated HSL-84 on 1 March 1984. The 'Thunderbolts' support the Naval Air Reserve antisubmarine effort with the Kaman SH-2F Seasprite LAMPS Mk I. The squadron's nickname is shared with a Marine Corps Hornet user, VMFA-251.

HSL-94 'Titans'
NAS North Island, CA: 'NW'
SH-2F

HSL-94, established 1 October 1985, is a Naval Air Reserve squadron equipped with the Kaman SH-2F Seasprite LAMPS Mk I antisubmarine helicopter. In 1991, for the second consecutive year, the 'Titans' were awarded the Admiral Alfred M. Pride ASW Award as the LAMPS Mk I squadron in the Naval Air Reserve demonstrating the highest mission readiness.

Left: HSL-49 flies the SH-60B from the main antisubmarine helicopter base at North Island.

HT (Helicopter Training Squadron)

Marked for Training Air Wing 5, this TH-57C flies from Whiting Field. The wing has two helicopter squadrons, HT-8 and HT-18.

HT-8
NAS Whiting Field, FL: 'E'
TH-57B

HT-8 traces its history to the establishment of HTU-1 on 3 December 1950. The Navy's first helicopter training unit was redesignated HTG-1 in March 1957, and became HT-8 on 1 July 1960. The squadron, part of TW-5 at NAS Whiting Field, FL, operates the Bell TH-57B helicopter to provide transitional training (between T-34C fixed-wing and advanced rotary-wing training with HT-18) to rotary-wing naval aviators. The two Whiting HT squadrons retired previous TH-57A aircraft in the late 1980s.

HT-18
NAS Whiting Field, FL: 'E'
TH-57B, TH-57C

HT-18 with TW-5 at Whiting Field, FL, established 1 March 1972, operates the Bell TH-57B to provide advanced flight training to rotary-wing naval aviators.

VA (Attack Squadron)

VA-34 'Blue Blasters'
NAS Oceana, VA: 'AG'
A-6E, KA-6D

VA-34 is the medium attack component of CVW-7 on USS *Dwight D. Eisenhower* (CVN-69). The current VA-34, not the first Navy squadron with this designation, was established on 1 January 1970. The 'Blasters' fly Grumman A-6E Intruders and KA-6D tankers.

The squadron is perhaps best known for its role in the rapid coalition response to the Iraqi invasion of Kuwait on 2 August 1990. In the early part of Desert Shield, *Eisenhower* and its air wing transited the Suez Canal, proceeded to the Gulf region, and began flying missions aimed at deterring an Iraqi thrust into Saudi Arabia. VA-34 helped to pioneer 'mirror image' strikes which simulated actual attacks on Iraqi targets. This show of force may have contributed to the coalition having time to build up, which in turn resulted in 'Ike', CVW-7 and VA-34 departing the region before the conflict began on 17 January 1991.

In the post-Desert Storm 1990s, VA-34 maintains its role as a key medium attack squadron committed to Atlantic Fleet/ Mediterranean operations.

VA-34 became the first Fleet A-6E squadron to fire an AGM-65E laser-guided Maverick missile during an 11 February 1992 exercise in the Arabian Sea. One missile was fired by a laser-designating aircraft which then designated the target for another A-6E firing a second Maverick. Both missiles hit the target.

VA-35 'Black Panthers'
NAS Oceana, VA: 'AA'
A-6E

VA-35, callsign RAYGUN, is one of the oldest squadrons in the US Navy, having employed its Panther emblem since the mid-1930s and winning fame under its earlier designation, VB-3, at the Battle of Midway. Its history began with the establishment of VF-3B on 1 July 1934. The squadron was redesignated VB-4 on 1 July 1937, VB-3 on 1 July 1939, VA-3A on 15 November 1946, VA-34 on 7 August 1948 and, finally, VA-35 on 15 February 1950. The squadron operates the A-6E Intruder and operated from *Saratoga* with CVW-17 during the first combat strikes of Desert Storm, beginning 17 January 1991.

The squadron lost two Intruders on the first day of the war. The first A-6E (BuNo. 161668, coded AA-510) was shot down on the evening of 17 January on a strike against Iraq's H-3 airfield. Pilot Lieutenant Robert Wetzel and bomber/navigator Lieutenant Jeffrey N. Zaun ejected at high speed and low altitude, and were taken prisoner and released after the war. A second A-6E (BuNo. 158539) returned safely but was damaged beyond economical repair. During this combat cruise in the Red Sea, the 'Panthers' made extensive use of night

vision goggles. Just after the war, it was reported that the squadron had accumulated 1,000 NVG hours since acquiring them in May 1988. Some 300 NVG hours were logged during combat missions in Iraq and Kuwait.

In the postwar 1990s, the squadron is scheduled to transition to the A-6E SWIP Intruder.

VA-36 'Roadrunners'
NAS Oceana, VA: 'AJ'
A-6E, KA-6D

VA-36 is part of CVW-8 aboard *Roosevelt*. The carrier air wing is unusual in having two medium attack squadrons of Grumman A-6E and KA-6D Intruders. Only one other air wing, CVW-2 on *Ranger*, has a double dose of Intruders.

Roosevelt's battle group participated in the Gulf conflict, with VA-36 flying day and night strike and interdiction missions against Iraqi targets. On 2 February 1991 the squadron suffered the combat loss of an A-6E Intruder (BuNo. 155632, coded AJ-531) and its crew, Lieutenant Patrick K. Connor and Lieutenant Commander Barry T. Cooke.

The squadron has resumed its Mediterranean/Atlantic Fleet commitment.

VA-42 'Green Pawns'
NAS Oceana, VA: 'AD'
KA-6D, A-6E, TC-4C, T-34C

VA-42 began life as VF-42 on 1 September 1950 and received its current designation on 1 November 1953. VA-42 is the East Coast FRS squadron for flight crews and

maintenance people en route to Fleet assignments in the KA-6D and A-6E Intruder. The squadron operates several versions of the Intruder including the A-6E SWIP Intruder, which is the latest block in service in the Fleet.

In connection with bombardier/navigator training, the squadron also provides training in four Grumman TC-4C Academe turboprop aircraft. In 1990, VA-42 acquired three Beech T-34C Turbo-Mentors, reflecting an excess of this type in primary training squadrons, to use for general pilot proficiency.

Above: A-6Es of VA-34, carrying full loads of Mk 83 LDGPs with ablative coating.

VA-52 'Knight Riders'
NAS Whidbey Island, WA: 'NL'
A-6E, KA-6D

VA-52 traces its history to Reserve squadron VF-884 which was established and called to active duty on 20 July 1950, less than a month into the Korean War, flying

Above: One of the US Navy's best-known unit insignias is the black panther, now carried by VA-35. The squadron is a night attack specialist, as witnessed in the Gulf War.

A large roadrunner's head is the unit insignia for VA-36, shore-based at Oceana but normally part of Air Wing 8 aboard USS Theodore Roosevelt.

The two A-6 FRS units have a small number of TC-4C Academes assigned for B/N training. The nosecone houses the A-6E radar and has the TRAM turret underneath.

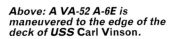

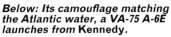

F-4U Corsairs. The squadron was redesignated VF-144 on 4 February 1953 and became VA-52 on 23 February 1959. Even with this long history, the squadron is, in fact, the second in Navy history to be designated VA-52. The 'Knight Riders' fly Grumman A-6E and KA-6D Intruders with CVW-15 aboard *Kitty Hawk*.

VA-55
This unit was disestablished 22 February 1991.

VA-65 'Tigers'
NAS Oceana, VA: 'AJ'
A-6E, KA-6D
VA-65 began its life as VT-74, established 1 May 1945, at which time the prefix denoted a torpedo squadron. The squadron was redesignated VA-2B on 15 November 1946, VA-25 on 1 September 1948, and VA-65 on 1 July 1959. The squadron has a long history in the Intruder, having flown A-6As in Vietnam. VA-65 is part of CVW-8 aboard *Roosevelt*, whose air wing is unusual in having two A-6E medium attack

Below: A-6E of VA-85 'Buckeyes'.

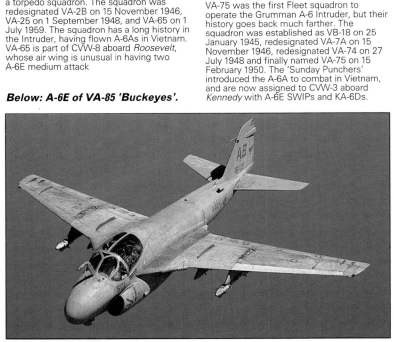

Above: This A-6E of VA-65 'Tigers' carries a D-704 buddy refueling pod on the centerline pylon.

squadrons. KA-6D Intruder tankers are also in inventory. Only one other air wing, CVW-2 on *Ranger*, has two Intruder squadrons. *Roosevelt*'s battle group participated in the Gulf conflict, VA-65 flying strike and interdiction missions against Iraqi targets. The squadron has since remained with *Roosevelt* during more prosaic Mediterranean/Atlantic Fleet operations.

VA-75 'Sunday Punchers'
NAS Oceana, VA: 'AC'
A-6E, KA-6D
VA-75 was the first Fleet squadron to operate the Grumman A-6 Intruder, but their history goes back much farther. The squadron was established as VB-18 on 25 January 1945, redesignated VA-7A on 15 November 1946, redesignated VA-74 on 27 July 1948 and finally named VA-75 on 15 February 1950. The 'Sunday Punchers' introduced the A-6A to combat in Vietnam, and are now assigned to CVW-3 aboard *Kennedy* with A-6E SWIPs and KA-6Ds.

Above: A VA-52 A-6E is maneuvered to the edge of the deck of USS Carl Vinson.

Below: Its camouflage matching the Atlantic water, a VA-75 A-6E launches from Kennedy.

Kennedy was one of the principal actors in the Gulf conflict. VA-75 carried out a heavy commitment of combat against Iraqi forces in Iraq and Kuwait, and is credited with the first operational use of the AGM-84E SLAM during Desert Storm. The SLAM strike against a hydroelectric plant north of Baghdad on the Tigris River resulted in the four missiles, fed mid-course corrections after launch, literally entering the turbine hall of the plant's powerhouse. A squadron member, after looking at a videotape of this current example of 'smart' weaponry, said, ''It reminds you of the joke in [the cartoon strip] *Doonesbury* about a missile rattling around inside a laboratory, looking for the director's office, knocking on his door, and blowing him away.'' The squadron also flew SEAD missions with the AGM-88B HARM missile, which the A-6E SWIP Intruder is equipped to carry.

VA-85 'Buckeyes'
NAS Oceana, VA: 'AB'
A-6E, KA-6D
Today's VA-85, though it has a long history, is not the first Navy squadron to hold the VA-85 designation. VA-85 owes its origin to Reserve Squadron VA-859 which was established and called to active duty on 1 February 1951, during the Korean War. VA-859 was redesignated VA-85 on 4 February 1953.

Today's VA-85 is part of CVW-1 aboard *America* with Grumman A-6E and KA-6D Intruder aircraft. The carrier and squadron flew in combat during Desert Storm, and have since resumed less dramatic Mediterranean/Atlantic Fleet operations.

VA-95 'Green Lizards'
NAS Whidbey Island, WA: 'NH'
A-6E, KA-6D
VA-95, established 1 April 1972, operates the Grumman A-6E and KA-6D Intruder as part of CVW-11 aboard *Lincoln*, and flew in the Gulf region in mid-1992 immediately following Desert Storm. The squadron sent three detachments to Sheik Isa air base, Bahrain, during this period.

VA-115 'Eagles'
NAS Whidbey Island, WA: 'NF'
A-6E
VA-115 has a long history, beginning as torpedo squadron VT-11, established on 10 October 1942. The squadron was redesignated VA-12A on 15 November 1946, and VA-115 on 15 July 1948. The squadron has an unusual footnote: it was inactive from August 1967 to 1 January 1969 but was not disestablished during this time and retained a very limited number of personnel, located at NAS Lemoore, CA. Thus, the squadron identity was continued when VA-115 was reactivated 1 January 1970. For many years, the squadron was nicknamed the 'Arabs' until modern-day sensibilities dictated a change.

The 'Eagles', as VA-115 is now nicknamed, transitioned from *Midway* to *Independence* at Pearl Harbor in August 1991, when the former aircraft carrier was en route to the US for retirement and the latter became home-ported with CVW-5 at Yokosuka, Japan. At this time, VA-115 acquired several A-6E SWIP Intruders, the latest model of the Intruder in the fleet, and gave up its KA-6D Intruder tankers.

Left: A-6 squadrons normally have KA-6D tankers assigned, this being an example from VA-95.

Above: The oriental-style tailcode celebrates the fact the VA-115 flies from the Japan-based 'Indy'.

Above: *VA-196 is a Pacific Fleet A-6E unit, all of which are shore-based at Whidbey Island.*

Below: *VA-205 is a Reserve squadron. This is one of its KA-6D tankers, carrying a D-704 pod.*

Above: *VA-128 'Golden Intruders' are the Pacific Fleet replenishment squadron.*

Below: *As might be expected from their tail markings, VA-145 is known as the 'Swordsmen'.*

Above: *Receiving maintenance on deck is an A-6E of VA-155. The opened radome reveals the Norden attack radar and mounting for the TRAM turret.*

Below: *An Intruder launches from the waist cat of* Nimitz. *The full-span flaps enable the A-6E to haul a heavy load from the carrier deck.*

VA-128 'Golden Intruders'
NAS Whidbey Island, WA: 'NJ'
A-6E, TC-4C

VA-128, established 1 September 1967, is the West Coast FRS squadron for the Grumman A-6E Intruder and has been associated with the Intruder since its inception, when the A-6A version was in use. The squadron trains air crews and maintenance personnel operating Intruders with the Pacific Fleet. The squadron also provides bombardier/navigator training in Grumman TC-4C Academe turboprop aircraft.

VA-145 'Swordsmen'
NAS Whidbey Island, WA: 'NE'
A-6E, KA-6D

VA-145 originated when Reserve squadron VA-702 was established and called to active duty on 20 July 1950, less than a month into the Korean War. The squadron has operated F-4U Corsairs and AD-1 Skyraiders. It was redesignated VA-145 on 4 February 1953,

and shares its nickname with Tomcat operator VF-32.

The squadron is part of CVW-2 aboard *Ranger* and operates the Grumman A-6E Intruder in the medium attack role. The squadron participated in combat during Desert Storm, when it carried out the first combat firings of the AGM-88B HARM by an Intruder unit.

VA-145 was scheduled to receive the last production A-6E Intruder (BuNo. 164385, the 205th A-6E and 708th Intruder), which was delivered to the US Navy on 3 February 1992. Delivery of this aircraft ended 31 years of continuous Intruder production.

VA-155 'Silver Foxes'
NAS Whidbey Island, WA: 'NE'
A-6E, KA-6D

VA-155 is an Intruder squadron assigned to CVW-2 aboard *Ranger*, the only Pacific Fleet carrier with two Intruder squadrons on board. Both squadrons flew perilous missions during Desert Storm. On 18 January 1991, the 'Silver Foxes' lost an A-6E Intruder (BuNo. 152928) and its crew, Lieutenants William T. Costen and Charles J. Turner. The aircraft, the number two in a four-ship strike package, was hit and the crew apparently did not eject.

After the war, the squadron received its first A-6E SWIP Intruders on 19 August 1991. VA-155 was the last West Coast Intruder squadron to acquire the SWIP version.

VA-165 'Boomers'
NAS Whidbey Island, WA: 'NG'
A-6E, KA-6D

VA-165, established 1 September 1960, operates the Grumman A-6E and KA-6D Intruder as part of CVW-9 aboard *Nimitz*.

VA-176

This unit was disestablished in 1992.

VA-185

This unit, formerly aboard *Midway* with A-6E Intruders, was disestablished in August 1991.

VA-196 'Main Battery'
NAS Whidbey Island, WA: 'NK'
A-6E

VA-196 began life on 15 July 1948 as VF-153. The squadron was redesignated VF-194 on 15 February 1950 and VA-196 on 4 May 1955. VA-196 operates Grumman A-6E and KA-6D Intruders as part of CVW-14, formerly aboard USS *Constellation* (CV-64) and recently assigned to *Carl Vinson*.

VA-205 'Green Falcons'
NAS Atlanta, GA: 'AF'
A-6E, KA-6D

VA-205 is a Naval Air Reserve operator of the Grumman A-6E Intruder in the medium attack role, with KA-6D tanker support. The squadron was established 1 July 1970, coinciding with the assignment of more important duties to Reserve squadrons.

VA-304 'Firebirds'
NAS Alameda, CA: 'ND'
A-6E, KA-6D

VA-304, established 1 July 1970, is a Naval Air Reserve operator of the Grumman A-6E and KA-6D Intruder medium attack aircraft. VA-304 made a successful two-week deployment to NAS Fallon, NV, in June 1991, its first in the Intruder.

Below: *VA-304 is a Reserve unit at Alameda. The nearby Golden Gate bridge is an obvious photo-location.*

VAQ (Tactical Electronic Warfare Squadron)

VAQ-33 'Firebirds'
NAS Key West, FL: 'GD'
ES-3A, EP-3A/B/J

VAQ-33 performs electronic warfare and electronic aggressor duties with a mix of Lockheed ES-3A Viking, EP-3A, EP-3B and EP-3J Orion, and Vought EA-7L Corsair II aircraft. The squadron was scheduled to retire its EA-7Ls, among the last Corsairs in the US Navy, by 1 April 1992.

The squadron has a convoluted history. It began as composite squadron VC-33 on 31 May 1949 and was redesignated VA(AW)-33 on 2 July 1956. Further changes renamed the squadron VAW-33 on 30 June 1959 and VAQ-33 on 1 February 1968.

Together with VAQ-34 and VAQ-35, the squadron is part of the Fleet Electronic Warfare Support Group. Its most recent acquisitions are two EP-3J Orions (BuNos 152719 and 152745). The EP-3J designation was announced at the beginning of 1992 for this duo of Orions which have USQ-113 communications intrusion deception and jamming set, AST-4/6 stimulator pods, AN/ALQ-167 jamming pods and ALE-43 chaff dispensers. The EP-3Js play the role of hostile patrol and reconnaissance aircraft to test radar operators, electronic warfare techniques and air defenses during Fleet exercises.

VAQ-34 'Flashbacks'
NAS Lemoore, CA: 'GD'
F/A-18A/B

Established on 1 March 1983, VAQ-34 has recently abandoned its former nickname of 'Electric Horsemen' and, in 1991, moved

Above: EA-6B of VAQ-130 'Zappers'.

from NAS Point Mugu, CA. The squadron began operating McDonnell Douglas F/A-18A and B Hornets in late 1991 after being, for many years, an operator of the Vought EA-7L Corsair II. The squadron carries out an aggressor role to train land-based and shipboard radar operators in tracking hostile aircraft. Because its mission is not classified as 'combat', the squadron has traditionally offered female air crews the US Navy's only opportunity to fly high-performance jet aircraft. In its electronic defensive role, the squadron joins VAQ-33 and VAQ-35 as part of the FEWSG.

VAQ-35 'Graywolves'
NAS Whidbey Island, WA: 'GD'
EA-6B

VAQ-35 was formed 1 June 1991 at Whidbey Island, using personnel and equipment from VA-142 which had been disestablished two months earlier. Like other VAQ squadrons, the 'Graywolves' have an aggressor mission with their Grumman EA-6B Prowlers. The squadron's job is to operate the EA-6B to train shipboard radar operators in countering electronic jamming. In this role, the squadron joins VAQ-33 and VAQ-34 as part of the FEWSG.

VAQ-129 'New Vikings'
NAS Whidbey Island, WA: 'NJ'
EA-6B

VAQ-129 is the FRS squadron for the EA-6B Prowler. The squadron began life as VAH-10, operating the A-3 Skywarrior, and was established 1 May 1970. It acquired its current designation on 1 September 1970. VAQ-129 operates several Prowler sub-variants in training EA-6B crews for operations with both Fleets.

VAQ-130 'Zappers'
NAS Whidbey Island, WA: 'AC'
EA-6B

VAQ-130 was established as VW-13 on 1 September 1959, initially operating the

Above: VAQ-34 previously flew ERA-3Bs and EA-7Ls, but now uses F/A-18As for EW work.

Below: VAQ-129 undertakes the FRS role for the entire EA-6B community.

P4M-1Q Mercator. The squadron was redesignated VAQ-130 on 1 October 1968, to become the first operator of the Grumman EA-6B Prowler. The squadron customarily deploys with CVW-3 aboard *Kennedy*. The jamming capabilities of the EA-6B were proven during Desert Storm, when VAQ-130 was cited for its operations against Iraqi targets.

VAQ-131 'Lancers'
NAS Whidbey Island, WA: 'NE'
EA-6B

VAQ-131 flies the Grumman EA-6B Prowler as part of CVW-2 on *Ranger*. The squadron was established and called to active duty as VP-931 on 3 September 1950; it was redesignated VP-57 on 4 February 1953, became VAH-4 on 3 July 1956 and VAQ-131 on 1 November 1968. The 'Lancers' were active in electronic warfare operations against Iraq during Desert Storm.

VAQ-132 'Scorpions'
NAS Whidbey Island, WA: 'AA'
EA-6B

VAQ-132 flies the Grumman EA-6B Prowler as part of CVW-17 on *Saratoga*. The squadron began as VAH-2 on 1 November 1955 and picked up its current designation on 1 November 1968. The squadron flew electronic warfare missions during Desert Storm.

VAQ-133

This unit was disestablished in June 1992.

VAQ-134 'Garudas'
NAS Whidbey Island, WA: 'NL'
EA-6B

VAQ-134, established 17 June 1969, flies the Grumman EA-6B Prowler as part of CVW-15 on *Kitty Hawk*.

Left: VAQ-132 was part of the Forrestal wing, but now flies from Saratoga.

Below: The 'Garudas' of VAQ-134 have survived the squadron cuts in the EA-6 community.

Below: EA-6B of VAQ-135 'Black Ravens', from Abraham Lincoln.

Above: The 'Rooks' of VAQ-137 are deployed aboard USS America with Air Wing One.

Below: VAQ-136 is part of the Atsugi-based CVW-5, which flies aboard the Independence.

Below: VAQ-141 'Shadowhawks' fly from Theodore Roosevelt.

Above: VAQ-138 'Yellowjackets' are assigned to Nimitz.

VAQ-135 'Black Ravens'
NAS Whidbey Island, WA: 'NH'
EA-6B

VAQ-135, established 15 May 1969, flies the Grumman EA-6B Prowler as part of CVW-11 aboard Lincoln. The squadron flew electronic support missions when 'Abe' arrived in the Gulf region in mid-1991 following Desert Storm.

VAQ-136 'Gauntlets'
NAF Atsugi, Japan: 'NF'
EA-6B

VAQ-136, established 6 April 1973, transitioned from Midway to Independence at Pearl Harbor in August 1991, when the former aircraft carrier was en route to the US for retirement and the latter became home-ported with CVW-5 at Yokosuka.

VAQ-137 'Rooks'
NAS Whidbey Island, WA: 'AB'
EA-6B

VAQ-137, established 14 December 1973, flies the Grumman EA-6B Prowler as part of CVW-1 aboard America and was active in Desert Storm.

VAQ-138 'Yellowjackets'
NAS Whidbey Island, WA: 'NG'
EA-6B

VAQ-138, established 27 February 1976, flies the Grumman EA-6B Prowler as part of CVW-9 aboard Nimitz.

VAQ-139 'Cougars'
NAS Whidbey Island, WA: 'NK'
EA-6B

VAQ-139, established 1 July 1983, flies the EA-6B as part of Vinson's CVW-14.

VAQ-140 'Patriots'
NAS Whidbey Island, WA: 'AG'
EA-6B

VAQ-140 (established 1 October 1985) flies the Grumman EA-6B Prowler as part of CVW-7 aboard USS Dwight D. Eisenhower (CVN-69). The squadron flew electronic support missions during Desert Shield and, like 'Ike' and its air wing, withdrew before the beginning of the war with Iraq.

VAQ-141 'Shadowhawks'
NAS Whidbey Island, WA: 'AJ'
EA-6B

VAQ-141 flies the Grumman EA-6B Prowler as part of CVW-8 aboard Roosevelt. The squadron flew SEAD missions during Desert Storm.

VAQ-142

This unit, based at Whidbey Island, WA, was disestablished 31 March 1991.

VAQ-209 'Star Warriors'
NAF Washington, MD: 'AF'
EA-6B

VAQ-209 is a relatively new Naval Air Reserve squadron, established 1 October 1977 at NAF Washington (Andrews AFB, MD) and equipped with Grumman EA-6B Prowlers. The squadron's insignia is a likeness of Star Wars' Darth Vader.

VAQ-309 'Axemen'
NAS Whidbey Island, WA: 'ND'
EA-6B

VAQ-309, established 1 February 1979, is a Naval Air Reserve operator under CVWR-30 of the Grumman EA-6B Prowler. The squadron patch shows a Paul Bunyan-like woodsman holding a lightning bolt and an axe.

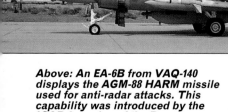

Above: An EA-6B from VAQ-140 displays the AGM-88 HARM missile used for anti-radar attacks. This capability was introduced by the ICAP-2 version of the Prowler.

Right: Both Reserve air wings have a Prowler squadron assigned, this aircraft being from CVWR-20's VAQ-209. This unit flies from Andrews AFB (NAF Washington).

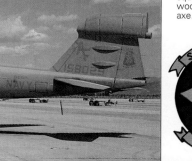

VAW (Carrier Airborne Early Warning Squadron)

VAW-78 'Fighting Escargots'
NAS Norfolk, VA: 'AF'
E-2C

VAW-78, established 1 July 1970, is a Naval Air Reserve operator of the Grumman E-2C Hawkeye early-warning aircraft. Squadron emblem shows the snail for which the unit is named against a lightning bolt.

VAW-88 'Cottonpickers'
NAS Miramar, CA: 'ND'
E-2C

VAW-88, established 1 June 1970, is a Naval Air Reserve operator of the Grumman E-2C Hawkeye early-warning aircraft.

VAW-110 'Firebirds'
NAS Miramar, CA: 'NJ'
E-2C, C-2A

VAW-110 began life as RVAW-110 on 20 April 1967; the squadron became VAW-110 on 1 May 1983. The 'Firebirds' is the West Coast FRS squadron for the Grumman E-2C Hawkeye and C-2A Greyhound aircraft, providing training to aircrews and maintenance personnel who work with these types in the Pacific Fleet. In early 1992, VAW-110 began fleet replenishment training in the E-2C Group II updated version of the Hawkeye, in preparation for Fleet squadron VAW-113 becoming the first to operate this improved variant.

VAW-112 'Golden Hawks'
NAS Miramar, CA: 'NG'
E-2C

VAW-112, estabished 20 April 1967, operates the Grumman E-2C Hawkeye. The squadron is part of CVW-9 aboard *Nimitz*.

VAW-113 'Black Hawks'
NAS Miramar, CA: 'NK'
E-2C

VAW-113, established 20 April 1967, is part of CVW-14 which has recently been assigned to *Vinson* following a long association with USS *Constellation* (CV-64). Long equipped with the Grumman E-2C Hawkeye early warning aircraft, the squadron was scheduled to become the US Navy's first to operate the E-2C Group II improved version beginning in 1993.

VAW-114 'Hormel Hawgs'
NAS Miramar, CA: 'NL'
E-2C

VAW-114, established 20 April 1967, operates the Grumman E-2C Hawkeye aircraft. The squadron is part of CVW-15 aboard *Kitty Hawk*.

Below: VAW-115 is part of the forward-deployed Air Wing 5, this example being seen on the wing's former carrier, USS Midway.

VAW-115 'Sentinels'
NAF Atsugi, Japan: 'NF'
E-2C

VAW-115 (until recently known as the 'Liberty Belles'), established 20 April 1967, transitioned from USS *Midway* (CV-41) to USS *Independence* (CV-62) at Pearl Harbor in August 1991, when the former aircraft carrier was en route to the US for retirement and the latter became home-ported with CVW-5 at Yokosuka, Japan. The squadron's shore base is NAS Atsugi.

On 24 September 1991, when a squadron E-2C (BuNo. 163027, coded NF-603) underwent repairs at a Japanese base in Gifu Prefecture, 150 miles (225 km) southwest of Tokyo, it became the first US military aircraft to land at Gifu since 1954.

VAW-116 'Sun Kings'
NAS Miramar, CA: 'NE'
E-2C

VAW-116, established 20 April 1967, operates the Grumman E-2C Hawkeye as part of CVW-2 aboard USS *Ranger* (CV-61). The squadron flew early warning missions during Desert Storm.

VAW-117 'Wallbangers'
NAS Miramar, CA: 'NH'
E-2C

VAW-117, established 1 July 1974, flies the Grumman E-2C Hawkeye as part of CVW-11 aboard *Lincoln*. The squadron participated in Gulf operations beginning mid-1991.

Above: Reserve unit VAW-78 has an inspired nickname: the 'Fighting Escargots'!

Below: VAW-88 is the second Reserve unit, flying with the Pacific Fleet's CVWR-30.

Above: E-2C Hawkeye of VAW-112.

Below: E-2C of VAW-116.

Above: VAW-120 trains Greyhound crews in addition to E-2 aviators, and consequently has a few C-2As.

Below: A runaway victor in the 'World's Largest Unit Insignia' competition is VAW-123.

Above: E-2C Hawkeye of Kennedy-based VAW-126.

VAW-120 'Cyclones'
NAS Norfolk, VA: 'AD'
C-2A, E-2C

VAW-120 is located at the East Coast Hawkeye base of Norfolk, and operates as the fleet replenishment squadron for Atlantic/Mediterranean units. In addition to training Hawkeye crews and maintenance personnel, the 'Cyclones' also provide instruction for the small Greyhound COD fleet, and consequently operates a handful of C-2As.

VAW-121 'Bluetails'
NAS Norfolk, VA: 'AG'
E-2C

VAW-121, established 1 April 1967, is part of CVW-7 aboard *Eisenhower* and operates the Grumman E-2C Hawkeye early-warning aircraft.

VAW-122 'Steeljaws'
NAS Norfolk, VA: 'AE'
E-2C

VAW-122, established 1 April 1967, operates the Grumman E-2C Hawkeye airborne early-warning aircraft and has long been associated with CVW-6 which operated aboard USS *Forrestal* (CV-59) before the carrier was reassigned to training duties in 1991. The squadron has made frequent Mediterranean deployments, using its E-2Cs to provide radar warning of threats to the *Forrestal* battle group.

The 'Steeljaws' suffered a bizarre incident on 8 July 1991 when one of their E-2C Hawkeyes had to be shot down over the Mediterranean after the crew bailed out to escape an uncontrollable engine fire. This is believed to be the only time a five-man E-2C crew has successfully parachuted from the Hawkeye, which is a difficult aircraft to get out of. While the crew was being rescued by helicopters from *Forrestal* and USS *Yorktown* (CG-48), an F/A-18A Hornet from VFA-132 was ordered to shoot down the E-2C to prevent it from crashing into civilian personnel or property. Cannon fire from the Hornet racked up this unique air-to-air 'kill'.

In early 1992, the US Navy announced that, as a result of *Forrestal*'s changed status, VAW-122 would be disestablished during 1992. The squadron was subsequently given a two-year reprieve and has been assigned drug-interdiction duties.

VAW-123 'Screwtops'
NAS Norfolk, VA: 'AB'
E-2C

VAW-123, established 1 April 1967, operates the Grumman E-2C Hawkeye as part of CVW-1 aboard USS *America* (CV-66). The squadron participated in Desert Storm.

VAW-124 'Bear Aces'
NAS Norfolk, VA: 'AJ'
E-2C

VAW-124, established 1 September 1967, is part of CVW-8 aboard USS *Theodore Roosevelt* (CVN-71), flying the Grumman E-2C Hawkeye. The carrier and the squadron participated in Desert Storm.

VAW-125 'Tigertails'
NAS Norfolk, VA: 'AA'
E-2C

VAW-125, established 1 October 1968, operates the Grumman E-2C Hawkeye in the airborne early warning role as part of CVW-17 aboard USS *Saratoga* (CV-60).

The carrier and its air wing were heavily involved in Desert Storm. An E-2C Hawkeye of the squadron (BuNo. 159107, coded AA-600) directed two VFA-81 'Sunliner' F/A-18C Hornets which shot down two Iraqi MiG-21s on 17 January 1991, this Hawkeye subsequently having the distinction of wearing two MiG-21 silhouettes on its forward fuselage. The E-2C crew was credited with making the calls that enabled the two Hornet pilots to shoot down the MiGs and resume their bombing mission.

'Sara' and VAW-125 were preparing for a subsequent Mediterranean cruise in the post-Desert Storm period.

VAW-126 'Seahawks'
NAS Norfolk, VA: 'AC'
E-2C

VAW-126, established 1 April 1969, operates the Grumman E-2C Hawkeye as part of CVW-3 aboard USS *John F. Kennedy* (CV-67). The carrier, often called 'Big John', was a critical participant in Desert Storm, during which time the 'Seahawks' flew early warning and combat support missions. Following the Gulf conflict, the squadron has resumed its Mediterranean/Atlantic Fleet commitment.

VC (Fleet Composite Squadron)

VC-1 'Blue Alii'
NAS Barbers Point, HI: 'UA'
A-4E, TA-4J

VC-1 is an archetypal composite squadron performing a range of transport and utility tasks in support of Fleet operations in the Hawaiian islands. Not the first Navy squadron to bear this designation, the current VC-1 was established as W-1 on 20 July 1951 and became VC-1 on 1 July 1965.

The squadron operates a mix of Douglas A-4E and TA-4J Skyhawks. On 1 October 1991, the squadron retired three Sikorsky CH-53A Sea Stallion transport helicopters which had contributed to its support mission, and has since retired its single VP-3A Orion.

VC-5 'Checkertails'
NAS Cubi Point, Philippines
TA-4J, SH-3G

VC-5 serves as the Navy's principal composite squadron in the Southeast Asia. The current squadron began as VU-5 on 16 August 1950 and received its current designation on 1 July 1965.

In 1992, the 'Checkertails' were operating 13 Douglas TA-4J Skyhawks, five Sikorsky SH-3G Sea Kings, AQM-37C and BQM-74 target drones, and QST-33/35 target missile boats. The squadron had a range of assignments which included dissimilar air combat training, war-at-sea exercises, target towing, drone recovery, and insertion of Marine, rescue or SEAL special operations forces by helicopter.

Following the 15 June 1991 eruption of Philippine volcano Mount Pinatubo, the squadron undertook extensive rescue and humanitarian flying. As the only US military squadron flying regularly in the Philippines during the aftermath of the disaster, VC-5 flew US Geological Survey teams to the volcano to lay seismic sensing equipment. VC-5's helicopters also provide the only SAR

VC-1 operates a handful of TA-4J Skyhawks for adversary and target facilities tasks.

capability in the Philippines and supported Operation Fiery Vigil, the evacuation of American dependants from the naval base at Subic Bay.

Left: Based at Cubi Point, VC-5 was on hand to provide immediate support following the eruption of Mount Pinatubo, including the transport of seismological teams.

Above: The Skyhawk is fast and nimble, and makes an ideal platform for simulating anti-ship missiles during attacks to test the defenses of US Navy vessels.

With the US withdrawal from the Philippines, VC-5 was scheduled to be disestablished 31 August 1992 and most of its A-4 Skyhawks sold for scrap. In early 1992, VC-5 was operating a detachment at NAS Atsugi, Japan.

VC-6 'Skeet of the Fleet'
NAS Patuxent River, MD
no aircraft assigned

VC-6, aptly named after the sport of shooting at flying objects, was established 1 March 1952 as VU-6 and became VC-6 on 1 July 1965. It is not the first US Navy squadron to bear the latter designation.

Today, VC-6 qualifies as a naval aviation squadron even it has no aircraft. The squadron employs Pioneer RPVs and places detachments at US Navy land bases and on surface warships. 'Skeet of the Fleet' was given an opportunity to demonstrate the usefulness of RPVs during Desert Storm.

The squadron provided detachments aboard the battleships USS *Missouri* (BB-63) and USS *Wisconsin* (BB-64). The VC-6 crews launched small, radio-controlled Pioneer drones over the Kuwaiti shore, using television cameras to relay gun-firing coordinates back to ships. Battleships were able to operate effectively in the narrow Gulf, where carriers rarely venture, and the RPVs proved a highly effective way of directing their powerful 16-in naval guns.

VC-8 'Redtails'
NAS Roosevelt Roads, PR: 'GF'
TA-4J, SH-3G

VC-8 was formed on 1 July 1958 as GMSRON-2 (Guided Missile Service

Squadron 2). On 1 July 1960 it became VU-8 and on 1 July 1965 VC-8, not the first squadron with that designation.

VC-8 operates Douglas TA-4J Skyhawk and Sikorsky SH-3G Sea King aircraft in its composite role of supporting Fleet operations in the Caribbean region. Uniquely, the job of commanding VC-8 is rotated between helicopter and fixed-wing pilots.

The helicopters of VC-8 drew the hapless

task of recovering the dead from the 1989 disaster aboard USS *Iowa* (BB-61), which killed 47 people when an ammunition magazine exploded.

VC-10 'Challengers'
NAS Guantanamo Bay, Cuba:
'JH'
TA-4J

VC-10 operates the Douglas TA-4J

Above: VC-8 is based in Puerto Rico, from where it flies this SH-3G.

Skyhawk in support of Fleet operations in the Caribbean area. VC-10 was established as VJ-16 on 1 December 1943, became VU-10 on 15 November 1946, and was redesignated VC-10 on 1 July 1965. The squadron's designation has been used previously and VC-10 shares its nickname with VF-43.

VF (Fighter Squadron)

VF-1 'Wolfpack'
NAS Miramar, CA: 'NE'
F-14

VF-1 (callsign WICHITA) was established at Miramar, CA, on 14 October 1972. Squadron insignia is a red wolf. Following crew training, the squadron received its first F-14 Tomcats on 1 July 1973. Together with VF-2 'Bounty Hunters', VF-1 deployed aboard USS *Enterprise* as part of CVW-14 beginning in September 1974, on a cruise which culminated in combat air patrols during Operation Frequent Wind, the 30 April 1975 evacuation of Saigon which ended the Vietnam War. The 'Wolfpack' shifted to CVW-2 and *Ranger* in September 1980 and remained with the same air wing on subsequent cruises with USS *Kitty Hawk* (CV-63) beginning in 1984. VF-1 returned to *Ranger* and, during a 1988 cruise, escorted Soviet MiG-23 'Flogger' fighters flying from Cam Ranh Bay, Vietnam.

VF-1 is currently part of CVW-2 assigned to *Ranger*. The air wing and carrier participated in the Gulf conflict, and a Tomcat (BuNo. 162603, coded NE-103) flown by pilot Lieutenant Stuart Broce and

RIO squadron commander Commander Ron McElraft scored the Grumman fighter's only Desert Storm aerial victory on 6 February 1991, shooting down a Mil Mi-8 helicopter using an AIM-9 Sidewinder missile.

Fittingly, VF-1 was the first Fleet squadron to operate the F-14 Tomcat, and it continues to fly the type 20 years later. Most of the squadron's aircraft have toned-down gray-on-gray unit markings, but the CAG-bird and this example, marked for the squadron CO, wear the full-color 'Wolf Pack' markings.

Left: Illustrating just how drab current US Navy schemes are is this pair of VF-2 Tomcats, the squadron CO's machine retaining the original full-color scheme.

Paired with VF-31, VF-11 joined CVW-3 aboard Kennedy in January 1982. VF-11 flew combat air patrols during the 4 December 1983 US air strike on Lebanon, in which two aircraft from a 28-strong Alpha Strike force were downed. On 1 April 1985, the 'Red Rippers' shifted to CVW-6 aboard Forrestal. When Forrestal completed its final cruise as a Fleet carrier on 21 December 1991 and subsequently became the Navy's training carrier, VF-11 moved to Miramar, CA, and transitioned to the F-14D. The squadron subsequently joined Vinson's CVW-14.

VF-14 'Top Hatters'
NAS Oceana, VA: 'AC'
F-14A

VF-14 (callsign CAMELOT) is the oldest US Navy squadron, with a continuous history dating to September 1919. A full history of the squadron's names and effective dates: Air detachment, Pacific Fleet, September 1919; VT-5, 15 June 1920; VP4-1, 7 September 1921; VF-4, 23 September 1921; VF-1, 1 July 1922; VF-1B, 1 July 1927; VB-2B, 1 July 1934; VB-3, 1 July 1937; VB-4, 1 July 1939; VS-41, 15 March 1941; VB-41, 1 March 1943; VB-4, 4 August 1943; VA-1A, 15 November 1946; VA-14, 2 August 1948; and, finally, VF-14, 15 December 1949. The squadron insignia shows a grinning tomcat in white tie and top hat leaning on his walking cane.

VF-14 began receiving its first F-14A Tomcats in January 1973, replacing F-4B Phantoms. Following three Mediterranean cruises with CVW-1 aboard Kennedy while paired with VF-32, the 'Top Hatters' shifted to CVW-6 aboard Independence in 1982. In 1983-84, Independence warplanes had the distinction of serving in two conflicts on the same cruise, in the US invasion of Grenada known as Operation Urgent Fury in October and the 4 December 1983 air strike on Lebanon. In 1985, the squadron was reassigned to CVW-3. Operating from Kennedy with CVW-3, VF-14 flew combat missions during Operation Desert Storm. Since then, the squadron has resumed Mediterranean deployments.

VF-21 'Freelancers'
NAS Miramar, CA: 'NF'
F-14A

VF-21 was established 2 March 1944 as VF-81, was redesignated VF-13A on 15 November 1946, became VF-131 on 2 August 1948, became VF-64 on 15 February 1950, and acquired its current designation on 1 July 1959. It is the second US Navy squadron to bear the VF-21 designation.

The squadron accepted its first F-14A Tomcat in November 1983 and was designated an F-14A squadron on 15 March 1984, replacing its previous F-4N Phantoms. Paired throughout its Tomcat career with VF-154, The 'Freelancers' served with CVW-14 aboard USS Constellation (CV-64) and later aboard Independence. A 1987 Constellation cruise took VF-21 to Gonzo Station near the Gulf of Oman. 1989 marked a return to the same location and landings at Diego Garcia. In August 1990, Independence, with her two Tomcat squadrons, was the first carrier to reach the Gulf region during Desert Shield, though the carrier completed its cruise before the outbreak of fighting on 17 January 1991.

In August 1991, VF-21 joined CVW-5 aboard Independence, which relieved Midway as the sole aircraft carrier home-ported at Yokosuka, Japan.

Left: Previously on Forrestal with F-14As, VF-11 was transferred to the Pacific Fleet to become the first front-line F-14D squadron. The squadron is assigned to Carl Vinson.

VF-2 'Bounty Hunters'
NAS Miramar, CA: 'NE'
F-14

VF-2 (callsign BULLET) was established at Miramar, CA, on 14 October 1972. Squadron insignia shows a shield replete with two biplanes, a skull and stars. Following crew training, the squadron received its first F-14 Tomcats on 1 July 1973. VF-2's markings, colorful in the 1970s and toned down in the 1990s, include a skull and stars (taken from the squadron's emblem in the 1920s and 1930s when it was composed primarily of enlisted pilots and was known as the 'Chief's squadron') on a gray Langley stripe (symbolizing the US Navy's first aircraft carrier) bordered by two stars. VF-2 is a TARPS squadron, its Tomcats configured to carry the reconnaissance pod.

Paired with VF-1 'Wolfpack', VF-2 deployed aboard USS Enterprise as part of CVW-14 beginning in September 1974 and flew combat air patrols during Operation Frequent Wind. The 'Bounty Hunters' shifted to CVW-2 and Ranger in September 1980 and became the second TARPS-equipped squadron to deploy to the western Pacific and Indian Ocean. The squadron remained with the same air wing on a subsequent cruise with USS Kitty Hawk (CV-63) beginning in 1984, then returned to Ranger. On 2 June 1984, the 'Bounty Hunters' achieved an obscure 'first' as the first F-14A squadron to launch from the flight deck of an aircraft carrier while towing an air-to-air gunnery banner. During a 1986 Ranger western Pacific cruise, the squadron intercepted Soviet Su-15 'Flagon' and MiG-23 'Flogger' fighters as well as 'Badger' and 'Bear' bombers. During a 1987 cruise, Ranger's 260,000th landing was logged.

Above: Claiming to be the Navy's oldest squadron, the 'Top Hatters' fly the Tomcat with Air Wing 3, partnered by VF-32 in 'Big John'.

VF-11 'Red Rippers'
NAS Miramar, CA: 'NK'
F-14D

VF-11 (callsign RIPPER) transitioned to the F-14A Tomcat in the summer of 1980, replacing the F-4J Phantom. The squadron was established as VF-43 on 1 September 1950, and was redesignated VF-11 on 16 February 1959. VF-11 adopted the insignia used by the previous VF-11, which had been disestablished the day before (15 February 1959). Today's VF-11 carries on the insignia and tradition of the 'Red Ripper' squadron dating to 1 February 1927, but not the lineage.

Left: VF-21 'Freelancers' has been a Tomcat unit since 1983 and has now settled aboard Independence, based in Japan. The carrier and unit saw Desert Shield service but did not take part in any fighting.

Above: Like its partner, VF-11, VF-31 transferred from Oceana to Miramar, and from F-14A to F-14D.

VF-24 'Fighting Renegades'
NAS Miramar, CA: 'NG'
F-14A

VF-24 (callsign NICKEL) began converting to the F-14A Tomcat in November 1975, replacing the F-8J Crusader. Not the first VF-24 in the US Navy, the squadron dates to its establishment as VF-211 in June 1955 and was given its current designation on 9 March 1959.

The squadron made its first cruise with the F-14A Tomcat as part of CVW-9 aboard USS *Constellation* (CV-64) in 1978-79, paired with VF-211. Still with CVW-9, the squadron shifted to *Ranger* for a 1983-84 cruise, then returned to 'Connie'. In the mid-1980s and well into its Tomcat era, the squadron's nickname was changed to 'Fighting Renegades' from its former 'Red Checkertails'. On 20 May 1985, a Fighting Two Four Tomcat (BuNo. 159593) became the first F-14 to log 3,000 flight hours. During a 1985 *Kitty Hawk* western Pacific/ Indian Ocean cruise, VF-24 became the first Tomcat squadron to be mission capable for 45 consecutive days.

Still with CVW-9, the 'Renegades' shifted in 1988 to *Nimitz*. The squadron transitioned to the F-14A+ (A Plus) beginning with receipt of its first example in April 1989. This model has since been redesignated F-14B. VF-24 has subsequently reverted to the F-14A due to a shortage of F-14Bs.

VF-31 'Tomcatters'
NAS Miramar, CA: 'NK'
F-14D

VF-31 'Tomcatters' (callsign BANDWAGON), the second oldest US Navy fighter squadron, began training at Oceana on 8 September 1980 to convert to the F-14A Tomcat as a replacement for its F-4J Phantoms.

The squadron began as VF-1B on 1 July 1935 and was subsequently designated VF-6 on 1 July 1937; VF-3 on 15 July 1943; VF-3A on 15 November 1946; and VF-31 on 7 August 1948. The squadron is not the first in the US Navy to hold the VF-31 appellation. Squadron markings include the well-known Felix (from the *Felix the Cat* cartoons), designed by Emile Chourre.

VF-31 received its first Tomcat on 22 January 1981 and stood up with the new fighter on 4 June 1981. With VF-11, the 'Tomcatters' joined CVW-3 aboard *Kennedy* in January 1982. On the Indian Ocean cruise which followed, VF-31 pioneered use of the TARPS-configured Tomcat for the reconnaissance role. In a subsequent 'Big John' cruise, which included combat operations in Lebanon in November-December 1983, the squadron flew TARPS missions over Syrian positions near Beirut, including the 3 December 1980 air strike in which Syrian anti-aircraft and missile fire were encountered. During this cruise, two F-14As were lost in non-combat incidents.

Right: Seen during Desert Shield, this is VF-32's 'boss-bird'. The squadron is the assigned TARPS unit in Kennedy.

The squadron shifted to CVW-6 aboard *Forrestal* on 1 April 1985.

When *Forrestal* completed its tour and became the US Navy's training carrier in early 1992, VF-31 was scheduled to relocate to Miramar and to transition to the F-14D Super Tomcat. The squadron has since joined Air Wing 14 on the USS *Carl Vinson*.

VF-32 'Swordsmen'
NAS Oceana, VA: 'AC'
F-14A

The squadron was established as VBF-3 on 1 February 1945. It was redesignated VF-4A on 15 November 1946, and VF-32 on 7 August 1948. VF-32's insignia shows a yellow lion wielding sword and shield with a yellow slash in the background, and the squadron shares its nickname with Intruder operator VA-145. VF-32 (callsign GYPSY) transitioned to the F-14A Tomcat from the F-4B Phantom in 1974.

Paired with VF-14, the squadron carried out three Mediterranean cruises with CVW-1 aboard *Kennedy*, beginning in 1981, before shifting to CVW-6 aboard *Independence* in 1982. In an exercise called Harpoonex '82, in mid-1982, VF-32 made early use of the TARPS to record Harpoon missile strikes on an actual warship used as a target. In 1983-84, *Independence* warplanes served in two conflicts on the same cruise, Operation Urgent Fury in October and the 4 December 1983 air strike in Lebanon. During operations in Grenada and Lebanon, TARPS-equipped 'Swordsmen' F-14As provided photography for Fleet planners.

The squadron was reassigned to CVW-3 aboard *Kennedy* on 1 April 1985. In January 1989 during a Mediterranean cruise aboard 'Big John', VF-32 crews engaged and shot down two Libyan MiG-23 'Flogger' fighters over international waters near Libya.

VF-32 was deployed with CVW-17 on *Kennedy* during Desert Shield/Storm. The squadron carried out combat air patrols in the Persian Gulf and made a major contribution to the coalition effort with TARPS flights. A VF-32 Tomcat crew on a TARPS mission on 4 March, five days after the cessation of hostilities, laid claim to being the last US Navy air crew over Baghdad.

VF-32 has resumed Mediterranean deployments.

VF-33 'Starfighters'
NAS Oceana, VA: 'AB'
F-14A

VF-33 (callsign TARBOX), established 12 October 1948, was known as the 'Tarsiers' until a name change in the mid-1980s. In late 1981, the squadron transitioned to the F-14A Tomcat after operating the F-4J Phantom. The squadron first went to sea with the Tomcat as part of CVW-1 aboard *America*, at first during workups and later on a Mediterranean and Indian Ocean cruise which culminated in June 1983. A second *America* cruise followed in 1984.

VF-33 Tomcats flew in Operation Prairie Fire operations against Libya in March 1986 and Operation El Dorado Canyon, the air strikes on Libya on 15 April 1986. Paired with VF-102, the 'Starfighters' continued to serve aboard *America* with Air Wing One and carried out combat operations during Desert Storm. In September 1991, the squadron participated in Operation North Star, a NATO joint exercise involving 10 ships in America's

Above: An F-14B from VF-24 prepares to launch from USS Nimitz.

Above: This smart CAG-bird is from VF-33 'Starfighters'.

battle group and British Sea Harriers from HMS *Invincible*.

America was a key participant in Desert Storm and VF-33 did its share. The squadron returned to Oceana following the conflict.

Right: Most of VF-33's aircraft wear this far more restrained scheme, with the star in dark gray outline only. The unit was previously known as the 'Tarsiers'.

Above: VF-45 at Key West has among its fleet this two-seat F-5F adversary aircraft.

Below: Both East Coast adversary units fly the F-16N, this example wearing the red star of VF-45.

Left: VF-41's finest hour in recent years came when the unit downed two Libyan Su-22s.

Left: The backbone of the USN adversary program is the Skyhawk. VF-43 flies both A-4F and TA-4J (illustrated).

VF-41 'Black Aces'
NAS Oceana, VA: 'AJ'
F-14A

VF-41 (callsign FAST EAGLE) was established 1 September 1950 and is the fourth US Navy squadron to bear the VF-41 designation. The squadron began transition to the F-14A Tomcat in April 1976, giving up its F-4N Phantoms. The squadron joined CVW-8 and in December 1977 began the first of several cruises aboard *Nimitz*. The 1980 cruise included a detour to the Arabian Sea where, on 24 April, *Nimitz* launched the ill-fated attempt to rescue US hostages in Iran.

On 19 August 1981, two 'Black Aces' F-14As downed two Libyan Sukhoi Su-22 'Fitter' fighters after being attacked during a freedom of navigation exercise. During 1985 *Nimitz* operations, the squadron tested minor improvements in the M61A1 'Gatling Gun' cannon. 1985 saw 68 days of contingency operations off Lebanon and desert warfare rehearsals in Egypt in Exercise Bright Star '85. A 1986 *Nimitz* North Atlantic deployment included operations with the Norwegian air force. Still with CVW-8, the squadron shifted in October 1987 to *Roosevelt*. During Exercise Teamwork '88, the squadron worked out with British and French fighters in the North Atlantic.

The squadron and the air wing shifted to *Lincoln*, which arrived for 'clean up' operations in the Persian Gulf region following the end of Desert Storm.

VF-43 'Challengers'
NAS Oceana, VA: 'AD'
A-4F, TA-4J, F-5E/F, F-16N, TF-16N, T-2C

VF-43 was established on 1 May 1945 as VF-74A. Subsequent changes in designation were VF-74 on 1 August 1945, VF-1B on 15 November 1946, VF-21 on 1 September 1948, VA-43 on 1 July 1959, and VA-43 on 1 June 1973. The 'Challengers' share their nickname with VC-10.

Left: A pair of VF-43 F-16Ns launches for an ACM hop in parallel with an F-14A of VF-14.

Below: VF-51 was planned to be the first F-14D unit, but instead remained with A models.

Above: VF-43 has a mixed fleet for adversary work at Oceana. This is a Northrop F-5E.

The squadron operates a mix of Douglas A-4F and TA-4F Skyhawks, Northrop F-5E and F-5F Tigers, General Dynamics F-16N and TF-16N Fighting Falcons, and North American T-2C Buckeyes, all for the purpose of providing air combat training to Fleet fighter squadrons.

VF-45 'Blackbirds'
NAS Key West, FL: 'AD'
A-4F, TA-4J, F-16N, TF-16N, F-5E/F

VF-45 was established on 15 February 1963 as VA-45 and given its current designation on 7 February 1985. The squadron operates a mix of Douglas A-4F and TA-4J Skyhawk, General Dynamics F-16N and TF-16N Fighting Falcon, and Northrop F-5E and F-5F Tiger aircraft for air combat training of Fleet fighter squadrons. VF-45 maintains a detachment at NAS Cecil Field, FL.

VF-51 'Screaming Eagles'
NAS Miramar, CA: 'NL'
F-14A

VF-51 (callsign EAGLES) took delivery of its first F-14A Tomcat on 16 June 1978 after relinquishing its F-4N Phantoms. Squadron designations have been VF-1 on 15 February 1943, VF-5 on 15 July 1943, VF-5A on 15 November 1946, and VF-51 on 16 August 1948.

In May 1979, the squadron embarked on a western Pacific cruise with CVW-15 aboard the USS *Kitty Hawk* (CV-63). After two further *Kitty Hawk* cruises, the squadron remained with CVW-15 but, together with sister squadron VF-111, detoured to the East Coast in March 1983 to participate in the first operations conducted aboard the newly-commissioned USS *Carl Vinson*. A March-October 1983 world cruise aboard *Vinson* has been followed by additional deployments by the 'Screaming Eagles' on *Vinson's* decks with the Pacific Fleet. VF-51 claims to be the first US Navy squadron (in 1984) to carry out the first F-14A day and night Automatic Carrier Landings and the first to intercept Soviet Tu-26 'Backfire' bombers and armed MiG-23 'Flogger' and Su-15 'Flagon' fighters, these being engaged with the help of the Tomcat's Television Camera Set during 1985.

Also in 1985, part of VF-51 was at Miramar to film most of the flying scenes for the motion picture *Top Gun*. In December 1991, the US Navy cancelled plans for VF-51 and sister squadron VF-111 to be the first Fleet squadrons to operate the F-14D Super Tomcat.

VF-74 'Bedevilers'
NAS Oceana, VA: 'AA'
F-14B

VF-74 (callsign DEVIL) was established as VBF-20 on 16 April 1945. Subsequently, it was VF-10A on 15 November 1946, VF-92 on 12 August 1948, and VF-74 on 15 January 1950 (though not the first VF-74 in the US Navy). The squadron began training in February 1983 to operate the Grumman F-14A Tomcat as a replacement for the F-4S Phantom. The first Tomcat was received in June 1983 and the squadron became fully operational in October 1983. Fighting Seven Four took their Tomcats to sea aboard *Saratoga* in April 1984. The squadron flew against Libya in Operation Prairie Fire in March 1986 and Operation El Dorado Canyon on 15 April 1986.

Paired with VF-103, the squadron began operating the F-14A+ (A Plus) in 1989. This version was redesignated F-14B on 1 May 1991. VF-74 flew numerous F-14B combat air patrols during the 1991 Gulf War.

VF-84 'Jolly Rogers'
NAS Oceana, VA: 'AJ'
F-14A

The squadron was established as VA-86 on 1 July 1955 but, in one of those bizarre historical quirks, was redesignated VF-84 on the same day. It is the second squadron in the US Navy to bear the VF-84 designation. The squadron's markings include a distinctive skull and crossbones. In October 1975, VF-84 (callsign VICTORY) began preparations to convert to the F-14A Tomcat, giving up F-4N Phantoms. The squadron's first sea cruise with the Tomcat came in December 1977 as part of CVW-8 aboard the new *Nimitz* while paired with VF-41. The second encompassed the 24 April 1980 attempt to rescue American hostages in Iran, mounted from *Nimitz*'s deck.

Subsequently, during the 1981 cruise when sister squadron VF-41 shot down two Libyan Su-22s, VF-84 became the first US

Below: VF-101 acts as the Atlantic Fleet Tomcat FRS. It flies both the F-14A and F-14B (illustrated).

Right: VF-74 'Bedevilers' used to fly the F-14A, but have now upgraded to the F-14B.

Navy squadron to deploy the TARPS-equipped F-14A Tomcat for the reconnaissance mission. 1985 included training in desert warfare in Egypt during Exercise Bright Star '85. A 1986 *Nimitz* North Atlantic cruise included exercises with the Norwegian air force. In 1988, CVW-8 and VF-84 shifted to *Roosevelt*. During Exercise Teamwork '88, the squadron worked out with British and French fighters in the North Atlantic.

A 'Jolly Rogers' F-14A made the first Fleet arrested landing aboard *Lincoln* on 1 December 1989. *Lincoln* arrived in the Persian Gulf region immediately after Desert Storm, and VF-84 flew combat air patrols in the region.

VF-101 'Grim Reapers'
NAS Oceana, VA: 'AD'
F-14A/B

VF-101 (callsign GUNFIGHTER) is the East Coast FRS and trains Tomcat pilots, RIOs and maintenance people before they join the Fleet.

A different squadron, designated VF(N)-101, flew night fighters during World War II, but today's is the first squadron to bear the VF-101 designation and was established 1 May 1952. The 'Grim Reapers' began in late 1975 to take over training Tomcat personnel, although it continued to operate some F-4J Phantoms as late as 1977. The 'Grim Reapers' received their first F-14A Tomcats in 1976 and began training aircrews in the autumn of that year. The squadron received F-14A+ (A Plus) aircraft, since redesignated F-14B, beginning in 1988.

VF-102 'Diamondbacks'
NAS Oceana, VA: 'AB'
F-14A

The squadron (callsign DIAMONDBACK) was established on 1 July 1955 as VA-36 and redesignated VF-102 on the same day. A footnote in naval history archives points out that ''on the same day, 1 July 1955, the old VF-102 was redesignated VA-36. This unit is

separate from [today's VF-102].'' The 'Diamondbacks' began transitioning to the F-14A Tomcat, to replace the F-4J Phantom, in July 1981.

By May 1982, the squadron made some landings aboard *America* during workups off the East Coast. From the outset, the squadron equipped with both 'vanilla' F-14As and with TARPS-equipped F-14As for the reconnaissance role. In December 1982, the squadron deployed to the Mediterranean and Indian Ocean as part of CVW-1 aboard USS *America*. Paired with VF-33, the squadron continues to operate from *America* as part of Air Wing One.

'Diamondbacks' combat air patrol Tomcats were fired on by Soviet-built SA-5 missiles and anti-aircraft artillery during Operation Prairie Fire operations against

Libya in March 1986. VF-102 flew top cover during Operation El Dorado Canyon, the air strikes on Libya on 15 April 1986. The squadron, operating from *America*, participated in Exercise Solid Shield '87 (1987), which included ACM maneuvering against USAF F-15s.

The squadron flew in combat during Desert Storm in 1991. VF-102 later participated in Operation North Star in Norwegian waters in late 1991.

Below and bottom: Two shots of VF-102's Tomcats depict the high- and low-visibility color schemes.

Above: The 'Sluggers' have adopted a new insignia for their F-14Bs, incorporating the 'Clubleaf'.

VF-103 'Sluggers'
NAS Oceana, VA: 'AA'
F-14B

VF-103 (callsign CLUBLEAF) was established 1 May 1952 and is not the first US Navy squadron with this designation. The 'Sluggers' began in January 1983 to transition to the F-14A Tomcat from the F-4S Phantom. The first cruise with the F-14A was made with CVW-17 aboard *Saratoga* to the Mediterranean, beginning in April 1984 and concluding in October. The squadron's deployment on this cruise began its reconnaissance role with TARPS-equipped Tomcats. During a 1987 'Sara' cruise, the squadron did extensive TARPS flying, including overflights of the Soviet carrier *Kiev*, as well as ACM training with French Super Etendards. On 15 August 1988, the squadron temporarily left *Saratoga* for operations aboard *Independence* during an eight-week deployment around the horn of South America to San Diego.

The squadron flew against Libya in Operation Prairie Fire in March 1986 and Operation El Dorado Canyon on 15 April 1986. The squadron converted to the F-14+ (A Plus) in 1989. VF-103 is teamed with sister squadron VF-74 aboard 'Sara' and both participated in Desert Storm. A squadron F-14A+ (BuNo. 161430, coded AA-212, callsign CLUBLEAF 212) was downed during combat against Iraq on 21 January 1991. Pilot Lieutenant Devon Jones was rescued by two USAF A-10 Thunderbolts and an MH-53J Pave Low III helicopter. RIO Lieutenant Lawrence Randolph 'Rat' Slade was a POW until war's end. Reports indicate the casualty was a TARPS Tomcat downed by a derivative of the SA-2 developed by the Iraqis with a ground-guided optical tracker.

The squadron continues its Atlantic Fleet/Mediterranean commitment with its aircraft, which were redesignated F-14B on 1 May 1991.

VF-111 'Sundowners'
NAS Miramar, CA: 'NL'
F-14A

VF-111 (callsign SUNDOWNER) dates to its establishment as VA-156 on 4 June 1956. It was redesignated VF-111 on 20 January 1959. The squadron adopted the insignia of the old VF-111 which had been disestablished on 19 January 1959, but while the new VF-111 can carry on the traditions of the old VF-111, which dates to World War II, it cannot claim that squadron's lineage.

The squadron began F-14A Tomcat operations in 1978, replacing its F-4J Phantoms, and deployed aboard USS *Kitty Hawk* (CV-63) in May 1979. This cruise with CVW-15 was extended to enable *Kitty Hawk* to operate in the Arabian Sea when American hostages were seized in Iran. Following a second cruise with the same carrier, the 'Sundowners' and the rest of CVW-15, including sister squadron VF-51, shifted to *Vinson*, carrying out a world cruise in March-October 1983. The squadron acquired TARPS capability soon after and is now back on *Kitty Hawk*.

In December 1991, the US Navy cancelled plans for VF-111 and sister squadron VF-51 to be the first Fleet squadrons to operate the F-14D Super Tomcat.

VF-114 'Aardvarks'
NAS Miramar, CA: 'NH'
F-14A

VF-114's (callsign AARDVARK) history

Above: VF-111 (along with VF-51) was due to receive F-14Ds, but the honor went instead to VF-11 and VF-31.

Below: The quirky beast on the tails of VF-114 Tomcats is the 'Aardvark' of their name.

includes its designations as VBF-19 on 20 January 1945, VF-20A on 15 November 1946, VF-192 on 24 August 1948, and VF-114 on 15 February 1950. The squadron's mascot, named Zot, is a replica of the *B.C.* comic strip aardvark. A 2-ft replica carved out of wood is encased and prominently displayed in the squadron ready room – and scrupulously guarded against incursions by tricksters in other squadrons.

The squadron began transitioning to the F-14A Tomcat on 15 December 1975, from the F-4J Phantom. Transition to the Tomcat was completed 1 January 1977, and the 'Aardvarks' made their first cruise with CVW-11 aboard USS *Kitty Hawk* (CV-63) in the western Pacific in 1977. Mediterranean cruises aboard *America*, again with CVW-11, followed in 1979 and 1981. With the same air wing, the squadron subsequently joined USS *Enterprise* (CVN-65) from 1982 on. The 'Aardvarks' are paired with VF-213.

VF-124 'Gunfighters'
NAS Miramar, CA: 'NJ'
F-14A/D, T-34C

VF-124 (callsign GUNSLINGER) was established as VF-53 on 16 August 1948 and became VF-124 on 11 April 1958. The 'Gunfighters' are the West Coast/Pacific

Below: VF-124 was the first US Navy service squadron to get the F-14D, for the training mission.

Fleet FRS with the task of training Tomcat pilots and RIOs. In 1970, the former F-8 Crusader training squadron became the first Tomcat FRS, though the first F-14A did not arrive until 8 October 1972. VF-124 has trained F-14A Tomcat aircrews since 1973. In 1991, VF-124 acquired a small number of Beech T-34C Turbo-Mentors for use as spotter aircraft on target ranges.

The squadron accepted its first F-14D Super Tomcat on 16 November 1990 at Miramar and is now the sole F-14D FRS. The squadron sent four of the new F-14D Super Tomcats aboard *Nimitz* on 2 October 1991 for the D model's first Fleet carrier qualifications.

Below: VF-124 is the Pacific Fleet Tomcat FRS, and operates a few T-34Cs on range spotting duties.

Above: Projecting from underneath this VF-111 F-14 are dummy weapons for a bombing exercise.

Below: VF-124 crews regularly undertake air shows, creating spectacular pressure clouds.

VF-126 'Bandits'
NAS Miramar, CA: 'NJ'
A-4E/F, TA-4J, F-16N, TF-16N

VF-126 is the US Navy's West Coast adversary squadron, equipped with Douglas A-4E/F and TA-4J Skyhawks, and General Dynamics F-16N and TF-16N Fighting Falcons.

VF-142 'Ghostriders'
NAS Oceana, VA: 'AG'
F-14B

VF-142 was established as VF-193 on 24 August 1948, and was redesignated VF-142 on 15 October 1963. The 'Ghostriders' (callsign DAKOTA) transitioned to the F-14A Tomcat at Miramar, CA, in 1974.

While becoming an F-14 user, the squadron shifted from the Pacific to Atlantic Fleet with Oceana, VA, as home base. Formerly, the squadron had flown the F-4J Phantom. As part of CVW-6, the 'Ghostriders' made their first carrier deployment aboard *America*, beginning April 1976. After a subsequent cruise, the 'Ghostriders' shifted in 1979 to CVW-7 aboard USS *Dwight D. Eisenhower* (CVN-65).

The squadron converted to the F-14A(Plus), which was redesignated F-14B on 1 May 1991. Paired with VF-143, the squadron remained with 'Ike' and CVW-7 during Desert Shield on a cruise which included a 7 August 1991 transit of the Suez Canal. The carrier, air wing and squadron withdrew from the Persian Gulf region before the start of the war with Iraq.

VF-143 'Pukin' Dogs'
NAS Oceana, VA: 'AG'
F-14B

VF-143 (callsign TAPROOM) traces its history to VF-871, a Reserve squadron called to active duty for the Korean War on 20 July 1950. The squadron flew the F-4J Phantom before becoming a Tomcat user, transitioning to the F-14A Tomcat at Miramar, CA, in 1974 while converting from the Pacific to Atlantic Fleet. The 'Pukin' Dogs' are now home-ported at Oceana, VA.

As part of CVW-6, VF-143 made its first F-14 carrier deployment aboard *America*, beginning in April 1976. After a subsequent cruise, VF-143 shifted in 1979 to CVW-7 aboard USS *Dwight D. Eisenhower* (CVN-69). During a 29 February to 29 August 1988 'Ike' Mediterranean cruise, the squadron used its TARPS capability to photograph the Soviet warship *Baku*, a 'Kiev'-class carrier. On 26 May 1989, VF-143 began transitioning to the F-14A+ TARPS-equipped Tomcat with the delivery of its first aircraft (BuNo. 161441), and soon thereafter became fully equipped with A+ models. Paired with VF-142, the squadron remained

Below: VF-154 live up to their 'Black Knights' nickname with a heraldic fin-marking.

with the same carrier and air wing during Desert Shield. All were withdrawn before the start of the war with Iraq.

The squadron, its aircraft now designated F-14B, has resumed Mediterranean/Atlantic Fleet operations.

VF-154 'Black Knights'
NAS Miramar, CA: 'NF'
F-14A

VF-154 was established 1 February 1951 when Reserve squadron VF-837 was called to active duty for the Korean War. The squadron was designated VF-154 on 4 February 1953.

The emblem of the 'Black Knights', showing an armored knight at parade rest holding shield and sword, was designed by Lieutenant Junior Grade John Miottel in 1957 and drawn by cartoonist Milton Caniff of *Steve Canyon* fame. VF-154 (callsign BLACKKNIGHT) transitioned to the F-14A Tomcat, including TARPS-equipped aircraft, at Miramar, giving up F-4S Phantoms. The 'Black Knights' made their first cruise in 1985 as part of CVW-14 aboard USS *Constellation* (CV-64). A 1987 'Connie' cruise took VF-154 to Gonzo Station near the Gulf of Oman and included intercepts of Iranian P-3F Orions. Paired with VF-21, the squadron has more recently operated aboard *Independence*, the first carrier to arrive for Desert Shield in August 1990.

In August 1991, VF-21 joined CVW-5 aboard *Midway*, which relieved *Midway* as the sole aircraft carrier home-ported at Yokosuka, Japan.

VF-201 'Hunters'
NAS Dallas, TX: 'AF'
F-14A

VF-201 (callsign HUNTER), established 25 July 1970, is one of two Naval Air Reserve squadrons at NAS Dallas which operate the F-14A Tomcat. Squadron insignia is a sword against a Texas flag and a formation of four aircraft.

VF-201 and VF-202 are part of Reserve Air Wing 20. The squadron converted to the F-14A in 1987. One aircraft received by the 'Hunters' was the last F-14A built (BuNo. 162711) before production shifted to the F-14A+ (now F-14B) model.

Below right: Part of the unofficial 'Texas air force', VF-201 is based at Dallas.

Above: A VF-142 aircraft receives maintenance on deck. Above left is the unit's insignia.

Below: The 'Pukin' Dogs' are operational in the F-14B. The insignia is supposed to be a griffin!

US Navy Units

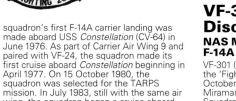

VF-202 'Superheats'
NAS Dallas, TX: 'AF'
F-14A

VF-202, established 1 July 1970, is one of two Reserve squadrons at Dallas which replaced the F-4S Phantom with the F-14A Tomcat. Squadron insignia is a horse's head chess piece against a tan star and yellow field.

The squadron accepted its first F-14A on 10 April 1987. In May 1988, VF-202 concluded the transition to Tomcats with carrier qualification aboard *America* off the Virginia coast. The 'Superheats' are the TARPS squadron for Reserve Air Wing 20. The squadron participated in the USAF-sponsored 1988 Reconnaissance Air Meet (RAM '88) at Bergstrom AFB, TX.

VF-211 'Flying Checkmates'
NAS Miramar, CA: 'NG'
F-14A

VF-211 (callsign CHECKMATE) traces its history to VB-74, established 1 May 1945, and acquired its current designation on 9 March 1959. The 'Checkmates' stood up as an F-14A squadron at Miramar on 1 December 1975, following months of preparation and after operating the F-8J Crusader. The squadron's maiden flight in a Tomcat was made 23 December 1975. The

Below: Also bearing allegiance to the 'Lone Star State', VF-202 partners VF-201 in CVWR-20.

Above: Famous from their days as a Crusader squadron, the 'Flying Checkmates' operate the F-14B.

Below: The XO's aircraft from VF-211 has embellished markings with stylized trim.

squadron's first F-14A carrier landing was made aboard USS *Constellation* (CV-64) in June 1976. As part of Carrier Air Wing 9 and paired with VF-24, the squadron made its first cruise aboard *Constellation* beginning in April 1977. On 15 October 1980, the squadron was selected for the TARPS mission. In July 1983, still with the same air wing, the squadron began a cruise aboard *Ranger*. In 1985, the squadron operated with CVW-9 aboard USS *Kitty Hawk* (CV-63).

VF-211 began transition to the F-14A(Plus) (now designated F-14B) Tomcat in April 1989, but has since reverted to the F-14A due to a lack of F-14Bs. VF-211 remains TARPS capable.

VF-213 'Black Lions'
NAS Miramar, CA: 'NH'
F-14A

VF-213 (callsign BLACKLION), established 22 June 1955, stood up with the F-14A Tomcat at Miramar in September 1976, replacing the F-4B Phantom. In October 1977, the squadron embarked on its first cruise with Tomcats as part of CVW-11 aboard USS *Kitty Hawk* (CV-63). Mediterranean cruises aboard USS *America* (CV-66, again with CVW-11) followed in 1979 and 1981. In 1982, the squadron acquired the tactical reconnaissance role and took delivery of its first TARPS-equipped aircraft. With the same air wing, the squadron subsequently went on a cruise with USS *Enterprise* (CVN-65) in 1982-83, and again in 1984. The TARPS-capable 'Black Lions' are paired with VF-114.

VF-301 'Devil's Disciples'
NAS Miramar, CA: 'ND'
F-14A

VF-301 (callsign DEVIL), which is also called the 'Fighting Infernos', was established 1 October 1970 and is a Reserve squadron at Miramar and part of Reserve Air Wing 30. Squadron patch shows a smiling satanic figure holding a pitchfork. The squadron began the transition to the F-14A Tomcat in 1985. On 21 April 1985, VF-301 made the first Reserve deployment of the Tomcat, taking five aircraft to Yuma, AZ, for air-to-air training. The first deployment at full squadron strength was made for training at NAS Fallon, NV, beginning 4 August 1985. The squadron subsequently practiced carrier operations aboard *Ranger*.

VF-302 'Stallions'
NAS Miramar, CA: 'ND'
F-14A

VF-302 (callsign STALLION), established 21 May 1971, is a Reserve squadron at Miramar. The squadron began the transition to the F-14A Tomcat in 1985, giving up its F-4S Phantoms. VF-302 is paired with VF-301 as part of CVWR-30. Unlike its sister squadron, Fighting Three Zero Two was assigned the TARPS reconnaissance mission. During 10-22 August 1988, all of CVWR-30 carried out flight deck operations aboard USS *Enterprise* (CVN-65). The squadron participated in the USAF-sponsored 1988 Reconnaissance Air Meet (RAM '88) at Bergstrom AFB, TX.

Above: If a VF-213 Tomcat can have two fins, then why can't a 'Black Lion' have two tails?

Below: VF-302 is part of the Pacific Reserve CVWR-30, and wears the stylized 'ND' tailcode.

Left: The 'Devil's Disciples' may have a frightening nickname, but the squadron marks are muted.

VFA (Strike Fighter Squadron)

VFA-15 'Valions'
NAS Cecil Field, FL: 'AJ'
F/A-18A

VFA-15, a former A-7 Corsair II unit established 1 August 1968 and given its current designation on 1 October 1986, became a strike fighter squadron and McDonnell Douglas F/A-18A Hornet user on the latter date at NAS Cecil Field. The squadron's emblem shows a lion riding on a bomb falling towards the sea. The squadron is part of CVW-8 aboard USS *Theodore Roosevelt* (CVN-71) and participated in the Gulf War of 1991.

Following the Persian Gulf deployment, VFA-15 took delivery of its first F/A-18C Lot 14 Hornet night attack aircraft. The squadron was transitioning to this aircraft in mid-1992.

VFA-22 'Fighting Redcocks'
NAS Lemoore, CA: 'NH'
F/A-18C

VFA-22, with a history dating to 28 July 1948, operates the McDonnell Douglas F/A-18C Hornet with CVW-11 aboard *Lincoln*. The squadron participated in post-Desert Storm operations in the Persian Gulf.

VFA-25 'Fist of the Fleet'
NAS Lemoore, CA: 'NK'
F/A-18C

VFA-25, dating to 1 January 1943, operates the McDonnell Douglas F/A-18C Hornet at Lemoore with CVW-14. The squadron received its first Lot 14 version of the night attack F/A-18C Hornet in late 1991, transitioning from earlier-block F/A-18C airplanes. The 'Fist', together with VFA-113, were scheduled to complete transition in 1992 to the upgraded Hornet, which features night-vision goggles, an onboard oxygen-generating system, a ring-laser inertial navigation system, and the NACES ejection seat.

VFA-27 'Chargers'
NAS Lemoore, CA: 'NL'
F/A-18C

VFA-27 operates the McDonnell Douglas F/A-18C Hornet with *Kitty Hawk*'s CVW-15.

VFA-37 'Bulls'
NAS Cecil Field, FL: 'AC'
F/A-18C

VFA-37, a former Vought A-7 Corsair II operator, flies the McDonnell Douglas F/A-18C Hornet as part of CVW-3 aboard *Kennedy*. The squadron flew combat sorties in Desert Storm and has since resumed traditional Mediterranean/Atlantic Coast activities.

VFA-81 'Sunliners'
NAS Cecil Field, FL: 'AA'
F/A-18C

VFA-81 operates the F/A-18C Hornet as part of CVW-17 aboard *Saratoga*. The former A-7 operator stood up with Hornets on 4 February 1988.

Saratoga was deployed to the Persian Gulf region and participated in the Desert Storm conflict from the beginning on 17 January 1991. On that date, two VFA-81 pilots, Lieutenant Commander Mark Fox and Lieutenant Nick Mongillo (in BuNos 163508 and 163502, coded AA-401 and AA-410), scored the US Navy's only fixed-wing aerial victories of the war when they shot down two MiG-21s while en route to a target. These first-ever kills for the Hornet did not prevent Fox and Mongillo from completing a bombing mission, demonstrating the Hornet's dual-role capability.

VFA-82 'Marauders'
NAS Cecil Field, FL: 'AB'
F/A-18C

VFA-82 converted from the A-7 on 15 July 1987 and became the first Fleet squadron equipped with the F/A-18C version of the Hornet strike fighter. Assigned to CVW-1

aboard *America*, the squadron participated in Desert Storm.

VFA-83 'Rampagers'
NAS Cecil Field, FL: 'AA'
F/A-18C

VFA-83 made the transition from the A-7 to become a McDonnell Douglas F/A-18C Hornet strike fighter squadron on 1 February 1988. As part of CVW-17 on *Saratoga*, the squadron flew in combat during Desert Storm.

Right: Black fin trim applied to the F/A-18s of VFA-15 heightens the aircraft's attractive lines. The unit now has night attack aircraft.

Above: VFA-25 is proud of its nickname, even to the point of carrying 'Fist' on the root fillet.

Below: The 'Bulls' of VFA-37 fly from Kennedy, and took part in Desert Storm.

Above: F/A-18C of VFA-83 'Rampagers'.

Above: Carrying three ferry tanks and no weapons, an F/A-18C of VFA-82 'Marauders' lands on USS America.

Right: VFA-81 flew in Desert Storm, scoring the Hornet's first two air-to-air kills.

Above: VFA-94's CAG-bird is seen during weapons training at Fallon, armed with live Mk 82s.

Left: A 'Sidewinder' Hornet lines up for launch from America, bearing the snake of the same name on the fin.

VFA-94 'Mighty Shrikes'
NAS Lemoore, CA: 'NH'
F/A-18C

VFA-94, established 26 March 1952, operates the McDonnell Douglas F/A-18C Hornet with CVW-11 aboard *Lincoln* and operated in the Persian Gulf region in mid-1991 following Desert Storm.

VFA-97 'Warhawks'
NAS Lemoore, CA: 'NL'
F/A-18C

This squadron operates the F/A-18C aboard USS *Kitty Hawk* with CVW-15.

VFA-105 'Gunslingers'
NAS Cecil Field, FL: 'AC'
F/A-18C

VFA-105, established 4 March 1968, operates the McDonnell Douglas F/A-18C Hornet as part of CVW-3 aboard *Kennedy*. The squadron flew strike missions during the Gulf War of 1991.

VFA-106 'Gladiators'
NAS Cecil Field, FL: 'AD'
F/A-18A/B/C/D

VFA-106 traces its history to an establishment date of 27 April 1984. The squadron became the East Coast FRS squadron for the Hornet on that date. The 'Gladiators' operate a mix of F/A-18A, B, C, and D aircraft in their training mission.
In 1991, VFA-106 acquired a small number of Beech T-34C Turbo-Mentors for use as range clearance aircraft.

Above: The fuel tank and tail badge leave little doubt as to which unit this F/A-18C belongs to.

Left: An important task of the Hornet force is SEAD, for which the aircraft carries the AGM-88 anti-radiation missile. This pair is from VFA-97.

VFA-113 'Stingers'
NAS Lemoore, CA: 'NK'
F/A-18C

VFA-113 was established as VF-113 on 15 July 1948, became VA-113 in March 1956, and was redesignated VFA-113 on 25 March 1983. The squadron was a long-time user of the A-7 Corsair II before receiving Hornets.
VFA-113 acquired its first Lot 14 version of the night attack McDonnell Douglas F/A-18C Hornet on 18 October 1991, transitioning from earlier-block F/A-18C airplanes. The 'Stingers', together with VFA-25, were scheduled to complete transition in 1992 to the upgraded Hornet. The squadron operates with CVW-14 aboard USS *Carl Vinson*.

VFA-86 'Sidewinders'
NAS Cecil Field, FL: 'AB'
F/A-18C

VFA-86 operates the McDonnell Douglas F/A-18C Hornet as part of CVW-1 aboard *America*, and flew combat missions in the 1991 Gulf War. Squadron emblem, not surprisingly, is a rattlesnake poised to strike from its perch on a top hat.
The 'Sidewinders' participated in Operation North Star in September 1991, a major NATO joint exercise.

VFA-87 'Golden Warriors'
NAS Cecil Field, FL: 'AJ'
F/A-18C

VFA-87 traded in the Vought A-7E Corsair II for the McDonnell Douglas F/A-18C Hornet on 15 July 1987. Established 1 February 1968 and given its current identity on 1 May 1986, the squadron belongs to CVW-8 aboard *Roosevelt*, and participated in Desert Storm.
Following the Persian Gulf deployment, VFA-87 took delivery of its first F/A-18C Lot 14 Hornet night attack aircraft. The squadron was transitioning to the latter aircraft in mid-1992.

VFA-125 'Rough Riders'
NAS Lemoore, CA: 'NJ'
F/A-18A/B/C/D

VFA-125 was established 13 November 1980 as the US Navy's first Hornet user. The 'Rough Riders' are the West Coast FRS squadron for F/A-18 Hornet training, as well as the first squadron to fly the Hornet type. The squadron has a mixture of F/A-18A/B/C/D aircraft.
In 1991, VFA-125 acquired a small number of Beech T-34C Turbo-Mentors for use as range clearance aircraft.

Above: Despite the 'Marines' title, VFA-106 is the Navy's East Coast Hornet FRS.

Below: VFA-125 is the West Coast FRS, and with VFA-106 operates most of the Navy's two-seaters.

VFA-127 'Cylons'
NAS Fallon, NV: 'NJ'
F-5E/F, F/A-18A/B

VFA-127 is an adversary squadron equipped with Northrop F-5E/F Tigers. In mid-1992, the squadron began to transition to the McDonnell Douglas F/A-18A/B, becoming the first adversary squadron to operate the Hornet.

VFA-131 'Wildcats'
NAS Cecil Field, FL: 'AG'
F/A-18C

VFA-131 (established 3 October 1983) belongs to CVW-7 aboard USS *Dwight D. Eisenhower* (CVN-69). The squadron's history dates to 3 October 1983 when it was formed as a brand-new Hornet squadron. The squadron participated in Operations Prairie Fire and El Dorado Canyon against Libya in March and April 1986, at which time the 'Wildcats' were operating from the since-retired USS *Coral Sea* (CV-43).

Together with VFA-136, the squadron converted to the McDonnell Douglas F/A-18C Hornet from the F/A-18A version in 1991. *Eisenhower* subsequently played a key role in Desert Shield, but was withdrawn before Desert Storm began in January 1991. VFA-131 has since resumed Mediterranean deployments aboard 'Ike'.

VFA-132 'Privateers'
NAS Lemoore, CA: 'AE'
F/A-18C

VFA-132 (established 3 January 1984), operating the F/A-18C Hornet, began operations at Lemoore on 9 January 1984 and made the 1986 CVW-13/*Coral Sea* cruise which threw the squadron into combat during Operations Prairie Fire and El Dorado Canyon against Libya. More recently, the 'Privateers' were associated with CVW-6 aboard *Forrestal* until the end of 1991.

Right: VFA-127's adversary aircraft include this Iraqi-schemed F-5E.

On 8 July 1991, this Hornet squadron was called upon to achieve an unusual aerial 'kill' when pilot Lieutenant Bill Reilly was tasked to shoot down a crippled Grumman E-2C Hawkeye over the Mediterranean after the E-2C crew had parachuted out safely following an inflight emergency.

Following *Forrestal*'s change of status to become the US Navy's training carrier in early 1992, VFA-132 was disestablished on 1 June 1992.

VFA-136 'Knighthawks'
NAS Cecil Field, FL: 'AG'
F/A-18C

VFA-136 (established 1 July 1985) is part of CVW-7 aboard USS *Dwight D. Eisenhower* (CVN-69). The 'Knighthawks' were established as a new Hornet squadron on 1 July 1985, initially with the F/A-18A version. The squadron badge shows a taloned hawk descending against a night sky. VFA-136 received its first F/A-18C night attack Hornet (BuNo. 164206) on 13 November 1990, and subsequently reached full strength with the upgraded F/A-18C.

'Ike' and its carrier air wing made an important contribution to the Desert Shield build-up but departed the Persian Gulf region before actual fighting with Iraq began. In the post-Desert Storm era, the 'Knighthawks' resumed deployments to the Mediterranean.

Below right: Recently disestablished, VFA-132 served aboard **Forrestal.**

Below: For a squadron named the 'Wildcats', VFA-131 have a suitably fierce tail badge.

Above: An F/A-18C of VFA-146 lands aboard USS **Nimitz.**

VFA-137 'Kestrels'
NAS Lemoore, CA: 'NE'
F/A-18C

VFA-137 was established on 1 July 1985. The squadron operates the F/A-18C Hornet and was associated with CVW-6 aboard USS *Forrestal* through the end of 1991. The squadron badge is a simple outline of the bird after which VFA-137 is named, shaped to resemble an arrowhead.

In 1992, the 'Kestrels' left CVW-6 and Cecil Field and transferred to Lemoore to become the sister squadron of VFA-151 with CVW-2 aboard the USS *Ranger*.

VFA-146 'Blue Diamonds'
NAS Lemoore, CA: 'NG'
F/A-18C

VFA-146 was established 1 February 1956 and operated FJ-4B Fury and A-7 Corsair II aircraft before becoming a strike fighter squadron with the Hornet. The 'Blue Diamonds' are one of the most recent McDonnell Douglas F/A-18C Hornet strike fighter units and are assigned to CVW-9 aboard *Nimitz*.

Right: VFA-137 CAG-bird and 'boss-bird' show the 'Blue Angels' that they don't have a monopoly on mirror flying.

197

VFA-147 'Argonauts'
NAS Lemoore, CA: 'NG'
F/A-18C

VFA-147 were established 1 February 1967 as VA-147, the first Fleet squadron to operate the A-7A Corsair II. In the mid-1980s, the squadron became a Hornet strike fighter unit and now flies McDonnell Douglas F/A-18C Hornets and is assigned to CVW-9 aboard *Nimitz*.

VFA-151 'Vigilantes'
NAS Lemoore, CA: 'NE'
F/A-18C

VFA-151 was established 6 August 1948 as VF-23, became VF-151 on 23 February 1959 as an operator of F-3B Demons until 1964, followed by F-4B Phantoms until 1973, F-4N Phantoms until 1977, F-4J Phantoms until 1980, and F-4S Phantoms until 1986. The squadron was redesignated VFA-151 on 1 June 1986, and converted to strike fighter squadron status as an operator of the F/A-18A Hornet. Beginning in 1972, the squadron was associated with CVW-5 on *Midway*, long the only US aircraft carrier home-ported abroad, with its home base at Yokosuka, Japan.

When *Midway* was retired from service and replaced at Yokosuka by *Independence*, the actual transition taking place at Pearl Harbor in August 1991, the 'Vigilantes' returned to US soil for the first time in nearly two decades, transferring to Lemoore. VFA-151 was joined at Lemoore by a new sister squadron, VFA-137, moving from the East Coast. As late as March 1992, a typical 'Vigilantes' Hornet (BuNo. 162896/coded NM-304) still had the name of the retired *Midway* painted on its fuselage. Since then, the squadron has been assigned to *Ranger*'s CVW-2. A decision is expected as to whether the squadron will convert to newer F/A-18C Hornets.

Below: VFA-195 is famed as the 'Dam Busters' after the squadron attacked the Hwachon dam with AD Skyraiders during the Korean War. The unit is still in the Far East, shore-based at Atsugi with CVW-5.

VFA-192 'World Famous Golden Dragons'
NAS Atsugi, Japan: 'NF'
F/A-18C

VFA-192 dates to the establishment of VF-153 on 26 March 1945. The squadron became VA-192 on 10 March 1956 and subsequently flew FJ-4B Furies and A-7 Corsair IIs. Redesignated VFA-192 on 10 January 1985, the 'Dragons' formed as a Hornet strike fighter squadron in 1985 at Lemoore and moved to NAS Atsugi, Japan, in November 1986. The squadron made frequent cruises on *Midway*, from which it transferred to *Independence* at Pearl Harbor in August 1991, when the former aircraft carrier was en route to the US for retirement and the latter became home-ported with CVW-5 at Yokosuka, Japan. At this time, the squadron also converted from the F/A-18A to F/A-18C Hornet.

VFA-195 'Dam Busters'
NAS Atsugi, Japan: 'NF'
F/A-18C

VFA-195 dates to the establishment of torpedo squadron VT-19 on 15 August 1943. Redesignated VA-195 on 24 August 1948, the squadron drew its nickname from the last occasion in history when aerial torpedoes were used in battle, dropped by AD Skyraiders on dams on the Yalu River during the Korean War. Later an operator of the A-7 Corsair II, the 'Dam Busters' acquired their current designation and became a Hornet strike fighter squadron on 1 April 1985. VFA-195 reached NAS Atsugi, Japan, on 10 November 1986, permanently forward-deployed with CVW-5 on *Midway*. With the same air wing, the squadron transferred to *Independence* at Pearl Harbor in August 1991, when the former aircraft carrier was en route to the US for retirement and the latter became home-ported with CVW-5 at Yokosuka, Japan. At this time, the squadron also converted from the F/A-18A to F/A-18C Hornet.

VFA-203 'Blue Dolphins'
NAS Cecil Field, FL: 'AF'
F/A-18A

VFA-203, established 1 July 1970 at Cecil Field, is a Naval Air Reserve former A-7 squadron operating the McDonnell Douglas F/A-18A Hornet. The squadron emblem is a leaping dolphin.

VFA-204 'River Rattlers'
NAF New Orleans, LA: 'AF'
F/A-18A

VFA-204, established on 1 July 1970, is a Naval Air Reserve former A-7 squadron operating the McDonnell Douglas F/A-18A Hornet. The squadron emblem shows a venomous rattlesnake coiled around a loaded bomb.

Above: Another unit to feature a sword in their badge is VFA-147 'Argonauts'.

Below: A VFA-192 F/A-18C displays the TINS pod mounted on the port Sparrow pylon.

VFA-303 'Goldenhawks'
NAS Lemoore, CA: 'ND'
F/A-18A

VFA-303 was established 1 July 1970 as the first Naval Air Reserve operator of the A-7 Corsair II, and acquired its current designation on 1 January 1984 as the first Reserve strike fighter squadron. The 'Goldenhawks' received their first eight McDonnell Douglas F/A-18A Hornets on 19 October 1985. The squadron emblem shows a hawk against a hostile sky. The Lemoore-based Reservists have been at sea for brief periods, including a deployment aboard USS *Enterprise* (CVN-65) in August 1988.

VFA-305 'Lobos'
NAS Point Mugu, CA: 'ND'
F/A-18A

VFA-305 (established 1 July 1970) became the Naval Air Reserve's second strike fighter squadron on 18 January 1987. The squadron badge, not surprisingly, depicts a baying wolf. The 'Lobos' have spent brief periods at sea, including a deployment aboard *Enterprise* with VFA-303 in August 1988.

Below: This VFA-203 F/A-18A carries an AGM-62 Walleye EO-guided missile.

Left: The Navy Reserve has four squadrons of F/A-18As, this aircraft being from VFA-204.

Below: Representing the Pacific Reserve wing (CVWR-30) is this F/A-18A from VFA-305.

VFC (Fighter Composite Squadron)

VFC-12 'Fighting Omars'
NAS Oceana, VA: 'JY'
A-4F/M

VFC-12 is a Naval Air Reserve light attack squadron equipped with the Douglas A-4F ('Super Fox') and A-4M Skyhawk. The squadron carries out a variety of fighter and support duties, including air combat training for Fleet squadrons.

VFC-13 'Saints'
NAS Miramar, CA: 'UX'
A-4F/M

VFC-13 is a Naval Air Reserve operator of Douglas A-4F ('Super Fox') and A-4M Skyhawks.

Both VFC units fly the Skyhawk on adversary duties. Above right is an A-4F of VFC-12, while below is a TA-4J of VFC-13.

VP (Patrol Squadron)

VP-1 'Screaming Eagles'
NAS Barbers Point, HI: 'YB'
P-3C

VP-1 traces its history to 15 February 1943. The squadron was making a routine deployment to NAS Cubi Point, Philippines, with its Lockheed P-3C Orions when Iraq invaded Kuwait on 2 August 1990. The squadron claims to be the first in US aviation to have responded to the invasion, having moved a two-plane temporary detachment already at Diego Garcia to Al Masirah, an island off the coast of Oman, on 4 August. Thus, VP-1 was flying operational missions in response to the Kuwait invasion two days before Desert Shield began on 6 August 1990. The remainder of VP-1 subsequently deployed to Diego Garcia. A detachment was also stationed at Jeddah and was relieved there in October 1990 by VP-23.

Like all Orion squadrons, the 'Screaming Eagles' are dedicated to long-range antisubmarine patrol. During the crisis with Iraq, which has no submarines, the aircraft ranged over the Persian Gulf and Red Sea as key elements of the Maritime Interdiction Force, locating and identifying shipping and vectoring coalition warships to intercept vessels.

In August 1991, VP-1 completed the transition from its early P-3Cs to the P-3C Update III Retrofit variant.

VP-4 'Skinny Dragons'
NAS Barbers Point, HI: 'YD'
P-3C

VP-4 traces its lineage to establishment on 1 July 1943. The squadron operated P2V Neptunes from 1947, and P-3A Orions from 1966. In 1974, the P-3B Orion came on board. The squadron then operated the P-3B(MOD), or 'Super Bee', from May 1979, beginning with a difficult deployment to Cubi Point, Philippines. In December 1989, the squadron transitioned to the P-3C Update I.

During Desert Shield, the squadron deployed to Diego Garcia and Al Masirah (an island off Oman) on 10 November 1990 to relieve VP-1 in Desert Shield. When the war began on 17 January 1991, the squadron had a key role in supporting air strikes and conducting maritime surveillance. A group of 15 Iraqi vessels heading for Maridim Island, an outpost in Kuwaiti hands, was detected by a VP-4 crew, who vectored strike aircraft against the force, resulting in five ships sunk and seven or more damaged.

Hours later, another VP-4 crew detected a group of Iraqi vessels attempting a rapid transit from Iraqi ports around Bubiyan Island, apparently seeking refuge in Iranian waters. P-3s from VP-4 and two other

squadrons provided target locations for strike aircraft, including Marine AH-1T Sea Cobra gunships, which destroyed 11 Iraqi vessels.

In August 1991, the 'Dragons' completed the transition from P-3C Update Is to the P-3C Update III Retrofit variant of the familiar Orion.

VP-5 'Mad Foxes'
NAS Jacksonville, FL: 'LA'
P-3C

VP-5 traces its history to 2 January 1937 and now operates the Lockheed P-3C Orion Update III aircraft. Late in Desert Shield, the squadron deployed to Rota, Spain, for maritime surveillance of vessels thought to be moving to or from Iraq.

VP-6

This unit was disestablished in 1992.

VP-8 'Tigers'
NAS Brunswick, ME: 'LC'
P-3C

VP-8 (established 1 September 1942) operates the Lockheed P-3C Orion Update II.5. The squadron flew PBM Mariners in the Atlantic during World War II and P2V

Below: This VP-8 P-3C was at Eielson AFB for 'Icex 92', training over the ice pack.

Above: The 'Screaming Eagles' of VP-1 have reinstated unit insignia.

Neptunes thereafter, relinquishing its last P2V-5F in October 1962. That month, the squadron became the Fleet's first operational user of the P3V-1 (P-3A) Orion. The P-3B version was subsequently employed until the current aircraft was received.

During Desert Shield, the interdiction of vessels included maritime surveillance of shipping in the Mediterranean, a task which VP-8 carried out for several months beginning 7 December 1990, when it deployed aircraft to NAS Sigonella, Italy, to relieve VP-11.

VP-9 'Golden Eagles'
NAS Moffett Field, CA: 'PD'
P-3C

VP-9 (established 15 March 1951) flew PB4Y-2 Privateers in the Korean War. The squadron acquired P2V Neptunes in the mid-1950s and flew P-3B Orions in the combat zone off the coast of South Vietnam, 1966-69. The squadron transitioned to the Lockheed P-3C Orion Update III Retrofit antisubmarine aircraft from the P-3C Update I version in 1991. The squadron carries out long-range antisubmarine patrols along the West Coast and in the Pacific.

With the closing of Moffett Field, the squadron was scheduled to move to Barbers Point in November 1992.

VP-10 'Red Lancers'
NAS Brunswick, ME: 'LD'
P-3C

VP-10 operates the Lockheed P-3C Orion on antisubmarine patrol missions in the Atlantic Fleet. The squadron insignia is a compass rose on a background over which are superimposed the Big Dipper and the North Star. The squadron was established on 19 March 1951 and at first flew Lockheed P2V Neptunes from Jacksonville. VP-10 moved to Brunswick and received its first P-3A Orion in 1965, its first P-3B in 1966, and its first P-3C Update II in 1980.

VP-11 'Pegasus'
NAS Brunswick, ME: 'LE'
P-3C

VP-11 dates to 15 May 1952. The squadron operated P2V Neptunes before transitioning to the P-3A Orion in 1964. VP-11 now operates Lockheed P-3C Orion Update II.5.

VP-11 is known as the 'Pegasus' squadron, and carries the winged horse on the tail of their aircraft.

antisubmarine patrol aircraft. Deployed to NAS Sigonella, Italy, at the outset of Desert Shield, the squadron sent a detachment to Jeddah, Saudi Arabia, on 31 October 1990 to relieve VP-23.

Orion missions in the confrontation with Iraq included using hand-held VHF radios to interrogate thousands of merchant ships on their identities and cargoes. During Desert Shield, Orion missions by several squadrons resulted in the interception of over 6,300 ships.

VP-16 'Eagles'
NAS Jacksonville, FL: 'LF'
P-3C

VP-16 dates to 1 May 1951. Initially, the squadron was a Reserve operator of the PBY Catalina. Subsequently, VP-16 flew P2V Neptunes and in February 1962 flew the first aircraft over the 'Friendship Seven' space capsule when astronaut John Glenn returned from orbit.

In July 1964, the squadron received its first P-3A Orion. Since then, the squadron has flown several versions and now operates the Lockheed P-3C Orion on antisubmarine operations in the Atlantic. In the summer of 1990, VP-16 transitioned to the P-3C Update III version.

VP-17 'White Lightnings'
NAS Barbers Point, HI: 'ZE'
P-3C

VP-17, established 1 September 1950, now flies the Lockheed P-3C Orion Update III Retrofit aircraft on antisubmarine patrols in the Pacific. The squadron is scheduled to receive new P-3C Update III aircraft in September 1993.

VP-19 'Big Red'

This unit, based at NAF Misawa, Japan, was disestablished in 1991.

This P-3C is from VP-24.

VP-22 'Blue Geese'
NAS Barbers Point, HI: 'QA'
P-3C

VP-22 (established 15 February 1943) operates the Lockheed P-3C Orion Update II.5 on antisubmarine patrol operations in the Hawaiian Islands and western Pacific. The 'Blue Geese' had the distinction of operating the last P-3B model in the active-duty Navy, relinquishing it on 11 September 1990 in a move which left all VP squadrons except those in the Reserve operating C models. The squadron completed its transition to the current model in early 1991, and was scheduled to transition to the P-3C Update IIIR in May 1992.

VP-23 'Sea Hawks'
NAS Brunswick, ME: 'LJ'
P-3C

VP-23, established 17 May 1946, now operates Lockheed P-3C Orion Update II antisubmarine patrol aircraft. The squadron was established on 17 May 1946 and acquired its current designation on 1 September 1948. In recent times, the squadron became the third Orion operator to participate in Desert Shield/Storm (after VP-1 and the since-disestablished VP-19) when it deployed three aircraft to relieve the VP-1 detachment at Jeddah, Saudi Arabia, in October 1990.

VP-23 was scheduled to be disestablished at the end of 1992.

VP-24 'Batmen'
NAS Jacksonville, FL: 'LR'
P-3C

VP-24, established 10 April 1943, now operates the Lockheed P-3C Orion on antisubmarine patrol missions in the Atlantic.

VP-26 'Tridents'
NAS Brunswick, ME: 'LK'
P-3C

VP-26, established 26 August 1943, now flies Lockheed P-3C Orions. The squadron has a popular nickname; HS-3, HSL-32 and VP-65 are also graced with this nautical appellation. The squadron flew P2V Neptunes from 1970 to 1974, when it transitioned into the P-3A Orion. P-3C models were adopted in the mid-1980s. VP-26 was expected by mid-1992 to operate one of the US Navy's two P-3C 'Outlaw Hunter' aircraft which uses OTH technology to pinpoint surface targets.

VP-30 'Pros'
NAS Jacksonville, FL: 'LL'
P-3C, UP/TP-3A

VP-30, established 30 June 1960, is the East Coast FRS squadron for the Lockheed P-3 Orion type, and operates a mix of UP-3A, TP-3A and P-3C aircraft. In addition to training Atlantic Fleet Orion personnel, the squadron has the task of training foreign operators of the Orion.

Immediately after its founding, the squadron trained crews in the P2V Neptune and P5M Marlin aircraft. In June 1962, a detachment of VP-30 began measures to train crews in the P-3A Orion. The P-3C version arrived from June 1969.

The squadron is proud possessor of a UP-3A (BuNo. 149673, coded LL-25), the most modified Orion in the P-3 fleet in terms of the number of changes it has undergone. The UP-3A began life as a P-3A patrol aircraft in August 1962, one of the first in the US Navy, participated in a CIA project during which it was painted black for special operations in Southeast Asia (1964-67), later became the first EP-3A at the Pacific Missile Test Center, and subsequently was used by VX-1 to test look-down radar systems. Still later, this craft was employed for training duties. Modified at Jacksonville as a UP-3A, the aircraft is scheduled for retirement in 1993.

The squadron on 22 January 1992 drew the thankless task of ferrying three P-3C Update II.5 Orions (BuNos 164467/164469, Pakistani Navy numbers 26/28) which had been purchased by the Pakistani Navy under an FMS (Foreign Military Sales) contract not to their owner but to the AMARC storage 'boneyard' at Davis-Monthan AFB, AZ. Congressional legislation connected with Pakistani nuclear developments precluded delivery of these Orions to Pakistan, and the aircraft were expected to be stored. VP-30 was also required to cease training Pakistani Navy aircrews.

The first contingent of Republic of Korea Navy airmen were scheduled to join VP-30 in the spring of 1994 for training to operate Korea's eight P-3C Update III Orions.

VP-30 has a mix of Orion variants for the FRS role. It also maintains CINCLANT's VP-3A.

VP-31 'Black Lightnings'
NAS Moffett Field, CA: 'RP'
P-3C, UP/TP-3A

VP-31 was established 30 June 1960 at North Island as the replacement air group for the P5M Marlin and P2V Neptune. With the introduction of the P-3A Orion to the Pacific Fleet, VP-31 detachment Alpha was established on 4 January 1963 at Moffett Field to commence Orion training.

In 1967, the squadron phased out SP-5B (P5M-2) training, left a detachment at North Island, and moved to Moffett Field. Training in the SP-2H (P2V-7) was phased out in 1969 and the North Island detachment closed down in 1970.

VP-31 is the West Coast Orion FRS squadron. The squadron uses TP-3A and P-3C Orions, including Update I, II.5 and III subvariants, to train patrol crews and personnel destined for operations in support of the Pacific Fleet. In connection with the Navy's force reductions and the closing of Moffett Field, the Navy plans to reduce Orion FRS squadrons from two to one, by having VP-31 gradually surrender its assets to VP-30 at Jacksonville. VP-31 was scheduled to be disestablished by November 1993.

VP-40 'Fighting Marlins'
NAS Moffett Field, CA: 'QE'
P-3C

VP-40 was established 20 January 1951 at North Island with PBM Mariners. In April 1953, the squadron transitioned to the P5M-1 Marlin. After being assigned to Sangley Point, Philippines, with Marlins, the squadron moved to Moffett Field and transitioned to the P-3B Orion.

Transition to the P-3C came in mid-1975, and the squadron now operates Lockheed P-3C Orion Update IIIs. This patrol squadron contributed aircraft and crews to the vast maritime surveillance effort which was a part of Desert Shield/Storm.

VP-40 was expected by mid-1992 to operate one of the US Navy's two P-3C 'Outlaw Hunter' aircraft. With the closing of Moffett Field, VP-40 is scheduled to move to Brunswick, ME, and to transfer to the P-3C Update II.5 in May 1993.

VP-44 'Golden Pelicans'

This unit, based at NAS Brunswick, ME, was disestablished 31 May 1991.

VP-45 'Pelicans'
NAS Jacksonville, FL: 'LN'
P-3C

VP-45, established 1 November 1942, operates the Lockheed P-3C Orion Update III aircraft. The squadron flew PBM Mariners during World War II and, from 1951, operated P5M Marlin seaplanes. VP-45 began transitioning to the P-3A Orion in September 1963, becoming fully operational by May 1964. In April 1972, VP-45 began transitioning to the P-3C and completed the process in October 1972. In 1987, the 'Pelicans' became the first active-duty patrol squadron on the East Coast to acquire the P-3C Update III package.

The squadron participated in Operation Market Time, the surveillance of seaborne infiltration during the Vietnam War. Legend holds that in the 1980s during a deployment to Kinloss, Scotland, VP-45 sighted the elusive Loch Ness Monster and tracked Nessie for two hours using radar and sonobuoys. Late in Desert Shield, the squadron deployed to Rota, Spain, to take over much of the task of maritime surveillance of Mediterranean shipping thought to be heading to or from Iraq.

VP-46 'Gray Knights'
NAS Moffett Field, CA: 'RC'
P-3C

VP-46 was established 1 September 1931. The squadron's history includes P5M-2 and P2Y aircraft in the 1930s, PBY Catalinas in the 1940s, PBM Mariners thereafter, and finally P2V Neptunes, before shifting to the P-3A Orion in January 1964. The squadron transitioned to the P-3B Orion in December 1966. Today, VP-46 operates Lockheed P-3C Orion Update IIIs, having transitioned from the P-3C Update I version in 1991.

This patrol squadron contributed aircraft and crews to the vast maritime surveillance effort which was a part of Desert Shield/Storm. Crews from VP-46 pinpointed Iraqi vessels transiting Bubiyan Island during the war with Iraq, helping strike aircraft to destroy 11 of these vessels in combat.

VP-46 is scheduled to move to Jacksonville in November 1993.

Right: Along with the rest of the P-3 community, the 'Fighting Marlins' of VP-40 have returned to carrying unit markings.

VP-47 'Golden Swordsmen'
NAS Moffett Field, CA: 'RD'
P-3C

VP-47, established 1 June 1944, began flying PBM Mariners. In 1953, it acquired the P5M-2 (SP-5B) Marlin. With Marlins, it was the first patrol squadron to be deployed to Vietnam. In March 1965, moving to Moffett after half a dozen previous homes, VP-47 transitioned into the P-3A Orion and in 1971 to the P-3C, the first Pacific Fleet squadron to do so, and now operates the type on Pacific antisubmarine missions. In 1989, the squadron had a successful deployment to

Above: A pair of VP-31 Orions in the high-gloss finish. Established as the West Coast FRS, VP-31's role is to be amalgamated with the East Coast FRS unit.

Kadena AB, Okinawa.
VP-47 is scheduled to move to Barbers Point in November 1993.

VP-48 'Boomerangers'

This unit, based at Moffett Field, CA, was disestablished 31 August 1991.

VP-49 'Woodpeckers'
NAS Jacksonville, FL: 'LP'
P-3C

VP-49, established 1 February 1944, flies the Lockheed P-3C Orion Update III Retrofit antisubmarine aircraft in Atlantic operations.

Left: VP-45 'Pelicans' are famous as the alleged trackers of the Loch Ness Monster.

Below: VP-49 flies the P-3C Update IIIR, a conversion of earlier models.

US Navy Units

Right: A recent casualty of defense cutbacks, VP-50 flew 'SG'-coded P-3Cs from Moffett Field.

VP-50 'Blue Dragons'
NAS Moffett Field, CA: 'SG'
P-3C

VP-50 was established 4 August 1950 and was known as the 'Ancient Mariners'. The squadron flew PBM Mariners from 1951, P5M-2 (SP-5B) Marlins from 1958, and P-3A Orions from 1967. In 1967, the squadron made the Navy's last Marlin deployment. In May 1971, VP-50 transitioned to the P-3C Orion. Until recently, the squadron operated Lockheed P-3C Orion Update III aircraft on Pacific operations.

VP-50 suffered one of the US Navy's worst recent tragedies on 21 March 1991, 60 miles (97 km) off San Diego when two aircraft (BuNos 158930 and 159325) came together in mid-air while one was relieving the other on station. Both Orions were lost and all 27 crew members of both aircraft were killed.

VP-50 was scheduled for disestablishment on 30 June 1992.

Right: Part of the Naval Reserve, VP-62 previously flew P-3Bs (illustrated) but now has P-3Cs.

Left: VP-66 is the 'Liberty Bell' squadron, and commemorates the fact on the fins of its P-3Bs.

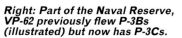

VP-56 'Dragons'

This unit, based at NAS Jacksonville, was disestablished 28 June 1991.

VP-60 'Cobras'
NAS Glenview, IL: 'LS'
P-3B

VP-60, established 1 November 1970, is a Naval Air Reserve user of the P-3B Orion.

VP-62 'Broadarrows'
NAS Jacksonville, FL: 'LT'
P-3C

VP-62, established 1 November 1970, is a Naval Air Reserve operator of the Lockheed P-3C Orion antisubmarine patrol aircraft.

VP-64 'Condors'
NAS Willow Grove, PA: 'LV'
P-3B

One of two Naval Air Reserve Orion units headquartered at NAS Willow Grove, VP-64 was established 1 November 1970 and flies the Lockheed P-3B Orion in support of Atlantic Fleet operations. VP-64 is scheduled to be disestablished during FY 1993 as part of the Navy's overall force reduction scheme.

VP-65 'Tridents'
NAS Point Mugu, CA: 'PG'
P-3C

VP-65, established 16 November 1970, is a Naval Air Reserve antisubmarine patrol squadron and enjoys the same nickname as HS-3, HSL-32 and VP-26. The squadron received its first of eight Lockheed P-3C Orions on 2 August 1991, beginning a transition from the P-3B version which is expected to continue until March 1993.

VP-66 'Liberty Bell'
NAS Willow Grove, PE: 'LV'
P-3B

VP-66, established 1 November 1970, is a Naval Air Reserve user of the Lockheed P-3B Orion in support of Atlantic Fleet antisubmarine efforts.

VP-67 'Golden Hawks'
NAS Memphis, TN: 'PL'
P-3B

VP-67, established 1 November 1970, is a Naval Air Reserve user of the Lockheed P-3B Orion. VP-67 was scheduled to be disestablished during FY 1993 as part of the Navy's overall force reductions.

Below left: VP-65 is based at Point Mugu, flying the P-3C as part of the Reserve.

Below: With tactical paint scheme applied and unit markings removed, this VP-67 Orion is very drab.

Above left: Identifying Orion units can be an exasperating business. This one is from VP-68.

Above: VP-69 only recently disposed of its P-3As, and now has B models (illustrated).

VP-68 'Blackhawks'
NAF Washington, MD: 'LW'
P-3C

VP-68, established 1 November 1970, is a Naval Air Reserve antisubmarine patrol squadron. In late 1991, the squadron took delivery of its full complement of eight Lockheed P-3C Orion Update I aircraft, replacing the P-3B version, and is scheduled to be fully operational in the newer model by May 1993.

VP-69 'Totems'
NAS Whidbey Island, WA: 'PJ'
P-3B

VP-69, established 1 November 1970, is a Naval Air Reserve operator with nine Lockheed P-3B Orion antisubmarine patrol aircraft. The squadron briefly flew SP-2H Neptunes before acquiring P-3A Orions in the early 1970s.

VP-69 had the distinction of disposing of the last P-3A model in US Navy service on 12 October 1990, when the 'Totems' delivered their final P-3A to the National Museum of Naval Aviation, Pensacola, FL.

VP-90 'Lions'
NAS Glenview, IL: 'LX'
P-3B

VP-90, established 1 November 1970, is a Naval Air Reserve user of the Lockheed P-3B Orion. VP-90 was scheduled to be disestablished during FY 1993 as part of the Navy's overall force reductions.

VP-91 'Stingers'
NAS Moffett Field, CA: 'PM'
P-3C

VP-91, established 1 November 1970, is a Naval Air Reserve squadron operating the Lockheed P-3C Orion Update III. The squadron was the first Reserve operator of the Orion and gave up its last P-3B model in October 1990, making it the second Reserve unit equipped with the Update III variant. In connection with the closing of Moffett Field, VP-91 is scheduled to be relocated.

The 'Stingers' contributed one aircraft and crew to the multi-squadron Orion effort in Desert Shield/Storm.

VP-92 'Minutemen'
NAS South Weymouth, MA: 'LY'
P-3C

VP-92, established 1 November 1970, is a Naval Air Reserve squadron operating the Lockheed P-3C Orion. On 26 January 1991, the squadron became the first in the Reserve force to support ASW operations mounted on a rotational basis from Bermuda, a task previously set aside for active-duty squadrons. The rotational Bermuda deployment has since been taken over entirely by the Reserve.

Later in 1991, the 'Minutemen' began converting from the 'non-Update' variant of the P-3C Orion to the P-3C Update II version, a process which was completed in December 1991.

VP-93 'Executioners'
NAF Detroit, MI: 'LH'
P-3B

VP-93, founded 1 July 1976, operates Lockheed P-3B Orion antisubmarine patrol aircraft as part of the Reserve. VP-93 was

Below: Unit markings have made a comeback to the Orion community, as evidenced by this VP-93 P-3B.

Above: PATRON 90 has the lion as its badge and its nickname. The unit flies P-3Bs.

Above is the tail of VP-92 'Minutemen'; below is that of VP-94 'Crawfishers'.

scheduled to be disestablished during FY 1993 as part of the Navy's overall force reductions.

VP-94 'Crawfishers'
NAS New Orleans, LA: 'LZ'
P-3B

VP-94, established 1 November 1970, carries out its Naval Air Reserve commitment with Lockheed P-3B Orions.

Below: VP-91 is in the vanguard of Reserve units in being equipped with the P-3C Update III. It was another participant in 'Icex 92'.

VPU (Patrol Squadron, Special Operations)

VPU-1 'Pirates'
NAS Brunswick, ME
P-3B

VPU-1, established 1 July 1982, is tasked by Naval Air Systems Command for 'unconventional' maritime operations. The unit operates Lockheed P-3B Orions. The 'Pirates' have a patch with a buzzard about to pounce, accompanied by the words

'Special Operations'. The squadron reportedly employed laser dazzler devices in the 1980s, used to blind adversaries, until a treaty banned these devices. The squadron's exact mission has not been disclosed, and it routinely employs tailcodes and BuNos assigned to other squadrons and has the authority to take over prosecution of an attack on a submarine from a Fleet VP squadron on request.

VPU-2 'Wizards'
NAS Barbers Point, HI: 'SP'
P-3B, UP-3A

VPU-2, established 1 July 1982, shares with VPU-1 the 'unconventional' maritime operations mission. The unit's precise mission has not been disclosed but it employs P-3B and UP-3A Orions in special-operations activities against maritime

threats. The unit deploys worldwide and frequently appears with aircraft having bogus tailcodes and BuNos.

VQ (Fleet Air Reconnaissance Squadron)

VQ-1 'World Watchers'
NAS Agana, Guam: 'PR'
EP-3E

During the 1950s, VQ-1, established 1 June 1955, operated the P4M-IQ Mercator, one of which was badly damaged by North Korean MiG-17s on 16 June 1959. The squadron retired the Navy's final Mercator on 23 July 1960. VQ-1 operated EA-3B Skywarriors, EC-121M Super Constellations and EP-3B Orions during the Vietnam era. A VQ-1 EC-121M was shot down by North Korean MiG-17s on 14 April 1969 with the loss of 31 men aboard.

Today, VQ-1 is equipped with Lockheed EP-3E Aries I and II Elint/radar intelligence aircraft used to maintain surveillance of Soviet naval communications and to perform other intelligence duties. The EP-3E Aries II is the result of a CILOP program awarded to Lockheed Aircraft Services in June 1986 which resulted in five aircraft conversions. The CILOP program was taken over by NADC Alameda, CA, on 31 July 1991, and will convert the final seven of 12 P-3Cs selected to become EP-3E Aries IIs to replace aging EP-3B/E Aries Is. The program will replace all Aries I models by 1994. Through a variety of antennas, operators aboard the EP-3E Aries I and II receive and identify signals for threat analysis. VQ-1's mission is to find airborne, shipborne and land-based hostile radars.

The squadron operates a detachment in Japan which, in 1991, moved to NAF Misawa in northern Honshu island, after more than 20 years at NAF Atsugi, Japan. The entire squadron had also been based until the 1980s at Atsugi. During Desert Shield, VQ-1 established an EP-3E detachment at Bahrain. In time, both VQ-1 and VQ-2 from Rota, Spain, were completely committed to the Gulf War effort. EP-3E aircraft provided round-the-clock coverage for sea- and land-based strikes throughout Desert Storm.

As new career fields open for women in flying roles which come close to being defined as 'combat', VQ-1 in 1991 took on the first female EP-3E Senior Evaluator (Lieutenant Sondra Even) and the first female pilot designated as an Electronic Warfare Aircraft Commander (Lieutenant Lisa Rathjen).

VQ-2 'Batmen'
NAS Rota, Spain: 'JQ'
EP-3E

VQ-2, established 1 September 1955, operates Lockheed EP-3E Aries I electronic warfare aircraft. In November 1990, the squadron sent a detachment to Bahrain to join VQ-1 in 24-hour coverage of land- and sea-based strikes throughout Desert Storm. VQ-2 also provided a Douglas EA-3B Skywarrior detachment to Jeddah, Saudi Arabia. (The EA-3Bs of VQ-2 were the last operational 'Whales' in the US Navy and were subsequently retired in September 1991.) Completing the total commitment of VQ-2's aircraft to the war effort, in January 1991 the squadron flew EP-3E reconnaissance missions in connection with coalition air strikes originating from Turkey. VQ-2 also continued to fly reconnaissance missions over the Mediterranean to monitor potential threats to deploying forces. At the end of hostilities and with the commencement of Operation Provide Comfort in April 1991, VQ-2 flew EP-3E missions which assisted the humanitarian

Above: A rare sight indeed: a trio of EP-3E aircraft from VQ-1. Note that all have slightly differing antenna fits, something common to several Sigint aircraft fleets.

Right: An EP-3E-II Aries II of the 'Spanish spooks' from VQ-2. The Aries II was introduced during 1991 just after the unit saw Gulf service.

effort for Kurdish refugees along the Turkey-Iraq border.

VQ-2, back home at Rota, then began to convert from EP-3E Aries I to EP-3E Aries II aircraft.

VQ-3 'Iron Men'
NAS Barbers Point, HI: 'TC'
E-6A

VQ-3, previously known as 'Tacamopac', was established 1 July 1968. The squadron is one of two (with VQ-4) US Navy operators of the Boeing E-6A Mercury, the former Hermes TACAMO strategic communications aircraft. The E-6A force will be consolidated by the mid-1990s, with both squadrons moving to Tinker AFB, OK, to serve under the Commander, Strategic Communications Wing One.

VQ-4 'Shadows'
NAS Patuxent River, MD: 'HL'
E-6A

VQ-4, established 1 July 1968, is one of two (with VQ-3) US Navy operators of the Boeing E-6A Mercury (formerly Hermes) TACAMO strategic communications aircraft. VQ-4 accepted its first E-6A in January 1991, replacing the Lockheed EC-130Q Hercules in the mission of communications support of Fleet ballistic missile submarines. The squadron retained one TC-130Q Hercules, which it contributed to Desert Shield to haul cargo around the Mediterranean during the build-up of forces confronting Iraq.

The E-6A force will be consolidated by the mid-1990s with both squadrons moving to Tinker AFB, OK, where the US Air Force

Below: VQ-3 was the first of the two TACAMO squadrons to get the E-6A. Originally the unit was known as the 'Tacamopac', but has now changed to the 'Iron Men'.

operates other aircraft types based on the Boeing 707-320B airframe. Though the Navy acquired 16 E-6A Mercury aircraft for its TACAMO fleet, it was expected that the number of E-6As in service might be reduced to go along with a reduction in tensions in the 1990s. It has been speculated that VQ-4 may turn some of its E-6As over to the USAF to take on other duties.

Above: Both E-6 squadrons are scheduled to concentrate at Tinker AFB alongside USAF E-3s.

VQ-5 'Black Ravens'
NAS Agana, Guam: 'SS'
ES-3A

VQ-5 was established at NAS Agana on 15 April 1991 as the US Navy's first squadron to operate the Lockheed ES-3A Viking electronic warfare aircraft. The squadron was scheduled to operate eight ES-3As carrier-based electronic reconnaissance aircraft on detachments with Pacific Fleet carriers. The ES-3A performs Elint and Comint missions in support of battle group and air wing operations.

As of March 1992, conversion of existing S-3A airframes to ES-3A standard was proceeding slowly and the squadron was not scheduled to be fully operational with its inventory of aircraft until about January 1993. It already operates a handful of 'TA'-coded S-3A Vikings.

VQ-6 'Sea Shadows'
NAS Cecil Field, FL: 'ET'
ES-3A

VQ-6, established 8 August 1991, was scheduled to operate eight Lockheed ES-3A Viking carrier-based electronic reconnaissance aircraft on detachments with Atlantic Fleet carriers. Replacing the retired Douglas EA-3B Skywarrior, the ES-3A is a Viking converted to carry out Elint and Comint missions, including intercept of enemy communications. The squadron was operating a handful of S-3A aircraft while awaiting receipt of its first operational ES-3A in late 1992.

The US Navy has violated its own regulations by assigning VQ-6 the 'ET' tailcode already used by Marine squadron HMM-262.

Above: The ES-3A electronic reconnaissance variant of the Viking is the mission equipment of VQ-5 and VQ-6.

VR (Fleet Logistic Support Squadron)

VR-22 'Med Riders'
NAS Rota, Spain: 'JR'
KC/C-130F

VR-22, established 15 October 1984, operates Lockheed C-130F and KC-130F transport/tankers to provide airlift support to US Navy forces in the Mediterranean region.

VR-24 'Lifting Eagles'
NAS Sigonella, Italy: 'JM'
C-2A, CT-39G

VR-24, which calls itself 'The Biggest Little Airline', was established 3 December 1946 as VRU-4, acquired its current designation on 1 September 1948, and now carries out transport duties with Grumman C-2A Greyhound and North American CT-39G Sabreliner aircraft. The squadron's duties include COD support for aircraft carriers in the Mediterranean.

VR-24 began its role in Desert Storm operating between Ben Gurion Airport, Israel, and USS *Dwight D. Eisenhower* (CV-69) with its C-2As. The squadron's detachment Romeo began operations in Jeddah, Saudi Arabia, as early as 13 August 1990. In eight months of operation in the Persian Gulf area, VR-24 logged 2,227 flight hours, transporting 8,015 personnel, 1,017,797 lb of mail, and 1,253,181 lb of cargo. The squadron subsequently gave support to Operation Provide Comfort.

VR-24 became the first COD squadron to operate behind the former 'Iron Curtain' when its C-2A Greyhounds flew in 4,000 lb of foodstuffs to the American Embassy in Bucharest, Romania, in November 1991. The squadron's CT-39G Sabreliners also supported the supply operation.

VR-46 'Peach Airlines'
NAS Atlanta, GA: 'JS'
DC-9

VR-46 (established 1 March 1981) operates

Right: Dedicated to carrier support in the Mediterranean, VR-24 operates the C-2A for COD work.

Right: VR-22 is based permanently in the Mediterranean, and has the KC-130F for tanker/transport duties.

two Douglas DC-9 transports to support US Navy logistics operations on the East Coast. All of the Navy's DC-9 and C-9B squadrons provided substantial assistance to Desert Shield/Storm.

VR-48
NAF Washington, MD: 'JR'
C-20G, C-130T

Lacking an assigned nickname but calling itself the 'Sky Pigs', Naval Air Reserve squadron VR-48 was established 1 October 1980. VR-48 had the distinction of operating the last Convair C-131 Samaritan in US military service. VR-48 transferred its last C-131H (BuNo. 550299, originally US Air Force serial number 55-0299) to the Department of State on 30 August 1990.

The squadron has since equipped with the

Grumman C-20G Gulfstream III to provide VIP transportation and logistics support originating from the US capital, and will use its C-130Ts to train crews for VR-53, slated to stand up at Martinsburg, WV.

Below: As befitting a transport unit based in Georgia, VR-46 calls itself the 'Peach Airlines'. Two DC-9s are on strength.

Below: An East Coast support unit is VR-56 'Globemasters', stationed at Norfolk.

Above: VR-55 is based at Alameda, flying the C-9B.

Right: The 'RX' tailcode denotes VR-57 'Conquistadors'.

VR-51 'Flamin' Hookers'
NAS Glenview, IL: 'RV'
C-9B

VR-51, established 1 November 1970, operates two Douglas C-9B Skytrain transports as a Naval Air Reserve logistics squadron. Since the C-9B is incapable of lowering a tailhook for a carrier landing, it must be assumed that VR-51 derives its appellation from ladies of the night.

Above: 'JV' is the tailcode for Florida-based VR-58, appropriately named the 'Sun Seekers'.

Above: The 'Lone Star Express' aircraft wear a 'TX' tailcode for Texas instead of the previous 'RY'.

VR-52 'Taskmasters'
NAS Willow Grove, PA: 'JT'
DC-9

VR-52, a Naval Air Reserve unit, was established 24 June 1972 as the second US Navy squadron to hold this designation. VR-52 flies two Douglas DC-9 transports.

VR-54 'Revelers'
NAS New Orleans, LA: 'CW'
C-130T

VR-54 was established on 1 June 1991 as the Naval Air Reserve's first fleet air logistics support squadron. The squadron received its first Lockheed C-130T Hercules (BuNo. 164762) on 20 August 1991 and was scheduled to have an inventory of six C-130Ts for tactical and long-range logistics missions.

VR-55 'Bicentennial Minutemen'
NAS Alameda, CA: 'RU'
C-9B

VR-55, established 1 April 1976, is a Naval Air Reserve logistics unit operating two Douglas C-9B Skytrains from Alameda.

VR-56 'Globemasters'
NAS Norfolk, VA: 'JU'
C-9B

VR-56, established 1 July 1976, is a Naval Air Reserve operator of two Douglas C-9B Skytrains stationed at Norfolk.

VR-57 'Conquistadors'
NAS North Island, CA: 'RX'
C-9B

VR-57, established 1 November 1977, is a Naval Air Reserve unit operating three C-9Bs.

Above: This DC-9 serves with VR-61 in Washington state.

Below: Most Reserve DC-9/C-9 units have two or three aircraft. VR-62 has two with the 'JW' tailcode.

VR-58 'Sun Seekers'
NAS Jacksonville, FL:'JV'
C-9B

VR-58, established 1 November 1977, contributes to the Naval Air Reserve logistics effort with three Douglas C-9Bs.

VR-59 'Lone Star Express'
NAS Dallas, TX: 'TX'
C-9B

VR-59 was established 1 October 1982 and is a Naval Air Reserve user of three C-9Bs.

VR-60 'Volunteer Express'
NAS Memphis, TN: 'RT'
DC-9

VR-60 was established 3 October 1982 and operates two Reserve DC-9s.

VR-61 'Islanders'
NAS Whidbey Island, WA: 'RS'
DC-9

VR-61 was established 1 October 1982 and is a Naval Air Reserve operator of two Douglas DC-9s in the logistics support role.

VR-62 'Motowners'
NAS Detroit, MI: 'JW'
DC-9

VR-62, established 1 October 1982, joins the Reserve logistics effort with two DC-9s.

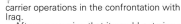

VRC (Fleet Tactical Support Squadron)

VRC-30 'Providers'
NAS North Island, CA: 'RW'
C-2A, UC-12B, CT-39E

VRC-30 provides COD and intra-theater airlift support for Pacific Fleet forces. The squadron began life on 1 October 1966 as VR-30 and was redesignated VRC-30 on 1 October 1978. The squadron is equipped with Grumman C-2A Greyhound, Beech UC-12B and North American CT-39E Sabreliner aircraft.

VRC-40 'Rawhides'
NAS Oceana, VA: 'JK'
C-2A

VRC-40, previously known as 'Codfish Airlines', was established 1 July 1960. The squadron operates the Grumman C-2A Greyhound for COD support in the Atlantic Fleet.

VRC-50 'Foo Dogs'
NAS Cubi Point, Philippines: 'RG'
C-2A, US-3A

VRC-50 (established 1 October 1966) operates Grumman C-2A Greyhound and Lockheed US-3A Viking aircraft in the COD role, supporting aircraft carrier operations in the 7th Fleet and western Pacific.

On 17 November 1990, with a landing aboard *Lincoln*, the squadron's Lieutenant Commander Larry Smith claimed a unique record, the first pilot to make an arrested landing on every US Navy carrier currently on active duty.

During Desert Shield, VRC-50 deployed its sole US-3A to Diego Garcia to support US

Below: VRC-40 is the East Coast COD squadron, supporting carriers in the Atlantic.

carrier operations in the confrontation with Iraq.

After announcing that it would not give up Subic Bay naval base and the associated Cubi Point air station, the US Navy was instructed by the Philippine government to leave by the end of 1992. VRC-50 was scheduled to transfer to Anderson AFB, Guam, in August 1992.

Right: In addition to Greyhounds, VRC-30 also has Sabreliners for staff transport duties.

Below: VRC-50 performs COD tasks in the Far East with C-2As (illustrated) and one US-3A.

VS (Air Antisubmarine Squadron)

VS-21 'Fighting Redtails'
NAS Atsugi, Japan: 'NF'
S-3B

VS-21 dates to 26 March 1945 and has had several designations before acquiring its current name on 23 April 1950. The 'Redtails' are part of CVW-5 aboard *Independence* and is shore-based at NAS Atsugi. In 1991, the squadron completed the transition from the Lockheed S-3A Viking to the S-3B variant.

VS-22 'Vidars'
NAS Cecil Field, FL: 'AC'
S-3B

VS-22, established 18 May 1960, is part of CVW-3 aboard *Kennedy* and operates the Lockheed S-3B Viking antisubmarine aircraft.

During Desert Storm, confronted with an enemy who had no submarines, the 'Vidars' employed their 'Hoovers', as the S-3B is nicknamed, in other roles. In VS-22 (as well as VS-30), the S-3B's electronic warfare suite, designed for maritime use, was pressed into a new role overland as a threat warning system. All Viking units in the conflict discovered that their aircraft, though not designed for the purpose, made an excellent bomber. Typical of VS-22's war participants was an S-3B Viking (BuNo. 160152, coded AC-702) which ended the conflict wearing 'kill' markers for two Iraqi radar stations destroyed by bombing.

VS-24 'Scouts'
NAS Cecil Field, FL: 'AJ'
S-3B

VS-24, established 25 May 1960, operates the Lockheed S-3B Viking antisubmarine

aircraft as part of CVW-8 aboard *Roosevelt*. *Roosevelt* was a participant in Desert Storm, and VS-24's Vikings engaged Iraqi ground and sea targets with Mk 82 500-lb (227-kg) bombs and other ordnance. Several important sorties were flown against anti-aircraft artillery sites in southern Iraq. Squadron members created a humorous cartoon to commemorate the 'Ground Attack Viking', which performed very well at a mission for which it had not been designed.

Above: VS-22 is shore-based at Cecil Field but takes its S-3Bs aboard Kennedy.

VS-27 'Seawolves'
NAS Cecil Field, FL: 'AD'
S-3B

VS-27 is the East Coast FRS squadron for the Lockheed S-3B Viking. (All East Coast Viking squadrons are equipped with S-3Bs.)

Above: Illustrating the old and new paint schemes is this pair of S-3s from VS-24.

Right: Training for the East Coast Viking community is provided by VS-27. This is an S-3B.

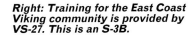

Left: VS-29 is no longer aboard Carl Vinson, serving now with CVW-11 on Abraham Lincoln.

Above: VS-30 was one of the units which used its Vikings for bombing duties during Desert Storm.

Below: Wearing special markings for Air Wing One, this is VS-32's CAG-bird.

Above: VS-31 was one of the Viking units to be disestablished, its S-3Bs passing to other units.

VS-28 'Gamblers'

This unit was disestablished in 1992.

VS-29 'Screaming Dragon Fires'
NAS North Island, CA: 'NH'
S-3A

This VS-37 'Sawbucks' Viking carries a refueling pod under the port wing.

VS-29, established 1 April 1960, operates the Lockheed S-3A Viking with CVW-11 aboard *Lincoln*. VS-29 maintained the carrier's antisubmarine effort in the Persian Gulf region in mid-1991 following Desert Storm.

Lincoln, its air wing and VS-29 participated in the evacuation of Subic Bay naval base following the June 1991 volcanic eruption of Mount Pinatubo.

VS-30 'Diamondcutters'
NAS Cecil Field, FL: 'AA'
S-3B

VS-30 (callsign DYMON), which dates to 9 April 1951, is part of CVW-17 aboard *Saratoga* and operates the Lockheed S-3B Viking antisubmarine aircraft.

In the Persian Gulf conflict, confronted with an enemy with no submarines, VS-30 used its S-3Bs in other roles. In VS-30 (as well as VS-22), the S-3B's electronic warfare suite, designed for maritime use, was pressed into a new role overland as a threat warning system. VS-30 Vikings routinely carried out air-to-surface missions with Rockeye cluster bombs and other ordnance not associated with their usual ASW mission.

VS-32 'Maulers'
NAS Cecil Field, FL: 'AB'
S-3B

VS-32 has a history dating to establishment on 31 May 1949. Its current designation as an air antisubmarine squadron came on 20 April 1950. The 'Maulers' are now part of CVW-1 on *America*. The squadron operates the Lockheed S-3B Viking antisubmarine aircraft.

America was part of the Gulf War from its start on 17 January 1991. On 20 February 1991, a VS-32 crew engaged a small Iraqi vessel and attacked it with 500-lb (227-kg) bombs, scoring what is believed to be the first surface ship 'kill' by a Viking. Another VS-32 crew achieved the dubious honor of crippling an Iraqi vessel after the pilot pulled the wrong pickle switch and mistakenly dropped not a bomb but a refueling pod (!) on it.

VS-33 'Screwbirds'
NAS North Island, CA: 'NG'
S-3A

VS-33, established 1 April 1960, now flies the Lockheed S-3A Viking with CVW-9 on *Nimitz*.

VS-35 'Blue Wolves'
NAS North Island, CA: 'NK'
S-3A

VS-35 was established on 4 April 1991 as an operator of the Lockheed S-3A Viking carrier-based antisubmarine aircraft. Temporarily allocated a 'VS' tailcode while awaiting assignment to a carrier air wing, the squadron converted to the S-3B in 1992 and transferred to CVW-14 aboard USS *Carl Vinson*, picking up that carrier's code.

VS-37 'Sawbucks'
NAS North Island, CA: 'NL'
S-3A

VS-37 began life when VS-871 Reserve squadron was called to active duty for Korea on 1 July 1951, and was redesignated VS-37 on 24 June 1953. The squadron now operates the Lockheed S-3A Viking ASW aircraft, transferred on 1 April 1991 from CVW-14 (a Navy air wing not then assigned to a specific aircraft carrier and now on *Vinson*) to CVW-15 aboard *Kitty Hawk*. The squadron has flown the S-3A in its carrier-based antisubmarine mission on numerous deployments.

In 1992, the squadron began transitioning from the S-3A to the S-3B version of the Viking.

VS-38 'Red Griffins'
NAS North Island, CA: 'NE'
S-3A

VS-38 flies the Lockheed S-3A Viking with CVW-2 aboard *Ranger*. The squadron dates to 20 July 1950 and acquired its current designation on 4 February 1953. The squadron, air wing and carrier fought in Desert Storm.

VS-41 'Shamrocks'
NAS North Island, CA: 'NJ'
S-3B

VS-41, established 30 June 1960, is the West Coast FRS squadron for the Lockheed S-3B Viking. The squadron shares its nickname with the Marine Corps' VMFA-333, which was disestablished in 1992. The S-3B squadron trains air crews and ground personnel in Viking operations for the Pacific Fleet.

VT (Training Squadron)

VT-2 'Doer Birds'
NAS Whiting Field, FL: 'E'
T-34C

VT-2 was established when BTG-2 (Basic Training Group 2) was redesignated VT-2 on 1 May 1960. The 'Doer Birds' are one of three squadrons at Whiting Field (with VT-3 and VT-6), which operate the Beech T-34C Turbo-Mentor to provide primary flight training to naval aviators.

VT-3 'Red Knights'
NAS Whiting Field, FL: 'E'
T-34C

VT-3, formerly BTG-3 and established 1 May 1960, provides primary training for naval aviators in the T-34C.

VT-4 'Rubber Ducks'
NAS Pensacola, FL: 'F'
T-2C

VT-4, formerly BTG-9 and established on 1 May 1960, shares with VT-6 at Pensacola the mission of employing the North American T-2C Buckeye to provide basic jet instruction to NFOs and to some naval aviators taking the special syllabus required for E-2 Hawkeye/C-2 Greyhound aircraft. The term 'NFO' encompasses naval officers who are flight crew members but not pilots, and includes radar intercept officers (F-14), bombardier/navigators (A-6E), navigators (P-3) and electronic warfare officers (EA-6B, EP-3E, E-6A). The term 'naval aviator' refers to pilots only.

VT-6
NAS Whiting Field, FL: 'E'
T-34C

VT-6, once known as MultiEngine Training Group (METG) and established on 1 May 1960, provides intermediate training in fixed-wing aircraft, using the T-34C Turbo-Mentor for those naval aviators who are scheduled to become rotary wing pilots.

VT-7 'Eagles'
NAS Meridian, MS: 'A'
TA-4J

VT-7, established 1 June 1958, serves with TW-1 at McCain Field and operates the Douglas TA-4J Skyhawk to provide advanced jet training to naval aviators.

VT-10 'Cosmic Cats'
NAS Pensacola, FL: 'F'
T-34C, TA-4J, T-2C

VT-10 came into existence when the BNAO (Basic Naval Aviation Officers School) was redesignated VT-10 on 15 January 1968. VT-10 provides intermediate flight training for naval flight officers. The squadron operates Beech T-34C Turbo-Mentors, Douglas TA-4J Skyhawks and North American T-2C Buckeyes.

VT-10 was for some years the only operator of the T-2B version of the Buckeye trainer and has retired B models twice. The 14 T-2B Buckeyes in service with VT-10 were retired for the second time at the end of October 1991. Having once been replaced

by the T-2C for flight training in the early 1970s, the T-2Bs were returned to service for NFO training during the 1980s to alleviate a shortage of T-2Cs. Given reduced pilot training requirements and the introduction of the T-45A Goshawk, the US Navy now has sufficient T-2Cs for NFO training.

A small number of T-45As will be introduced into NFO training operations in the late 1990s.

Above: The 'E' tailcode is worn by the Whiting-based T-34Cs of VT-2, VT-3 and VT-6.

Right: A long way from their Florida base, a pair of VT-3 T-34Cs overflies the Grand Canyon.

Above: In non-standard camo, this VT-7 TA-4J is marked for TW-1's commander.

Below: VT-10 has a mixed fleet for the training of naval flight officers. This is a T-2C.

Above: VT-7 flies the advanced training syllabus at Meridian using the TA-4J.

Below: VT-4 is another unit dedicated to providing training for NFOs, using T-2Cs.

Above: Students progressing from T-34 schools to TW-2 at Kingsville first fly the T-2C with VT-23 for intermediate training. TA-4 training with VT-21 or VT-22 follows.

Left: A T-34C 'Tormentor' of VT-27, one of a pair of Mentor squadrons flying primary training sorties from Corpus Christi.

VT-19 'Fighting Frogs'
NAS Meridian, MS: 'A'
T-2C

VT-19 with TW-1 at McCain Field was established 2 August 1971. The squadron flies the North American T-2C Buckeye to provide intermediate strike training for naval aviators.

VT-21 'Red Hawks'
NAS Kingsville, TX: 'B'
TA-4J

VT-21 with TW-2 was established as ATU-202 in April 1951 and received its current designation on 1 May 1960. The squadron first trained student naval aviators in the Grumman F6F Hellcat. In May 1954, the F9F-2 Panther was introduced for flight training. The Panther was replaced in January 1958 by the Grumman F9F-8T Cougar. After 12 years of service the Cougar was replaced by the Douglas TA-4J Skyhawk. The first Skyhawks arrived in June 1969, and final transition was completed by October of that year.

VT-21 was scheduled to receive the first operational McDonnell T-45A Goshawk in January 1992, with 12 more to follow by January 1993. The US Navy plans to replace all T-2C and TA-4J aircraft used for intermediate and advanced strike training with the T-45A by 2002.

VT-22 'King Eagles'
NAS Kingsville, TX: 'B'
TA-4J

VT-22 with TW-2, established 1 May 1960, traces its history to 13 June 1949, when Advanced Training Unit Six (ATU-6) was formed at NAS Corpus Christi, Texas. Soon afterward, the unit was tranferred to NAS Whiting Field, FL. There, ATU-6 was redesignated Jet Training Unit One (JTU-1). In 1950, the Navy's famed 'Blue Angels' joined JTU-1 for jet transition training into the F9F Panther.

On 20 August 1951, JTU-1 was transferred to Kingsville and redesignated ATU-3. The name changed again over the next four years, first to ATU-200 and then to ATU-212. In 1959, the squadron became the first operator of the F9F-8T Cougar to log 10,000 accident-free hours.

VT-22 assisted in evaluating the two-seat Vought F8U-IT Crusader, which was not adopted by the Navy. In August 1970, the squadron transitioned from TF-9J (F9F-8T) to TA-4J Skyhawk, and now operates the TA-4J for advanced strike training of naval aviators.

Above: This VT-22 TA-4J is marked for USS Lexington, although Forrestal is now the training carrier.

Above left: VT-19 flies the T-2C Buckeye from Meridian.

Left: A VT-21 TA-4 Skyhawk approaches the training carrier for an arrested landing.

VT-23 'Professionals'
NAS Kingsville, TX: 'B'
T-2C

VT-23 with TW-2 was established in November 1958 as ATU-222 and picked up its current designation on 1 May 1960. The first squadron in the Naval Air Training Command to employ supersonic aircraft, ATU-222 instructed selected student pilots in advanced air-to-air gunnery in the Grumman F11F-1 Tiger. VT-23 transitioned to the TF-9J Cougar in 1965. In 1970, the squadron changed aircraft type again, shifting to the TA-4J Skyhawk.

VT-23 received a new mission of intermediate strike training in 1972. In this capacity, the squadron flies the North American T-2C Buckeye in the intermediate strike training syllabus for naval aviators. Those who graduate move onward to the TA-4J in squadrons VT-21 or VT-22, also at Kingsville. Over some years, the dual intermediate/advanced roles handled by separate T-2/TA-4J squadrons will be incorporated into a single syllabus in the T-45A Goshawk.

VT-24 'Bobcats'

This unit was disestablished in 1992.

VT-25 'Cougars'

This unit was disestablished in 1992.

VT-26 'Tigers'

This unit was disestablished in 1992.

VT-27 'Boomers'
NAS Corpus Christi, TX: 'G'
T-34C

VT-27 initially stood up on 11 July 1951 as Advanced Training Unit B at NAS Corpus Christi. The squadron moved to NAS Kingsville, TX, in 1952, and to NAS New Iberia, Louisiana, in 1960. In July 1964, the squadron returned to Corpus Christi. On 1 August 1973, the unit began to phase out advanced multi-engine training in the Grumman TS-2A Tracker and received its first North American T-28 Trojan for its new (and continuing) role in primary training.

The squadron took on its first Beech T-34C Turbo-Mentor in August 1983 and gave up the last T-28 ever used for naval flight training in March 1984. With TW-4, the 'Boomers' operate the T-34C, alias the 'Tormentor,' for primary flight training of naval aviators. All Corpus-based squadrons previously had a 'D' tailcode which was dropped because, when rendered phonetically as 'Delta' in radio communications, it was often confused with Delta Air Lines. The 'Boomers' average well over 17,000 training missions a year and more than 100 sorties per training day.

VT-28 'Rangers'
NAS Corpus Christi, TX: 'G'
T-44A

VT-28 was established 1 May 1960 and serves with TW-4. The unit operates the Beech T-44A Pegasus for advanced training of aviators destined for multi-engine careers.

VT-31 'Wise Owls'
NAS Corpus Christi, TX: 'G'
T-44A

VT-31, formerly ATU-601, was established 1 May 1960 and serves with TW-4. The unit operates the T-44A for advanced training of naval aviators.

VT-86 'Sabre Hawks'
NAS Pensacola, FL: 'F'
T-39N, T-2C

VT-86 with VT-6 was established 5 June 1972 and provides advanced flight training to NFOs, with the exception of those who will become navigators and are trained by the US Air Force. The squadron operates Rockwell T-39N Sabreliner and North American T-2C Buckeye aircraft.

The squadron derives its nickname from the North American T-39D Sabreliner equipped with APS-94 radar similar to that of the F-8 Crusader fighter. The T-39D launched the advanced NFO training program in 1963 and served until 1982. When a replacement for the T-39D's vacuum-tube radar was needed, the Navy solicited bids for a new training aircraft and system in 1982, handled ever since on a contract basis. Rockwell (formerly North American) was at that time selling the Sabreliner design to what became the Sabreliner Corporation, so no T-39 variant was offered. The service selected a program

Right: Advanced NFO radar training is provided by VT-86, with civilian-operated T-39Ns.

Below right: VT-28 and VT-31 (illustrated) use the T-44A for multi-engine training.

based on the Cessna T-47A Platypus (Citation II) with APG-167 radar similar to that of the Northrop F-5E Tiger fighter.

In turn, the T-47A was replaced in 1990 by the T-39N Sabreliner Model 40 with APG-66NT coherent, multi-mode, digital fire-control radar. The T-39N is a refurnished ex-civil aircraft provided by the Sabreliner Corporation. The first two T-39Ns (registered N301NT and N303NT) were delivered at the manufacturer's Perryville, MO, facility on 14 June 1991. The T-39N is part of a $242-million multi-year training services contract which also includes ground-based air-to-air radar intercept, and air-to-ground navigation training simulators, logistics, maintenance and training services. The T-39N is structurally modified to increase service life to 30,000 hours, and carries Westinghouse APG-66NT radar to train NFO candidates in air-to-air intercept and air-to-ground navigation.

A legal challenge to the award of the T-39N contract was mounted by Flight International, which had proposed a version of the Learjet 35. A 3 July 1991 out-of-court agreement gave Flight International 18 months to prepare to take over this NFO

program. It was not clear in early 1992 whether Sabreliner or Flight International would be handling VT-86's training function when the 18-month contract expired in 1993.

In 1991, VT-86 phased out the Douglas

TA-4J Skyhawk which had been in use since 1974. It had been determined that the high cost of operating the TA-4J justified the transition to the North American T-2C Buckeye.

VX (Air Test and Evaluation Squadron)

VX-1 'Pioneers'
NAS Patuxent River, MD: 'JA'
P-3, S-3, SH-2, SH-3, SH-60B, SH-60F

VX-1 was established 1 April 1943 and assumed its current mission on 15 March 1946. In the 1950s, the squadron tested AD Skyraider, P2V Neptune, S2F Sentinel (Tracker), P5M Marlin, and HRP helicopter aircraft, as well as ASW weaponry. More recently, the squadron was involved in development of the US Navy's current fleet of ASW aircraft.

The 'Pioneers' fly a remarkable mix of

Lockheed P-3 Orion, Lockheed S-3 Viking, Kaman SH-2 Seasprite, Sikorsky SH-3 Sea King and Sikorsky SH-60B and SH-60F Seahawk aircraft in test and evaluation duties for the US Navy.

In June 1990, the prototype SH-60F proved its SAR capabilities when it rescued the crew of a VF-84 F-14 Tomcat who had ejected following an inflight emergency during a routine training flight near USS *John F. Kennedy* (CV-67) in the Atlantic. VX-1 happened to have the first SH-60F on the scene, traveled to the rescue site, and lowered a swimmer who assisted in saving the two-man Tomcat crew.

Above: 'Fighter Test' sums up VX-4's work, for which it has Hornets (illustrated) and Tomcats.

Right: The Playboy bunny symbol adorns the fins of VX-4's aircraft, including this F-14A.

Left: The 'JA' code on the nosewheel door identifies this P-3C as being from VX-1.

VX-4 'Evaluators'
NAS Point Mugu, CA: 'XF'
F-14A/B/D, F-18A/C/D

VX-4 (callsign VANDY) was established 15 September 1952, the second US Navy squadron given this designation, and is the Navy's operational test and evaluation squadron. VX-4 has operated a number of F-14 Tomcats since 1972. In its role as the Navy and Marine Corps evaluator of fighter and strike fighter combat systems, the 'Evaluators' at the outset of 1992 had seven F-14A/B Tomcats, two F-14D Super Tomcats and a seven-plane mix of F/A-18A/C/D Hornets.

The squadron is relatively large, with 39 officers including three Marines and a US Air Force exchange officer, 281 enlisted people and five civilians. Its test mission was

Above: VX-1 is mainly involved in ASW test work, and has this SH-60B on charge.

described in vivid terms by Commander Tom Hejl, operations officer in 1992, who said, "We test it, rock it, roll it, slam it, jam it, beat it, drop it and ram it aboard the boat [aircraft carrier]."

VX-4 was first to operate the Tomcat's TCS (Television Camera System), a passive electro-optical system which extends the 'eyeball' range of Tomcat pilots up to 100 miles (161 km). Since the F-14D Super Tomcat incorporates air-to-ground capability, the squadron has evaluated the 'Bombcat' in ordnance separation tests. The squadron has done extensive work with missile avionics for the Tomcat and Hornet. A recent achievement was making the newly-developed AN/ALR-67 radar warning receiver ready for use in time for Desert Storm.

US Navy Units

VX-5 'Vampires'

NAWC China Lake, CA: 'XE'
TA-4J, A-6E, AV-8B, F/A-18,
OV-10A/D, AH-1J/T/W

VX-5, established 18 June 1957, has long been a key US Navy operational test and evaluation squadron, located at the Naval Air Warfare Center Weapons Division (formerly the Naval Weapons Test Center) at China Lake, CA, and heavily involved in developments of ordnance and tactics. The 'Vampires' have operated most tactical warplanes in US Navy inventory. In early 1992, the squadron was able to boast a fleet which included Douglas TA-4J Skyhawk,

Grumman A-6E Intruder, McDonnell AV-8B Harrier, McDonnell F/A-18 Hornet, North American OV-10A/D Bronco (being phased out), and Bell AH-1J/T/W SeaCobra/ SuperCobra aircraft.

Right: VX-5 evaluates Marine aircraft as well as Navy machines. This is a Night Attack AV-8B.

VXE (Antarctic Development Squadron)

VXE-6 'Puckered Penguins'

NAS Point Mugu, CA: 'XD'
LC-130F/R, HH-1N

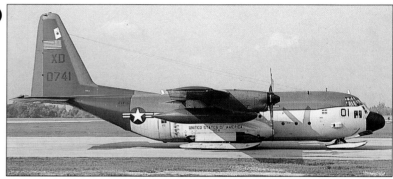

VXE-6 began life as VX-6 on 17 January 1955 and became VXE-6 on 1 January 1969. The 'Penguins' operate two Lockheed LC-130F Hercules, four LC-130R ski-equipped models and six Bell HH-1N Huey aircraft in Antarctic exploration.

The squadron is well known for resurrecting an LC-130F (BuNo. 148321) which spent 16 years buried in snow before being retrieved and turned over to the Naval Aviation Depot, Cherry Point, NC, for refurbishment which began in 1990 and was expected to take 2½ years.

In mid-1991, an LC-130 of VXE-6 landed at McMurdo Station, Antarctica, to complete the first mid-winter medical evacuation of critically ill personnel since 1966. A scientist was flown 2,400 miles (3860 km) to a

medical facility in Christchurch, New Zealand, for care. This was the first such rescue in 30 years carried out in the austral winter in complete darkness, at sub-zero temperatures, in strong winds.

25 October 1991 marked the first time an aircraft with an all-female crew flew in Antarctica. An LC-130, from VXE-6, with a seven-woman crew, made a sortie carrying passengers and supplies to the Amundsen-Scott South Pole station. The operators of

Above: One of the more unusual tasks of the US Navy is to support scientific research in Antarctica. The LC-130Rs of VXE-6 deploy to New Zealand during the fall/winter for this task.

LC-130F/R and HH-1N aircraft in the Antarctic have received much attention for their work at the bottom of the world, and were the

subject of a recent novel, *The Icemen*. The squadron is expected to continue supporting Antarctic operations in the 1990s.

VXN (Oceanographic Development Squadron)

VXN-8 'World Travelers'

NAS Patuxent River, MD: 'JB'
P-3B

VXN-8 is the US military's only squadron dedicated to airborne geophysical surveying (known to the Navy as Project Birdseye). The squadron was established 1 July 1965 as OASU (Oceanographic Air Survey Unit),

became VX-8 on 1 July 1967, and was redesignated VXN-8 on 1 January 1969.

The squadron has performed its job for many years with versions of the Lockheed P-3 Orion. The squadron retired its last

Left: VXN-8 has operated various P-3s over the years on research programs. The nickname reflects the many overseas deployments.

RP-3A Orion, the 'Arctic Fox' (BuNo. 150500) on 11 July 1991. This aircraft is to be replaced by a P-3B (BuNo. 154587), being converted to RP-3D standard and expected to be operational in January 1993, resurrecting the 'Arctic Fox' nickname. VXN-8's full inventory is to be five RP-3D aircraft, including two which preserve well-known nicknames, 'Roadrunner' and 'El Coyote'.

Left: VXN-8's aircraft have always featured cartoon characters.

Miscellaneous units

Base Flights

The US Navy operates 32 base flights employing support aircraft for its naval air stations around the world. Most of these units have one or two Beech UC-12B/M support aircraft. A few also have helicopters. The base flight at NAS Patuxent River, MD, operates Sikorsky SH-3D/G Sea King helicopters.

Left: Pensacola's Base Flight UC-12B was pressed into Gulf service during Desert Storm.

Above: Whidbey Island has this colorful SH-3D assigned for SAR duties.

Fighter Weapons School

The Fighter Weapons School at Miramar, CA, is more colloquially known as 'Top Gun' and was created to provide Fleet fighter crews with air combat training. The school operates Douglas A-4E Skyhawk, General Dynamics F-16N and TF-16N Fighting Falcons, and Northrop F-5E and F-5F Tigers.

212

Above: Among 'Top Gun's' collection of adversary aircraft are several F-16Ns.

Above right: Latest NFWS adversary aircraft is the F-14A, this being the plain-colored example.

Right: An FEWSG NKC-135A follows the EC-24A on to a Norwegian runway during an EW exercise.

Fleet Electronic Warfare Support Group

The FEWSG at Waco Field, TX, flies the US Navy's sole EC-24A (a Douglas DC-8) and two Boeing NKC-135A Stratotankers providing electronic warfare support and training for the Fleet.

Fleet Logistics Support Wing

The Naval Air Reserve's Fleet Logistics Support Wing maintains its detachment NOLA at NAS Orleans, LA, with one North American CT-39G Sabreliner, and detachment WASH at NAF Washington, MD, with C-20D Gulfstream and CT-39G Sabreliner transports.

Naval Coastal Systems Center

The Naval Coastal Systems Center at Panama City, FL, operates a Sikorsky H-53 Sea Stallion helicopter for support duties to transport personnel and equipment.

Naval Strike Warfare Center

The NSWC, commonly called 'Strike University' and established in 1984 to provide realistic combat training to the attack and strike fighter community, has a few McDonnell Douglas F/A-18 Hornets on charge.

Below is FLSW det WASH's C-20D, while at bottom are two Hornet operators: the US Navy's Test Pilot's School (left) and the 'Blue Angels' display team (right).

Navy Flight Demonstration Team

The Navy Flight Demonstration Team, or 'Blue Angels', provides displays of flying capabilities at air shows, open days and other events using modified McDonnell Douglas F/A-18A Hornets. The 'Blue Angels' are supported by a Marine Corps KC-130F Hercules transport.

Pacific Missile Range Facility

The Pacific Missile Range Facility operates Beech RC-12F and Sikorsky UH-3A Sea King aircraft in support duties at Barking Sands, HI.

Test Pilot's School

The Test Pilot's School at NAS Patuxent River, MD, operates various aircraft types to train test pilots who evaluate Navy warplanes. T-38A Talons, a U-1 Otter and three U-6A Beavers are among aircraft types on charge.

In 1991, TPS acquired four Hughes OH-6B Cayuse helicopters on loan from the US Army for use in training rotary-wing test pilots.

Above: This CT-39G is operated by det WASH of the FLSW. Det NOLA also has a Sabreliner.

Below: Among the diverse types assigned to 'Strike U' at Fallon is this SH-3H for range support.

US MARINE CORPS UNITS

HMA (Attack Helicopter Squadron)

HMA-773 'Cobras'
NAS Atlanta, GA: 'MP'
AH-1J

HMA-773 is a Marine Air Reserve operator of the Bell AH-1J Sea Cobra, reporting to MAG-42 at MCAS Atlanta, GA. The squadron was scheduled to convert to the AH-1W in 1993. Elements of HMA-773 were activated for Operation Desert Storm under MAG-50 and flew combat missions in the Persian Gulf region.

HMA-775 'Coyotes'
Camp Pendleton, CA
AH-1J

HMA-775 is a Marine Air Reserve user of the Bell AH-1J SeaCobra, reporting to MAG-46 at nearby El Toro. The 'Coyotes' were scheduled to receive the AH-1W in 1993. Elements of HMA-775 were activated for Operation Desert Storm and flew combat missions from King Abdul Aziz air base, Saudi Arabia.

Right: The last remaining AH-1J Cobras are flown by two Reserve units, including HMA-775 at Camp Pendleton.

HMH (Marine Helicopter Squadron, Heavy)

HMH-361 'Pineapples'
MCAS Tustin, CA: 'YN'
CH-53E

HMH-361 under MAG-16 operates the Sikorsky CH-53E Super Stallion after converting from the CH-53D Sea Stallion in September 1990. With this transition, no fewer than four CH-53E squadrons were located at the Tustin airfield near Twentynine Palms, CA, where Marine ground forces routinely exercise.

HMH-362 'Ugly Angels'
MCAS New River, NC: 'YL'
CH-53D

HMH-362 under MAG-26 operates the Sikorsky CH-53D Sea Stallion to support ground combat forces of the 2d Marine Division at Camp Lejeune, NC.

HMH-363 'Red Lions'
MCAS Tustin, CA: 'YZ'
CH-53D

HMH-363 under MAG-16 operates the Sikorsky CH-53D Sea Stallion transport helicopter in support of ground forces.

Above: This HMH-363 CH-53D provides a good comparison with the CH-53E in the background.

HMH-461 'Sea Stallions'
MCAS New River, NC: 'CJ'
CH-53E

HMH-461 under MAG-26 operates the Sikorsky CH-53E Super Stallion heavylift helicopter and routinely deploys to support Marine operations.

A detachment aboard the amphibious ship USS *Guam* (LPH-9), while en route to the Persian Gulf, played a key role in Operation Eastern Exit, the non-combatant evacuation of the American Embassy in Mogadishu, Somalia, in January 1991. CH-53Es brought Marines and SEALs into the Somali capital and, after inserting the security force, assisted in the evacuation. This activity was carried out at long range; although the CH-53E is not normally fitted with a refueling probe, probes were installed for the operation and refueling was carried out by Lockheed KC-130 Hercules dispatched from the Desert Storm contingent at Bahrain.

HMH-462 'Heavy Haulers'
MCAS Tustin, CA; 'YF'
CH-53D

HMH-462 under MAG-16 operates the Sikorsky CH-53A Sea Stallion transport helicopter in support of ground forces. The squadron deployed to King Abdul Aziz naval air base, Saudi Arabia, under MAG-16 during Operation Desert Storm.

Far right: The three-engined CH-53E greatly enhanced USMC lift capability. This example is from HMH-464.

HMH-463 'Heavy Haulers'
MCAS Kaneohe Bay, HI: 'YH'
CH-53D, UH-1N

HMH-463 reports to MAG-24 and flies Sikorsky CH-53D Sea Stallion and Bell UH-1N Huey helicopters to support ground forces. Elements of the squadron deployed to King Abdul Aziz naval air base, Saudi Arabia, under MAG-16 during Operation Desert Storm.

The 'Haulers' operate a detachment at Futemma with CH-53Ds and UH-1Ns.

HMH-464 'Condors'
MCAS New River, NC: 'EN'
CH-53E

HMH-464 under MAG-29 operates the Sikorsky CH-53E Super Stallion for heavylift and ground combat support duties.

HMH-465 'Warhorses'
MCAS Tustin, CA: 'YJ'
CH-53E

HMH-465 operates the Sikorsky CH-53E Super Stallion transport helicopter in support of ground forces.

HMH-466
MCAS Tustin, CA: 'YJ'
CH-53E

HMH-466 operates the Sikorsky CH-53E Super Stallion transport helicopter in support of ground forces. Serving under MAG-16 temporarily, the squadron operated from Ras Al Gar during Operation Desert Storm.

Above: HMH-462 flies the early-generation CH-53 from Tustin.

HMH-772 'Flying Armadillos'
NAS Willow Grove, PA: 'MT'
CH-53A/D

HMH-772 is equipped with the Sikorsky CH-53A/D Sea Stallion helicopter. Detachment A of the squadron ('MS' tailcode, now HMH-769) is at NAS Alameda, CA, and detachment B ('QM' tailcode, now HMH-777) at NAS Dallas, TX, both also equipped with CH-53A/Ds for cargo, transport and medical evacuation duties. This Marine Air Reserve squadron, which was activated during Operation Desert Shield/Storm, normally reports to MAG-49 at Willow Grove.

Detachment A of HMH-772 operated from the assault ship USS *Tarawa* (LHA-1) during Operation Desert Storm. Returning from the

war, *Tarawa* was diverted on 15 May 1991 to assist survivors of a devastating cyclone in Bangladesh in Operation Productive Effort. Helicopters from the squadron participated in this humanitarian effort.

HMH-772 was temporarily deployed aboard USS *Midway* (CV-41) for the carrier's final cruise to provide medical and humanitarian relief as part of Operation Fiery Vigil following the 10 June 1991 eruption of Mount Pinatubo in the Philippines. CH-53D helicopters belonging to the squadron supported the carrier's SH-3H Sea Kings from HS-12 in providing support for the beleaguered naval base at Subic Bay during the volcano disaster.

Above: HMH-772 is a Reserve squadron headquartered at Willow Grove, flying early CH-53s. It also has two detachments, det A ('MS' tailcode – illustrated) at Alameda and det B ('QM' tailcode) at Dallas.

Left: HMH-466 flies the CH-53E from Tustin.

Right: CH-53Es from HMH-465 cluster on the deck of USS New Orleans. The unit is shore-based at Tustin.

HML (Marine Helicopter Squadron, Light)

HML-771
NAS South Weymouth, MA: 'QK'
UH-1N

HML-771 appears to be the only existing HML squadron and is a Marine Air Reserve unit flying the Bell UH-1N Huey helicopter.

HMLA (Marine Helicopter Attack Squadron, Light)

HMLA-167
MCAS New River, NC: 'TV'
UH-1N, AH-1W

HMLA-167 under MAG-26 operates Bell UH-1N Huey and AH-1W SuperCobra helicopters in support of ground combat troops of the 2d Marine Division.

HMLA-169 'Vipers'
MCAS Camp Pendleton, CA: 'SN'
UH-1N, AH-1W

HMLA-169 under MAG-39 operates Bell UH-1N Huey and AH-1W SuperCobra helicopters in direct support of ground combat troops of the 3d Marine Division. Originally an HMA squadron (AH-1J), the squadron has previously operated AH-1J, AH-1T, and AH-1T (TOW). HMLA-169 is considered the West Coast 'float' squadron, a role it took on beginning in 1977, and would operate all of the assets on an assault ship when deployed on a cruise.

UH-1Ns and AH-1Ws from the squadron were deployed aboard the assault ship USS *Tarawa* (LHA-1) during Operation Desert Storm. Returning from the war, *Tarawa* was diverted on 15 May 1991 to assist survivors of a devastating cyclone in Bangladesh in Operation Productive Effort. Helicopters from the squadron participated in this humanitarian effort.

Left: Most HMLA units have both UH-1N Hueys and Cobras. This Huey is from HMLA-167 based at New River.

Below: AH-1W Cobras partner Hueys with HMLA-267 at Camp Pendleton.

HMLA-269 'Sea Cobras'
MCAS New River, NC: 'HF'
AH-1W, UH-1N

HMLA-269 under MAG-29 traces its history to HMA-269 which flew AH-1J SeaCobra helicopters during the Vietnam years.

The squadron deployed to Operation Desert Shield/Storm to fly rear area security missions for Marines arriving in Saudi Arabia, using the Bell AH-1T SeaCobra. The squadron reached Dhahran on 16 August

HMLA-267 'Black Aces'
MCAS Camp Pendleton, CA: 'UV'
UH-1N, AH-1W

HMLA-267, which is also known as the 'Stingers', under MAG-39 operates Bell UH-1N Huey and AH-1W SuperCobra helicopters in support of the 3d Marine Division. The squadron formerly was HML-267 flying Huey helicopters only.

Right: Looking suitably battered, this AH-1W is a Gulf War veteran from HMLA-169 'Vipers'.

Above: Supporting the Cobras of the 'Scarface' unit are Bell UH-1N Twin Hueys.

1990. Beginning 12 November 1991, the squadron deployed 12 AH-1Ts aboard USS *Shreveport* (LPD-12), six aboard USS *Raleigh* (LPD-1), and 12 aboard USS *Nassau* (LHA-4), all in preparation for the amphibious invasion of Kuwait which was expected but never came. HMLA-269 AH-1T SeaCobras operated from *Nassau* to attack Iraqi forces

on Bubiyan Island on 26 February 1991 after US Navy Orion patrol aircraft pinpointed enemy troops.

Subsequently, the 'Gunrunners' became the last operator of the AH-1T version of the SuperCobra helicopter. On 7 August 1991, the squadron returned to New River from the AH-1T's last deployment in which USS *Guadalcanal* (LPH-7) supported Kurdish relief operations from the eastern Mediterranean. All remaining AH-1T aircraft in Marine Corps inventory were scheduled to be upgraded to AH-1W standard by the end of 1992.

The squadron now operates Bell UH-1N Hueys and Bell AH-1W SuperCobras. HMLA-269 trains regularly at the Marine reservation at Camp Lejeune, NC, to support Marine ground combat forces.

HMLA-367 'Scarface'
MCAS Camp Pendleton, CA: 'VT'
UH-1N, AH-1W

HMLA-367 under MAG-39 operates Bell UH-1N Huey and AH-1W SuperCobra helicopters in support of the 3d Marine

Left: Wearing a split desert/gray camouflage, this AH-1W serves with HMLA-367 'Scarface'.

Above: This HMLA-369 UH-1N displays a limited attack capability in the form of rocket pods.

Division. The squadron's detachment B operates permanently at Kaneohe Bay, HI. 'Scarface' is a former HML squadron (UH-1N) and flew Huey gunships in Vietnam. Before its current nickname, the squadron had the cartoon character 'Yosemite Sam' as its emblem.

HMLA-367 and HMLA-369 deployed to Jubail airfield, the closest Saudi base to the Kuwait border, during Operation Desert Storm, and flew anti-armor missions.

HMLA-369 'Gunfighters'
MCAS Camp Pendleton, CA: 'SM'
UH-1N, AH-1W

HMLA-369 under MAG-39 operates Bell UH-1N Huey and AH-1W SuperCobra helicopters in support of the 3d Marine Division. The squadron is a former HMA (AH-1J) attack unit. HMLA-367 and HMLA-369 deployed to Jubail airfield, the closest Saudi base to the Kuwait border, during Operation Desert Storm, and flew anti-armor missions against Iraqi forces.

HMM (Marine Helicopter Squadron, Medium)

HMM-161
MCAS Tustin, CA: 'YR'
CH-46E

HMM-161 under MAG-16 operates the Boeing CH-46E Sea Knight in support of the 3d Marine Division at Camp Pendleton. The squadron deployed to King Abdul Aziz naval air base under MAG-16 and flew combat support missions during Operation Desert Storm.

HMM-162
MCAS New River, NC: 'YS'
CH-46E

HMM-162 under MAG-29 operates the Boeing CH-46E Sea Knight in support of ground forces of the 3d Marine Division at Camp Lejeune, NC.

HMM-163 'Ridgerunners'
MCAS Tustin, CA: 'YP'
CH-46E

HMM-163 under MAG-16 is a long-established operator of the Boeing CH-46E Sea Knight used for vertical insertion of Marine combat troops on the battlefield and for other duties. The squadron had a detachment embarked aboard the assault ship USS *Peleliu* (LHA-5) in the aftermath of the Persian Gulf.

Below: HMM-263 flew Desert Storm missions, this CH-46E looking decidedly war-weary.

In 1991, the 'Ridgerunners' and companion squadron HMM-166, also at Tustin, became the first to receive the 'Bullfrog' version of the CH-46E helicopter. The 'Bullfrog' features enlarged sponsons which double the fuel capacity, allowing for longer range. Flotation devices and a modified flight computer are also included in the helicopter.

HMM-164
MCAS Tustin, CA: 'YT'
CH-46E

HMM-164 under MAG-16 operates the Boeing CH-46E Sea Knight helicopter to support ground forces. During Operation Desert Storm, the squadron embarked on USS *Okinawa* (LPH-3) and other warships in the Persian Gulf region.

HMM-165
MCAS Kaneohe Bay, HI: 'YW'
CH-46E

HMM-165 under MAG-24 operates the Boeing CH-46E Sea Knight helicopter to support ground forces. The squadron participated in Operation Desert Storm.

HMM-166
MCAS Tustin, CA: 'YX'
CH-46E

HMM-166 under MAG-16 operates the Boeing CH-46E Sea Knight helicopter to support ground forces.

HMM-261
MCAS New River, NC: 'EM'
CH-46E

HMM-261 under MAG-26 operates the Boeing CH-46E Sea Knight to support ground combat forces of the 2d Marine Division at Camp Lejeune, NC.

Below: In recent years the Marine helicopter force has appeared in a wide array of colors. This sand and gray CH-46E is from HMM-165.

Above: New River is the main East Coast base for the CH-46, housing six HMM squadrons and a training unit. This 'Frog' is from HMM-162.

HMM-262
MCAS Kaneohe Bay, HI: 'ET'
CH-46E

HMM-262 under MAG-24 operates the Boeing CH-46E Sea Knight helicopter to support ground forces. The US Navy has

mistakenly assigned the 'ET' tailcode to two squadrons, the other being VQ-6.

HMM-263
MCAS New River, NC: 'EG'
CH-46E

HMM-263 under MAG-29 flies the Boeing CH-46E Sea Knight in support of ground combat forces of the 2d Marine Division at Camp Lejeune. HMM-263 contributed helicopters to vessels at sea during Operation Desert Storm.

HMM-264
MCAS New River, NC: 'EH'
CH-46F

HMM-264 under MAG-26 flies the Boeing CH-46F Sea Knight in support of ground forces of the 2d Marine Division at Camp Lejeune, NC.

HMM-265
MCAS Kaneohe Bay, HI: 'EP'
CH-46E

HMM-265 under MAG-24 is one of numerous operators of the Boeing CH-46E Sea Knight helicopter and is frequently deployed on naval vessels to support Marine operations.

The squadron was aboard the assault ship USS *Tarawa* (LHA-1) during Operation Desert Storm and carried out VOD, transport, utility and other duties, although these Marine helicopters were never called upon to make an amphibious assault as had been expected. Returning from the war, *Tarawa* was diverted on 15 May 1991 to assist survivors of a devastating cyclone in Bangladesh under Operation Productive Effort. Helicopters from the squadron participated in this humanitarian effort for two weeks.

HMM-266
MCAS New River, NC: 'ES'
CH-46E

HMM-266 under MAG-26 flies the Boeing CH-46E Sea Knight helicopter to support ground forces with the 2d Marine Division at Camp Lejeune, NC. During Operation Desert Storm, the squadron operated from Abdul Aziz air base, Saudi Arabia.

HMM-268
MCAS Tustin, CA: 'YQ'
CH-46E

HMM-268 under MAG-16 is a long-established operator of the Boeing CH-46E Sea Knight, and had the distinction of being one of the last US Marine Corps participants in Operation Desert Storm to return home. Embarked on the assault ship USS *New Orleans* (LPH-11), the squadron reached the US only on 24 August 1991, some six months after the end of the Gulf War.

Below: HMM-764 is a USMCR unit, based at El Toro. It was called to duty for Desert Storm.

Above: HMM-262 'The Flying Tigers' is based at Kaneohe Bay with CH-46Es.

During the war, the squadron had carried out ship-to-shore operations and supported Marine amphibious forces.

HMM-364
MCAS Kaneohe Bay, HI: 'PF'
CH-46E

HMM-364 under MAG-24 operates the Boeing CH-46E Sea Knight in support of ground forces.

HMM-365
MCAS New River, NC: 'YM'
CH-46E

HMM-365 under MAG-29 operates the Boeing CH-46E Sea Knight in support of ground forces of the 2d Marine Division at Camp Lejeune. The squadron supplied CH-46Es to assault ships and other vessels in the Persian Gulf during Operation Desert Storm.

HMM-764
MCAS El Toro, CA: 'ML'
CH-46E

HMM-764 under MAG-46 is a Marine Air Reserve operator of the Boeing CH-46E Sea Knight helicopter. The squadron was activated and flew combat missions in Operation Desert Storm.

HMM-767
NAS New Orleans, LA: 'MM'
UH-1N

HMM-767 is a Marine Air Reserve operator of the Bell UH-1N Huey helicopter,

Right: The only HMM unit to fly the UH-1N is HMM-767 of the Reserve, based at New Orleans.

Above: 'Frogs' in low visibility markings operate in France. The unit is HMM-266 from New River.

Below: A CH-46E from HMM-268 demonstrates the standard three-tone camouflage.

US Marine Corps Units

and reports to MAG-46 at El Toro. During Operation Desert Storm, these Reservists were activated and flew their UH-1Ns at King Abdul Aziz air base, Saudi Arabia.

Far right: Another Reserve CH-46E operator is HMM-774, which flies from NAS Norfolk.

HMM-774
NAS Norfolk, VA: 'MQ'
CH-46E

HMM-774 operates the Boeing CH-46E Sea Knight as a Marine Air Reserve squadron, reporting to MAG-42 at Atlanta. HMM-774 was activated and flew combat missions during Operation Desert Storm.

HMT (Marine Helicopter Training Squadron)

HMT-204
MCAS New River, NC: 'GX'
CH-46E, CH-53D

HMT-204 is the Marine Corps' training squadron for personnel who will fly and maintain Boeing CH-46 Sea Knight and Sikorsky H-53 Sea Stallion helicopters. The squadron trains personnel using the CH-46E and CH-53D variants.

HMT-301
MCAS Camp Pendleton, CA: 'SU'
CH-46E

HMT-301 operates the Boeing CH-46E

Two USMC training units are HMT-204 (CH-46E) and HMT-302 (CH-53E).

Sea Knight in training and support duties for the 3d Marine Division.

HMT-302
MCAS Tustin, CA: 'UT'
CH-53A/E

HMT-302 operates the Sikorsky CH-53A/E Sea Stallion transport helicopter.

HMT-303
MCAS Camp Pendleton, CA: 'QT'
UH-1N, AH-1J/W, OV-10A/D

HMT-303 is the Marine Corps' training squadron for personnel who will fly and maintain Bell UH-1 Huey and AH-1 Cobra

helicopters. The squadron operates UH-1N, AH-1J and AH-1W models in carrying out its training duties.

On 1 October 1991, HMT-303 took on an additional task, becoming the Marine Corps replacement training squadron for its North American OV-10A/D Bronco forward air control aircraft. The Marines had previously sent Bronco people for training to the US Air Force's 22nd Tactical Air Control Training Squadron at Davis-Monthan AFB, AZ. The USAF had assumed all Bronco training for all service branches in 1981. When the OV-10 was removed from USAF inventory on 30 September 1991 and the 22nd TASTS was given a new designation (333rd Fighter Squadron) and a new aircraft (OA-10 'Warthog'), the Marines were left as the only US service operating the Bronco. HMT-303 operates a mix of OV-10A and OV-10D(Plus) Broncos in addition to its rotary-wing fleet. The Corps was scheduled to phase out all Bronco operations by the end of FY 1994, however, and on 13 March 1992 HMT-303 terminated training of replacement personnel for the aircraft.

In addition to training AH-1/UH-1 crews, HMT-303 has responsibility for OV-10 instruction.

HMX (Marine Helicopter Squadron)

HMX-1
MCAS Quantico, VA: 'MX'
VH-46, VH-3D, VH-53, VH-60

HMX-1 provides VIP transport with a mixed fleet of Boeing VH-46 Sea Knight, Sikorsky VH-3D Sea King and VH-53 Sea Stallion, and Sikorsky VH-60 Seahawk helicopters. The squadron operates a detachment at Anacostia in Washington,

DC, which provides presidential and other VIP transport. HMX-1 recently retired six Bell VH-1N Hueys to the AMARC storage facility at Davis-Monthan AFB, AZ.

The Marine Corps has responsibility for helicopter transport of the President and his staff, employing the VH-60.

MALS (Marine Aviation Logistics Squadron)

MALS-32
MCAS Cherry Point, NC: 'DA'
TA-4J

MALS-32 operates Douglas TA-4J Skyhawks for support purposes.

MALS-24 'Bandits'
MCAS Kaneohe Bay, HI: 'EW'
TA-4F

MALS-24 operates the Douglas TA-4F Skyhawk in support duties.

MALS-31
MCAS Beaufort, SC: 'EX'
TA-4F/J

MALS-31 operates Douglas TA-4F/J Skyhawk aircraft in support duties.

MALS-42
NAS Alameda, CA: 'MW'
TA-4J

MALS-42 is a Marine Air Reserve operator of the Douglas TA-4J Skyhawk.

MALS-49
NAS Willow Grove, PA: 'QZ'
TA-4J

MALS-49 operates under MAG-49 as a Marine Air Reserve unit with the Douglas TA-4J Skyhawk.

Left: This strikingly marked TA-4J is on the strength of MALS-32 from Cherry Point.

Above: The MALS units are equipped with two-seat Skyhawks for general duties. This TA-4F is from MALS-31 at Beaufort.

MWHS (Marine Headquarters Squadron)

VMA (Marine Attack Squadron)

VMA-124 'Whistling Death'
NAS Memphis, TN: 'QP'
TA-4J, A-4M
VMA-124 is a Marine Air Reserve operator of the Douglas TA-4J and A-4M Skyhawk, reporting to MAG-41 (headquartered at Dallas).

VMA-131 'Diamondbacks'
NAS Willow Grove, PA: 'QG'
A-4M
VMA-131 is a Marine Air Reserve squadron reporting to MAG-49 at Willow Grove and operating the Douglas A-4M Skyhawk.

VMA-211 'Wake Island Avengers'
MCAS Yuma, AZ: 'CF'
AV-8B
VMA-211 under MAG-13 operates the McDonnell AV-8B Night Attack Harrier.

VMA-214 'Black Sheep'
MCAS Yuma, AZ
AV-8B
VMA-214 under MAG-13 traces its history to the heady days of Pacific conflict in World War II, when the squadron was headed up by air ace and Medal of Honor recipient Gregory 'Pappy' Boyington and flew F4U-1 Corsairs. The squadron operated A-4 Skyhawks before acquiring Harriers early in the Harrier program. In 1990, it became one of two (together with VMA-211) squadrons to transition from the AV-8B Harrier II day attack aircraft to the AV-8B Night Attack Harrier.

The squadron took the Night Attack Harrier on its first overseas deployment when it departed Yuma for a rotational tour at MCAS Iwakuni, Japan, in October 1991. Harrier duty at Iwakuni is customarily six months in duration, with each squadron returning to its home base after such a tour.

VMA-223 'Bulldogs'
MCAS Cherry Point, NC: 'WP'
AV-8B
VMA-223 under MAG-32 operates the McDonnell AV-8B Harrier in the day attack

Below right: This pair of VMA-231 AV-8Bs demonstrates the original green/gray camouflage.

Below: This VMA-311 AV-8B displays a variation of the two-tone gray scheme.

role. VMA-223 provided a detachment which supported Operation Sharp Edge, the evacuation of foreigners from war-torn Liberia. In January 1991, the squadron sent a six-plane detachment to Rota, Spain, as a contingency for Operation Desert Shield/Storm. The detachment saw no action in Desert Storm and returned on 23 February 1991. In June 1991, the squadron dispatched 10 aircraft in a detachment aboard USS *Wasp* (LHD-1) for a Mediterranean and Persian Gulf area cruise.

VMA-231 'Ace of Spades'
MCAS Cherry Point, NC: 'CG'
AV-8B
VMA-231, callsign SHANK, under MAG-32 operates the McDonnell AV-8B Harrier in the day attack role. The squadron, its aircraft temporarily painted in non-regulation two-tone gray, was forward-deployed at MCAS

VMA-211 (right) is based at Yuma with Night Attack AV-8Bs, while VMA-223 (below) flies the regular Harrier II from Cherry Point.

MWHS-1
MCAS Futemma, Okinawa: 'SZ'
CT-39G

MWHS-1 under MAG-36, in recent years the Corps' final operator of the Douglas C-117D 'Gooney Bird', now operates the North American CT-39G Sabreliner in support duties.

Iwakuni, Japan, when Operation Desert Shield began and deployed directly to Sheik Isa air base, Bahrain, in December 1990. After participating in the Desert Storm conflict as part of MAG-13, the Marines of VMA-231 had been away from home for a full 11 months.

On 9 February 1991, an 'Ace' Harrier

Above: A-4Ms are flown by USMCR units, including VMA-131.

(BuNo. 162081, coded CG-09, callsign JUMP 57) was shot down by a SAM over southern Kuwait. Captain Russell A. C. ('Bart') Sanborn was captured and was a POW until war's end.

Above: Outliving the Phantom, the Skyhawk clings to service with the USMCR. VMA-322 is illustrated.

Below: The yellow stripes on the fin identify this Harrier as being from VMA-542 'Flying Tigers'.

Above: A 'Flying Nightmares' AV-8B releases a pair of Mk 84 LDGP bombs over the Yuma range.

VMA-311 'Tomcats'
MCAS Yuma, AZ: 'WL'
AV-8B

VMA-311 under MAG-13 flies the McDonnell AV-8B Harrier in the day attack role and is slated to receive the Night Attack Harrier.

The squadron participated in Operation Desert Storm from King Abdul Aziz airfield, Saudi Arabia. One combat loss of an AV-8B Harrier (BuNo. 163518) occurred on 28 January 1991 and pilot Captain Michael C. Berryman was held prisoner until war's end.

VMA-322 'Gamecocks'
NAS South Weymouth, MA: 'QR'
A-4M

VMA-322 is a Marine Air Reserve operator of the Douglas A-4M Skyhawk serving under MAG-49 at Willow Grove.

VMA-331 'Bumblebees'
MCAS Cherry Point, NC: 'VL'
AV-8B

VMA-331 under MAG-32 operates the McDonnell AV-8B Harrier in the day attack

role. The squadron participated in Operation Desert Storm as the only Harrier unit to fly in combat from a ship deck, operating from USS *Nassau* (LPH-4) in the Persian Gulf. On 27 February 1991, the 'Bumblebees' suffered the loss of an AV-8B (BuNo. 162740) and pilot Captain Reginald C. Underwood was killed.

VMA-513 'Flying Nightmares'
MCAS Yuma, AZ: 'WF'
AV-8B

VMA-513, one of four McDonnell AV-8B Harrier squadrons under MAG-13, is a one-time World War II night-fighter squadron and Vietnam-era fighter squadron (F-4B Phantoms), but became part of the Harrier community early in the program.

The squadron returned to Yuma on 24 October 1991 following a nearly 11-month deployment to MCAS Iwakuni, Japan. The squadron's normal six-month rotational tour in Japan was extended because of Operation Desert Storm. A detachment of VMA-513 served in the Persian Gulf conflict.

VMA-542 'Flying Tigers'
MCAS Cherry Point, NC: 'WH'
AV-8B

VMA-542 with MAG-32 operates the McDonnell AV-8B Harrier in the day attack role.

The squadron deployed to King Abdul Aziz air base, Saudi Arabia, and flew hazardous combat missions during Operation Desert Storm. On 23 February 1991, the 'Tigers' sustained a combat loss of an AV-8B Harrier (BuNo. 161573) and its pilot, Captain James N. Wilbourne. The only Marine squadron to experience two combat losses, VMA-542 on 25 February 1991 saw Iraqi forces claim another AV-8B Harrier (BuNo. 163190). Pilot Captain Scott Walsh was rescued.

Left: VMA-331 Harriers wear a small badge on the nose showing a bumblebee carrying a bomb.

VMA(AW) (Marine Attack Squadron, All-Weather)

VMA(AW)-224 'Bengals'
MCAS Cherry Point, NC: 'WK'
A-6E

VMA(AW)-224 under MAG-14 operates the Grumman A-6E Intruder in the medium-attack role. The squadron has a long history in the venerable Intruder, which it flew in Vietnam. Its final combat in the Intruder was

from Sheik Isa air base, Bahrain, during Operation Desert Storm.

In 1990, the Corps decided to relinquish its entire Intruder fleet in favor of the F/A-18D Hornet. The 'Bengals' are expected to be disestablished in the mid-1990s rather than to convert to the newer aircraft.

Below: The days of the Intruder in USMC service are numbered. This A-6E TRAM is with the 'Bengals'.

VMA(AW)-332 'Polka Dots'
MCAS Cherry Point, NC: 'EA'
A-6E

VMA(AW)-332 under MAG-14 flies the Grumman A-6E Intruder. The squadron is expected to convert to the F/A-18D Hornet in the mid-1990s.

VMA(AW)-533 'Hawks'
MCAS Cherry Point, NC: 'ED'
A-6E

VMA(AW)-533 under MAG-14 flies the Grumman A-6E Intruder. The squadron deployed to Sheik Isa air base, Bahrain, for combat during Operation Desert Storm. The squadron is expected to convert to the F/A-18D Hornet in the mid-1990s.

Above: Two of the A-6 units will convert to F/A-18Ds, including VMA(AW)-332 'Polka Dots'.

VMAQ (Marine Tactical Electronic Warfare Squadron)

VMAQ-2 'Playboys'
MCAS Cherry Point, NC: 'CY'
EA-6B

VMAQ-2 under MAG-14 is the Marines' primary operator of the Grumman EA-6B Prowler electronic warfare aircraft, to which the squadron converted from the EA-6A model in the mid-1980s. The 'Playboys' work closely with US Navy VAQ Prowler squadrons and frequently provide carrier-

based detachments, as was done during Operations Prairie Fire and El Dorado Canyon against Libya in 1986.

Operating from Sheik Isa air base, Bahrain, beginning in August 1990, VMAQ-2 carried out electronic warfare operations during Operation Desert Shield/Storm. During the same period, VMAQ-2's remaining six EA-6Bs were deployed with detachment X-Ray in the western Pacific, covering Marine contingencies in that part of

the world.

VMAQ-2 long maintained three Prowler detachments (X, Y and Z) to meet rotating overseas deployment commitments, including a detachment at Iwakuni under MAG-12. On 1 July 1992, VMAQ-2 was scheduled to be split to form VMAQs 1, 2 and 3. These were to be joined at Cherry Point by VMAQ-4, which was to deactivate as a Reserve squadron and join the active Marine force.

VMAQ-4 'Seahawks'
NAS Whidbey Island, WA: 'RM'
EA-6B

VMAQ-4 is the sole Marine Air Reserve squadron operating the EA-6B Prowler electronic warfare aircraft, reporting to MAG-46 at El Toro. Beginning 14 November 1991, the squadron was 'at home' at Whidbey from a months-long stint at MCAS Iwakuni, Japan, its first operational deployment site.

This Reserve squadron was called to active duty and replaced its EA-6As with

VMAQ-2 has been the sole active-duty EW squadron for some time, but is to split into three separate squadrons in late 1992.

EA-6Bs, deploying in June 1991 to replace a VMAQ-2 detachment that was extended at Iwakuni because of Operation Desert Storm. On 30 September 1992, VMAQ-4 was scheduled to deactivate as a Reserve squadron and to be reactivated on 1 October 1992 as an active squadron, moving from Whidbey Island to Cherry Point.

VMAQ-4 is currently a Reserve unit based at Whidbey Island. It is to become an active-duty squadron.

VMAT (Marine Attack Training Squadron)

VMAT-203 'Hawks'
MCAS Cherry Point, NC: 'KD'
AV/TAV-8B

VMAT-203 is the East Coast training squadron for the McDonnell AV-8B Harrier. The squadron operates a mix of AV-8Bs and two-seat TAV-8Bs in training crews and maintenance personnel.

The role of training Marine Corps Harrier pilots is entrusted to VMAT-203 at Cherry Point. The unit has many TAV-8B two-seaters.

VMAT (AW) (Marine Attack Training Squadron, All-Weather)

VMAT(AW)-202

This unit has been disestablished.

VMFA (Marine Fighter Attack Squadron)

VMFA-112 'Cowboys'
NAS Dallas, TX: 'MA'
F/A-18A

Marine Air Reserve squadron VMFA-112 under MAG-41 converted from the F-8A Crusader to the F-4N Phantom in 1976. VMFA-112 had earlier been known as the 'Wolf Pack.' In July 1983, the Reserve squadron made another change when it transitioned from F-4N to F-4J. Just 18 months later, in December 1984, the squadron began to transition from F-4J to F-4S.

This squadron has the distinction of being the very last Navy or Marine Corps unit to operate the F-4 Phantom, and was participating in live bomb drops with its F-4S aircraft at the Chocolate Mountains range as late as May 1991. The Dallas-based Marine Reservists continued to fly the F-4 Phantom until 1992. One of the squadron's aircraft (BuNo. 157293), which had shot down a MiG-21 in Vietnam while serving as a Navy F-4J, became the last Phantom in the Marine Corps and was scheduled for preservation at the Fort Worth Aviation Museum. The unit converted to the F/A-18A Hornet in 1992.

VMFA-115 'Silver Eagles'
MCAS Beaufort, SC: 'VE'
F/A-18A

VMFA-115 under MAG-31 flew F-4 Phantoms in Vietnam and transitioned to the McDonnell F/A-18A Hornet from the F-4S model in 1985. VMFA-115 has a distinctive eagle fin badge. The squadron has made deployments at MCAS Iwakuni, Japan, and at Vandel, Denmark, during Exercise Northern Wedding in September 1986. The 'Silver Eagles' joined the land-based Marine effort in the Persian Gulf region during Operation Desert Storm.

VMFA-122 'Crusaders'
MCAS Beaufort, SC: 'DC'
F/A-18A

VMFA-122 under MAG-31 became the second East Coast McDonnell F/A-18A Hornet squadron in the Corps when it converted from the F-4S early in 1986. The squadron has a shield as its tail badge. The 'Crusaders' have deployed to MCAS Iwakuni, Japan, and to Norway during Exercise Northern Wedding in March 1987.

VMFA-134 'Smokes'
MCAS El Toro, CA: 'MF'
F/A-18A

VMFA-134 is a Marine Air Reserve operator of the McDonnell F/A-18A Hornet, reporting to MAG-46 at Atlanta.

VMFA-142 'Flying Gators'
NAS Cecil Field, FL: 'MB'
F/A-18A

VMFA-142 underwent a very unusual change in recent Marine Corps Air Reserve history, shifting from the Douglas A-4M Skyhawk to the McDonnell F/A-18A Hornet on 21 December 1990.

The squadron provides the only Marine presence in the very active Hornet strike fighter community at Cecil, and routinely trains in the Hornet's dual-role, air-to-air and air-to-ground missions.

VMFA-212 'Lancers'
MCAS Kaneohe Bay, HI: 'WD'
F/A-18C

VMFA-212 under MAG-24 at operates the McDonnell F/A-18C Hornet after a long history in the F-4 Phantom.

Above: The F/A-18 Hornet has established itself as the Marine Corps' principal strike fighter, nearing the completion of replacement of the A-4, A-6, F-4 and RF-4. VMFA-115 'Silver Eagles' was a Phantom user prior to re-equipment.

Below: The shield badge on the fin is a suitably heraldic device for VMFA-122, known as the 'Crusaders'.

VMFA-134 (above) is a Reserve unit flying the F/A-18A, while VMFA-212 (right) is part of MAG-24 at Kaneohe Bay.

Left: VMFA-235 are the 'Death Angels', flying the Hornet from Kaneohe Bay.

Above: VMFA-212 'Lancers' aircraft carry individual names on the fin-tip, this being 'Rif Raf'.

Left: Marine air power: a KC-130 leads an AV-8B and a VMFA-312 F/A-18C on a live-drop exercise.

VMFA-232 'Red Devils'
MCAS Kaneohe Bay, HI: 'WT'
F/A-18C

VMFA-232 under MAG-24 operates the McDonnell F/A-18C Hornet after a long history in the F-4 Phantom. The 'Red Devils' deployed to Bahrain for combat in Operation Desert Storm.

VMFA-235 'Death Angels'
MCAS Kaneohe Bay, HI: 'DB'
F/A-18C

VMFA-235 under MAG-24 operates the McDonnell F/A-18C Hornet after a long history in the F-4 Phantom.

Above: VMFA-314 has the distinction of being the first squadron to be operational with the Hornet. Flying from Midway with VMFA-323, it took part in the raid on Libya.

VMFA-251 'Thunderbolts'
MCAS Beaufort, SC: 'DW'
F/A-18A

VMFA-251 under MAG-31 became the third East Coast Marine operator of the McDonnell F/A-18A Hornet in 1986, after a long history in Phantoms concluding with the F-4S model. The squadron has a lightning flash on its fin and shares its nickname with the Navy's HSL-84.

VMFA-312 'Checkerboards'
MCAS Beaufort, NC: 'DR'
F/A-18C

VMFA-312 has a long history with the F-4 Phantom and F/A-18 Hornet. On 8 August 1991, the squadron began to receive F/A-18C night attack Hornets, replacing its F/A-18A versions, and reached full strength with 12 aircraft apparently in November 1991.

VMFA-314 'Black Knights'
MCAS El Toro, CA: 'VW'
F/A-18A

VMFA-314 under MAG-11 shifted from the F-4S Phantom to the McDonnell F/A-18A Hornet and became operational in the Hornet on 7 January 1983. In 1986, the squadron made a cruise aboard USS *Coral Sea* (CV-43) and participated in Operations Prairie Fire and El Dorado against Libya. Deployments to Egypt for Exercise Bright Star and a rotational assignment to Iwakuni followed.

VMFA-321 'Hell's Angels'
NAF Washington, MD: 'MG'
F/A-18A

VMFA-321 (known as the 'Black Barons' during a temporary name change while flying F-8K Crusaders), is a Marine Air Reserve squadron under MAG-49. The squadron transitioned from Crusaders to F-4B Phantoms on 9 December 1973, to F-4N models in 1977 and to F-4S Phantoms beginning September 1984.

VMFA-321 held ceremonies at Andrews AFB on 13 July 1991 to mark the departure of the squadron's last F-4S Phantom, displaying the F-4S Phantom it plans to keep as an exhibit (BuNo. 153904).

VMFA-321 was without aircraft until January 1992, when it received its first two F/A-18A Hornets (BuNos. 161981/161982, coded MG-5/6). With the departure of this squadron's last Phantom, VMFA-112 'Cowboys' became the last squadron in Navy/Marine aviation to operate the F-4.

Above: As might be gathered from the fin badge, VMFA-251 are known as the 'Thunderbolts'.

Left: VMFA-323 'Death Rattlers' was the second USMC F/A-18 squadron, and also took part in Operation El Dorado Canyon.

VMFA-323 'Death Rattlers'
MCAS El Toro, CA: 'WS'
F/A-18A

VMFA-323 under MAG-11 converted to the McDonnell F/A-18A Hornet in 1983, after a long history in Phantoms. Together with VMFA-314, the squadron flew in combat against Libya from *Coral Sea* in 1986, deployed to Egypt in Exercise Bright Star in 1987, and has carried out a rotational stint at MCAS Iwakuni, Japan.

VMFA-333 'Shamrocks'
MCAS Beaufort, SC: 'DN'
F/A-18A

VMFA-333 had a long history in the Marine Corps, in recent years as an operator of the F-4 Phantom.

During July-December 1971, the squadron deployed on USS *America* (CV-66) with CVW-8, becoming the first Marine F-4J squadron to go aboard an aircraft carrier. On a subsequent combat cruise, on 11 September 1972, Major Thomas 'Bear' Lasseter and Captain John Cummings shot down a MiG-21, the only kill of the Vietnam War by a Marine crew flying a Marine aircraft.

The 'Shamrocks', also known as 'Triple Trey', flew the F-4S Phantom variant before converting to the F/A-18A Hornet in the late 1980s. The squadron deployed to Sheik Isa air base, Bahrain, during Operation Desert

Above: A 'Triple Trey' Hornet from VMFA-333 displays the three-shamrock unit markings.

Storm, and VMFA-333 flew numerous close air support and interdiction sorties against Iraqi forces. The 'Shamrocks' also employed AGM-88B HARM missiles in SEAD strikes against Iraqi air defense radars.

VMFA-333 was disestablished on 31 March 1992.

VMFA-451 'Warlords'
MCAS Beaufort, SC: 'VM'
F/A-18C

VMFA-451 under MAG-31 adopted the McDonnell F/A-18C Hornet in 1987 after a long history with F-4 Phantoms. The squadron was assigned to CVW-13 for a Sixth Fleet Mediterranean cruise in USS *Coral Sea* (CV-43) in 1989.

VMFA-531 'Gray Ghosts'
MCAS El Toro, CA: 'EC'
F/A-18A

VMFA-531 under MAG-11 had a long history as an F-4 Phantom operator. The 'Gray

Above: A 'Gray Ghosts' Hornet from VMFA-531 features an air superiority load-out with Sparrows.

Ghosts' became the first Marine Corps fixed-wing squadron committed to Southeast Asia, arriving at Da Nang on 10 April 1965.

In 1983, the squadron converted from F-4N to F/A-18A Hornet. The squadron was scheduled to be decommissioned on 31 March 1992.

Below: A pair of Hornets from VMFA-451 takes off from a Norwegian base.

VMFA(AW) (Marine All-Weather Fighter Attack Squadron)

VMFA(AW)-121 'Green Knights'
MCAS El Toro, CA: 'VK'
F/A-18D

VMFA(AW)-121, callsign COMBAT, under MAG-11 were the first Marine Corps squadron to operate the two-seat McDonnell F/A-18D Hornet Night Attack aircraft.

During Operation Desert Storm, 'Green Knights' F/A-18Ds operating from Bahrain, with no advance training for the job, carried out the fast FAC mission. In the fast FAC role, the Hornet is equipped with a Laser Spot Tracker/Strike Camera and a Hughes AN/AAR-50 FLIR pod on opposite sides of the fuselage. The squadron also flew night attack sorties.

VMFA(AW)-225 'Vagabonds'
MCAS El Toro, CA: 'CR'
F/A-18D(CR)

VMFA(AW)-225, under MAG-11, formerly called the 'Vagabonds', became the Marine Corps' third F/A-18D Hornet squadron when it was reactivated on 1 July 1991. Although not a direct result of the Corps' decision to give up its fleet of A-6E Intruders in favor of the McDonnell fighter, the squadron's colors had been folded on 30 June 1991, at which time it was designated VMA(AW)-225 and operated the A-6A Intruder. The squadron's history dates to 1 January 1943, and it flew F4U Corsairs at Guam during the Pacific War.

VMFA(AW)-225 operates the two-seat F/A-18D(CR) night attack/combat reconnaissance aircraft which the Corps now favors over the Intruder solely to reduce the number of aircraft types in its inventory. Following the example of the first such squadron to take on the F/A-18D, namely VMFA(AW)-121 which was tasked with fast FAC in Operation Desert Storm, the 'Vikings' employ Hornets at night and in

bad weather to support Marine combat troops on the ground.

VMFA(AW)-225 took delivery of its first Lot 14 F/A-18D Hornet on 14 February 1992. The Lot 14 F/A-18D is the first aircraft capable of operating the Advanced Tactical Aerial Reconnaissance System. VMFA(AW)-225 was scheduled to be fully equipped with 12 of these aircraft by July 1992.

VMFA(AW)-242 'Batmen'
MCAS El Toro, CA: 'DT'
F/A-18D

VMFA(AW)-242 under MAG-11 transferred its last Grumman A-6E Intruder to VA-128 in December 1990 and subsequently began to operate the 12 McDonnell F/A-18D Hornet night attack aircraft following a long Intruder history.

With the F/A-18D, the squadron trains for night attack aided by NVGs, navigation and targeting FLIR, and other equipment unique to the two-seat night attack version.

Above right: VMFA(AW)-225 is the chosen recipient of the F/A-18D(CR) aircraft.

Right: VMA(AW)-242 transitioned from the A-6E to the F/A-18D in 1990.

Below: Another ex-Intruder unit now flying the F/A-18D is VMFA(AW)-121.

US Marine Corps Units

VMFAT (Marine Fighter Attack Training Squadron)

VMFAT-101 'Sharpshooters'
MCAS El Toro, CA: 'SH'
F/A-18A/B

VMFAT-101, after a long history with the F-4 Phantom, is now the Marine Corps' FRS squadron for the training of aircrews and maintenance personnel in the McDonnell F/A-18 Hornet. In early 1992, the squadron was still providing Hornet training with F/A-18A/B aircraft, although some operational Marine squadrons employ the F/A-18D.

In 1991, VMFAT-101 acquired a small number of Beech T-34C Turbo-Mentors to maintain instructor proficiency and as target range spotter aircraft.

Above: VMFT-401 was well-known as the USMC's operator of the IAI F-21A Kfir, which it used for the dissimilar air combat training role. Today the unit continues this task, equipped with the Northrop F-5E/F Tiger II, flying from Yuma where most of the Marines' tactical training takes place.

Left: VMFAT-101 is based at El Toro to provide type training on the Hornet for Marine units. This is an F/A-18B.

VMFT (Marine Fighter Training Squadron)

VMFT-401 'Snipers'
MCAS Yuma, AZ
F-5E/F

VMFT-401 is an adversary squadron operating the Northrop F-5E/F Tiger. The squadron was the last in US forces to fly the Israeli Aircraft Industries F-21A Kfir in the adversary role.

VMO (Marine Observation Squadron)

VMO-1 'Yazoo'
MCAS New River, NC: 'ER'
OV-10A/D(Plus)

VMO-1 under MAG-29 operates North American OV-10A and OV-10D(Plus) Bronco forward air control aircraft. VMO-1 received the first operational OV-10D in February 1980. The two active-service squadrons, VMO-1 and VMO-2 at Camp Pendleton, use a mix of OV-10As and OV-10D(Plus). Conversion of 42 OV-10As to the newer OV-10D(Plus) standard was performed by the Naval Aviation Depot at Cherry Point. The OV-10D(Plus) is characterized by structural and systems improvements, a quick-detach rear door for paradrops, AN/ALQ-144 infra-red countermeasures, and AAS-37 FLIR, retaining the same engine as the OV-10D, the T-420/421.

Both Marine active-duty OV-10 squadrons deployed to the Persian Gulf during Operation Desert Shield/Storm. Ferrying of the aircraft to the war zone was, itself, the longest deployment of the OV-10 type ever made. The Broncos performed FAC work, initially under severe restrictions because of a belief that they were vulnerable to Iraqi defenses. VMO-1 lost one aircraft in combat, an OV-10A (BuNo. 155424, coded ER-15) hit by a SAM on 25 February 1991. Pilot Major Joseph J. Small became a POW and was released after hostilities. Observer Captain David M. Spellacy was killed.

A 16 December 1991 decision by the Commandant of the Marine Corps will deactivate the Corps' two active-duty and one Reserve Bronco squadrons by the end of FY 1994, and will mean the end of the Bronco's service in US forces.

VMO-2
MCAS Camp Pendleton, CA: 'UU'
OV-10A/D(Plus)

VMO-2 under MAG-39 operates a mix of North American OV-10A and OV-10D(Plus) Bronco forward air control aircraft. The squadron, which has no nickname, uses the callsign HOSTAGE. On 1 July 1988, VMO-2 took delivery of the first operational OV-10D(Plus) Bronco (BuNo. 155473). The D(Plus) is described in the entry for the Corps' other active-duty Bronco squadron, VMO-1.

Both Marine active-duty OV-10 squadrons deployed to the Persian Gulf during Operation Desert Shield/Storm. VMO-2 lost one aircraft in combat. The OV-10A (BuNo. 155435, callsign HOSTAGE ONE) was claimed on 18 January 1991 and the two-man crew, including squadron commander Lieutenant Colonel Clifford Acree, were held prisoner until the end of hostilities.

Below: VMO-2 has fashioned its 'UU' tailcode into horseshoes. This is an OV-10A.

Above: An active-duty Bronco unit is located on each coast, this OV-10D(Plus) serving with VMO-1 at New River.

Returning from the Persian Gulf, VMO-2 Broncos supported evacuation efforts following the 10 June 1991 volcanic eruption of Mount Pinatubo in the Philippines.

A 16 December 1991 decision by the Commandant of the Marine Corps will deactivate the Corps' two active-duty and one Reserve Bronco squadrons by the end of FY 1994, and will mean the end of the Bronco's service in US forces.

Below: VMO-4 flies a mix of OV-10As (illustrated) and OV-10D (Plus).

VMO-4
NAS Atlanta, GA: 'MU'
OV-10D(Plus)

VMO-4, the Marine Corps' only Reserve observation squadron, accepted its first OV-10D(Plus) Bronco in a 29 May 1991 ceremony. The squadron has for many years operated the OV-10A Broncos and its entire OV-10A fleet was scheduled for upgrade to OV-10D(Plus) status.

It is unclear whether the upgrade was to proceed in the meanwhile, pending the result of a 16 December 1991 decision by the Commandant of the Marine Corps to deactivate VMO-4, together with the Corps' two active-duty Bronco squadrons, by the end of FY 1994. The decision will mark the end of the Bronco's service in US forces.

VMGR (Marine Aerial Refueler Transport Squadron)

VMGR-152
MCAS Futemma, Okinawa: 'QD'
KC-130R

VMGR-152 under MAG-36 operates the Lockheed KC-130R Hercules tanker/transport to support tactical air units in the region and ground forces of the First Marine Division.

VMGR-234 'Thundering Herd'
NAS Glenview, IL: 'QH'
KC-130F/T

VMGR-234 under MAG-41 operates Lockheed KC-130F/T tanker/transports in Marine Air Reserve duties. The squadron, together with VMGR-452, was activated and flew more than 3,000 hours in support of Persian Gulf operations in 1990-91. Missions included air refueling, DASC/A (Direct Air Support Center/Airborne), and aerial delivery.

VMGR-252 'Heavy Haulers'
MCAS Cherry Point, NC: 'BH'
KC-130F/R

VMGR-252 under MAG-14 carries out inflight refueling and tactical airlift duties in the Lockheed KC-130F/R Hercules. The

Below: Reserve unit VMGR-452 flies the KC-130T, one of which is seen here at Bahrain.

Right: VMGR-152 is based on Okinawa to provide refueling to Marine aircraft in the Far East.

squadron dispatched aircraft to Bahrain during Operation Desert Shield/Storm. In addition, Hercules from VMGR-252 (joined by VMGR-352), while operating from Bahrain, supported Operation Eastern Exit, the non-combatant evacuation of the American Embassy in Mogadishu, Somalia, in January 1991.

VMGR-352
MCAS El Toro, CA: 'QB'
KC-130F/R

VMGR-352 under MAG-11 performs inflight refueling and tactical airlift duties with the Lockheed KC-130F/R Hercules. During Operation Desert Storm, the squadron operated its Hercules from Bahrain. During this period, in January 1991, VMGR-352 played a key role (with VMGR-252) in Operation Eastern Exit, the non-combatant evacuation of the American Embassy in Mogadishu, Somalia, in January 1991.

VMGR-452
Stewart IA, NY: 'NY'
KC-130

VMGR-452, under MAG-49 at Stewart International Airport, New York, is a Reserve unit which reports to the 4th Marine Aircraft Wing. The squadron was activated for Operation Desert Storm and flew seven KC-130s from Jubail air base, Saudi Arabia. One of these aircraft was the newly

designated Comint platform named Senior Warrior.

Subsequently, VMGR-452 became the first squadron in any branch of the US armed services to fly a 'stretched' version of the Lockheed C-130 Hercules. This occurred on 29 October 1991, when the squadron took delivery of the first of two KC-130T-30

'stretched' Hercules tankers (BuNo. 164597) to complement the shorter-fuselage KC-130Ts already in service.

Below: The East Coast active-duty Hercules squadron is VMGR-252, flying both KC-130Fs and KC-130Rs from Cherry Point.

VMGRT (Marine Transport/Air Refueler Training Squadron)

VMGRT-253
MCAS Cherry Point, NC: 'GR'
KC-130F

Right: Although type conversion is handled by the USAF, Marine C-130 crews also receive instruction from VMGRT-253 on KC-130Fs.

VMGRT-253 is the Marine Corps' training squadron for the service's only multi-engine aircraft, the Lockheed C-130 Hercules. Basic Hercules flight training is provided by the US Air Force at Little Rock, AR, after which future Hercules crews receive additional training, including air refueling training, with VMGRT-253, which operates the KC-130F version.

Base Flights

The Marine Corps operates base flights and SAR flights which report directly to its Marine Corps air stations at five locations. These local support units employ Beech UC-12B, Bell UH-1N Huey and Boeing HH-46D Sea Knight aircraft. A Douglas C-9B

Skytrain is operated by the base flight at Cherry Point. During Operation Desert Storm, UC-12Bs from El Toro and Yuma flew support missions from Bahrain.

Below: Marine air stations have base flights and SAR flights. This HH-46D flies from Kaneohe Bay.

Headquarters, United States Marine Corps

HQ USMC maintains a VIP flight at NAF Washington (Andrews AFB, Maryland) equipped with Douglas C-9B Skytrain and North American CT-39G Sabreliner

transports. The C-9B is customarily employed for VIP transport of the Commandant of the Marine Corps.

A single C-9B is operated by the SOES based at Cherry Point.

USN/USMC TAILCODES

The US Navy and Marine Corps have applied a single or double letter tailcode to their aircraft and helicopters as a form of unit identification since the late 1940s. The initial system consisted of double letter codes displayed on patrol, transport, utility, composite and a number of miscellaneous squadrons, as well as all Marine Corps units. In addition, the 13 carrier air groups were allocated a single letter identity which was applied to the majority of aircraft assigned during cruises. The gradual increase in the total number and variety of Navy and Marine Corps squadrons during the early 1950s saw an expansion in the quantity of tailcodes. Most codes were allocated at random with very little coordination or sequence system, although all utility squadrons were appropriately prefixed with the letter U, while test and development squadrons began with the letter X.

During FY 1958 the carrier air groups, which numbered no less than 25 to include attack and antisubmarine aircraft carriers, were realigned, with two letter codes assigned. At the same time, the air groups were assigned the system of identification codes which is in use today, with A signifying the Atlantic and N the Pacific. Many shore-based squadrons were recoded to reflect their assignment to either the Atlantic or Pacific Fleets. Among these were the prefix letters H, J, L and M for the Atlantic squadrons, while the Pacific Fleet included P, Q, R, S, T and Z. This system has remained, although many codes have disappeared as the number of squadrons has shrunk.

The following year Naval Air Training Command and the Naval Air Reserve applied tailcodes to their squadrons, although their systems consisted of a number and letter combination. Squadrons operated by Naval Basic Training Command were prefixed with the number 2, while the Advanced Training Squadrons commenced with the number 3. Operational aircraft with the technical training units had the prefix 4. Some naval air stations had basic training and technical training units in residence, such as NAS Memphis, TN, with Basic Training Group 7 (BTG-7) allocated tailcode 2M, while the Techical Training Center had code 4M.

The Naval Air Reserve was allocated a similar system which commenced with 6 or 7, with the individual tailcode applied to the all aircraft irrespective of the role. The Reserve was assigned a variety of aircraft types including patrol, transport, fighter and communications/trainers, with tailcodes such as 6M, 7R and 7V for Memphis, TN, Floyd Bennett, NY, and Glenview, IL, respectively.

In 1975 Naval Training Command abandoned the number/letter combination in favor of a single letter tailcode for all aircraft at their six flying training stations.

Marine Corps tailcode allocation was on a random basis with any letter combination available, provided it was not already assigned to a Navy squadron. For more than 40 years the Marine Corps has remained with this system, with none allocated specifically to determine assignment to either Fleet Marine Force Atlantic or Pacific.

The vast majority of Marine Corps aircraft and helicopters display their tailcode despite the introduction of low-visibility gray camouflage schemes. However, this is not the case with Navy squadrons as many patrol and aggressor units have for many years flown without a tailcode or with this form of identity presented small on the fintip or on the nosewheel door. The anonymity of the patrol units is gradually being addressed as the tailcode is being reapplied to both front-line and Reserve P-3 Orions.

Code	Sqn	Type	Station
'A'	VT-7	TA-4J	Meridian, MS
	VT-19	T-2C	Meridian, MS
	BF	HH-1N	Meridian, MS
'B'	VT-21	TA-4J to T-45A	Kingsville, TX
	VT-22	TA-4J	Kingsville, TX
	VT-23	T-2C	Kingsville, TX
'E'	HT-8	TH-57B	Whiting Field, FL
	HT-18	TH-57B/C	Whiting Field, FL
	VT-2	T-34C	Whiting Field, FL
	VT-3	T-34C	Whiting Field, FL
	VT-6	T-34C	Whiting Field, FL
'F'	VT-4	TA-4J, T-2C	Pensacola, FL
	VT-10	T-2C	Pensacola, FL
	VT-86	T-34C, T-39N	Pensacola, FL
	BF	UC-12B, T-39D	Pensacola, FL
'G'	VT-27	T-34C	Corpus Christi, TX
	VT-28	T-44C	Corpus Christi, TX
	VT-31	T-44C	Corpus Christi, TX
'AA'	HS-9	SH-3H	Jacksonville, FL
	VA-35	A-6E, KA-6D	Oceana, VA
	VAW-125	E-2C	Norfolk, VA
	VAQ-132	EA-6B	Whidbey Island, WA
	VF-74	F-14B	Oceana, VA
	VF-103	F-14B	Oceana, VA
	VFA-81	F/A-18C	Cecil Field, FL
	VFA-83	F/A-18C	Cecil Field, FL
	VS-30	S-3B	Cecil Field, FL
'AB'	HS-11	SH-3H	Jacksonville, FL
	VA-85	A-6E, KA-6D	Oceana, VA
	VAQ-137	EA-6B	Whidbey Island, WA
	VAW-123	E-2C	Norfolk, VA
	VF-33	F-14A	Oceana, VA
	VF-102	F-14A	Oceana, VA
	VFA-82	F/A-18A	Cecil Field, FL
	VFA-86	F/A-18A	Cecil Field, FL
	VS-32	S-3A	Cecil Field, FL
'AC'	HS-7	SH-3H	Jacksonville, FL
	VA-75	A-6E, KA-6D	Oceana, VA
	VAQ-130	EA-6B	Whidbey Island, WA
	VAW-126	E-2C	Norfolk, VA
	VF-14	F-14A	Oceana, VA
	VF-32	F-14A	Oceana, VA
	VFA-37	F/A-18C	Cecil Field, FL
	VFA-105	F/A-18C	Cecil Field, FL
	VS-22	S-3B	Cecil Field, FL
'AD'	VA-42	A-6E, TC-4C, T-34C	Oceana, VA
	VAW-120	C-2A, E-2C	Norfolk, VA
	VF-43	A-4E/F, TA-4J, F-5E/F, F-16N, T-2C	Oceana, VA
	VF-45 det	A-4E, TA-4J, F-16N	Cecil Field, FL
	VF-45 det	A-4E, TA-4J, F-5E/F, F-16N, TF-16N	Key West, FL
	VF-101	F-14A/B	Oceana, VA
	VFA-106	F/A-18A/B/C/D, T-34C	Cecil Field, FL
	VS-27	S-3A	Cecil Field, FL
'AE'	HS-15	SH-3H to SH-60F	Jacksonville, FL
	VA-176	A-6E, KA-6D	Oceana, VA
	VAQ-133	EA-6B	Whidbey Island, WA
	VAW-122	E-2C	Norfolk, VA
	VFA-132	F/A-18C	Lemoore, CA
	VFA-137	F/A-18A	Cecil Field, FL
	VS-28	S-3B	Cecil Field, FL
'AF'	VAQ-209	EA-6B	Washington, DC
	VAW-78	E-2C	Norfolk, VA
	VF-201	F-14A	Dallas, TX
	VF-202	F-14A	Dallas, TX
	VFA-203	F/A-18A	Cecil Field, FL
	VFA-204	F/A-18A	New Orleans, LA
	VA-205	A-6E, KA-6D	Atlanta, GA
'AG'	HS-5	SH-3H	Jacksonville, FL
	VA-34	A-6E, KA-6D	Oceana, VA
	VAQ-140	EA-6B	Whidbey Island, WA
	VAW-121	E-2C	Norfolk, VA
	VF-142	F-14B	Oceana, VA
	VF-143	F-14B	Oceana, VA
	VFA-131	F/A-18C	Cecil Field, FL
	VFA-136	F/A-18C	Cecil Field, FL
	VS-31	S-3B	Cecil Field, FL
'AJ'	HS-3	SH-60F, HH-60H	Jacksonville, FL
	VA-36	A-6E	Oceana, VA
	VA-65	A-6E, KA-6D	Oceana, VA
	VAQ-141	EA-6B	Whidbey Island, WA
	VAW-124	E-2C	Norfolk, VA
	VF-41	F-14A	Oceana, VA
	VFA-15	F/A-18A	Cecil Field, FL
	VFA-87	F/A-18A	Cecil Field, FL
	VS-24	S-3A	Cecil Field, FL
'AR'	HS-1	SH-3H, SH-60F	Jacksonville, FL
'BF'	HC-16	HH-1N, SH-3D/H	Pensacola, FL
'BH'	VMGR-252	KC-130F/R	Cherry Point, SC
'BJ'	HM-14	MH-53E	Norfolk, VA
'BR'	HC-8	CH-46D, HH-46D, UH-46D	Norfolk, VA
('CD')	VRC-40	C-2A, CT-39E	Norfolk, VA
'CE'	VMFA(AW)-225	F/A-18D	El Toro, CA
'CF'	VMA-211	AV-8B	Yuma, AZ
'CG'	VMA-231	AV-8B	Cherry Point, SC
'CJ'	HMH-461	CH-53E	New River, NC
('CN')	MALS-14	TA-4F	Cherry Point, SC
'CW'	VR-54	C-130T	New Orleans, LA
'CY'	VMAQ-2	EA-6B	Cherry Point, SC
'DB'	VMFA-235	F/A-18C	Kaneohe Bay, HI
'DC'	VMFA-122	F/A-18A	Beaufort, SC
'DH'	HM-12	MH-53E	Norfolk, VA
'DN'	VMFA-333	F/A-18A	Beaufort, SC
'DR'	VMFA-312	F/A-18A	Beaufort, SC
'DT'	VMFA(AW)-242	F/A-18D	El Toro, CA
'DW'	VMFA-251	F/A-18A	Beaufort, SC
'EA'	VMA(AW)-332	A-6E	Cherry Point, SC
'EC'	VMFA-531	F/A-18A	El Toro, CA
'ED'	VMA(AW)-533	A-6E	Cherry Point, SC
'EG'	HMM-263	CH-46E	New River, NC
'EH'	HMM-264	CH-46E	New River, NC
'EM'	HMM-261	CH-46E	New River, NC
'EN'	HMH-464	CH-53E	New River, NC
'EP'	HMM-265	CH-46E	Kaneohe Bay, HI
'ER'	VMO-1	OV-10A/D	New River, NC
'ES'	HMM-266	CH-46E	New River, NC
'ET'	VQ-6	ES-3A	Cecil Field, FL
'EZ'	MWHS-4	UC-12B	New Orleans, LA
'GD'	VAQ-33	EA-6A, EP-3A, EP-3J	Key West, FL
	VAQ-34	F/A-18A/B	Lemoore, CA
	VAQ-35	EA-6B	Whidbey Island, WA
'GF'	VC-8	TA-4J, SH-3G	Roosevelt Roads, PR
'GR'	VMGRT-253	KC-130F	Cherry Point, SC
'GX'	HMT-304	CH-46E, CH-53A	New River, NC
'HC'	VR-24	CH-53E	Sigonella, Sicily
'HF'	HMLA-269	AH-1W, UH-1N	New River, NC
'HK'	HSL-40	SH-60B	Mayport, FL
'HN'	HSL-42	SH-60B	Mayport, FL
'HP'	HSL-44	SH-60B	Mayport, FL
'HQ'	HSL-46	SH-60B	Mayport, FL
'HR'	HSL-48	SH-60B	Mayport, FL
'HT'	HSL-30	SH-2F	Norfolk, VA
'HU'	HC-2	VH-3A, SH-3G/H, CH-53E	Norfolk, VA
'HV'	HSL-32	SH-2F	Norfolk, VA
'HW'	HC-6	VH-3A, CH-46A/D, HH-46A	Norfolk, VA
'HX'	HSL-34	SH-2F	Norfolk, VA

Code	Squadron	Aircraft	Location
'HY'	HSL-36	SH-2F	Mayport, FL
'JA'	VX-1	SH-2F, SH-3H, SH-60B/F, P-3C, S-3A/B	Patuxent River, MD
'JB'	VXN-8	P-3B, RP-3D	Patuxent River, MD
'JH'	VC-10	EA-4F, TA-4J, OA-4M	Guantanamo Bay, Cuba
'JM'	VR-22	C-130F, KC-130F	Rota, Spain
	VR-24	C-2A, CT-39G	Sigonella, Sicily
'JQ'	VQ-2	EP-3E	Rota, Spain
'JS'	VR-46	C-9B	Atlanta, GA
'JT'	VR-52	C-9B	Willow Grove, PA
'JU'	VR-56	C-9B	Norfolk, VA
'JV'	VR-58	C-9B	Jacksonville, FL
'JW'	VR-62	C-9B	Detroit, MI
'JY'	VFC-12	A-4F, TA-4J	Oceana, VA
'KC'	VMAT(AW)-202	A-6E, TC-4C	Cherry Point, SC
'KD'	VMAT-203	AV-8B, TAV-8B	Cherry Point, SC
'LA'	VP-5	P-3C	Jacksonville, FL
'LC'	VP-8	P-3C	Brunswick, ME
'LD'	VP-10	P-3C	Brunswick, ME
'LE'	VP-11	P-3C	Brunswick, ME
'LF'	VP-16	P-3C	Jacksonville, FL
'LH'	VP-93	P-3B	Detroit, MI
'LJ'	VP-23	P-3C	Brunswick, ME
'LK'	VP-26	P-3C	Brunswick, ME
'LL'	VP-30	TP-3A, P-3C	Jacksonville, FL
'LM'	VP-44	P-3C	Brunswick, ME
'LN'	VP-45	P-3C	Jacksonville, FL
'LP'	VP-49	P-3C	Jacksonville, FL
'LQ'	VP-56	P-3C	Jacksonville, FL
'LR'	VP-24	P-3C	Jacksonville, FL
'LS'	VP-60	P-3B	Glenview, IL
'LT'	VP-62	P-3C	Jacksonville, FL
'LU'	VP-64	P-3B	Willow Grove, PA
'LV'	VP-66	P-3B	Willow Grove, PA
'LW'	VP-68	P-3C	Washington, DC
'LX'	VP-90	P-3B	Glenview, IL
'LY'	VP-92	P-3C	South Weymouth, MA
'LZ'	VP-94	P-3B	New Orleans, LA
'MA'	VMFA-112	F/A-18A	Dallas, TX
'MB'	VMFA-142	F/A-18A	Cecil Field, FL
'ME'	VMA-133	A-4M	Alameda, CA
'MF'	VMFA-134	F/A-18A	El Toro, CA
'MG'	VMFA-321	F/A-18A	Washington, DC
'ML'	HMM-764	CH-46E	El Toro, CA
'MM'	HML-767	UH-1N	New Orleans, LA
'MP'	HMA-773	AH-1J	Atlanta, GA
'MQ'	HMM-774	CH-46E	Norfolk, VA
'MS'	HMH-772 det	RH-53D	Alameda, CA
'MT'	HMH-772	CH-53A	Willow Grove, PA
'MU'	VMO-4	OV-10A/D	Atlanta, GA
'MW'	MALS-42	TA-4J	Atlanta, GA
('MX')	HMX-1	VH-3D, CH-53E, VH-60N	Quantico, VA
'ND'	VAQ-309	EA-6B	Whidbey Island, WA
	VAW-88	E-2C	Miramar, CA
	VF-301	F-14A	Miramar, CA
	VFA-303	F/A-18A	Lemoore, CA
	VA-304	A-6E, KA-6D	Alameda, CA
	VFA-305	F/A-18A	Point Mugu, CA
'NE'	HS-14	SH-3H	North Island, CA
	VA-145	A-6E, KA-6D	Whidbey Island, WA
	VA-155	A-6E	Whidbey Island, WA
	VAQ-131	EA-6B	Whidbey Island, WA
	VAW-116	E-2C	Miramar, CA
	VF-1	F-14A	Miramar, CA
	VF-2	F-14A	Miramar, CA
'NF'	HS-12	SH-3H	Atsugi, Japan
	VA-115	A-6E	Atsugi, Japan
	VAQ-136	EA-6B	Atsugi, Japan
	VAW-115	E-2C	Atsugi, Japan
	VF-21	F-14A	Atsugi, Japan
	VF-154	F-14A	Atsugi, Japan
	VFA-192	F/A-18C	Atsugi, Japan
	VFA-195	F/A-18C	Atsugi, Japan
	VS-21	S-3B	Atsugi, Japan
'NG'	HS-2	SH-60F, HH-60H	North Island, CA
	VA-165	A-6E, KA-6D	Whidbey Island, WA
	VAQ-138	EA-6B	Whidbey Island, WA
	VAW-112	E-2C	Miramar, CA
	VF-24	F-14B	Miramar, CA
	VF-211	F-14B	Miramar, CA
	VFA-146	F/A-18C	Lemoore, CA
	VFA-147	F/A-18C	Lemoore, CA
'NH'	HS-6	SH-60F, HH-60H	North Island, CA
	VA-95	A-6E, KA-6D	Whidbey Island, WA
	VAQ-135	EA-6B	Whidbey Island, WA
	VAW-117	E-2C	Miramar, CA
	VF-114	F-14A	Miramar, CA
	VF-213	F-14A	Miramar, CA
	VFA-22	F/A-18C	Lemoore, CA
	VFA-94	F/A-18C	Lemoore, CA
'NJ'	VA-128	A-6E, KA-6D, TC-4C	Whidbey Island, WA
	VAQ-129	EA-6B	Whidbey Island, WA
	VAW-110	C-2A, E-2C, TE-2C	Miramar, CA
	VF-124	F-14A/D, T-34C	Miramar, CA
	VFA-125	F/A-18A/B/C/D, T-34C	Lemoore, CA
	VFA-125 det	F/A-18C/D	Fallon, NV
	VF-126	A-4E/F, TA-4J, F-16N, T-2C	Miramar, CA
	VFA-127	TA-4J, F-5E/F	Lemoore, CA
	VFA-127 det	F-5E/F	Fallon, NV
	VS-41	S-3A/B	North Island, CA
'NK'	HS-8	SH-60F, HH-60H	North Island, CA
	VA-196	A-6E, KA-6D	Whidbey Island, WA
	VAQ-139	EA-6B	Whidbey Island, WA
	VAW-113	E-2C	Miramar, CA
	VF-11	F-14D	Miramar, CA
	VF-31	F-14D	Miramar, CA
	VFA-25	F/A-18C	Lemoore, CA
	VFA-113	F/A-18C	Lemoore, CA
'NL'	HS-4	SH-60F, HH-60H	North Island, CA
	VA-52	A-6E, KA-6D	Whidbey Island, WA
	VAQ-134	EA-6B	Whidbey Island, WA
	VAW-114	E-2C	Miramar, CA
	VF-51	F-14A	Miramar, CA
	VF-111	F-14A	Miramar, CA
	VFA-27	F/A-18C	Lemoore, CA
	VFA-97	F/A-18C	Lemoore, CA
	VS-37	S-3A	North Island, CA
'NW'	HCS-4	HH-60H	Norfolk, VA
	HCS-5	HH-60H	Point Mugu, CA
	HM-18	RH-53D	Norfolk, VA
	HM-19	RH-53D	Alameda, CA
	HS-75	SH-3H	Jacksonville, FL
	HSL-74	SH-2F to SH-2G	South Weymouth, MA
	HSL-84	SH-2F to SH-2G	North Island, CA
	HSL-94	SH-2F to SH-2G	Willow Grove, PA
'NY'	VMGR-452	KC-130T	Stewart, NY
'PC'	VP-6	P-3C	Barbers Point, HI
'PD'	VP-9	P-3C	Moffett Field, CA
'PE'	VP-19	P-3C	Moffett Field, CA
'PF'	HMM-364	CH-46E	Kaneohe Bay, HI
'PG'	VP-65	P-3C	Point Mugu, CA
'PJ'	VP-69	P-3B	Whidbey Island, WA
'PL'	VP-67	P-3B	Memphis, TN
'PM'	VP-91	P-3C	Moffett Field, CA
'PR'	VQ-1	EP-3E, P-3B	Agana, Guam
'QA'	VP-22	P-3C	Barbers Point, HI
'QB'	VMGR-352	KC-130F/R	El Toro, CA
'QD'	VMGR-152	KC-130F	Futemma, Okinawa
'QE'	VP-40	P-3C	Moffett Field, CA
'QG'	VMA-131	A-4M	Willow Grove, PA
'QH'	VMGR-234	KC-130T	Glenview, IL
'QK'	HML-771	UH-1N	South Weymouth, MA
'QL'	HML-776	UH-1N	Glenview, IL
'QM'	HMH-772 det	CH-53D	Dallas, TX
'QP'	VMA-124	A-4M, TA-4J	Memphis, TN
'QR'	VMA-322	A-4M	South Weymouth, MA
'QT'	HMT-303	AH-1W, UH-1N, OV-10A	Camp Pendleton, CA
'RA'	HS-10	SH-3H, SH-60F	North Island, CA
'RC'	VP-46	P-3C	Moffett Field, CA
'RD'	VP-47	P-3C	Moffett Field, CA
'RG'	VRC-50	C-2A, C-130F, US-3A, CT-39E	Cubi Point, RP
'RM'	VMAQ-4	EA-6B	Whidbey Island, WA
'RP'	VP-31	P-3C	Moffett Field, CA
'RS'	VR-61	C-9B	Whidbey Island, WA
'RT'	VR-60	C-9B	Memphis, TN
'RU'	VR-55	C-9B	Alameda, CA
'RV'	VR-51	C-9B	Glenview, IL
'RW'	VRC-30	C-2A, UC-12B/F, CT-39E	North Island, CA
'RX'	VR-57	C-9B	North Island, CA
'RY'	VR-59	C-9B	Dallas, TX
'SA'	HC-3	CH-46D, HH-46D	North Island, CA
'SD'	NAWC/AD	A-6E, F-14D, F/A-18C, AV-8B, TAV-8B	Patuxent River, MD
'SF'	VP-48	P-3C	Moffett Field, CA
'SG'	VP-50	P-3C	Moffett Field, CA
'SH'	VMFAT-101	F/A-18A/B/C/D, T-34C	El Toro, CA
'SM'	HMLA-369	AH-1W, UH-1N	Camp Pendleton, CA
'SN'	HMLA-169	AH-1W, UH-1N	Camp Pendleton, CA
'SS'	VQ-5	ES-3A	Agana, Guam
'SU'	HMT-301	CH-46E	Tustin, CA
'TA'	HSL-51	SH-60B	Atsugi, Japan
'TB'	HM-15	MH-53E	Alameda, CA
('TC')	VQ-3	E-6A	Barbers Point, HI
'TD'	HSL-31	SH-2F	North Island, CA
'TF'	HSL-33	SH-2F to SH-2G	North Island, CA
'TG'	HSL-35	SH-2F	North Island, CA
'TH'	HSL-37	SH-2F, SH-60B	Barbers Point, HI
'TL'	BF	UC-12B	Point Mugu, CA
'TS'	HSL-41	SH-60B	North Island, CA
'TT'	HSL-43	SH-60B	North Island, CA
'TV'	HMLA-167	AH-1W, UH-1N	New River, NC
'TX'	HSL-49	SH-60B	North Island, CA
'TY'	HSL-47	SH-60B	North Island, CA
'TZ'	HSL-45	SH-60B	North Island, CA
'UA'	VC-1	A-4E, TA-4J, SH-3G	Barbers Point, HI
'UE'	VC-5	A-4E, TA-4J, UH-3A, SH-3G, CH-53E	Cubi Point, RP
'UP'	HC-1	SH-3D/G/H, CH-53E	North Island, CA
'UT'	HMT-302	CH-53D/E	Tustin, CA
'UU'	VMO-2	OV-10A/D	Camp Pendleton, CA
'UV'	HMLA-267	AH-1W, UH-1N	Camp Pendleton, CA
'UX'	VFC-13	A-4F, TA-4J	Miramar, CA
'VE'	VMFA-115	F/A-18A	Beaufort, SC
'VK'	VMFA(AW)-121	F/A-18D	El Toro, CA
'VL'	VMA-331	AV-8B	Cherry Point, SC
'VN'	VMFA-451	F/A-18A	Beaufort, SC
'VR'	HC-11	CH-46D, HH-46D, UH-46D	North Island, CA
'VT'	HMLA-367	AH-1W, UH-1N	Camp Pendleton, CA
'VW'	VMFA-314	F/A-18A	El Toro, CA
'WD'	VMFA-212	F/A-18C	Kaneohe Bay, HI
'WE'	VMA-214	AV-8B	Yuma, AZ
'WF'	VMA-513	AV-8B	Yuma, AZ
'WH'	VMA-542	AV-8B	Cherry Point, SC
'WK'	VMA(AW)-224	A-6E	Cherry Point, SC
'WL'	VMA-311	AV-8B	Yuma, AZ
'WP'	VMA-223	AV-8B	Cherry Point, SC
'WR'	HMA-775	AH-1J	Camp Pendleton, CA
'WS'	VMFA-323	F/A-18A	El Toro, CA
'WT'	VMFA-232	F/A-18C	Kaneohe Bay, HI
'WX'	MALS-36	OV-10A/D	Futemma, Okinawa
'XD'	VXE-6	LC-130F/R, HH-1N	Point Mugu, CA
'XE'	VX-5	A-4M, TA-4J, A-6E, EA-6B, F/A-18D, AV-8B, OV-10D	China Lake, CA
'XF'	VX-4	F-14A/B/D, F/A-18A/C	Point Mugu, CA
'YB'	VP-1	P-3C	Barbers Point, HI
'YD'	VP-4	P-3C	Barbers Point, HI
'YF'	HMH-462	CH-53D	Tustin, CA
'YH'	HMH-463	CH-53D	Kaneohe Bay, HI
'YJ'	HMH-465	CH-53E	Tustin, CA
'YK'	HMH-466	CH-53E	Tustin, CA
'YL'	HMH-362	CH-53D	New River, NC
'YM'	HMH-365	CH-46E	New River, NC
'YN'	HMH-361	CH-53E	Tustin, CA
'YP'	HMH-163	CH-46E	Tustin, CA
'YQ'	HMM-268	CH-46E	Tustin, CA
'YR'	HMM-161	CH-46E	Tustin, CA
'YS'	HMM-162	CH-46E	New River, NC
'YT'	HMM-164	CH-46E	Tustin, CA
'YW'	HMM-165	CH-46E	Kaneohe Bay, HI
'YX'	HMM-166	CH-46E	Tustin, CA
'YZ'	HMM-363	CH-53D	Tustin, CA
'ZE'	VP-17	P-3C	Barbers Point, HI
'5A'	HQ USMC Flt	UC-12B	Washington, DC
'5B'	MARTD	UC-12B	Beaufort, SC
'5C'	MARTD	UC-12B	Cherry Point, SC
'5D'	MARTD	UC-12B, HH-46D	New River, NC
('5F')	MARTD	UC-12B	Futemma, Okinawa
('5G')	MARTD	UC-12B, HH-46D	Iwakuni, Japan
'5T'	MARTD	HC-12B, HH-1N	El Toro, CA
'5Y'	MARTD	UC-12M, HH-1N	Yuma, AZ
'7B'	BF	UC-12B	Atlanta, GA
'7C'	BF	UC-12B/M	Norfolk, VA
'7D'	BF	A-4M, UC-12B	Dallas, TX
'7E'	BF	UC-12B, SH-3H	Jacksonville, FL
'7F'	BF	UC-12B, HH-1N	Brunswick, ME
'7G'	BF	C-12B, SH-3D	Whidbey Island, WA
'7H'	BF	UC-12B, HH-1N	Fallon, NV
'7J'	BF	UC-12B	Alameda, CA
'7L'	BF	UC-12B	Memphis, TN
'7M'	BF	UC-12B	North Island, CA
'7N'	BF	UC-12B	Washington, DC
'7Q'	BF	UC-12B, SH-3D	Key West, FL
'7R'	BF	UC-12B, SH-3G	Oceana, VA
'7S'	BF	UC-12B, HH-1N	Lemoore, CA
'7T'	BF	UC-12B	Moffett Field, CA
'7U'	BF	UC-12B	Cecil Field, Fl
'7W'	BF	UC-12B	Willow Grove, PA
'7X'	BF	UC-12B	New Orleans, LA
'7Z'	BF	UC-12B	South Weymouth, MA
('8A')	BF	UC-12F	Atsugi, Japan
('8B')	BF	UC-12B	Cubi Point, RP
('8C')	BF	UC-12M	Sigonella, Sicily
('8D')	BF	UC-12M	Rota, Spain
('8E')	BF	UC-12M	Roosevelt Roads, PR
('8G')	BF	UC-12M	Mildenhall, UK
('8H')	BF	UC-12B	Kadena, Okinawa
'8K'	HQ CMEF	UC-12B	Bahrain IAP, Bahrain
('8M')	BF	UC-12B	Misawa, Japan
'8N'	BF	UC-12B	El Centro, CA

BF = Base Flight

INDEX

Glossary

Index

Picture credits

Front cover: George Hall/Check Six Productions. **6:** US Navy via Peter B. Mersky. **7:** US Navy via Peter B. Mersky, Randy Jolly. **8:** Lockheed, Sikorsky via Robert L. Lawson. **9:** via Peter B. Mersky, D.L. Killingsworth. **10:** McDonnell Douglas. **11:** Paul W. Langshaw. **12:** US Navy via Peter B. Mersky. **13:** US Navy via Peter B. Mersky (two). **14:** US Navy. **15:** US Navy via Peter B. Mersky (two). **16:** US Navy, US Navy via Peter B. Mersky. **17:** US Navy via Robert L. Lawson. **18:** US Navy, Robbie Shaw. **19:** US Navy, Newport News. **20:** Newport News, US Navy via Peter B. Mersky, US Navy. **21:** US Navy, Robert F. Dorr. **22:** Randy Jolly, US Navy via Peter B. Mersky. **23:** Randy Jolly, US Navy, US Navy via Peter B. Mersky. **24:** Randy Jolly, US Navy via Peter B. Mersky. **25:** McDonnell Douglas. **26:** McDonnell Douglas. **27:** Randy Jolly (two). **28:** Randy Jolly, Michael M. Anselmo, US Navy via Peter B. Mersky. **29:** US Navy, Robbie Shaw, Michael M. Anselmo. **30:** Yves Debay. **31:** T. Malcolm English, Werner Münzenmaier, Jeff Rankin-Lowe. **32:** via Peter B. Mersky. **33:** via Peter B. Mersky, McDonnell Douglas. **34:** US Navy via Peter B. Mersky, Robert L. Lawson. **35:** McDonnell Douglas, VF-1/US Navy. **36:** P.G. Barker, Jeff Rankin-Lowe. **37:** Peter B. Mersky. **38:** Rick Mullen. **39:** Randy Jolly (two). **40:** Rick Mullen, Randy Jolly. **41:** Randy Jolly. **42:** Rick Mullen (two). **43:** Randy Jolly (two). **44:** Yves Debay, Randy Jolly. **45:** Randy Jolly, Yves Debay, Jeff Rankin-Lowe. **46:** Barry D. Smith. **47:** US Coast Guard, Richard Gennis, Jeff Wilson, John Gourley, Barry D. Smith. **48:** US Coast Guard (three). **49:** Joe Towers, Richard Gennis. **50:** P.G. Barker. **52:** Richard Gennis, B. Redfern, Robert L. Lawson. **53:** Peter B. Mersky, B. Redfern. **54:** US Navy via Peter B. Mersky. **55:** Robert L. Lawson. **56:** Robert L. Lawson, US Navy. **57:** Yves Debay, Robert L. Lawson. **58:** Robert L. Lawson. **60:** Peter B. Mersky, Yves Debay. **61:** T. Malcolm English. **62:** Rick Linares/MAPS, Randy Jolly. **63:** Randy Jolly. **64:** Yves Debay, Stefan Petersen, Randy Jolly. **65:** US Navy via Peter B. Mersky. **66:** Rick Linares/MAPS. **68:** David Donald. **69:** US Coast Guard. **70:** Robbie Shaw, Beech via Robert L. Lawson. **71:** David Donald. **72:** Vern Pugh via Robert L. Lawson, Robert L. Lawson. **73:** Ray Rivard via Robert L. Lawson. **74:** Randy Jolly. **75:** David Donald, Jeff Rankin-Lowe, Austin J. Brown/APL, Robbie Shaw. **76:** Randy Jolly, US Coast Guard, Lockheed. **78:** Simon Watson. **79:** via Peter B. Mersky, US Navy via Robert L. Lawson, US Coast Guard. **80:** Grumman. **81:** US Navy, Michael M. Anselmo. **82:** US Navy via Peter B. Mersky, Jeff Rankin-Lowe, US Coast Guard. **84:** Boeing. **85:** Boeing (two). **86:** Robert Archer. **87:** Randy Jolly, via Peter B. Mersky. **89:** US Navy via Peter B. Mersky. **90:** VF-1/US Navy, NAS Point Mugu, US Navy. **91:** US Navy, Robert L. Lawson, via Peter B. Mersky. **92:** US Navy via Peter B. Mersky, Richard Gennis. **93:** D.L. Killingsworth. **94:** Michael M. Anselmo, Richard Gennis, Stephen J. Brennan. **95:** Randy Jolly. **96:** P.G. Barker, Dr. J.G. Handelman. **97:** McDonnell Douglas. **98:** Werner Münzenmaier, Rick Linares/MAPS, Randy Jolly. **100:** Robert Archer, US Navy. **101:** US Coast Guard. **102:** Rick Mullen. **103:** Randy Jolly (two). **104:** Yves Debay, B. Redfern. **105:** Rick Mullen. **106:** Randy Jolly, Stephen J. Brennan. **107:** US Navy via Peter B. Mersky, Yves Debay. **108:** Kaman. **109:** via Peter B. Mersky. **110:** Randy Jolly, Barry D. Smith. **111:** Graham Robson, USNTPS. **112:** Rick Mullen. **113:** David Donald, Robbie Shaw, Rick Mullen. **114:** Rick Mullen. **115:** Randy Jolly, Jeff Rankin-Lowe. **116:** Robert L. Lawson, Rick Mullen. **118:** Rick Mullen, Sikorsky. **119:** Jeff Rankin-Lowe. **120:** Peter B. Mersky, Robert L. Lawson. **121:** US Navy. **122:** US Navy, Barry D. Smith. **124:** Sikorsky, USNTPS, John Gourley, US Navy. **125:** Joe Towers. **126:** Lockheed, Stephen J. Brennan, Mark Attrill. **128:** Richard Gennis (two), Neil Dunridge. **129:** Austin J. Brown/APL, Peter B. Mersky. **130:** David Donald, via Peter B. Mersky. **131:** US Navy, M.J. Gault. **132:** US Navy, Robbie Shaw, Lockheed. **134:** Hendrik J. van Broekhuizen. **135:** Peter B. Mersky (two), USNTPS. **136:** Robbie Shaw, via Robert L. Dorr. **137:** Graham Robson, T. Malcolm English. **138:** Jack Callaway via Robert F. Dorr. **139:** Jeff Rankin-Lowe. **140:** McDonnell Douglas. **141:** Dr. J.G. Handelman, USNTPS. **143:** Joe Towers. **144:** US Coast Guard, Mike Verier. **145:** B. Redfern, Yves Debay. **146:** Randy Jolly, Bell, Douglas A. Zalud. **147:** Robert L. Lawson. **148:** US Navy (three). **149:** US Navy, via Peter B. Mersky. **150:** Peter B. Mersky, Anderson via Peter B. Mersky, US Navy. **152:** US Navy. **153:** General

Electric. **154:** via Peter B. Mersky, US Navy, Steven D. Eisner. **155:** US Navy, McDonnell Douglas. **156:** David Donald (two), McDonnell Douglas (two), US Navy. **157:** Bell, US Navy (three). **158:** Peter B. Mersky. **159:** McDonnell Douglas, Michael M. Anselmo, US Navy. **160:** USMC via Mike Verier. **161:** Kaman, US Navy. **162:** US Navy. **163:** W.G. Turner. **164:** Rick Linares/MAPS, W.G. Turner. **166:** US Navy via Peter B. Mersky, T. Malcolm English. **168:** Randy Jolly, Mike Verier, Jeff Wilson. **170:** US Coast Guard. **173:** David Donald, Paul W. Langshaw, T. Malcolm English. **174:** US Navy via Peter B. Mersky, Robbie Shaw, B.Redfern, Peter B. Mersky, US Navy, Pat Martin. **175:** Robbie Shaw, Jeff Wilson (two), Michael M. Anselmo, Robert F. Dorr. **176:** Robbie Shaw, Peter R. Foster, Dana Bell. **177:** Randy Jolly (two), Mark Attrill, Jeff Rankin-Lowe, Hendrik J. van Broekhuizen. **178:** Robbie Shaw (three), Richard Gennis (two). **179:** Stephen J. Brennan, Robert F. Dorr, US Navy (two), Peter B. Mersky. **180:** US Navy, Grumman, Robbie Shaw, Jeff Wilson. **181:** Robbie Shaw, Michael M. Anselmo, Dana Bell, Randy Jolly. **182:** Jeff Wilson, Grumman, Rick Linares/MAPS, Graham Robson, Mark Attrill, Mike Lumb, via Peter B. Mersky. **183:** Werner Münzenmaier, B. Redfern, Peter B. Mersky, David Donald, Stephen J. Brennan. **184:** Randy Jolly, Paul W. Langshaw, M.J. Gault, W.G. Turner, Richard Gennis, Douglas D. Olson via René J. Francillon, Peter B. Lewis via René J. Francillon. **185:** Stephen J. Brennan, Mike Lumb, Mark Attrill, Jeff Wilson. **186:** Robbie Shaw (two), Jeff Rankin-Lowe, Peter B. Mersky. **187:** via Peter B. Mersky (two), Austin J. Brown/APL, Lt. N.B. Jones. **188:** Dave Baranek, Robert L. Lawson, Rick Linares/MAPS, Jeff Puzzullo. **189:** Robert L. Lawson, Mike Lumb, Douglas D. Olson via René J. Francillon, US Navy via Peter B. Mersky (two). **190:** Peter B. Mersky (two), Rick Linares/MAPS, B. Redfern, Michael M. Anselmo, US Navy via Peter B. Mersky, Grumman. **191:** VF-84/US Navy, US Navy, Jeff Puzzullo (two), Douglas D. Olson via René J. Francillon, Randy Jolly. **192:** Douglas D. Olson via René J. Francillon (two), Stephen J. Brennan, P.G. Barker. **193:** N. Donald via René J. Francillon, Richard Gennis (three), Rick Linares/MAPS, M.J. Gault, W.G. Turner. **194:** Jeff Rankin-Lowe, US Navy, Jeff Puzzullo (three), Robert Archer. **195:** McDonnell Douglas (two), P.G. Barker, Dana Bell, Randy Jolly, Robbie Shaw. **196:** Randy Jolly, Douglas D. Olson via René J. Francillon (three), Dana Bell, Tom Kaminski. **197:** Rick Linares/MAPS, Mike Lumb, B. Redfern (two), McDonnell Douglas. **198:** Michael M. Anselmo, M.J. Gault (two), Peter B. Lewis via René J. Francillon (two), Stephen J. Brennan. **199:** Peter B. Mersky, P.G. Barker, David Donald (two). **200:** Tom Ross, Robbie Shaw, John Gourley. **201:** US Navy via Peter B. Mersky, M.J. Gault, John Gourley, Robbie Shaw. **202:** Stephen J. Brennan, Greg Kromhout, Robbie Shaw (two). **203:** Robbie Shaw (four), B. Redfern, David Donald, Jeff Rankin-Lowe. **204:** Lockheed, David Donald, Werner Münzenmaier. **205:** Boeing, Lockheed, Austin J. Brown/APL, Pat Martin, via Peter B. Mersky. **206:** Robert L. Lawson (three), Pat Martin (three), Jeff Rankin-Lowe. **207:** Stephen J. Brennan, Jeff Rankin-Lowe (two), Robbie Shaw, Dana Bell, US Navy. **208:** Robbie Shaw (two), David Donald, via Peter B. Mersky, Jeff Wilson. **209:** VT-3/US Navy via Peter B. Mersky, Peter B. Mersky, B. Redfern, Randy Jolly, Robbie Shaw, Hendrik J. van Broekhuizen. **210:** B. Redfern, David Donald, Stephen J. Brennan. **211:** Douglas D. Olson via René J. Francillon, Jeff Rankin-Lowe (two), Robbie Shaw, Paul W. Langshaw, VX-4/US Navy. **212:** Pat Martin, Jeff Puzzullo, T. Malcolm English (two), David Donald, Mark Munzel. **213:** D.L. Killingsworth, Yves Debay, Aerophoto, René J. Francillon, Robbie Shaw (two), T. Malcolm English. **214:** B. Redfern, Mike Verier (two), Graham Robson. **215:** Stefan Petersen, via Robert L. Lawson, Aerophoto, B. Redfern, M.P. Hopper. **216:** M.P. Hopper (two), Mike Verier, Salvador Maf Huertas, Yves Debay, Graham Robson. **217:** Randy Jolly, Yves Debay, Mike Verier, B. Redfern, Stefan Petersen. **218:** Jeff Wilson, John Gourley, David Donald, B. Redfern, Sikorsky, Peter R. Foster, Yves Debay. **219:** Shirley Rankin-Lowe, Randy Jolly (two), Michael M. Anselmo, Stefan Petersen. **220:** Randy Jolly, Robbie Shaw, Mike Verier, Yves Debay, M.J. Gault, Greg Meggs. **221:** via Peter B. Mersky, Jeff Rankin-Lowe, John Gourley, Tom Kaminski, B. Redfern, Randy Jolly, Graham Robson. **222:** Randy Jolly (two), Michael M. Anselmo, Hendrik J. van Broekhuizen, Stephen J. Brennan, McDonnell Douglas. **223:** Robbie Shaw, McDonnell Douglas, Yves Debay, Robert L. Lawson, Peter B. Lewis via René J. Francillon, Hughes. **224:** P.G. Barker, Randy Jolly, Chris Ryan, Pat Martin, Stephen J. Brennan. **225:** Greg Meggs, David Donald, Stephen J. Brennan, Yves Debay, Robbie Shaw, via Robert L. Lawson.